Philadelphia Pres

Published with the
Philadelphia Historical Commission

The Historic American Buildings Survey
is a program of
the National Park Service,
United States Department
of the Interior.

Philadelphia Preserved

Catalog of
the Historic American
Buildings Survey

Richard J. Webster

With an Introduction by
Charles E. Peterson

Temple University Press
Philadelphia

Temple University Press, Philadelphia 19122
© 1976 by Temple University. All rights reserved
Published 1976. Second edition 1981.
Printed in the United States of America

Library of Congress Cataloging in Publication Data

Historic American Buildings Survey.
    Philadelphia preserved.

    Includes bibliographical references and index.
    1. Historic buildings—Pennsylvania—Philadelphia—
Conservation and restoration—Catalogs. 2. Architec-
ture—Pennsylvania—Philadelphia—Conservation and
restoration—Catalogs. I. Webster, Richard J.
II. Philadelphia Historical Commission. III. Title.
NA108.P5H57   1980   720′.9748′11   80-26661
ISBN 0-87722-089-1
ISBN 0-87722-215-0 (pbk.)

Contents

Illustrations

Shippen-Wistar and Norris-Cadwalader Houses
Water Trough and Fountain
Joseph Wharton House
William H. Winder Houses

Penn's City: Old City

Page 38:
Map of Old City

Following page 102:
Arch Street Friends Meeting
Athenaeum of Philadelphia
John Brock Sons & Co. Warehouse
Christ Church
Elfreth's Alley Area Study
Farmers' and Mechanics' Bank
First Bank of the United States
Independence Hall, Assembly Room, tabernacle frame
Independence Hall, Central Hallway
Insurance Patrol
Leland Building
Pennsylvania Fire Insurance Company Building
Philadelphia Bourse
Philadelphia Exchange Company (Merchants Exchange)
Philadelphia Fire Department, Engine Co. No. 8
Philosophical Hall
Provident Life and Trust Company Bank
Reynolds-Morris House
Second Bank of the United States

Penn's City: Center Square

Page 104:
Map of Center Square

Following page 150:
Academy of Music
Bulletin Building
Girard Trust Corn Exchange Bank
Harrison Building
Market Street National Bank Building
Pennsylvania Academy of the Fine Arts
Pennsylvania Institution for Deaf and Dumb
Pennsylvania Railroad, Broad Street Station
Philadelphia and Reading Railroad, Terminal Station, Train Shed

Delaware River Corridor

Foreword

Since the creation of the Philadelphia Historical Commission in 1955, the Commission and the Historic American Buildings Survey have maintained a continuously evolving relationship. Together they have striven to identify and protect the historically and architecturally significant structures of Philadelphia. They have also sought to preserve at least an archival record of the tremendous variety of buildings which make this city one of the nation's richest sources of architectural, social, and cultural history. Finally, the Commission and the Survey have collaborated in compiling the historical data essential to the scholarly utility of a comprehensive collection of measured drawings and photographs. After twenty-one years, their collaboration has reached fruition in this excellent publication, *Philadelphia Preserved: Catalog of the Historic American Buildings Survey*.

In the beginning, the already long established Survey provided a documented base for the Commission's first efforts, and lent stature to the recommendations and decisions of the municipal agency. The Commission also adopted several of the Survey's proven procedures and methods for the preparation of an inventory of buildings. As the Commission and its reputation grew, and as its staff (under the supervision of Dr. Margaret B. Tinkcom, the Commission's first historian) undertook fundamental research, the Survey and this Catalog came to rely increasingly on the resources of the Commission. Without the scores of eighteenth-, nineteenth-, and twentieth-century insurance surveys, the hundreds of chains-of-title, and the countless notes on builders and architects in the Commission's files, the Catalog as it now appears simply would have been an impossibility.

The participation of the Philadelphia Historical Commission in the publication of this work extends far beyond the sharing of information. It made office space and services available to Richard Webster, the editor. It alerted the Survey to the approaching demolition of important buildings, such as Moyamensing Prison and the entire neighborhood of early houses now replaced by the Delaware Expressway, so that these structures could be recorded. Through its own local activities, it contributed to the expansion of the Survey's listings in Philadelphia from some 60 primarily eighteenth-century structures in 1959 to the present 600 buildings of every period and genre, including a castiron sidewalk. And, perhaps most importantly, it agreed in 1969 to publish the Catalog and to raise the necessary subvention.

Much of the credit for the Commission's constant involvement with the Catalog and for the quality of the Catalog itself belongs to Margaret B. Tinkcom. She persuaded the Commission to underwrite its publication and directed the staff research which complements Mr. Webster's work. Her vision of preservation and significance brought professional standing to a much larger appreciation of the City's architecture. She played an instrumental part in securing the service of Mr. Webster as editor and acted as his unfailing advisor. Finally, she handled much of the requisite administrative detail which resulted in *Philadelphia Preserved: Catalog of the Historic American Buildings Survey.*

Richard Tyler
Philadelphia Historical Commission
Philadelphia, Pennsylvania

Preface

Since 1933, when the Histŏric American Buildings Survey was established as a Works Progress Administration program, HABS has grown into a national archive of significant American architecture. Under a tripartite agreement dating from 1934, HABS administers the program and is responsible for qualitative standards, selection of subjects for recording, and organization of the recording projects. The Library of Congress is the depository of the records, which are serviced by the Prints and Photographs Division, and the American Institute of Architects provides professional advice.

The Survey's goal is to develop the broadest possible coverage for all areas, periods, styles, and types of American architecture. Structures represented in the Survey span the period from both prehistoric and colonial times to the early twentieth century and include examples from all fifty states, the District of Columbia, Puerto Rico, and the Virgin Islands. The collection now includes approximately 16,000 buildings represented by more than 31,000 drawings, 47,000 photographs, and 23,500 pages of written data.

Those who are interested in consulting the HABS records may either visit the Division of Prints and Photographs of the Library of Congress, or consult the published HABS catalogs. A comprehensive, geographically arranged *Catalog* was published in 1941, and was updated by a *Supplement* in 1959. More recently, because of the extensiveness of HABS holdings, new catalogs are being published for states and metropolitan areas. To date, state catalogs have appeared for New Hampshire (1963), Massachusetts (1965), Wisconsin (1965), Michigan (1967), Utah (1969), Maine (1974), and Texas (1974). The catalogs for Chicago and nearby Illinois areas and for Washington,

D.C., were published in 1966 and 1976 respectively. Most of these publications can be found in major university or public libraries. Further questions regarding the consultation of records and ordering of reproductions may be addressed to:

> Division of Prints and Photographs
> Library of Congress
> Washington, D.C. 20540.

Questions regarding HABS recording and publishing programs or materials temporarily held in HABS offices may be addressed to:

> Historic American Buildings Survey
> National Park Service
> Washington, D.C. 20240.

In 1970 the National Park Service published *Recording Historic Buildings*, compiled by Professor Harley J. McKee. Based on the Survey's long experience and widely regarded as the definitive work in the field, this volume establishes standards and procedures for gathering both historic and architectural documentation. Copies may be purchased from:

> Superintendent of Documents
> U.S. Government Printing Office
> Washington, D.C. 20402.

More than 600 examples of Philadelphia's structures and street furniture are listed in this catalog. They represent the total number of items in the city that have been recorded by the Historic American Buildings Survey through the summer of 1976. The Philadelphia survey includes all of the entries from the national 1941 *Catalog* and the 1959 *Supplement*, which have been updated and expanded to provide more useful information. During the 1960's and 1970's, approximately 550 structures were added to the Survey to make it more comprehensive and illustrative of the city's multiplicity of building types. Most of the additions of the 1960's resulted from two major cooperative projects that recorded buildings in the path of Interstate Route 95 (Delaware Expressway). The Southwark Project, funded by the American Philosophical Society and executed by HABS and the Philadelphia Historical Commission, led to the publication of Margaret B. Tinkcom's excellent architectural history of the area in the August 1970 *Proceedings of the American Philosophical Society*. The

Pennsylvania Historical Salvage Council, a joint project of HABS, the Philadelphia Historical Commission, and the University of Pennsylvania, centered its attention on Northern Liberties and Kensington, north of the original city limits.

The catalog is arranged much as a museum script. The central focus is on the material objects, or, more accurately, the catalog entries, which are organized alphabetically within nine historical-geographical districts. Preceding each group of entries is an architectural history of that district which relates its buildings to the district's social and economic development. Following each section is a gallery of illustrations, also arranged alphabetically for the convenience of the reader.

As far as possible, both the introductions and entries reflect the latest historical research. In many cases it has been possible to correct dates for buildings or to note them more precisely. More historically accurate names have been assigned to some buildings, and abundant cross-references under formerly or popularly used names have been employed. The identification and history of the buildings are based on a variety of sources, but the most frequently used sources were briefs of title, fire insurance surveys, building permits, newspapers, and old maps and atlases. While briefs of title (compiled for the most part by the Philadelphia Historical Commission), newspapers, and maps are familiar sources, the fire insurance survey remains a frequently overlooked but invaluable research tool. There is an abundance of surveys for Philadelphia buildings in particular, because of the early and prosperous history of fire insurance companies in the city, dating from the 1752 founding of the Philadelphia Contributionship for Insuring Houses against Loss by Fire. Surveys and re-surveys often possess detailed information on buildings' functions, plans, materials, and technology, which is useful for both the historian and the restorer. Building permits, on the other hand, are useful for only the twentieth century. Although surviving permits date from the late 1880's, an index system was not begun until 1902.

The format of the entries consists of: the historic name; HABS number; address; brief physical description, including construction materials, dimensions, number of stories, roof type, and important interior and exterior details; statement of architectural significance; date of erection; architect and builder, if known; alterations and additions; statement of historical significance; citations by public agencies; and a listing of the measured drawings, photographs, photocopies, and data pages available in the HABS archives.

The following abbreviations, terms, and symbols have been used in the catalog entries:

PA-100

All structures recorded by the Survey are assigned a Historic American Buildings Survey number. These numbers have no historical significance but serve only to facilitate processing. They should be used when inquiring about a structure or ordering reproductions.

London house plan

Adopted from William Murtagh's article on the Philadelphia row house in the December 1957 issue of the *Journal of the Society of Architectural Historians*, this term applies to a house plan two rooms deep with a side hall leading to stairs between the two rooms.

city house plan

Also from Murtagh's article, this plan consists of a one-room front building and a rear ell which includes a piazza, or stair tower.

town house plan

The largest and most sophisticated of Philadelphia house plans, the town house plan contains a wide front section with two rooms and a stair hall and narrower backbuildings.

certified, PHC

The building has been judged historic by the Philadelphia Historical Commission, affording the building an element of protection from wanton demolition and inaccurate or unsympathetic alteration.

Pennsylvania Register

The building has been entered on the Pennsylvania Register of Historic Sites and Landmarks.

NR

The building has been entered on the National Register of Historic Places.

sheets

The number of sheets of measured drawings available for study and reproduction is cited near the end of the catalog entry. Sheets are a standard size, 15½ inches by 20 inches inside border lines. The number of sheets in the set and kinds of drawings (plans, elevations, sections, details) are listed.

Prints of measured drawings are made at actual size.

photos

The number of exterior and interior photos available for reproduction is also cited near the end of the entry. HABS negatives normally are 5 by 7 inches, but are sometimes in other sizes, especially 4 by 5 inches or 8 by 10 inches. Duplicate prints of HABS photographs are the same size as the originals.

data pages

Data pages include information on the structure, ideally its physical history and a technical architectural description. Original data pages are typewritten and may be duplicated.

HABSI form

The Historic American Buildings Survey Inventory form is a single-page record that provides for identification of the structure, concise written historical and/or architectural data, a small photograph, a location diagram, and source references. HABSI forms are duplicated at actual size (8 by 10½ inches).

n.d.

The date is not ascertainable.

*

An asterisk after a date indicates that the measured drawings, photographs, or data pages made on the indicated date are temporarily being held for editing and processing at the Washington, D.C., office of the Historic American Buildings Survey, prior to transmittal to the Library of Congress.

I am indebted to many people and institutions who have helped to make this book possible. First tribute must go to Dr. Margaret B. Tinkcom, former historian of the Philadelphia Historical Commission, for her valuable counsel and scholarly direction. I am also indebted to the Philadelphia Historical Commission staff for its many favors, and especially to Mrs. Beatrice Kirkbride for sharing with me her expert knowledge of Philadelphia insurance surveys. I appreciate the generosity of the many contributors to the Harry A. Batten Memorial Fund of the Philadelphia Historical Commission, which made the book's publication economically possible. Some of the city's leading business institutions that made major contributions are First Pennsylvania Banking and Trust Company, Germantown Savings Bank, Girard Bank, Mutual Assurance Company for Insuring Houses against Loss by Fire, Old Original Bookbinder's, Penn Mutual Life Insurance Company, Philadelphia Contributionship for Insuring Houses against Loss by Fire, Philadelphia Saving Fund Society, Daniel J. Walsh's Sons, and Western Saving Fund Society. Major individual contributors include Dorothy Collins, C. Jared Ingersoll, Olan Lowry, Esq., Lawrence M. C. Smith, Charles R. Tyson, members of the Washington Square Association, Henry M. Watts, Jr., and members of the Philadelphia Historical Commission staff.

I also appreciate the cooperation of the many present and former members of the Historic American Buildings Survey staff, particularly James C. Massey, John C. Poppeliers, S. Allen Chambers, Jr., and Christine St. Lawrence; Allen Weinberg, John Daly, and Ward Childs of the Philadelphia City Archives; Joseph McDevitt of Philadelphia Records Storage; Lee Nelson and Penelope Hartshorne Batcheler, architects with the National Park Service; Carolyn Pitts of the Historic Sites Survey, National Park Service; Isadore Lichstein, formerly of the *Evening and Sunday Bulletin;* Reeves Wetherill, Public Relations Director of John Wanamaker; John F. Harbeson, F.A.I.A.; Charles E. Peterson, F.A.I.A.; George E. Thomas; the staffs of the Philadelphia City Planning Commission, Free Library of Philadelphia, Historical Society of Pennsylvania, Library Company of Philadelphia, and Philadelphia Museum of Art; and three fine men and excellent photographers, Jack E. Boucher, George A. Eisenman of James Dillon and Company, and Cortlandt V. D. Hubbard.

I am also grateful for the nearly three centuries of Philadelphia architects, builders, craftsmen, and patrons who have produced a city rich in material culture to be enjoyed by all who care to look about them.

And for my cheerful and loving wife, Yvonne Sanwald Webster, I reserve the last and most grateful credit line.

Richard J. Webster
West Chester State College
West Chester, Pennsylvania

HABS—In and Out of Philadelphia

For more than forty years the Historic American Buildings Survey has been an active institution and a source of ready aid to a large community scattered from coast to coast, and beyond. But published accounts of the Survey are scarce—perhaps because few architects write for publication and the founders of the Survey were all architects.[1] In addition to architects in different parts of the country, an energetic and dedicated Park Service staff in Washington was essential to the success of the new enterprise. The tiny headquarters staff worked up directives to the men in the field, collected the harvest of drawings, and pushed it on to the Library of Congress, where it was and still is available to all. A distinguished Advisory Commission, early appointed and convened, lent prestige and support to HABS, the bureau's first national venture into historiography.

Those pioneers of the 1930's and their successors with antlike industry built, and have never stopped building, the great collection of architectural drawings, photographs, and historical data in the Library of Congress. But many of the official files that dealt with administration and personnel have been dispersed and for the time being at least are out of reach. To assemble a definitive chronicle of the HABS achievement now would entail major archival campaigns.[2] But the *architectural* records, far from lying forgotten, have been actively used from the first days of their arrival at the Library. It has been shown that HABS is one of the most actively consulted archives in that vast collection of collections. As works of graphic analysis, they are more than just mindless mechanical exercises; they provide a basic understanding and appreciation of the American builders' art.

The original proposal still works as a comprehensive, loose-fit charter that in later years has allowed development in several directions. Notably, since 1957, the interpretive and artistic standards of HABS photography have been built up. The policy was then developed that photographs should be of publishable quality, with great care being taken as to camera position, lighting, and other technical details. And the historical research that supplies the textual component of the Survey has come to incorporate some of the best-informed work being done today.

Much of the Survey as now conducted follows procedures and techniques developed at Philadelphia in the period 1950–1962. The program was deliberately used at that time for the recruitment and training of young architects considering the field of historic conservation as a career. Some of them stayed with the Survey and others moved into the field of restoration; a number are today in important positions nationally.

From Philadelphia the new wave of HABS spread to San Francisco and then from the Virgin Islands and Puerto Rico to Hawaii and Alaska. The Survey is now well rooted and promises to flourish indefinitely. Certainly there is plenty to do as public moneys flow into historic conservation programs. Today hard data are more needed than ever before.

Early Portraits of Philadelphia

The reader consulting this catalog will soon note that the buildings of Philadelphia have had an extraordinary amount of attention from HABS. With more than six hundred items, the collection for this city is more extensive than for any other; more buildings were recorded here than in many states. The Philadelphia collection was not made too soon, for there have been mighty changes in the architectural face of the city in the last twenty-five years. At best, our fine old buildings have been carefully restored, HABS drawings often serving as the base upon which the architects' plans were developed. At worst, a tragic number have been removed, among several reasons, for highway rights of way, by the lethal hand of urban renewal, and through the negligence—if not animosity—of city planners. In more than one case HABS was on hand during the last agonies of buildings under demolition.

Appreciation of Philadelphia's landmarks as such took time to develop. We do have one exceptionally early example reported by

Peter Kalm, the agricultural explorer from Upsala, who spent much time here. In the year 1749 he wrote that Philadelphians were already preserving an old structure—the Swanson house—as a reminder of pioneer days![3] Unfortunately, we have no sure record of it, and afterward it disappeared.

We have very few portraits of individual buildings during Philadelphia's first century. But beginning in 1750 the situation improved. In that year Scull and Heap's map of the city carried an engraved view of the State House. Then came the "East Prospect" of the city drawn by George Heap in 1752 from a point across the Delaware River.[4] In the Heap view (as engraved, over seven feet long) the steeples are identifiably portrayed and the warehouses on the river bank have a characteristic gambrel-roofed individuality. A splendid start.[5]

First Records by Architects

Scale drawings—floor plans, elevations, sections and details— are the architect's peculiar idiom. Such precise documents are required to fix building projects that can then be turned over to mechanics for execution at the site. They have other uses, too. When an architect wants to analyze an existing building closely, he makes a measured drawing of it. This reveals to him the peculiar relationship between what the eye sees in perspective and how the facts appear when formally projected on a sheet of paper. Plans and sections speak to the professional of things not seen by the eye.

European architects had long been making measured drawings of the buildings that survived antiquity. First Roman structures, and then Greek, provided a treasury of details that could be copied or adapted in new buildings across Britain and Europe. Their books, published in London, could be found in American libraries, and details from engraved plates might be seen on new American buildings.[6] But while the measuring of antiquities did not start early in America, we do have the example of a Boston architect picking up ideas in Philadelphia. In 1789, Charles Bulfinch carried home an elevation of William Bingham's new and fashionable house on South Third Street,[7] which he used soon afterward as the design for the Harrison Gray Otis House on Cambridge Street, Boston, for many years now the headquarters of the Society for the Preservation of New England Antiquities.

Picture books of Philadelphia began in earnest at the end of the eighteenth century, when the English-trained William Russell Birch engraved his attractive and well-known set of *Views* intended as "a memorial of progress for the first century." Today highly prized by collectors and often reproduced, these charming perspectives delineate buildings now regarded as historic which in their time were just a part of the contemporary scene.

The first outright *antiquarian* record by an *architect* may well have been William Strickland's drawing of Anthony Benezet's house on Chestnut Street commissioned by Roberts Vaux just before it was pulled down in March, 1818. The street elevation appeared as a frontispiece to *The Port Folio* of Philadelphia for October, 1818. The thought was expressed that it was gratifying to look upon the buildings that our ancestors occupied. "There remains," according to the anonymous staff writer, "scarcely a vestige of the style of architecture adopted by our goodly and adventurous predecessors. It is but a few months since one of the oldest, *if not the first brick house* erected in Philadelphia, was torn down, to give space to a more spacious structure, and we believe that edifice to have been the last *specimen* in this city, toward which the curious inquirer in these matters, might have been directed."[8]

In 1824, the triumphant return of General Lafayette to America on its fiftieth anniversary triggered waves of patriotic nostalgia that have continued to inspire writers and artists. At that point there fortunately appeared in Philadelphia an Englishman—William L. Breton—who had, he said, learned to draw on the way across the Atlantic. Soon after his arrival he sketched the Stritzel house in Church Alley and the Carpenter house on Chestnut, both soon to be torn down.[9] Breton's views first appear in *The Casket* (another local magazine) for 1827 and they quickly became familiar to the reading public in the form of engravings, woodcuts, and lithographs.

Local historians, beginning with Robert Proud, did not seem to fancy architectural landmarks. It remained for John Fanning Watson, shopkeeper, banker, and railroad executive immigrating here from Burlington County, New Jersey, to become the tireless antiquarian investigator of "Olden Time Philadelphia," as he liked to call it. Watson's avocation was interviewing oldtimers, salvaging documents, and souveniring all kinds of relics. In 1824, the historian proposed a scheme for purchasing and rehabilitating the old Rising Sun Tavern (which he called the Letitia Penn House) to "preserve its exterior walls with inviolate faithfulness," at the same time adapting its interior as a historical museum. Realizing the value and interest of pictures for promoting his project, Watson engaged Breton to make a sketch of the tavern in 1828.[10] Watson's grand ambition was heralded in *The Casket* for June, 1828, in a little article on the Old Court House then still standing in the middle of Market Street at Second but pulled down shortly afterward.[11] Watson's answer to such threats was his book, the now famous *Annals* of 1830, one of the first illustrated American city histories.[12] In it old buildings became heroes and they have remained so to many people.

An interesting architectural record of the year 1824 was the floor plan of Wyck in Germantown drawn by the office of William Strickland just before he enlarged the house, completely denaturing its original seventeenth-century character (illus.).[13]

More Measured Drawings: Photography Arrives

A few years later, Mrs. Louisa C. Tuthill, a popular Connecticut writer, took on the whole world of architecture from its beginning. In a work published here and inscribed "to the Ladies of the United States of America, the acknowledged Arbiters of Taste," she presented a chapter on the current "State of Architecture," including a blue-ribbon roll call of Philadelphia buildings. But beyond citing the layout of Babylon as prototype for William Penn's city plan, she says little about Philadelphia history. Her lions were the new buildings admired at the time.[14] Another variety of historian, Benson J. Lossing, came from New York, systematically seeking out Revolutionary War landmarks and personally sketching "physical vestiges of that struggle." He tells us that he traveled eight thousand miles to build up his "pictorial field book." He did well by Philadelphia and his indignant description of Carpenters' Hall in 1848—then in use as an auction house—may well have led directly to its restoration by the Carpenters' Company nine years later.[15]

On September 25, 1839, Joseph Saxton, following directions from France and using a homemade box camera, took what is believed to be the first American outdoor photograph. A scruffy specimen, though historic, it is a small daguerreotype view from a window in the first U.S. Mint looking toward the high school in Center City. The next year an Englishman, Fox Talbot, invented the calotype or talbotype. This process was brought to Philadelphia in 1849 by William and Frederick Langenheim who introduced it commercially—though not successfully.[16] The "Langenheim Talbotypes" give us some remarkable views of local landmarks, usually circular in shape.[17] Other daguerreotypes followed, and then glass plates. The collections of the 1850's and later are so vast—so far—as to defy all attempts at comprehensive listing. As a record of what meets the eye the camera cannot be beat. But the eye cannot see everything, and the architect and his drawings are still needed.

As the Victorian rage for complicated effects was topping out— and probably in reaction to it—architects became interested for the first time in early American buildings. The Colonial Revival began formally when Richard Upjohn of New York, president of the American Institute of Architects, addressing its third annual convention in 1869, recommended the collection of information on our early buildings and a close study of remaining examples. By 1872, when Charles Follen McKim of New York had restored a colonial room in Newport,[18] the need by draftsmen for details in the old/new style— such as sections of moldings and other ornament—must have been evident.[19]

The centennial celebration at Philadelphia quickened popular interest. *The Historic Mansions and Buildings of Philadelphia* by Thompson Westcott (Philadelphia, 1877) was a product of the times and a prototype for many later works. But it didn't do much for the architectural offices expected to imitate the best features of the eighteenth-century mansions still standing in numbers. *The American Architect and Building News* of Boston took up the challenge. In 1881, it published a piece on "colonial architecture" illustrated with sketches and a few measured floor plans and elevations. Two issues carried the report by George Champlin Mason, Jr., of Newport, Rhode Island, chairman of a committee of the American Institute of Architects, titled "Practice of American Architects and Builders during the Colonial Period and the first Fifty Years of our Independence." The first installment (August 13) referred to origins of style in England, laid out the lines for an American architectural history, reproduced twelve sketches of old Newport houses and some fireplace details. The second part (August 20) carried eight more drawings, a detailed specification from an early contract to build a house. It concluded with a wistful hope that "the little we have done may serve as an incentive for fuller investigation and research, begun and carried on in a systematic and business-like manner."[20]

Books by and for Architects

Two Philadelphia architects produced a book of measured drawings exclusively aimed at drafting rooms: *Old Colonial Architectural*

Details in and around Philadelphia. 50 Plates of Scaled and Measured Drawings, offered to William Helburn's architectural publishing house in New York on October 31, 1890.[21] In it William Davenport Goforth and William J. McAuley presented a collection of "as good specimens . . . of their respective classes as could be found in and around Philadelphia . . . arranged as nearly as possible in Historical order." The plates reproduced competently executed drawings of about twenty buildings—mostly houses—in Philadelphia and Germantown. The shaky identification by names and dates and the scant textual content reflect the undeveloped historiography of the times.[22]

Such studies did not come too soon. The buildings on Independence Square, an early focus of historic sentiment, were about to be restored *again.* Unfortunately, the earlier work there, designed by capable *modern* architects such as William Strickland and John Haviland, was not considered acceptable by later standards of authenticity and most of it was fated to be removed.

Today, early restoration drawings—as elsewhere—are scarce. We have little more than artists' views and photography to explain those pioneer restorations. Perhaps the oldest working drawing surviving is on a single sheet of paper of the period 1895–97 done by George C. Mason. The Newport architect had by that time opened an office in Philadelphia where City Councils invited the various "patriotic hereditary societies" to restore some of the historic rooms on the Square. Mason's drawing proposed certain details including that special Yankee feature—the open, twisted stair newel.[23] Although executed, such work was not at home in Philadelphia and much of it was removed a few years later. Mason may have used the wrong book; perhaps he did not realize that New England details, however attractive they may be, are not always exportable.[24]

The architects in many American cities did not have old Georgian buildings to study first hand, and the importance of scale drawings to the revival of colonial architecture sweeping the country can hardly be exaggerated. The demand for such architecture continues even now, when there are fewer and fewer professionals who can meet it with confidence. It takes extreme skill to produce a good Georgian building—though our leading campus theoreticians (among others) hardly admit that their former students now facing apprenticeship often do not even know what a molding is. The truly competent restorationist today, practicing what might be called the geriatrics of the building business, has become a rare breed indeed.

More books came forth to meet the need. William Rotch Ware's great three-volume work, *The Georgian Period, A Collection of Papers*

Dealing with "Colonial" or XVIII-Century Architecture in the United States, together with References to Earlier Provincial and True Colonial Work, was a collection of photographs, sketches, and measured drawings published in 1901, 1902, and 1908. It illustrates English precedents and carries thoughtful essays on many subjects. Philadelphia is represented by some of its well-known eighteenth-century structures, such as Christ Church, Old Swedes', Carpenters' Hall, Mount Pleasant, and Woodford Mansion, many of which were recorded by that skilled draftsman Charles L. Hillman.[25]

The well-known "White Pine Series of Monographs," begun in 1915 under the direction of Russell F. Whitehead and continued for many volumes, provided measured drawings and photographs distributed from New York to as many as ten thousand addresses. The "Monographs" did not include any Philadelphia buildings,[26] but our city is well represented in twentieth-century publications—as twelve pages in the Roos bibliography attest.[27] *Old Philadelphia Colonial Details* (New York, 1914), by Joseph Patterson Sims and Charles Willing, is a notable example of a book useful to practitioners of the Georgian style. And the photographic picture books of Philip B. Wallace include fine measured drawings by William Allen Dunn and M. Luther Miller.[28]

The reports of the historical committee of the Philadelphia AIA Chapter have not all been located, but the collection they built up included Independence Hall (drawings of 1898, 1918, 1921, 1923), Congress Hall (1901, 1912), the Bartram House on the west bank of the Schuylkill (undated), the Blue Bell Tavern (1916) and Washington's Headquarters at Valley Forge (1931). At least some of this material is in The Historical Society of Pennsylvania.

Local architects had become deeply involved with our early buildings during the early twentieth century. One of the high points was another restoration of Independence Hall, this time under the direction of Horace Wells Sellers in the 1920's. Notably, it was backed up by the architect's extensive historical scholarship. But the great stock market crash of 1929 signaled the end of an era in many fields, including architecture.

The Old Philadelphia Survey

The dank winds of the Great Depression did blow some good. The architectural profession, badly hit all over the world, found measures to relieve its distress by setting up various campaigns for recording historic architecture. Those operating independently in London, New York, Pittsburgh, and Philadelphia were notably successful.[29]

The movement here had begun in the 1920's with Frances A. Wister, President of the Civic Club of Philadelphia and kingpin of "The Old Philadelphia Survey." Miss Wister had firsthand knowledge of the old parts of the city, which she felt could be rehabilitated "in harmony with the traditional architecture of the City." Housing and zoning agencies got interested, but when Miss Wister read in the newspapers of September 17, 1929, that Mayor Mackey was having his *engineers* work on plans for the reconstruction of the district, she realized that the rehabilitation program was in serious trouble. She and others like her began a campaign that led to the harmonious restoration she advocated.

As a part of that early proposal for "urban renewal" it was felt that a systematic collection of historical and architectural data was needed for reference. But an attempt to involve the students at the School of Architecture at the University of Pennsylvania failed and the program was temporarily shelved. Conditions in 1930 nevertheless cried for action. The Philadelphia AIA Chapter set up a temporary committee with D. Knickerbacher Boyd as chairman. A comprehensive survey of what they called "Old City"—the Delaware to Ninth Street and Spring Garden Street to Washington Avenue— was proposed. Mrs. Cyrus H. K. Curtis, widow of the publisher, gave $5,000 and a committee of architects was appointed.[30] The committee met in December, studied old maps and assigned a schedule of field work to twenty-two members of the chapter. Sydney E. Martin succeeded to the chairmanship and by October, 1931, the work as originally projected was substantially completed.[31] Fifty-seven draftsmen produced 407 excellent measured drawings of outstanding structures in the Old City and along the banks of the Schuylkill. Reports covering the whole area were made: 125 photographs had been taken, and architect William M. Campbell, a mapmaker of note and later an important HABS team supervisor, was engaged to compile the results on an attractive map.[32]

A book with a selection of the new drawings, such as New York City had, was planned.[33] Mr. Martin prepared a foreword and Horace Wells Sellers an extended essay, "Philadelphia's Early Architecture and Architects."[34] Although the book never did appear, the original drawings survived and are carefully preserved in the Art Department of the Free Library.[35] And through the Old Philadelphia

Survey the architectural community of Philadelphia was readied for
the Historic American Buildings Survey, which was soon to follow.

The Beginnings of HABS

Washington, D.C., was agog with excitement in 1933. President
Roosevelt, after his inauguration on March 4, immediately began his
dramatic war against the Depression. New Deal agencies, administrators, and idea men rose, spoke, and faded month by month. New
schemes were regularly announced in the press and on the radio.
Some of them were to change the American way of government for
good. Just how much was pure idealism will be debated long into the
future. But there is no question that a real spirit of innovation was in
the air and some profitable experiments were made. On November 9,
the President by executive order established the Civil Works
Administration with Harry L. Hopkins as Administrator. His
mandate was to create four million jobs to help the vast army of
unemployed over the winter. The executive departments were
invited to bring forth programs for those needing work, including
professional people. Speed was essential, and four days later the National Park Service proposed a comprehensive operation calling for
work by architects and architectural draftsmen, titled *The Historic
American Buildings Survey*. Dated November 13, 1933, it proposed the
allocation of $448,000 to employ 1,200 persons under the National
Recovery Act.[36]

The proposal moved along rapidly. On November 17, the
program was approved by Secretary of the Interior Harold Ickes and
on December 1, by Hopkins, with the full backing of the Executive
Committee of the American Institute of Architects.[37] The Advisory
Committee of the Williamsburg Restoration endorsed it, too.[38] A picture story in the *Washington Post* for November 29 predicted that work
would start immediately—and it did, with HABS under the broad authority of the National Recovery Act.

The original work outline proposed to employ the thousand
persons for a period of six months, the time limit then specified for all
such programs. One of the very first steps was to contact Dr.
Leicester B. Holland, Philadelphia scholar and architect then in
Washington. Fortuitously, he was both head of the Fine Arts Depart-
ment of the Library of Congress and Chairman of the AIA's national
Committee on Historic Buildings. Dr. Holland had been active in
Philadelphia's own campaign and he had already initiated a collection

at the Library called "The Pictorial Archives of American Architecture."[39] He was ready to undertake a national project,[40] and at the request of Holland and myself, Edward C. Kemper, the alert and able AIA Executive Secretary, sent out urgent telegrams to the presidents of the chapters across the country asking each to nominate a district officer to direct HABS work in his respective area.

By December 27, E. Perot Bissell of Philadelphia had been appointed District Officer for Eastern Pennsylvania (east of the West Fork of the Susquehanna and the Genessee) and was assigned forty-two men. Philadelphia work began at once in the Germantown area, with care not to repeat the drawings made by the Old Philadelphia Survey. Among the first buildings tackled were "Wister's Big House"—now called Grumblethorpe—Vernon, Wyck, Germantown Academy, and the Blair House, all along Germantown Avenue or north of the Old City.[41]

The Survey Made Permanent

On January 8 and 9, 1934, the first meeting of the National Advisory Committee was held in Washington. It was a distinguished group, the majority architects, and the first committee of historical advisors ever assembled by the Park Service. Many problems of policy and technique encountered by the new Survey were discussed. The report reveals many issues of the moment, some of bureaucratic nature, rather than professional.[42] Drafting-room techniques were reviewed. The standard paper selected for final record drawings was of a 40-pound weight and 100% rag content—considered the most permanent drawing base available—and a uniform sheet size was established.[43]

Each district was encouraged to assemble its own advisory committee. The budget for photography was small. While the drawings would be government property, they were in the public domain and therefore available at the Library of Congress for consultation and copying. Some doubt was expressed by the committee that architects could make measured records of prehistoric remains without help from archaeologists.

Apprehension that the program might have to terminate as early as February 15 motivated a recommendation that field men make up lists of important buildings remaining to be documented. The sessions closed with a recommendation to the Secretary of the Interior for a "reasonable extension and enlargement of the present program."[44] The life expectancy of the Survey was precarious indeed. On February 13, the staff was advised of the imminent end of the project, but working with inspired desperation, the men in the field matched wits with local administrators, and HABS somehow came through.[45]

At the peak of employment 772 men were at work but no more than $196,267.63 had been spent. Telegrams from concerned architects and preservationists urged that the Survey be continued under the authority of the states using federal funds.[46] An exhibition of the new records from the entire nation was promptly assembled and hung at the National Museum in Washington from April 5 to 26. Panels displayed drawings supplemented by photographs, texts, and maps. Instructions to the field had advised that "this will be a public exhibition. Although it is naturally assumed that its greatest appeal will be to architects and historians, a distinct effort will be made to give also a strong popular appeal."[47] It was a success.

A nationwide total of 880 buildings represented by over five thousand ink-on-paper drawings of good quality and three thousand photographs had been made—all in four months. Index cards for two thousand subjects showed that much more work was in prospect. The pay for the field work was only $39.60 per 32-hour week, but the program had made a hit—men were working at something they could like and value.[48]

By July 23, a consensus national in scope between the National Park Service,[49] the American Institute of Architects, and the Library of Congress was reached. Known as "The Tripartite Agreement," it survives today with only modest changes, as the cooperative base on which HABS rests.[50]

It has not been possible to trace in detail Philadelphia operations under Joseph P. Sims, who had been active in the Old Philadelphia Survey and succeeded Mr. Bissell in 1935 as District Officer. The 1938 *Catalog* of HABS measured drawings in the Library of Congress lists substantial contributions such as those for Trinity Church, Oxford (6 sheets), Old Swedes' Church (10 sheets) and the Cove Cornice House at the foot of Spruce Street. Other structures, such as those in Workman Place (Southwark), in Fort Mifflin, and nearby Cannonball Farm, were represented by only a few photographs.

A comprehensive report by staff architect Waterman dated May 19, 1937, showed that in the whole state of Pennsylvania 156 buildings had already been measured (total, 1034 sheets of drawings) and 151 photographed (616 negatives).[51] Waterman was particularly pleased that the eighteenth-century mansions Port Royal and Chalkley Hall in the Frankford area of Philadelphia could be recorded at that time. He pointed out that, although they had been abandoned and their fine woodwork stripped, it was possible to locate the missing parts and reassemble them on paper for HABS.[52]

The National Parks Come East

The presence of National Park Service architects in the east was a new development. Until 1930, the bureau had been almost exclusively a western outfit with its professional branches centered in field headquarters in San Francisco. But in that year, as the result of much promotion, two new projects emerged in Virginia: the George Washington Birthplace and the Colonial National Monument (the latter at Jamestown-Williamsburg-Yorktown).[53] A minimal staff of landscape architects, architects, and engineers was set up to plan and supervise. But that staff was vastly augmented from 1933 on by temporary appointees engaged to direct New Deal ventures, such as the great Civilian Conservation Corps program. And under the Roosevelt reorganization the War Department gave up its historic battlefield parks, adding new responsibilities from Maine to Louisiana. All this came about while the three scenic national parks—the Great Smoky Mountains, the Shenandoah, and the Mammoth Cave—were coming into official existence.

Many historic sites and buildings were involved. Where architectural study was required, HABS records were made early in the process. In each case structures were measured and drawn preparatory to making new plans: for example, at Morristown, New Jersey, in 1934–35, the Tempe Wick House in Jockey Hollow (13 sheets of drawings), the Guerin House (9 sheets), and the Ford Mansion (called "Washington's Headquarters," 26 sheets). In quite another field, the extensive seventeenth-century remains being excavated at Jamestown Island, Virginia, were recorded in detail. Another archaeological project undertaken by the CCC was digging the foundations of Mannsfield, a great plantation house on the Rappahannock River below Fredericksburg that had burned in the Civil War.

One of the most intensive architectural studies of all was undertaken at St. Louis, beginning in 1936. Incidental to it, the local HABS collection was extended by a great addition of records made in the old riverfront area on the Levee.[54] Many of the interesting old structures on those eighty acres were soon to be removed as de-

manded by the local sponsors who wanted to create a "City Beautiful" development, vintage 1900, on the site.[55]

The Independence National Park

The first Philadelphia restoration project of the federal government, in what was to become Independence Park, was the rehabilitation of the old Custom House (now called the Second Bank of the
United States) on Chestnut Street. Abandoned by the Treasury Department, it was transferred in order to save it. The Carl Schurz
Foundation agreed to occupy the building and provided most of the
cash needed. Park Service architects working out of the Washington
office drew the plans and, as a matter of course, first prepared a fine
set of nineteen drawings of existing conditions for—and deposited in
1939 with—HABS, along with thirty-five record photographs.

A dozen years (and one war) later, the Park Service set up in
Philadelphia a project office to acquire the land necessary to create the
great Independence Park.[56] An intensive study of the existing buildings in the area was undertaken and measured drawings were begun
in order to analyze the condition and needs of those that could be
proven "historic." The postwar prosperity of 1951 kept architects
generally busy, so the office expediently employed gifted young
draftsmen, whose first efforts produced conspicuously valuable
results.[57] When it was discovered that the U.S. Army Engineers had
been authorized to hire undergraduate professional students during
their summer academic recess, the HABS Philadelphia office decided
to invoke the same privilege.[58] Accordingly, in the summer of 1952
teams of architectural students were organized to make detailed scale
drawings, systematically, building by building, on the new lands being acquired. Supervisors were selected on the basis of their personal
interest in American buildings as well as their ability to lead. Students
were individually recruited for their drafting ability and/or their tenta-
tive interest in history, and they were deliberately chosen from
among different schools. Gradually, HABS won the confidence of architectural faculties, who recommended their best students to
compete for its jobs.

While both quality and quantity of draftsmanship was exacted,
the careful study of each fabric was emphasized. The difference
between surviving original features and later modifications was to be
observed and reflected in the drawn record. Lecturers on
Philadelphia architectural history were brought in to give depth to the
summer's experience and, when actual restoration work was started,

the students had the chance to become acquainted with building mechanics and their work.

Through the summer of 1962, and later, valuable files of analytical drawings were built up for the use of the architectural planners at a minimum cost. Best of all, young architects had developed a fund of experience.[59]

In 1954, the Park Service opened a new professional office to handle planning and construction work in Philadelphia for the eastern half of the United States. This consortium of architects, landscape architects, and engineers was called the Eastern Office of Design and Construction (EODC). The architects from the Independence Park staff were assimilated and their geographic responsibilities greatly increased. HABS was then exported to other National Park areas where restoration work was programmed. In the summer of 1955, for instance, a team was placed at the Adams Mansion, Quincy, Massachusetts, a complex more than two centuries old that had been recently given to the nation. Another was set up at Harpers Ferry, West Virginia, a picturesque industrial village on the Potomac. The historical project sent architectural teams to make the basic drawings on which plans for restoration would be based. A team was placed at Greenville, Tennessee (1957), where the home of President Andrew Johnson was to be restored, another at Appomattox Courthouse, where General Robert E. Lee surrendered, and one at Gettysburg Battlefield (1957), which still had farmhouses surviving the great Civil War battle. Their work in accumulating the necessary records was financed by the Interior Department's annual construction appropriation as a preliminary step toward plans for preservation. Measured drawings of government-owned buildings continued to be made with an eye, whenever suitable, for deposit in HABS.[60]

In 1957, HABS was suddenly catapulted to a new level of responsibility by the on-coming program known as "Mission 66," which required that the architectural stock of the country as a whole be reviewed.

Mission 66

"Mission 66" was a promotional package to obtain funds for bringing the National Parks, neglected during the years of World War II, up to physical standards by 1966, the fiftieth anniversary of the Park Service. Congress appropriated annual funds for a vast ten-year program.

The Historic Sites and Buildings Act of 1935 had granted

permanent authority to HABS to make records of historic architecture—either in or out of federal ownership—but no financing had been provided. In the Mission 66 appropriation HABS was now allocated $200,000, a staggering sum considering that no personnel were on hand for such an enterprise. All the new money was to be spent in one fiscal year by the Philadelphia office, the only one with relevant experience. While there had always been a certain amount of loose talk (not shared by this writer) about "finishing" HABS, that is, completing drawings, photographs, and write-ups for *all* historic buildings in the whole country, nobody seemed to know how many such buildings there were.

In the emergency, Agnes Addison Gilchrist, an experienced architectural historian, was brought from New York to help the writer analyze the situation. On a large blank county map of the United States the statistics for HABS work already done were compiled, state by state.[61] Large areas across the country still had no records at all, but none of them was entirely without "historic" buildings. No fixed and accepted standards of judgment, probably wisely, had ever been established. And a quarter-century had increased the published knowledge of American places and the spectrum of architectural appreciation.[62] The Survey in 1957 could not be reactivated on its original basis of unemployment relief. So the successful annual summer student program at Philadelphia was emulated on a large scale.

Because it seemed then (as it does now) that to prepare detailed, elaborate drawings for *all* historic buildings in the United States worth attention would be impossible, it was decided to develop a wide coverage by photography and to emphasize quality so that the pictures could be used by writers and editors for publication. Each picture published can do as much good as hundreds that merely exist in archives. The problem was to get good negatives at a reasonable cost. Well-known lensmen like Fritz Henle and Cervin Robinson of New York and Cortlandt Van Dyke Hubbard of Philadelphia were induced to undertake sample projects at modest rates. Jack E. Boucher, then of Pleasantville, New Jersey, became the in-house architectural photographer. A large photographic project under outside contract was arranged for Providence, Rhode Island, where the redevelopment of College Hill was in prospect. Another New England project was inspired by the threatened abandonment of a branch of the Boston & Albany Railroad with a fine series of H. H. Richardson stations. The so-called "photo-data book" concept was developed, in which a selected community having a group of interesting buildings would provide the historical data and the government would arrange for photography.

One way of estimating the work needed to "complete" HABS was to consider one county at a time and multiply the number of counties by the estimated number of historic buildings in each. For a sample, we chose nearby Chester County, Pennsylvania, where the county's historical society had built up a splendid file on local building history. The society and HABS selected one hundred buildings of varied type and period, for which the former wrote up the historic data, and HABS engaged a photographer, Ned Goode of Frazer. Cooperation was excellent, and the project concluded with an exhibition of salon prints and a celebratory dinner at West Chester.

Of course, Chester County had more than a hundred buildings worth recording, whereas a county in the west would probably have many less. But the arbitrary figure of one hundred each for all three thousand American counties produced a tremendous total of three million buildings. Because no one could recommend recording on such a scale the idea of "finishing HABS" was quietly dropped. Instead the term "open-end archive" was adopted.[63]

Society Hill and Other Places

During the 1950's, urban renewal was getting under way on Society Hill, where a large number of buildings was scheduled to come down in line with city planning. Many good ones did. HABS was able to make last-minute records before some disappeared; other buildings probably survived as a result of the attentions of the Survey. HABS under James O'Gorman made drawings of the great Neave and Abercrombie houses (both from 1759) on Second Street after they had been emptied through urban renewal and while the original woodwork was nightly being stolen.[64] In another case HABS junior architect John Milner was dispatched to record a small but choice eighteenth-century house on Delancey Street that had retained much good woodwork. The new owner, his architect, and his builder were inexperienced but willing to learn, so that the active presence of HABS saved a great deal of the original fabric that might otherwise not have been kept in place.

As the idea got around that an HABS record in the Library of Congress was a real distinction, we were called to many places besides Philadelphia to confer that form of immortality. Many owners were surprised to learn that the Secretary of the Interior and the Library of Congress found their houses to be of significance, but the little certificate conferred generated a new pride by both owners and occupants.

We found that cooperative projects could be set up with the local people footing part of the bill, especially for historic research. In the summer of 1959 we mounted three projects in the middle Connecticut Valley. In a sort of barter process Dartmouth College agreed to provide a drafting room, inexpensive summer housing for the team in a faculty house, and other considerations. The team measured a selection of buildings on campus and in the nearby countryside on both sides of the river. Professor Frank J. Roos of the University of Illinois prepared data for buildings around Bellows Falls later recorded by our photographer. And lower down in the Valley a team was operating in Old Deerfield under the direction of Professor Harley J. McKee of Syracuse University.

Two notable New England projects were those on Cape Cod in 1959 and 1962 where studies and records were made under Ernest A. Connally's direction while the acquisition of lands for the National Seashore project was just beginning. The anxiety of the local people (who feared that a federal agency from out of the Wild West would thoughtlessly destroy all the old houses they had treasured) was much alleviated. Another attractive scene of operations was the American Virgin Islands, where eighteenth- and nineteenth-century Danish architecture had made a picturesque compromise with tropical needs and practices. The Royal Academy of Fine Arts of Copenhagen was sending an architectural expedition to survey the scene (with Rockefeller assistance) and we were able to field an American team of students to work alongside them.

New Techniques

During this activity, the original field handbook, "Specifications for . . . Measurement and Recording"—hurriedly mimeographed in December, 1933, and added to and revised in bits up until July, 1958—was re-examined and found wanting. The original criteria for selecting buildings had become somewhat dated and field techniques had been more highly developed. Professor McKee was brought in to Philadelphia for the summers of 1960–62 to work on a new manual.

Various aspects of the recording process were written up individually and issued in parts for testing in the field. For instance, very few people, even architects, can describe a building systematically, succinctly, and thoroughly. For that purpose a form called the "Architect's Work Sheet" was devised as well as "Historian's Work Sheet," handy checklists of the many parts that make up even the simplest building. The *Manual*—generously illustrated with samples of drawings and photographs—was completed by 1962.[65]

At the same time, experiments were made in photographing existing architectural drawings onto plastic sheets which could thus be built into HABS like new drawings. The Philadelphia Blueprint Company showed that duPont's "Cronar"—believed to be of archival permanence—was suited to this purpose and that technique of adding valuable material drawn by others became standard procedure.

We were proud to have a part in introducing architectural photogrammetry to the recording of historic American buildings in 1957. Photogrammetry makes possible quite accurate scale drawings of details impossible to reach without architectural steeplejacks or extensive scaffolding. The highly specialized technique was originally brought here by Perry E. Borchers of the School of Architecture at Ohio State University, who had studied it in Europe.[66]

Our first order to his department was for sixteen drawings of a tavern in Lancaster, Ohio, the Congregational Church in Oberlin, and the facade of Isaac M. Wise (Plum Street) Temple in Cincinnati. Professor Borchers's recording of the lofty oriental minarets of the temple was a spectacular contribution to HABS that would have been impossible to produce by any other technique.[67] Also included were sixty-four "stereopairs," or photographic records on glass to include other buildings.[68] The expensive equipment of Ohio State's Engineering Experiment Station was rented and used by Mr. Borchers's architectural students.[69] This pilot project was a decided success and led to another contract the following year. In 1959, the Ohio team made stereopairs of the great row of banks at 407–431 Chestnut Street, Philadelphia, opposite the Independence Park.[70] It was done by good fortune shortly before Frank Furness's great Provident National Bank (No. 407) was demolished.

In the summer of 1962, when this chronicle ends, faculty and students from twenty-three architectural schools across the country were working on HABS teams under the direction of the Philadelphia central office. A small but growing body of young architects had earned their stripes in this unique opportunity to acquire a healthy respect for native design and construction. And the value of the Survey's work—both in the treatment of buildings nationally owned and to the preservation community as a whole—had been demonstrated. At the end of that summer, an all-day "Carpenters' Carnival" was staged when the Building Restoration Specialists of the Independence Park gave an outdoor exhibition with the men at work. By invitation people came from all over the east to see it. [71]

Architect James C. Massey, who first worked at the Independence Park as a student, took over HABS in the east, assisted by historian John Poppeliers. In 1966, when EODC was closed down, Mr. Massey moved to Washington to direct the whole national program, continuing HABS with notable energy and imagination until 1972.

Charles E. Peterson, F.A.I.A.
Philadelphia, Pennsylvania

Notes

1. The leading figures from the beginning, most of whom I have known, have been interesting people. Among the first generation was Leicester B. Holland of Philadelphia, classical archaeologist, teacher, and inventor as well as architect. William Graves Perry and Frank Chouteau Brown were from Boston. Perry, the architectural genius of the Williamsburg Restoration, was the first chairman of the HABS Advisory Committee. Brown, a well-known master draftsman, though dying of cancer, produced sheet after sheet of fine drawings—as long as he could hang on to his drafting board. Charles Morse Stotz of Pittsburgh, after completing his outstanding Western Pennsylvania Architectural Survey, was invited to join us. Albert Simons of Charleston, well established as an authority in South Carolina, put his shoulder to the wheel. Richard Koch of New Orleans—practically indestructable, it seemed—built up his post of operations on the lower Mississippi. Earl H. Reed of Chicago was to become a national figure in the Preservation movement. And then there was that squad of Denver architects who went into the desert to join John Gaw Meem of Santa Fe and make pioneer records of the Indian pueblos. Through all the years from 1933 until he left Washington in 1961, Thomas C. Vint, though basically a landscape architect, was a tireless and effective proponent of HABS.

2. It is hoped that the notes in this brief history will encourage others to develop the story more fully. This sketch relates chiefly to the period before October, 1962, when I left the Park Service. I am indebted to Dr. Margaret B. Tinkcom for suggestions.

3. It was probably a cabin of horizontal logs, a type introduced to the Delaware Valley by the Swedes. Kalm called it "a wretched old wooden building . . . preserved on purpose as a memorial to the poor condition of the place before the town was built on it. . . . Its antiquity gives it a kind of superiority over all the other buildings. . . . But . . . [it] is ready to fall down" (Adolph B. Benson, ed., *Peter Kalm's Travels in North America*, New York, 1966, pp. 33–34).

4. Published in 1752, see Nicholas B. Wainwright, "Scull and Heap's East Prospect of Philadelphia," *PMHB*, 73 (Jan., 1949), 16–25. Engraved by Gerard Vandergucht of London. The crude delineations in the much-reproduced Peter Cooper painting "ca 1720" at the Library Company of Philadelphia can hardly be regarded as reliable architectural portraits.

5. Five valuable books of old Philadelphia views available today are Theodore B. White, ed., *Philadelphia in the Nineteenth Century*, Philadelphia, 1953 and 1973; Nicholas B. Wainwright, *Philadelphia in the Romantic Age of Lithography*, Philadelphia, 1958; George B. Tatum, *Penn's Great Town*, Philadelphia, 1961; Martin P. Snyder, *City of Independence*, New York, 1975; Edwin Wolf 2nd, *Philadelphia, Portrait of an American City*, Harrisburg, Pa., 1975.

6. The first American building to bring Europeans across the Atlantic was the Walnut Street Jail by Robert Smith. But the eighteenth-century interest in that remarkable pre-Revolutionary fireproof building was for its experiments in penology rather than its design or construction.

7. Designed by an unidentified London architect (Robert C. Alberts, *The Golden Voyage, the Life and Times of William Bingham*, Boston, 1969, pp. 157–63).

8. Benezet was a well-known Quaker philanthropist who had died years before. The house, according to the article, was built by David Breitnall and was later rented to the Governor of Bermuda. It stood on the right bank of Dock Creek and directly between Benjamin Franklin's mansion and Carpenters' Hall.

9. Martin P. Snyder, "William L. Breton, Nineteenth-Century Philadelphia Artist", *PMHB*, LXXXV, 2. At the same time C. G. Childs, Philadelphia engraver, published a collection called *Views in Philadelphia from Original Drawings Taken in 1827–30* by several artists. But in their own time they were not historical subjects.

10. See Deborah Dependahl Waters, "Philadelphia's Boswell: John Fanning Watson," *PMHB*, XCVIII (Jan., 1974), 38–41. The project proved to be fifty years ahead of its time, but the building was suffered to remain and was eventually moved to Fairmount Park in honor of the City's 200th anniversary.

11. Watson's project was described in *The Casket:* "This once venerable building, long divested of its original honours . . . had long been regarded by us and others, as a rude and *undistinguished* edifice: But our feelings and sympathies in its favour, have been strongly awakened by seeing its former renown and even greatness depicted in a lively manner in the MS. "Annals of Philadelphia", by J. F. Watson, Esq. at some future day to be published with pictorial embellishments, when we venture to pronounce, that our cotemporaries [*sic*] will be surprised, amused and charmed with the hidden facts reserved for his amusement and gratification. . . ."

12. John F. Watson, *Annals of Philadelphia*, Philadelphia, 1830, p. 147, first of several well-thumbed editions. Somewhere in this period B. R. Evans began his colorful series of watercolors of Philadelphia street views of which some three hundred survive for the period 1830–1879. And from David Kennedy, even more prolific, we have about nine hundred watercolors from the years 1838–1873.

13. Published here, courtesy Thomas Wistar, Jr., The Wyck Charitable Trust, and the Athenaeum of Philadelphia.

14. *The History of Architecture from the Earliest Times*, Philadelphia, 1848, said to be the first American architectural history. Illustrated with competent perspectives were Girard College, the mansions of James Dundas and Mathew Newkirk (all by Thomas U. Walter), the Athenaeum (John Notman), Monument Cemetery Chapel, and the Bank of North America. Mrs. Tuthill had the use of Ithiel Town's library at New Haven (Agnes Addison Gilchrist in *Notable American Women 1607–1950*, Cambridge, Mass., 1971, pp. 487–88).

15. Benson J. Lossing, *The Pictorial Field Book of the Revolution*, New York, 1851, Vol. II, pp. 521–23. Lossing reproduced two views of the Hall. His interior is the oldest known. On its restoration, see Charles E. Peterson, "Carpenters' Hall," *Transactions*

American Philosophical Society, Vol. 43, Part I, pp. 113, 114. No drawings have been found for that operation.

16. Beaumont Newhall, *The History of Photography,* New York, 1964, pp. 20, 31–44.

17. Charles van Ravenswaay, then Director of the Missouri Historical Society, St. Louis, kindly loaned us in 1951 an album of Langenheim paper prints and permitted us to photocopy them. They turned out to be the oldest known sets of photographs of Philadelphia, Washington, and Mount Vernon.

18. For a chronology see Charles E. Peterson, *Antiques Magazine,* February, 1966, pp. 229–32.

19. That such work could be well done up that way is illustrated by the excellent record drawings by John H. Sturges of the Hancock House on Beacon Hill, Boston, just before it was torn down in 1863. These were not published until November, 1926, in *Architecture,* pp. 333–36.

20. In the *AABN* issue for August 27 (p. 102), A. J. Bloor of New York claimed credit for proposing the committee at the Thirteenth AIA convention. Bloor was a national secretary of the AIA and a founding member of the Metropolitan Museum of Art.

21. The book is now scarce and its compilers little known. Goforth appears in Gopsill's Philadelphia directories for 1891–97 as an architect-partner of Albert E. Yarnell at 14 South Broad. He is listed as living in Jenkintown but disappears by 1900. McAuley appears in 1889 as a draughtsman at 3711 Powelton, in 1895 as an architect but is not listed after 1896.

22. The "Thomas House at Angora, Pa." turned out (after some detective work) to be Whitby Hall on Cobb's Creek near Kingsessing. In this century the building was taken apart and two paneled rooms and the main stairway sent to the Detroit Institute of Arts, some parts to Haverford, Pennsylvania, and the rest to the dump.

23. Mason's report on this work appeared in *The American Historical Register* (issue not located).

24. For an evaluation of Mason's work as an architect and restorationist in Newport, see Antoinette F. Downing and Vincent J. Scully, *The Architectural Heritage of Newport, Rhode Island,* 2d ed., New York, 1967, p. 5. Not to be outdone, T. Mellon Rogers, for the Daughters of the American Revolution, went ahead and installed some woodwork in Independence Hall reminiscent of early McKim, Mead and White "Colonial," but it, too, was removed soon afterward. For the story of recent architects' work at Independence Hall, see Lee H. Nelson and Penelope Hartshorne Batcheler in *Building Early America,* Radnor, Pa., 1976, pp. 277–318.

25. Issued serially, those dates according with the title pages in this writer's set. The Hillman drawings exist, at least in part, at the Free Library of Philadelphia.

26. This seems surprising now—in view of the fact that Whitehead was a native of Trenton and studied at Drexel Institute. See Charles Magruder, "The White Pine Monograph Series," *Journal of the Society of Architectural Historians,* XXII (March, 1963), 39–41.

27. Frank J. Roos, *Bibliography of Early American Architecture,* 2d ed., Urbana, 1968, pp. 179–90.

28. Dunn, in *Colonial Ironwork in Old Philadelphia,* New York, 1930; Miller, in *Colonial Houses, Pre-Revolutionary Period,* New York, 1931.

29. "The Work of the R.I.B.A. Unemployment Committee," *Journal of the Royal Institute of British Architects,* June 23, 1934. In the background were the Society for Photographing Relics of Old London (1875) and the London Survey Committee (1893).

Hermione Hobhouse, *Lost London*, New York, 1971, p. 7. For New York, see note 33. For Pittsburgh, see Charles Morse Stotz, *The Early Architecture of Western Pennsylvania. A Record of Buildings before 1860 Based upon the Western Pennsylvania Architectural Survey a Project of The Pittsburgh Chapter of the American Institute of Architects . . .,* New York, 1936, pp. 280–83.

30. Half of the Curtis fund was allocated for the purpose, and $13,500 was raised by the Chapter's Unemployment Committee. Members were Walter H. Thomas, H. Louis Duhring, Leicester B. Holland, Horace Wells Sellers, Franklin D. Edmunds, and Charles S. Hillman.

31. "Mr. Martin organized and conducted all of the work of the Chapter that has been done along these lines in the last two years" (C. C. Zantzinger to L. B. Holland, November 28, 1933, Library of Congress [MS], Prints & Photographs file).

32. Copies were sold to benefit the program; the map is still in print.

33. The New York "Architects' Emergency Committee" published two handsome volumes of measured drawings and photographs of buildings scattered from Maine to Louisiana in 1933 and 1937. Though they were titled *Great Georgian Houses of America*, the examples extended into the Greek Revival period. The books have recently been re-published by Dover.

34. He also wrote an unpublished history of the Survey which is the basis of this account. A copy is in my possession.

35. They have just been photocopied under the direction of Miriam L. Lesley, head of the Art Department, where prints may be ordered.

36. The original longhand draft is still in my possession. It had the old-fashioned title "The Relief Employment Under the Civil Works Administration of a Substantial Number of the Architectural Profession in a Program Recording Interesting and Significant Specimens of American Architecture." It is published in full in "American Notes," *Journal of the Society of Architectural Historians*, XVI (Oct., 1957), 29–31. Although the word "Survey" was loosely used for promotional reasons, as surveys were popular at the time, the index cards used from the beginning did perform a true survey function. But they can be consulted only at the Library of Congress and few people know about them.

37. AIA Document No. 259, p. 7. Special meeting, Nov. 18–21, 1933.

38. The telegram, signed by perhaps the most distinguished group of American restorationists that ever met, seems well worth reproducing in full:

WESTERN UNION
STRAIGHT MESSAGE
CHG.PSH, WMSBG.

                                                           WILLIAMSBURG, VIRGINIA
                                                           NOVEMBER 16, 1933

CHARLES E. PETERSON
3065 NAVY BUILDING
WASHINGTON, D.C.

RESOLVED THAT THE UNDERSIGNED COMMA MEMBERS OF THE ADVISORY COMMITTEE OF ARCHITECTS FOR AND OTHERS ASSOCIATED WITH THE RESTORATION OF WILLIAMSBURG VIR-GINIA COMMA HAVING RECEIVED THE PLAN OF MAKING A NATIONAL SURVEY AND RECORD OF EXISTING BUILDINGS AND OTHER STRUCTURES WORTHY OF PRESERVATION COMMA EITHER PHYSICALLY OR BY SUITABLE RECORD COMMA HEREBY EXPRESS APPROVAL OF THE

PROJECT STOP THE PLAN AS DETAILED IMPRESSES US AS AN ADMIRABLE METHOD OF AC-
COMPLISHING A WORK OF HISTORIC IMPORTANCE STOP

SIGNED: [ROBERT P.] BELLOWS, [EDMUND S.] CAMP-
BELL, DR. [W.A.R.] GOODWIN, [ANDREW H.]
HEPBURN, [A. LAWRENCE] KOCHER, [W.
DUNCAN] LEE, MRS. [SUSAN HIGGINSON]
NASH, [WILLIAM G.] PERRY, [THOMAS MOTT]
SHAW, [ARTHUR A.] SHURCLIFF, [HAROLD R.]
SHURTLEFF, [PHILIP N.] STERN, [THOMAS E.]
TALLMADGE, [R.E. LEE] TAYLOR, [D. EVERETT]
WAID, [MARCELLUS E.] WRIGHT.

39. *American Institute of Architects Journal of Proceedings,* 1930, pp. 130–31. *The
Octagon,* June, 1930, pp. 7–8. That collection, though of considerable size, remains obscure and it's still hard to find out what's in it.

40. In *The Octagon, A Journal of the AIA,* for February, 1933 (Vol. 5, No. 2), pp. 15,
16, Dr. Holland called for nominations for a national list of historic buildings—with
what success has not been determined.

41. For a complete list, see John P. O'Neill, comp. and ed., *Historic American Buildings Survey Catalog* . . ., January 1, 1938, Washington, GPO, n.d., pp. 186–87.

42. For instance, rulings handed down from the Civil Works Administration first
declared HABS personnel as "skilled workers instead of technicians." However, when
such persons could not be found locally they could be imported from other places, in
which case they would be classified as "technical or supervisory employees."

43. Dr. Holland explained the format adopted: "There are three reasons for using
these small size drawing sheets: (1) It is possible to take it on the ground for field work.
(2) It can be bound up in albums for consultations at the Library of Congress. (3) When
it is reduced to one half it makes a page which is about standard for architectural books
at the present time." The idea of publishing the drawings was to keep coming up again
and again for years. At one point there was word that Dr. Nicholas Murray Butler of
Columbia had asked Secretary Ickes if the Survey could be published in toto and for
how much. The answer came, as I remember it, to a couple of million dollars, which
sum ended the discussion.

44. A copy of the report of the proceedings was distributed as "HABS Bulletin No.
20" dated February 8, 1934, and is found in a collection of circular letters for the years
1933–1938 kept by the late Earl H. Reed (xerox in HABS office, Washington).

45. An "informal communication" by Thomas C. Vint, Chief Architect, to the district officers on February 19 gives a good idea of the hectic atmosphere within the
federal establishment. Herewith an excerpt: "The status of the Survey was completely
changed almost hourly. Instructions wired to District Officers on February 15, were the
result of a ruling by the Federal Civil Works Administrator's office that the HABS
would be classed as a Statistical Project and was therefore to operate after February 15,
without having personnel reduced. On the night of February 15, that ruling was re-
scinded by the Federal Civil Works Administration, and the HABS was immediately
placed under the classification of a Federal Project operating upon Public Property. According to this classification the HABS was to accept an immediate reduction in personnel of approximately 50% of present work force and to continue operations for ten
weeks following February 15, reducing the total personnel 10% each week. As a result
of further negotiations with the Supervisors of other National Parks Projects the National Headquarters of the HABS was enabled to alleviate this drastic reduction of 50%

by the addition of more than two hundred persons to the reduced rolls of the Survey."

46. The same district officers were continued, and still under the direction of Washington.

47. HABS Bulletin No. 22, March 5, 1934. *Journal of the American Institute of Architects*, April, 1934, pp. 15, 16.

48. The ingenuity and skill of the staff in Washington was provided by three young architects: Thomas T. Waterman of Virginia, a veteran of the early days of Williamsburg; John P. O'Neill, a graduate of Notre Dame with some experience in archaeology; and Dudley C. Bayliss of Minnesota.

49. On March 2, 1934, Congress changed the name of the bureau back to the original "National Park Service," much to everyone's gratitude.

50. The "Memorandum of Agreement" was published in a 15-page "Circular of Information" by the U.S. Department of the Interior (U.S. Government Printing Office, Washington, 1936).

51. Washington National Archives, Record Group No. 64, WPA, Division of Information, Primary File A 36–42—785, HABS (typescript).

52. Both houses were demolished but Chalkley Hall not before 1950. Mr. Waterman was then working for Henry Francis du Pont at Winterthur where some of the Port Royal woodwork ended up. Waterman was able to use a lot of his HABS studies in *The Dwellings of Colonial America*, (Chapel Hill, 1950).

In 1941, early in World War II when we were both in the Navy Department, Waterman would bring out of hiding in his drafting table the illustrations for *Mansions of Virginia* (Chapel Hill, 1946) then in preparation.

53. For some of the earliest ventures of the National Park Service in the field of history, see Horace M. Albright, "Origins of National Park Service Administration of Historic Sites" (a pamphlet), Eastern National Park & Monument Association, Philadelphia, 1971.

54. For instance, before the Old Courthouse was restored we extended the original set of 17 HABS drawings to over one hundred. The area was then being developed as the Jefferson National Expansion Memorial. HABS documented many interesting structures now gone, including the Old Rock House or Manuel Lisa Warehouse, the oldest building in St. Louis that was demolished *after* it was completely restored.

55. A progress report of that period is Charles E. Peterson, "Our National Archives of Historic Architecture," *The Octagon*, July, 1936.

56. A land purchasing office was opened late in 1949; I reported as Resident Architect soon afterward.

57. David Krumbhaar of the University of Pennsylvania and Richard E. Pryor, graduate of the University of Miami (Ohio), recommended by Dr. Holland, were the first.

58. I recently noted that the fine drawings in Part VII (1900) of Ware's *Georgian Period* were made by "Sundry Pupils of the Architectural Department of the M.I.T. during the Summer Schools of 1894–95."

59. A report on this subject is Ernest A. Connally, "Preserving the American Tradition," *Journal of the American Institute of Architects*, May, 1961.

60. At the same time, the work of summer teams was being brought to National Park areas such as Fort McHenry, Baltimore (1958), Christiansted, St. Croix (1959), and the Minute Man park, Lexington to Concord (1961), among others.

61. Four special field offices complete with station wagons and travel money had been active in 1940–41.

62. Even the Greek Revival was hardly well established as a subject. When HABS began, the only volume on the subject was Howard Major, *Domestic Architecture in the Early American Republic,* Philadelphia, 1926.

63. In a somewhat parallel project Robert L. Raley of Wilmington, Delaware worked on a complete sweep of buildings in neighboring Mill Creek Hundred. He used the new Historic American Buildings Survey Inventory forms but the project was never completed and HABSI (familiarly called "Habsy") eventually fizzled out as a national program.

HABSI was formed in answer to the challenge of Frederick L. Rath of the National Trust who was then proposing to start a new national survey of his own. He needed a wider coverage than could be afforded by HABS. For quite a period large numbers of people used to meet in Washington and haggle over the mechanics of the proposed operation. It finally got started and Earl Reed of Chicago became its chief salesman. But although extensive work was done in a few areas, the records were hard to handle, were seldom looked at in the Library and the program eventually expired.

64. At the time I lived in the area and was serving on the Philadelphia Historical Commission, on the board of The Landmarks Society, and on the boards of the two successive neighborhood associations during this traumatic period. Fifty-nine certified historic houses came down within two blocks of my house.

65. It was subsequently published in letterpress under the title *Recording Historic Buildings,* Harley J. McKee, comp., by the Washington office in 1970. Available from the Superintendent of Documents, U.S. Government Printing Office, Washington, D.C. 20402—I 29.2H62/12, $6.50.

66. The procedure is very complicated though Prof. Borchers won't admit it. The more he explains, the more obscure it becomes. See *JSAH,* XVI (Dec., 1957), 29.

67. Illustrated in "American Notes", *JSAH,* XVII (May, 1958), 27 as "Photogrammetry, the Magic Scaffold."

68. From such pairs the architectural drawings are made. It is thus possible to make emergency records on glass which can be transposed to drawings at any time later.

69. The first contract amounted to $6,824.00 and included a report on the cost and practicability of such work.

70. The value of the new technique was by then well demonstrated, and we helped the group obtain the commission to record Trinity Church and St. Paul's Chapel in Manhattan. The latest (1976) is a series of record drawings of Indian pueblos in the Southwest—huge complexes on many levels and with few, if any, right angles, a draftsman's nightmare by conventional methods of measurement.

71. A report issued in that period is Charles E. Peterson, "Thirty Years of HABS," *Journal of the American Institute of Architects,* November, 1963.

Preface to the Revised Edition

When the first printing of *Philadelphia Preserved* appeared five years ago, many hoped that the enthusiasm for the nation's bicentennial would yield a golden age for historic preservation in the city of the country's founding. Unfortunately that did not occur. Although many eighteenth-century relics have benefited from their often remote association with the founding fathers, nineteenth-century buildings have not been as uniformly fortunate in arousing the public's imagination and investors' interests. On the positive side, tax reforms and scholarly research have encouraged some rehabilitation projects; the Bellevue-Stratford Hotel, the Drexel Building, the Philadelphia Bourse, and a number of Old City lofts stand out as the more visible examples of a new market. Significant losses, however, have matched these gains. In many cases fire proved the malefactor, and destroyed such landmarks as the cast-iron Brock warehouse, the richly picturesque Widener mansion, and the gargantuan Bromley mills. In other cases vacant buildings have simply collapsed from neglect.

Interwined with economics and politics, historic preservation frequently faces disputes and must accept, sometimes even welcome, compromises. Two highly publicized incidents in particular illustrate the pragmatism of preservation. The Northern Saving Fund controversy resulted in the demolition of all additions to the bank building as a device to maintain the original 1872 section. In the other instance the facades of a range of houses on Spruce Street west of Washington Square were saved in order to preserve the neighborhood's ambience, but their interior walls and fine rooms fell to make way for the needed expansion of Pennsylvania Hospital. In two other cases landmarks were saved by moving them, a preservation of last resort. The Sims-Bilsland House, the final survivor on Franklin Row, escaped the developer's bulldozer by being moved one block at considerable expense. Similarly the cast-iron sidewalk on North Seventh Street, slowly disappearing piece by piece under the cover of darkness, was torn up to save it (in Catch-22 fashion); some of its elements went to Germantown where they serve as a conservatory floor in a historic house museum.

Other compromises touched on the deliberate double entendre of our title. These were the buildings that have been demolished, but before their demise they were recorded by photographs and measured drawings for the collections of the Historic American Buildings Survey. Admittedly this is not preservation as understood by most people or preferred by the Historic American Buildings Survey, but it does afford one means of preserving a record of the nation's built environment while inevitable change destroys its physical presence. It is what James C. Massey, a former head of HABS, has called preservation through documentation. These records have proven their worth innumerable times to historians, architects, preservationists, and journalists, and will continue to do so in the future.

The decision to publish a revised paperback edition of *Philadelphia Preserved* offered an opportunity to update the catalog and add a street index in order to make the book more usable. These changes and corrections are included as addenda. The introductory essays stand unchanged.

As in the case of the book's first printing, the addenda are a product of the Philadelphia-Washington connection, the cooperation between the Philadelphia Historical Commission and the Historic American Buildings Survey in Washington, D.C. In Philadelphia I thank Richard Tyler, historian of the Philadelphia Historical Commission, and his excellent staff, Patricia Siemiontkowski, Jefferson M. Moak, and Hillary Browne; in Washington I thank Carolyn Pitts, S. Allen Chambers, Jr., John Burns, and Kim Hoagland. Collectively and individually they proved to be storehouses of information, advice, and good will.

Richard J. Webster
West Chester, Pennsylvania
February 1981

Independence Hall, Chestnut Street front. *Engraving, 1750, the first of a Philadelphia building.*

Bingham House. *Drawing by Charles Bullfinch, 1789, courtesy Library of Congress.*

Second Bank of the United States, iron gates. *Drawing by Samuel Richards, Philadelphia ironmonger, for Charles Bullfinch, 1827, courtesy Library of Congress.*

Anthony Benezet House. *Engraving published in* The Port Folio *for October, 1818, from a drawing by William Strickland, courtesy Historical Society of Pennsylvania.*

Wyck. *Drawing by William Strickland before remodeling, 1824, courtesy Wyck Charitable Trust.*

Oldest surviving American exterior daguerreotype view, of Central High School cupola from United States Mint. *Daguerreotype by Joseph Saxton, September 16, 1839, courtesy Historical Society of Pennsylvania.*

Second Bank of the United States. *Langenheim "talbotype," 1850, courtesy Missouri Historical Society.*

Philadelphia Exchange Company (Merchants Exchange). *Langenheim "talbotype," 1850, courtesy Historical Society of Pennsylvania.*

Whitby Hall, chimney wall paneling details. *Plate 7 in W. Davenport Goforth and William J. McAuley,* Old Colonial Architectural Details, *1890, a pioneer work.*

Vernon, mantelpiece woodwork and composition ornament details. *Pencil drawing from one of the first HABS field notebooks used in Philadelphia, January 29, 1934.*

Four Philadelphia HABS architects: *Upper left:* Leicester B. Holland, FAIA (1882–1952), former chairman of the HABS Advisory Committee. *Upper right:* E. Perot Bissell, FAIA (1873–1944), first District Officer for HABS in eastern Pennsylvania. *Lower left:* Joseph P. Sims, FAIA (1890–1953), second Philadelphia District Officer. *Lower right:* James C. Massey (1932–   ), director of the HABS national program from Washington between 1966 and 1972 and currently Vice President of the National Trust for Historic Preservation in charge of Historic Properties.

1 Society Hill
2 Old City
3 Center Square
4 South Philadelphia
5 West Philadelphia
6 Fairmount Park
7 Northwest Philadelphia
8 North Philadelphia
9 Delaware River Corridor

Penn's City

Society Hill

1

Introduction

"The brick walls, as well as the framework of the houses, are painted yearly. The doors are usually white, and kept delicately clean, which, together with the broad slabs of white marble spread before them, and the trees, now gay with their first leaves, which, with some intervals, line the pavements, give an air of cheerfulness and elegance to the principal streets quite unknown to the black and crowded streets of Europe."[1]

*F*RANCES WRIGHT'S description of residential Philadelphia in the spring of 1819 conforms closely to the present state of Society Hill, an area whose origins go back to the founding of the Quaker Commonwealth. Shortly after William Penn launched his Holy Experiment, he deeded to the Free Society of Traders a raised strip of land between the present Spruce and Pine streets and extending west from the Delaware River to the Schuylkill River. The Free Society was a joint-stock company organized in London to stimulate settlement in Pennsylvania. It overextended itself and was dissolved in 1723,[2] but the neighborhood of its property is still called Society Hill.

Society Hill in conjunction with neighboring Independence National Historical Park is popularly known today as historic Philadelphia. Such terminology betrays an eighteenth-century bias, of course, but, as a living museum of early American architecture, Society Hill has few peers. The boundaries of Society Hill depend largely on who is describing them. The National Register of Historic Places defines Society Hill as the area between Walnut and Lombard streets and Front and Eighth streets. In this catalog, however, the area is defined as that between Locust and South streets and the Delaware River and Ninth Street. This includes buildings east of Front Street that were surveyed by HABS but are now gone, and it runs the boundary to the southern limits of Penn's original city to encompass an area that is in general socially and architecturally homogeneous.

Much of Philadelphia's early development was concentrated along the Delaware River and to the north in Old City. Among the earliest houses built in Society Hill are the two matching dwellings at 117–19 Lombard Street (illus.), which were erected about 1743.[3] Their verticality, intensified by abutting the third-story windows against the plain box cornice, combine with the segmental arches above the 9 over 9 windows and the plain, transomed doorways to illustrate the relative awkwardness of early Georgian proportions. Slightly later in date, between 1743 and 1745, are the two-and-a-half-story bandboxes (that is, one room to a floor) at 220–22 Spruce Street. Since they were built for William Arbour, laborer and porter, they are more modest than the Lombard Street examples, which were built for skilled craftsmen, John Palmer, bricklayer, and Joseph Wharton, cooper. Originally separate but similar houses, the Spruce Street dwellings were made into one during their 1958 rehabilitation when one door was remodeled into a window.[4]

About a decade later, sometime between 1750 and 1758, the master builder and politician Samuel Rhoads built a comfortable two-and-a-half-story dwelling on an empty lot at 217 Delancey Street, and in 1758 sold it to Alexander Barclay, who had just become comptroller of the Port of Philadelphia.[5] Although the Rhoads-Barclay House retains the shed dormer, pent eave, and simple, transomed doorway of the Arbour House, it reflects a growing sophistication in the use of Georgian architectural elements. Its greater width and pent eave combine with the water-table at the street level and a line of bricks between the second-story windows and the modillion cornice to give it a greater horizontality and more classical proportions than the earlier houses exhibited.

The random distribution of these early houses—all built on vacant lots—suggests that the development of Society Hill was not a systematic march from either the north or the east. For many years during the mid-eighteenth century dwellings stood by themselves, surrounded by empty land. For example, a 1762 map of the city shows only two dwellings on Third Street between Spruce and South.[6] Beginning in the late 1750's and lasting until the outbreak of the American Revolution, a burst of construction filled many of the empty spaces east of Fourth Street.

Two of the finest town houses of this period are the Abercrombie House at 268 South Second Street and the Powel House (illus.) at 244 South Third Street. The Abercrombie House is the older and the larger of the two. It was built about 1759 for Captain James Abercrombie, a prosperous seagoing merchant, and was one of the tallest dwellings in the city, four-and-a-half stories high with a decked gable roof capped by a balustrade. It was a self-conscious expression of Georgian architecture complete with a Doric frontispiece and mutule cornice.

Although the Powel House was not as large, the English traveler Nicholas Pickford in 1786 found that it was "of admirable Design both without and within, and might do credit to London. It is evident that no expense was spared that might contribute to either Elegance or Comfort."[7] Its owner, "typical and best of Philadelphia's cosmopolitan gentry," was Samuel Powel, a successful merchant and evidently an equally successful politician who served as the city's last mayor under the monarchy and its first mayor under the new Republic.[8] Unlike the Abercrombie House, which later became a warehouse and was gutted, the Powel House, although used commercially, preserved its elegant interiors. When the house was threatened with demolition in the 1920's, the paneling and woodwork from several rooms were removed and installed in the Philadelphia Museum of Art and New York's Metropolitan Museum of Art.[9] After the Powel House was saved, its missing interior elements were carefully reconstructed beginning in 1931 and its exterior restored, and today it is open to the public as a historic house museum; even the two-hundred-year-old pear tree in the garden of the Powel House remains and blooms each spring probably much as it did when it was enjoyed by Washington and Adams and other notables who visited the Powels.

Contrasting with merchants' town houses were workingmen's bandboxes, often set back from the street in courts.[10] A good example is Drinker's Court at 236–38 Delancey Street. In about 1765 John Drinker erected his dwelling on Pine Street and five income-producing bandboxes at the rear of his lot facing Delancey Street; other apartments were added during the early nineteenth century.[11] This practice was an obvious deviation from Penn's original plan of single dwellings and large garden lots, but it provided cheap housing for workingmen close to their places of employment and gave the area an economic mix.

Post-Revolutionary Society Hill saw a resumption of construction, most of it farther west, that is, on Fourth Street and westward. Some of the new residences were grand and were freestanding within large lots. The Hill-Physick House at 321 South Fourth Street was built in 1786 for the prosperous wine merchant Henry Hill.[12] It ranks among the city's finest examples of the Federal style that became so popular after the Revolution. During this period the robust sculptural quality of the colonial houses was replaced by delicate, flat surfaces, attained in this house by the use of a flat, finely carved frontispiece and windows without lintels. Its large leaded fanlight with delicately wrought muntins serves as the focal point of the street facade and coordinates other large-scale elements to indicate the house's great size: thirty-two rooms within three-and-a-half stories.

Closer to Philadelphia's row house tradition is the town house of the merchant-banker John Clement Stocker, which was built at 402 South Front Street during the early 1790's.[13] Although it was constructed on a much larger scale than its colonial neighbors and had an abundance of delicately carved ornamentation on its fireplaces and ceilings, it adjoined houses on both sides and continued the earlier town house plan of side hall and rear stairtower, or piazza, as Philadelphians called this small ell which enclosed two or three flights of stairs. The house still stands, starkly alone, awaiting restoration.

By the end of the eighteenth century, Society Hill's population had grown to the point that the market stalls at Second and Lombard streets had to be extended along the middle of Second Street, first to South Street in 1797 and then to Pine Street in 1804. There the present Head House was erected to house a volunteer hose company and a volunteer engine company.[14]

Another response to the city's population growth was the extension of the Pennsylvania Hospital (illus.) at Eighth and Pine streets, then on the fringes of the city. Outskirts were favorite sites for hospitals since they afforded the open spaces and tranquil settings that were believed to be the most healthful for body and mind and reduced the threat of fire, an ever present menace to early cities. Pennsylvania Hospital is another product of the indefatigable Benjamin Franklin, this time working in conjunction with Dr. Thomas Bond, and is another Philadelphia first—the country's earliest public hospital. Its eastern wing had been standing since 1757, and in 1794 work was begun on the center and western sections. In 1805 the splendid Adamesque-Federal center section with its circular surgical amphitheater (the nation's oldest) was completed.[15] The result was not only a physical plan that was to be emulated in American hospitals for a century but also an outstanding medical institution that helped to make Philadelphia a center of medicine.

Part of Society Hill's post-Revolutionary growth was created by the migration of free Negroes into the area. The nucleus of this early black neighborhood, which still exists, was Bethel African Methodist Episcopal Church (illus.).[16] In 1787 the Reverend Richard Allen, a former slave who would later become the first bishop of the African Methodist Episcopal Church, led his fellow blacks out of St. George's Methodist Episcopal Church in protest against its segregation practices and bought a lot at 419 South Sixth Street, north of Lombard.[17] The present late-nineteenth-century Romanesque Revival church, the third built on this site by the congregation of Mother Bethel, stands on what is thought to be the oldest piece of ground continuously owned and occupied by blacks in the United States.[18]

Society Hill remained relatively stable throughout most of the nineteenth century. Physical changes were minimal. Shops were put in the ground stories of some dwellings, particularly those at corners. Some new churches went up to accommodate growing congregations, and some new warehouses were built along the waterfront. Because of Philadelphians' continuing affinity for brick and the buildings' relatively low height, the new structures blended into the older cityscape. The Norris-Cadwalader House (Mutual Assurance Company) (illus.) at 240 South Fourth Street, for example, was built about 1828, yet it fits well with its colonial neighbor, the Shippen-Wistar House (illus.).[19] It was such homogeneity and regularity, with its "air of cheerfulness, cleanliness, and comfort," that gave Frances Wright "so much satisfaction" during her visit to the city in 1819.[20]

After the Civil War and particularly after electric trolleys were introduced in the 1890's, Society Hill residents started moving to Rittenhouse Square and farther out to the new residential "suburbs." Their homes were taken by the immigrants who began flooding into Philadelphia from southern and eastern Europe after 1880. The shift can be traced in the changing ownership of old churches and the erection of new houses of worship. In 1900, for example, Chevia B'nai Aviohome Mi Russe began its synagogue at 523 Lombard Street; in 1912 a Rumanian congregation converted Spruce Street Baptist Church into a synagogue; in 1922 St. Andrew's Protestant Episcopal Church became St. George's Greek Orthodox Church.[21]

Dwellings throughout the area were altered to accommodate stores, warehouses, light manufacturing establishments, or tenements, but because Society Hill became a low-rent district quickly there was little demolition or rebuilding. That left the material culture of an earlier era under galvanized iron shopfronts, layers of wallpaper, and bricked-up fireplaces to be uncovered when Society Hill's rebirth would come a half-century later.

That renaissance occurred during the late 1950's and 1960's. Through the cooperation of three government agencies and one nonprofit corporation, Society Hill became known as one of the nation's most successful urban renewal projects. The Philadelphia City Planning Commission prepared the comprehensive plan; the Redevelopment Authority acquired the properties for development; the Philadelphia Historical Commission certified historically significant buildings and collected the materials needed for accurate restorations; and the Old Philadelphia Development Corporation made many of these houses available for purchase and restoration.[22] Through this system nearly eight hundred houses have been restored and approximately two hundred new houses have been built. Visually anchoring the revitalized neighborhood are the Society Hill Towers. These three high-rise apartment buildings designed by Ieoh Ming Pei serve not only as focal points for Society Hill in relation to its primary historic sites and open spaces but also in relation to the rest of downtown Philadelphia and its traffic flow.[23] In spite of their radically different scale and style they relate to the older buildings about them through their articulated fenestration and adjacent town houses.

Society Hill today stands as a fine example of how a historically significant square mile can be restored from slum status, its old buildings integrated with modern structures, and converted into one of the most desirable living areas in the region.

Catalog

Abercrombie, Captain James, House (now Perelman Antique Toy Museum)

(PA-1315), 268–70 S. Second St. Museum. Brick with marble trim, 30'-5" (four-bay front) × 45'-2¹/₂" originally with two-story rear ell, four-and-a-half stories, decked gable roof with balustrade, Doric frontispiece, mutule cornice, arched alleyway to rear yard, side-hall town house plan.

Notable Georgian town house unusual for its height. Built c. 1759; ground-story storefront built before 1857; ground story rebuilt later. Rear ell rebuilt 1913, enlarged 1922, 1929. Rear ell demolished, front section restored 1967–68; John Lloyd and Associates, architects. Certified, PHC 1957. 5 sheets (1959–60, including plot plan, plans, elevations, section);* 9 ext. photos (1957, 1959, 1972),* 4 int. photos (1960);* 4 data pages (1957, including 1770 insurance survey).*

Apartment Building

(PA-1316), 113–17¹/₂ South St. Five brick dwelling units with ground-story shops, each approx. 16' (three-bay front) × 60', three stories, flat roof, projecting upper-story molded metal bay with pilasters and pediment on each unit, every ninth row of bricks recessed to simulate rustication, originally one-family apartment on each upper floor, L-plan for each unit.

Example of modest early-20th-century apartment building in a degenerate expression of the classical tradition. Built 1913–14; Solomon Brothers, contractors. New storefront for No. 113 built 1941; permastone facade added to No. 115, 1950. 1 ext. photo (1967);* 3 data pages (1973, including 1913 building permit).*

9

Arbour, William, House

(PA-1051), 220 Spruce St., at S.E. corner American St. Brick, 14'-10" (two-bay front) × 18'-1", two-and-a-half stories on raised basement, gable roof, one room to a floor. Built 1743–45; two-story rear ell added c. 1746, demolished 1958; front section rehabilitated 1958. Probably the oldest surviving house in Society Hill. Certified, PHC 1957. 1 sheet (1959, including plot plan, plans, details); 2 ext. photos (1957), 1 int. photo (1957); 4 data pages (1959).

Bake House and Oven

(PA-1317), Rear of 423 S. Second St. House: brick, approx. 35' (four-bay front) × 17', two stories, shed roof, one room to a floor. Oven in basement: brick, recessed approx. 3' within low arch approx. 9' wide × 6' high. Built before 1796. Certified, PHC 1957. 1 ext. photo (1963),* 1 int. photo (1963);* 5 data pages (1961, including 1802 insurance survey).*

Bethel African Methodist Episcopal Church (now Mother Bethel African Methodist Church). Illustrated

(PA-1318), 419 S. Sixth St., at S.E. corner Addison St. Brick with random rough-hewn granite front and rusticated base, approx. 64' (three-bay front) × 82' with three-story rear Sunday-School building, two stories, gable roof with two cross-gables, four-story square corner tower and belfry with gargoyles and clustered-colonette pinnacles, large semicircular entrance arch on clustered columns, large semicircular window on three sides, three-aisle plan with balconies, hexagonal chancel.

Church with architectural emphasis on its Romanesque Revival facade. Built 1889–90; Hazlehurst and Huckel, architects. The fourth African Methodist Episcopal church building on this lot, purchased 1787 and the oldest piece of real estate owned by blacks in the United States. Richard Allen, first ordained black man in America and founder of the African Methodist Episcopal Church, is buried in basement crypt. Certified, PHC 1964; Pennsylvania Register 1970; designated National Historic Landmark 1974. 2 ext. photos (1973);* 3 data pages (including 1890 insurance survey);* HABSI form (1971).*

Blackwell, Reverend Robert, House (now St. Peter's Church House)

(PA-1319), 313 Pine St. Brick with granite trim, approx. 24' (three-bay front) × 38' with three-story rear ell, three-and-a-half stories on raised basement, gable roof, arch-head entrance with fanlight, first- and second-story windows set in blind arches with recessed solid tympanums, side-hall plan, large columnated parlor.

Fine Federal-style urban dwelling. Built 1809; possibly by Robert Mills, architect. Ground-story interior altered, kitchen ell enlarged c. 1840; west wall altered 1965. St. Peter's Church House since 1922. Certified, PHC 1956; Pennsylvania Register 1970. 1 ext. photo (1972);* 6 data pages (1958, including 1809, 1880 insurance surveys);* HABSI form (1971).*

Bridges, Robert, House

(PA-1320), 507 S. Front St. Brick, approx. 22' (three-bay front) × 40', three-and-a-half stories on raised basement, gable roof, brick string-courses, London house plan. Built c. 1791; altered to tavern 1865; store and dwelling after 1918; demolished 1966. Certified, PHC 1957. 1 ext. photo (1958);* 7 data pages (1961, including 1791–1918 insurance surveys);* HABSI form (1957).*

Bridges-LaTour House

(PA-1321), 509 S. Front St. Brick, approx. 18' (two-bay front) × 40', three-and-a-half stories on raised basement, gable roof, brick string-courses, round-arch entrance with fanlight and Adamesque frontis-piece, probably London house plan. Built 1791; demolished 1966. Between 1813 and 1850 home of John LaTour, merchant, who owned dwelling and rear adjoining lot with warehouse (PA-1056). Certified, PHC 1957. 2 ext. photos (1958, 1961),* 8 int. photos (1966);* 7 data pages (1957, including 1791 insurance survey);* HABSI form (1957).*

Burgin, Dr. George H., House

(PA-1322), 319 S. Fifth St. Brick with stone trim, approx. 16' (two-bay front) × 36' with three-story rear ell, three-and-a-half stories, gable roof, originally side-hall town house plan.

Built between 1821 and 1823; rear kitchen ell raised to two stories 1827; altered to store and rear ell raised to three stories after 1912; demolished 1964. Built for George H. Burgin, physician, druggist, glass manufacturer, and public servant who served as director of public schools 1838–53, manager of Wills Eye Hospital 1848–56, trustee of Philadelphia Gas Works 1842–60. Burgin lived here c. 1825–31, rented house 1831–70. Certified, PHC 1957. 1 ext. photo (1960);* 6 data pages (1959, including 1823–1912 insurance surveys).*

Bussey-Poulson House

(PA-1323), 320 S. Fourth St. Brick, 18'-0" (three-bay front) × 26'-8" with three-story rear ell, three-and-a-half stories, gable roof, side-hall plan. Built 1783; rehabilitated 1967–70. Certified, PHC 1957. 4 sheets (1959, including plot plan, plans, elevations, details)* courtesy of Philadephia Historical Commission; 3 ext. photos (1959, 1972);* 5 data pages (1957, including 1796–1908 insurance surveys);* HABSI form (1958).*

Cove Cornice House. See Man Full of Trouble Tavern

Currie, Dr. William, House

(PA-191), 271 S. Fifth St. Brick, approx. 23' (three-bay front) × 40', three-and-a-half stories, gable roof, side-hall plan. Built 1811; entire ground story removed later; demolished 1957. 2 ext. photos (1957); 2 data pages (1957, including 1811 insurance survey).

Davis-Lenox House

(PA-1324), 217 Spruce St. Brick, approx. 22' (three-bay front) × 30' with two-story rear ell, three-and-a-half stories on raised basement (originally two), gable roof, originally side-hall London house plan.

Built c. 1758; James Davis, house carpenter. Raised one-and-a-half stories, kitchen altered to stair tower, new two-story kitchen built 1784; kitchen altered to dining room, new one-story kitchen built 1848; kitchen raised one story later. Restored to 1784 state 1960; George B. Roberts, architect. Major David Lenox, Revolutionary hero and later president of Bank of the United States and American minister to the Court of St. James, lived here 1779–1810. Certified, PHC 1957. 2 ext. photos (1959, 1961);* 6 data pages (1958, including 1781–1848 insurance surveys).*

Drinker, John, House

(PA-1325), 241 Pine St. Brick, approx. 18' (two-bay front) × 30' with three-story rear ell (originally two stories), three-and-a-half stories, gable roof, pent eave between first and second stories, side-hall plan.

Fine example of modest Philadelphia town house whose lot originally included rear tenement court (Drinker's Court) behind 236–38 Delancey St. Built c. 1765; John Drinker (bricklayer), builder. Rear ell enlarged before 1870. Restored 1956–57; Edward Parnum, architect. Certified, PHC 1957; Pennsylvania Register 1970. 1 ext. photo (1973),* 2 int. photos (1959);* 6 data pages (1957, including 1806, 1870 insurance surveys).*

Drinker's Court

(PA-1326), 236–38 Delancey St. A complex of two front buildings and six rear apartments and a rear building flanking a courtyard.

No. 236: brick, 16'-4" (two-bay front) × 14'-9", two-and-a-half stories, half-gambrel roof, pent eave, one room to a floor; three brick rear apartments (originally four), each approx. 14' (two-bay front) × 12', two stories, shed roof, one room to a floor.

No. 238: brick, 15'-2" (two-bay front) × 16'-10", two-and-a-half stories, half-gambrel roof, one room to a floor; three brick rear apartments, each approx. 16' (two-bay front) × 11', two stories, shed roof, one room to a floor; rear brick building, 13'-3" (two-bay front) × 15'-7", three stories, shed roof, one room to a floor. Originally balanced by three-story rear building at rear of apartments of No. 236.

The construction of small row houses on a court with one row facing the other was a common building practice in 18th-century and early 19th-century Philadelphia, as the large city blocks were subdivided by secondary streets. These buildings were on the northern extremity of a lot owned by John Drinker and on which he built his dwelling at 241 Pine St. See Drinker, John, House (PA-1325). Court later known as Deimling Place, later as Bodine St.

No. 236 and rear kitchen (later northernmost apartment), No. 238 and three rear apartments built c. 1765; probably by John Drinker, bricklayer. Rear apartments of No. 236 built after 1806. Three-story rear building of No. 238 built between 1827 and 1829. No. 236 altered to store c. 1870; reverted to dwelling between 1920 and 1931. Southernmost three-story apartment of No. 236 demolished after 1939. No. 238 and apartments rehabilitated 1958–59; No. 236 and apartments rehabilitated 1965–66. Shutters, window and door elements at Architectural Study Collection, Museum Division, Independence National Historical Park. Certified, PHC 1956; Pennsylvania Register 1970; NR.

4 sheets (1958, 1959, including plot plan, plans, elevations, section, details)* courtesy of Philadelphia Historical Commission; 5 ext. photos (1959, 1972),* 1 int. photo (1959);* 13 data pages (1958, including 1806–70 insurance surveys);* HABSI form (1957).*

Eastburn Mariners' Bethel (Presbyterian) Church (also known as Mariners' Bethel)

(PA-1327), 328–30 S. Front St., at S.W. corner Delancey St. Brick, approx. 54' (three-bay front) × 76', two-and-a-half stories, gable roof originally with square clock tower near front peak, name stone in gable, chapel and reading rooms on ground story, three-aisle sanctuary on second story.

Built 1868–69; possibly by Stephen D. Button, architect. Clock tower removed after 1912; building vacated 1959; interior destroyed by fire 1963. Organized by Joseph Eastburn 1819, Mariners' Bethel was one of the oldest seamen's churches in the country; merged with Third Presbyterian Church 1959. Certified, PHC 1957. 2 ext. photos (1961),* 1 photocopy of ext. photo (1959),* 9 photocopies of int. photos (1959);* 19 data pages (1959).*

Estlack, Thomas, House

(PA-1328), 413 Lombard St. Brick, approx. 16' (two-bay front) × 35' with three-story rear stair tower, three-and-a-half stories on raised basement, gable roof, arch-head entrance, side-hall plan. Built 1821; probably by Thomas Estlack, bricklayer. Demolished 1964. Certified, PHC 1957. 1 ext. photo (1960);* 3 data pages (1959, including 1822 insurance survey).*

Fitzgerald, Thomas, House

(PA-1329), 437 Lombard St. Brick with marble trim, approx. 19' (three-bay front) × 30' with three-story rear ell, three-and-a-half stories, gable roof, side-hall town house plan. Built 1799; rear ell built 1844; demolished 1964. Certified, PHC 1957. 1 ext. photo (1960);* 5 data pages (1959, including 1811, 1845 insurance surveys).*

Girard Row

(PA-1330), 326–34 Spruce St. Five brick row houses with marble ground story and trim, each approx. 21' (two-bay front) × 40' with two- and three-story rear ell, three-and-a-half stories on raised basements, gable roofs. Row houses built as investment for Stephen Girard, early millionaire merchant and financier. Built 1831–33; William Struthers, marble mason. Nos. 332–34 restored 1954–   ; Charles E. Peterson, architect. Certified, PHC 1957. 1 sheet (1958, downspout detail);* 2 ext. photos (1959),* 4 int. photos (1959, including 4 fireplaces);* 20 data pages (1964, including 1845 insurance survey).*

Hall, John, House

(PA-1331), 327 S. Third St., at N.E. corner Delancey St. Brick, 16'-0" (two-bay front) × 35'-4", three-and-a-half stories, gable roof, brick stringcourses. Built between 1783 and 1799; John Hall, house carpenter. Ground story altered to store c. 1854; rehabilitated 1965–

66. Certified, PHC 1957. 5 sheets (1957, 1959, including plot plan, plans, elevations, section, details)* courtesy of Philadelphia Historical Commission; 3 ext. photos (1959, 1972),* 2 int. photos (1959);* 2 data pages (1958);* HABSI form (1959).*

Hall-Wister House

(PA-1332), 330 S. Third St. Brick, approx. 16' (two-bay front) × 20' with two-story rear ell, two-and-a-half stories, gable roof, brick stringcourse, well-preserved interior woodwork, one-room ground story. One of a pair of row houses. Built between 1771 and 1774; John Hall, house carpenter. Altered c. 1890. Restored, rear ell replaced 1959–61; Robert T. Trump, restorer. In possession of Wister family 1778–1853. Certified, PHC 1957. 2 ext. photos (1959, 1972),* 1 int. photo (1959);* 3 data pages (1958, including 1774 insurance survey).*

Hill, David, House

(PA-1333), 309 S. Third St. Brick with marble trim, 25'-5¹/₂" (three-bay front) × 49'-6¹/₂" with three-story rear ell, three-and-a-half stories on raised basement, gable roof, round-arch entrance with fanlight, side-hall town house plan. Built 1831–39; ground story altered to store later. Restored 1970–71; Hugh M. Zimmers, architect. Certified, PHC 1957. 6 sheets (1958, including plans, elevations, section, details)* courtesy of Philadelphia Historical Commission; 4 ext. photos (1959, 1973),* 3 int. photos (1959);* 2 data pages (1958);* HABSI form (1958).*

Hill-Physick House

(PA-1334), 321 S. Fourth St., at S.E. corner Cypress St. Historic house museum. Brick with marble trim, approx. 48' (three-bay front) × 51', three-and-a-half stories on raised basement, hipped roof, round-arch entrance with sidelights and notable fanlight, center-hall plan, springhouse extends from cellar under Cypress St. sidewalk.

Notable example of a large Federal-style residence. Built 1786 incorporating earlier house into its northeast end; one-story wing built at rear of north side, interior remodeled 1815; one-story wing extended to front c. 1838; interior extensively remodeled 1850's; three-story rear ell demolished before 1868; interior remodeled probably c. 1920; three-story elevator shaft built on south side 1921; elevator shaft, two-story rear stable demolished 1966. Restored by Philadelphia Society for Preservation of Landmarks 1965–66; George B. Roberts, architect.

Home of Col. Henry Hill, wine merchant active in Revolutionary affairs, 1786–98, and of Dr. Philip Syng Physick, father of American surgery, 1815–37. Headquarters of the Society of the Cincinnatus of Pennsylvania since 1966. Certified, PHC 1957; Pennsylvania Register 1970. 3 ext. photos (1972, 1976),* 1 int. photo (1959);* 17 data pages (1958, 1964, including 1815–1921 insurance surveys).*

Hilyard, Eber, House

(PA-1335), 427 Lombard St. Brick with marble trim, approx. 16' (two-bay front) × 40', three-and-a-half stories on raised basement, gable roof, side-hall plan. One of a pair of houses. Built 1807; probably by Eber Hilyard, bricklayer. Demolished 1964. Certified, PHC 1957. 1 ext. photo (1960);* 4 data pages (1959, including 1807, 1919 insurance surveys).*

Holy Trinity (German) Roman Catholic Church

(PA-1336), 601–9 Spruce St., at N.W. corner Sixth St. Brick, approx. 100' (five-bay front) × 60', one story, hipped roof, round-arch windows, three-aisle plan, polygonal chancel. Built 1789; damaged by fire, altered 1860. Altered 1902; George I. Lovatt, architect. 3 ext. photos (1973),* 1 photocopy of int. lithograph (c. 1880);* 1 data page (1964).*

House

(PA-1809), 532 S. Water St., at N.W. corner South St. Brick with marble trim, approx. 18' (two-bay front) × 38', three-and-a-half stories, rusticated marble flat-arch lintels with keystones, brick stringcourse. Built c. 1790; altered to store before 1860; demolished 1959. Certified, PHC 1958. 1 ext. photo (1958).*

Houses

(PA-1337), 319–21 S. Front St. Brick covered with plaster, approx. 18' (three-bay front) × 40', three-and-a-half stories, gable roof. Built late 18th century; altered to store before 1861; demolished 1967. 2 ext. photos (1961).*

House

(PA-1338), 532 S. Front St., at N.W. corner South St. Brick with stone trim, approx. 18' (two-bay front) × 36', three-and-a-half stories, gable roof. Built late 18th century; altered to store later; demolished 1959. Certified, PHC 1957. 1 ext. photo (1958);* HABSI form (1957).*

Houses

(PA-1339), 722–30 Spruce St., at S.E. corner Eighth St. Eight brick houses with marble trim, each approx. 25' (three-bay front) × 50' with two-, three-, four-story rear ells, three-and-a-half stories (No. 730 four stories), mansard, gable, flat roofs, side-hall plans (No. 730 center-hall plan). Nos. 722–26 built before 1845, mansard added later; No. 728 built before 1860; No. 730 built 1837. Demolished 1958. Certified, PHC 1958. 5 ext. photos (1958, including two of iron stair railing);* 26 data pages (1963, including 1837–1937 insurance surveys).*

Jefferson, Joseph, House

(PA-1340), 600 Spruce St., at S.W. corner Sixth St. Brick with marble trim, approx. 20' (two-bay front) × 42', three-and-a-half stories, gable roof. Built 1804–5; probably by Edward Bonsall, house carpenter. Altered to store 1835; renovated c. 1905; two-story rear ell demolished 1969; rehabilitated 1969–70. Joseph Jefferson, perhaps America's most celebrated 19th-century actor and comedian, was born here 1829. Certified, PHC 1957. 1 ext. photo (1958);* 4 data pages (1958, including 1805–1914 insurance surveys).*

Jordan-Stoddart House

(PA-1341), 409 S. Fifth St., at N.E. corner Addison St. Brick with stone trim, approx. 16' (two-bay front) × 38' with two-story rear wing, three-and-a-half stories, gable roof, originally London house plan. Built between 1804 and 1806; rear two-story wing built 1885; altered to store 1909; demolished 1964. Certified, PHC 1957. 1 ext. photo (1960);* 5 data pages (1959, including 1811–1909 insurance surveys).*

Kosciuszko, General Thaddeus, House

(PA-1342), 301 Pine St., at N.W. corner Third St. (originally 342 S. Third St.), Independence National Historical Park. Museum. Brick, approx. 31' (three-bay front) × 15', three-and-a-half stories, gable roof, London house plan. Built 1774–75; probably by Joseph Few, carpenter. Altered to tavern 1865; altered to store and dwelling later; altered to dwelling 1942. Restored by National Park Service 1974–76. Gen. Thaddeus Kosciuszko, Polish patriot and chief engineer of the Continental Army 1780–83, lived here 1797–98 while in exile. Certified, PHC 1957; Pennsylvania Register 1971; NR. 2 ext. photos

(1972);* 6 data pages (1957, including 1775–1922 insurance surveys);* HABSI form (1971).*

LaTour Warehouse

(PA-1056), 508 S. Water St. Brick, 21' (three-bay front) × 50'-6", two-and-a-half stories, gambrel roof, double doors on first and second stories front and rear, hooded dormer covering hoist tackle, one room to a floor.

Notable early-19th-century warehouse. Built 1817–18; demolished 1967. Certified, PHC 1957. 8 sheets (1958, including plot plan, plans, elevations, sections, details); 6 ext. photos (1958), 3 int. photos (1958); 5 data pages (1959, 1960); HABSI form (1957).*

Lombard Street Area Study

(PA-1678), 323–33 Lombard St. Six adjoining brick houses with marble trim (No. 331 with coral stone rear ell and cellar), each approx. 18' (two-bay front) × 38' with two- or three-story rear ell (except No. 333), three-and-a-half stories on raised basement (No. 331 originally two-and-a-half stories), gable roofs (No. 331 originally gambrel), side-hall plans.

No. 331 built 1763–66, enlarged and interior altered 1818, raised to three stories and new front built 1927; No. 333 built 1813, altered to store later, reverted to dwelling 1928; No. 325 built 1817; Nos. 327–29 built c. 1835; No. 323 built 1839, renovated as part of St. Peter's Choir School after 1888. All but No. 323 demolished 1964. Certified, PHC 1958. 4 ext. photos (1960);* 18 data pages (1959, 1963, including 1763–1849 insurance surveys).*

McDonald, Malcolm, Houses

(PA-1343), 315–17 S. Fifth St. Brick with stone trim, each approx. 20' (three-bay front) × 45' with two- and three-story rear ell, three-and-a-half stories, gable roof, originally side-hall town house plan. Built between 1795 and 1797; altered to stores before 1912; demolished 1964. Certified, PHC 1957. 1 ext. photo (1960);* 5 data pages (1959, including 1799 insurance survey).*

McKean, Thomas, Jr., House

(PA-190), 269 S. Fifth St. Brick, approx. 23' (three-bay front) × 30', three stories on raised basement, flat roof, side-hall plan. Built c. 1816; demolished 1957. 1 sheet (1957, including details); 2 ext. photos

(1957), 3 int. photos (1957); 4 data pages (1957, including 1837 insurance survey).

McMullin, Robert, House

(PA-1344), 411 Pine St. Brick with marble trim, 19' (two-bay front) × 35'-6" with three-story rear ell, three-and-a-half stories on raised basement, gable roof, arch-headed entrance with fanlight, side-hall plan. Built c. 1831; exterior restored 1965. Certified, PHC 1957. 2 ext. photos (1965),* 6 int. photos (1965);* 3 data pages (1963).*

Man Full of Trouble Tavern (also known as Cove Cornice House and Stafford's Tavern). Illustrated

(PA-128), 127 Spruce St., at N.W. corner Mattis St. Historic house museum. Brick, approx. 22' (two-bay front) × 20', two-and-a-half stories, gambrel roof with original cove cornice, front pent eave with cove cornice, balcony on east end, two rooms to a floor.

Fine example of 18th-century city tavern. Built 1760; projecting one-story frame shed built at northeast corner before 1835; interior altered 1879, 1900. Frame shed demolished c. 1963. Restored by Knauer Foundation for Historic Preservation 1963–65; W. Nelson Anderson, architect. Wallpaper sample (c. 1785) in Architectural Study Collection, Museum Division, Independence National Historical Park. Certified, PHC 1957.

4 sheets (1936, 1958, including plans, elevations, details); 10 ext. photos (1958, 1961, 1973),* 3 int. photos (1958, 1959),* 1 photocopy of old wash drawing (1835),* 1 photocopy of old ext. photo (1850);* 26 data pages (1958, 1966, including 1769–1900 insurance surveys).*

Manning Street Area Study. See Marshall's Court Area Study

Mariners' Bethel. See Eastburn Mariners' Bethel (Presbyterian) Church

Marshall's Court Area Study (also known as Manning Street)

(PA-1345), 403–11 Marshall's Court, between 256–58 S. Fourth St. and 275–77 S. Fifth St. N. of Spruce St. Independence National Historical Park. Five contiguous brick houses, each approx. 15' (two-bay front) × 32', three-and-a-half stories, gable roofs, London house plans. Built c. 1812; demolished 1959. Mantels, stairway elements, shingles in Architectural Study Collection, Museum Division, Independence National Historical Park. Certified, PHC 1957. 5 ext. photos

(1958),* 9 int. photos (1958);* 3 data pages (including 1816, 1837 insurance surveys).*

Mears-Heaton House
(PA-1070), 240 Delancey St. Brick, 14'-11$^{1}/_{2}$" (two-bay front) × 30'-6" with two-story rear brick stair tower and two-story brick-pane (half-timber frame with brick nogging) rear ell, two stories, mansard roof (originally gable), originally pent eave, two rooms to a floor. The rear ell was the only known extant brick-pane building in Philadelphia. Rear ell probably built before 1765. Front building built 1765–66; John Mears (joiner), builder. Mansard added later. Demolished 1954. 4 sheets (1954, 1962, including plot plan, plan, section, details); 5 data pages (1962, including 1782 insurance survey).*

Mellon, Thomas, House
(PA-1346), 716 Spruce St. Brick with marble trim, approx. 25' (three-bay front) × 54' with three- and four-story rear ell, four stories, flat roof, side-hall town house plan, notable Greek Revival interior woodwork. Built 1836; demolished 1959. Certified, PHC 1957. 2 sheets (1959, including plan, details)* courtesy of Philadelphia Historical Commission; 1 int. photo (1959),* 7 photocopies of int. photos (1959);* 3 data pages (1958, including 1836 insurance survey).*

Mifflin, John, Houses
(PA-1347), 521–23 S. Front St. Brick, each approx. 14' (two-bay front) × 35', three-and-a-half stories, gable roof, round-arch entrances with fanlights, London house plans. Built before 1779; demolished 1966. Certified, PHC 1957. 13 data pages (1961, including 1784, 1785 insurance surveys);* 3 HABSI forms (1957).*

Mitchell, Thomas, House
(PA-1348), 276 S. Third St., at N.W. corner Spruce St. Brick, approx. 18' (two-bay front) × 30' with rear addition, four stories on raised basement, half-hipped roof, blind arch with recessed tympanum above second-story window, elliptical windows at fourth story. Built c. 1815; probably by Robert Mills, architect. Flat-roof addition along Spruce St. built c. 1850. Demolished 1964. Certified, PHC 1957. 3 ext. photos (1961, 1962),* 4 int. photos (1961),* 1 aerial photo (1962);* 1 data page (1957).*

Mother Bethel African Methodist Episcopal Church. See Bethel African
Methodist Episcopal Church

Mutual Assurance Company. See Norris-Cadwalader House

Neave, Samuel, House and Store
(PA-1349), 272–74 S. Second St., at N.W. corner Spruce St. Brick with
marble trim, 29'-9" (three-bay front) × 44'-2¹/4" originally with one-
and two-story rear ell, three-and-a-half stories on raised basement,
gable roof, pent eave on south facade (not original), pedimented frontispiece, originally side-hall town house plan with store in front.
   Fine Georgian house of a prominent merchant. Built c. 1759; rear
ell raised to three stories 1829; ground-story interior extensively altered, one-story lateral rear addition built 1841; ground-story
storefront built before 1857; rear ell, storefront rebuilt 1905; three-
story rear ell demolished 1959. Front section restored 1967–70; Carl
Massara and Associates, architects. Certified, PHC 1957.
   10 sheets (1959, 1960, including plot plan, plans, elevations, section, details);* 9 ext. photos (1957, 1959, 1960, 1972),* 11 int. photos
(1959, 1960);* 9 data pages (1957, including 1760–1841 insurance surveys).*

Nevel, Thomas, House
(PA-1350), 338 S. Fourth St. Brick, approx. 22' (three-bay front) × 37'
with two-story rear ell, two-and-a-half stories, gambrel roof with
mutule cornice, round-arch entrance with fanlight and Tuscan frontispiece, side-hall plan.
   Fine Georgian house originally with shop in front. Built 1770;
Thomas Nevel, house carpenter. Rear ell enlarged and altered 1844;
interior altered 1865; altered to tavern 1888. Exterior restored 1961;
John A. Bower, architect. Certified, PHC 1957. 3 ext. photos (1964,
1972),* 3 int. photos (1964);* 13 data pages (1960, including 1770–1880
insurance surveys).*

"New Market"
(PA-1351), in middle of Second St. between S. side Pine St. and N.
side Lombard St. Market House (originally quarters of Hope Hose
Co. No. 6 and Fellowship Engine Co. No. 29, later known as Head
House): brick with marble trim, approx. 30' (three-bay front) × 28',
two stories, gable roof with octagonal cupola, arched passage

through center of ground story to shambles (open market sheds). Shambles: brick piers, approx. 30' × 245', one story, gable roof, vaulted plaster ceiling.

Probably the oldest extant firehouse and market structure in the United States. First eight stalls built at Lombard St. 1745; extended north to Stamper's Alley 1795–97; extended north to Pine St. and Head House built 1804. Shambles widened 1809, enclosed 1921. Head House restored 1959–61; shambles restored 1962–63. Certified, PHC 1956; Pennsylvania Register 1970; designated National Historic Landmark 1966. 2 ext. photos (1963).*

Norris-Cadwalader House (now Mutual Assurance Company). Illustrated (PA-1352), 240 S. Fourth St. Brick with marble trim, approx. 30' (three-bay front) × 50' with three- and four-story rear ell, four-and-a-half stories, gable roof; notable interior paneling and plasterwork, side-hall town house plan with ground-story offices.

Fine early-19th-century residence-office. Built c. 1828 for attorney Joseph P. Norris, Jr., and after 1837 home of prominent attorney John Cadwalader. Interior altered 1912; rear ell enlarged 1941, 1947. In possession of Cadwalader family until 1912 when it became offices of Mutual Assurance Company for Insuring Houses from Loss by Fire. Certified, PHC 1957. 1 ext. photo (1972),* 8 int. photos (1959, of fireplaces),* 2 photocopies of old ext. photos (c. 1900),* 8 photocopies of int. photos (c. 1900);* 3 data pages (1959, including 1837 insurance survey).*

Old Pine Street Church. See Third Presbyterian Church

Old St. Mary's. See St. Mary's Church

Palmer, John, House
(PA-1353), 117 Lombard St. Brick, approx. 18' (three-bay front) × 32' with two- and three-story rear ell, three-and-a-half stories, gable roof, segmental-arch heads over windows, brick stringcourse with glazed headers, alleyway through ground story to rear yard, originally London house plan.

One of a pair of row houses. Built 1743; probably by John Palmer, bricklayer. Rear kitchen and stair ell built c. 1763; altered and enlarged c. 1809. Exterior restored 1966–68; interior rehabilitated 1973. Certified, PHC 1957. 1 ext. photo (1973);* 5 data pages (1961, including 1764, 1810 insurance surveys).*

Pancake, Philip, House

(PA-1354), 333 S. Fifth St. Brick, approx. 20' (two-bay front) × 34' with three-story rear ell, three-and-a-half stories, gable roof, side-hall plan. Built c. 1775; two-story rear kitchen built 1773; rear kitchen raised to three stories, ground story altered to store, new dormer and galvanized metal cornice added 1911. Demolished 1964. Certified, PHC 1957. 1 ext. photo (1960);* 3 data pages (1964).*

Pancoast-Lewis-Wharton House

(PA-1083), 336 Spruce St. Brick with marble trim, approx. 20' (three-bay front) × 36' with three-story rear ell, three-and-a-half stories, gable roof, round-arch entrance with fanlight and Tuscan frontispiece, side-hall town house plan.

Fine Federal-style town house. Built 1790; probably by Samuel Pancoast, house carpenter. Rear ell enlarged 1834; house enlarged and altered 1916–17. Restored 1962; George A. Robbins, architect. Birthplace and home of Joseph Wharton, founder of the Wharton School of Finance and Commerce, University of Pennsylvania. Christ Church Rectory since 1962. Certified, PHC 1957.

7 sheets (1932, including elevations, sections, details) from Survey, Philadelphia Chapter, A.I.A., 4 sheets (1961, including plot plan, plans); 2 ext. photos (1961, 1962), 4 int. photos (1962), 1 photocopy of old ext. photo (c. 1890); 10 data pages (1961, 1964).

Paschall, Benjamin, House. Illustrated

(PA-1355), 129A Spruce St. Brick, approx. 16' (two-bay front) × 20', two-and-a-half stories, half-gambrel roof with cove cornice, front pent eave with cove cornice, one room to a floor. Built 1760; altered to store c. 1827; altered to warehouse before 1931. Restored 1963–65; W. Nelson Anderson, architect. Certified, PHC 1957. 2 sheets (1957, including plans, elevation, details);* 2 ext. photos (1958, 1961),* see Man Full of Trouble Tavern (PA-128) for 1 ext. photo (1973),* 1 int. photo (1968);* 15 data pages (1958, 1966).*

Pennsylvania Hospital. Illustrated

(PA-1123), N.W. corner Eighth and Pine sts. Museum. Brick with granite and marble trim, approx. 285' (twenty-three-bay front) × 110' including wings, two-and-a-half and three stories on raised basement, hipped roof with circular balustraded skylight on octagonal base on center section, gable and hipped roofs with octagonal cupolas on wings, marble ground story and six giant pilasters at second and third stories of center section, round-arch entrance with fanlight and modified Corinthian frontispiece on center section, central-hall plan with offices and library in center section and wards in wings.

Notable architectural complex whose center building is an outstanding example of American Adamesque architecture and whose plan influenced later hospital design. East wing built 1755–57; Samuel Rhoads, architect. West wing built 1794–96, center section built 1794–1805; David Evans, Jr., architect. West wing altered 1846–47, center section altered 1848, east wing altered 1853; John McArthur, contractor; John McArthur, Jr., superintendent. East and west wings altered 1896; Addison Hutton, architect. Founded 1751 by Benjamin Franklin and Dr. Thomas Bond, Pennsylvania Hospital is the earliest established hospital in the United States with the country's oldest surgical amphitheater. It pioneered in psychotherapy from its beginning and established one of the country's first mental health clinics 1885. Nursing museum in east wing since 1976. Certified, PHC 1956; designated National Historic Landmark 1965.

19 sheets (1940, including plans, elevations, section, details) from Survey, Philadelphia Chapter, A.I.A. (1931–32); 4 ext. photos (1974),* 3 int. photos (1976),* 3 photocopies of measured drawings (1897),* 19 photocopies of architectural competition drawings for building never erected (1834, including four by John Haviland, four by Samuel H. Kneass, four by William Strickland, three by John C. Trautwine, four by Thomas U. Walter),* 1 photocopy of heating plans by Morris, Tasker & Morris (1846);* 23 data pages (including 1761–1896 insurance surveys).*

Perelman Antique Toy Museum. See Abercrombie, Captain James, House

Physick-Conner House
(PA-1356), 240 Pine St. or 401 S. Third St., at S.E. corner Third and Pine sts. Brick with marble trim, approx. 20' (two-bay front) × 43' with two-story rear ell, three-and-a-half stories, gable roof, elliptical window in gable end, side entry hall. Built c. 1830; altered to store c. 1900; rehabilitated 1967–68. Certified, PHC 1957. 1 photocopy of old ext. photo (c. 1890),* 5 photocopies of old int. photos (c. 1890);* 2 data pages (1958).*

Pickands, Thomas, House
(PA-1357), 307 S. Third St. Brick with marble trim, 26'-3" (three-bay front) × 42'-9" with three-story rear ell, three-and-a-half stories on

raised basement, gable roof, round-arch marble entrance with fan-light, marble lintels with keystones, originally side-hall town house plan.

Fine early-19th-century town house. Built 1808–9; Thomas Pickands, house carpenter. Altered to store 1868; reverted to dwelling 1895. Restored 1966–68; Hugh D. Zimmers, architect. Hallway arches at Smithsonian Institution, Washington, D.C. Certified, PHC 1957.

6 sheets (1958, including plans, elevations, section, details)* courtesy of Philadelphia Historical Commission; 3 ext. photos (1959, 1972),* 1 int. photo (1959);* 8 data pages (1958, including 1813–96 insurance surveys);* HABSI form (1958).*

Piles, John, House
(PA-1358), 328 S. Third St. Brick, approx. 16' (two-bay front) × 20', two-and-a-half stories, gable roof, brick stringcourse, one-room ground story. One of a pair of row houses. Built 1772; John Piles, house carpenter. Restored 1959–61. Certified, PHC 1957. 2 ext. photos (1959, 1973);* 3 data pages (1958, including 1772 insurance survey).*

Powel, Samuel, House. Illustrated
(PA-1359), 244 S. Third St. Historic house museum. Brick with stone trim, approx. 30' (three-bay front) × 50' with two- and three-story rear ell, three-and-a-half stories, gable roof, Doric frontispiece, stone stringcourses, side-hall town house plan, notable interior.

One of the finest Georgian town houses in Philadelphia. Built 1765 for Charles Stedman, merchant. Interior altered 1770; Robert Smith, builder. Ground-story interior altered mid-19th century; interior elements removed 1921, 1925. Restored 1931–33; Louis Duhring, architect. Ballroom woodwork and ornamental plaster ceiling in Philadelphia Museum of Art; rear parlor woodwork in Metropolitan Museum of Art, New York; reproductions in house. Home of Samuel Powel, city's last mayor under the Crown and first mayor in the New Republic, 1769–93. Owned by Philadelphia Society for the Preservation of Landmarks since 1931. Certified, PHC 1956; Pennsylvania Register 1970.

5 ext. photos (1967, 1969, 1972),* 14 int. photos (1958, 1962, 1967),* 2 photocopies of int. photos (1925, 1929);* 5 data pages (including 1769–1859 insurance surveys).*

Reed Houses

(PA-1615), 518–20 S. Front St. Two brick row houses with stone trim, each approx. 24' (three-bay front) × 42' with original two-story rear ell and later one-story additions, three-and-a-half stories, gambrel roofs, originally frontispiece with columns, stone stringcourses, lintels with keystones, side-hall town house plans.

Fine merchants' town houses with later alterations. Built 1796–98. No. 518 altered to store, one-story rear side brick addition built 1913–14; Herman H. Kline, architect. No. 520 interior altered to warehouse later. Certified, PHC 1957; Pennsylvania Register 1970. 3 ext. photos (1958, 1961, 1966);* 8 data pages (1960, including 1798 newspaper advertisement and 1803, 1851 insurance surveys);* 2 HABSI forms (1957).*

Rhoads-Barclay House

(PA-1057), 217 Delancey St., at N.E. corner Philip St. Brick, 22'-6" (three-bay front) × 37'-0" with two-story rear ell, two-and-a-half stories, gambrel roof, pent eave, notable interior woodwork and staircase, side-hall London house plan.

Fine example of mid-18th-century Philadelphia dwelling originally with detached kitchen. Built between 1750 and 1758; Samuel Rhoads, builder. Rear ell demolished 1959. One-story rear kitchen wing built, exterior restored, interior altered 1960; W. Nelson Anderson, architect; Robert T. Trump, restorer. Built by Samuel Rhoads, master builder and Mayor of Philadelphia 1774, for Alexander Barclay, Comptroller of Port of Philadelphia 1758–71. Certified, PHC 1957; Pennsylvania Register 1970.

7 sheets (1961, including plot plan, plans, elevations, details); 4 ext. photos (1959, 1973*), 3 int. photos (1959); 6 data pages (1959, 1963).

Rich-Truman House

(PA-1074), 320 Delancey St. Brick, 18'-11" (two-bay front) × 18' with two-story rear kitchen ell, two-and-a-half stories, gable roof, pent eave, one-room ground story. Fine example of modest craftsman's house built as one of a pair of row houses. Rear ell built before 1771. Front section built 1771; John Rich (plasterer), builder. Restored 1962; Joseph A. Praissman, architect. Certified, PHC 1957; Pennsylvania Register 1970. 12 sheets (1962, including plot plan, plans, elevations, sections, details); 2 ext. photos (1963), 1 int. photo (1963), 1 photocopy of old ext. photo (n.d.); 8 data pages (1963).

Richardson, Nathaniel, House

(PA-1360), 524 S. Front St. Brick, approx. 20' (three-bay front) × 37' with two- and three-story rear ell, three-and-a-half stories, gable roof, originally side-hall town house plan. Built 1792–93; altered to store before 1860; two-story rear brick addition built 1919; interior altered 1920. Certified, PHC 1957; Pennsylvania Register 1970. 1 ext. photo (1967);* 5 data pages (1961, including 1893 insurance survey);* HABSI form (1958).*

Robinson, William, House

(PA-1361), 23 Clymer St. Wood frame with clapboard sides and rear, approx. 16' (two-bay front) × 18' with one-story rear wing, two-and-a-half stories, half-gambrel roof. Built c. 1795; demolished 1967. 1 ext. photo (1966);* 9 data pages (1966).*

St. Andrew's (Protestant Episcopal) Church (now St. George's Greek Orthodox Cathedral)

(PA-1362), 250–54 S. Eighth St. Brick covered with rough cast to simulate ashlar blocks, approx. 65' × 89', two stories on raised basement, gable roof, Ionic hexastyle portico, notable iron fence, three-aisle plan with balconies.

Fine Greek Revival church with historical antecedents. Built 1822–23; John Haviland, architect. Three-story rear Sunday School and vestry building built 1840. Haviland belonged to this congregation and was buried under the church; body reinterred at Philadelphia Divinity School 1922. Acquired by St. George's Greek Orthodox congregation 1922; became Cathedral 1971. Certified, PHC 1956; Pennsylvania Register 1970. 1 ext. photo (1958);* 13 data pages (1965, including 1824–54 insurance surveys).*

St. George's Greek Orthodox Cathedral. See St. Andrew's (Protestant Episcopal) Church

St. Mary's (Roman Catholic) Church (also known as Old St. Mary's)

(PA-1363), 244 S. Fourth St. Brick with marble trim, 71'-7" (three-bay front) × 110'-10", one story, gable roof, rectangular front facade with Gothic-, Tudor-, ogee-arch windows and entrance, round-arch side and rear windows; three-aisle plan, galleries, semicircular chancel.

Built 1763; interior renovated 1782. Enlarged 1810–11; Charles Johnson (master carpenter), architect. Crucifix carved by William Rush c. 1810; new organ front designed by Thomas U. Walter (architect) 1839. Altar moved to western end, rounded bay added 1886; church remodeled 1963. The chief Roman Catholic house of worship during the Revolutionary period, St. Mary's in 1779 was the site of the first public religious service in commemoration of the Declaration of Independence. Commodore John Barry, father of the American Navy, is buried in the churchyard. Cathedral Church of the See of Philadelphia 1808–38. Certified, PHC 1957. 1 ext. photo (1972),* 1 photocopy of old int. lithograph (c. 1880),* 1 photo (1958)* of crypt; 1 data page (1959).*

St. Peter's Church House. See Blackwell, Reverend Robert, House

St. Peter's (Protestant Episcopal) Church. Illustrated
(PA-1118), S.W. corner Third and Pine sts. Brick with marble trim, approx. 61' (three-bay front) × 95', two stories with six-story square tower and octagonal spire (originally only octagonal cupola), gable roof, round-arch windows with large Palladian window in eastern end, quoins; three-aisle plan with box pews, galleries, rectangular chancel.

Fine Georgian church design. Built 1758–61; Robert Smith, architect. Organ loft built over chancel 1789. Tower and spire built 1842; William Strickland, architect. Iron spiral staircases installed c. 1846; Thomas U. Walter, architect. Interior altered 1960. Many members of this congregation were prominent in Revolutionary politics and military affairs. Certified, PHC 1957.

17 sheets (1940, including plot plan, plans, elevations, sections, details) from Survey, Philadelphia Chapter, A.I.A. (1932); 6 ext. photos (1976),* 3 photocopies of old ext. photos (1898, c. 1910),* 4 photocopies of old int. photos (1898, c. 1910);* 3 data pages (1965, including 1843 insurance survey).*

Schively, Henry, House
(PA-1364), 329 S. Third St., at S.E. corner Delancey St. Brick, approx. 17' (two-bay front) × 30', three stories on raised basement, gable roof. Built c. 1826; altered to store 1877; rehabilitated 1969. Certified, PHC 1957. 3 ext. photos (1961);* 3 data pages (1958, including 1877 insurance survey).*

Shippen-Wistar House. Illustrated
(PA-1365), 238 S. Fourth St., at S.W. corner Locust St. Brick, approx. 33' (three-bay front) × 42' originally with two-story back buildings on

Locust St. attached by stair tower, three-and-a-half stories, gable roof, Tuscan pilaster frontispiece with fanlight, side entrance foyer.

Fine example of corner-house plan with its more efficient use of interior space. Built c. 1765; back buildings demolished 1912. Between c. 1765 and 1797 the home of William Shippen, a leading colonial physician and medical educator who headed the medical department of the Continental Army 1777–81. Caspar Wistar, a physician and chemistry professor who served as third president of the American Philosophical Society, lived here 1798–1809. Offices of Mutual Assurance Company for Insuring Houses from Loss by Fire since 1912. Certified, PHC 1956; Pennsylvania Register 1970. 1 ext. photo (1963),* 2 int. photos (1959);* 12 data pages (1959, including 1785–1913 insurance surveys).*

Sink-Burgin House
(PA-1366), 331 S. Fifth St. Brick with marble trim, approx. 20' (three-bay front) × 38' with two-story rear wing, three-and-a-half stories, gable roof. Built between 1810 and 1815; altered to store, new cornice and dormers added after 1890; shopfront altered 1941; demolished 1964. Built for Lawrence Sink, cabinetmaker. Between 1831 and 1870 home of George H. Burgin, physician-druggist known for his glass manufacturing and civic activities, which included roles in the founding of Philadelphia College of Pharmacy 1821 and Women's Medical College 1853. Certified, PHC 1957. 1 ext. photo (1960);* 3 data pages (1964).*

Smith, Daniel, Jr., House
(PA-1367), 505 S. Front St. Brick with marble trim, approx. 20' (two-bay front) × 40', three-and-a-half stories on raised basement, gable roof, arch-head entrance with fanlight, two rooms and entry with rear stair ell. Built 1828; demolished 1966. Certified, PHC 1957. 1 ext. photo (1961);* 3 data pages (1961, including 1828 insurance survey);* HABSI form (1957).*

Society Hill Synagogue. See Spruce Street Baptist Church

South Water Street Area Study
(PA-1619), 516–26 S. Water St., W. side Water St. in block between Lombard and South sts. Six contiguous brick houses, each approx. 14' (two-bay front) × 30', two-and-a-half and three-and-a-half stories, gable roofs, probably London house plans except No. 526

(side-hall plan with rear stair tower). Nos. 516–18 built 1819–20; Nos. 520–22 built between 1779 and 1783; No. 524 built 1784; No. 526 built 1832–34. Demolished 1967. Certified, PHC 1957. 3 photocopies of ext. photos (1957, c. 1960);* 13 data pages (1961);* 5 HABSI forms (1957).*

Southern Loan Company of Philadelphia (later known as Tradesmen's National Bank of Philadelphia)

(PA-1368), 300 S. Second St., at S.W. corner Spruce St. Brick with marble ground story (now covered with scored stucco) and stucco top story, approx. 16' (two-story front) × 60', four stories, flat roof. Built c. 1837; ground story altered 1922; rehabilitated 1967–68. First home of Tradesman National Bank. 2 ext. photos (1959, 1973);* 3 data pages (1960).*

Southwark Hose Company No. 9

(PA-1369), 512 S. Third St. Brick with stone and iron trim, approx. 20' (three-bay front) × 75', three stories, flat roof, round-arch doors and windows, vertical emphasis to facade from projecting piers and recessed spandrels. Built 1858; possibly by Stephen D. Button, architect; Charles T. Brown, superintendent of construction. Altered to store later; shopfront remodeled 1906, 1914, 1934; renovated 1972. 1 ext. photo (1963).*

Spruce Street Baptist Church (now Society Hill Synagogue)

(PA-1370), 426 Spruce St., at S.W. corner Lawrence St. Brick with smooth-rusticated granite basement and scored-plastered granite front, approx. 60' (three-bay front) × 82' with rear projection, one story on raised basement with square corner towers (originally with cupolas), gable roof, front windows with granite surrounds and lintels on corbels; three-aisle plan, rear balcony (originally balconies on three sides), rectangular chancel with elliptical arch.

An early work of a major early-19th-century architect. Built 1829–30; Thomas U. Walter, architect. Enlarged, new front built 1851; Thomas U. Walter, architect; R. Morris Smith, supervisory architect. Interior altered, two-story rear projection built 1871; rear projection replaced by larger one 1877; interior altered 1901; cupolas removed after 1911. Exterior restored (except for cupolas) 1968; Henry J. Magaziner, architect. Interior restored 1971– ; Francis, Cauffman, Wilkinson and Pepper, architects, in association with John D. Milner, architect. Synagogue since 1912. Certified, PHC 1957; Pennsylvania Register 1970. 1 ext. photo (1976),* 1 photocopy of old ext. print (c. 1860);* 6 data pages (1963, including 1852–77 insurance surveys).*

Stafford's Tavern. See Man Full of Trouble Tavern

Stewart, Thomas, House
(PA-189), 410 Locust St., Independence National Historical Park. Brick, 17'-8" (two-bay front) × 18'-10" with one- and three-story rear ell, three-and-a-half stories, gable roof, round-arch entrance with fanlight, city house plan. Built c. 1824; rehabilitated 1954. Hardware samples, cornice and molding elements in Architectural Study Collection, Museum Division, Independence National Historical Park. Certified, PHC 1957. 6 sheets (1957, including plot plan, plans, elevations, section, details); 2 ext. photos (1957); 7 data pages (1957).

Stiles, William, House
(PA-1371), 310 Cypress St. Brick with marble trim, approx. 20' (three-bay front) × 20' with two- and three-story rear ell, three-and-a-half stories, gable roof, side-hall plan. Built before 1792; probably by William Stiles, stonecutter. Certified, PHC 1957. 2 ext. photos (1962);* 5 data pages (1963, including 1810 insurance survey).*

Stocker, John Clement, House
(PA-1068), 402 S. Front St. Brick with marble trim, 27'-2" (three-bay front) × 45'-0" with two- and three-story rear wing, three-and-a-half stories on raised basement, gable roof, originally round-arch entrance with fanlight and frontispiece with columns and pediment, side-hall town house plan.

Fine example of a wealthy merchant's Federal town house. Built between 1791 and 1795; rear addition built c. 1803; altered to store before 1910; altered to warehouse c. 1936. Certified, PHC 1957. 6 sheets (1960, 1961, including plot plan, plan, elevation, section, details); 2 ext. photos (1961), 7 int. photos (1961), 2 photocopies of old ext. photos (c. 1910), 4 photocopies of measured drawings of second-floor fireplace walls and details (1914); 11 data pages (1962).

Stride-Madison House
(PA-1073), 429 Spruce St. Brick, 17'-7" (three-bay front) × 32'-3½" with three-story rear ell (originally two- and three-story ell), three-and-a-half stories, gable roof, round-arch entrance with fanlight and pedimented frontispiece, side-hall plan.

Built c. 1791; altered to warehouse 1916. Exterior restored, interior rehabilitated 1962–63; W. Nelson Anderson, architect. James Madison, fourth President of the United States, and his wife Dolley rented this house 1795–96 when he was a member of Congress.

Certified, PHC 1957. 6 sheets (1961, including plot plan, plans, sections, details); 4 ext. photos (1961, 1965), 5 int. photos (1962, 1965), 1 photocopy of old ext. photo (c. 1914); 8 data pages (1964).

Sully, Thomas, House

(PA-1372), 530 Spruce St. Brick with marble trim, approx. 22' (three-bay front) × 44' with one- and three-story rear ell, three-and-a-half stories, gable roof, rear bow, floor-to-ceiling second-story windows with iron screens, side-hall town house plan. Built 1797; Griffith Coombe, house carpenter. Remodeled, three-story rear ell built 1842; one-story rear kitchen built 1896. Rehabilitated 1965. Thomas Sully, famous and prolific 19th-century portraitist, lived here 1828–29. Certified, PHC 1957; designated National Historic Landmark 1965. 1 ext. photo (1967),* 5 int. photos (1967);* 5 data pages (1957, including 1841–96 insurance surveys).*

Summers-Worrell House

(PA-1373), 505 Delancey St., at N.E. corner Reese St. Brick, approx. 14' (two-bay front) × 19' with two-story rear ell, three stories, gable roof, one room to a floor. Built 1796; George Summers and Joseph Worrell, house carpenters. Demolished 1964. Certified, PHC 1957. 1 ext. photo (1960);* 5 data pages (1964, including 1810, 1893 insurance surveys).*

Third Presbyterian Church (also known as Old Pine Street Church)

(PA-1374), 422 Pine St. Stuccoed brick, approx. 63' (three-bay front) × 93', two stories with Corinthian octastyle portico (originally with pedimented frontispiece and Palladian window above), gable roof, pilasters on side walls, three-aisle plan with galleries.

Colonial church with fine 19th-century classical revival remodeling. Built 1766–68; interior remodeled, exterior stuccoed 1837. Exterior remodeled 1857; John Fraser, architect; A. Catanach, carpenter. Interior renovated 1867, 1952. Many members of this congregation served in the American Revolution. With the merger of Holland-Scots Church 1953 and Eastburn Mariners' Bethel Church 1958, the church's corporate name is now Third, Scots, and Mariner's Church. Certified, PHC 1957. 1 ext. photo (1974),* 4 photocopies of int. photos (1956);* 2 data pages (1965).*

Tradesman National Bank of Philadelphia. See Southern Loan Company of Philadelphia

U.S. Bonded Warehouse
(PA-1375), 415–19 S. Front St. and 416–18 S. Water St., at S.E. corner Front and Lombard sts. Brick with stone trim, approx. 150' (sixteen-bay front) × 130', three stories on Front St., five stories on Water St., flat roof, segmental-headed windows and doorways, chamfered stone piers on ground-story front, rectangular plan. Built 1853; John McArthur, Jr., architect. Demolished 1967. 4 ext. photos (1960, including one of iron sign hook).*

Waln, Isaac, House
(PA-1376), 259 S. Third St. Brick with marble trim, approx. 27' (three-bay front) × 44' with three-story rear ell, three stories, low gable roof, Ionic frontispiece with pediment, side-hall plan. Built 1791; altered to store later; demolished 1960. Certified, PHC 1957. 2 ext. photos (1960),* 4 int. photos (1960);* 5 data pages (1960, including 1791–1849 insurance surveys).*

Warehouse
(PA-1377), 105 Delancey St. Brick with stone trim, approx. 18' (three-bay front) × 40', three stories, half-gambrel roof, rectangular plan. Built early 19th century; demolished 1961. 1 ext. photo (1961).*

Warehouse
(PA-1378), 329 S. Water St. and 330 S. Delaware Ave., at N.E. corner Water and Panama sts. Brick with stone trim, 29'-11" (three-bay front) × 44'-7" with four-story rear addition, three stories, gable roof, rectangular plan with interior wood columns. Built c. 1810; rear addition built c. 1830; demolished 1967. 5 sheets (1966, including plot plan, plans, elevations, section);* 3 ext. photos (1966).*

Water Trough and Fountain. Illustrated
(PA-1379), E. side Ninth St. between Spruce and Pine sts., opposite Clinton St. Granite, carved monolithic fountain pedestal (approx. 5'-6" height) with attached trough on west (street) side, pedestal approx. 4'-9" × 1', trough approx. 4'-9" × 2', gadrooned fountain basin on east (sidewalk) side; "Edward Wetherill 1821–1908" inscribed above fountain, "A Merciful Man/Is Merciful To His Beast" inscribed above trough. Fine example of functional street furniture before the age of the auto. Built c. 1910. 2 photos (1975).*

Wetherill, Joseph, House

(PA-1380), 233 Delancey St. Brick with marble trim, approx. 17' (two-bay front) × 40', three-and-a-half stories on raised basement, gable roof, arch-head entrance, London house plan. Built 1811. Certified, PHC 1957. 1 ext. photo (1972),* 3 int. photos (1959, of fireplaces);* 3 data pages (1959, including 1824 insurance survey).*

Wharton, Isaac, House

(PA-1381), 510 S. Front St., at S.W. corner Naudain St. Brick, approx. 23' (three-bay front) × 40' with two- and three-story rear ell, three-and-a-half stories on raised basement, round-headed entrance, brick stringcourse, side-hall town house plan.

A merchant's town house built for rental income in a commercial-residential neighborhood. Built 1793; interior altered 1871. Certified, PHC 1957; Pennsylvania Register 1970. 2 ext. photos (1958, 1967);* 5 data pages (1961, including 1793–1879 insurance surveys);* HABSI form (1957).*

Wharton, Joseph, House. Illustrated

(PA-1382), 119 Lombard St. Brick, approx. 18' (three-bay front) × 32' with two-story rear ell, three-and-a-half stories, gable roof, segmental-arch heads over windows, brick stringcourse with glazed headers, alleyway through ground story to rear yard, London house plan.

One of a pair of row houses. Built c. 1743; possibly by John Palmer, bricklayer. Rear ell built c. 1767. Restored 1964–66; Duncan W. Buell, architect. Certified, PHC 1957. 2 ext. photos (1962, 1972),* 4 int. photos (1962);* 3 data pages (1961, including 1767 insurance survey).*

Williams-Hopkinson House

(PA-1084), 338 Spruce St. Brick, approx. 18' (three-bay front) × 36' with two- and three-story rear ell, three-and-a-half stories, gable roof, pedimented frontispiece, brick stringcourses, side-hall town house plan.

Modest Federal town house. Built between 1785 and 1791; rear addition built 1907; altered to store 1909; restored 1959–64. Old wallpaper samples in Architectural Study Collection, Museum Division, Independence National Historical Park. Joseph Hopkinson, writer of "Hail, Columbia!" lived here 1794–1800. Certified, PHC 1957.

5 sheets (1932, including elevations, details) from Survey,

Philadelphia Chapter, A.I.A., 3 sheets (1961, including plot plan, plans); 2 ext. photos (1961, 1962), 5 int. photos (1959, 1961, 1962), 3 photocopies of measured drawings of second-floor fireplace walls and details (1914); 10 data pages (1961, 1964).

Williams-Mathurin House

(PA-1383), 427 Spruce St. Brick with marble trim, 22'-9" (three-bay front) × 34'-5" with three-story rear ell, three-and-a-half stories, gable roof, round-arch entrance with fanlight and Adamesque frontispiece, marble stringcourses and lintels with keystones, mutule cornice, side-hall town house plan.

Fine Federal-style town house. Built 1791; William Williams, house carpenter. Altered to warehouse c. 1920. Exterior restored 1969–72; Carl Massara, architect. Antoine René Charles Mathurin, French Consul General, lived here 1791–93. Certified, PHC 1957. 3 ext. photos (1961, 1972),* 6 int. photos (1961);* 6 data pages (1959, including 1793, 1812 insurance surveys).*

Winder, William H., Houses. Illustrated

(PA-1384), 232–34 S. Third St. Two brick row houses with marble trim, each approx. 20' (four-bay front) × 49' with three- (originally two-) and four-story rear ell, four-and-a-half stories with marble ground story, gable roofs, Ionic frontispieces, notable ornamental ironwork balcony at second story, side-hall plans.

Fine Greek Revival row; originally a unit of three. Built 1843–44; possibly by Thomas U. Walter, architect. Rear ell raised to three stories 1855; exterior restored, interior rehabilitated 1962–64. No. 232 houses Executive Offices of Episcopal Community Services. Certified, PHC 1957. 4 ext. photos (1962, 1972);* 10 data pages (1958, including 1844, 1855 insurance surveys).*

Winemore, Phillip, House

(PA-1050), 222 Spruce St. Brick, 15'-5" (two-bay front) × 21'-10" with two-story rear ell, two-and-a-half stories, gable roof, one room to a floor. Built c. 1746; rear ell built later; rehabilitated 1958. Certified, PHC 1957. 1 sheet (1959, including plot plan, plans, section); 2 ext. photos (1957), 1 int. photo (1957); 5 data pages (1959).

Wood, George, Houses

(PA-1385), 335–37 S. Fifth St. Brick with stone trim, each approx. 20' (two-bay front) × 35' with three-story rear ell (originally two stories), three-and-a-half stories, gable roof, side-hall plan. Built after 1767; probably by George Wood, house carpenter. Rear ell raised to three stories c. 1853; altered to stores, cornices and dormers changed later; demolished 1964. Certified, PHC 1957. 1 ext. photo (1960);* 8 data pages (1959, including 1851–53 insurance surveys).*

Woods, Captain John, House
(PA-1111), 500 S. Front St., at S.W. corner Lombard St. Brick, approx. 21' (two-bay front) × 44', originally with two- and three-story rear wing, three-and-a-half stories on raised stone basement, gable roof, round-arch side entrance with fanlight, center-hall plan. Built 1783; originally a store in east room. Communicated with adjacent house on Front St. 1904; destructively altered and reduced to two stories 1955. 9 sheets (1940, including elevations, details) from Survey, Philadelphia Chapter, A.I.A. (1932); 3 data pages (including 1783, 1785, 1918 insurance surveys).*

Bethel African Methodist Episcopal Church. *Jack E. Boucher photo, 1973.*

Man Full of Trouble Tavern *(right)* and Benjamin Paschall House *(left)*. *Jack E Boucher photo, 1972.*

Pennsylvania Hospital. *Cortlandt V. D Hubbard photo, 1976.*

Samuel Powel House. *Jack E. Boucher photo, 1972.*

St. Peter's (Protestant Episcopal) Church. *James L. Dillon & Co. photo, 1976.*

Shippen-Wistar *(right)* and Norris-Cadwalader *(left)* Houses. *Cortlandt V. D. Hubbard photo, 1963.*

Water Trough and Fountain. *Jack E. Boucher photo, 1974.*

Joseph Wharton House. *Jack E. Boucher photo, 1972.*

William H. Winder Houses. *Jack E. Boucher photo, 1972.*

Penn's City

Old City

2

Introduction

*O*LD CITY IS ONE of Philadelphia's richest neighborhoods in terms of history, architectural diversity, and potential development. Its history incorporates the history of the city from its beginning; its architecture includes examples of nearly every type of building erected since the mid-eighteenth century; its future could be that of a combined New York Greenwich Village and Washington Georgetown. Old City's georgaphical limits are arbitrarily defined to include the area bounded by the Delaware River on the east, Vine Street on the north, Ninth Street on the west, and Locust Street on the south. It encompasses Independence National Historical Park, two historic districts listed by the National Register of Historic Places, and eight National Historic Landmarks, among them the U.S.S. *Olympia,* Admiral Dewey's flagship at the Battle of Manila in 1898.[1]

Part of the original (1682) plan of the city of Philadelphia as laid out by Thomas Holme, William Penn's surveyor-general, this neighborhood was the center of much of the early political history of Pennsylvania. The first site of city and provincial government was the Old Court House, or Town Hall, which in the medieval English fashion stood in the middle of High Street, at Second Street, with market stalls extending westward behind it. Built in 1701–10, the Old Town Hall was demolished in 1837 during renovation of the market sheds, and the sheds, in turn, were removed in 1859 in favor of a street railway.[2]

Always functionally separate, city and colonial governments were physically separated in 1748, when the new State House (Independence Hall) (illus.) opened on what was then the western edge of the city at Sixth and Chestnut streets. This latter building, an outstanding example of Georgian public architecture, was to play an even greater role in the founding of the American nation when it served as the meeting place for the Second Continental Congress and saw the adoption of the Declaration of Independence and in 1787 the drafting of the United States Constitution. It has been a national shrine ever since.[3] In 1791 the city government moved to the same site, when City Hall was built as an eastern wing to the State House, balancing the County Court Building, built two years earlier on the western end. Both buildings were also used for federal purposes when Philadelphia served as the nation's capital during the 1790's. Local government offices began moving out of the two buildings and into the present City Hall at Center Square after 1877.[4]

The city's early commercial district concentrated in this area and has done so ever since the first wharf was built along the Delaware River at Walnut Street in 1685. Contrary to Penn's intentions (he had planned a promenade there), the waterfront by the mid-eighteenth century was congested with buildings catering to maritime needs.[5] All these eighteenth-century structures between the river and the east side of Front Street and their later replacements fell to Interstate 95 (Delaware Expressway) in the late 1960's. HABS, however, recorded some examples, such as the warehouse of Paul Beck, Jr., on the waterfront at Delaware Avenue and two eighteenth-century houses on North Water Street.

Beck's warehouse was generally thought to be a rare eighteenth-century structure, and at one point its removal to another site was under consideration.[6] Fire insurance surveys uncovered by Mrs. Earle Kirkbride of the Philadelphia Historical Commission, however, show the building to have been newly built in December, 1805.[7] The gambrel roof, thought to have been its eighteenth-century hallmark, was actually added about 1870, presumably for the same reasons it was used in the eighteenth century—to save building materials and provide more space in the garret.[8] The warehouse had a simple rectangular plan with open stairs to the upper floor and was divided by a solid brick wall that extended the length of the building on both stories. The dividing walls were evidently standard features at the time. For example, three warehouses in Philadelphia's Southwark section were similarly built: Thomas Penrose's three-story warehouse on Water Street below South (c. 1797), the 1810 warehouse at 329 South Water Street, and Jesse Godley's extensive structure at 19–27 Queen Street, built as late as 1868.[9] Such interior walls offered two advantages. First, the wall enabled the owner to rent the parts separately, as is suggested in Beck's warehouse by the presence of four plastered counting rooms, presumably one on each floor of each section, and, second, it made the warehouse more fire-resistant. Evidently the latter was also its intent, since iron window shutters were put up along the sides and the flat dormers of the sailmaker's loft were cased with iron, an early use of this material.[10]

The colonial houses at 113–15 North Water Street, on the other hand, were initially dwellings. It was not unusual for eighteenth-century merchants to live along the waterfront, either next to or above their stores; in fact, in the 1790's, Stephen Girard, the wealthiest of these entrepreneurs, had his dwelling built at 23 North Water Street with a private counting room on the ground floor and a public counting room in the adjacent building. These houses were not temporary quarters to be endured until the merchant could afford to move to a more fashionable address. They were first-class dwellings, well built and handsomely finished, as seen in the case of the Dowers-Okill House at 115 North Water Street, which had carved mantles and cornices, stucco and gilt decoration, and a balcony overlooking the river. These appointments had been removed long before the house's demolition in the early 1960's, but its rare scalloped lintels suggested its earlier elegance.[11] As the only known surviving example of scalloped lintels in Philadelphia, they were removed to the Museum Division of Independence National Historical Park when the building gave way to the Delaware Expressway.[12]

With the rise of business activity along the waterfront came the need for a common meeting place where merchants could exchange information on cargoes, prices, and sales. The first of these was the London Coffee-House, which was built in 1702 as a residence at the southwest corner of Front and Market streets. In 1754 it began twenty years' service as a merchants' exchange and center of commercial and political activity, until it was overshadowed by the newer, more modish City Tavern, which opened in 1773, on Second Street above Walnut.[13] While merchants gathered at City Tavern, the old London Coffee-House spent a brief period as a printing and bookseller's shop before it was put to mercantile use in 1789 by the retail hardware merchant, James Stokes; it remained a store, albeit one with a declining status, until it was demolished in 1884.[14]

The eastern end of Old City Philadelphia continued to develop and to increase its commercial diversity during the first half of the nineteenth century. In addition to the maritime commerce and retail trade of the eighteenth century, light manufacturing, wholesale houses, and the financial institutions needed to underpin these entrepreneurial activities, banks and insurance companies, began to fill the area.[15]

This increasingly complex commercial and financial activity quickly exceeded the limited space and facilities the old coffee houses had afforded Philadelphia's merchants. In response to the new needs, the Philadelphia Exchange Company (illus.) was organized in 1831 and the next year it commissioned William Strickland to design a building on the raised triangular lot bounded by Third, Walnut, and Dock streets.[16] Its location a block west of City Tavern reflected the westward shift of commerce and the concern to be as accessible to the city's three major financial institutions—Girard's Bank (illus.) on Third Street and the Bank of North America and the Second Bank of the United States (illus.) on Chestnut Street—as to the waterfront warehouses. As the exchange was opening in 1834 the formerly splendid City Tavern had degenerated into a rooming house, its elegant interior extensively altered.[17] The Exchange Building, on the other hand, with its curved Corinthian colonnade and lantern copied after the Choragic Monument of Lysicrates, was to dominate the neighborhood architecturally as well as financially for the next two generations. It housed the Philadelphia Merchants' Exchange, the Maritime Exchange, and the Stock Exchange intermittently until the end of the century, but its fortunes declined after the Civil War. An attempt to revitalize the building's commercial prospects in 1900 by gutting and rebuilding the interior proved an eventual failure, and in 1922 the former exchange became the center of the wholesale food market district.[18]

Part of the difficulties of the Philadelphia Exchange after the Civil War was the consolidation of a group of grain and flour dealers who inaugurated the Commercial Exchange, a reorganization of the earlier Corn Exchange, and challenged the primacy of the older Philadelphia Exchange. For their new building the Commercial Exchange acquired and cleared a lot at the southeast corner of Second and Sansom streets, then the site of the Slate Roof House, the city's oldest building and once the residence of William Penn. Cosmic retribution struck in December, 1869, when the new exchange was severely damaged by fire, less than a year after it had opened. It was rebuilt in 1870 from the designs of James H. Windrim, who salvaged most of the original walls but gave the building a stylish mansard and a more impressive tower. Thereafter, the Commercial Exchange emerged as one of the city's largest and most important commercial organizations until its building was enlarged and altered to house a telephone exchange and offices in 1901–2, accounting for its later ungainly proportions.[19]

By this time mercantile hopes and interests had shifted to a new organization and building, the Philadelphia Bourse (illus.) on Fifth Street below Market. Literally as big as a city block, this steel-frame pile could boast of a handsome interior court, industrial exhibition halls, and a grain and stock exchange. Its great size and special accommodations bore ample testimony to the scale of the city's commerce and industry.[20]

Another reflection of the growing specialization of industrialism was the practice of concentrating one kind of business activity within a one- or two-block area. Front Street north of Market evolved into a wholesale warehouse district and almost the whole block was rebuilt during the 1830's, giving it remarkable visual homogeneity. The style, a utilitarian classicism, was popular for nearly a quarter-century. Its architectonic features, granite or marble piers with molded caps and a plain granite or marble architrave, were limited to the ground story; above it rose a simple brick superstructure, often with stone sills and lintels and a molded brick cornice. Although the North Front Street stores were probably designed by builders, some later examples with clustered stone columns on the second story were architect-designed.[21] Built as warehouses, these buildings have ample dimensions, sometimes as wide as twenty-six feet and as deep as eighty feet, and except for an area partitioned off on the first or second floors for the counting-room and fire-proof, there is but one large room to a floor. Straight stairs rise along one wall for four or five stories, and a hoist machine is on the top floor with hatchways cut through each floor at the front of the building or, if it parallels an alley, at the side.[22] Probably the finest of these warehouses today is that of Nathan Trotter and Company. Built in 1833, it has been altered only slightly and still has its cast-iron columns extending along the middle of the large rooms of the first two floors.[23] While this is an early example of structural cast iron, it is not the earliest. Iron piers were used on the ground-story front of two warehouses around the corner on Church Alley in 1831, and as early as 1829 William Strickland had incorporated iron columns into the balconies of the United States Naval Asylum.[24]

As America entered the modern world of industrial technology in the second quarter of the nineteenth century, architects groped toward an appropriate historical style that would gratify the aesthetic and social needs of merchants as well as the economic and functional demands of their businesses. In Philadelphia John Haviland employed the immutable Egyptian in 1838 to suggest the permanence of the Pennsylvania Fire Insurance Company (illus.); Samuel Sloan used the castellated Gothic to make Bennett and Company's Tower Hall one of the most distinctive stores of its day; John Fraser applied the exotic Moorish in 1854 to one of Caleb Cope's dry goods bazaars.[25] Yet they all failed to provide the adaptable formula that would gratify the ego as well as the eye. Instead, that formula was found in Europe's more recent past: "There had never before been any considerable amount of architecturally ambitious commercial building; and the Renaissance cities of Italy seemed to provide the most impressive architectural results of the patronage of a rich merchant class."[26] Designers turned to the Italian style for its flexibility in attaining the proper impression of conservatism and stability, yet with a spirit of progressive enterprise and liberality. In fine, the objective was to make every merchant a miniature Medici.

During the 1850's Chestnut Street between Second and Third streets became a showcase for the Italianate, as the many forms of the Italian became known. The south side of the street has been demolished by the federal government, the east end in the 1930's for the Customs House and the west end in the 1950's for Independence National Historical Park. The north side remains, however, as a fine example of a mid-nineteenth-century center of dry goods commission merchants. Because of the wholesale nature of the block's business many stores were rendered in a utilitarian Italianate. This mode was handled either as an updating of the utilitarian Greek Revival or a variant of the orthodox Italian Renaissance Revival. The former, best illustrated by the store at 233 Chestnut, employed a more elaborate ground story, either in iron or stone, and a modest console cornice instead of the molded brick.

More innovative is the other handling of the utilitarian Italianate, sometimes called Philadelphia Functionalism.[27] The Jayne Building, which stood across the street at 242–44 Chestnut until early 1958, was in the Venetian Gothic style rather than the Italianate, but it probably was the source of inspiration for the utilitarian Italianate examples that followed its erection in 1849–50.[28] Two extant examples of this latter style can be seen side by side at 235–37 Chestnut Street, the Elliott and Leland buildings respectively, and at 239–41 Chestnut Street, the Lewis Building.[29] Designed by Stephen D. Button in 1852, the Lewis Building is the more radical departure from the norm. At a time when M. Field, a published New York spokesman on good taste in urban architecture, was pointing out "the unnecessary insertion of perpendicular lines as the prevalent fault of street architecture,"[30] Button went to extremes to stress perpendicular lines. Field suggested that "to produce real as well as apparent solidity, the solid parts should preponderate" in a building, allowing a rich variety of architectural elements to ornament the street front,[31] as in the case of the brownstone store at 229 Chestnut Street at the west corner of Bank Street. Button, on the other hand, stripped the wall of excessive ornament and designed thin piers and wide voids to open the wall to light. To indicate a skeletal framework, the spandrels were recessed to emphasize the continuous upward flow of the plain piers.

Less extreme examples of Philadelphia Functionalism are the Elliott and Leland buildings, built in 1854 and 1856.[32] On these identical buildings the architect, Joseph C. Hoxie, employed many elements of the Italianate but, by recessing the spandrels and restricting the stone carving, he made the design simpler and more coherent than was common for commercial buildings at the time.

Like the Front Street warehouses a generation earlier, these stores were built with one room to a floor with one or two counting rooms partitioned off, usually at the rear. The stores of the 1850's, however, were larger and incorporated many new appointments made available by the Industrial Revolution. The depth of the Leland Building, for example, was twice that of Nathan Trotter's warehouse, which gave it more than double the storage space since it was a story higher. Equally significant was the difference in fire-proofs, or safes. Fire-proofs in the Front Street stores were not described by insurance surveys of the 1830's except to mention that they were in the counting rooms, hence no bigger than closets. By the 1850's, however, fire-proofs had become large and separate parts of the buildings. Although most fire-proofs of this period were only one story high, the one in the Leland Building was two stories high and measured 7 feet 6 inches by 11 feet 8 inches. Like most commercial buildings of the time, the Leland store had a water closet, washstand, and urinal on the ground story, a skylight whose illumination extended into the basement, and plate-glass front windows protected at night by iron sliders rather than iron shutters.[33]

Around the corner on Third Street was Brokers' Row. Within the two-block square area of Third Street between Market and Walnut streets were 94.7 per cent of the city's brokers and investment bankers during the 1850's. The greatest concentration was on Third

Street between Market and Chestnut where 33.6 per cent of the city's 113 brokerage houses were located.[34] The architecture of mid-nineteenth-century brokers' offices was not significantly different from that of wholesale dry goods stores. The offices of Hutchinson and Company at 20 South Third Street were in a structure that had once served as a dwelling and shop but that was remodeled in late 1847 into a four-story, flat-roofed commercial building whose brownstone storefront featured battered Egyptian Revival doors, a not so subtle suggestion of the firm's sobriety.[35]

Drexel and Company, on the other hand, under the leadership of Francis M. Drexel, commissioned G. Runge in 1853 to design a new building at 34 South Third. The architect produced "one of the most imposing business edifices" in that part of the city.[36] Its chaste marble front was executed in the Tuscan mode of the Italianate, in which a balance of horizontal and vertical lines was attained through the use of molded pilasters and cornices at each floor.

Most brokers, however, rented office space. For example, both Edwin Booth and B. W. Tingley and Company found accommodations in the new building at 37–39 South Third, (illus.) which had been built for Charles Leland in 1855. As the finest example of Stephen D. Button's utilitarian Italianate,[37] it stands in vivid contrast to the Drexel Building across the street. Evidently in appreciation of the building's office functions, the elements of the Leland Building are more subtly synthesized than in the Lewis Building around the corner. The upward thrust of the Leland Building's granite piers gracefully terminate at the fourth story in round arches with plain moldings that are duplicated by the arcade on the ground story.

The interiors of these office buildings were similarly finished with higher quality materials and craftsmanship, reflecting the different nature and status of their functions. The Tuscan mode of the Drexel Building's front was continued in the large banking room, which was impressively furnished with a fifty-foot-long counter with a built-in ventilator near the encaustic tile floor. The rear of the building was illuminated by a large skylight that extended into the basement restaurant and the sub-basement's furnace room. The two wainscoted offices on the second story were finished with stucco cornices, ceiling centerpieces for gas lamps, and figured and painted glass in the paneled partitions.[38] As a rental property, the Leland Building across the street was done more plainly. Yet its two ground-story rooms were finished with pilasters, brackets, and enriched cornices, and deeply set square panels graced the foyer and stairway.[39] In both buildings water closets and iron wash basins were placed on nearly every floor, and sometimes there were two to a floor; and throughout both the windows were cased and finished with architraves rather than simply plastered to the sashes as in the Chestnut Street wholesale stores.[40]

Bank Row had eighteenth-century beginnings at 307 Chestnut Street with the Bank of North America, chartered in 1781 as America's first commercial bank, and followed in 1797 with the opening of Samuel Blodgett's architectural and Alexander Hamilton's financial masterpiece, the First Bank of the United States (illus.) on Third Street below Chestnut.[41] The institution that determined the nineteenth-century development of the row, however, was the Second Bank of the United States (illus.).[42] Chartered by Congress in 1816 and headquartered in Philadelphia, the Second Bank was to play a prominent role in both national politics and architecture, as a chartered monopoly with a unique and lucrative relationship to the federal government and as one of the country's first public buildings in the Greek Revival style. The former role aroused the presidential wrath of Andrew Jackson and led to the bank's financial demise, and the latter role established the popularity and viability of this variant of Romantic Classicism, catapulting the building's young architect, William Strickland, into the profession's front ranks.[43] In Philadelphia it was to cement banking functions on Chestnut Street, where they stayed even after the Second Bank became the United States Customs House in 1844. This was evidenced by the decision of the Bank of North America in 1847 to erect a new building at its original site there.[44]

Afterward, a series of granite and marble banks designed by a host of notable Philadelphia architects rose on the street.[45] John M. Gries was responsible for the two fine examples of the 1850's, the Philadelphia Bank and the Farmers and Mechanics Bank (illus.), adjacent to each other at 421 and 427 Chestnut Street respectively. The Farmers and Mechanics Bank, built in 1854–55, is the earlier of the two structures, and is significant not only for its "highly enriched white marble front" but also for its initial interior plan.[46] Instead of placing the banking room in the front, as was customary at the time, Gries followed a plan that was reminiscent of the nearby Second Bank of the United States. The front section had three doorways, two at the ends (since converted to windows) opening onto stairways and one in the middle with Corinthian pilasters that led down a passage to the rear, skylighted banking room. Richly decorated to echo key exterior elements, this room rose the full three stories to the arched ceiling.[47] Iron was used throughout the building, as part of the structure in the arched girders of the roof and straight girders of floor joists, as part of the furnishings in the iron counter with its built-in vents, and as decorative elements in the form of lions' heads on the front door that matched the marble examples on the keystones of the flanking windows.[48]

Although built of granite rather than marble and less elaborately carved, the Philadelphia Bank is the more imposing building.[49] This is partly because it is greater in size and scale, fifteen feet wider across the front and an additional story taller. Its Venetian Italianate style, "boldly modelled and open in feeling," gives the building a vertical articulation and less ornate appearance that complements its bulk.[50] Its plan was very similar to that of the Farmers and Mechanics Bank. The rear banking room rose the building's full height to an iron dome, whose top was sixty-five feet above the floor, giving an impressive interior space.[51]

Undaunted by the Panic of 1873, Philadelphia bankers added the greatest number of new banks to the row during the 1870's. Frank Furness, who was then emerging as the city's leading architect, contributed two banks, the Guarantee Trust and Safe Deposit Company at 318 Chestnut (1874–75) and the Provident Life and Trust Company (illus.) at 409 Chestnut (1876–79).[52] James H. Windrim designed two in 1874, the Philadelphia Trust, Safe Deposit and Insurance Company, 415 Chestnut, and the Peoples Bank, 435 Chestnut;[53] and Addison Hutton, the talented Quaker, was responsible for the finely modeled Pennsylvania Company for Insuring Lives and Granting Annuities, 431 Chestnut, in 1872–73.[54] All except Hutton's granite building are gone now, but for nearly eighty years these banks made this one of the most imposing stretches of streetscape in the city. Furness's banks, eyesores to some, were the visual anchors for the blocks.[55] Their robust detailing and monumental scale evoked the free-wheeling dynamism of a sanguine era. The last nineteenth-century addition to the row was the third Bank of North America, another Windrim work, this time designed in conjunction with his son, John T. Windrim.[56] Until it fell to make space for a parking lot in 1972, its Roman facade related well to John McArthur's chaste Italianate design for the First National Bank (1865–67) at 315 Chestnut.[57]

Insurance Row, the area on Walnut Street and adjacent streets between Third and Fifth, evolved around the venerable Philadelphia

Contributionship for the Insuring of Houses from Loss by Fire, organized by Benjamin Franklin in 1752, the nation's oldest mutual fire insurance company. Its present offices at 212 South Fourth Street were erected in 1835–36 from the Greek Revival designs of Thomas U. Walter.[58] Its domestic scale fits its original function of both dwelling and office. The insistence of the company's directors on the dual role was initially a point of contention between them and the architect, but Walter appears to have given his clients what they wanted, that is, a house with ground-story offices, a cellar kitchen, and upper chambers.[59] After the Civil War the company hired Collins and Autenreith to replace the porch, whose low-quality marble was deteriorating rapidly, and to add a mansard in order to gain an additional five rooms.[60] To take advantage of new technology, more alterations were made in the 1890's. Furness, Evans and Company drew up the designs for a new cellar kitchen and toilet room and other alterations to accommodate telephones in the offices and toilet rooms on the upper floors, with the top story remodeled into a well-appointed apartment.[61]

Meanwhile, other insurance companies moved into the neighborhood. Buildings to house their operations were erected along Walnut Street well into the twentieth century. Not much larger than the Philadelphia Contributionship, usually only four stories high, they were nevertheless unmistakably commercial buildings with ciphers or plaques or distinctively grotesque facades to make them stand out among their competitors. Yet the practice of maintaining an apartment on the top floor was continued, at least in the Reliance Insurance Company, 429 Walnut Street, and apparently in the adjacent Spring Garden Insurance Company.[62]

The availability of structural steel allowed early-twentieth-century office buildings to rise higher and be distinctive for that reason alone, but the inertia of nineteenth-century taste meant that they would be finished in an historical style. The Irvin Building (formerly the Fire Association of Philadelphia) at 401 Walnut Street, for example, was built in 1911–12 from the restrained classical designs of Edgar V. Seeler.[63] The Doric distyle portico in antis and other classical elements were proportionately scaled and low enough to be easily viewed by pedestrians. When an addition was required seventeen years later, however, another architect carried the new section to seventeen stories, piled another ten stories on the old part, and introduced a series of juxtaposed elements to produce what might be called a modernistic classicism.[64] A Greek fret frieze above the seventh story and freestanding spread eagles at the corners of the tenth story were suggestive of an imperial Greek style, while recessed bays with rounded corners and the building's name carved in shallow relief made the building very up-to-date.

The Irvin Building illustrates not only shifting taste but also changes in building technology and scale of business. Whereas the Philadelphia Contributionship employed traditional building materials and techniques, brick-bearing walls with oak joists and heart pine floors, the Irvin Building had a steel frame with brick and limestone curtain walls and concrete floors, construction materials that did not exist in 1835.[65] Building costs embody similar contrasts. Philadelphia Contributionship cost $20,946, while the Irvin Building was estimated to cost $300,000, or more than fourteen times the former.[66] These figures testify to the tremendous expansion of the national economy in general and the insurance business in particular during the last three-quarters of the nineteenth century, as well as to a company's willingness to spend its earnings on notable architecture.

But like Bank Row, Insurance Row has known architectural change in recent years. When the National Park Service tore down the Irvin Building in 1974, it completed the decimation of the north side of the 400 block of Walnut Street, while the former American Fire Insurance Company Building, with one of Furness, Evans and Company's more restrained business facades, is one of the last two insurance company buildings to survive in the 300 block. One member of the row, however, has put its best face forward and remains a part of the streetscape. As a result of the imagination and determination of the Penn Mutual Life Insurance Company and its architects, Mitchell and Giurgola Associates, the Egyptian Revival facade of the Pennsylvania Fire Insurance Company's old building (illus.) at 508–10 Walnut Street has been preserved as a courtyard screen in front of a new high-rise office building.[67]

Despite the onslaught of automobiles and bulldozers, the commercial row pattern persists. Clothing jobbers, for example, have been on Third Street above Market since the middle of the last century, Jewelers' Row still occupies the 700 block of Sansom Street and much of the north side of Walnut Street in that block as well, and the Washington Square neighborhood has been known as Publishers' Square for nearly eighty years. Among the major publishing companies still on the Square are J. B. Lippincott and Company, W. B. Saunders Company, the Farm Journal, and Lea and Febiger, the nation's oldest continuous publishing house.[68]

By the time of the Civil War, commercial Philadelphia was beginning to encroach upon what had been residential Old City. Starting in the 1850's, the brick dwellings along Arch and Cherry streets were replaced by factories and commercial buildings as far west as Fifth and Sixth streets. Most of these buildings stood for nearly a century. Joseph C. Hoxie's stark and imposing Horstmann Factory (1852–53) at the northeast corner of Fifth and Cherry streets, for example, was not replaced until the 1930's.[69] Others, such as the Schenck Building at the southeast corner of Sixth and Arch, survived until they were demolished in order to create a vista in front of Independence Hall.[70]

Farther south, the shopping district moved westward along Market and Chestnut streets. Three retail stores devoted to the carriage trade, for example, opened on Chestnut Street west of Eighth in 1857 alone, including the elegant L. J. Levy & Co. and Sharpless Brothers, whose interior arrangement anticipated the modern department store.[71] About the same time the first of the former dwellings in the 700 block of Market Street was replaced by a five-story commercial building for James M. Maris and Company at 711 Market, followed two years later by J. B. Lippincott's adjacent marble-fronted bookstore with its rear printing shop and bindery.[72] Although a retail district by the time of the Civil War, this block's appearance changed more slowly than did some of the wholesale blocks during the 1850's. Change became more rapid after 1893 when the Lit brothers began to expand their dry goods business, which within a remarkably short time grew from a single store at the northeast corner of Eighth and Market to a department store occupying the entire block by 1907, consolidating the hitherto disparate elements composing that block into one of the city's great architectural monuments and department stores.[73] Evidently pleased with Collins and Autenreith's design for the new corner store in 1893, they retained the architects to continue this design on 731–33 Market in 1895, 723–29 Market in 1896, and the other end of the block, 701–7 Market, in 1907.[74] Lit Brothers' reputation as a great example of cast-iron architecture, however, is exaggerated. (It received a plaque from the Philadelphia Chapter of the Victorian Society of America in 1973, commemorating the store as a great surviving example of the nineteenth-century building material.) The only two cast-iron buildings in the group are the former Joel Bailey store at 719 Market and its neighbor to the west.

Old City also retains some of the nation's most famous eighteenth-century residences. The twenty-nine brick houses of Elfreth's Alley (illus.), a six-foot-wide alley between Front and Second streets above Arch, illustrate the typical side-street dwellings

of eighteenth-century artisans on the oldest continuously inhabited
street in Philadelphia. It is one of the best known and, through the
joint efforts of the Elfreth's Alley Association and the Philadelphia
Historical Commission, one of the best researched streets in the city.
Since late 1957 Hannah Benner Roach, the historian and researcher of
the Association, has been poring over a wide variety of documentary
materials to develop an accurate history of this byway. Opened
between 1702 and 1704, it was initially called Gilbert's Alley, after
John Gilbert, who owned the land on the north side of the alley. By
the time that Jeremiah Elfreth acquired title to properties on both
sides of the street and it accordingly became known as Elfreth's Alley
in the mid-eighteenth-century, most of the houses on the south side
and six on the north side had been built.[75] During this time the
residents' livelihoods were tied to the water, as they were mariners,
river pilots, shipwrights, and the like. After the Revolution, when
houses at each end and in the middle of the north side were built,
most of the occupants were employed in domestic trades, such as
carpentry, furniture-making, and pewtering.[76] In spite of Elfreth's
Alley's reputation for its eighteenth-century charm, a few houses
were erected in the nineteenth century, and one, Number 125, not
until the late 1830's, as suggested by its fanlight transom, symmetry
of fenestration, and flat gable roof.[77]

   Less famous than Elfreth's Alley but equally significant is the
German Reformed Church district on North Fourth Street below
Race. Many of these properties, including a school at 327 Cherry
Street, were owned by German Reformed or Lutheran parishes that
played a prominent role in this predominantly German neighborhood for more than a century after the 1730's. The finest of these
dwellings is the three-and-a-half-story house at the corner of Fourth
and Cherry, next to the German School and opposite the site of the
Zion Lutheran Church, which was demolished in 1869. Built in 1787
for the German Lutheran congregation, its ample proportions,
modillion returning cornice, and circular window in the gable cause it
to stand out from its older neighbors,[78] which were built during the
colonial period, as suggested by the pent eaves and lower ceilings.[79]
The German Lutheran Church acquired four of these properties, 129–
35 North Fourth, during the 1760's and 1770's and for more than
seventy years used one as a parsonage and rented the others to
people of modest means: tailors, barbers, a laborer, and a huckster.[80]
The Fourth Street houses and the German Reformed Church at
Fourth and Race are currently being restored, and it is expected that

the area will become the kind of mixed neighborhood of dwellings, workshops, and stores that it was two hundred years ago.

Another kind of neighborhood development, one that would become increasingly familiar to Philadelphians during the nineteenth century, was begun at the very end of the eighteenth century west of Seventh Street along Walnut and Sansom streets. This was Sansom's Row, the city's first speculative row development in which the entire block was planned and built as a row rather than as individual houses built at different times adjacent to one another. In about 1799 William Sansom had Benjamin Latrobe design a row of brick houses with traditional London house plans for Walnut Street and a year or two later Thomas Carstairs did similar drawings for Sansom Street.[81] Although eventually an apparent financial success, the row was an aesthetic disappointment. Instead of treating the row as a unit, the designers planned the dwellings with individual but identical Georgian facades. The only concession to comprehensive planning was the pairing of doorways and placing of battlements at extreme ends of every pair to create the impression of ten pairs of dwellings. Whereas Elfreth's Alley has the charm of houses with varying widths and heights, and different street lines, doorways, and brickwork, Sansom's Row was a flat, repetitive expanse, pointing out one of the major design problems that has plagued speculative developments ever since.

Robert Mills, America's first professionally trained native-born architect,[82] tried to solve this problem in Franklin Row (illus.), a stretch of ten row houses on Ninth Street above Locust being promoted by John Savage and John Meany. In the spring of 1809 Mills prepared two sets of plans, one with doorways alternating and the other with doorways paired under a large arch, but both with the traditional London house plan and cellar kitchen. The houses were built according to the first plan, Mill's second choice, but he "gave it added grandeur by placing a tripartite window and its recessed arch on the second floor as well as on the first floor."[83] For the first time a conscious effort had been made to lend some distinction to a practical row development. Later examples in other parts of the city, Thomas U. Walter's Portico Square and John Haviland's Colonnade Row, would employ freestanding porticoes to give rows even greater plasticity.

Old City also had a number of comfortable town houses, most of which have been removed as the real estate has been put to other uses. Two of the finest late-eighteenth-century town houses to be found anywhere, however, survive in this area and have been recorded by HABS. They are the Reynolds-Morris House (illus.), 225 South Eighth Street, and Bishop William White's House, 309 Walnut Street, both built in 1787. Bishop White's three-and-a-half-story house follows the pattern of most Philadelphia town houses of its time, with a side entrance hall, a sitting room and dining room to the side, and a rear ell consisting of a piazza, or stairwell, two-story kitchen with scullery and laundry below, and a two-story nursery. It was a large house with a comfortable twenty-six-foot front and unusually large windowpanes, and it was an elegantly designed house with a pedimented Doric frontispiece, marble lintels with keys, and decorative scrolls flanking its dormers. In fine, it was a proper residence appropriately placed for one of the nation's leading Episcopal clergymen, who served both Christ Church to the north and St. Peter's to the south. [84]

The facade of the Reynolds-Morris House incorporates the same elements found on the bishop's house, but the former's great size is unusual, made possible by the double lot on which it was built. The house's interior lived up to its exterior dimensions, having a central hall with stairs, rare for a town house. [85] Each floor was finished with chimney breasts, wainscoting, and double architraves on the doors and single architraves on the windows, luxurious appointments for its day. [86] The rear has been changed over the years and today only the facade remains of the original, expressing the elegance of an early merchant-manufacturing class. [87]

In response to Penn's call for industrious family men and his assurance of religious liberty, a wide range of religious sects arrived during the early years of the province, a fact that is materially represented by a series of religious structures in Old City that were built through the first half of the nineteenth century. Later, the area's commercial-industrial development militated against the growth of residential neighborhoods that support churches. Reflecting both the city's Quaker origins and later crises of state and soul are the Arch Street Friends Meeting (illus.) at the southeast corner of Fourth and Arch and the Free Quakers Meeting House at the southwest corner of Fifth and Arch. The former, although begun as late as 1803 (late for the faith that founded the colony in 1682), is the city's oldest extant Quaker meeting house and a notable example of the Quaker plain style. The Free Quakers Meeting House vividly illustrates the impact of the American Revolution on the pacifist Society of Friends and of the subsequent spirit of nationalism on the Quaker plain style. It is the older of the two, erected in 1783–85, but as its name implies, it was never an orthodox Quaker meeting house, since it was built for Friends who had been disowned by their meetings for participating in the Revolutionary War. Its interior plan followed the general plan of Friends meeting houses of the time except for the introduction of wine storage vaults beneath the street, an income-producing feature for the enterprising congregation. The building's significance, however, rests in its exterior design, which in addition to its up-to-date architectural details includes a stone tablet in the north gable that patriotically proclaims:[88]

> By General Subscription
> for the
> FREE QUAKERS
> Erected in the YEAR
> of OUR LORD 1783
> of the EMPIRE 8.

Many of the pietist sects did not stay in the city but moved into the fertile countryside where they could remain farmers. The more worldly Anglicans, however, settled in and about the city, where as early as 1695 they built their first church on Second Street north of Market. Beginning in 1727 this structure was replaced by the present Christ Church (illus.), a *tour de force* of Palladian church architecture strongly influenced by the London city churches of Sir Christopher Wren.[89] Within a decade after the Anglicans' beginnings in the Quaker city, Philadelphia's first Presbyterian congregation organized and in 1704 moved into a frame building at Market and Bank streets that served as its church throughout the colonial period. It was replaced in 1793 by a handsome structure with a Corinthian portico, but when the columns rotted, the congregation in 1822 left the noise and stench of the market sheds extending along the middle of Market Street for the open air and fashionable address of Washington Square, where John Haviland had designed a Greek Revival church. Out of the evangelical turbulence of the Great Awakening emerged Philadelphia's second Presbyterian congregation, which in 1750 built its church at Third and Arch streets. Its spire, which rivaled that of nearby Christ Church for half a century until it had to be dismantled in 1803, suggested that the congregation was as devoted to public display as to the new Calvinist preaching. This trait was repeated as the congregation moved westward with the city's expansion, first in 1837

to a comfortable classical church on Seventh below Arch and again in
1872 to its present site at Twenty-first and Walnut streets.[90]

Other houses of worship were erected in the area by a host of
faiths, many of them, like the German Lutherans, reflecting the city's
ethnic pluralism. Lutherans outgrew St. Michael's within a generation after they built it at Fifth and Appletree streets in the 1740's, and
in 1766 they began the Zion Church, one of the colonies' largest
churches, at Fourth and Cherry.[91] Meanwhile the German Reformed
Church, which had been renting space in the neighborhood since
1727, began its own structure, a hexagonal church with a tall cupola,
in 1747 at the southeast corner of Fourth and Race streets, where its
third structure still stands.[92] Philadelphia's Methodists also located
nearby, at Fourth and New streets. Architecturally plain but historically significant as the world's oldest Methodist church in
continuous use, St. George's dates from 1769, when it was acquired
from a Presbyterian congregation that lacked the funds to finish
construction.[93] Across Fourth Street from St. George's stands St.
Augustine's Roman Catholic Church, which was rebuilt in 1848 as a
living monument to the triumph over religious persecution. The dis-
crimination suffered by Philadelphia's Jews (a traditionally
persecuted people) in the erection of the first Mikveh Israel Synagogue (1782) on Cherry near Third was mild compared to that
endured by the city's Catholics during the eighteenth and early
nineteenth centuries. St. Joseph's, located on Willing's Alley where
Old City merges with Society Hill, was threatened by anti-Catholic
mobs twice during the colonial era and again during the most violent
outburst of intolerance, the "Native American" riots of 1844, which
led to the burning of St. Michael's in Kensington and the late-
eighteenth-century St. Augustine's.[94]

Despite its religious origins and multiplicity of faiths, Philadelphia easily assumed the secular ways of the Enlightenment
and became a center for the exchange of ideas as well as goods.
Benjamin Franklin, the Boston-trained printer who retired to become
one of the foremost theoretical physicists of his day, played a key role
in this stage of the city's history. Aware that the scientific society had
offered a successful means of promoting the arts and sciences ever
since the founding of England's Royal Society in 1662, he helped to
establish the American Philosophical Society in 1743, making it now
the oldest learned society in the country. Because of local apathy the
society languished until it was reorganized in the 1760's. After the
Revolutionary War, the society built its hall (illus.) on South Fifth

Street, in what is now Independence National Historical Park,[95] while directly across the street another pioneer intellectual institution begun by Franklin and his friends was going up. Founded in 1731, the Library Company of Philadelphia built a handsome new library in 1789–90 from the designs of Dr. William Thornton, later the architect of the United States Capitol. The present structure is not affiliated with the Library Company and instead houses the library of the Philosophical Society. It is a reconstruction, since the original Library Company building was razed in 1887 and replaced by the Drexel Building.[96]

Similar institutions continued to be established in the neighborhood during the early nineteenth century. Two of the most notable examples, quite different in goals and membership, were the Franklin Institute and the Athenaeum of Philadelphia (illus.). The former was founded in 1823 as part of the early-nineteenth-century Lyceum Movement, an effort to provide a practical scientific education for workingmen. The institute's first building still stands at 15 South Seventh Street as a major example of the Greek Revival. By basing the small building on the Choragic Monument of Thrasyllus, architect John Haviland produced a compact monumental facade whose romantic allusions to democratic learning remain appropriate for its present use as the Atwater Kent Museum.[97] The Athenaeum was organized in 1814 by a group of literate young gentlemen in order to provide a "place of common resort" with a reading room and library. In 1847 it moved from its Philosophical Hall quarters to Washington Square, where its new brownstone Renaissance Revival building helped to popularize locally both the material and the style. Since then the basic design and function of the Athenaeum has not changed, making it a notable example of the Italian style and the city's oldest library building in continuous use.[98]

The theater was one expression of secularism that was opposed throughout most of the eighteenth century, but after Philadelphia was designated the temporary capital of the new nation in 1789, the last ordinance that had prohibited—but had not prevented— theatrical performances was repealed. As the governmental and economic center of the nation at the time, Old City also became the nucleus of the city's theater district when the Chestnut Street Theatre was begun west of Independence Hall in 1791. It was followed four years later by Ricketts' Circus, which, until it burned down in 1799, presented drama, pantomime, and equestrian acts, diagonally across Chestnut Street.[99]

The 1820's were an even busier period of theater construction. In that decade William Strickland designed three theaters: a second Chestnut Street Theatre to replace the burned-out original, the Arch Street Theatre two blocks to the north, and the Musical Fund Society's Hall at 808 Locust Street. At about the same time John Haviland remodeled into the Walnut Street Theatre the blank brick Olympic Theatre, which had been built at Ninth and Walnut streets in 1809. The latter two buildings still stand, both with long and varied theatrical and architectural histories. The Walnut Street Theatre has recently had its Haviland facade restored and carries on its active life as the oldest theater in continuous use in the English-speaking world. The Musical Fund Hall, however, has not been as fortunate. Although it was saved from humiliating service as a tobacco warehouse in 1964, it has remained empty and unused, its famous acoustics wasted and its fabric deteriorating.[100]

As the city's commercial district moved westward during the late nineteenth and early twentieth centuries, the eastern end of Old City declined. Although this was a blow to the neighborhood's economy, it was a blessing for its historic preservation. Surviving examples of urban Philadelphia include relics of its early commerce, such as the 1806 Singer Warehouse at the rear of 319 Market Street, the city's oldest extant warehouse; significant but obscure examples of architectural history, such as the Brock Warehouse (illus.) at 242–44 North Delaware Avenue, the country's oldest known surviving cast-iron building; and modest dwellings of common folk, such as Henry Harrison's little known mid-eighteenth-century row on Cuthbert near Front.[101]

The creation of Independence National Historical Park in 1948 and urban renewal and highway projects beginning in the 1960's have destroyed some of this Old City, but they have also revitalized other segments, particularly in the area of Franklin Court and along Independence Mall, a three-block expanse north of Independence Hall now lined with government buildings and commercial structures.[102] The restoration of the nineteenth-century commercial-residential Old City Historic District is going forward; a major contribution to the section's renaissance will be Penn's Landing, a thirty-acre, $30 million development of offices, shops, hotels, museum, marina, and promenades along the Delaware River waterfront.[103]

Catalog

American Fire Insurance Company Building

(PA-1386), 308–10 Walnut St. Brick with stone and terra cotta trim, approx. 46' (five-bay front) × 60' with three-story rear ell, five stories (originally four), mansard roof (originally gable), rectangular plan. Built 1840. Altered 1881; Furness and Evans, architects. Remodeled, enlarged 1886; Furness, Evans & Co., architects; Jacob Myers, builder. Certified, PHC 1973. 1 ext. photo (1958);* 6 data pages (including 1840 insurance survey, 1886 news article).*

American Life Insurance Company Building (also known as the Manhattan Building)

(PA-1064), 330–36 Walnut St. Gray stone ashlar with interior iron columns and beams, 46'-9" (four-bay front) × 101'-3", eight stories with three-story tower, mansard roof with semicircular projecting hoods, offices disposed around central stair, elevator, and fire-escape shaft.

Early Philadelphia skyscraper. Built 1888; Thomas P. Lonsdale, architect. Exterior partially remodeled c. 1891; probably by Will Decker, architect. Demolished 1961. 7 ext. photos (1960, 1961), 1 int. photo (1960), 1 photocopy of old ext. print (n.d.); 10 data pages (1960).

American Philosophical Society. See Philosophical Hall

Arch Street Area Study

(PA-1387), 501–27 Arch St., on N. side Arch St. between Fifth and Sixth sts. Twelve contiguous commercial buildings ranging from three-and-a-half-story late-18th-century house with gable roof to mid- and late-19th-century brick and cast-iron buildings of two, four, and six stories. Includes Insurance Patrol (PA-1433) and Robert Ralston House (PA-1016). Representative of the architectural variety of a Philadelphia commercial block. Built at various times between late 18th and late 19th centuries; demolished 1959. 4 ext. photos (1959).*

Arch Street Friends Meeting. Illustrated

(PA-1388), 330 Arch St. Brick, approx. 180' (thirteen-bay front) × 85', two stories, hipped roof with cross-gable, projecting central pavilion, three porches with Tuscan columns across north side and two each on east and west sides, 1804 date stone in gable end.

Notable example of Quaker plain style. East wing and center building built 1803–5; Owen Biddle, architect. West wing built 1810–11. One-story addition behind west wing built 1896; demolished 1968. Two-story addition behind center building built 1902, 1906; demolished 1968. Interior east wing renovated and two-story addition behind center building built 1968–69; Cope and Lippincott, architects. Structural, exterior, interior elements in Architectural Study Collection, Museum Division, Independence National Historical Park. Oldest Friends Meeting in the city and headquarters of the Philadelphia Yearly Meeting of the Society of Friends. On ground owned by Friends since the city's beginning. Certified, PHC 1956; Pennsylvania Register 1970; NR. 4 ext. photos (1958, 1974).*

Armory of the National Guards. See National Guard's Hall

Athenaeum of Philadelphia. Illustrated

(PA-1389), 219 S. Sixth St., at S.E. corner St. James St. on E. side of Washington Sq. Stuccoed brick and coursed brownstone ashlar, approx. 50' (three-bay front) × 128', three stories, flat roof, projecting lintels, balustrade between first and second stories, quoins, center-hall plan.

An early and influential example of the Italian Renaissance Revival style. Built 1845–47; John Notman, architect. Interior altered (A.I.A. Meeting Rooms) 1870; Frank Furness of Frazer, Furness and Hewitt, architect. Exterior restored 1975–76; John Dickey, architect. Interior restored, mechanical systems renovated 1975–76; George D. Batcheler, Jr., architect. Founded 1814 as a private literary association. Certified, PHC 1956; Pennsylvania Register 1970; NR. 3 ext. photos (1972),* 2 photocopies of architectural drawings (1845, one by Notman, one competition drawing by John Haviland);* 9 data pages (including architect's agreement and specifications).*

Athenaeum of Philadelphia, Privy
(PA-1092), rear of 219 S. Sixth St. Brick, approx. 8' × 10', one story, low gable roof, six private compartments arranged in two back-to-back rows of three. Built c. 1847; John Notman, architect. Demolished by falling tree 1962. 1 sheet (1962, including plot plan, plan, detail);* 2 ext. photos (1962);* 2 data pages (1962, including architect's specifications).*

Atwater Kent Museum. See Franklin Institute

Ayer, N. W., & Son, Inc., Building (later N. W. Ayer & Company)
(PA-1390), 204–12 S. Seventh St., at S.W. corner St. James St., on W. side Washington Sq. Steel skeleton, brick curtain walls faced with dressed limestone ashlar, approx. 105' (ten-bay front) × 115', fifteen stories with setbacks, flat roof, two carved three-story limestone figures on each facade above first setback, notable brass sculpture on entrance and in lobby.

Fine example of Art Deco mode integrating sculpture with design of the tall office building. Built 1927–29; Ralph B. Bencker, architect; J. Wallace Kelly and Raphael Sabatini, sculptors; Ketcham and McQuade, contractors. Founded 1869, N. W. Ayer & Company is the oldest advertising company in the United States. 2 ext. photos (1976).*

Bank of North America
(PA-1391), 305–7 Chestnut St. Brick with steel joists, Jonesboro granite front with polished Scotch granite trim, 56'-6" (three-bay front) × 118'-4" with four-story rear wing, one story (two-story facade), flat roof with front pediment, smooth rusticated ground story, central balcony with balustrade supported by coupled Tuscan columns.

Built 1893–95; James H. and John T. Windrim, architects; George Watson & Son, contractors. Demolished 1972. Bank of North America was chartered 1781 as the nation's first commercial bank, and occupied this site until it merged with Pennsylvania Company for Banking and Trusts 1929. Certified, PHC 1970. 4 ext. photos during demolition (1972),* 2 photocopies of old ext. photos (c. 1900, 1959);* 9 data pages (including 1894–1945 insurance surveys);* HABSI form (1971).*

Bank of Pennsylvania (also known as Philadelphia Bank)

(PA-1392), 421 Chestnut St. Brick with Quincy granite ashlar front, approx. 70' (five-bay front) × 45' with four- and six-story rear additions, four stories originally with cast-iron dome, flat roof, monolithic pilasters and round arches on ground story, tall arches with carved keystones rise through second and third stories, rusticated quoins, originally center corridor to rear banking room in one story.

Fine example of mid-19th-century Renaissance Revival style in Venetian mode. Built 1857–59; John M. Gries, architect; H. C. Oram & Co., iron work. Four-story addition built between front and rear buildings 1892, rear banking room demolished and replaced by five-story office building 1892–93, raised one story 1903; Theophilus Parsons Chandler, Jr., architect. Bank of Pennsylvania failed during Panic of 1857 and building was completed by Philadelphia Bank. Certified, PHC 1969; Pennsylvania Register 1970. 4 ext. photos (1972),* 1 photogrammetric stereopair (1959),* 1 photocopy of old ext. photo (c. 1910).*

Baugh Warehouse. See Beck Warehouse

Beck Warehouse (also known as Baugh Warehouse)

(PA-1188), 18–20 S. Delaware Ave. Brick, 40' (four-bay front) × 75'-8", three-and-a-half stories (originally two-and-a-half stories), gambrel roof (originally gable roof), rectangular plan with longitudinal brick partition.

Fine example of early-19th-century waterfront warehouse. Built 1805; raised one story, gambrel roof built before 1870; No. 18 altered to storefront 1915. Demolished 1967. Paul Beck, Jr., a prominent, civic-minded merchant, owned building until his death 1844. Headquarters of Baugh & Sons Co., fertilizer manufacturers, 1860–1954. 5 sheets (1965, 1968, including plot plan, plans, elevation, hoist machinery);* 2 ext. photos (1958, 1965), 3 int. photos (1965); 3 data pages (including 1805–1915 insurance surveys).*

Berry-Coxe House

(PA-1062), 413 Locust St., Independence National Historical Park. Brick with marble trim, approx. 24' (three-bay front) × 44' with two- and three-story rear ell, three-and-a-half stories, gable roof, Tuscan frontispiece with fanlight, side-hall town house plan.

Fine early-19th-century town house. Built c. 1802–4; probably by Peter L. Berry, house carpenter. Interior extensively remodeled 1959–60. Tenanted 1804–7 by Tench Coxe, political economist and father of American cotton industry. Certified, PHC 1957; Pennsylvania Register 1970; NR. 10 sheets (1954, 1962, including plot plan, plans, elevations, sections, details); 3 ext. photos (1958, 1973*), 12 int. photos (1958); 8 data pages (1958).

Blair, Reverend Samuel, House

(PA-1063), 415 Locust St., Independence National Historical Park. Brick with marble trim, approx. 23' (three-bay front) × 45' originally with one-story rear ell, three-and-a-half stories, gable roof, Adamesque frontispiece with fanlight, side-hall town house plan. Built c. 1807; possibly by Peter L. Berry, house carpenter. Rear ell raised to three stories, two-story addition built before 1860; ground story altered to store before 1890. Rear ell demolished, exterior restored, interior extensively rebuilt 1959–60. Hardware samples in Architectural Study Collection, Museum Division, Independence National Historical Park. Certified, PHC 1957; Pennsylvania Register 1970; NR. 2 ext. photos (1958), see also ext. photo (1973)* of Berry-Coxe House (PA-1062); 4 data pages (1959).*

Blight Warehouse

(PA-1393), 101–3 S. Front St., at S.E. corner Chestnut St. Brick with marble trim, approx. 40' (five-bay front) × 40', five stories, flat roof, marble-pier storefront, 1840 date stone in end parapet. Built 1840; demolished 1967. 1 ext. photo (1966);* 9 data pages (1966).*

Bonsall, John, House

(PA-1394), 706 Locust St., on S. side of Washington Sq. Brick with marble trim, approx. 24' (three-bay front) × 42' with four-story rear ell, three-and-a-half stories on raised basement, gable roof. One of

five row houses. Built c. 1818–19. Certified, PHC 1957. 1 ext. photo
(1975),* 5 int. photos (1959);* 2 data pages (1959).*

Brock, John, Sons & Co. Warehouse. Illustrated

(PA-1395), 242–44 N. Delaware Ave. and 243–45 N. Water St. Brick
with cast-iron front on Delaware Ave. and cast-iron storefront on
Water St. (rear), approx. 42' (six-bay front) × 148' (originally approx.
136' × 148'), five stories on Delaware Ave., four stories on Water St.,
flat roof, originally balcony with iron railing at second story, rectangular plan.

Fine early example of cast-iron design with iron plates simulating
smooth rusticated masonry; perhaps nation's oldest iron-front building. Built 1850; Hoxie and Button, architects; William and N. W. Ellis,
contractors; iron work by Reeves, Buck & Co., Cresson & Co., J. & S.
Field; Robert Wood, iron railing. Iron railing and balcony removed
1865; first- and second-story doors and windows bricked up 1951.
Southern section (Nos. 238–40) demolished 1939; northern section
(Nos. 246–48) demolished 1959. 5 ext. photos (1972, 1973);* HABSI
form (1970).*

Butcher & Brother Warehouse

(PA-1396), 142–44 N. Front St., at N.W. corner Quarry St. Brick with
granite trim, approx. 27' (four-bay front) × 33', five stories, flat roof,
storefront of granite piers and lintel, rectangular plan. Built between
1853 and 1861; demolished c. 1970. 1 ext. photo (1967);* 12 data pages
(1968).*

Carpenter, Joshua, House (also known as Carpenter's Mansion)

(PA-1397), 615–19 Chestnut St., originally grounds occupied N. side
Chestnut St., between Sixth and Seventh sts. Brick, approx. 36' × 24'
with rear stair tower, two-and-a-half stories, jerkin-head roof, pent
eaves at first and second stories, originally three rooms to a floor.

Built between 1701 and 1722; Joshua Carpenter, builder. Remodeled and gable-roof front addition built for John Dickinson 1774.
Demolished 1826. Occupants included Provincial Governor George
Thomas 1738–47, Pennsylvania Chief Justice William Tilghman 1798–
1826, and the French legation 1779–85. 1 photocopy of old watercolor
drawing (c. 1826); 3 data pages (including 1766–85 insurance surveys).*

Carpenters' Hall

(PA-1398), 320 Chestnut St., Carpenters' Court, Independence National Historical Park. Museum. Brick, approx. 50' (five-bay front) × 50', two stories on raised basement, gable roof with cross-gables on north and south sides, projecting central pavilion on north and south sides, pedimented frontispiece, round-arch entrance with fanlight, round-arch windows with false balustrades on second story of north pavilion, octagonal cupola, cruciform plan.

Fine colonial example of Georgian guild hall whose cruciform plan gives it four distinct facades. Built 1770–74; Robert Smith, architect. Interior renovated 1857, 1904; south doorway restored 1964; interior restored 1967–68. Interior and exterior architectural elements in Architectural Study Collection, Museum Division, Independence National Historical Park. Founded 1724, Carpenters' Company is the oldest builders' organization in the United States and still owns and maintains the Hall. First Continental Congress met here 1774. Offices of Secretary of War 1790–91; offices and vaults of First Bank of the United States 1791–97; used by Musical Fund Society 1821–24, by Franklin Institute 1824–26; site of country's first exhibit of American manufactures 1824; auction hall 1828–56; opened to public as museum 1857. Certified, PHC 1956; Pennsylvania Register 1970; designated National Historic Landmark 1970. 3 sheets (1932, including elevation, section, details);* 8 ext. photos (1939, 1975,* including 1 of reconstructed Pemberton House on east side of court), 1 int. photo (1975),* 1 photocopy of ext. stereo view (n.d.),* 1 photocopy of int. stereo view (n.d.),* 4 photocopies of measured drawings (1897),* 1 photocopy of proposed plan for Carpenters' Court (c. 1768);* 1 data page (including 1773 insurance survey).*

Front Store. (PA-1399), 322 Chestnut St. Stuccoed brick (originally brick), 26'-6" (three-bay front) × 71' (originally 26'-6" × 44' with three-story back building), four stories, hipped roof, monolithic stone piers and Doric cornice at ground story, projecting corbeled lintels, corbeled cornice. Built 1810–11. New storefront, mastic added to upper stories, interior altered 1846; William Johnston, architect. New front, interior alterations, fourth story added to rear 1861; Collins and Autenreith, architects. Demolished 1957. 3 sheets (1958, including plot plan, plan, elevations, details);* 4 ext. photos (1957),* 1 aerial photo (1957);* 7 data pages (1954, including 1811 insurance survey).*

New Hall. (PA-1400), rear of 322 Chestnut St., on W. side of Carpenters' Court, Independence National Historical Park. Museum. Brick, approx. 61' (eight-bay front) × 20', four stories (originally two stories), flat roof (originally hipped roof). Built 1791; third story added

1833; fourth story added 1861; demolished 1957–58; reconstructed 1958–60 to 1791 appearance for U.S. Marine Corps Museum. 2 ext. photos (1957);* 6 data pages (1960, including 1791–1857 insurance surveys).*

Carriage House
(PA-1401), rear of 212 S. Fourth St. and 422 Walnut St. on E. side of Lawrence St. (not cut through), Independence National Historical Park. Brick, 46'-11^1/$_2$" (three-bay front) × 30'-2^3/$_8$", two stories, shed roof, rectangular plan. Example of colonial vernacular architecture. Built mid-18th century; demolished 1960. Shutter, door in Architectural Study Collection, Museum Division, Independence National Historical Park. 2 sheets (1958, including plans, elevations, sections);* 2 ext. photos (1959),* 9 int. photos (1959).*

Chamber of Commerce. See Commercial Exchange

Chestnut Street Area Study
(PA-1402), 213–43 Chestnut St., on N. side Chestnut St. between Strawberry and Third sts. Thirteen contiguous commercial buildings, brick with brick, brownstone, granite, and cast-iron fronts, mostly three- and four-bay fronts, four and five stories, flat roofs, rectangular plans.

One of the few surviving examples of a formerly stylish mid-19th-century wholesale-retail block. Includes: Keen Building (No. 217), built 1851, Samuel Sloan, architect, cast-iron storefront by Architectural Iron Works (Daniel D. Badger), New York; Gendell and Landreth Buildings (Nos. 219–21), built c. 1853 with cast-iron front by Architectural Iron Works; Elliott Building (No. 235), built 1856, Joseph C. Hoxie, architect; Leland Building (No. 237), built 1854, Joseph C. Hoxie, architect; Lewis Building (Nos. 239–41), built 1852, Stephen D. Button, architect, cast-iron storefront by Architectural Iron Works; Borie Brothers Bank (No. 243), built 1897, Wilson Eyre, Jr., architect. 2 ext. photos (1972),* 1 photocopy of old ext. photo (1930);* HABSI form (1970).*

Christ Church (Protestant Episcopal). Illustrated
(PA-1071), 22–26 N. Second St., at N.W. corner Church St. Brick, 87'-0^1/$_2$" (eight-bay side) × 61'-6", two stories with square tower and three-stage spire, gable roof, round-arch windows, notable Palladian window at east end, Doric frieze, mutule cornice, balustrade with

urns; three-aisle plan, clerestory, galleries, rectangular chancel framed by Doric pilasters and pediment.

An outstanding example of Palladian church architecture in the United States. Built 1727–44; Dr. John Kearsley (physician), supervisor and probable architect. Steeple built 1751–54; John or Daniel Harrison, designer; John Palmer, mason; Robert Smith and John Armstrong, carpenters. West gallery enlarged 1732, 1782. Interior altered 1834; Thomas U. Walter, architect. Interior altered 1852. Interior altered 1882; G. W. Hewitt, architect. Steeple rebuilt after fire 1908. Certified, PHC 1956; Pennsylvania Register 1970, designated National Historic Landmark 1970.

21 sheets (1933, c. 1959,* 1971, including plot plan, plans, elevations, spire section, spire plan, sections, details, conductor head*); 21 ext. photos (1939, 1965, including 6 of tower renovations*), 9 int. photos (1965, 1969, including one of tower),* 1 photocopy of old ext. photo (c. 1910),* 2 photocopies of measured drawings (1897).*

Commercial Buildings
(PA-1404), 105–11 N. Water St. and 106–12 N. Delaware Ave. Four adjoining brick stores with granite trim, each approx. 25' (three-bay front) × 123', four stories, flat roofs, Tuscan granite piers and architraves at ground story, rectangular plans. Built c. 1835–40; demolished 1968. 1 ext. photo (1967).*

Commercial Buildings
(PA-1405), 125–27 S. Second St., at S.E. corner Gatzmer St. Two brick stores, northern one (No. 125) with cast-iron front, southern one with granite-pier storefront, each approx. 20' (three-bay front) × 125' (No. 125) and 85' (No. 127), five stories, flat roof. No. 127 built c. 1840. No. 125 built 1852 for J. Howell and Co.; John Riddell, architect. Storefront elements altered later; both demolished 1974. 1 sheet (1974, including plot plan, elevation).*

Commercial Exchange (also known as Chamber of Commerce)
(PA-1406), 135 S. Second St., at S.E. corner Sansom St. Brick with brownstone and granite trim, approx. 105' (seven-bay front) × 150', six stories (originally with central tower), flat roof (originally mansard as sixth story), central four-story entrance pavilion.

A post–Civil War office building that has retained its character in spite of later alterations. Built 1867–68; John Crump, architect.

Partially destroyed by fire 1869. Rebuilt 1870; James H. Windrim, architect; Benjamin Ketchum, builder. Cupola added before 1875. Tower removed, interior extensively altered 1901–2; Seymour Davis, architect; George Kessler, contractor. Mansard removed 1910. Interior altered, reinforced 1927; Clarence E. Winder, architect. Demolished 1976. Largest and most important commercial organization in late-19th-century Philadelphia; site of world's first automatic telephone exchange during occupancy of Keystone Telephone Co. 1902–44. Vacated 1961. Certified, PHC 1970. 2 ext. photos (1972);* HABSI form (1970).*

Commercial Union Assurance Company Building
(PA-1076), 416–20 Walnut St. Brick with limestone trim, 54'-5" (three-bay front) × 80', eight stories, gable roof with flat roof over rear wings, central service core with iron and marble stairs rising height of building. Built 1888–89; Theophilus Parsons Chandler, Jr., architect; J. E. and A. L. Pennock, contractors. Demolished 1963. 4 ext. photos (1962, 1963), 3 int. photos (1962); 6 data pages (1963).

Cooper, Jacob, House
(PA-1407), 118 Cuthbert St. Brick, approx. 12' (two-bay front) × 20', two-and-a-half stories, gable roof, cove cornice, originally pent eave. One dwelling in an original unit of three. Built late 18th century. Certified, PHC 1957. 2 ext. photos (1958);* 2 data pages (1958).*

Cope, Caleb, & Co. Store (late Goldberg's Army-Navy Store)
(PA-1408), 429 Market St. Brick with granite front, approx. 28' (four-bay front) × 205', five stories, flat roof, arcaded windows at second and fifth stories, corbeled cornice, parapet, rectangular plan. Fine example of mid-19th-century retail store built for a leading dry goods merchant and later banker. Built 1853; Joseph C. Hoxie, architect; Charles Rubicam, builder; Solomon K. Hoxsie, granite-cutter. Demolished 1970. 2 ext. photos (1970);* 7 data pages (including 1854–92 insurance surveys).*

Dilworth-Todd-Moylan House (also known as Dolley Madison House)
(PA-1409), 343 Walnut St., at N.E. corner Fourth St., Independence National Historical Park. Historic house museum. Brick, approx. 16' (two-bay front) × 35' with two-story rear kitchen ell, three stories, gable roof, brick string-course, London house plan.

Fine Georgian row house. Built c. 1775; Jonathan Dilworth,

house carpenter. Altered to store before 1859; new storefronts built 1909, 1923, 1931. Restored by National Park Service and two adjacent 1775 houses rebuilt 1958–70. John Todd, Jr., lawyer, lived here 1791–93; his widow, Dolley, married congressman James Madison 1794, who leased the house to Stephen Moylan, merchant and Continental Army officer. Certified, PHC 1956; NR. 4 sheets (1961, including floor and framing plans);* 1 ext. photo (1974).*

Dock Street Sewer
(PA-1072), beneath Dock St. between Third St. and Delaware River. Elliptical brick vault, span approx. 50'. Built for Girard Estate c. 1900; James H. Windrim, architect. Demolished 1962. 1 sheet (1962, including plot plan, sections).*

Dowers-Okill House
(PA-1410), 115 N. Water St. Brick, approx. 23' (three-bay front) × 45', three stories, gable roof, flat-arch brick lintels with scalloped edges at second story, London house plan. Built between 1747 and 1750; demolished c. 1963. Lintel in Architectural Study Collection, Museum Division, Independence National Historical Park. 4 ext. photos (1957).*

Drexel & Co. Building
(PA-1411), 34 S. Third St. Brick with coursed marble ashlar front, approx. 20' (three-bay front) × 83', four stories with one-story rear extension, flat roof, carved Tuscan pilasters and projecting cornice at each story, acroteria on pediment, "Drexel & Co." carved on ground-story cornice, rectangular plan.
    Fine example of Tuscan mode of Italianate style office building. Built 1853–54; G. Runge, architect. Altered later. Founded 1837 by Francis M. Drexel, Drexel & Co. became one of the nation's foremost 19th-century investment banks; at this site 1854–85. Certified, PHC 1973; Pennsylvania Register 1975; NR. 2 ext. photos (1975),* 1 phtocopy of old ext. photo (c. 1900).*

Drinker, John, House (later known as Krider Gun Shop)
(PA-1055), 133–35 Walnut St., at N.E. corner Second St. Brick, 27'-1 1/2" (four-bay front) × 47'-1 1/2", three-and-a-half stories, gable roof, pedimented west end. Built 1751 as two dwellings in one unit; demolished 1955. Served as gun shop 1856–97. 16 sheets (1953, including plans, elevations, sections, details), 2 sheets (1953, including ele-

vation, sections, isometric assembly of casement window);* 4 ext. photos (1953, 1958, including details of original casement window), 1 int. photo (1953), 1 photocopy of old ext. photo (n.d.); 9 data pages (1963).

Duncannon Iron Company Warehouse and Office

(PA-1412), 122–24 Race St. Brick, approx. 36' (four-bay front) × 76'with two-story rear extension, two stories, gable roof, large vehicle door on ground story, rectangular plan with counting room in northeastern quarter. Built c. 1867; cornice, vehicle door altered after 1893; wooden trusses replaced by steel beams 1914; rear extension enlarged 1920–21; demolished c. 1969. Duncannon Iron Company here 1868–1909. 1 ext. photo (1967);* 4 data pages (including 1893 insurance survey, 1914–20 building permits).*

Elfreth, Jeremiah, House

(PA-1413), 126 Elfreth's Alley. Historic house museum. Brick, approx. 16' (two-bay front) × 22' with two-story rear ell, two-and-a-half stories, gambrel roof, pent eave, originally one room to a floor. Fine example of a mid-18th-century artisan's house. Built between 1741 and 1762; rear ell added later. Partially restored by Elfreth's Alley Association 1958–66. One of many houses on the alley owned by Elfreth for rental income. Elfreth's Alley Association Headquarters since 1962. Certified, PHC 1956. 2 ext. photos (1959),* 3 int. photos (1959),* 1 photocopy of old ext. photo (n.d.);* 1 data page (including 1762 insurance survey).*

Elfreth's Alley Area Study. Illustrated

(PA-1103), both sides of Elfreth's Alley between Front and Second sts., including Bladen's Court. Twenty-nine adjoining brick houses, mostly two-bay fronts, two, two-and-a-half, and three-and-a-half stories, gable and gambrel roofs. Includes Jeremiah Elfreth House (PA-1413).

Built at various times between mid-18th and early 19th centuries. The six-foot-wide street is the oldest unchanged and continuously inhabited street in Philadelphia and illustrates the typical side-street urban dwellings of 18th-century artisans. Residents included cabinetmaker Daniel Trotter, silversmith Philip Syng, pewterer William Will. Alley opened between 1702 and 1704; Bladen's Court opened between 1749 and 1753. Certified, PHC 1956; Pennsylvania Register 1970; designated National Historic Landmark 1963.

19 sheets (1940, including plans, elevations, sections, details) from Survey, Philadelphia Chapter, A.I.A. (1932); 9 ext. photos (1972, 1976),* 1 aerial photo (1965);* 40 data pages (1960, 1961, including insurance surveys).*

Ellison, John B., & Sons, Building
(PA-1414), 22–26 S. Sixth St. Brick with brownstone trim and cast-iron storefront, approx. 49' (five-bay front) × 173', five stories, mansard roof, floral patterns between third and fourth stories. Built 1881; demolished 1961. One of the largest cloth-importing houses in late-19th-century America. 1 ext. photo (1961),* 1 photocopy of old ext. photo (c. 1890).*

Farmers' and Mechanics' Bank. Illustrated
(PA-1415), 427 Chestnut St. Brick with marble ashlar front, approx. 55' (five-bay front) × 45' with two-story passage and three-story rear building, three stories, flat roof, round-arch windows with corbeled lintels, bracketed cornice with parapet, notable iron front door, originally stairs in front building and center corridor to rear three-story banking room in one story with skylight.

Fine Italianate bank design for one of three surviving banks on what was known as Bank Row. Built 1854–55; John M. Gries, architect; John Rice, builder; William Struthers, marble mason; Robert Wood, iron work. Interior altered 1873. Interior altered, basement enlarged 1903; W. Woodward Potter, architect. Rear one-story addition built 1917; C. Henry Wilson, architect. Interior altered 1919; William Steele and Sons Co., architects and builders. Altered to museum c. 1965. Owned by Philadelphia National Bank since 1918. Site of Philadelphia Maritime Museum 1965–74. Certified, PHC 1969; Pennsylvania Register 1970.

4 ext. photos (1972),* 1 photogrammetric stereopair (1959),* 2 photocopies of old ext. photos (c. 1910, n.d.),* see also photogrammetric stereopair of Pennsylvania Company for Insurances on Lives and Granting Annuities (PA-1452);* 8 data pages (including 1855–1904 insurance surveys, 1915–19 building permits).*

Fife, Matthew, House
(PA-1416), 136 Race St. Brick with marble trim, approx. 16' (two-bay front) × 25' with three-story rear ell, three stories on raised basement, flat roof, round-arch entrance with fanlight and arched marble hood on carved marble corbels, carved lintels, heavy bracketed

cornice, side-hall plan with rear stairwell. Fine example of mid-19th-century city dwelling. Built 1854–55 for Matthew Fife, box manufacturer. 1 ext. photo (1967);* 2 data pages (including 1855 insurance survey).*

Fire Association Building. See Irvin Building

Fireman's Hall. See Philadelphia Fire Department, Engine Company No. 8

First Bank of the United States (also known as Stephen Girard's Bank).
Illustrated
(PA-1417), 120 S. Third St., Independence National Historical Park. Brick with marble front and trim, 90'-11" (seven-bay front) × 81'-9", three stories with Corinthian hexastyle portico, hipped roof with balustrade and gable skylight over dome (not original), notable mahogany pediment sculpture.

Notable early example of Classical monumental building. Built 1795–97; Samuel Blodgett, Jr., architect; Claudius LeGrand, sculptor. Extensive interior renovations and dome added 1901; James H. Windrim, architect; Doyle and Doak, contractors. Restored by National Park Service 1974–76. Origional iron entrance gates at Henry Francis duPont Winterthur Museum, Delaware. Construction elements, pieces of tympanum carving, parts of galvanized iron cornice (1901) in Architectural Study Collection, Museum Division, Independence National Historical Park. One of the nation's oldest bank buildings, it served as the Bank of the United States until 1812 and then as Stephen Girard's Bank and its successor, Girard National Bank, 1812–1926. Certified, PHC 1956; Pennsylvania Register 1970; designated National Historic Site 1948.

17 sheets (1958, 1960, including plot plan, plans, elevations, truss section, portico framing plan, details);* 22 ext. photos (1939, 1959,* 1961,* 1965,* 1975* including 1 photo of lantern, 11 photos of entrance gates), 2 int. photos (c. 1975, 1956),* 1 aerial photo (c. 1965),* 1 photocopy of old ext. photo (n.d.).*

First German Reformed Church Area Study
(PA-1418), 129–51 N. Fourth St., between Cherry and Race sts., and 322–30 Race St. Seven contiguous brick houses (Nos. 129–39, 151), each approx. 18' (two-bay front) × 18'with two- or three-story rear ells, three-and-a-half stories (No. 131 originally two-and-a-half stories), gable roofs, brick stringcourses or second-story pent eaves (Nos. 133–35).

First (German) Reformed Church (322–30 Race St.): brick with stone trim, approx. 64' (three-bay front) × 82', two stories, gable roof, round-arch windows, three-aisle plan, galleries. This church with the nearby school (327 Cherry St.) and dwellings served as a center of the city's German community for a century and a half.

Houses built at various times between 1745 and 1804; Nos. 129, 131 raised one story c. 1865, c. 1800 respectively; all altered to shops later. Restored 1969–; P. Richard Frantz, architect. Dwellings (Nos. 129–35) owned by German Lutheran Church 1771–1848. Church built 1836–37; altered to factory 1882. Restored 1967–; P. Richard Frantz, architect. Plaster ceiling ornament, wallpaper sample in Architectural Study Collection, Museum Division, Independence National Historical Park. Church founded 1727; congregation's third house of worship on this site; now called Old First Reformed Church, United Church of Christ. Certified, PHC 1965. 5 ext. photos (1974);* 15 data pages (1965, including 1769–1819 insurance surveys).*

First National Bank
(PA-1011), 315 Chestnut St. Brick with Quincy granite ashlar front, approx. 60' (three-bay front) × 82', two stories, flat roof with balustrade, central round-arch entrance with engaged columns and piers, round-headed windows, originally central banking room with balustraded galleries.

Restrained Italian Revival design. Built 1865–67; John McArthur, Jr., architect; John Rice, builder. Rear addition built 1912; interior remodeled 1953. First national bank chartered in the United States; now First Pennsylvania Banking and Trust Company. 1 ext. photo (1957), 1 photocopy of old int. photo (n.d.); 4 data pages (1958).

First Presbyterian Church (also known as Washington Square Presbyterian Church)
(PA-1117), S.E. corner Seventh and Locust sts., on S. side of Washington Sq. Stuccoed brick with stone trim, approx. 71' (five-bay front) × 88', two stories with Ionic hexastyle portico, gable roof, octagonal cupola; four-aisle plan, galleries, apsidal chancel.

Early use of radiating seating on inclined floor in a significant Greek Revival church. Built 1820–22; John Haviland, architect; John Clark, builder; John Struthers, stonecutter. Vacated 1928; demolished 1939. 15 sheets (1940, including plans, elevations, sections, details) from Survey, Philadelphia Chapter, A.I.A. (1932); 1 photocopy of old photolithograph (c. 1900).*

Franklin Institute (now Atwater Kent Museum)

(PA-121), 15 S. Seventh St. Museum. Brick with marble ashlar front and interior cast-iron columns, 61'-1¹/₂'' (three-bay front) × 98'-6¹/₄'', three stories on raised basement, flat roof, four Tuscan piers, wreathes along frieze, originally front offices flanked center hall leading to auditorium.

Greek Revival building with ancient design precedents. Built 1825–27; John Haviland, architect. Interior renovated, two-story rear wing built 1897; John R. Wiggins, contractor. Rear wing removed later, interior renovated 1937–38. Between 1827 and 1933 headquarters of Franklin Institute, scientific research and study center named in memory of Benjamin Franklin, which also offered draftsmanship and architecture instruction during its early decades. Since 1939 it has served as Atwater Kent Museum, devoted to the history of Philadelphia. Certified, PHC 1956; Pennsylvania Register 1970; NR.

7 sheets (1936, 1937, including plans, elevation, sections, details); 2 ext. photos (1972),* 1 photocopy of architect's drawing (c. 1825);* 1 data page (including 1867 insurance survey).*

Free Quakers Meeting House

(PA-1120), 500 Arch St., at S.W. corner Fifth St., Independence National Historical Park. Historic museum. Brick, 48'-4'' (three-bay front) × 36'-3'', two stories, gable roof, pedimented doorway, rusticated stucco lintels, dentil cornice, inscribed stone plaque in north gable; auditorium plan with galleries along three interior walls.

Fine example of nationalist influences on traditional Quaker plain style. Built 1783; Samuel Wetherill and Timothy Matlack, architects. Renovated, second floor installed 1788. Interior altered 1858, 1868. Two-story western addition built 1868; Stephen D. Button, architect. Masonry vaults and basement demolished when building was moved 33' west and 8' south 1961. Restored 1961–69; F. Spencer Roach, architect. Free Quakers were Friends who were expelled from the Religious Society of Friends for participation in the American Revolution; they proposed no new doctrines and dissolved 1836. Building served as Apprentices' Library 1841–97. Maintained by Junior League of Philadelphia, Inc., whose headquarters are in basement. Certified, PHC 1956; Pennsylvania Register 1970; NR.

2 sheets (1940, including elevation, details) from Survey, Philadelphia Chapter, A.I.A. (1932), 21 sheets (1963–64, including plot plan, plans, elevations, sections, details);* 9 ext. photos (1961,

1976*), 3 int. photos (1961), 1 aerial photo (1961), 3 photocopies of architectural drawings (1783); 4 data pages (including 1795–1882 insurance surveys).*

Garden, C. H., & Co. Building
(PA-1419), 606 Market St. Brick with cast-iron front, approx. 40' (five-bay front) × 118', six stories (originally five), mansard roof (originally flat with ornamental parapet), arcaded windows above ground story, originally columned ground story. Built c. 1866. Mansard added, interior altered 1899; Collins and Autenreith, architects. Ground story altered 1940; Israel Demchick, architect. Demolished c. 1965. 1 ext. photo (1962);* 1 photocopy of old ext. print (n.d.).*

Godley's Stores. See Granite Street Vaults

Goldberg's Army-Navy Store. See Cope, Caleb, & Co., Store

Gordon, George, Building
(PA-1065), 300 Arch St., at S.W. corner Third St. Cast iron with brick party walls, 15'-9" (two-bay front) × 37'-4", five stories, flat roof, arcaded windows above ground story. Fine early example of mid-19th-century cast-iron commercial building. Built 1856; demolished 1963. 4 sheets (1963, including plan, elevations, cast-iron structural details); 4 ext. photos (1959, 1962, 1963), 1 int. photo (1963); 5 data pages (1961, 1963).

Granite Street Vaults (also known as Godley's Stores)
(PA-1420), 100–12 and 101–27 Granite St., beneath sidewalks and street, between Front and Dock sts. Rubble-and-brick walls, longitudinal brick-arch arcade, granite-slab ceiling (street floor above), approx. 25' × 300', approx. 9' height.

An unusual example of granite-covered storage vaults under the length and width of a street. East section built 1849–50; John Rice, builder and superintendent of construction. West section built 1850–53; Jessee Godley, superintendent of construction. Demolished 1960. 2 ext. photocopies (1959),* 2 int. photocopies (1959).*

Hansell, John, House
(PA-1012), 153 N. Sixth St. Brick, approx. 18' (two-bay front) × 45' with three-story rear ell, three-and-a-half stories, gable roof. Built between 1788 and 1802; altered to store later; demolished 1959. 1 ext. photo (1959); 4 data pages (1959).

Harrison, Henry, Houses

(PA-1421), 112–16 Cuthbert St. (originally Coombe's Alley). Three brick row houses, each approx. 14' (two-bay front) × 37', two-and-a-half stories, gambrel roofs, cove pent eaves, two rooms to a floor with rear stair tower.

Fine example of 18th-century Philadelphia side-street rental properties. Built c. 1760. Fireplace and paneling of No. 116 in Queen Anne Bed Room, Henry Francis duPont Winterthur Museum, Delaware. Certified, PHC 1957; Pennsylvania Register 1970. 8 sheets (1957, 1959, including plot plan, plans, elevations, sections, details)* courtesy of Philadelphia Historical Commission; 1 ext. photo (1951),* 3 int. photos (1951);* 9 data pages (1957, including 1781–1850 insurance surveys);* 3 HABSI forms (1957).*

Hensel, Colladay & Co. Factory

(PA-1422), 45–51 N. Seventh St. Brick with cast-iron storefronts, approx. 90' (five-bay front) × 100', six stories, steep mansard roof, large windows with thin piers and spandrels, dark brick bands and carved stone panels on piers at each story, rectangular plan. Built 1881; Allen B. Rorke, contractor. Demolished 1965. Hensel, Colladay & Co. were manufacturers of dress trimmings. 2 ext. photos (1965);* 1 data page (1965).*

House

(PA-1423), 620, Arch St. Brick with cast-iron storefront, approx. 25 (three-bay front) × 65', three-and-a-half-stories, gable roof. Built late 18th century; renovated to store later; demolished 1965. 1 ext. photo (1965);* 1 data page (1965).*

House

(PA-1424), 628–30 Arch St. Brick with wooden and pressed metal storefronts, approx. 35' (four-bay front) × 45', three-and-a-half stories, gable roof. Built late 18th century; renovated to store later; demolished 1965. 1 ext. photo (1965);* 1 data page (1965).*

House

(PA-1425), 113 N. Water St. Brick, approx. 25' (three-bay front) × 46', three stories, gable roof. Built mid-18th century; demolished c. 1963. 2 ext. photos (1957).*

House

(PA-1426), 523–25 Quarry St., at N.E. corner Fairhill St. Brick, approx. 38' (four-bay front) × 18' with two-story rear ells, two-and-a-half stories, gable roof, two dwellings in one unit. Built mid-18th century; demolished c. 1960. 1 ext. photo (1959).*

Houses

(PA-1427), 113–15 Summer St. (originally Swarthmore Pl.). Two contiguous brick houses, each approx. 15' (two-bay front) × 30' with rear two-story ell, three stories, gable roof. Originally part of a row of six tenement houses on court extending east from between 229 and 231 N. Second St. Built early 19th century; demolished 1968. Swarthmore Pl. became Summer St. 1911. 1 ext. photo (1967).*

Howell & Brothers Building

(PA-1428), 12–14 S. Sixth St. Brick with iron front, approx. 41' (six-bay front) × 173', five stories, flat roof, straight-arch windows. Built c. 1870; demolished 1961. Howell & Brothers were one of the country's largest manufacturers of paper hangings. 1 ext. photo (1961).*

Independence Hall (originally known as the State House of Pennsylvania).
Illustrated

(PA-1430), S. side Chestnut St. between Fifth and Sixth sts., Independence National Historical Park. Brick with marble and soapstone trim, approx. 107' (nine-bay front) × 45', two stories, decked gable roof with balustrade; on north facade are marble panels between marble stringcourses at second story, marble keystones, soapstone quoins, wooden Corinthian cornice with carved modillions; south facade dominated by brick-veneered stone tower with wooden steeple and octagonal cupola, Doric frontispiece, Palladian window, Doric, Ionic, Corinthian pilasters on successive stories, urns and balustrade mark setbacks of steeple; open triple-arch arcades connect main building to flanking two-story hipped-roof wings. Central Hallway with engaged Doric columns and entablature flanked by Assembly Room (east room) fully paneled on east wall with fluted Ionic pilasters and cove ceiling and Supreme Court Room (west room) fully paneled on all walls with fluted Doric pilasters; Long Room extends length of second floor.

An outstanding colonial example of Georgian public architecture. Built 1732–48; Edmund Wooley (master carpenter) and Andrew

Hamilton (lawyer), architects. Tower and steeple built 1750–53; steeple removed 1781. Clock on soapstone case structure built on west end 1752. Wings and arcades removed, replaced with office wings 1813–15; Robert Mills, architect. Soapstone clock case structure removed 1815. Steeple reconstructed, clock on west end of Hall removed 1828; William Strickland, architect. Assembly Room and second story renovated 1802; Assembly Room remodeled c. 1818. Assembly Room "restored" 1831; John Haviland, architect. Second story renovated 1828 for federal courts 1828–54; John Haviland, architect. Second story renovated 1854 for City of Philadelphia Councils' Chambers 1854–95. Interior "restored," wings and arcades reconstructed by Philadelphia Chapter, Daughters of American Revolution 1896–98; T. Mellon Rogers, architect. Second story restored by City of Philadelphia 1922, plans and supervision by committee of Philadelphia Chapter, A.I.A.; Horace Wells Sellers, chairman. Restored by National Park Service 1951–73.

Pennsylvania State House 1735–99, housing Assembly, Council, and Supreme Court of the Province and later Commonwealth. Second Continental Congress and Congress of Confederation held most of their sessions here. Site of the adoption of Declaration of Independence 1776, enactment of Articles of Confederation 1781, drafting of U.S. Constitution 1787. Charles Willson Peale's museum (Philadelphia Museum), America's first modern museum, occupied second story 1802–28. Owned by City of Philadelphia since 1818, administered by National Park Service. Certified, PHC 1956; Pennsylvania Register 1970; designated National Historic Site 1943.

18 ext. photos (1939, 1959,* 1975*), 4 ext. photos of tower (1959),* 14 int. photos of tower (1959),* 47 photos of Central Hallway (1959, 1975),* 27 photos of Assembly Room (1959, 1969, 1975),* 11 photos of Supreme Court Room (1959, 1975),* 7 photos of second floor (1959, 1975),* 6 photos of garret (1959),* 33 photos of stairhall (1959),* 1 photocopy of old drawing (c. 1732),* 58 photocopies of measured drawings (1898, 1899, 1918, 1923, n.d.),* 1 photocopy of old ext. photo (c. 1865–69);* 4 data pages (including 1818–29 insurance surveys).*

Congress Hall (originally known as Philadelphia County Court House). (PA-1431), S.E. corner Sixth and Chestnut sts., Independence National Historical Park. Brick with marble trim, approx. 50' (five-bay front) × 98', two-and-a-half stories with slightly projecting three-bay pedimented pavilion and round-arch entrance with fanlight,

hipped roof with open octagonal cupola, rear two-story semioctagonal bay, round-arch windows on ground story; House Chamber on
ground floor, four semicircular tiers, gallery on north wall, Senate
Chamber on second floor.

Fine example of Federal-style public architecture complementary
to notable adjacent Georgian building. Built 1787–89; enlarged to accommodate U.S. Congress 1793–95. Senate Chamber restored by Society of Colonial Dames in Pennsylvania 1895–96; George C. Mason,
architect. House of Representatives Chamber restored by City of
Philadelphia 1912–13, plans and supervision by committee of
Philadelphia Chapter, A.I.A.; Frank Miles Day, chairman. Restored
by National Park Service 1959–62. Cornice and interior elements in
Architectural Study Collection, Museum Division, Independence National Historical Park.

U.S. Congress met here 1790–1800, making it the oldest extant
building in which U.S. Congress has met. Site of the ratification of
the Bill of Rights 1791, of Washington's second inauguration 1793 and
his Farewell Address 1797, and of John Adams's inauguration 1797.
Philadelphia County Court House 1800–1890; later public uses.
Certified, PHC 1956; Pennsylvania Register 1970; designated National
Historic Site 1948. 3 ext. photos (1975),* 14 int. photos (1963, 1964,
1975),* 13 photocopies of measured drawings (1901, 1912);* 4 data
pages (including 1823, 1851 insurance surveys).*

Philadelphia City Hall (also known as U.S. Supreme Court Building). (PA-
1432), S.W. corner Fifth and Chestnut sts., Independence National
Historical Park. Brick with marble trim, approx. 50' (five-bay
front) × 70', two-and-a-half stories with slightly projecting three-bay
pedimented pavilion and round-arch entrance with fanlight,
hipped roof with open octagonal cupola, exterior appearance same as
Congress Hall.

Built 1790–91; David Evans, master carpenter. Restored by City
of Philadelphia 1921–22; plans and supervision by committee of
Philadelphia Chapter, A.I.A.; Horace Wells Sellers, chairman. Restored by National Park Service 1951–74. U.S. Supreme Court, U.S.
Circuit Court, U.S. District Court met here 1791–1800. Used as
Philadelphia City Hall 1791–c. 1895. Certified, PHC 1956; Pennsylvania Register 1970; designated National Historic Site 1948. 2 sheets
(1961, including elevations);* 1 ext. photo (1975),* 4 int. photos
(1975),* 18 photocopies of measured drawings (1918);* 1 data page
(including 1821 insurance survey).*

Independence National Historical Park. See Carpenters' Hall, Dilworth-Todd-Moylan House, First Bank of the United States, Independence Hall, Philadelphia Exchange Company, Philosophical Hall, Second Bank of the United States, Bishop William White House

Insurance Patrol. Illustrated
(PA-1433), 509 Arch St. Brick with cast-iron front, approx. 27' (three-bay front) × 205', two stories, flat roof. Built c. 1879; demolished 1965. Sponsored by insurance companies, the Insurance Patrol protected property during and after fires. 1 ext. photo (1959),* 1 photocopy of old ext. photo (n.d.);* 3 data pages (1964).*

Irvin Building (originally known as Fire Association Building)
(PA-1434), 401–13 Walnut St., at N.W. corner Fourth St. Steel frame, brick curtain walls faced with coursed limestone ashlar, approx. 128' (ten-bay front) × 100' originally 53'-3¹/₂" × 80'-3³/₄"), ten, fourteen, seventeen stories (originally seven), flat roof, two ground-story flat Doric distyle porticoes in antis, second-story windows with bold lintels and Ionic pilasters, recessed center bay above sixth story, carved spread eagle on fasciae at ninth-story corners, fluted panels at seventh and eighth stories, rectangular plan with elevators at rear wall.
    Fine example of evolution of an early-20th-century office building in a late Victorian eclectic classicism complementary to neighboring structures. Built 1911–12; Edgar V. Seeler, architect; Cramp and Company, contractors. Raised four stories, lateral fourteen- and seventeen-story and rear ten-story additions built 1928–30; Ernest J. Matthewson, architect; Doyle and Company, contractors. Mezzanine floor filled in to create another floor 1955; C. H. Woolmington, architect. Demolished 1974. 6 ext. photos (1974),* 1 photocopy of old ext. photo (1915);* 2 data pages (including building permits 1911–55).*

Iungerich Warehouse
(PA-1403), 147 S. Front St. Brick with sandstone and granite trim, approx. 28' (four-bay front) × 25'; four stories, mansard roof, squat central tower with pointed roof, rectangular plan. Built after 1867; demolished 1967. 1 ext. photo (1966);* 7 data pages (1966).*

Jayne Building
(PA-188), 242–44 Chestnut St. Brick with granite front and interior iron columns and wooden girders supporting floors, 42'-2" (seven-

bay front) × 133'-6", eight stories with two-story castellated tower (destroyed 1872), flat roof, clustered-column piers terminate with pointed arches at seventh story and quatrefoil windows at eighth story, rectangular plan.

Prototype skyscraper design. Built 1849–50; William Johnston, architect; Thomas U. Walter, architect, finished building at Johnston's death 1849; ironwork by J. K. and E. K. Smith (Tamaqua, Pa.). Six-story side wings (238–40 and 246 Chestnut St.) added 1851; Thomas U. Walter, architect. Interior rebuilt, rear granite wall replaced by brick, steam elevator installed after fire 1872. Altered 1907; Furness, Evans & Co., architects. Demolished 1957–58. Dr. David Jayne was a prominent patent-medicine producer and real estate developer.

16 sheets (1957, including plot plan, plans, elevations, sections, details); 15 ext. photos (1951, 1957, 1958), 2 photocopies of insurance survey plans (c. 1862, 1873);* 3 data pages (1957).

Jefferson Fire Insurance Company Building

(PA-1435), 423 Walnut St. Brick with stone and tile trim, approx. 22' (three-bay front) × 76' with three-story rear addition, four stories, flat roof, parapet with acroterion. Built c. 1885. Interior altered, three-story addition built 1907; Arnold H. Moses, architect. Demolished 1959. 2 ext. photos (1959),* 1 photocopy of old ext. photo (1915).*

Keystone Telephone Company Building. See Commercial Exchange

Kid-Chandler House

(PA-1436), 323 Walnut St., Independence National Historical Park. Brick with marble trim, approx. 21' (three-bay front) × 42', three-and-a-half stories, gable roof, notable interior details. Originally apothecary shop on ground story with separate entrance at eastern (right) end and entrance hall to rear stair tower at western end.

Early Philadelphia example of use of second story as main living floor. Built c. 1810–15; altered c. 1840, c. 1870, c. 1880, c. 1909; rear kitchen wing demolished 1959; interior extensively remodeled and exterior restored 1963–64. Shutter and many elements of top-floor woodwork in Architectural Study Collection, Museum Division, Independence National Historical Park. Present quarters of Pennsylvania Horticultural Society and Philadelphia Society for Promoting Agriculture. Certified, PHC 1957; Pennsylvania Register 1970; NR. 9 ext. photos (1959, 1960, 1961, 1972, 1975),* 36 int. photos (1959, 1961);* 35 data pages (1959, 1961).*

Kid-Physick House

(PA-1437), 325 Walnut St., Independence National Historical Park. Brick with marble trim, approx. 18' (two-bay front) × 42', three-and-a-half stories, gable roof; originally side-hall plan with two counting rooms on ground story, living quarters on second story.

Built c. 1811–12; altered c. 1865, c. 1909; rear wing demolished 1959; interior extensively remodeled and exterior restored with 18th-century-style garden 1963–64. With adjacent dwelling this house has been headquarters of Pennsylvania Horticultural Society and Philadelphia Society for Promoting Agriculture since 1964. Certified, PHC 1957; NR. 2 ext. photos (1959),* see also ext. photo (1973)* of Kid-Chandler House (PA-1436), 18 int. photos (1959);* 46 data pages (1958, 1959).*

Krider Gun Shop. See Drinker, John, House

Lee, Robert M., House and Law Office

(PA-1052), 109–11 N. Sixth St. Brick, approx. 34' (four-bay front) × 28' with three-story rear ell, three-and-a-half stories, gable roof, handsome Greek Revival interior details. Built between 1769 and 1774 as two dwellings; remodeled into one building with Greek Revival detailing c. 1840; demolished 1959. 3 sheets (1959, including plot plan, second-floor plan, details); 1 ext. photo (1959), 6 int. photos (1959), 1 photocopy of old ext. photo (c. 1870); 11 data pages (1959, 1960).

Leland Building. Illustrated

(PA-1086), 37–39 S. Third St. Brick with granite ashlar front, approx. 34' (five-bay front) × 80', five stories, flat roof, rectangular plan with rear ell, facade has vertical emphasis from continuous granite piers and recessed spandrels. One of a complex of buildings around a central courtyard. Early architectural solution for tall, narrow commercial building. Built 1855; Stephen D. Button, architect; Solomon K. Hoxsie, granite-cutter; John Kilgore and John R. Hudders, carpenters. Certified, PHC 1971. 5 ext. photos (1963, 1965), 1 int. photo (1965); 7 data pages (1964).

Lit Brothers

(PA-1438), 701–39 Market St., composing block bounded by Seventh, Market, Eighth, Filbert sts. Brick end pavilions with terra cotta and galvanized iron trim (701–7 and 723–39 Market St.), brick center buildings with painted granite and marble ashlar fronts, reinforced concrete and buff brick building on northeast end (10–34 N. Seventh St.), approx. 400' (fifty-bay front) × 350', five, six, and seven stories, flat roof, semihexagonal bays at three corners, at third-story rear arched concrete bridge with brick walls and carved limestone trim over Filbert St.

Outstanding example of the architectural and business evolution of a major Philadelphia department store. No. 711 Market St. built for J. M. Maris & Co. 1859; Nos. 715–17 Market St. built for J. B. Lippincott & Co. 1861; Nos. 723–25 Market St. built c. 1865; No. 709 Market St. built c. 1870; No. 713 Market St. built 1872. Nos. 719–21 Market St. built for Joel J. Bailey & Co. 1873; William D. Price, architect. Nos. 737–39 Market St. built 1893, Nos. 727–35 Market St. and Nos. 7–13 N. Eighth St. built 1895–96; Collins and Autenreith, architects. Interior of Nos. 715–21 Market St. altered 1898–99, Nos. 15–21 N. Eighth St. built 1900; Collins and Autenreith, architects. Nos. 701–7 Market St. built 1907; Charles M. Autenreith, architect. Bridge at 720 Filbert St. built 1912; Stearns and Castor, architects. Nos. 10–34 N. Seventh St. built 1917–18; Simon and Bassett, architects. Many later interior alterations.

Enterprise expanded from store at N.E. corner Eighth and Market sts. (37' × 96') 1893 to include three store lots 1895, another three 1897, and three stores 1898 to measure 236' × 231'. By 1907 twenty-three more stores were incorporated at Seventh and Market sts. and along Seventh St. to give present dimensions. 3 ext. photos (1972, 1973, including 1 of bridge).*

McClare-Hutchinson Building
(PA-1439), 20 S. Third St. Stuccoed brick with brownstone storefront (originally brick), approx. 20' (three-bay front) × 36' with one-story rear extension (originally three-story kitchen ell), four stories (originally three-and-a-half stories), flat roof (originally gable), lotus-leaf piers, battered doors, rectangular plan (originally two shops and parlor on ground story).

Fine example of 18th-century shop-dwelling remodeled to mid-19th-century office building with notable Egyptian Revival doors. Built for Samuel McClare 1789; raised one story, new front built 1847–48 for Hutchinson & Co., stockbrokers; rear ell replaced later. Certified, PHC 1973. 2 ext. photos (1958, 1972).*

McCrea, James, House

(PA-1440), 108–10 Sansom St. Brick, approx. 47' (six-bay front) × 28' with three-story rear ell, four stories (originally three), shed roof, pedimented round-arch entrances. Built between 1794 and 1812 as two dwellings in one unit. Certified, PHC 1959; Pennsylvania Register 1970. 1 ext. photo (1959);* 4 data pages (1965).*

Manhattan Building. See American Life Insurance Company Building

Market Street Area Study

(PA-1441), 621–35 Market St., on N. side of Market St. between Sixth and Seventh sts. Nine contiguous brick and cast-iron commercial buildings, three- and four-bay fronts, four, five, and six stories, flat and mansard roofs. Typical late-19th-century retail block. Built at various times during the last half 19th century; demolished 1965. 5 ext. photos (1965);* 4 data pages (1965).*

Mason, James S., & Co., Store

(PA-1442), 138–40 N. Front St., at S.W. corner Quarry St. Brick with granite ashlar front and interior iron columns and wooden girders supporting floors, approx. 28' (five-bay front) × 95', five stories, flat roof, large Tudor-arch windows with engaged clustered columns on second-story front, flat-arch lintels on upper-story windows, rectangular plan.

Notable example of mid-19th-century wholesale store. Built 1850–51; demolished 1973. James S. Mason & Co., a prominent manufacturer of blacking and inks, was here until 1919. 5 ext. photos (1973),* 1 int. photo (1973),* 1 photocopy of old ext. print (1855).*

Mechanics Bank (now Norwegian Seamen's Church)

(PA-1443), 22 S. Third St. Coursed granite ashlar front and stuccoed brick sides and rear, approx. 33' (three-bay front) × 58', two stories (originally one) with Corinthian distyle portico in antis, gable roof, originally one-story banking room with square skylight.

Fine Greek Revival bank, one of Strickland's last designs in Philadelphia. Built 1837; William Strickland, architect; John Struthers, stonemason. Interior renovated 1874; James H. Windrim, architect. Interior altered, two-story rear brick addition built 1930; Edwards and Green, architects. Norwegian Seamen's Church since 1930. Certified, PHC 1961; Pennsylvania Register 1970. 2 ext. photos (1958);* 5 data pages (1958, 1965, including 1837, 1855 insurance surveys).*

Megargee Brothers Building

(PA-1444), 18–20 S. Sixth St. Brick with iron storefront, approx. 41′ (four-bay front) × 173′, five stories, flat roof. Built c. 1868; upper stories replaced c. 1880; demolished 1961. 1 ext. photo (1961).*

Merchants' Exchange. See Philadelphia Exchange Company

Merchants' Hotel

(PA-1445), 40–50 N. Fourth St. Brick with marble trim, 88′ (nine-bay front) × 190′, five stories, flat roof, colonnade at ground story, recessed five-bay balcony at second story, central-hall plan. Built 1837; William Strickland, architect. Destroyed by fire 1966. Columns, part of iron balcony railing in Architectural Study Collection, Museum Division, Independence National Historical Park. At the time of construction it was the largest, most distinguished hotel in the city, and served as James Buchanan's presidential campaign head-quarters 1856. Certified, PHC 1956. 6 ext. photos (1962),* 5 int. photos (1962),* 1 photocopy of old print (1857);* 19 data pages (1962, 1963, including 1837 news article and 1837–51 insurance surveys).*

Meredith House. See Stone-Penrose House

Morris Brewery Vaults

(PA-1446), 210 Chancellor St., at S.E. corner American St. Rubble foundation and piers with galleting and brick-vaulted ceiling, approx. 35′ × 85′, approx. 11′ height. Built 1789; demolished 1961. 6 photocopies of int. photos (1959);* 3 data pages (1962, including 1790–1831 insurance surveys).*

Musical Fund Society Hall

(PA-1447), 808 Locust St. Brick with buff brick front and copper and terra cotta trim, approx. 76′ (three-bay front) × 94′ (originally approx. 60′ × 110′), three stories (originally two), flat roof with pediment, giant Corinthian pilasters on upper stories, large arched entrance.

Fine 19th-century music hall whose appearance and function reflect changes in architectural styles and the city's cultural life. Built 1824; William Strickland, architect; John O'Neill, builder; Daniel Groves, master mason. Enlarged, new front built, stage moved to rear 1847; Napoleon LeBrun, architect. New front built, interior re-modeled into three saloons and one banquet room 1891; Addison Hutton, architect. Entrance altered, interior converted to warehouse 1946; Howard Carter Hill, architect.

Oldest surviving music hall in the United States, noted for its acoustics. Site of first Republican Party National Convention 1856. Musical Fund Society was formed 1820 to cultivate musical taste and help needy musicians and used hall for concerts and lectures until 1924 when it became Philadelphia Labor Institute; used for various social and athletic events 1934–45; warehouse 1946–64; vacated 1964. Certified, PHC 1957; Pennsylvania Register 1970; designated National Historic Landmark 1974.

1 ext. photo (1976);* 15 data pages (1959, including architects' estimates and specifications 1825, 1847).*

National Guard's Hall (also known as Armory of the National Guards)

(PA-1015), 518–20 Race St. Brick, approx. 60' (five-bay front) × 130', three stories, flat roof, round-arch windows. Built 1856–57; demolished 1959. 3 ext. photos (1959), 4 int. photos (1959, including chandelier), 1 photocopy of old ext. print (n.d.); 6 data pages (1959).

North Front Street Area Study

(PA-1448), 2–66 N. Front St., on W. side Front St. between Market and Arch sts. Twenty-six contiguous commercial buildings, brick with granite storefronts (one with cast-iron facade), mostly two- and three-bay fronts, four and five stories, flat, gable, and mansard roofs, rectangular plans.

Well-preserved block of early-19th-century wholesale stores and warehouses. Three-and-a-half story Nos. 16, 46 built c. 1780, 1785; Nos. 2–6, 14, 18–44, 48–66 built between 1828 and 1836; five-story iron-front No. 8 built c. 1855. Nos. 10–12 demolished c. 1915; No. 54 demolished between 1960 and 1969. Nos. 18–30 part of Stephen Girard estate since 1830. Nos. 46, 50 certified, PHC 1960, 1970. 9 ext. photos (c. 1958, 1974);* 40 data pages (1960, including 1829–1933 insurance surveys).*

North Seventh Street Area Study

(PA-1449), 21–33 N. Seventh St., on E. side Seventh St. between Commerce and Filbert sts. Six contiguous brick and cast-iron commercial buildings, three- and four-bay fronts, two, three, four, and five stories, flat and gable roofs. Includes Philadelphia Hose Company (PA-1460). Built at various times during last half of 19th century; demolished 1965. 1 ext. photo (1965).*

North Third Street Area Study
(PA-1450), 17–63 N. Third St., E. side Third St. between Church and Arch sts. Twenty-two contiguous brick commercial buildings with brick, granite, brownstone, and cast-iron fronts, mostly three-bay fronts, three-and-a-half, four, and five stories, gable and flat roofs.

A treasury of mid-19th-century stores. Built between c. 1840 and 1875. Includes Nos. 47–49 built 1853, Joseph C. Hoxie, architect; Nos. 61–63 built 1852; John Riddell, architect. Nos. 53–55 enlarged, new fronts added 1913–14, Sauer and Hahn, architects; new front added to No. 59 1926. No. 49 demolished 1964–65. Certified, PHC 1974. 7 ext. photos (1974),* 1 photocopy of old lithograph (c. 1855).*

Norwegian Seamen's Church. See Mechanics Bank

Old Customs House. See Second Bank of the United States

Old St. Paul's. See St. Paul's (Protestant Episcopal) Church

Penn Mutual Life Insurance Company Building (known as Penn Mutual Building)
(PA-1451), 129 S. Third St. and 241 Dock St., at N.E. corner Third and Dock sts. Cast-iron with brick party walls, 19'-11½" (three-bay front) × 32'-10", five stories, flat roof, originally cast-iron statue of William Penn in second-story niche, round-arch windows, rectangular plan.

One of the earliest cast-iron buildings in the country, introducing a new method of jointing and bolting cast-iron plates. Built 1850–51; G. P. Cummings, architect; Joseph Singerly, builder. Demolished 1956. William Penn statue removed to lobby of Penn Mutual Building, 530 Walnut St., Philadelphia 1945. 1 ext. photo (1951).*

Pennsylvania Company for Insurances on Lives and Granting Annuities
(PA-1452), 431 Chestnut St. Brick with Quincy granite ashlar front, approx. 30' (three-bay front) × 164', three stories, flat roof, three-arch arcades with foliated carvings on keystones on first and second stories, third-story six-arch arcade with squat columns, front two-story banking room with skylights in vaulted ceiling.

Only extant post–Civil War bank on Bank Row. Built 1871–73; Addison Hutton, architect; William A. Armstrong, builder. Interior remodeled 1880; Addison Hutton, architect. Chartered 1812, Pennsylvania Company is the oldest institution of its kind in the United States. Pennsylvania Company here 1873–90, Tradesmen's National Bank 1910–30, Philadelphia National Bank since 1940. Certified, PHC 1958.

2 ext. photos (1959),* 2 photogrammetric stereopairs (1959),* 1 photocopy of old ext. photo (1929),* 1 photocopy of old int. photo (c. 1910).*

Pennsylvania Company for Insurances on Lives and Granting Annuities

(PA-1453), 304 Walnut St. Brick with Pictou stone front, approx. 25' (three-bay front) × 97', two stories, flat roof, incised pilasters and spandrels on ground story, smooth rusticated upper story, round-arch windows and entrance with carved keystones, large one-room banking room with galleries and rectangular skylight.

Fine Italianate bank design. Built c. 1859. Restored 1966–67; Stewart, Noble, Class & Partners, architects. Now a branch bank of First Pennsylvania Banking and Trust Company. Certified, PHC 1961; Pennsylvania Register 1970. 3 ext. photos (1958, 1961),* 3 int. photos (1961);* 13 data pages (1961, including 1859–75 insurance surveys).*

Pennsylvania Fire Insurance Company Building. Illustrated

(PA-1454), 508–10 Walnut St. Brick with marble front, approx. 45' (six-bay front) × 138' (originally approx. 22' × 50' with three-and four-story rear ell), four stories, flat roof, fluted papyrus-leaf columns at ground story, windows with battered surrounds and winged orb on cavetto lintels at second story, fluted cavetto parapet with winged orb and company's name (not original).

Fine example of Egyptian Revival architecture with later matching addition. No. 510 built c. 1839; probably by John Haviland, architect. No. 508 built, No. 510 enlarged 1902; Theophilus Parsons Chandler, Jr., architect; Doyle and Doak, contractors. Building demolished, facade preserved as courtyard screen before twenty-one-story office building 1971–74; Mitchell/Giurgola Associates, architects. Certified, PHC 1962. 8 ext. photos (1959, 1974, 1976).*

Perseverance Hose Company No. 5

(PA-1455), 316 Race St. Brick with Pictou stone ashlar front, approx. 16' (one-bay front) × 75', two stories, flat roof, large straight-arch equipment door, triple-arch window above, rectangular plan. Built 1867; upper story removed 1948; demolished 1959. 1 photocopy of old ext. photo (c. 1935).*

Philadelphia Bank. See Bank of Pennsylvania

Philadelphia Bourse. Illustrated

(PA-1456), 11–21 S. Fifth St., composing block bounded by Fifth, Ludlow, Fourth, Ranstead sts. Steel frame, rusticated sandstone lower stories and buff brick curtain walls with terra cotta trim, approx. 132' (eleven-bay front) × 362', nine stories, flat roof, giant columns and piers mark two-story entrance, rusticated quoins on lower three stories; long central interior court with gallery and skylights, originally exhibition halls in basement and eighth story.

Built 1893–95; G. W. and W. D. Hewitt, architects; Allen B. Rorke, contractor. Interior court altered later. Ground-story interior and exterior west (Fifth St.) and south sides altered 1973–74; Thalheimer and Weitz, architects. Modeled after European bourses, it was the only American institution of its kind when built. Certified, PHC 1971. 6 ext. photos (1973, 1974, 1976),* 1 photocopy of old ext. photo (c. 1925);* 4 data pages (including 1933 insurance survey).*

Philadelphia Contributionship for the Insuring of Houses from Loss by Fire

(PA-1457), 212 S. Fourth St. Brick with marble trim, approx. 50' (three-bay front) × 54', four stories (originally three) with Corinthian tetrastyle porch, mansard roof (originally flat), double-entry stairway, double windows with marble lintels and pilasters, center-hall plan.

Fine example of Greek Revival office-dwelling. Built 1835–36; Thomas U. Walter, architect; Daniel Knight, Robert Knight, and Joseph S. Walter, builders. Mansard added and porch replaced 1866–67; Collins and Autenreith, architects; J. Struthers and Son, marble masons; Michael Errickson, carpenter. Interior altered 1898; Furness, Evans & Co., architects; John Duncan, contractor. Renovated and partially restored 1930, 1970. Formed by Benjamin Franklin in 1752, the Philadelphia Contributionship is the nation's oldest mutual fire insurance company. Certified, PHC 1956; Pennsylvania Register 1970; NR.

2 ext. photos (1958),* 3 int. photos (1958),* 1 photocopy of architect's drawing (1835);* 34 data pages (1959, including 1835–37, 1866–67 correspondence with architect and marble mason).*

Philadelphia Exchange Company (later known as Merchants' Exchange). Illustrated

(PA-1028), 143 S. Third St., on triangular lot bounded by Third, Walnut, Dock Sts., Independence National Historical Park. Brick faced with marble ashlar, 95'-4³/4" (five-bay front) × 152'-8¹/2", three stories, hipped roof, notable semicircular Corinthian prostyle portico on east facade flanked by stairs, circular lantern with engaged Corinthian columns, plain sides with tripartite windows, Corinthian tetrastyle portico in antis with pediment on west facade.

A masterpiece of Greek Revival architecture that exploits the break in the city's grid afforded by its irregular lot. Built 1832–33; William Strickland, architect; John Struthers, marble mason. Recumbent marble lions imported from Italy 1838. Interior altered 1891; Frank Miles Day, architect. Interior gutted and rebuilt 1901–3; Louis C. Hickman, architect. Exterior and lantern tower restored 1964–65. For over half a century Philadelphia's commercial center, replacing earlier taverns. Certified, PHC 1956; Pennsylvania Register 1970; designated National Historic Site 1948. 14 sheets (1954, including plot plan, plans, portico plan, section, elevation, details);* 19 ext. photos (1939, 1964,* 1975*), 1 photocopy of old ext. print (c. 1835);* 17 data pages (including 1834–1903 insurance surveys).*

Philadelphia Fire Department, Engine Company No. 8 (now known as Fireman's Hall). Illustrated

(PA-1459), 149 N. Second St., at N.E. corner Quarry St. Museum. Brick with stone trim, approx. 30' (three-bay front) × 105', two-and-a-half stories, stepped gable roof with triple dormer, diapering above second story, rectangular plan. Built 1898; Thomas M. Seeds, Jr., contractor. Altered later. Fire Department Museum since 1967, known as Fireman's Hall since 1975. 1 sheet (1974, including elevation);* 1 ext. photo (1976).*

Philadelphia Hose Company No. 1

(PA-1460), 33 N. Seventh St., at S.E. corner Filbert St. Brick with brownstone ashlar front, approx. 15' (two-bay front) × 58', three stories, flat roof, paired windows framed by Tuscan pilasters and architrave, quoins. Built 1849–50; demolished 1965. Established 1803 as the first hose company in the United States and in 1857 became the country's first regular fire company to employ a steam fire engine. 1 ext. photo (1965),* 3 photocopies of old ext. photos (c. 1880, c. 1935);* 1 data page (1965).*

Philadelphia Saving Fund Society

(PA-1461), 306 Walnut St. Brick with marble ashlar front, approx. 28' (three-bay front) × 94', two stories (originally one) with Ionic distyle portico in antis with pediment (originally balustrade), flat roof.

Fine example of small Greek Revival bank design. Built 1839–40; Thomas U. Walter, architect; J. Struthers & Sons, masons. Pediment added 1881; rear raised to two stories 1896. Interior of front altered to two stories, remodeled 1950–51; Leopold Hauf, Jr., architect. Founded 1816 as the first savings bank in the United States, Philadelphia Saving Fund Society was here until 1881. Certified, PHC 1957; Pennsylvania Register 1970.

2 ext. photos (1958),* 1 photocopy of old ext photo (n.d.),* 1 photocopy of old engraving (n.d.);* 6 data pages (1959, including 1882–96 insurance surveys, 1907–50 building permits).*

Philadelphia Saving Fund Society

(PA-1462), 700–710 Walnut St., at S.W. corner Seventh St. Brick faced with granite ashlar, approx. 152' (eight-bay front) × 170' (originally approx. 55' × 125' with three-bay front), two stories, flat roof with balustrade, symmetrical facade with two round-arch rusticated entrances, two-story banking room with gallery.

Fine Italianate bank building with complementary additions. Built 1868–69; Addison Hutton of Sloan and Hutton, architect. Rear addition built 1885–86; Addison Hutton, architect. Western addition built 1888; Addison Hutton, architect. Another western addition built 1897–98; Furness, Evans & Co., architects. Interior altered 1919; Furness, Evans & Co., architects. Gallery erected 1925, altered 1927; Mellor, Meigs and Howe, architects. Interior altered 1929–31; Howe and Lescaze, architects. Second headquarters of the bank. Certified, PHC 1957; Pennsylvania Register 1970. 2 ext. photos (1975);* 17 data pages (1959, including 1869 news article and 1888 insurance survey);* HABSI form (1970).*

Philadelphia Trust, Safe Deposit and Insurance Company

(PA-1181), 415 Chestnut St. Brick with marble ashlar front, approx. 50' (three-bay front) × 164', two stories in front, seven stories in rear, flat roof, projecting central bay with grouped pilasters, statuary at cornice, round-arch entrance and windows, rusticated quoins. Built 1873–74; James H. Windrim, architect; William A. Armstrong, builder. Rear raised one story 1898, interior remodeled 1908; John T. Windrim, architect. Rear raised four stories 1922. Demolished 1959. 1 sheet (1965, including elevation);* 2 ext. photos (1959),* 1 photogrammetric stereopair (1959),* 1 photocopy of old ext. photo (c. 1910).*

Philosophical Hall (also known as American Philosophical Society).
Illustrated

(PA-1464), 104 S. Fifth St., Independence National Historical Park. Brick with marble trim, approx. 70' (five-bay front) × 50', two-and-a-half stories, hipped roof, flat lintels with keystones, round-arch entrance with keystone and fanlight, oculus above entrance, central-hall plan.

Restrained Federal style that complements adjacent public buildings. Built 1785–89; Samuel Vaughan, architect. Third floor added 1890; Wilson Brothers & Co., architects; Charles McCaul, contractor. Building restored and third floor removed 1948; Sydney Martin, architect. Founded in 1743 by Benjamin Franklin, the oldest learned society in the United States; reorganized 1769 and officially entitled American Philosophical Society, held at Philadelphia, for Promoting Useful Knowledge. Certified, PHC 1956; Pennsylvania Register 1970; designated National Historic Landmark 1965. 3 ext. photos (1967, 1975),* 6 int. photos (1967);* 14 data pages (including 1828–1908 insurance surveys).*

Provident Life and Trust Company Bank. Illustrated

(PA-1058), 409 Chestnut St. Granite ashlar with marble and tile trim, approx. 40' (three-bay front) × 160', one story, flat roof, gigantic ornamental membering and projecting center bay; one monumental skylighted story inside with decorated iron trusses, tiled walls and floors, notable and unusual ornament, L-plan with a front at 44 S. Fourth St.

One of the most significant works of Frank Furness. Built 1876–79; Frank Furness, architect. Ten-story eastern addition (401–7 Chestnut St.) built 1888–90; Furness, Evans & Co., architects. Extended north on Fourth St. to Ranstead St. 1892, 1895, 1902; Furness, Evans & Co., architects. Buildings on Fourth St., 401–7 Chestnut St. demolished 1945; bank demolished 1959–60.

2 sheets (1962, including elevations, details); 7 ext. photos (1959), 3 int. photos (1959), 8 photogrammetric stereopairs (1959), 1 photocopy of old view (c. 1880); 11 data pages (1960); HABSI form (1962).*

Ralston, Robert, House

(PA-1016), 521 Arch St. Brick, approx. 27' (three-bay front) × 50' with one-story rear addition, three-and-a-half stories on raised basement, gambrel roof, Tuscan pilaster frontispiece, Greek Revival interior details. Built between 1804 and 1838; altered to office, rear one-story warehouse built 1920; demolished 1959. Ralston was a prominent merchant; George R. Graham, publisher of *Graham's Magazine,* lived here 1843–48. 3 ext. photos (1959, including photo of iron work), 5 int. photos (1959); 3 data pages (1959).

Reliance Insurance Company of Philadelphia Building
(PA-1465), 429 Walnut St. Brick with brownstone front, approx. 22′ (three-bay front) × 50′ with two- and three-story rear ell, four-and-a-half stories, gable roof with cross-gable and gargoyles at roofline, apartment on top floor. Built 1881–82; Furness, Evans & Co., architects. Interior altered, two-story rear ell addition built 1907; Brockie and Hastings, architects. Demolished 1960. 1 ext. photo (1959),* 2 int. photos (1959),* 2 photocopies of old ext. photos (c. 1895, 1915).*

Reynolds-Morris House. Illustrated
(PA-1107), 225 S. Eighth St. Brick with marble trim, approx. 42′ (five-bay front) × 24′ with three-story rear ell, three-and-a-half stories, gable roof with modillion cornice, pedimented round-arch entrance with fanlight, marble lintels with keystones, central-hall plan.

Notable Georgian town house. Built 1786–87; restored 1959. Certified, PHC 1956; Pennsylvania Register 1970; designated National Historic Landmark 1967. 9 sheets (1940, including plans, elevations, details) from Survey, Philadelphia Chapter, A.I.A. (1932); 2 ext. photos (1972),* 2 photocopies of measured drawings (1897);* 9 data pages (1960, 1964, including 1830 insurance survey).*

Riggs & Brother, Navigator Statue
(PA-1466), 310 Market St. Painted wooden statue of navigator sighting sextant, approx. 5′ height, originally anchored on exterior at second story. A notable example of 19th-century advertising sculpture. Carved c. 1875; Samuel Sailor, woodcarver. Probably moved to Market St. from S.E. corner of Dock and Walnut sts. 1896; dismantled and deposited at Philadelphia Maritime Museum 1973. Riggs & Brother, chronometer and nautical instrument-makers, were in business 1818–1973 and at this site since 1896. Certified, PHC 1962. 1

photocopy of photo (c. 1970);* 6 data pages (1962);* HABSI form (1970).*

Roney, John, House

(PA-1017), 117 N. Sixth St. Brick, approx. 17' (two-bay front) × 30' with three-story rear ell, three-and-a-half stories, gable roof. Built early 19th century; altered to store later; demolished 1959. 1 ext. photo (1959); 3 data pages (1959).

Rowley-Pullman House

(PA-1467), 238 S. Third St. Brick, approx. 20' (two-bay front) × 44' with two- and three-story rear ell, three-and-a-half stories, gable roof, round-arch entrance with fanlight, side-hall town house plan. Built c. 1823–25. Remodeled and notable new facade added c. 1888; Wilson Eyre, Jr., architect. Restored to 1825 facade 1963; Joseph A. Praissman, architect. Certified, PHC 1963. 5 ext. photos (1962, 1963, 1972);* 2 data pages (1961).*

Royal Insurance Company Building

(PA-1468), 212 S. Third St. Brick with stone trim, approx. 26' (four-bay front) × 97', four-and-a-half stories, gable roof, facade dominated by piers ending in pointed arches. Built 1882; demolished 1960. 3 ext. photos (1960).*

Rumpp, C. F., & Sons, Inc., Factory

(PA-1469), 114–30 N. Fifth St., at S.W. corner Cherry St. Buff brick with blue Indiana limestone and terra cotta trim, approx. 83' (five-bay front) × 103' (originally approx. 55' × 103'), seven stories, flat roof, rusticated first and second stories, giant pilasters at third and fourth stories, arches at fifth story, rectangular plan. Built 1893; Hazlehurst and Huckel, architects; John R. Wiggins, contractor. Two seven-story southern additions (122–24 and 114–20 N. Fifth St.) built 1902, 1912; Carl P. Berger, architect. Rear three-story boiler–engine house built 1910; Carl P. Berger, architect. Demolished 1965. Manufacturers of pocketbooks and fancy leather goods since 1850, C. F. Rumpp & Sons were here 1893–1958. 1 ext. photo (1959),* 2 photocopies of old ext. photos (1894, c. 1905).*

Russell Building

(PA-1797), 152–54 N. Front St., at S.W. corner Race St. Brick with iron shopfront and stone trim, approx. 52' (six-bay front) × 48', five stories (originally four stories), flat roof, rectangular plan. Built c. 1868; ground story altered, raised to five stories between 1935 and 1945; demolished c. 1969. 1 ext. photo (1967),* 1 photocopy of old ext. photo (1919).*

Russell, Captain James, House
(PA-1470), 113 Spring St. (originally 6 Brooks Court). Brick, approx. 16' (two-bay front) × 18' with two-story rear ell (originally tenements), three stories, gable roof, brick stringcourses at second and third stories, probably originally London house plan. Built c. 1752 as house in court extending west between 206 and 208 N. Front St.; excavated around basement to make four-story house c. 1922; demolished 1973. Brooks Court became Augusta Place 1858, Spring St. 1911. 1 ext. photo (1967);* 3 data pages (1960).*

St. Augustine's Roman Catholic Church
(PA-1471), N.W. corner Fourth and New sts. Brick with granite trim, approx. 61' × 152', one story, gable roof, center square three-stage tower with stone quoins and small dome steeple on octagonal lantern, carved limestone volutes between tower and parapet, blind arch on each side of tower, large Doric pedimented frontispiece, three-aisle plan, galleries, rectangular chancel with dome (not original).

Example of Italian Revival architecture in Palladian mode. Built 1847–48; Napoleon LeBrun, architect; William Moroney, supervisor of construction. Steeple added 1867; Edwin F. Durang, architect. Frescoes by Philip Costaggini 1882, 1884; shrine of Our Lady of Good Counsel added to north side of sanctuary 1891, extensively renovated 1911–12. Interior renovated including dome over sanctuary c. 1895, c. 1923; entrance altered when street was lowered 1924. Three-story brick school built on north side 1870; Edwin F. Durang, architect. Three-and-a-half-story brick and limestone rectory built adjoining southwest corner 1924; Folsom, Stanton and Graham, architects. Certified, PHC 1963. 1 ext. photo (1974).*

St. Charles Hotel
(PA-1472), 60–66 N. Third St. Brick with cast-iron front and interior iron columns, approx. 66' (nine-bay front) × 31', five stories, flat roof, ornamental lintels, balcony at second story originally with ornamental iron railing, ground story originally in one room with three vestibules. Rare surviving early hotel. Built 1851; Charles A.

Rubicam, builder. Ground story altered to store 1920; second floor rehabilitated as offices 1975. 3 ext. photos (1962);* 5 data pages (including 1851–1905 insurance surveys).*

St. George's Methodist Episcopal Church
(PA-1473), S.E. corner Fourth and New sts. Brick, approx. 50' (three-bay front) × 80', three stories on raised basement, gable roof; three-aisle plan, shallow rectangular apse, balconies. Built c. 1769; balconies built 1792; basement added 1804, enlarged 1836; street lowered 1924. St. George's is the world's oldest Methodist church in continuous service. Francis Asbury, first Bishop of American Methodism, preached his first sermon in America here 1771; Richard Allen, founder of the African Methodist Episcopal Church, licensed here as first Negro Methodist to preach in America. Historical center and museum adjoins church. Certified, PHC 1956; Pennsylvania Register 1970; NR. 2 ext. photos (1974),* 3 int. photos (1972);* HABSI form (1970).*

St. James Street Area Study
(PA-1474), 202–14 St. James St., on S. side St. James St. between Second and American Sts. Seven contiguous brick houses, each approx. 16' (two-bay front) × 20', three-and-a-half stories, gable roofs (No. 202 shed roof). Built middle and late 18th century; demolished 1959. 4 ext. photos (1959),* 3 int. photos (1959).*

St. Paul's (Protestant Episcopal) Church (also known as Old St. Paul's)
(PA-1475), 225 S. Third St. Brick with stone trim, approx. 65' (three-bay front) × 90', two stories, gable roof, stone Tuscan pilaster frontispiece, round-arch windows, originally three-aisle plan with galleries.

Built 1760–61; John Palmer (bricklayer), architect; Robert Smith, builder. Organ installed 1806, its wooden figures carved by William Rush 1812; Palladian window in east end walled up 1822. Altered 1830; William Strickland, architect; interior details by Thomas U. Walter, architect. Altered to three stories of offices, organ figures removed to St. Peter's Protestant Episcopal Church 1904; Duhring, Okie & Ziegler, architects. Since 1904 headquarters of Episcopal Community Services of the Diocese of Pennsylvania. Certified, PHC 1960. 1 ext. photo (1959);*3 data pages (including 1823, 1831 insurance surveys).*

Sansom, William, House

(PA-1476), 707 Walnut St., on N. side Washington Sq. Brick with marble trim, approx. 20' (three-bay front) × 40' with three-story rear ell (not original), three-and-a-half stories, gable roof, side-hall town house plan (originally London house plan).

Built c. 1799; Benjamin Henry Latrobe, architect. Renovated and enlarged in mid-19th century. One of an original row of twenty houses on Walnut St. and twenty-two on Sansom St. known as Sansom's Row; first example of large-scale speculative development in the city. Certified, PHC 1957. 1 ext. photo (1958),* 1 photocopy of architectural plan and elevation (c. 1800);* 6 data pages (1958).*

Schenck Building

(PA-1078), 535–37 Arch St., at N.E. corner Sixth St. Cast iron on south and west facades, brick party walls on north and east facades, approx. 45' (nine-bay front) × 81', five-and-a-half stories with central mansard tower, mansard roof, arcades on all stories, four truncated towers. Built c. 1869–72; Stephen D. Button, architect. Upper stories removed 1938; surviving ground story demolished 1959. 2 ext. photos (1958), 1 photocopy of old ext. print (c. 1875); 3 data pages (1963).

Second Bank of the United States (also known as the Old Customs House). Illustrated

(PA-137), 420 Chestnut St., Independence National Historical Park. Museum. Brick faced with Pennsylvania marble ashlar, approx. 87' (three-bay front) × 161', two stories with Doric octastyle porticoes at each end, gable roof, barrel-vaulted ceiling supported by double range of six Ionic columns in central one-story banking room.

As the first public building based on the design of the Parthenon, the bank was widely acclaimed and established the popularity and viability of the Greek Revival in the United States. The original interior was an outstanding example of classical progression of space. Built 1818–24; William Strickland, architect; John Struthers, marble mason. Rehabilitated 1844; William Strickland, architect. Interior altered 1864–72; John McArthur, Jr., architect. Partially restored by Works Progress Administration 1939–41; partially restored by National Park Service 1964–73. Served as Second Bank of the United States until 1836 and Philadelphia Customs House 1844–1935; since 1975 portrait gallery of eminent early Americans. Certified, PHC 1956; Pennsylvania Register 1970; designated National Historical Site 1939.

19 sheets (1939, including plans, elevations, sections, details, iron gates); 27 ext. photos (1939, 1975,* including 2 of iron gates), 11 int. photos (1939, 1975*), 1 aerial photo (1965),* 2 photocopies of competition drawings (plan, section) by Benjamin Henry Latrobe (1818),* 1 photocopy of elevation drawing by William Strickland (c. 1821).*

Singer, John, Warehouse

(PA-1478), 319½ Market St., at rear of 319 Market St. Brick, approx. 16' (two-bay front) × 58', three-and-a-half stories, gable roof. Built 1806; altered to dwelling c. 1848; reverted to warehouse between 1911 and 1928. Oldest known extant warehouse in the city. Certified, PHC 1970. 1 ext. photo (1972);* 4 data pages (including 1806–81 insurance surveys);* HABSI form (1970).*

Smythe Building

(PA-1479), 101–5 Arch St., at N.W. corner Front St. Brick with cast-iron front, approx. 75' (nine-bay front) × 73' (originally approx. 150' × 73' and 97'), five stories, flat roof, arcade on each story (originally with Corinthian caps), rectangular plan.

Fine example of cast-iron commercial architecture in Northern Italian Renaissance style. One half of original building which extended through 111 Arch St. Built 1855–57; Brown and Allison, carpenters; George Creely, bricklayer; Tiffany and Bottom (Trenton, N.J.), iron work. No. 107 demolished for trolley loop 1913; cornice removed after 1920; No. 101 demolished 1975, its front dismantled and stored by Fairmount Park Commission. Certified, PHC 1976. 1 ext. photo (1966);* 6 data pages (including 1873–95 insurance surveys);* HABSI form (1970).*

Sons of Temperance Fountain

(PA-1480), octagonal cast-iron water fountain with Gothic motifs, approx. 6' high. Made 1876, errected by Grand Division of Sons of Temperance on Centennial grounds at Belmont and Fountain aves.; removed to Independence Sq. 1877–1969; now in storage. 1 photo (1961).*

Souder, Charles F., House

(PA-1018), 514 Race St. Brick, approx. 18' (two-bay front) × 58', three-and-a-half stories, gable roof. Built 1834–35; altered to store later; demolished 1959. 1 ext. photo (1959); 3 data pages (1959).

South Water Street Area Study
(PA-1810), 100-50 S. Water St., W. side Water St. between Chestnut and Walnut sts. Twenty-four contiguous brick warehouses, each approx. 25' (two- or three-bay front) × 27' or 35', four, five, and six stories, gable and flat roofs, rectangular plans. Includes Blight Warehouse (PA-1393). Built early and mid-19th century. 1 ext. photo (c. 1967).*

Southeast Square. See Washington Square Area Study

Spring Garden Insurance Company Building
(PA-1481), 431 Walnut St. Brick with marble facade, approx. 25' (four-bay front) × 42' with three-story rear ell, three-and-a-half stories, mansard roof. Built 1880–81; Theophilus Parsons Chandler, Jr., architect. Extensive interior alterations 1897; Addison Hutton, architect. Demolished 1960. 1 ext. photo (1959),* 1 photocopy of old ext. photo (1915).*

State House of Pennsylvania. See Independence Hall

Stephen Girard's Bank. See First Bank of the United States

Stiles, Edward, House
(PA-1482), 128 N. Front St., at N.W. corner Elfreth's Alley. Brick with marble trim, approx. 23' (three-bay front) × 85' (originally approx. 23' × 42' with three- and two-story rear ell), four stories (originally three-and-a-half), flat roof (originally gable), cast-iron storefront, marble stringcourse and flat-arch lintels, rectangular plan (originally side-hall plan with rear stair tower).

Built 1787–88; altered to store before 1860; enlarged and converted to manufacturing use before 1875; demolished c. 1969. Built for rental income for Edward Stiles, prominent merchant. 1 ext. photo (1967);* 4 data pages (1960, including 1787–88 insurance surveys).*

Stone-Penrose House (also known as Meredith House)
(PA-1483), 700 Locust St., at S.W. corner Seventh St., on S. side of Washington Sq. Brick with marble trim, approx. 27' (three-bay front) × 70', three-and-a-half stories on raised basement, gable roof, side-hall plan, rear addition with veranda. Built c. 1818–23; altered

later. Restored 1967–68; Henry J. Magaziner, architect. Residence of British Consul General since 1968. 3 ext. photos (1975),* 1 photocopy of old photolithograph (c. 1900);* 5 data pages (1959, including 1877 insurance survey);* HABSI form (1970).*

Stortz, John, & Son, Store
(PA-1484), 210 Vine St. Brick with molded galvanized metal trim, approx. 17' (two-bay front) × 48' with three-story rear wing, four stories, flat roof, molded metal cornice and pedimented parapet capped by spread eagle. Built c. 1885; ground story altered later. Owned by family cutlery firm since it was built. 1 ext. photo (1967).*

Tutleman Brothers & Faggen Building
(PA-1485), 56–60 N. Second St., at N.W. corner Cuthbert St. Brick with cast-iron front, approx. 44' (six-bay front) × 50', five stories (originally four), flat roof, articulated front with continuous piers and wide spandrels, scroll-shaped posts on upper stories, center parapet with small swag-decorated pediment, rectangular plan. One of the last cast-iron fronts erected in the country. Built as three brick stores before 1836. Altered to factory, raised one story, cast-iron front built 1900–1901; Thomas Stephen (Camden, N.J.), architect. Ground story altered later. 1 ext. photo (1976).*

U.S. Supreme Court Building. See Independence Hall, Philadelphia City Hall

Vaults
(PA-1486), beneath sidewalks at S.W. corner Front and Walnut sts. Rubble walls and brick-vaulted ceiling, approx. 12' × 40' along Front St., approx. 12' × 80' along Walnut St., approx. 8' height. Storage vaults under sidewalks at basement or sub-basement levels were common in the 19th century but extant examples are rare. Built c. 1840; demolished 1959. 7 photocopies of int. photos (1959).*

Walnut Street Theatre
(PA-1487), 829–33 Walnut St., at N.E. corner Ninth St. Brick faced with marble ashlar, approx. 90' (six-bay front) × 140', two stories, flat roof with balustrade (originally dome), smooth rusticated ground story with Doric colonnade flanked by round-arch niches, second-story windows set in blind arches.

Fine example of the Greek Revival style applied to theater design. Built 1808–9 as circus; altered to theater 1816. Extensively renovated, new front built 1827–28; John Haviland, architect; John Randall (master carpenter), builder. Interior renovated 1852; Joseph C. Hoxie, architect. Interior renovated c. 1903; Willis G. Hale, architect. Exterior, interior renovated 1920–21; William Lee, architect. Exterior restored to 1828 appearance 1970–72; Dickey, Weissman, Chandler and Holt, architects. Interior remodeled 1970–72; F. Bryan Loving, architect. Oldest surviving theater in the United States; began presenting legitimate drama 1811. Certified, PHC 1957; Pennsylvania Register 1970; designated National Historic Landmark 1968.

26 ext. photos (1958, 1969, 1972),* 51 int. photos (1969),* 1 photocopy of 1830 ext. drawing, 1 photocopy of 1831 ext. engraving, 10 photocopies of old ext. photos (n.d., 1865, c. 1890, c. 1900. c. 1905, 1913).*

Washington Hose Company No. 10
(PA-1488), 35 N. Ninth St. Brick with cast-iron front, approx. 15' (three-bay front) × 55', three stories, flat roof, originally arched pediment with bust of George Washington, rectangular plan. Built c. 1852; altered to store after 1872; storefront altered 1918. New storefront installed, upper stories altered to office and dwelling 1939–40; Sidney Laub, architect. New storefront installed, interior altered to store 1946; Walter Russell, architect. 1 photocopy of old ext. photo (c. 1935).*

Washington Square Area Study (originally known as Southeast Square)
(PA-1489), Block bounded by Sixth, Seventh, Walnut, Locust sts. Twenty-one commercial and domestic buildings ranging from the three-and-a-half-story brick William Sansom House (1799) to the thirty-two-story concrete Hopkinson House (1962–63). Includes Athenaeum of Philadelphia (PA-1389), N.W. Ayer & Son, Inc., Building (PA-1390), John Bonsall House (PA-1394), Philadelphia Saving Fund Society (PA-1462), William Sansom House (PA-1476), Stone-Penrose House (PA-1483), and between 1822 and 1939 First Presbyterian Church (PA-1117).

One of four original squares established as parks by William Penn, it served as potter's field and pasturage 1706–c. 1813. Landscaped as park 1816–18; George Vaux (merchant), director; George Bridport (decorative painter), designer. Officially named Washington Square 1825, and residential in nature until after Civil War. Noted for law offices in last quarter of 19th century and for publishing houses after c. 1900. Landscaped 1913–15; Olmsted Brothers and Co.

(Boston), landscape architects. Revived as residential square since 1957. 2 aerial photos (1965),* 2 photocopies of ext. photos (c. 1957, c. 1962),* 4 photocopies of old photolithographs (c. 1900, 1914),* 1 photocopy of 1842 plot map.*

Washington Square Presbyterian Church. See First Presbyterian Church

White, Bishop William, House
(PA-1490), 309 Walnut St., Independence National Historical Park. Historic house museum. Brick with marble trim, approx. 26′ (three-bay front) × 44′ with two- and three-story ell, three-and-a-half stories, gable roof, pedimented Doric frontispiece, round-arch entrance with fanlight, marble lintels with keystones, large glass panes, side-hall town house plan.

Fine example of a post-Revolution town house. Built 1786–87; ground story altered to commercial use c. 1858, c. 1880, 1946. Restored by National Park Service 1951–63. Bishop White, rector of Christ Church and St. Peter's, was instrumental in restructuring Anglicanism in the form of the Episcopal Church after the American Revolution. Certified, PHC 1957; NR. 1 ext. photo (1974);* 1 data page (including 1795 insurance survey).*

Arch Street Friends Meeting. *Jack E. Boucher photo, 1974.*

Athenaeum of Philadelphia. *Jack E. Boucher photo, 1972.*

John Brock Sons & Co. Warehouse. *Jack E. Boucher photo, 1972.*

Christ Church. *James L. Dillon & Co. photo, 1969.*

Elfreth's Alley Area Study. *Jack E. Boucher photo, 1972.*

Farmers' and Mechanics' Bank. *Jack E. Boucher photo, 1972.*

First Bank of the United States. *Jack E. Boucher photo, 1965.*

Independence Hall, Central Hallway.
James L. Dillon & Co. photo, 1969.

Insurance Patrol. *Photo c. 1880,
courtesy Historical Society of Pennsylvania.*

Independence Hall, Assembly Room tabernacle frame. *Jack E. Boucher photo,
1959.*

Leland Building. *Jack E. Boucher photo, 1965.*

Philadelphia Exchange Company (Merchants Exchange). *Jack E. Boucher photo, 1973.*

Pennsylvania Fire Insurance Company Building. *Cortlandt V. D. Hubbard photo, 1976.*

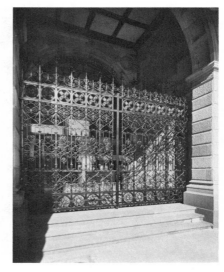

Philadelphia Bourse. *James L. Dillon & Co. photo, 1976.*

Philadelphia Fire Department, Engine Co. No. 8. *Hugh McCawley, del., 1974.*

Philosophical Hall. *Cortlandt V. D. Hubbard photo, 1967.*

Provident Life and Trust Company
Bank. *Photogrammetric drawing, 1959,
plotted by Perry E. Borchers 1962,
Dellas H. Harder, del., 1962.*

Reynolds-Morris House. *Jack E.
Boucher photo, 1972.*

NORTH (CHESTNUT) ELEVATION

SOUTH (SANSOM ST) ELEVATION

Second Bank of the United States. *A. G. Guttersen, del., 1939.*

Penn's City

Center Square

3

Introduction

$\mathcal{P}$HILADELPHIA'S CITY HALL (illus.), a marble masterpiece of High Victorian Picturesque Electicism, fills Center Square and visually challenges every edifice in the vicinity. Once the largest structure in the United States, it consumes all of the Square's five acres, and with its tower and statue of William Penn it rises 584 feet, still the tallest building in the city. By erecting City Hall in Center Square, one of the city's original five public places, Philadelphians strategically placed it in the middle of the intersection of their two main thoroughfares, Broad and Market streets. Its location also put it in the geographical center of the original city, a point reinforced by the massive brass compass inlaid in the center of City Hall courtyard. Because of its central location and massive size, City Hall fixes the city's central design scheme between the Delaware and Schuylkill rivers and serves as a beacon for those approaching the city from any direction. It also has contributed to a rare American use of the term "center city," which for Philadelphia makes more sense than the more common American designation, "downtown."

Three decades in the making, City Hall is the paragon of the French Renaissance style that became the rage for public buildings after the Civil War. It was begun in 1871 with John McArthur, Jr., as its chief architect, in association with the highly respected Thomas U. Walter. Both men had died, however, before the building was officially completed in 1901 under the supervision of W. Bleddyn Powell.[1] Its plan is quite simple: a squarish rectangle whose interior court is one of the finest urban public spaces in the country. It is entered through four vaulted portals that are large enough to accommodate buses that pass through them each weekday to deliver prisoners for trial in the building's county and state courts, which occupy more than half of City Hall's fourteen and a half acres of floor space. Its exterior walls are bristling with symbolic sculpture: caryatids, bas-reliefs, statues, all from the designs of Alexander Milne Calder.[2] As Nature abhors a vacuum, City Hall abhors a blank surface; even the windows are filled—with air conditioners. Its spacious interior is equal to its exterior. Many of its finest rooms are the work of George Herzog, the best local interior designer of the day. Gilded ornament and opulent materials, such as polished marbles, encaustic tiles, and mother-of-pearl inlays, become all the more impressive within such great volumes. In fine, City Hall is the central structure of the Center Square area, a part of the original city with arbitrary boundaries at Ninth Street on the east, South Street on the south, Schuylkill River on the west, and Vine Street on the north.

City Hall was not the first structure to occupy Center Square.[3] In 1800, when most of the present Center Square area was undeveloped, the engine house for the city's water system was erected here. Benjamin Henry Latrobe's plans for the waterworks established his national reputation as an engineer and his bold design for the Pump House promoted both the Greek Revival style and his reputation as an architect.[4] After the Fairmount Waterworks on the Schuylkill superseded Latrobe's system, the Pump House was torn down and the square appears to have remained vacant for the next fifty years. At the time of its demolition in 1827 the Pump House was no longer isolated; the city's westward development had extended beyond Ninth Street. The area's earliest construction of note was Franklin Row (illus.), a range of ten dwellings designed by Robert Mills for John Savage and John Meany in 1809. Mills's plan for the development that extended along the west side of Ninth Street north of Locust expanded upon the practice begun a decade earlier in Sansom's Row in the Old City area. Instead of designing each house separately, as was the case of all Philadelphia rows up to that time, Mills treated the entire row as a design project. Through the use of large recessed blind arches over the tripartite windows on the first and second stories, Mills was able to impart an element of plasticity to each facade and a visual unity to the row.[5] The only survivor, the Sims-Bilsland House at 228 South Ninth Street, is being restored for Thomas Jefferson University.

It was Thomas U. Walter and John Haviland, however, who made the Greek Revival an overt part of the row house design and carried the Philadelphia row development to new heights of gran-

deur. Walter was just emerging as a young architect when he
received the commission from John Savage in 1830 to erect another of
his rows, sixteen dwellings along the south side of Spruce Street
between Ninth and Tenth.[6] The source of its name, Portico Row,
originally Portico Square, is obvious. A flat portico supported by
three Ionic marble columns graced each of the paired doorways. This
scheme gives the development both symmetry and monumentality,
no mean feat for speculative housing. Haviland, on the other hand,
was well established in his profession when he designed Colonnade
Row on the south side of Chestnut Street between Fifteenth and
Sixteenth in the same year that Walter was working on Portico
Square. By running an Ionic colonnade the length of the ten-house
row he was able to achieve even greater grandeur and continuity.[7]
While Colonnade Row was replaced by commerical buildings long
ago, Portico Square still stands as an example of how regal the row
house can look.

When fashionable Philadelphians began moving west of Broad
Street into the Rittenhouse Square neighborhood in the mid-
nineteenth century, the row development followed. Some of these
later examples, such as Samuel Sloan's 1856 Harrison Row on Locust
Street east of Eighteenth, were as visually impressive as the Walter
and Haviland examples.[8] Harrison Row is gone now, however, and
more representative of the mid-century housing construction is the
brick row on the south side of Delancey Street between Eighteenth
and Nineteenth. The ten easternmost dwellings, 1800–1818 Delancey
Street, were built with a common plan and design between 1854 and
1856 by different carpenters for three different clients, who promptly
sold the completed houses to gentlemen, attorneys, and merchants.[9]
The western end of the block was similarly developed from
somewhat different plans in 1857 for John McCrea, gentleman.[10]
After a hundred and twenty years the block retains much of its old
character and has been enlivened with some later "modernizations,"
particularly the delicate detailing and carved caryatids by Eyre and
McIlvaine on Number 1810 and the robust Georgian Revival front by
Wilson Eyre, Jr., on Number 1824.[11]

After the Civil War, real estate developers in the neighborhood
became more style-conscious, probably in response to the tastes of
their prospective clients. Row developments of the 1870's and 1880's
appear to be the work of architects rather than builders or house
carpenters. The twelve dwellings on the north side of Delancey Street
between Twenty-third and Twenty-fourth, for example, are stylis-

tically quite sophisticated, in the up-to-date High Victorian Gothic.
They were built c. 1875 as a carefully conceived unit with contrasting
colors, textures, and silhouettes.[12] A four-story brick and brownstone
house stands at each end, and four of them anchor the center of the
block, flanked by three two-and-a-half-story dwellings of random
Trenton sandstone. This composition is an improvement over the
repetitive brick rows to be found in less affluent parts of the city.

In addition to the attractive rows in the Rittenhouse Square
neighborhood were many fine individual dwellings. Each decade of
the last half of the nineteenth century seems to have spawned a new
generation of domestic architecture. Some of the finest examples of
the 1850's and 1860's have fallen to later development. Joseph Harrison's magnificent Italian mansion, for example, designed by Samuel
Sloan in 1855, on the east side of Rittenhouse Square gave way to an
apartment building in 1925.[13] Yet some brownstones can still be
found along Locust Street. One of the finest is the four-story town
house at 1618 Locust, built c. 1850 for Charles C. Harrison. It is
particularly interesting because it has a bay window added in 1888
from the arabesque designs of Wilson Eyre, Jr.[14] One of Philadelphia's finest town houses of the 1870's is the 1875 Thomas Hockley
House at 235 South Twenty-first Street. Frank Furness, who was just
emerging as the leading and most innovative local architect of his
generation, applied to this High Victorian Gothic house expressive
brick patterns and bold details to make a heavy and uncommon
design all the more massive and eccentric.[15]

The fashion *au courant* in the 1880's is exhibited in the Scott-
Wanamaker House (illus.) at 2032 Walnut Street. The popular and
prolific Theophilus Parsons Chandler, Jr., designed this Jacobean
Revival mansion in 1883 for James P. Scott, head of a sugar-refining
firm. In 1894 the great department-store pioneer John Wanamaker
purchased it and made it his city home until his death in 1922.[16] The
original exterior has remained intact and its richly textured granite
front with bays, minarets, and intricately carved balustrades makes it
an architectural gem of its era. Although the upper floors were altered
to make apartments in the 1930's and elements of the ground story
were vandalized in 1972, its present owners are restoring the main
floor and the massive open stairway to their former grandeur. Beaux-
Arts Classicism was the vogue of the 1890's, and one of its most
patrician examples is the Fell–Van Rensselaer House at the northwest
corner of Eighteenth and Walnut streets. Peabody and Stearns of
Boston, arbiters of architectural good taste of the time, were com-

missioned by Mrs. Sarah Drexel Fell in 1896 to design this Renaissance palace.[17] Mrs. Fell was the widow of the president of A. Pardee & Company, a leading Pennsylvania coal operator, but shortly after the house was completed in 1898 she married Alexander Van Rensselaer of the baronial New York family.[18] Although the Scott-Wanamaker House and the Fell–Van Rensselaer House are stylistic opposites—the stippled granite walls and medieval elements of the former are diametrically opposed to the smooth marble surfaces and classical details of the latter—they have shared similar fates. Both houses have changed very little on the outside and very much on the inside. Until it was gutted in October, 1974, the Fell–Van Rensselaer House had one of the richest residential interiors in the city. All that is left is the stained-glass dome in the entrance hall and the spectacular Doge Room, a dining room whose ceiling is filled with ninety-four portrait medallions of Venetian doges.[19] Nearly all of its original interior may be gone, but the building still stands on the corner of Rittenhouse Square, a marble monument to the luxurious life of inherited wealth and high fashion in the days before income taxes and regulatory commissions.

Churches were always highly visible parts of Victorian communities, and the status of the community usually determined the sect, if not the style of the churches. The upper strata were generally Episcopalians and Presbyterians, and below them were the Baptists and Methodists.[20] Consequently, it is not surprising to find a plethora of Episcopal and Presbyterian churches in the Center Square area. One of the earliest examples is the 1822 St. Stephen's Protestant Episcopal Church at Tenth and Ludlow streets. To worshipers St. Stephen's is best known for its healing services and work with the sick. To architectural historians it is recognized as an early and significant Gothic Revival design by an architect best remembered for his fine Greek Revival works, William Strickland.[21] To most Philadelphians, however, it is an unchanging center city landmark. Its twin octagonal towers with their crenelated fringes and connecting granite screen have been part of the streetscape for more than 150 years. The same cannot be said about the interior, which has a history of many redecorations, additions, and alterations, including a number of notable pieces of sculpture and stained glass.

St. Mark's Protestant Episcopal Church at 1625 Locust Street serves as another chapter in the architectural and religious history of Center Square. St. Mark's was formed in June, 1847, as an early American response to the religious revival that began in the Anglican faith during the 1830's. This movement attempted to restore to Anglican practice elements of Roman Catholicism that had been purged during the Reformation. Directed by the Camden Society, later called the Ecclesiological Society, the movement identified Gothic architecture with "High Church" rituals. Accordingly, the architect of St. Mark's, John Notman, was directed to design an archaeologically accurate church for the congregation. The result, completed in 1851, is one of America's finest Gothic Revival churches in the English decorated and perpendicular styles.[22] The architectural history of the church did not end with Notman's masterpiece. Of the later additions the most notable is the sensitive rendering by Cope and Stewardson of the Lady Chapel at the east end of the church.[23] As in the case of medieval abbeys there was no attempt to hide the fact that it was an addition; its version of the Gothic, executed in red sandstone, is distinctive but not discordant. The magnificence of the interior of both the church and the chapel is enhanced by one of the country's finest collections of ecclesiastical treasures. Of these the most splendid is the 1908 sterling silver altar in the Lady Chapel.

Notman designed two other Episcopal churches in the area, St. Clement's (illus.) at Twentieth and Cherry streets and Church of the Holy Trinity at Nineteenth and Walnut streets, both completed in 1859.[24] St. Clement's spire was dismantled ten years later,[25] and the church is not as imposing as Notman had intended; yet its bowed chancel and Romanesque arcade remain to impress the careful observer. Holy Trinity still has its tower and although it no longer looms over its neighborhood, since high-rise apartment buildings are all about it, it overshadows them architecturally. Holy Trinity has long been considered a permanent fixture on Rittenhouse Square. Other buildings have disappeared with barely a whimper, but when it was rumored in 1968 that Holy Trinity was to be replaced by a thirty-three-story apartment-office tower, parishioners, preservationists, neighbors, and strangers rallied to its cause.[26] As a result, this seminal work of the Romanesque Revival still graces Rittenhouse Square.

In spite of the preponderance of Episcopal churches, the Center Square area was not an Episcopal ghetto in the nineteenth century. In 1853 the First Baptist congregation began its brownstone church from the designs of Stephen D. Button at the northwest corner of Broad and Arch streets, and in 1869 the Arch Street Methodist Episcopal Church was erected diagonally across the intersection.[27] The Baptist Church was demolished in 1898 to make room for the UGI Building,[28] and the congregation now worships in Edgar V. Seeler's Byzantine gem at Seventeenth and Sansom, but Arch Street Methodist still gleams in the shadow of City Hall. Presbyterians built earlier and farther west. Three fine examples of their churches are still standing: Joseph C. Hoxie's 1853 West Arch Street Presbyterian (illus.) at Eighteenth and Arch, John McArthur's 1854 West Spruce Street Presbyterian at Seventeenth and Spruce (now Tenth Presbyterian), and Henry Sims's 1869 Second Presbyterian Church (now First Presbyterian) at Twenty-first and Walnut.[29] The prefix "West" for the former church differentiated it from the Arch Street Presbyterian, which once stood near Tenth and Arch, and where, according to romantic theory, the young Emily Dickinson swooned over its minister, the Reverend Charles Wadsworth.[30] Romantic tales of unrequited love and secret poets, however, are not part of the lore of Joseph C. Hoxie's West Arch Street church. It does not need them to be noteworthy; its architecture alone does that. It was built at a cost of $100,000,[31] a great sum for a church in its day, but it brought results. Praised for its architectural beauty and convenience in 1855,[32] and, although its bell towers and central cupola are now gone, it still has probably the richest Italianate interior in the city. Part of the reason this well-proportioned church is often overlooked by Philadelphians is that it is dwarfed by its neighbor at Eighteenth and Race streets, the Cathedral of SS. Peter and Paul. Three architects, John Notman, John T. Mahoney, and Napoleon LeBrun, and two priests, Mariano Maller and John B. Tornatore, worked on the cathedral's plans, and all can take some credit for this great brownstone pile.[33] No one, however, may care to take credit for the interior renovations, lateral protrusions, and northern chapel addition of the 1950's, since they have destroyed the cathedral's former symmetry.

The fashionable mid-nineteenth-century neighborhood that built so many splendid churches also supported a host of social and cultural institutions. Many of them can still be found extending along Broad Street north and south from Center Square. One of the earliest, at the corner of Pine Street, is the former Pennsylvania Institution for the Deaf and Dumb (illus.), which in spite of many later additions still suggests the spirit of the ancient Greek style. It was built in the 1820's from the designs of John Haviland[34] when the area was sufficiently underdeveloped to possess qualities of a pastoral countryside, which was considered the ideal environment for such well-intentioned projects. Probably the best known of Philadelphia's cultural institutions is the Academy of Music (illus.) at Broad and Locust streets.

World-famous for its acoustics since its opening in January, 1857, the
Academy was the work of LeBrun and Runge, who won the architectural competition in 1854.[35] Marble facing was intended for the exterior walls but a shortage of funds caused the directors to postpone
this final step,[36] and like so many temporary solutions, it has become
permanent. Consequently, the "Old Lady of Locust Street," as the
Academy is affectionately known, remains clothed in modest brick.
Yet its lavish interior and unsurpassed acoustics make it a suitable
home for the Philadelphia Orchestra, one of the world's greatest.
Perhaps not as well known but equally significant is the Pennsylvania
Academy of the Fine Arts (illus.) at Broad and Cherry streets, the nation's oldest art school and museum. The Academy is a notable
expression of America's High Victorian Gothic and the most important and best-known work of Furness and Hewitt, a Philadelphia
architectural partnership that ended in 1875, a year before the
Academy's completion.[37] Both men, Frank Furness and George W.
Hewitt, continued their energetic work throughout the last quarter of
the century in other partnerships. The exterior of the Academy was
cleaned in 1966, exposing to even the most casual observer a fascinating variety of forms, materials, and decorations. A restoration project
completed in 1976 brought back the same richness to the interior and
replaced some missing elements on the front. No nineteenth-century
theaters have survived on Broad Street, but an extant example in the
area is the former Arch Street Opera-House at 1005 Arch Street. It
was rather casually named, since it was originally built in 1870 for
minstrelsy, which made its conversion to a burlesque house in 1896
barely noticeable.[38] It now holds the dubious distinction as the oldest,
if not the only, burlesque theater in Philadelphia, but its long tenure
in this barely remunerative enterprise has preserved it from ruinous
remodelings.

Clubs and fraternal societies were also part of nineteenth-century
social life. The oldest and most prestigious of the city social clubs is
the Philadelphia Club at Thirteenth and Walnut streets.[39] Built in
1836 as a city mansion and the club's headquarters since 1850,[40] the
building's scale is so great and its condition so pristine that many
casual observers mistake it for a twentieth-century example of the
Georgian Revival. Architecturally more conspicuous is the Union
League of Philadelphia at Broad and Sansom streets. The Union
League was founded in 1862 as a semipolitical organization of businessmen and civic leaders who pledged "unqualified loyalty to the
government of the United States and unwavering support of its

measures for the suppression of the Rebellion." In this effort they raised a half-million dollars and 10,000 volunteers for the Civil War's battlefields. Originally a third of its members were Democrats, but in 1898 it became explicitly a Republican club, allowing the Union League to call itself the oldest Republican Party club in continuous existence in the United States.[41] John Fraser designed the house in 1864 and it was completed the next year as one of the city's early examples of the new "Mansard Mode."[42] Its striking but lugubrious brick and brownstone eminence inspired the late Philadelphia wit Alfred Bendiner to suggest that club members hang black crepe to cheer it up.[43] A large granite and steel-frame annex was built at the rear between 1908 and 1911 from the designs of Horace Trumbauer,[44] but the Broad Street front has changed little. The ornamental iron roof fringe and the tower's mansard were removed during the 1920's, but everything else is intact, including one of the handsomest sweeping stairs to be found anywhere.

Equally prominent for its architecture and history is the Philadelphia Masonic Temple at Broad and Filbert streets. James H. Windrim won the architectural competition in 1868, but it was five years before the construction ended, primarily because all the stone had to be cut, squared, and marked at the quarries according to Masonic tradition. The design is a fine academic rendering of the Norman style and the asymmetrical towers and splendidly carved entrance porch are especially noteworthy. Yet its reputation as one of the world's greatest Masonic temples rests more on its rich interior, which took more than fifteen years to complete. Great rooms are decorated in different historical styles intended as symbolic instruction in the principles of Freemasonry.[45]

Other notable clubs and fraternal headquarters also stood along Broad Street, such as the Odd Fellows Hall at Race Street, the Manufacturers Club at Walnut Street, and the Philadelphia Art Club at Chancellor Street. Since it was built as a high-rise office building, the Manufacturers Club building has a bright future, but the others are gone. The last to fall was the Art Club. This notable Italian design was the first major work of Frank Miles Day, who won the architectural competition in 1887 shortly after returning from Europe.[46] The club fell victim to the Great Depression, and many present-day Philadelphians knew the building only as the Keystone Automobile Club, which had its headquarters there between 1946 and 1968.[47] After that, it endured long periods of vacancy broken by occasional occupancies, often as political campaign headquarters. Finally in late 1975 came the final blow, one suffered by so many historic buildings: the Art Club was demolished to make space for a parking lot.[48]

As churches and clubhouses went up along Broad Street and to the west, commercial Philadelphia started to edge into the Center Square area, primarily along Market and Chestnut streets. Partly because a railroad did not run down the middle of Chestnut Street as it did down Market Street, Chestnut Street attracted greater investment in commercial structures, and its stores became known for their carriage trade. Except for the chaste Italianate stores at 920–22 Chestnut Street, designed by Stephen D. Button in 1853,[49] examples of the 1850's have been replaced by later buildings. Many fine stores of the 1860's and 1870's could be found in the 1000 block of Chestnut Street until the greater part of its south side was torn down in 1975.[50] Still standing at the northwest corner of Tenth and Chestnut, however, is the imposing New York Mutual Life Insurance Company Building, or Victory Building, as it is almost universally known about the city. One of the country's largest insurance companies after the Civil War, New York Life retained New York architects to design its many office buildings across the land. In 1873 Henry Fernbach of New York was that architect, and it was he who was responsible for the French Renaissance design of the initial four-story office building.[51] Philip W. Roos of New York was the company's choice for architect in 1890, when three stories were sandwiched between the massive French roof and the lower three stories, accounting for its present appearance.[52]

Many Philadelphians were surprised and perplexed when John Wanamaker converted the old Pennsylvania Railroad Freight Depot at Thirteenth and Market into the Grand Depot Store in time for the centennial celebration. It seemed then to be on the western outskirts of the city's shopping area. Indeed it was. Wanamaker, however, had observed the westward movement of the commercial district since he had opened his Oak Hall Store at Sixth and Market less than fifteen years earlier, and he suspected that the erection of the new City Hall in Center Square would stimulate this shift.[53] Also, he evidently expected that the removal of the rails from Market Street (which made the Freight Depot available, of course) would enhance its value as a retail street. So Wanamaker both anticipated and contributed to the continuation of the westward direction of the retail district.

Two other responses and stimuli to the area's commercial development were the Broad Street Station (illus.) at the northwest corner of Broad and Market and the Reading Terminal at the

northeast corner of Twelfth and Market.[54] The Pennsylvania Railroad's Broad Street Station was completed in 1882, but the greatest
commercial development west of Broad Street coincided with the station's enlargement in 1892–94.[55] Nearly all these early skyscrapers,
such as Cope's and Stewardson's Harrison Building (illus.) and Furness, Evans and Company's Arcade Building at opposite corners of
Fifteenth and Market,[56] have been replaced by the extensive Penn
Center renewal project. The opening of the Terminal Station of the
Philadelphia and Reading Railroad in 1893 set off a similar flurry of
building activity on both sides of Market Street between Ninth and
Thirteenth streets. One of the finest was the six-story Monarch Building at Tenth and Filbert. It was designed by Cope and Stewardson as
twelve separate stores,[57] unified by a single monumental facade
whose classical ornament was sensitively scaled for the passing
pedestrian, while the deeply recessed windows punched out of the
plain brick upper stories emphasized its sense of mass. The greatest
of all, however, is the terminal itself. The Head House, whose florid
Renaissance style is executed in rich cream-colored terra cotta on
buff brick, is a peerless example of railroad grandeur, executed for a
company that went bankrupt within months after the station
opened. The cavernous train shed (illus.) extending from the rear of
the Head House to Arch Street is even more important because of its
engineering significance. Fundamental to its construction was the
three-hinged arch, which allowed engineers to bridge great distances
and bring under a single span unprecedented expanses of clear space.
Such single-span train sheds were not uncommon at the turn of the
twentieth century, and its architects and engineers, Wilson Brothers
and Company, built an even larger one for the Broad Street Station.[58]
Since the Broad Street shed burned in 1923, the rarity of the Reading
Terminal's shed has made it all the more valuable.

These building ventures continued into the early years of the
twentieth century, virtually remaking the center of the city. Some of
the offices and hotels are now gone, but many of the best still stand.
Among them is the Land Title Building by D. H. Burnham and Company of Chicago, one of America's great architectural firms and a
leader of commercial design at the time. The first stage, built in 1897–
98 at the southwest corner of Broad and Chestnut streets, is a fine
example of what became known in the 1890's as the Commercial
style.[59] This style had its roots in mid-nineteenth-century Philadelphia and New York but had come into its own in Chicago after 1890.
In fact, the first stage of the Land Title Building bears a close resem-

blance to the Fisher Building, which Burnham had built in Chicago a year earlier.[60] To maximize light and space Burnham designed bay windows into the steel frame of both buildings, but while in the Chicago building a balance of horizontal and vertical lines is maintained, in the Philadelphia example the frame construction was accentuated by recessing the spandrels to suggest a continuous upward thrust of the piers that end in arches at the next-to-top floor. Burnham also designed the twenty-two-story addition at the northwest corner of Broad and Sansom.[61] Built in 1902, it departs from the earlier Commercial style and incorporates classical elements into the facade, placing a range of giant pilasters along the ground story and giant engaged Corinthian columns at the top of the building. Nevertheless, Chicago influenced the later design as much as the early ones, for Chicago's Columbian Exposition in 1893 had turned the attention of many architects to an academic classicism. For want of a better term, the handsome 1902 section might be called a Neoclassical Revival skyscraper.

Burnham's other great work in Philadelphia is the John Wanamaker Department Store. Built in three stages between 1902 and 1910, this enormous building fills an entire city block, between Thirteenth and Juniper and Market and Chestnut streets.[62] Here Burnham turned for inspiration to the Renaissance Revival with great success. The traditional Renaissance division of a building into base, body, and top resolved the problem of organizing architectural elements over twelve stories, allowing the firm to bring to bear its experience and skill in handling familiar architectural motifs. At the lower level giant pilasters cover steel piers and form the necessary sense of support for the large show windows, and giant Tuscan columns mark the recessed entrances. The body of the four facades is composed of rusticated limestone ashlar with well-spaced fenestration, and to prevent top-heaviness the last three stories are finished in dressed ashlar and relieved by a two-story arcade and small square windows below the cornice. The large-scale grace of the exterior is continued inside. The five-story court is one of the city's grandest interior spaces. Its organ, the world's largest when acquired from the 1904 Louisiana Purchase Exposition in St. Louis, has been enjoyed by generations of Philadelphia shoppers, and its 2,500-pound bronze eagle, from the same exposition, has marked a favorite rendezvous since its installation in 1911.[63] The richness of the Egyptian Hall and Greek Hall has been diminished by alterations, but the Crystal Tea Room remains virtually unchanged as one of the city's largest and

most elegant public dining places. Philadelphia can be grateful to
John Wanamaker for his good taste. His store remains the handsome
offspring of a long relationship in which for sixty years citizens and
merchant patronized each other. The local prince of merchandising
got his Renaissance palace and the people of Philadelphia got an architectural monument that can be enjoyed with no purchase
necessary.

Of all Center Square's new-century buildings probably the most
eye-catching is the Girard Bank (illus.) at the northwest corner of
Broad and Chestnut streets, not because it is so large but because it is
so small and chaste, making it stand out among its tall neighbors. It is
Philadelphia's best example of the Neoclassical Revival traditionally
claimed by the noted New York firm of McKim, Mead and White.
Construction was begun in 1905 under the supervision of Allen Evans
of Furness, Evans and Company. When it was completed in 1908, a
glistening white marble version of Rome's second-century Pantheon
graced the center of the banking district.[64] To base the design of a
twentieth-century bank on an ancient temple to pagan gods suggests
satirical allusions that the architects probably never intended. Instead
they almost certainly were following the nineteenth-century architectural tradition of employing an historical style that would suggest a
bank's fiscal stability, an architectural venture into the subliminal that
seems to have done little in preventing bank failures. It was a practice
continued well into the twentieth century, even after the infamous
Crash of 1929.[65]

Probably the best of the later classically derived banks is the
Federal Reserve Bank of Philadelphia at the northeast corner of Tenth
and Chestnut streets, built in 1932–35.[66] It is a fine example of the
stripped classicism of Paul P. Cret, who in 1903 was induced to leave
his studies at the Paris Ecole des Beaux-Arts, then the fountainhead
of academic classicism, to come to Philadelphia, a city that at the time
seemed addicted to this architectural mode. The decision was never
regretted by Cret or by Philadelphia, or by hundreds of his devoted
architectural students at the University of Pennsylvania.[67] As in
much of Cret's work, the exterior design of the Bank is remarkably
simple. It is composed of two functional units: engaged piers and a
simplified classic cornice on the lower part suggest a classical temple
in which the large, carefully crafted banking room is located; and the
repetitive fenestration of the four-story upper section marks it as office space. Further, Cret's use of Boittau's sculpture makes the building's symbolism as clear as does its design. The bas-relief to the left of

the main entrance depicts the Federal Reserve Bank as advisor of the country's banking system, a figure representing the institution rests upon the shield of Athena, the goddess of wisdom, and looks to her idol for guidance while a rugged oak, the symbol of strength, fills the background. On the right, emblems of agriculture, industry, and trade suggest the foundations of national wealth, and overhead hovers a spread eagle, indicating the national scope of the Federal Reserve System.[68] The symbolism became incongruous, however, when the Federal Reserve Bank in 1976 moved into the new Federal Building at Seventh and Arch, a collaborative high-rise that for better or worse forsakes Philadelphia's tradition of bank architecture.

At the same time that Cret was updating Philadelphia's classical tradition at Tenth and Chestnut, two other architects were striking out in a new direction at Twelfth and Market. In 1929 George Howe, a Philadelphia architect with important social connections, and William Lescaze, a Swiss-born architect with European training and a New York practice, formed a partnership with the express intention of designing a new office building for the Philadelphia Saving Fund Society to be modeled on "the new system" then being practiced in Europe by such men as Walter Gropius, Mies van der Rohe, and Le Corbusier.[69] Even before its completion in 1932 it was being hailed as the country's only skyscraper that was thoroughly dedicated to the principles of what was then becoming known as the International style. By way of contrast, one of the best of its contemporaries, the nearby Market Street National Bank Building (illus.), with its modish Art Deco elements, was modernistic rather than modern. Howe's and Lescaze's building has worn well, and although it is now over forty years old, it still looks up-to-date, a tribute to the architects and to the bank's directors, whose architectural judgment over the institution's 160-odd years has compared favorably with their financial wisdom. Philadelphians have been calling it the PSFS Building ever since 1933, when its twenty-seven-foot red neon sign was perched atop its thirty-two stories.[70] A precursor of supergraphics, the sign remains one of the best examples of architectural advertising to be found anywhere; it is often imitated but rarely equaled.

While the PSFS Building is universally recognized as a trailblazer in American architecure—and accordingly was proclaimed the "Building of the Century" by the American Institute of Architects at their centennial in 1969—the Benjamin Franklin Parkway on the other side of Center Square is similarly acknowledged as a successful pioneer venture in urban planning. The first plans for the parkway were submitted in 1907 by Paul P. Cret. This should be expected since the nation was then swept up in the City Beautiful movement that had spun out of the Columbian Exposition, and Cret's credentials as a Beaux-Arts architect were impeccable. Cret was not the final designer, however. That distinction went to another Frenchman, city planner Jacques Gréber, who was indebted to a considerable degree to a host of local architects and art-conscious organizations who had contributed plans and opinions for nearly twenty years before Gréber got the nod.[71] The end result was a bold diagonal cutting across the city's restrictive grid plan, extending northwest from the appropriately French Renaissance City Hall through Logan Square, which was converted to a circle for ease of traffic flow, to the Neoclassical Revival Museum of Art on Fairmount, Philadelphia's own Acropolis. The parkway's earliest buildings, with low, classically derived facades parallel to the street, are compatible with its baroque design. Its post–World War II architecture, on the other hand, reflects the newer idea of buildings as large, isolated volumes surrounded by their own green space and oriented to one another rather than to the street.[72] Although these recent high-rise buildings violated the designers' original intent, the parkway's great width, combined with its abundant plantings and strategically placed fountains, enables it to hold its own as one of the nation's most spectacular and successful examples of baroque city planning.

The most recent urban renewal project in the Center Square area is Penn Center, a glass and steel menagerie for button-down businessmen and their minions. It was begun in 1956 on the fourteen-acre site of the Broad Street Station and its Chinese Wall, the elevated tracks that had carried trains and its own peculiar form of blight into the heart of the city. Lined with parking lots and decaying stores, the grim brick wall was less a fortress than a noose, strangling the city's westward commercial development.[73] When it was first proposed about 1952, the city hoped to stimulate private investment in the project by tearing down City Hall, then considered "dismal and depressing with an unfortunate psychological effect on all people who use it," and replace it with a "new and inspiring municipal building" on Reyburn Plaza.[74] The Municipal Services Building was indeed erected on Reyburn Plaza during the early 1960's and, while it may not be inspiring, it is well designed.[75] City Hall, however, was spared. It was found that cleaning the exterior and painting the interior was infinitely cheaper than demolition.[76] What psychological effects this has had on its occupants is still open to question. Because the Penn Center project was considered a high risk during its early years, the initial buildings are of the glass-slab genre, but later structures, particularly Vincent G. Kling's IBM Building at Seventeenth and Market and his Transportation Building at Eighteenth and Market, exhibit a more sanguine spirit and consequent investment. Most successful are the recently built office towers that came in the wake of Penn Center's financial achievements. One of the best is the Centre Square Towers at Fifteenth and Market, a Kling venture into the New Brutalism mode. It opened in 1974 on the site of the former Harrison Building (illus.) at the southwest corner of Fifteenth and Market, and shows that urban renewal does not necessarily mean uglification. Under the geodesic dome of its lobby bright brass and unfinished concrete contrast with great effectiveness. The handling of Penn Center's open space has followed a similar historical sequence. Although no one equates Penn Center with New York's Rockefeller Center, improvements have been made in recent years and it is now considered by some one of the more successful examples of extensive urban renewal. In the final analysis, the plan's one great virtue was the decision to work around City Hall, the city's focal point, which is where we came in.

Catalog

Academy of Music (originally known as American Academy of Music).
Illustrated
(PA-1491), 232–46 S. Broad St., at S.W. corner Locust St. Brick with sandstone trim, approx. 132' (seven-bay front) × 220', three stories, hipped roof, round-arch entrances and windows, cast-iron bracketed cornice, parapet with 1857 date stone, octagonal ventilation cupola, highly ornate interior.

Fine example of the Italianate mode with a neobaroque emphasis on interior. Built 1855–57; Napoleon LeBrun and G. Runge, architects; Charles Conrad, superintendent of construction; John D. Jones, contractor; Robert Wood, iron work. Planned exterior marble sheathing never erected. Interior altered 1940–41; Silverman and Levy, architects. Restored 1957–66; Robert A. Class of Martin, Stewart, Noble and Class, architect. Home of the Philadelphia Orcestra since 1900, the Academy is the oldest musical auditorium in the United States still in use and remains famous for its acoustics. Certified, PHC 1956; Pennsylvania Register 1970; designated National Historic Landmark 1963. 3 ext. photos (1957, 1963),* 15 int. photos (1967),* 2 photocopies of architects' drawings (1856),* 1 photocopy of architectural competition elevation by Stephen D. Button (1854);* 2 data pages (1965).*

Academy of Notre Dame
(PA-1492), 208 S. Nineteenth St. on W. side of Rittenhouse Sq. Brick with brownstone trim, approx. 53' (three-bay front) × 70' with four-story rear addition, three stories, flat roof. Built c. 1867. Four-story rear addition built 1896; Edwin F. Durang, architect. Demolished 1969. 4 ext. photos (1969);* 1 data page (1969).*

American Academy of Music. See Academy of Music

Arcade Building (also known as Commercial Trust Building)

(PA-1493), 1428–34 Market St., composing block bounded by Market, Broad, Fifteenth sts., S. Penn Sq. Steel frame with coursed dark ashlar and terra cotta curtain walls, aprox. 120′ (twelve-bay front) × 230′ (originally 50′ on Market St. × 230′ on Fifteenth St. × 120′ on S. Penn Sq.), thirteen stories with twenty-one-story tower, flat roof, originally L-plan, later developed into U-plan, pedestrian arcade along two sides, pedestrian bridge at second story over Market St. to Pennsylvania (Broad St.) Railroad Station.

Rare example of a highrise building designed to accommodate pedestrian traffic and to incorporate later expansion as adjoining properties were acquired. Built 1900–1902; Furness, Evans & Co., architects; Samuel Hart & Sons, contractors. Enlarged 1904–1906, tower added 1913, further additions until c. 1930; Furness, Evans & Co., architects. Demolished 1969. 7 ext. photos (1962–63, 1964),* 3 int. photos (1962–63),* 1 photocopy of architectural rendering (c. 1901);* 9 data pages (1962).*

Arch Street Methodist Episcopal Church

(PA-1494), S.E. corner Broad and Arch sts. Brick faced with coursed Massachusetts white marble ashlar, approx. 75′ (three-bay front) × 96′ with two-story rear random marble ashlar chapel (approx. 38′ × 76′), one story, gable roof with cross-gable of chapel, three-stage square corner entrance and bell tower with marble pinnacles and spire at northwest corner, pointed-arch windows with flanking buttresses, large pointed-arch window with tracery on front of church (north end) and chapel, aedicule at each end; four-aisle plan with galleries suspended on carved brackets, Gothic vaulted ceiling.

Fine "decorated" English Gothic Revival church whose landmark qualities have been enhanced by creation of open space about City Hall during the 1950's and 1960's. Chapel built 1864–65; Addison Hutton, architect. Church built 1869–70; Addison Hutton, architect. Chapel remodeled, new entrance door installed 1956; Charles L. Bolton, architect. 1 ext. photo (1974);* 2 data pages (1964).*

Arch Street Opera-House (now known as The Troc)

(PA-1495), 1003–5 Arch St. Brick, approx. 48′ (three-bay front) × 170′, two stories, flat roof, large round-arch windows with ornamental lintels, originally lyre-sculpture atop cornice, notable interior details. Built 1870; burned, rebuilt 1872; interior burned, rebuilt 1883. Interior altered 1891, 1894, 1896; George W. Plowman, architect. Built for minstrelsy; burlesque house since 1896. Name changed to Continental Theatre 1888, The Trocadero 1896, The Troc 1949. Certified, PHC 1972. 1 ext. photo (1973),* 1 photocopy of old ext. photo (1916).*

Arch Street Presbyterian Church. See West Arch Street Presbyterian Church

Baltimore and Ohio Railroad Station
(PA-1220), S.W. corner Twenty-fourth and Chestnut sts. Brick with iron girder and brownstone and copper trim, approx. 173' (twenty-bay front) × 132', three-and-a-half stories, hipped and gable roofs, porte-cochere and picturesque clock tower mark entrance, iron-beam arcade at lower level; irregular plan on two levels, ornamental iron and brick interior.

Notable urban railroad station whose eclectic design made it a landmark. Built 1886–88; Frank Furness of Furness, Evans & Co., architect. One-story steel-frame addition built 1912; M. A. Long (Baltimore), architect. Part of interior remodeled 1943; L. P. Kimball (Baltimore), architect. Demolished 1963. 4 sheets (1966, 1968, including plans, elevation); 3 ext. photos (1959), 3 int. photos (1959), 7 photocopies of old ext. photos (1940, n.d.), 4 photocopies of old int. photos (n.d.).

Bartram, John, Hotel. See Hotel Walton

Broad Street Station. See Pennsylvania Railroad, Broad Street Station

Bulletin Building (now Penn Square Building). Illustrated
(PA-1496), 1315–25 Filbert St., at N.E. corner Juniper St. Steel frame, brick curtain walls faced with enameled terra cotta on south and west upper stories and Indiana limestone ground story, 105'-4⁵/8" (nine-bay front) × 147'-4³/4" (originally 63'-1¹/2" × 147'-4³/4"), nine and ten stories, flat roof originally with balustrade, twelve-story round corner tower with green and white terra cotta dome, rounded corner, rectangular plan.

Fine example of an early-20th-century commercial building that complements neighboring City Hall and with later alteration making significant use of glass in design. Built 1906–8; Edgar V. Seeler, architect; Frank C. Roberts & Co., engineers; Doyle and Doak, contractors. Ten-story eastern addition (1315–17 Filbert St.) built 1915–16; Edgar V. Seeler, architect; Doyle and Co., contractors. Cornice removed 1936. Interior, ground-story exterior remodeled in glass blocks 1938–43; George Howe, architect. Offices and printing facilities of *The Evening and Sunday Bulletin* until 1955. 1 ext. photo (1973),* 1 photocopy of old ext. photo (1911);* 7 data pages (1973, including 1906–56 building permits).*

Butler, Thomas, House. See Philadelphia Club

Cathedral of SS. Peter and Paul (Roman Catholic)
(PA-1497), N.E. corner Eighteenth and Race sts., at intersection of Benjamin Franklin Parkway, on E. side Logan Sq. Coursed brownstone ashlar, approx. 130' (five-bay front) × 216', one story with large central copper dome, gable roof on nave, hipped roofs on transept, shed roofs on aisles, Corinthian tetrastyle portico on nave pavilion, statuary in pedimented niches, round-arch windows; cruciform plan with extended nave and semicircular chancel, three aisles with altars along sides, richly ornamented interior.

Outstanding Palladian Revival church that dominates Logan Sq. and serves as a major focal point along Benjamin Franklin Parkway. Built 1846–64; initial designs by Rev. Mariano Maller, C.M., and Rev. John B. Tornatore, C.M.; ext. plans by John Notman, architect, in association with John T. Mahoney, architect; int. plans by Napoleon LeBrun, architect; int. decorations by Constantino Brumidi. Interior renovated 1914–15; Henry D. Dagit, architect. Enlarged, interior extensively renovated 1957; Eggers and Higgins (New York), architects. Three-story steel-frame Bishop's House with brownstone ashlar curtain walls built at southeast corner (1723 Race St.) 1912; Henry D. Dagit, architect. One-story brownstone ashlar Chapel of Our Lady of the Blessed Sacrament built on north side 1954; Eggers and Higgins (New York), architects. Certified, PHC 1957; Pennsylvania Register 1971; NR. 2 ext. photos (1973),* 1 photocopy of old ext. photo (1928).*

Chestnut Street Bridge
(PA-1054), Chestnut St. across Schuylkill River. Cast iron with stone abutments and pier, approx. 390' × 42', two arches of six parallel tubular ribs, vertical supporting members composed of cast-iron Gothic Revival arches. As the third iron arch bridge in the United

States, it marked a notable advance in the evolution of tublar-arch construction; it was also considered one of the handsomest bridges in the country. Built 1861–66; Strickland Kneass, architect and engineer. Demolished 1958. 4 photos (1957), 1 photocopy of old photo (n.d.); 3 data pages (1957).

Chinatown YMCA (also known as Chinese Cultural and Community Center)

(PA-1498), 125 N. Tenth St. Museum. Brick, smooth stuccoed front with tile and enameled wood trim imported from Taiwan (Republic of China), approx. 25′ × 95′ (originally 20′ × 36′ with three-story rear ell), three-and-a-half stories with front tiled gable-roof penthouse, gable roof, balcony at second and third stories, projecting tile pent eaves with "clud" brackets at first and third stories, imported carved stone bas-reliefs and ornamentation flanking recessed entrance, entry foyer and large front room with imported wood-and-gilt tiles.

Rare and outstanding example of the Peking Mandarin Palace style in the United States. Built 1831–32. One-story side addition and three-story rear addition built 1906, new front with ground-story storefront and upper bay windows built and second story put onto side addition 1910; Clyde S. Adams, architect. New front built and interior extensively altered 1967–71; C. C. Yang (Taipei, Taiwan), architect; Stephen Burczynski, Jonathan Bugbee, and Joseph Nowicki, consulting architects. Houses Chinese Cultural and Community Center. 5 ext. photos (1974);* 3 data pages (1974, including 1906–10 building permits.)*

Church of the Holy Trinity (Protestant Episcopal)

(PA-1085), 200 S. Nineteenth St., at S.W. corner Walnut St., on W. side of Rittenhouse Sq. Brownstone ashlar, approx. 74′ (three-bay front) × 126′, two stories, gable roof, three-stage corner tower with pinnacles, round-arch triple entrances and windows; three-aisle plan, clerestory, balconies, apsidal chancel.

Pioneer example of the Romanesque Revival by a leading mid-19th-century church architect. Built 1857–59; John Notman, architect. Tower completed 1868; George W. Hewitt, architect. Interior renovated 1880, 1914, 1970. Three-and-a-half-story brick and stone parish house at west end built 1890–91; G. W. and W. D. Hewitt, architects. Small two-story stone choir building at southwest corner built 1898; Cope and Stewardson, architects. Certified, PHC 1958;

Pennsylvania Register 1970; NR. 3 ext. photos (1959), 3 int. photos (1959), 1 photocopy of architect's drawing (c. 1857); 7 data pages (1964).*

Church of St. Luke and the Epiphany (Protestant Episcopal) (originally Church of St. Luke)

(PA-1499), 330 S. Thirteenth St. Stuccoed stone and brick, approx. 65' (six-bay front) × 130', two stories, gable roof, Corinthian octastyle portico with cast-iron capitals, twin front doors with corbeled lintels; second-story auditorium, three-aisle plan, galleries, semicircular chancel.

Fine example of late Greek Revival church design with notable iron fence and gates. Built 1839–40; Thomas S. Stewart, architect. Parish house adjoining south side built 1874–75; Furness and Hewitt, architects. Addition to south rear corner 1891. Vestibule enlarged, new front doors and windows added, new furnishings for chancel 1906; probably by Charles M. Burns, architect; George M. Newhall Engineering Co. Ltd., engineer. Second-story organ loft added to north corner 1925. Church of the Epiphany (founded 1834) and Church of St. Luke (founded 1839) merged 1898. Certified, PHC 1961. 3 ext. photos (1974, including 1 of fence);* 7 data pages (1961, including 1885–1906 insurance surveys).*

Commercial Trust Building. See Arcade Building

Cope, Edward Drinker, Houses

(PA-1500), 2100–2102 Pine St., at S.W. corner Twenty-first St. Brick with green serpentine ashlar front, approx. 39' (six-bay front) × 37' with three-story rear wing, three-and-a-half stories on raised basement, mansard roof, semi-hexagonal bays extending full height, segmental-arch windows with carved lintels, round-arch entrances, side-hall plans.

Built c. 1876; interior altered to apartments 20th century. Edward Drinker Cope, one of America's greatest paleontologists and geologists, lived here 1878–97, leasing the corner house after 1886; properties owned by his descendants until 1950. No. 2102 on Pennsylvania Register 1975; designated National Historic Landmark 1975. 1 ext. photo (1976).*

Delancey Street Area Study

(PA-1501), 1800–36 Delancey St., on S. side Delancey St. between

Eighteenth and Nineteenth sts. Nineteen brick row houses with marble trim, each approx. 20' (two- and three-bay fronts) × 75', four stories on raised basements, flat roofs, side-hall plans.

Mid-19-century middle-class residential street that has retained its visual character in spite of subsequent remodelings. Nos. 1816–18 built 1854; Thomas Dugan, builder. Nos. 1800–1806 built 1855; Joseph Gilbert, builder. Nos. 1808–14 built 1856; Joseph M. Hancock, builder. Nos. 1820–36 built c. 1857; John McCrea, developer. Interior No. 1820 remodeled 1891; Furness, Evans and Co., architects. No. 1824 remodeled 1895; Wilson Eyre, Jr., architect. No. 1836 remodeled c. 1895; Cope and Stewardson, architects. Interior No. 1814 altered 1898; Charles M. Burns, architect. Interior No. 1826 altered 1900–1901; Mantle Fielding, architect. No. 1832 altered, two-story rear addition built 1906–7; Edgar V. Seeler, architect. No. 1818 remodeled, three-story rear addition built 1908; Lloyd Titus, architect. Interior No. 1810 remodeled, four-story rear addition built 1908; Baker and Dallett, architects; exterior remodeled 1923; Eyre and McIlvaine, architects. No. 1804 altered, four-story rear addition built 1910; Thomas, Churchman and Molitor, architects. Interiors Nos. 1816, 1818 altered 1940; Erling Pederson, architect. Certified, PHC 1971. 8 ext. photos (1974);* HABSI form (1970).*

Delancey Street Area Study

(PA-1502), 2301–23 Delancey St., on N. side Delancey St. between Twenty-third and Twenty-fourth sts. Six brick and six brownstone row houses with sandstone trim, each approx. 20' (two-bay front) × 75', three and four stories on raised basements, mansard roofs. A row-house development in the High Victorian Gothic style. Built c. 1874; Robert Kaighn, developer. 3 ext. photos (1973);* HABSI form (1970).*

Drexel & Company

(PA-1503), 135–43 S. Fifteenth St., at N.E. corner Walnut St. Steel frame, smooth-rusticated granite curtain walls with dressed granite trim, 96'-4" (five-bay front) × 73'-0³/₄", six stories with penthouse, flat roof, balustraded balcony at second story, bas-relief panels of signs of zodiac above ground-story windows, carved escutcheons at corners and above large round-arch entrance, heavily worked wood and brass door, notable marble banking floor. Fine example of Italian Renaissance palazzo manner adapted to 20th-century office use. Built 1925–27; Day and Klauder, architects; Doyle and Co., contractors.

Banking floor altered 1943; Charles Z. Klauder, architect. Drexel & Company here 1927–43; vacated 1957. 2 ext. photos (1976).*

Dunlap-Eyre House

(PA-1504), 1003 Spruce St. Brick with marble trim, approx. 20′ (two-bay front) × 38′ with three-story rear ell, three-and-a-half stories on raised basement, gable roof, round-arch entrance with fanlight, side-hall town house plan. Built between 1830 and 1835. Interior remodeled, three-story rear addition built 1909; Wilson Eyre, Jr., architect. Home and office of Wilson Eyre, Jr., prominent Philadelphia architect, 1909–40. Certified, PHC 1960. 1 ext. photo (1974);* 8 data pages (1962, including 1852 insurance survey);* HABSI form (1971).*

Far East Chinese Restaurant

(PA-1505), 907–9 Race St. Two adjoining brick houses, each approx. 18′ (two-bay front) × 40′ with one-, two- and three-story rear ells, three and four stories (originally two), flat and mansard roofs (originally probably gable), ornamented iron balcony across second stories, recessed balcony at third story of No. 907.

Earliest known work and originally dwellings of a prominent early-19th-century architect and his brother; later remodeled to fit the Chinatown image. Built as two-story houses c. 1827; Thomas U. Walter (bricklayer), builder. No. 909 raised two stories later; No. 907 raised one story after 1889. Second story of both altered to restaurant, iron balcony erected, rear ells enlarged 1906–7; storefront of No. 909 replaced 1922, altered to grocery 1963. Far East Chinese Restaurant 1908–52. Certified, PHC 1973. 2 ext. photos (1973),* 1 photocopy of wash drawing (1923);* 4 data pages (1973, including 1836–49 insurance surveys, 1906–22 building permits).*

Federal Reserve Bank of Philadelphia

(PA-1506), 921–39 Chestunt St., at N.E. corner Tenth St. Steel frame with Vermont blue marble ashlar walls, approx. 170′ (eleven-bay front) × 113′ with earlier rear wing and later rear addition, seven stories (originally six), flat roof with simplified classical cornice, lower unit of engaged piers and narrow windows with ornamental bronze grilles, plain four-story upper unit, bas-relief sculpture flank entrance, center entrance lobby with main banking room running depth of west side.

One of the finest examples of Paul P. Cret's stripped classicism, continuing the bank design tradition of the Second Bank of the

United States. Seven-story steel-frame northern wing with marble ashlar walls built c. 1925; William L. Baily of Baily and Bassett, architect. Main building built 1931–35; Paul P. Cret, architect; Irwin and Leighton, contractors; Alfred Boittau, sculptor. Seven-story steel-frame rear eastern addition with marble ashlar walls and front formal garden built 1940–42; Paul P. Cret, architect; Irwin and Leighton, contractors. Recessed seventh story added 1952–53; Harbeson, Hough, Livingston and Larson, architects. 3 ext. photos (1951, 1975),* 4 int. photos (1951).*

Fell-Van Rensselaer House (later known as Penn Athletic Club)
(PA-1507), 1801–3 Walnut St., at N.W. corner Eighteenth St., on N. side Rittenhouse Sq. Coursed Indiana limestone ashlar with smooth-rusticated ground story and pecked-rusticated raised basement, approx. 124' (ten-bay front) × 44' including two-story northern extension, three-and-a-half stories, low half-hipped roof behind balustrade, curved bays on east front, balustraded entrance porch with coupled Ionic columns, large recessed round-arch entrance, round-headed ground-story windows with carved side panels, carved swags in panels between second- and third-story windows, quoins; central-hall plan open to notable stained-glass dome, notable paneling, marble elements, and ceilings.

Notable example of Beaux-Arts domestic architecture and one of the last extant 19th-century mansions on Rittenhouse Square. Built 1896–98; Peabody and Stearns (Boston), architects; George Watson & Son, contractors. Door cut into south exterior wall, most of interior gutted and remodeled 1974–75. Penn Athletic Club established here 1922, remained until 1964. John Fell was president of A. Pardee & Co., a major anthracite coal operator; his widow married Alexander van Rensselaer 1898. Certified, PHC 1970. 1 ext. photo (1976),* 9 int. photos (1974).*

First Unitarian Church
(PA-1508), 2125 Chestnut St., at N.W. corner Van Pelt St. Coursed granite ashlar (originally rock-faced), approx. 73' (seven-bay front) × 150', one story with open stone porch, hipped roof with three cross-gables, rose window and aedicule on south (front) gable, originally massive square tower with porte-cochere at southeast corner; cruciform plan with short transepts, two aisles, exposed wood-and-iron trusses; two-story Chapel-Parish House at northeast corner.

Important High Victorian church whose interior has survived 20th-century renovations. Built 1885–86; Frank Furness of Furness, Evans & Co., architect. Church and Parish House altered 1902; Savery and Sheetz, architects. Tower removed before 1939; squat entrance arch demolished, rock-facing reduced 1955. Certified, PHC 1957; Pennsylvania Register 1971; NR. 2 ext. photos (1973);* HABSI form (1970).*

Franklin Row. See Sims-Bilsland House

George, Henry, House
(PA-1509), 413 S. Tenth St. Museum. Brick with marble trim, approx. 18' (two-bay front) × 16' with three-story rear ell (originally two-and-a-half stories), three stories on raised basement (originally two-and-a-half stories), mansard roof (originally gable), galvanized iron cornice and semihexagonal second-story bay window, one room to a floor with box entry.

Built c. 1820; Edward Harlan, carpenter. Bay window and mansard added, rear ell raised to three stories later; interior rehabilitated, partially restored 1957. Birthplace of Henry George, political economist, social philosopher, and author of single-tax theory. Acquired by Henry George Foundation 1926, Philadelphia Extension of Henry George School of Social Science since 1957. Certified, PHC 1958. 1 ext. photo (1974);* 5 data pages (1961, including 1831 insurance survey.)*

Girard Trust Corn Exchange Bank. Illustrated
(PA-1510), 34–46 S. Broad St., at N.W. corner Chestnut St. Steel frame with marble ashlar curtain walls, approx. 138' (five-bay front) × 144', two stories with Ionic hexastyle portico on east facade and Ionic tetrastyle portico in antis on south facade, flat roof with Roman dome, large two-story domed banking room with side galleries.

A fine example of a Classical Revival design reflecting the architectural influence of Chicago's Columbian Exposition 1893. Built 1905–8; design by Frank Furness of Furness, Evans & Co., architects; detailing by McKim, Mead and White (New York), architects; Allen Evans of Furness, Evans & Co., superintendent of construction. Name changed to Girard Trust Bank 1964; known as Girard Bank since 1969. Certified, PHC 1963; Pennsylvania Register 1970. 2 ext. photos (1973);* HABSI form (1970).*

Gladstone Hotel (later known as Greystone Apartments)

(PA-1511), 328–38 S. Eleventh St. and 1101–11 Pine St., at N.W. corner Eleventh and Pine sts. Brick with granite trim and steel floor beams, approx. 120' (eighteen-bay front) × 52', ten stories, flat roof, octagonal bays through sixth story, balconies at fourth and sixth stories, large arched entry to circular lobby, reversed L-plan with rear courtyard.

Philadelphia's first multistory apartment building. Built 1889–90; Theophilus Parsons Chandler, Jr., architect; J. E. and A. L. Pennock, contractors; Levering and Garrigues, steel contractors. Demolished 1971. Fashionable apartment hotel through 1920's; became Greystone Apartments 1958. 2 photocopies of ext. photos (1971).*

Greystone Apartments. See Gladstone Hotel

Harrison Building I. Illustrated

(PA-1088), 4 S. Fifteenth St., at S.W. corner Market St. Steel frame with dark ashlar and terra cotta curtain walls, approx. 115' (nine-bay front) × 40', eleven-and-a-half stories, hipped roof, central-hall plan, elaborate French Renaissance details. Built 1894–95; Cope and Stewardson, architects; Louis D. Havens, contractor. First floor altered 1902; Cope and Stewardson, architects. Demolished 1969. 7 ext. photos (1962), 3 int. photos (1964), 1 photocopy of old ext. photo (c. 1900), 4 photocopies of published prints of architects' drawings (1895); 7 data pages (1962, 1964).

Harrison Building. See Monarch Building

Hockley, Thomas, House

(PA-1512), 235 S. Twenty-first St., at N.E. corner St. James St. Brick with brownstone trim, approx. 35' (five-bay front) × 78', three stories on raised rusticated brownstone basement, mansard roof with brick dormers, shed roof on two-story rear ell, second-story bay on brackets with pointed hipped roof, notable carved stone floral ornament on corner entrance tympanums, bands of canted and black brick.

An early Furness town house that established a pattern of texture and silhouette copied by Philadelphia developers for the next two decades. Built c. 1875; Frank Furness of Furness and Hewitt, architect. Altered, enlarged 1894; Furness, Evans & Co., architects. Interior altered to apartments later. Certified, PHC 1962. 1 ext. photo (1973);* HABSI form (1962).*

Holy Redeemer Chinese Catholic Church and School

(PA-1513), 915 Vine St., at N.W. corner Ridge Ave. Cinder block faced with buff brick and limestone trim, approx. 42' × 72' with two-story rear wing (school), one story on raised basement, gable roof, entrance and oculus set within deeply recessed arch, straight double-entry stairs to entrance, three-aisle plan, auditorium in basement and communicating with school.

Built 1941; Henry D. Dagit and Sons, architects; McCloskey and Co., contractors. Founded 1941 as the first Chinese Roman Catholic church and school in the United States; remains the social and re-ligious center of Philadelphia's Chinatown. Not a parish but a mission of St. John's Roman Catholic Church. 2 ext. photos (1973).*

Hotel Metropole. See Hotel Walton

Hotel Walton (later John Bartram Hotel)

(PA-1091), 233–47 S. Broad St., at S.E. corner Locust St. Brick with brownstone trim, approx. 170' (seventeen-bay front) × 130', main (north) section ten-and-a-half stories, older (south) section eight-and-a-half stories, mansard and gable roofs, turrets at corners of main section, stylized Flemish gables, "standardized" plan with rooms arranged around rectangular light well.

Older (south) section, former Hotel Metropole, built c. 1892; Angus S. Wade, architect. Main (north) section built 1893–95; Angus S. Wade, architect. Interior renovated 1948; demolished 1966. 4 ext. photos (1963), 1 photocopy of old ext. photo (1896), 1 photocopy of architectural rendering of Hotel Metropole (1894); 11 data pages (1964).

Keystone Automobile Club. See Philadelphia Art Club

Land Title Building

(PA-1514), 100–118 S. Broad St., between S.W. corner Chestnut St. and N.W. corner Sansom St. Steel frame with buff brick (northern building) and pale granite-faced brick (southern building) curtain walls, approx. 230' (sixteen-bay front) × 120' (originally 105' × 100'), fifteen and twenty-two stories, flat roof, rusticated Ionic ground-story arcade and semihexagonal bays above on northern building, range of giant modified Tuscan pilasters at lower stories and giant en-gaged Corinthian columns and pilasters at upper stories of southern building.

Excellent study in the development of the "Commercial style" at

the turn of the 19th century by a leading designer of tall office buildings. Northern fifteen-story building and one-story connection built
1897–98; D. H. Burnham & Co. (Chicago), architects; Charles Mc-
Caul, contractor. Southern twenty-two-story building built 1902; D.
H. Burnham & Co., architects; Doyle and Doak, contractors. Banking
room altered 1907; Horace Trumbauer, architect. Banking room altered 1946; James S. Hatfield, architect. Banking room and entrance
altered 1955–56; Thalheimer and Weitz, architects. Banking room altered 1964; Vincent G. Kling and Associates, architects. Chartered as
The Real Estate Title Insurance Co. 1876, Land Title Bank and Trust
Co. is the world's oldest title insurance company. 1 ext. photo (1973),*
1 photocopy of architectural rendering (c. 1901);* 2 data pages (1973).*

Leidy, Dr. Joseph, Jr., House (now Poor Richard Club)

(PA-1515), 1319 Locust St. Brick with sandstone trim, approx. 46'
(three-bay front) × 80', three-and-a-half stories on raised basement,
gable roof with cross-gables, two semihexagonal bays, round-arch
entrance with projecting voussoirs, central-hall plan.

Fine example of the Georgian Revival. Built 1893–94; Wilson
Eyre, Jr., architect. Interior renovated, tiered stair tower added to east
wall 1925; interior renovated 1937. Since 1925 the quarters of the Poor
Richard Club, world's oldest club of advertising men. Certified, PHC
1963. 2 ext. photos (1972),* 1 photocopy of architect's plan and elevation (1894);* 2 data pages (1964);* HABSI form (1971).*

Lippincott, Joshua B., House

(PA-1516), 204 S. Nineteenth St., on W. side of Rittenhouse Sq. Brick
with marble front, approx. 25' (three-bay front) × 85', four stories,
mansard roof, side-hall plan. Example of comfortable town houses of
prominent Philadelphians that lined Rittenhouse Square in last half
of 19th century. Built 1869–70; Addison Hutton, architect. Demolished 1972. Joshua B. Lippincott, founder of J. B. Lippincott & Co.
publishing house, lived here 1870–86. 2 ext. photos (1969),* 6 int.
photos (1969);* 3 data pages (1969).*

Market Street National Bank Building (now One East Penn Square Building). Illustrated

(PA-1517) 1–21 N. Juniper St., at N.E. corner Market St. Steel frame,
yellow brick curtain walls with yellow terra cotta lower stories and
polychromatic terra cotta trim, approx. 180' (twenty-five-bay
front) × 58', seventeen, nineteen, twenty-one, twenty-three, and
twenty-four stories produced by setbacks, flat roofs, projecting piers,

simulated buttresses above nineteenth story, rectangular plan with second-story banking room.

Notable example of modernistic, or Art Deco, architecture with Mayan-inspired decoration. Built 1930; Ritter and Shay, architects; William Steele & Sons Co., contractors. Extensive interior alterations 1962; fenestration of lower stories altered 1971. Name changed to One East Penn Square Building 1962. 4 ext. photos (1973);* 3 data pages (1973).*

Mask and Wig Club

(PA-1518), 310 S. Quince St. Stuccoed brick with brick trim, approx. 28' (five-bay front) × 85', three stories, gable roof, shingled gable peak, large hood over entrance, hood over second-story windows, center-hall plan. Built as coach house and stable between 1843 and 1853. Remodeled into clubhouse 1894; Wilson Eyre, Jr., architect. Enlarged, altered 1901–3; Wilson Eyre, Jr., architect. Since 1894 the headquarters of the Mask and Wig Club, a University of Pennsylvania dramatic group. Certified, PHC 1961. 1 ext. photo (1975);* 11 data pages (1962, including 1853–1914 insurance surveys).*

Meeting House of Central Philadelphia Meeting of Friends. See Twelfth Street Meeting House

Mellor and Meigs Architectural Offices

(PA-1519), 205–7 S. Juniper St., at S.E. corner Chancellor St. Brick with stone trim, 50' (three-bay front) × 24', two stories, gable roof with cross-gables, large windows on north and west facades, center entry room with "Big Room" in one story in southern half.

Offices and studio of and by a noted early-20th-century architectural firm. Built as carriage house and stable mid-19th century. Extensively remodeled to architectural offices 1912; Mellor and Meigs, architects; A. H. Williams' Sons, contractors. Altered to restaurant 1946. Mellor and Meigs (Mellor, Meigs and Howe 1917–28) were known for their distinguished suburban house designs and had offices here 1912–40. Mitchell's Restaurant since 1947. Certified, PHC 1973. 2 ext. photos (1973).*

Monarch Building (also known as Harrison Building)

(PA-1520), 1001–23 Filbert St., at N.W. corner Tenth St. Pompeiian brick with terra cotta trim and interior iron columns, approx. 308' (thirty-six-bay front) × 135', six stories, flat roof, ground-story brick piers with terra cotta bands and ornamented terra cotta architrave, deeply recessed windows, round-arch windows at top story, rectangular plan divided into twelve sections or stores. Monumental commercial building with well-scaled ornament; part of area's development stimulated by construction of Reading Terminal. Built 1893–94; Cope and Stewardson, architects; William C. McPherson and Son, contractors. Later minor interior alterations. 2 ext. photos (1976).*

Moore, Clarence B., House

(PA-1521), 1321 Locust St., at N.E. corner Juniper St. Buff brick with limestone trim, approx. 26' (two-bay front) × 80', three-and-a-half stories (originally three-and-a-half), mansard roof (originally tiled roofs on corner towers, recessed pointed-arch windows, medallions and gargoyles at entrance, great-hall plan.

Notable eclectic Gothic design by an imaginative architect of city and country houses. Built 1890; Wilson Eyre, Jr., architect. Interior altered later. Certified PHC 1963; Pennsylvania Register 1970; NR. 1 ext. photo (1972),* see Dr. Joseph Leidy, Jr., House (PA-1515) for photocopy of architect's plan and elevation (1894);* 1 data page (1962);* HABSI form (1971).*

New Century Club

(PA-1522), 124 S. Twelfth St. Buff brick with Indiana limestone trim, approx. 40' (five-bay front) × 35' with three-story rear wing, four stories (originally three-and-a-half), mansard room (originally tiled hipped roof) and rear shed roof, asymmetrical facade with curved and semihexagonal bays, center cross-gable with crockets and large fanlight (originally open), center-hall plan with front stairs.

An early architectural work by a woman architect. Built 1891; Minerva Parker (later Minerva Parker Nichols), architect; J. E. and A. L. Pennock, contractors. Interior altered, dormers removed, recessed balcony and fanlight enclosed 1907; Horace Wells Sellers, architect. Demolished 1973. Founded 1877, the New Century Club of Philadelphia is one of the nation's oldest women's clubs devoted to protection and promotion of women's interests and general social questions. Certified, PHC 1965. 2 ext. photos (1973),* 5 int. photos (1973),* 1 photocopy of old ext. photo (c. 1892).*

New York Mutual Life Insurance Company Building (also known as Victory Building)

(PA-1523), 1001–5 Chestnut St., at N.W. corner Tenth St. Brick faced with Rhode Island granite rusticated on ground story, interior iron posts and girders, approx. 58' (five-bay front) × 176', seven stories on raised basement (originally four), high mansard roof, rounded corner, engaged Ionic and Corinthian columns, balustrade at each original story, mansard windows with heavy arched lintels and pilasters; reverse E-plan with court on each side of stair tower, ornate iron and marble longitudinal corridors.

An early office building in the Second Empire mode with well-integrated later enlargement and florid Beaux-Arts addition. Built 1873–75; Henry Fernbach (New York), architect. Raised three stories, old mansard preserved 1890–91; Philip W. Roos (New York), architect. Ten-story cream brick and terra cotta addition (1007–13 Chestnut St.) with interior steel posts built 1901–2; Roos and Brosam (New York), architects; J. E. and A. L. Pennock, contractors. Rear steel-frame addition with brick curtain walls built, corner building's interior altered 1940–41; Max A. Bernhart, architect. Regional headquarters of one of the nation's largest insurance companies 1875–1920. Certified, PHC 1972. 2 ext. photos (1975),* 1 photocopy of architectural rendering (1901).*

One East Penn Square. See Market Street National Bank Building

Parry, Charles T., House
(PA-1524), 1921 Arch St. Brick with brownstone ashlar front, approx. 45' (five-bay front) × 52' with three-story rear ell, four stories, flat roof, asymmetrical facade, two projecting bays of paired windows, elaborately carved interior woodwork and marble.

Fine example of post–Civil War town house. Built 1870–71; demolished 1968. Parts of interior architectural elements preserved in Philadelphia Museum of Art. Home 1871–87 of Charles T. Parry, president 1874–87 of Burnham, Parry, Williams & Co., proprietors of Baldwin Locomotive Works. 2 ext. photos (1968),* 15 int. photos (1968),* 1 ext. photo of carriage house (1968),* 2 photocopies of old ext. photos (c. 1900),* 4 photocopies of old int. photos (c. 1890).*

Penn Athletic Club. See Fell-Van Rensselaer House

Penn Square Building. See Bulletin Building

Pennsylvania Academy of the Fine Arts. Illustrated
(PA-1525), 118–24 N. Broad St., at S.W. corner Cherry St. Museum. Brick with sandstone, granite, marble, ceramic tile trim, approx. 100' (three-bay front) × 265', two stories, complex roof; textured,

polychromatic picturesque facade with pointed-arch windows and bas-relief panels; notable interior grand staircase, functional skylight system, notable interior ornament.

An outstanding work and an early example of expressed iron construction on the interior by an important late-19th-century architect. Built 1872–76; Frank Furness of Furness and Hewitt, architect; William A. Armstrong, builder. Galleries altered early 20th century; street lamps removed before 1930; statue in middle of center pointed-arch window removed c. 1935. Monitors over front galleries removed, lobby made smaller and simpler 1949; Harbeson, Hough, Livingston and Larson, architects. Roof cresting removed, door embrasures and grilles removed c. 1950. Restored 1973–76; Day and Zimmerman, Inc., architects.

Founded 1805, Pennsylvania Academy, a combined art museum and art school, is the oldest art institution in the United States. Certified, PHC 1956; Pennsylvania Register 1970; designated National Historic Landmark 1975. 3 ext. photos (1967),* 8 int. photos (1967),* 2 photocopies of architect's drawings (c. 1872).*

Pennsylvania Institution for the Deaf and Dumb (now Philadelphia College of Art). Illustrated
(PA-1526), 320 S. Broad St., composing block bounded by Broad, Pine, Fifteenth, Delancey sts. Coursed granite ashlar with plastered stone rear wings and brick back buildings, approx. 200' (fifteen-bay front) × 160' (originally approx. 96' × 92'), two and three stories, gable and low hipped roofs, two bays with two-story blind arches (niches) flank central Doric tetrastyle portico in antis, elongated O-plan with wings (originally U-plan).

Fine application of Greek Revival elements to an institutional building. Built 1824–26; John Haviland, architect. Rear three-story stone addition to center building built, rear wings extended 1838. Plastered stone lateral wings added to north and south ends of front 1852; possibly by William Strickland, architect. Rear wings raised to three stories 1863. Two three-and-a-half-story brick buildings with hipped roofs built on Fifteenth St. and connected to rear wings 1875; Furness and Hewitt, architects. Interior front building and lateral wings altered 1876; one-story hipped-roof brick building built between Fifteenth St. buildings 1879. Detached one-story brick and concrete-block buildings built in yard 1914, c. 1950, 1963, 1967. Pennsylvania Museum and School of Industrial Art (later known as Philadelphia Museum College of Art) 1893–1964; Philadelphia

College of Art since 1964. Certified, PHC 1956; Pennsylvania Register 1971; NR. 5 ext. photos (1973, 1974),* 1 photocopy of architectural drawing (n.d.);* 25 data pages (1965, including 1826–89 insurance surveys).*

Pennsylvania Railroad Station, Broad Street Station. Illustrated
(PA-1527), N.W. corner Broad and Market sts. Granite ashlar and brick with terra cotta trim, approx. 306' (thirteen-bay front) × 212' with three-hinged wrought-iron arch train shed approx. 600' × 300', north section five-and-a-half stories with eight-story tower, south section eleven stories with thirteen-story tower, gable roof with cross-gables, rusticated ground story, pointed arches, pedestrian arcade, enclosed pedestrian bridge over Market St. to Arcade Building, main entrance at base of thirteen-story tower at corner Broad and Market sts., waiting rooms on second story.

One of the world's great railroad terminals. North section built 1880–82; Wilson Brothers & Co., architects. Station expanded and south section built for executive offices 1892–94; Furness, Evans & Co., architects. Notable architectural sculpture in terra cotta and interior bas-relief in plaster by Karl Bitter, sculptor. Train shed built 1892–93; Wilson Brothers & Co., engineers. Pedestrian bridge built c. 1902; Furness, Evans & Co., architects. Train shed destroyed by fire 1923; Karl Bitter's bas-relief "Spirit of Transportation" removed to Thirtieth St. Station 1933; station demolished 1952–53. When built, the station was the world's largest railroad passenger terminal, and the train shed had the world's largest permanent roof with a span of 300'-8". 5 photocopies of old ext. photos (1893, c. 1894, 1903, c. 1925),* 1 photocopy of architectural rendering (1893).*

Philadelphia and Reading Railroad, Terminal Station (also known as Reading Terminal). Illustrated
(PA-1528), 1115–41 Market St., at N.E. corner Twelfth St. Pink brick with steel beams and posts and cream terra cotta trim, originally rusticated granite ground story, approx. 267' (thirteen-bay front) × 107' with two-story concourse approx. 267' × 50' to three-hinged wrought-iron arch train shed approx. 267' × 559', eight stories originally on raised basement, flat roof, front corners and central section above second story recessed, elaborately ornamented oriel window in northwest corner recess, originally roof balustrade and second-story open arcade in central section, "stub end" plan of head house (passenger facilities, shops, offices) and rear train shed, waiting room on second story and level with tracks.

Significant engineering work and rare use of a composite Renaissance style on a railroad terminal. Built 1891–93; train shed designed by Wilson Brothers & Co., architects and engineers; head house designed by Francis H. Kimball of Kimball and Thompson (New York), architect; Charles McCaul, general contractor; J. J. Ryan & Co., excavation contractor; Pencoyd Iron Works, steel contractor. Sidewalk canopy added at main entrance before 1906, replaced by cantilevered stainless steel canopy 1948. Skylights of train shed roofed over, head house interior and exterior altered 1948. Train shed is world's oldest long-span roof structure and America's only surviving single-span arched train shed. Reading Terminal Market, in shed's ground story, remains on market space dating from 1860. Pennsylvania Register 1972; NR.

5 ext. photos (1974),* 2 photocopies of old ext. photos (c. 1892 during construction, c. 1937),* 3 photocopies of old int. photos (c. 1893 of train shed, c. 1948 before alterations).*

Philadelphia Art Club (later Keystone Automobile Club)

(PA-1529), 220 S. Broad St., at S.W. corner Chancellor St. Buff brick with limestone trim, approx. 64' (four-bay front) × 116', four stories on raised basement with seven-story rear addition, low hipped tile roofs, veranda on three-story northeast corner, quoins, center-hall plan.

An early work of a noted late-19th-century architect making fine use of architectural ornament. Built 1887; Frank Miles Day, architect. Ground story altered 1891; Frank Miles Day, architect. Interior altered 1902; Watson, Huckel and Co., architects. Rear addition built 1907; Newman and Harris, architects. Interior altered 1926; Day and Klauder, architects. Interior altered 1946; George I. Lovatt, architect. Demolished 1975–76. Occupied by Keystone Automobile Club 1946–68. Certified, PHC 1966; Pennsylvania Register 1970. 4 ext. photos (1972);* HABSI form (1970).*

Philadelphia City Hall. Illustrated

(PA-1530), Penn Square, intersection of Broad and Market sts. First story of granite blocks, upper stories of brick faced with white marble, upper stages of tower of iron, approx. 486' (nineteen bays) × 470', seven stories with 548-foot tower, mansard roofs, square plan enclosing central courtyard, towered pavilions mark arched pedestrian passages to courtyard, truncated towers at corners, sculpture on all facades and tower, lavish interior of marble, mosaics, carved woodwork.

One of the finest American examples of picturesque eclectic architecture in the Second Empire style, City Hall remains the nation's largest municipal governmental building and its tower makes it the world's tallest bearing-wall building. Built 1871–1901; John McArthur, Jr., chief architect; Thomas U. Walter, consulting architect; John Ord, assistant architect; Alexander Milne Calder, sculptor; William C. McPherson, superintendent of construction; Struthers & Sons, marble contractor; George Herzog, decorator of Supreme Court Room and Judges' Consultation Room. John Ord, chief architect 1890–94; W. Bleddyn Powell, chief architect 1894–1901. Occupied in stages after 1877; William Penn statue placed on tower 1894. Rehabilitated 1963–. 15 ext. photos (1958, 1959, 1962, 1963, 1965),* 5 int. photos (1959),* 2 aerial photos (1965),* 1 photocopy of old ext. photo (c. 1925),* 1 photocopy of old photo of William Penn statue (1894),* 2 photocopies of architect's drawings (1872, 1897).*

Philadelphia Club (originally known as Thomas Butler House)
(PA-1531), 1301–3 Walnut St., at N.W. corner Thirteenth St. Brick with Quincy granite trim, approx. 70' (seven-bay front) × 58' with one- and three-story rear additions (originally with two-story rear ell at northwest corner), three-and-a-half stories, gable roof, large round-arch entrance with notable fanlight, side entrance with transverse corridor and two intersecting stairhalls.

Notable example of 19th-century urban mansion with traditional, large-scale Georgian facade. Built 1837; probably by William Strickland, architect. Interior altered, kitchen moved to cellar 1850; one-story billiard room attached to east side of ell and connected to house by passageway 1858. Rear ell, billiard room, and passageway raised to three stories with mansard roof and second-story elliptical bay window 1888–89; Furness, Evans & Co., architects. One-story rear addition built at northeast corner of house 1892. Since 1850 the quarters of the Philadelphia Club, America's oldest city social club; founded 1834. Certified, PHC 1956. 1 ext. photo (1976);* 10 data pages (1964, including 1837–92 insurance surveys).*

Philadelphia College of Art. See Pennsylvania Institution for the Deaf and Dumb

Philadelphia Masonic Temple
(PA-1532), 1 N. Broad St., at N.E. corner Filbert St. Granite ashlar, approx. 138' (five-bay front) × 250', three stories with five- and seven- story towers, hipped roof, elaborate one-story Norman en-

trance portico, rounded-headed windows, turrets, lavish interior with separate apartments in different historical architectural styles.

One of the world's outstanding Masonic structures. Built 1868–73; James H. Windrim, architect. Much of the interior decorated in 1890's; George Herzog, decorator of Egyptian, Ionic, and Norman halls. Serves as Grand Lodge for Pennsylvania Masonry. Certified, PHC 1962; Pennsylvania Register 1970; NR. 9 ext. photos (1963),* 4 int. photos (1963),* 11 photocopies of architectural competition drawings (1867),* 1 photocopy of architect's plan (n.d.),* 14 photocopies of old photos of construction and interior (c. 1870, c. 1900);* 12 data pages (1967, 1971).*

Philadelphia Saving Fund Society Building (also known as PSFS Building)

(PA-1533), 12 S. Twelfth St., at S.W. corner Market St. Steel frame with granite and glass curtain walls, 164'-4¼" (nine-bay front) × 134'-4¼", thirty-two stories and three mezzanines with penthouse, flat roof; twenty-seven-story office tower with horizontal ribs rises from five-story curved glass and polished granite banking rooms, black brick service spine rises thirty-six stories, great neon PSFS sign (27' height) incorporated into design at top, rectangular plan with second-story banking room.

In its reconciliation of architectural form with modern technology the building stands as a landmark in architectural evolution. Often considered the first modern skyscraper in 20th-century United States, it marked the early use on a large scale of stainless steel and central air-conditioning. Built 1930–32; Howe and Lescaze, architects; Walter Behrman, interior designer; George A. Fuller Co., contractors. Ground-story shops altered 1949; Alexander T. C. Hazell, architect. Judged "Building of the Century" by Philadelphia Chapter, A.I.A. 1969. Certified, PHC 1968; Pennsylvania Register 1970. 2 ext. photos (1976),* 2 photocopies of architectural renderings (1932).*

Poor Richard Club. See Leidy, Dr. Joseph, Jr., House

Portico Square (later known as Portico Row)

(PA-1534), 900–930 Spruce St., composing block bounded by Ninth, Spruce, Tenth, Cypress sts. Sixteen brick row houses with marble trim, each approx. 24' (three-bay front) × 50' with three-story rear ell, three-and-a-half stories on raised basements, gable roofs, each pair of houses with common Ionic tristyle porch, side-hall plans.

Philadelphia's last surviving stylish residential development of the Jacksonian era and an early plastic solution to row house design. Built 1831–33; Thomas U. Walter, architect. Exterior No. 922 remodeled after 1870; No. 928 altered to store 1924. Commodore Issac Hull, commander of U.S.S. *Constitution* during War of 1812, lived at No. 908 1842–43; Mrs. Sarah Josepha Hale, editor of *Godey's Lady's Book* and crusader for Thanksgiving as a national holiday, lived at No. 922 1859–61; No. 910 Philadelphia High School for Young Ladies 1836–41. Certified, PHC 1962. 5 ext. photos (1975);* 58 data pages (1962, including 1832–1920 insurance surveys).*

PSFS Building. See Philadelphia Saving Fund Society Building

Reading Terminal. See Philadelphia and Reading Railroad, Terminal Station

Reed's, Jacob, Sons
(PA-1535), 1424–26 Chestnut St. Reinforced concrete, diapered brick curtain walls with marble and polychromatic terra cotta trim, 50'-1" (seven-bay front) × 230'-5", four stories in front, five stories in rear, front low gable roof, rear flat roof, giant recessed arched entrance on monolithic Byzantine columns with terra cotta designs on extrados, open arcade at top story, marble cavetto cornice with terra cotta medallions, date stones (of founding and erection) at front corners, quoins, rectangular plan.

Notable example of early reinforced concrete building in an eclectic style. Built 1903–4; William L. Price of Price and McLanahan, architect; murals by C. T. Monaghan. Rear fifth story added 1909; Spencer Roberts, architect. Jacob Reed's Sons have been retail clothiers since 1824. Certified, PHC 1966. 2 ext. photos (1976).*

Restaurant and Apartment Building
(PA-1536), 110 N. Ninth St. Brick with granite ashlar front, approx. 18' (three-bay front) × 46', six stories including mansard roof, arcades of horseshoe-arch windows with "Moorish" details, rectangular plan originally with living quarters on upper floors. Built c. 1870; ground story altered later. 2 ext. photos (1963);* 3 data pages (including 1891 insurance survey).*

Rogers-Cassatt House
(PA-1537), 202 S. Nineteenth St., on W. side of Rittenhouse Sq. Brick with brownstone and copper trim, approx. 50' (five-bay front) × 140',

four stories, mansard roof (probably originally flat), bay windows, ornate interior woodwork.

Example of a remodeled mid-19th-century city mansion on a fashionable square. Built c. 1856. Remodeled, renovated c. 1888; probably by Wilson Brothers and Co., architects. Demolished 1972. Alexander J. Cassatt, president of the Pennsylvania Railroad 1899–1906 and brother of Mary Cassatt, expatriot painter and etcher, lived here 1888–1906. Home of Fairman Rogers, prominent scientist, civil engineering professor and horseman, c. 1856–87. Church House for Episcopal Diocese of Pennsylvania 1921–72. Certified, PHC 1963. 3 ext. photos (1969),* 6 int. photos (1969);* 2 data pages (1969).*

St. Clement's (Protestant Episcopal) Church. Illustrated

(PA-1538), 128 N. Twentieth St., at S.W. corner Cherry St. Brownstone ashlar, approx. 68' × 128', one story with two-story square tower at northeast corner (originally three-story tower with octagonal spire), gable roof, pronounced apse with smooth rusticated base on east end, round-arch windows; three-aisle plan, apsidal chancel.

Fine Romanesque Revival church by a noted mid-19th-century church architect. Built 1856–59; John Notman, architect. Crypt Chapel built beneath apse 1898; Horace Wells Sellers, architect; William Halsey Wood (architect), designer of altar. Clergy house built onto southwest corner 1901–2, parish house built onto northwest corner 1906–7, church's sanctuary altered, enlarged 1908; Horace Wells Sellers, architect. Interior renovated 1915. Church moved 40' west 1929. Certified, PHC 1963; Pennsylvania Register 1971; NR. 7 ext. photos (1974);* 8 data pages (including 1902–15 insurance surveys).*

St. Mark's (Protestant Episcopal) Church

(PA-1093), 1625 Locust St. Random brown freestone and red sandstone ashlar, approx. 147' (ten-bay front) × 60', one story with four-stage main entry side tower and spire, gable and side-aisle shed roofs; notable interior design, three-aisle plan with rectangular chancel and appended Lady Chapel.

One of the earliest American applications of the concepts of the Anglican "High Church" religious revival to an urban site, producing a notable Gothic Revival church. Built 1848–51; John Notman, architect. Parish house at west end built 1892–93; Hazlehurst and Huckel, architects. Lady Chapel at southeast end built 1899–1902;

Cope and Stewardson, architects. Certified, PHC 1956; Pennsylvania Register 1970. 4 ext. photos (1958), 3 int. photos (1958), 2 photocopies of architect's drawings (c. 1848, including plan, sections); 10 data pages (1964).

St. Stephen's Protestant Episcopal Church

(PA-1539), 19 S. Tenth St., at N.E. corner Ludlow St. Coursed granite ashlar front and towers, brick sides and rear walls faced with coursed granite ashlar, approx. 61' (five-bay front) × 102', one story, gable roof, twin five-stage octagonal towers, pointed-arch windows; three-aisle plan, galleries, rectangular chancel.

Rare surviving example of a Gothic Revival design by William Strickland, known for his Greek Revival architecture. Built 1822–23; William Strickland, architect; Daniel Groves, master mason; John Struthers, marble mason. Stenciled interior decorations added, transept and vestry room built on north side 1878–79; Frank Furness, architect. Three-story rusticated granite ashlar parish house built on west side (front) of vestry room 1888; George C. Mason & Son, architects. Interior stenciled decorations painted over 1940's. Interior highlighted by notable memorials, which include "Angel of Purity" sculpture by Augustus Saint-Gaudens (c. 1900) and three Tiffany stained-glass windows. Certified, PHC 1957. 3 ext. photos (1972);* 6 data pages (including 1823–88 insurance surveys).*

Schuylkill Hose, Hook & Ladder Company No. 24

(PA-1540), 1227 Locust St. Stuccoed brick, approx. 20' (three-bay front) × 58', four stories, flat roof, projecting lintels with corbels, rectangular plan. Built c. 1857. Ground-story storefront added, second-story iron balcony removed 1934–35; R. R. Neely, architect. Storefront closed up, interior altered to restaurant 1955. Vacated 1967, condemned 1969. 1 photocopy of old ext. photo (c. 1934);* 2 data pages (1972, including 1934–55 building permits).*

Scott-Wanamaker House. Illustrated

(PA-1531), 2032 Walnut St. Brick faced with rusticated granite ashlar, approx. 50' (five-bay front) × 100', three-and-a-half stories on raised deeply vermiculated basement, hipped and gable roofs, asymmetrical facade with two-story semihexagonal bays capped by elaborately carved stone balustrade, picturesque roofline; center-hall plan with large open staircase to third story, elaborately carved and paneled interior.

Notable example of Jacobean Revival style. Built 1883; Theophilus Parsons Chandler, Jr., architect. Altered to apartment house, exterior stair tower added to west side 1938; Gabriel B. Roth, architect. Vacated 1972; rehabilitated, ground story partially restored 1973–. John Wanamaker lived here 1894–1922. As a major contributor to the concept of department store merchandising, Wanamaker founded the John Wanamaker Department Store, and as an active participant in Republican politics he served as Postmaster General in President Benjamin Harrison's Cabinet 1889–93. James Scott, sugar-refiner, lived here 1884–94. Certified, PHC 1962; Pennsylvania Register 1971; NR.

3 ext. photos (1973),* 8 int. photos (1973);* 17 data pages (including 1883, 1894 insurance surveys);* HABSI form (1970).*

Sims, Joseph, House. See Sims-Bilsland House

Sims-Bilsland House (originally known as 2 Franklin Row). Illustrated
(PA-1186), 228 S. Ninth St. Brick with stone trim, 23'-6" (two-bay front) × 40'-3", three-and-a-half stories, gable roof, triple window on first and second stories set in blind arch with recessed solid tympanum, side-hall plan with two rooms to a floor.

Last survivor of an early ten-house speculative development known as Franklin Row, significant for its use of monumental forms within a unified architectural composition. Built 1809–10; Robert Mills, architect; John Savage and John Meany, developers. Doorway lowered, third-story window replaced by double window 1935. Vacated 1966. Restored 1975–. Fanlight, woodwork, and plaster elements in Architectural Study Collection, Museum Division, Independence National Historical Park. Investment property of merchant Joseph Sims; Ann Bilsland, widow, was first occupant 1811–29. Facilities of Booth, Garrett and Blair, America's oldest commercial chemical laboratory, here 1935–66. Certified, PHC 1961.

5 sheets (1965, including plot plan, plans, elevation, section, details); 3 ext. photos (1962, 1965), 4 int. photos (1962), 2 photocopies of old ext. photos (1870, 1917), 1 photocopy of architect's elevation drawing (1809); 14 data pages (1961, 1962, including 1811 insurance survey*).

Spruce Street Area Study. Illustrated
(PA-1532), 2009–47 Spruce St., on N. side Spruce St. between Twentieth and Twenty-first sts. Twenty brick row houses faced with

brownstone ashlar, seven easternmost houses approx. 22' (three-bay fronts) × 105', thirteen westernmost houses approx. 19' (two-bay fronts) × 72', three-and-a-half stories on raised basements, mansard roofs, side-hall plans.

Fine study of a decade's change in brownstone row-house design. Nos. 2009–21 built c. 1868; Nos. 2023–47 built c. 1880. No. 2037 altered 1894; Hazlehurst and Huckel, architects. No. 2039 altered 1910; Spencer Roberts, architect. Interiors altered to apartments and professional offices between 1925 and 1937. 11 ext. photos (1974);* 4 data pages (including 1905 insurance survey);* HABSI form (1970).*

Troc. See Arch Street Opera-House

Twelfth Street (Friends) Meeting House (also known as Meeting House of Central Philadelphia Meeting of Friends)
(PA-1533), 20 S. Twelfth St., at N.W. corner Clover St. Brick, 90'-8" (five-bay front) × 57'-4", two stories, gable roof, entry porch on east end, two entry porches on north and south sides; meeting room with three longitudinal aisles and two transverse aisles, balconies, rear room.

Fine example of traditional Philadelphia architecture in early 19th century. Built 1812–13; John D. Smith, master carpenter and builder. Six trusses, attic roof, and floor framing, and some first-floor joists salvaged from Market Street Meeting House, S.W. corner Second and Market sts. (built 1755, demolished 1809). Friends Institute built at S.W. corner 1892, second story added 1909, Walter Smedley, architect. Second story of Meeting House remodeled 1936. Dismantled 1972, re-erected on grounds of George School, Newtown, Bucks Co., Pa. Meeting House served as a center for dissenting reform groups ever since the abolition movement in 1840's. Certified, PHC 1956; Pennsylvania Register 1970.

9 sheets (1971, including plot plan, plans, elevations, sections, section and details of 1755 truss, profile details);* 9 ext. photos (1971),* 32 int. photos (1971, including 8 of trusses),* 2 photocopies of old ext. photos (c. 1885, 1902);* 8 data pages (1963, 1972, including 1876–1908 insurance surveys).*

Union League of Philadelphia
(PA-1534), 140 S. Broad St., at S.W. corner Sansom St. Brick with brownstone trim, approx. 100' (seven-bay front) × 130', two-and-a-half stories on raised basement, mansard roof, central Corinthian

porch with curved double-entry stairway, square tower, central-hall plan, notable interior.

Notable and early Philadelphia example of the Second Empire style. Built 1864–65; John Fraser, architect; John Crump, builder. Interior burned, remodeled 1889; James H. Windrim, Theophilus Parsons Chandler, Jr., Charles M. Burns, architects; George Herzog, decorator. Two-and-a-half-story brick rear annex built c. 1881; Theophilus Parsons Chandler, Jr., architect. Interior altered, rear addition built 1893; Robert G. Kennedy, architect. Annex enlarged 1896; Keen and Mead, architects. Annex demolished c. 1910. Five-story rear steel-frame annex with granite ashlar curtain walls built in two phases: west section on Fifteenth St. built 1909–10; Horace Trumbauer, architect; James G. Doak & Co., contractors; middle section built 1910–11; Horace Trumbauer, architect; Cramp & Co., contractors. Mansard roof on tower removed after 1927. Interior altered 1945, 1956, 1953; Ralph B. Bencker, architect. Interior altered 1963, 1972.

Organized 1862, the Union League is the oldest Republican Party club in continuous existence. Certified, PHC 1957; Pennsylvania Register 1970. 1 ext. photo (1972),* 1 photocopy of architectural rendering (1864);* 11 data pages (1965, including 1865–1911 insurance agreements and surveys).*

Victory Building. See New York Mutual Life Insurance Company Building

Wanamaker, John, Store

(PA-1535), 1300–1324 Market St., composing block bounded by Market, Thirteenth, Chestnut, Juniper sts. Steel frame, brick curtain walls faced with coursed granite ashlar on upper stories and limestone ashlar on two lower stories, approx. 250' (eleven-bay front) × 480', twelve stories, flat roof, modified Tuscan distyle entrance in antis on each facade, great arches at ninth and eleventh stories; notable interior volumes include spacious five-story Grand Court on ground floor, Egyptian Hall on third floor, Crystal Dining Room on ninth floor; fluted columns, piers, pilasters, and ornate friezes throughout store.

Fine application of Second Renaissance Revival style to a large department store by one the nation's leading architects at the turn of the century. Built in three stages 1902–10; Daniel H. Burnham & Co., architects. Organ, world's largest at the time, from Louisiana Purchase Exposition, St. Louis 1904, installed 1911. World's largest retail merchandising building when built. John Wanamaker Memorial

Museum on eighth floor includes Wanamaker's office as he left it in 1922. Certified, PHC 1963. 1 ext. photo (1973),* 1 photocopy of ext. photo (c. 1960),* 1 photocopy of int. photo of Grand Court (c. 1960).*

West Arch Street Presbyterian Church (now Arch Street Presbyterian Church). Illustrated

(PA-1536), 1726–32 Arch St., at S.E. corner Eighteenth St. Brick and stone covered with plaster, approx. 85' (six-bay front) × 150', one story with Corinthian tetrastyle portico, low gable roofs with central dome, round-arch windows; three-aisle plan, balconies, Corinthian tetrastyle portico with pediment at chancel.

One of Philadelphia's most elaborate examples of the Italianate Revival. Built 1853–55; Joseph C. Hoxie, architect; Joseph DeNegre, builder; Henry Pasco & Son, plaster work. Original balustrade, urns, bell towers, dome's cupola removed after 1895. Sunday School and lecture room remodeled 1900; Charles W. Bolton & Co., architects. Certified, PHC 1961; Pennsylvania Register 1970; NR. 5 ext. photos (1974),* 5 int. photos (1976);* 3 data pages (1964).*

Western Saving Fund Society

(PA-1537), 1000–1008 Walnut St., at S.W. corner Tenth St. Brick faced with granite ashlar, 164'-4" (six-bay front) × 120'-2" (originally approx. 88' × 120' with three-bay front), three stories (originally two), flat roof, cyclopean rusticated ground story, great arches on coupled red marble columns, two-story banking room with mezzanine.

Eastern section built c. 1887; James H. Windrim, architect; Allen B. Rorke, contractor. Exterior altered 1902; Furness, Evans & Co., architects. Renovated, western section built c. 1910; John T. Windrim, architect. Third story installed later; demolished 1967. 4 ext. photos (1964),* 1 photocopy of old ext. photo (n.d.);* 8 data pages (including 1889, 1909 insurance surveys).*

White Tower

(PA-1538), 159 N. Broad St., at S.E. corner Race St. Brick faced with white porcelain enamel (not original), approx. 27' (four-bay front) × 25', one story with low squarish tower at northwest corner, flat roof, large single-pane windows with stainless steel sashes, goose-neck lamps at roof line, public dining room, small rear storage and rest rooms.

Fine example of merging symbolism of a firm's advertising image with the modern ahistorical style. Built 1932; Charles J. Johnson (New York), architect. Porcelain enamel facade applied to three walls 1950; Erie Enamel Co. (Erie, Pa.), contractor. One of the oldest fast food chains in the country; founded 1926 in Milwaukee, Wisc. 1 ext. photo (1976).*

Academy of Music. *Cortlandt V. D. Hubbard photo, 1967.*

Bulletin Building. *Jack E. Boucher photo, 1973.*

Girard Trust Corn Exchange Bank. *Jack E. Boucher photo, 1973.*

Harrison Building. *Jack E. Boucher photo, 1962.*

Market Street National Bank Building. *Jack E. Boucher photo, 1973.*

Pennsylvania Academy of the Fine Arts. *Jack E. Boucher photo, 1965.*

Pennsylvania Institution for Deaf and Dumb. *Jack E. Boucher photo, 1973.*

Pennsylvania Railroad, Broad Street Station. *Drawing by Furness, Evans & Co., 1893, courtesy Pennsylvania Railroad.*

Philadelphia and Reading Railroad, Terminal Station, Train Shed. *Photo 1893, courtesy Free Library of Philadelphia.*

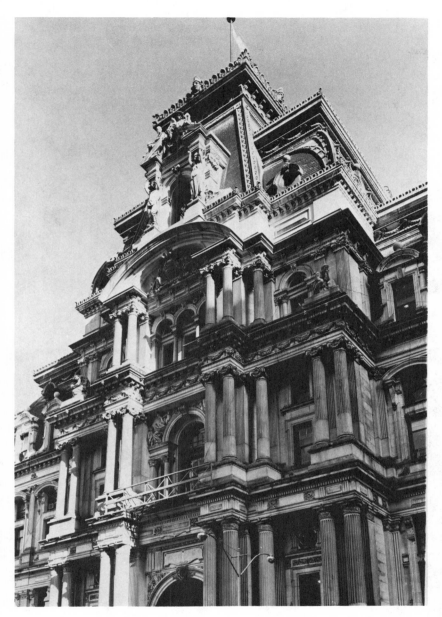

Philadelphia City Hall. *Cervin Robinson photo, 1958.*

Philadelphia City Hall, toilet stalls. *Cervin Robinson photo, 1959.*

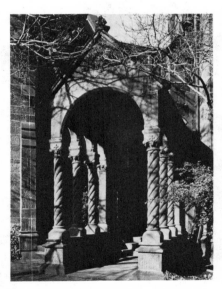

St. Clement's (Protestant Episcopal) Church. *Jack E. Boucher photo, 1974.*

Scott-Wanamaker House. *Cortlandt V. D. Hubbard photo, 1973.*

Sims-Bilsland House (Franklin Row). *Photo c. 1870, courtesy Historical Society of Pennsylvania.*

West Arch Street Presbyterian Church.
Cortlandt V. D. Hubbard photo, 1976.

Spruce Street Area Study. *Jack E. Boucher photo, 1974.*

South Philadelphia

Moyamensing and Passyunk
Townships

4

Introduction

$\mathcal{L}$ ONDON'S INFLUENCE on Philadelphia can be seen both in the material culture of the colonial city—its plan, pent-eaved houses in rows, and church spires—and in some of its place names—among these, Southwark. Named after that part of London south of the Thames, Philadelphia's Southwark was once a southern suburb that physically and commercially merged with the city but was politically separated from it until 1854 with South Street, then called Cedar Street, serving as the line of demarcation. Although always outside the city, Southwark emerged as a separate political entity within Philadelphia County in 1762, when it was organized as the District of Southwark.[1]

Other place names reveal an even earlier history for the District. The Lenni Lenape tribe called the area Wicaco, later spelled "Weccacoe." This name is sometimes translated as "pleasant place" or "at the pine tree camp," and was retained by early settlers from Europe.[2] The first of these immigrants were the Dutch, who in 1633 bought a tract along the river they called Schuylkill, meaning "hidden creek."[3] They were followed by the Swedes, who began to plan fur-trading posts in the area after 1638, thereby making it, in terms of recorded history, the oldest part of Philadelphia. The subsequent joint venture of Sweden and the Netherlands was marked more by competition than by cooperation, until in 1655 the Dutch forced the Swedish government out of the area.[4] Yet the mark of Sweden remains in such Southwark street names as Swanson (Andreas Swenson owned an 800-acre tract along the Delaware) and Christian (Christina succeeded Gustavus Adolphus as the Swedish monarch in 1632) and in the presence of the renowned Gloria Dei (illus.), affectionately known as

Old Swedes' Church. Built at the turn of the eighteenth century on the site of an earlier Swedish log church near the Delaware River, it has a Flemish bond with glazed headers and lozenge diaperwork that combine with its steep roof and valuted ceiling to give it a deceptively Swedish flavor. Its form, however, and most, if indeed not all, of its details are English.[5] It served as a mission of Sweden's state chruch until 1845, when it became a part of the Protestant Episcopal communion.[6]

After William Penn was granted his land, the claims of earlier inhabitants were recognized and adjusted, and the entire area south of the City of Philadelphia of the time was divided into Moyamensing Township and Passyunk Township, Indian names that together mean "pigeon droppings" "in the valley."[7] Moyamensing included approximately the eastern half of the territory and Passyunk the western half. Except for the creation of the District of Southwark in 1762, both townships retained their extensive sizes and sparse populations until 1848, when their boundaries were redrawn and Moyamensing was reorganized as a district adjacent to Southwark that extended from river to river.[8]

English colonists began to purchase Southwark land in the 1690's, but housing construction did not accelerate until the 1740's, when the city began to grow. The area quickly developed into a residential community whose people were closely tied to the river and the sea.[9] Representative of these early dwellings is the house at 770 South Front Street, which was built in 1745 by William Finlow as an investment property for two merchants, Maurice and Edmund Nichell. It was a plain house with a brick cornice, simple entrance, and pent eave, but it was comfortable, rising three-and-a-half stories and with a two-story rear ell for sitting room and kitchen.[10] Behind it was a court, one of those deep open spaces that was formed in the interior of large blocks in an effort to carve out more building lots.[11] During the eighteenth and early nineteenth centuries this space was filled with two facing rows of small housing units and was called Clymer's Court after George Clymer, a Philadelphia signer of the Declaration of Independence and United States Constitution. Over the span of two centuries both the house and the rear tenements deteriorated, until in 1969 the house was rehabilitated, its exterior restored, and the tenements rebuilt into middle-income dwellings and the open space landscaped.[12] It stands today as an example of imaginative integration of the old and the new, and a living testimony to the reasonableness of eighteenth-century living patterns.

A block to the north, at the southwest corner of Front and
Pemberton streets, is a variation on this plan, known as Workman
Place. Instead of the rear tenements being strung out along the length
of a single lot, the buildings are positioned roughly at right angles
across the width of three lots. The two oldest buildings were built in
1748 for George Mifflin, [13] which accounts for the date and initials laid
in glazed headers on the blank end walls facing what is now
Pemberton Street. These were separate two-and-a-half-story
bandboxes, each divided into two tenements, or apartments, with
corner winding stairs. [14] At a right angle to these earliest houses and
at the rear of the lots facing Front Street is a row of three two-and-a-
half-story bandboxes fronting onto the open courtyard. [15] These tenements probably were built at the same time as the three Front Street
houses (numbers 742–46); a fourth house, 740 South Front Street,
was demolished when Pemberton Street was cut through before
1849. These commodious three-and-a-half-story dwellings were built
along Front Street about 1812 for John Workman, who acquired this
extensive piece of real estate in 1810. [16] The compound yielded rental
income for the Workman family until 1906, when Lydia S. Clark acquired it as a philanthropic housing project, establishing a pattern
that has prevailed ever since. The Octavia Hill Association took over
the project in 1942, and acquired additional small dwellings facing the
courtyard from Fitzwater Street on the south. [17] By renting the units at
rates adjusted to the occupants' incomes and preserving the original
setting, the association has retained both the function and environment of Workman Place.

Also representative of Southwark housing is Nathaniel Irish's
house (illus.) at 704 South Front Street, built during the 1760's. [18] Its
masonry foundation, brick walls, dormer windows, and closets flanking the gable-end chimneys fit Peter Kalm's 1748 description of
Philadelphia houses. [19] Other features not mentioned by the Swedish
traveler but equally characteristic of colonial Philadelphia houses include the vaulted alleyway that is supported on brick arches in the
cellar and cuts through at the street level to the backyard; the London
house plan that places the winding stairs in the middle of a side wall
in order to best utilize a narrow but not excessively long lot; and the
ample use of decorative trim on the interior woodwork of an
otherwise modest dwelling.

The characteristics of Philadelphia dwellings related by Peter
Kalm and still to be seen in Southwark houses disguise, however, a
little known fact: the majority of Southwark houses were not brick

but frame, according to the 1811 statistics of Dr. James Mease, physician and amateur historian.[20] In fact, at the turn of the nineteenth century there was a great number of frame dwellings throughout the city, including a deceptively pretentious example on Market Street west of Tenth whose wooden siding was painted to imitate brick.[21] Consequently, George Pearson's (illus.) and Joseph Bird's two-and-a-half-story frame houses at 808–10 and 813–15 South Hancock Street respectively are probably more representative of early Southwark dwellings than was the Irish House. Neglect of the southernmost of Bird's two dwellings a couple of years ago led to the unfortunate decay of the tongue-and-groove weatherboards and to the unexpected discovery of a medieval construction technique evidently carried over from England—the use of brick nogging between the frame members. More representative of late-eighteenth-century frame construction was the house that until 1970 stood at the rear of 33 Catharine Street. Random-width board sheathing was nailed to the frame members and covered with the tongue-and-groove siding. It was much faster to build a house this way than with brick nogging and probably provided about the same degree of insulation.

As Southwark moved into the nineteenth century, it retained its ties to the maritime trade of the adjacent river and the nearby sea. This accounts for the great number of warehouses that stood east of Front Street until they fell to the I-95 expressway in the 1960's. Early in the century they were modestly scaled, as could be seen in John LaTour's 1818 warehouse on Water Street.[22] By the mid-nineteenth century, however, as the city became an industrial center as well as a commercial port, warehouses had become much larger. While LaTour's warehouse measured only 21 feet by 50 feet, for example, not much larger than a dwelling house, Jesse Godley's 1867 warehouse (illus.) at 19–27 Queen Street possessed more than eleven times the square footage. By this time a warehouse's site was determined by railroads as well as by the river, as illustrated by Godley's Argyle Stores, which until 1967 stood next to the Reading Company's tracks at 32–36 Kenilworth Street.

It should not be surprising that the earliest Southwark industry of note was shipbuilding. By the late 1790's Joshua Humphreys' shipyard was located just south of Gloria Dei, where he built a variety of ships, including the sailing frigates *United States* and *Philadelphia.* The United States Navy Yard was established nearby in 1801. Its two shiphouses, one rising 103 feet into the air, were built in 1821 and 1822 and remained the city's most conspicuous landmarks until the

Navy Yard was removed farther south to League Island in 1876.[23] Another famous Southwark landmark is Sparks's Shot Tower. It was the country's first shot tower when it was built in 1808 by Thomas Sparks and John Bishop, plumbers. As a conscientious Quaker, Bishop felt obligated to drop out of the partnership when the U.S. Army became a customer during the War of 1812. Sparks and his heirs carried on the business until 1907 when the tower was vacated; six years later it became part of a neighborhood recreation center,[24] preserving it both as a local landmark and visual reference point and as a rare relic of an extinct technology.

With the emergence of small industries unrelated to maritime activities, Southwark developed social aspects of a nineteenth-century industrial town. By the middle of the century low-rent housing was available; extant examples include William Harper's 1847 tenements at 621–23 South American Street and an 1880's rooming house at 115 Bainbridge Street.[25] Their appearance was followed by related public and quasi-public institutions such as soup kitchens and public bath houses. Until 1871 fire protection—and a good deal of neighborhood camaraderie—were provided by volunteer fire companies,[26] such as Hope Engine Company No. 17, whose exuberant Italianate hall at 733–35 South Sixth Street was built in 1851 from the designs of Hoxie and Button, a short-lived but prolific architectural partnership.[27] The Weccacoe Engine Company No. 9, which moved to 119 Queen Street about 1843, was one of the few volunteer companies to have had its hall continued as a municipal fire station in 1871.[28] Its present appearance is the result of an extensive remodeling with the addition of a police patrol house in 1893.[29] The only survivor of Southwark's public school buildings is the 1869 Ralston School at the northeast corner of American and Bainbridge streets. Until it was converted to commercial use in 1928, it was a fine example of the modified "Philadelphia Plan," a proposal of the noted Philadelphia architect Samuel Sloan, which provided flexible interior space and wide, safe front and rear exits.[30]

Churches increased in number and diversity during the nineteenth century. The Church of St. Philip de Neri at 220 Queen Street, built in 1840–41, was the first Roman Catholic church in the area. It survived the "Native American" riots of 1844 and a fire in 1897[31] and stands today opposite Mario Lanza Square as a fine example of a restrained church design based on Greek Revival principles. Not so fortunate, however, was the 1878 Church of the Redeemer for Seamen of the Port of Philadelphia at the northwest

corner of Front and Queen streets, which was destroyed by fire in
October, 1974.[32] The destruction of this bold expression of contrast-
ing colors, textures, and forms from the drawing boards of the great
Frank Furness[33] was a loss to both America's architectural history and
Southwark's visual diversity. The church's name described its
primary initial function—to serve as a mission church to seamen—
and is evidence that maritime activity in the neighborhood did not
diminish as manufacturing increased. Eastburn Mariners' Bethel
(Presbyterian) to the north at Front and Delancey streets and the
Baptist Mariners' Bethel (demolished 1966) and the Methodist
Mariners' Bethel to the south at 923 South Front Street and Washington and Moyamesing avenues reinforce the point.

During the eighteenth century and much of the nineteenth the
landscape west and south from Southwark was decidedly rural in appearance. Two of the best known architectural relics to survive from
the period are Bel Air and Stephen Girard's Gentilhommière. Both
are presently located in public parks: Bel Air in Franklin Delano
Roosevelt Park and Gentilhommière in Girard Park. Bel Air has stood
as an architectural mystery, or at least a curiosity, for many decades.
Much of this puzzle stems from its diversion from the standard appearance and plan of the eighteenth-century Philadelphia country
house. It has blank end and rear walls, for example, is only one room
deep, has its chimneys in the rear wall, and has a balcony over its
plain center entrance and projecting from the cove cornice a rounded
canopy over the balcony. These architectural irregularities on a
country house have led to claims of Swedish origin.[34] It is more
likely, however, that it was built about 1720 for former Philadelphia
mayor Samuel Preston, and that its design was determined by city
housing practices and English customs rather than by Swedish influence.[35] Unlike Philadelphia town houses, the country houses on
the city's outskirts did not conform to a pattern. In the openness of
the countryside the gentry seem to have felt free to express their individualism in taste. Gentilhommière, on the other hand, is a much
easier case to explain. When it became the country house of the famous merchant-financier Stephen Girard in December, 1797, only
the eastern eighteenth-century section was standing. Girard added
the finely proportioned center and western sections and the two versatile utility buildings before his death in 1831.[36] The house's interior
has been extensively altered through its use as a community center.

Because of its strategic location along the waterways leading to
Philadelphia, the area south of Southwark became a favorite site for

military installations at the turn of the nineteenth century. In 1798, while under the threat of war with France, the national government began building the Schuylkill Arsenal along the east bank of the Schuylkill River at Washington Avenue, and at the same time it opened a Navy Yard along the Delaware River in Southwark.[37] Also, beginning in the same year, the national government essentially re-built and enlarged Fort Mifflin on Mud Island, where American rebels had made a heroic but unsuccessful stand against the British in 1777.[38] A decade later, with the talk of war again facing the nation, the Commonwealth of Pennsylvania built a powder magazine in Passyunk,[39] not far from the fort. Except for Fort Mifflin, whose isola-tion has allowed it to stand unmolested over the years, these facilities are now gone, victims of modernized defense strategies and es-tablishments. The fort is undergoing restoration as a fine example of early-nineteenth-century fortifications.

By the second quarter of the nineteenth century, Moyamensing began to assume features of a pastoral countryside, a happy com-promise between urban congestion and wilderness. This made it a fa-vorite site for social institutions of the day. One of the most hand-some and serviceable of these is the United States Naval Asylum (illus.) for retired naval personnel at Gray's Ferry Avenue and Twenty-fourth Street, a short distance from the Schuylkill Arsenal's site. The main building, Biddle Hall (named for the Asylum's first Governor, Commodore James Biddle), was designed by William Strickland and built in 1827–33.[40] It is an exemplary piece of architec-ture and, in producing its design and plan, William Strickland drew upon his understanding of the history of his profession, his skill as an artist and draughtsman, his awareness of recent technological ad-vances, his knowledge of English and European building precedents, and his sensitivity to the current attitude about social reform. Stuart's and Revett's *Antiquities of Athens* was evidently the source for the broad Ionic octastyle portico that serves as both the focal point and central entrance for the large building. The manner in which the long dormitory wings extend from either side of this block is reminiscent of the European homes for service pensioners. Yet the heaviness that could result from such a large structure is alleviated by placing along the length of these wings piazzas or balconies supported by thin cast-iron columns. This not only solves a design problem but also an-ticipates a contemporary concern for the healthful effects of fresh air and ventilation. Furthermore, Strickland's early use of expressed cast-iron construction on these balconies illustrates his willingness to experiment with the new materials produced by the Industrial Revolution in an effort to construct as safe, economical, and modern a building as was then possible; in fact, it was reputed to be fireproof with its brick floors, vaulted ceilings, and slate and copper roofs. The beauty and usefulness of Biddle Hall are still evident in spite of the raised roof and dormers that altered its proportions in 1848[41] and raise questions about the soundness of the Navy's decision to vacate the building and neighboring facilities in 1976 in favor of a newly constructed high-rise in Gulfport, Mississippi.

The social theory that a pastoral setting was best for the rehabilitation of criminals helped to determine the site of the Philadelphia County Prison (illus.), or as it was commonly known, Moyamensing Prison or "Old Moko." Designed in 1831 by Thomas U. Walter,[42] it was an excellent representative of what Professor Alan Gowans calls early Victorian eclecticism of taste, making a visual statement through the careful selection of elements from a single historical style.[43] Like its predecessor, Eastern State Penitentiary in the city's Fairmount section, built in 1822–36, Moyamensing Prison was designed in the English Gothic castle style of architecture in order to create the impression of an invulnerable fortress with dismal dungeons within. Its heavy granite walls and octagonal towers served both as visual reminders of the certainty and permanence of punishment and as an effective means of detention and surveillance of prisoners. The adjacent Egyptian Revival Debtors' Prison, also designed by Walter, conveyed essentially the same message in another architectural style.[44] Both buildings were found to be unsuitable for the penal needs of the last half of the twentieth century and were demolished in 1968 without protests from their alumni.

The consolidation of Philadelphia in 1854 led to the division of South Philadelphia into four wards. The first encompassed the former Moyamensing District and Passyunk Township, while the old Southwark District was carved into the second, third, and fourth wards. The area's population grew consistently during the next sixty to eighty years, first westward along South Street and Washington Avenue, then down Broad Street, until by 1914 South Philadelphia included nine wards.[45] Some of these wards were congested and conditions of life there constituted a threat to public health. In 1910, for example, the third ward, between Fitzwater and Christian streets east of Broad Street, had a population density of 129,282 per square mile, a crowded situation as compared to Germantown's density of 14,000 per square mile at the same time.[46] Many of the residents were newcomers from Europe. Irish immigrants continued to flow into the city during the last half of the nineteenth century, some of them into this area. But the turn of the century an increasing number of eastern European Jews moved directly from disembarkation points on Delaware Avenue to the neighborhood below South Street, generally east of Eighth. Thousands of Italian immigrants settled throughout the area, with particularly dense concentrations west of Seventh Street between Bainbridge Street and Snyder Avenue.[47] Perhaps the most exciting living monument of the Italian presence in Philadelphia is the Italian Market, an open-air market extending along Ninth Street from just north of Christian Street to Federal Street. Here hucksters continue Old World merchandising practices that slowly disappeared in other parts of Philadelphia after the Civil War.

By 1920 most of South Philadelphia was filled with corridors of row houses and semidetached dwellings. Since these blocks were usually real estate developments, the houses possessed rigid uniformity. Some developers and builders ritualistically continued the colonial tradition of brick fronts and marble stoops, as can be seen along much of Federal Street. Others carried the classical manner one step beyond its early-nineteenth-century clarity and added hexagonal bays and open-columned porches to red and buff brick fronts. In some cases, architects were utilized to design these developments. One of the better examples is the well-preserved block on South Twentieth Street between Shunk and Porter streets where in 1910 John T. Windrim, working for the Trustees of the Girard Estate,[48] grafted the Colonial Revival style, then much used for suburban houses, onto modest semidetached city dwellings. The visual monotony of these neighborhoods was relieved by handsome churches, such as the Church of St. Charles Borromeo (1868–76) at Twentieth and Christian, St. Gabriel Roman Catholic Church (1902–12) at Twenty-ninth and Dickinson, and Church of St. Thomas Aquinas (1901–13) at Seventeenth and Morris streets.[49] All three were designed by Edwin F. Durang, who was responsible for many of the city's Roman Catholic churches between 1870 and the first World War.

An occasional square or playground provided open space and opportunities for off-street recreation. The most notable of these is Franklin Delano Roosevelt Park, known as League Island Park until 1955. Its development was begun in the early years of this century when the city began reclaiming land on the west side of Broad Street below Pattison Avenue. By 1923 the project was completed and the

365-acre park became the center of the Sesqui-Centennial Celebration in 1926.[50] In addition to stimulating the development of the south end of Broad Street, the Sesqui-Centennial accounted for two permanent structures of note, the American Swedish Historical Museum and the Municipal Stadium. In 1926 the museum, smaller than it is at present, was known as the John Morton Memorial Museum; it was completed in 1935, in time for the three-hundredth anniversary celebration of the arrival of the Swedes in Pennsylvania.[51] The Municipal Stadium on the east side of Broad Street was designed by the Philadelphia architects Simon and Simon to accommodate 73,073 persons, but 120,757 crowded in to see the first event to be staged there, the famous Dempsey-Tunney fight in 1926.[52] It was renamed the Philadelphia Stadium in 1959 and the John F. Kennedy Stadium in 1964. The biggest athletic event held there in recent years has been the annual Army-Navy football game, yet its presence near the Philadelphia Veterans Stadium, a baseball-football facility completed in 1971, and the Spectrum, a center for basketball, hockey, and boxing that opened in 1967, makes this corner of Philadelphia one of the nation's major sports complexes.

Broad Street has been the main thoroughfare of South Philadelphia for the past century. Many of the area's important social institutions are still to be found along its path: St. Agnes Hospital at Mifflin Street, South Philadelphia High School at Snyder Avenue, Methodist Hospital at Wolf Street, and the United States Naval Hospital at Pattison Avenue. The most impressive of these institutional structures architecturally is the Ridgway Branch of the Library Company of Philadelphia (illus.). The library, a gift from the estate of Dr. James Rush, son of the Signer Dr. Benjamin Rush, was constructed on Broad Street between Carpenter and Christian in anticipation of a strong southward development of the city. The directors of the Library Company, unhappy about the site chosen in 1869, interrupted construction for two years while they went to court in an unsuccessful effort to change the location of the branch library to one less inconvenient for its members.[53] The directors may have been selfishly motivated, but in hindsight they appear to have been prescient, since the presence of the Philadelphia, Wilmington and Baltimore Railroad tracks along Washington Avenue stymied residential development in the area until the advent of the automobile.[54]

Much in the manner of the Pharaohs who used their wealth to build both monuments to their memories and tombs for their bodies, Dr. Rush left a million-dollar trust for the erection of a library building, for the tomes of the Library Company, and tombs for himself and his wife. This may account for the library's morbid and redundantly monumental appearance. In search of overt allusions to erudition and the arts, architect Addison Hutton turned to ancient Greece for inspiration. Yet this building was to be grander than a mere classical temple, so Hutton abandoned the traditional single portico in favor of three: a central Doric octastyle portico and two flanking tetrastyle porticoes arrayed across the 220-foot front. Such pomposity combines blank areas of dark ashlar and heavy columns with exaggerated entasis and uncomely seams to make the building quite uninviting, perhaps a not altogether inappropriate appearance for a private library to have. The cavernous interior offered magnificent spaces and ample book stacks, but its great volume also made it nearly impossible to provide an appropriate environment for the preservation of the library's rare books and manuscripts, to say nothing of its staff and readers. Consequently, in 1966 the Library Company moved its collections, including the remains of Dr. and Mrs. Rush, to new quarters next to the Historical Society of Pennsylvania at Thirteenth and Locust streets,[55] where these two cooperating institutions form one of the nation's greatest private repositories of historical materials. Incidentally, the library's name was one of the conditions of Rush's generosity. Ridgway was the maiden name of his wife Phoebe Ann, the daughter of the prosperous merchant Jacob Ridgway, who was the principal source of James Rush's fortune.

South Philadelphia has shown remarkable resilience over the decades. Its residents take great pride in their neighborhoods. Probably the most disruptive force to attack the area in this century has been I-95, the express highway referred to earlier. Implicit in its construction was the destruction of many dwellings and warehouses, especially many fine old eighteenth-century buildings between Front Street and the Delaware River. In spite of this loss, the old Southwark area is making a comeback as Queen Village.[56] Helped by the success of adjacent Society Hill and by the decision not to construct the Crosstown Expressway along Bainbridge Street, Queen Village, with South Street as its revitalized northern boundary,[57] is a successful community effort at rehabilitation and restoration of many houses and the preservation of others that otherwise might have been lost.

Catalog

Annan, William, House

(PA-1539), 776 S. Front St. Brick with marble trim, approx. 20' (two-bay front) × 31' with two-story rear ell, three-and-a-half stories on raised basement, gable roof, London house plan. Built c. 1800; altered later. Certified, PHC 1957. 1 photocopy of ext. photo (1957);* 3 data pages (1961, including 1822 insurance survey);* HABSI form (1957).*

Arsenal on the Schuylkill (later known as the Schuylkill Arsenal)

(PA-1540), 2620 Gray's Ferry Ave., at N.W. corner Peltz St. at Washington Ave. Begun in 1799 as the nation's third arsenal, Schuylkill Arsenal expanded to include twenty-three buildings on its 8.6 acres when it was demolished in 1962. After 1816 it was used only for manufacturing Army clothing and blankets; during World War II and Korean conflict it became a barracks and recruiting and examination center. Certified, PHC 1957.

Building No. 1, Enlisted Men's Barracks (also known as Luding Hall): Approx. 100' W. of Gray's Ferry Ave. Brick with stone trim, approx. 100' (eleven-bay front) × 42' including wing, three-and-a-half stories, hipped roof, wing open at ground story, 1800 date stone. Built 1800; wing enclosed after 1876; demolished 1962. 4 ext. photos (1958);* 4 data pages (1958).*

Building No. 1A, Executive Officers' Quarters: Approx. 55' N. of Building No. 1. Brick with stone trim, approx. 50' (five-bay front) × 24' with two-story side wing (not original), three-and-a-half stories on raised basement (originally two), hipped roof, one-story entry porch, cornice between second and third stories, third-story round-arch windows. Built 1802; side wing added later; third story, porch added after 1876. 1 ext. photo (1958);* 1 data page (1958).*

Building No. 2, Mifflin Building: Approx. 55' S. of Building No. 1. Brick with stone trim, approx. 150' nine-bay front) × 60', four stories on Peltz St., three stories on courtyard, flat roof (originally hipped), three-story tower with portecochere and octagonal cupola (originally centered on building). Built 1804; alteration after 1876; demolished 1962. 2 ext. photos (1958).*

Building No. 6: Approx. 35' N.W. of Building No. 1. Brick with stone trim, approx. 145' (ten-bay front) × 45', two stories, hipped roof, Tuscan colonnade with balcony along south front, Palladian windows set in blind arches. Built 1804; balcony enclosed, interior altered after 1876; demolished 1962. 2 ext. photos (1958).*

Building No. 8, Powder Magazine: Rear of grounds on Peltz St., approx. 410' E. of Schuylkill River. Coursed granite ashlar ground story, brick upper story, approx. 100' (six-bay front) × 100', two stories, hipped roof, brick groined-arch ceiling on stone posts; surrounded by 10'-wide moat. Built c. 1799; upper story added 1802; demolished 1962. 1 ext. photo (1958),* 1 int. photo (1958).*

Askins-Jones Houses
(PA-1541), 720–24 S. Front St. Brick, Nos. 720–22 each approx. 12' (two-bay front) × 20' with one-story rear ell, No. 724 approx. 15' (two-bay front) × 25', two-and-a-half stories, half-gambrel roofs, London house plans. Built between 1762 and 1769; No. 720 altered to store before 1860, reverted to dwelling after 1931; exterior of No. 722 restored 1970. Certified, PHC 1957. 3 ext. photos (1961, 1967);* 9 data pages (1960);* HABSI form (1957).*

Beck Street Area Study
(PA-1542), 203–15 Beck St., on N. side Beck St., W. of Second St. Court of seven brick row houses, each approx. 16' (two-bay front) × 16' with two-story rear ell, two-and-a-half stories on raised basements (No. 215 three-and-a-half stories), gable roofs, probably city house plans. Built late 18th century. Certified, PHC 1965. 2 ext. photos (1961).*

Bel Air (also known as Belleaire, Singley House, Lasse Cock's Manor House)
(PA-1124), S.W. corner Twentieth St. and Pattison Ave., in Franklin Delano Roosevelt Park (known as League Island Park c. 1922–55). Brick with rubble foundation, approx. 42' (five-bay front) × 21', two-and-a-half stories, gable roof with cove cornice and pent eave around gable end, one-bay balcony over entrance, brick stringcourse, blank

end walls; central-hall plan, one room deep, notable interior panel-ing.

Notable early Georgian country house with distinctive early Philadelphia features. Built between 1714 and 1729, possibly incorporating an earlier building; interior probably remodeled c. 1735; restored 1934–41. Until 1735 country seat of Samuel Preston, Mayor of Philadelphia 1711–14, and Treasurer of the Province of Pennsylvania 1715–43. Maintained by Fairmount Park Commission, City of Philadelphia, since 1929. Certified, PHC 1956. 30 sheets (1940, including plans, elevations, section, details) from Survey, Philadelphia Chapter, A.I.A. (1932); 3 ext. photos (1936), 5 int. photos (1936).

Bellaire. See Bel Air

Bird, Joseph, Houses

(PA-1543), 813–15 S. Hancock St. Wood frame with clapboards, each approx. 14' (two-bay front) × 14' with one-story rear ell, two stories, gable roofs. Rare surviving frame dwellings with original brick nog-ging. Built after 1786. Certified, PHC 1966. 1 ext. photo (1961);* 3 data pages (1961).*

Bishop-Sparks House

(PA-1544), 948 S. Front St. Brick with marble trim, approx. 18' (two-bay front) × 32' with two-and-a-half-story rear ell, two-and-a-half stories on raised basement, gable roof. Built between 1808 and 1813. John Bishop and Thomas Sparks were initial owners of Sparks's Shot Tower (PA-1621). Certified, PHC 1957. 1 photocopy of ext. photo (1957);* 2 data pages (1961);* HABSI form (1958).

Byrne-Cavenaugh Houses

(PA-1545), 130–32 Queen St., at S.W. corner Hancock St. Brick, each approx. 15' (two-bay front) × 15' with two-story rear frame kitchen wing, three-and-a-half stories, shed roof, round-headed entrance (No. 132 altered to square head), one room to a floor. Built between 1813 and 1819 as tenements at rear of dwelling-tavern at S.E. corner Second and Queen sts. Certified, PHC 1958. 2 ext. photos (1961, 1974);* 6 data pages (1961, including 1835 insurance survey).*

Catharine Street Area Study

(PA-1811), 19–35 Catharine St., N. side Catharine St., in block between Swanson and Front sts. Eight contiguous brick houses and one frame house (No. 35), each approx. 20' (two-bay front) × 22' and

38', three houses with rear ells, two-and-a-half stories (No. 35 two stories), gable roofs, probably originally London house plans. Nos. 19–25 built between 1810 and 1830; Jesse Williamson and David Flickwer, house carpenters. Nos. 27–31 built c. 1791; No. 33 built before 1830; No. 35 built before 1810. Demolished 1967. Certified, PHC 1958. 1 ext. photo (1967).*

Church of the Redeemer for Seamen of the Port of Philadelphia
(PA-1077), 101–7 Queen St., at N.W. corner Front St. Trenton brownstone rubble, brick and frame, approx. 100' (nine-bay front) × 63', one and two stories with squat hipped-roof tower, intersecting gable roofs, Greek-cross plan with two-story school wing, elaborate interior truss work and framing system that eliminates columns between aisles and nave.

Innovative High Victorian Gothic church design. Built by Churchmen's Missionary Association for Seamen of the Port of Philadelphia 1878; Frank Furness, architect; Williams and McNichol, builders; Manly and Cooper, iron railing. Destroyed by fire 1974. Although interdenominational by charter, the church retained close ties with the Protestant Episcopal Church until it merged with the Seamen's Church Institute of Philadelphia and closed its doors 1922. Neighborhood boys' club 1925–68; vacated 1968. Certified, PHC 1957. 5 ext. photos (1961, 1962), 3 int. photos (1961); 5 data pages (1962).

Church of St. Charles Borromeo (Roman Catholic)
(PA-1546), 900 S. Twentieth St., at S.W. corner Christian St. Coursed brownstone ashlar with granite base and copper trim, approx. 75' (five-bay front) × 150', one story with three-stage French-roof tower on southeast corner and five-stage domed tower on northeast corner, gable roof; three-aisle plan, rectangular chancel, balconies.

Fine High Victorian baroque church design. Built 1868–76; Edwin F. Durang, architect; sanctuary and ceiling frescoes by Filippo Costaggini and Lorenzo C. Scataglia. Sandstone cupola with terra cotta dome put on northern tower 1901; Edwin F. Durang, architect; John McShain, contractor. 1 photocopy of old ext. photo (c. 1905),* 1 photocopy of old int. photo (c. 1905),* 1 photocopy of old lithograph (c. 1880).*

Church of St. Philip de Neri (Roman Catholic)
(PA-1547), 220–28 Queen St. Brick covered with coursed stucco, approx. 65' (three-bay front) × 115', two stories, gable roof, four giant

Doric pilasters on front, three-aisle plan. Built 1840–41. Interior extensively renovated after fire 1897; Frank R. Watson, architect. Interior altered 1908; Watson and Huckel, architects. Three-story brick rectory (218 Queen St.) built on east end 1902; Frank R. Watson, architect. Site of Philadelphia Native American riots 1844. Certified, PHC 1966. 2 ext. photos (1974),* 1 photocopy of old ext. lithograph (c. 1880).*

Clifton, John, House

(PA-1548), 852 S. Front St. Brick, approx. 16' (two-bay front) × 25' with two-story rear ell, two-and-a-half stories on raised basement, gable roof, side-hall plan. Built between 1745 and 1754; ground story altered to store 1860; altered to dwelling, new front wall added 1938. Certified, PHC 1957. 6 data pages (1961, including 1845, 1887 insurance surveys);* HABSI form (1957).*

Collins, Samuel, House

(PA-1549), 783 S. Front St. Brick with marble trim, approx. 22' (two-bay front) × 42', three-and-a-half stories on raised basement, gable roof, round-headed entrance, side-hall plan. Built between 1827 and 1842. Certified, PHC 1957. 1 ext. photo (1961);* 2 data pages (1961);* HABSI form (1958).*

Commandant's Quarters. See United States Naval Base, Quarters "A"

Curtis, John, House

(PA-1550), 785 S. Front St. Brick with marble trim, approx. 19' (three-bay front) × 30' with two-story rear ell, two-and-a-half stories, gambrel roof. Built between 1793 and 1840; altered later. Certified, PHC 1957. 1 photocopy of ext. photo (1957);* 3 data pages (1961);* HABSI form (1958).*

Donaldson, William, House

(PA-1551), 14–16 Queen St. Wood frame with clapboard siding, 23'-9½" (four-bay front) × 17–9" with one-story rear frame wing, two-and-a-half stories on raised basement, gable roof, originally one room to a floor.

Example of small dwelling of Southwark artisans who made their living on Delaware River. Built c. 1795; rear wing built after 1860; demolished 1967. Certified, PHC 1966. 4 sheets (1966, including plot plan, plans, elevation, section, detail);* 2 ext. photos (1966),* 3 int. photos (1966);* 12 data pages (1964).*

Duché House

(PA-1552), 24 Catharine St. Brick with marble trim, approx. 21' (two-bay front) × 33' with two-story rear ell, two-and-a-half stories on raised basement, gable roof, round-arch entrance with fanlight, side-hall plan. Built before 1827; kitchen added to ell 1855; demolished 1967. Certified, PHC 1963. 2 ext. photos (1966, 1967),* 4 int. photos (1967);* 15 data pages (1966, including 1831–55 insurance surveys).*

Duché-Walker House

(PA-1553), 26 Catharine St. Brick, approx. 19' (two-bay front) × 21' with one- and two-story rear ell, two-and-a-half stories on raised basement, gambrel roof, originally one room to a floor. Built c. 1774; rear ell added before 1831; rear frame kitchen added 1862; demolished 1967. Certified, PHC 1963. 1 sheet (1967, including plot plan, details);* 2 ext. photos (1966, 1967),* 2 int. photos (1967);* 14 data pages (1963, including 1831–71 insurance surveys).*

Eckert-Tarrant House

(PA-1554), 38 Catharine St. Wood frame with clapboard siding, 16'-1³/₄" (two-bay front) × 16'-4" with one- and two-story rear ell, two-and-a-half stories, gable roof, originally one room to a floor. Typical small dwelling of Southwark artisans who made their livings on the Delaware River. Built between 1794 and 1802; later rear additions; demolished 1967. Certified, PHC 1963. 3 sheets (1966, including plot plan, plans, elevation, section, details);* 2 ext. photos (1966, 1967),* 2 int. photos (1967);* 9 data pages (1963).*

Elliott, John, House

(PA-1555), 37 Queen St. Brick, approx. 17' (two-bay front) × 18' with two-story rear ell, three-and-a-half stories on raised basement, gable roof, round-arch entrance with fanlight, side-hall plan. Built c. 1813; demolished 1967. Certified, PHC 1957. 3 ext. photos (1961, 1966),* 4 int. photos (1967);* 10 data pages (1964, including 1813 insurance survey).*

Elwell, Henry, House

(PA-1556), 812 S. Front St. Brick with brownstone trim, approx. 18' (two-bay front) × 32' with two- and three-story rear ell, two-and-a-half stories on raised basement, gable roof, round-headed entrance, originally two rooms to a floor with rear stair tower, side-hall plan. Built 1822–23; interior altered later. Certified, PHC 1957. 1 photocopy of ext. photo (1957);* 4 data pages (1961, including 1823, 1850 insurance surveys);* HABSI form (1957).*

Ely-Osbourn Houses and Stores

(PA-1557), 136–38 South St., at S.W. corner Hancock St. Brick with marble trim, approx. 26' (four-bay front) × 60' with three-story wing on corner building and three- and two-story ell on other building (originally approx. 38' × 30' with rear stair tower), three-and-a-half stories, gable roof, rectangular plan with stores on ground story (originally front buildings divided into front shops and rear dwelling rooms with cellar kitchens).

Built as unit of three 1833–34; probably by Ebenezer Osbourn, house carpenter. Corner building altered to tavern, three-story rear wing built 1844; interior Nos. 138–40 altered, two-story kitchen ell built 1844; corner building's front upper stories, rear wing, and storefront replaced 1910; new storefront on No. 138 built 1922; westernmost building (No. 140) demolished between 1956 and 1958; Nos. 136–38 vacated 1967. 1 ext. photo (1967);* 6 data pages (1961, including 1834–44 insurance surveys).*

Finlow-Nichell House

(PA-1158), 770 S. Front St., at N.W. corner Clymer St. Brick, approx. 17' (two-bay front) × 19' with two-and-a-half-story half-gambrel roof rear ell, three-and-a-half stories, gable roof, pent eave between first and second stories, side-hall plan. Built 1745; restored 1969–70. Certified, PHC 1957. 2 ext. photos (1961);* 8 data pages (1961, including 1818, 1834 insurance surveys);* HABSI form (1957).*

First Polish Baptist Church. See Mariners' Bethel (Baptist) Church

Fitzwater Street Area Study

(PA-1559), 11–23 Fitzwater St., on N. side of Fitzwater St. between Swanson and Front sts. Seven contiguous brick houses, each approx. 18' (two-bay front) × 18' with one- or two-story rear ells, two-and-a-half stories on raised basements (No. 17 three stories), originally gable roofs, originally city house plans. Built at various times between 1761 and 1809; demolished 1967. Certified, PHC 1957. 4 ext. photos (1961, 1967);* 38 data pages (1961, 1966, including 1808, 1828 insurance surveys).*

Fitzwater Street Area Study

(PA-1560), 24–32 Fitzwater St., on S. side Fitzwater St. between Water and Front sts. Five brick row houses, each approx. 17' (two-bay front) × 17' with two-story rear ell, three stories, gable roofs, city house plans. Built between 1821 and 1830; demolished 1967. A row of houses built for rental income. Certified, PHC 1957. 2 ext. photos (1967);* 8 data pages (1961, including 1830 insurance survey).*

Flickwer-Williamson Houses

(PA-1561), 809–11 S. Hancock St. Wood frame, each approx. 11' (two-bay front) × 14' with one-story rear ell, two-and-a-half stories, gable roof. Built after 1802; probably by David Flickwer and Jesse Williamson, house carpenters. Certified, PHC 1966. 1 ext. photo (1961);* 3 data pages (1961).*

Franklin Sugar Refinery Warehouse (also known as Harrison, Frazier & Co.)

(PA-1562), 701–15 S. Front St., composing block bounded by Front, Kenilworth, Water, Bainbridge sts. Brick, approx. 122' (eleven-bay front) × 130' (originally approx. 82' × 130'), six stories with mezzanine, three gable roofs, brick-arch vaults under Front and Kenilworth sts. Eastern section built as one-story boiler house c. 1881; raised to six stories and mezzanine for storage purposes and enclosed bridge to buildings in next block built at third story c. 1886; western addition built after 1886, retaining exterior brick wall of adjoining building; bridge later raised three stories. Demolished 1967. 1 ext. photo (1967);* 2 photocopies of plans and views (1882, 1886).*

Fullerton, John, Houses

(PA-1563), 606–8 S. Front St. Two adjoining plastered brick houses, each approx. 14' (two-bay front) × 20' with one-story rear kitchen wing, two-and-a-half stories, half-gambrel roofs, originally one room to a floor. Evidently back buildings built in expectation of front buildings that were never built. Southern house (No. 608) built c. 1748; northern house built c. 1760. Certified, PHC 1957; Pennsylvania Register 1970. 2 ext. photos (1961, 1967);* 8 data pages (1961, including 1765 insurance survey);* HABSI form (1957).*

Gentilhommière (also known as Stephen Girard's Country House)

(PA-140), N.W. corner Twenty-first and Shunk sts. Girard Park. Brick with stucco on lateral wings, 80'-0" (ten-bay front) × 24'-4", two and two-and-a-half stories, gable and hipped roofs, one large room in central section, three-room plan in eastern section, central-hall plan in western section, French influence in casement windows and hardware of eastern section.

Fine example of the evolution of a country house. Eastern section built 1750; center section built c. 1800; western section built after 1825. Country house of Stephen Girard, French-born Philadelphia merchant, financier, and philanthropist 1798–1831. Administered by Department of Recreation, City of Philadelphia. Certified, PHC 1956. 11 sheets (1962, including plot plan, plans, elevations, partial section, details); 12 ext. photos (1940, 1962), 6 int. photos (1940, 1962), 5 photocopies of old ext. photos (c. 1900), 1 photocopy of old watercolor (1891); 20 data pages (1962).

Gentilhommière, Utility Building

(PA-1082), N.W. corner Twenty-first and Shunk sts. Girard Park. Approx. 35' N.E. of Country House. Brick, approx. 17' × 17', two stories with brick-domed cellar, pyramidal roof, upper smoke room, middle cooling room, lower root cellar. One of two identical buildings. Built early 19th century; probably from designs of Stephen Girard. Slightly altered 1901. Certified, PHC 1956. 3 sheets (1962, including plans, elevations, sections, details); 1 ext. photo (1965), 4 int. photos (1962); 4 data pages (1962, 1964).

Glebe House

(PA-139), Old River Road, south of Passyunk Ave. Bridge. Brick, 42'-4" (five-bay front) × 20'-3" with rear kitchen ell, two-and-a-half stories, gable roof with coved cornice, central-hall plan. Built 1698; interior damage by fire and partially rebuilt between 1800 and 1820; demolished before 1956. 14 sheets (1940, including plans, elevations, section, details); 2 ext. photos (1940).

Gloria Dei (Protestant Episcopal) (also known as Old Swedes Church).
Illustrated

(PA-120), 929 S. Water St. Brick, 30'-0¾" (three-bay front) × 79'-1½" with small side wings, one story with one-stage belfry and spire, gable roof with cross-gables, diamond patterns of glazed headers flank entrance; three-aisle plan (earlier two-aisle plan), galleries, semioctagonal chancel.

Notable early church whose English construction and details reflect the acculturation of its congregation. Built 1698–1700; Rev.

Andrew Rudman, builder. Side wings built 1703–5. Interior altered to three-aisle plan 1896; George C. Mason, architect. Wood details from original windows in Architectural Study Collection, Museum Division, Independence National Historical Park. Oldest extant church building in Pennsylvania and one of the oldest in the nation in continuous service. Mission of State Church of Sweden until 1845 when it became part of the Diocese of Pennsylvania of the Protestant Episcopal Church. Certified, PHC 1956; designated National Historic Site 1942. 10 sheets (1936, including plot plan, plans, elevations, sections, details); 10 ext. photos (1937, 1962, including 3 of c. 1830 rectory), 3 int. photos (1937), 4 photocopies of measured drawings (1897);* 2 data pages (1937).

Godley, Jesse, Warehouse. Illustrated
(PA-1564), 19–27 Queen St. Random ashlar with brick front, 109'-5" (nine-bay front) × 102'-2", three stories, flat roof, segmental-head windows, three interior sections with wood columns and stone walls.

Fine example of urban vernacular architecture. Built c. 1867; demolished 1967. Accessible to river and rail transportation, this warehouse was a major unit in Jesse Godley's storage business. Certified, PHC 1966. 5 sheets (1966, including plot plan, plans, elevation, section, details, hoist machinery);* 3 ext. photos (1961, 1966),* 2 int. photos (1966);* 8 data pages (1966).*

Godley's Argyle Stores
(PA-1565), 32–36 Kenilworth St. Stone with brick front, approx. 63' (seven-bay front) × 68', three stories, flat roof, segmental-arch doors and windows with stone keystones, rectangular plan. Built c. 1868; altered after 1868; demolished 1967. One of Jesse Godley's many warehouses, used for miscellaneous merchandise. 1 ext. photo (1967).*

Harmony Engine Company No. 6
(PA-1566), 730–32 S. Broad St. Brick with granite ashlar front, approx. 34' (three-bay front) × 60', four stories, mansard roof, projecting center semihexagonal bay at second story. Built c. 1868. Site of Franklin Hose Company No. 28 until 1867. Certified, PHC 1971. 2 ext. photos (1963).*

Harper, William, Jr., Houses
(PA-1567), 621–23 S. American St., at N.E. corner Harper's Pl. Two contiguous brick tenements, each approx. 15' (two-bay front) × 90',

three stories, flat roof, rectangular plan with seven dwellings in each building. Example of mid-19th-century low-cost housing. Built c. 1847. 1 ext. photo (1967).*

Harrison, Frazier & Co. See Franklin Sugar Refinery Warehouse

Hart, John, House
(PA-1568), 601 S. Front St., at S.E. corner South St. Brick, approx. 18' (three-bay front) × 36', three-and-a-half stories, gable roof, store in ground-story front room. Built between 1768 and 1771; altered to store before 1860; demolished 1966. Certified, PHC 1957. 1 photocopy of ext. photo (1957);* 6 data pages (1961, including 1771, 1840 insurance surveys);* HABSI form (1957).*

Hart-Patterson House
(PA-1569), 603 S. Front St. Brick, approx. 23' (three-bay front) × 36', three-and-a-half stories on raised basement, gable roof, wooden lintels carved to simulate stone voussoirs, London house plan. Built between 1768 and 1771; altered to store before 1860; demolished 1966. Certified, PHC 1957. 1 ext. photo (1961);* 6 data pages (1961, including 1771, 1840 insurance surveys);* HABSI form (1957).*

Hellings, Benjamin, House
(PA-1570), 931 S. Front St. Brick, approx. 14' (two-bay front) × 17', two-and-a-half stories, gable roof. Built c. 1762; demolished 1961. Certified, PHC 1957. 1 photocopy of ext. photo (1957);* 3 data pages (1961);* HABSI form (1958).*

Henderson, James, House
(PA-1571), 602 S. Front St. Brick, approx. 20' (two-bay front) × 30', three-and-a-half stories, gable roof, London house plan. Built c. 1795; altered to store before 1860; reverted to dwelling later. Certified, PHC 1957; Pennsylvania Register 1970. 3 data pages (1961, including 1795 insurance survey);* HABSI form (1957).*

Hope Engine Company No. 17
(PA-1572), 733 S. Sixth St. Stuccoed brick with cast-iron trim, approx. 17' (three-bay front) × 45', four stories, flat roof, round-arch windows with engaged columns, corbeling at each story, rectangular plan.
     Fine example of Italianate volunteer fire hall. Built 1851–52; Hoxie and Button, architects; Edward Storey, builder; William Trout

& Co. (Chester, Pa.), iron work. Ground-story interior and exterior altered 1907. Firehouse 1852–71; fraternal society lodge 1871–1920. Certified, PHC 1971. 2 ext. photos (1963);* 1 data page (1963).*

House

(PA-1573), 30 Catharine St. Brick with stone trim, approx. 16' (two-bay front) × 40' with two-story rear wing, three stories, flat roof. Built after 1871; demolished 1967. 2 ext. photos (1966).*

House

(PA-1069), 33¹/₂ Catharine St., at rear of 33 Catharine St. Wood frame with tongue-and-groove random width siding, 15'-4¹/₂" (two-bay front) × 14'-5⁷/₈", two-and-a-half stories, gable roof, one room to a floor. Built c. 1790; dismantled above ground story 1962; demolished 1970. Portions of siding preserved at Architectural Study Collection, Museum Division, Independence National Historical Park. 2 sheets (1961, including plot plan, plan, section, isometric detail of exterior corner);* 3 ext. photos (1961),* 2 int. photos (1961);* 4 data pages (1961, 1962).*

House

(PA-1574), 768 S. Front St. Brick, approx. 18' (two-bay front) × 19' with two-story rear ell, two-and-a-half stories, gable roof, originally one room to a floor. Built c. 1744; rehabilitated 1961. Certified, PHC 1957. HABSI form (1957).*

House

(PA-1575), 600 S. Second St., at S.W. corner South St. Brick with marble trim, approx. 20' (two-bay front) × 35', three-and-a-half stories, hipped roof, rectangular plan with ground-story restaurant (originally store). Built early 19th century; new storefront built 1914. Interior remodeled 1970; Venturi and Rauch, architects. 1 ext. photo (1967).*

Houses

(PA-1580), 125–27 Bainbridge St. Two contiguous brick houses, each approx. 20' (three-bay front) × 20' with two-story rear ell, two-and-a-half stories on raised basement, gable roof, arched ground-story alleyway between houses, probably originally city house plan. Modest dwellings of artisans who worked on the Delaware River. Built before 1784; altered later. Certified, PHC 1957. 1 ext. photo (1967);* 4 data pages (1961).*

Houses

(PA-1581), 111–13 Beck St. Brick, each approx. 12' (two-bay front) × 18', two-and-a-half stories, half-gambrel roof. Built mid-18th century. Certified, PHC 1965. 1 ext. photo (1961).*

Houses

(PA-1582), 102–18, 103–15 Clymer St., rear of 770 and 772 S. Front St. Court of seven and nine contiguous brick houses, each approx. 15' (two-bay front) × 15', three stories on raised basement, gable roof. Built early 19th century; rehabilitated 1969. Certified, PHC 1966. 1 ext. photo (1961).*

Houses

(PA-1583), 123–25 League St. Wood frame with clapboards, each approx. 15' (two-bay front) × 18' with rear ell, two-and-a-half stories, gable roof. Built between 1793 and 1806. Certified, PHC 1963. 1 ext. photo (1961).*

Houses

(PA-1584), 39–43 Norfolk St. Three contiguous brick houses, each approx. 14' (two-bay front) × 14', three stories, shed roof, one room to a floor. Built between 1830 and 1833; demolished 1967; 1 ext. photo (1967);* 12 data pages (1964, including 1832, 1833 insurance surveys).*

Houses

(PA-1585), 731–33 S. Front St. Two adjoining brick houses with marble trim, No. 731 approx. 25' (two-bay front) × 40', two stories, flat roof; No. 733 approx. 18' (two-bay front) × 44' with two-story rear wing, three stories on raised basement, flat roof, round-arch entrance. Built after 1860; new storefront added 1911; demolished 1967. 1 ext. photo (1967).*

Hutton, Nathaniel, House

(PA-1586), 814 S. Front St. Brick, approx. 14' (one-bay front) × 20' with three-story rear wing, three-and-a-half stories, half-gambrel roof. Probably a back building built in expectation of a front building. Built between 1785 and 1813; possibly by Nathaniel Hutton, shipwright. Certified, PHC 1964. 1 ext. photo (1961);* 3 data pages (1961).*

Irish, Nathaniel, House. Illustrated

(PA-1013), 704 S. Front St. Brick, 19'-7" (three-bay front) × 33'-10" with two-story rear ell, three-and-a-half stories on raised basement, gable roof, alleyway to rear yard, originally pent eave between first and second stories, originally London house plan, notable original woodwork.

Fine example of 18th-century Philadelphia dwelling. Built between 1762 and 1769; Nathaniel Irish, house carpenter. Interior altered later. Certified, PHC 1957; Pennsylvania Register 1970; NR. 1 sheet (1957, including plans, elevation, section)* courtesy of Philadelphia Historical Commission, 8 sheets (1966, including plot plan, plans, elevations, section, details);* 1 ext. photo (1959), 7 int. photos (1959, 1966*); 8 data pages (1959); HABSI form (1957).*

Keen, James, House
(PA-1587), 946 S. Front St. Brick, approx. 17' (two-bay front) × 30', two-and-a-half stories on raised basement, gable roof, round-headed entrance. Built between 1820 and 1834; wood cornice replaced by brick 1953. Certified, PHC 1957. 1 photocopy of ext. photo (1957);* 2 data pages (1961);* HABSI form (1958).*

Kenilworth Street Area Study
(PA-1588), 109–25 Kenilworth St., on N. side Kenilworth St. between Front and Second sts. Nine contiguous brick houses, each approx. 19' (two-bay front) × 23' with one-, two-, and/or three-story rear ells, two-and-a-half, three, or three-and-a-half stories, originally gable roofs, originally city house and side-hall plans. Built at various times between 1740 and 1800; Nos. 121–23 raised to three stories later. A residential community for waterfront workers for over two centuries. Certified, PHC 1957. 2 ext. photos (1961);* 25 data pages (1960, including 1757–1918 insurance surveys).*

Kitts, Captain John, House
(PA-1589), 609 S. Front St. Brick, approx. 18' (two-bay front) × 20' with two-story rear ell, two-and-a-half stories on raised basement, gambrel roof, city house plan. Built before 1789; altered to store before 1860; demolished 1966. 1 ext. photo (1961);* 2 data pages (including 1789 insurance policy).*

Lamb, Peter, House
(PA-1590), 28 Catharine St. Brick, approx. 16' (two-bay front) × 25' with two-story rear ell, two-and-a-half stories on raised basement, gable roof, round-arch entrance with fanlight. Built after 1821; demolished 1967. Certified, PHC 1963. 1 ext. photo (1966).*

Lasse Cock's Manor House. See Bel Air

Little, John, House
(PA-1591), 618 S. Front St. Brick, approx. 17' (two-bay front) × 30'
with two-story rear ell, two-and-a-half stories on raised basement,
gable roof, round-arch entrance with fanlight, London house plan.
Built 1774; renovated and enlarged c. 1833. Certified, PHC 1957. 1 ext.
photo (1966);* 7 data pages (1961, including 1774–1849 insurance surveys);* HABSI form (1957).*

Lyle-Newman Houses
(PA-1592), 905–7 S. Front St. Brick, each approx. 14' (two-bay
front) × 28', two-and-a-half stories, gable roof, originally London
house plan. Built 1815; demolished 1967. Certified, PHC 1957. 1
photocopy of ext. photo (1957);* 7 data pages (1961, including 1815,
1918 insurance surveys);* 2 HABSI forms (1958).*

McCraig, George, House
(PA-1593), 810 S. Front St. Brick with marble trim, approx. 18' (two-
bay front) × 18', three-and-a-half stories, gable roof. Built between
1784 and 1786; two-story rear ell removed after 1887. Certified, PHC
1957. 1 photocopy of ext. photo (1957);* 3 data pages (1961);* HABSI
form (1957).*

McDowell-Fritz House
(PA-1594), 808 S. Front St. Brick, approx. 18' (two-bay front) × 22'
with two-story rear ell, two-and-a-half stories on raised basement,
gable roof, probably London house plan. Built between 1754 and
1761; altered later. Certified, PHC 1957. 2 ext. photos (1961);* 2 data
pages (1961);* HABSI form (1957).*

Maloby, Thomas, House and Tavern
(PA-1595), 700 S. Front St., at S.W. corner Bainbridge St. Brick, approx. 17' (two-bay front) × 36', three-and-a-half stories, gable roof,
pent eave, originally London house plan. Built c. 1764; altered to store
before 1860; one-story rear wing removed later. Interior rehabilitated,
exterior partially restored 1972–74. Certified, PHC 1957; Pennsylvania
Register 1976; NR. 1 ext. photo (1966);* 10 data pages (1960, including
1774 insurance survey);* HABSI form (1957).*

Mariners' Bethel (Baptist) Church (later known as First Polish Baptist Church and Bethel Christian Center)

(PA-1596), 923 S. Front St. Brick, approx. 40' (three-bay front) × 70' two stories, gable roof. Built 1863; possibly by Stephen D. Button, architect. Small, one-story toilet wing added 1922. Demolished 1966. Certified, PHC 1963. 1 ext. photo (1961).*

Marks-Dunbar House

(PA-1597), 849 S. Front St. Brick, approx. 16' (two-bay front) × 17' with two-story rear ell, two-and-a-half stories on raised basement, gable roof, originally pent eave between first and second stories, originally one room to a floor, later city house plan.

Typical small dwelling of Southwark artisans. Built 1758; rear ell built before 1860, enlarged later; demolished 1967. Certified, PHC 1957. 4 sheets (1967, including plot plan, plans, elevation, section, details);* 2 ext. photos (1966),* 4 int. photos (1966);* 12 data pages (1961, including 1762 insurance survey);*HABSI form (1958).*

Marshall, Joseph, Houses

(PA-1598), 854–56 S. Front St. Brick, each approx. 16' (two-bay front) × 25' with one-story rear addition, two-and-a-half stories, gable roof, probably London house plan. Built c. 1831; altered to store before 1860; rear addition built between 1860 and 1887; new storefront 1930. Certified, PHC 1957. 1 photocopy of ext. photo (1957);* 7 data pages (1961);* 2 HABSI forms (1957).*

Marshall-Morris House

(PA-1599), 774 S. Front St. Brick, approx. 17' (two-bay front) × 34' (originally with two-story rear ell), three-and-a-half stories, gable roof, originally London house plan. Built between 1772 and 1777; altered to store c. 1841; altered to warehouse later. Certified, PHC 1957. 1 photocopy of ext. photo (1957);* 6 data pages (1961, including 1807–41 insurance surveys);* HABSI form (1957).*

Maxfield-Elliott House

(PA-1600), 35 Queen St. Brick, approx. 24' (three-bay front) × 18' with one- and two-story rear ell, three-and-a-half stories on raised basement, gable roof, round-arch entrance with pedimented frontispiece, side-hall plan. Built c. 1802; demolished 1967. Certified, PHC 1957. 2 sheets (1967, including plot plan, fireplace plans and elevations, details);* 4 ext. photos (1961, 1966, 1967),* 3 int. photos (1967);* 11 data pages (1964, including 1813 insurance survey).*

Mercer, Thomas, Houses
(PA-1601), 2–12 Christian St. Five contiguous brick houses, each approx. 15' (two-bay front) × 30' with three-story rear ell, and one adjoining brick house approx. 16' (two-bay front) × 18' with two-story rear ell, three stories on raised basements, gable roofs. Nos. 2–10 built c. 1833. No. 12 built c. 1844; probably by Alexander McMullin, bricklayer. Demolished 1962. Certified, PHC 1958. 2 ext. photos (1961–62),* 2 int. photos (1961–62),* 1 photocopy of ext. photo (1957);* 6 data pages (1961).*

Mikveh Israel Cemetery Gatehouse
(PA-1602), 1114 Federal St. Stuccoed brick, approx. 30' (three-bay front) × 20', two stories, flat roof, battered recesses flanking door with corbeled recess above, notable Egyptian Revival details. Built before 1849; demolished 1963. 2 ext. photos (1963).*

Moffett, Robert, House
(PA-1603), 35 Catharine St. Wood frame with clapboard siding, approx. 20' (three-bay front) × 32', two stories, gable roof. Built between 1793 and 1810; demolished 1967. Certified, PHC 1963. 1 ext. photo (1966);* 15 data pages (1963).*

Moore, Captain Thomas, House
(PA-1604), 702 S. Front St. Brick, approx. 18' (three-bay front) × 34' with two-story rear ell, three-and-a-half stories on raised basement, gable roof, originally pent eave between first and second stories, London house plan. Built between 1767 and 1779; possibly by Nathaniel Irish, house carpenter. Altered to store before 1860; reverted to dwelling and rear ell later raised to two stories. Certified, PHC 1957; Pennsylvania Register 1970; NR. 7 data pages (1960);* HABSI form (1957).*

Moore, John, House
(PA-1605), 734 S. Front St. Brick, approx. 16' (two-bay front) × 33' with three-story rear ell (originally one story), three-and-a-half stories (originally two), gable roof, originally London house plan. Built between 1770 and 1772; house and rear ell raised one story

between 1810 and 1820; ell raised to three stories after 1860. Demolished 1967. Certified, PHC 1957. 1 photocopy of ext. photo (1957);* 4 data pages (1960, including 1772 insurance survey);* HABSI form (1957).*

Moyamensing Prison. See Philadelphia County Prison

Murphy-Johnson House
(PA-1606), 42 Catharine St. Wood frame with clapboard siding, 19'-4¹/₂" (three-bay front) × 17'-4" with two-story rear brick addition and one-story rear ell, two-and-a-half stories, gambrel roof, originally one room to a floor.

Typical small dwelling of Southwark artisans who made their living on Delaware River. Built c. 1795; brick addition later; one-story ell built after 1860; demolished 1967. Certified, PHC 1957. 3 sheets (1966, including plot plan, plans, section);* 1 ext. photo (1967),* 1 int. photo (1967);* 14 data pages (1963).*

Old Swedes Church. See Gloria Dei

Paschall, Jonathan, House
(PA-1607), 36 Christian St. Brick, 16'-0" (two-bay front) × 16'-10" with one- and two-story rear frame ell, two-and-a-half stories, gambrel roof, pedimented frontispiece, originally one room to a floor. One of many small dwellings of Southwark artisans who made their living on Delaware River. Built c. 1749; rear frame ell and addition built later; frontispiece added c. 1800; demolished 1967. Certified, PHC 1963. 4 sheets (1966, including plot plans, elevation, details);* 2 ext. photos (1966);* 6 data pages (1960).*

Pearson, Anthony, House
(PA-1608), 806 S. Front St. Brick, approx. 14' (two-bay front) × 21' with two-story rear ell, two-and-a-half stories, gable roof, city house plan. Built 1754; probably by Anthony Pearson, bricklayer. Certified, PHC 1957. 2 ext. photos (1961);* 3 data pages (1961, including 1764 insurance survey);* HABSI form (1957).*

Pearson, George, Houses. Illustrated
(PA-1609), 808–10 S. Hancock St. Wood frame with clapboards, each approx. 10' (one-bay front) × 12' with one-story rear wing, two-and-a-half stories on raised basement, gable roof. Built late 18th century;

probably by George Pearson, carpenter. Certified, PHC 1966. 1 ext. photo (1961);* 2 data pages (1961).*

Philadelphia County Prison (also known as Moyamensing Prison).
Illustrated
(PA-1096), 1400 S. Tenth St., at S.W. corner Reed St. at Passyunk Ave. Front buildings (offices): Quincy granite ashlar with rubble rear wall, approx. 173' (seventeen-bay front) × 36', two and three stories, flat roofs, battlemented front corner turrets and central two-story octagonal tower on projecting center section, battlemented octagonal tower at front corners of side wings, recessed lancet windows, front part of U-plan.

Two rear buildings (convict quarters): rubble with granite ashlar trim, each approx. 53' × 380', three stories with clerestory skylights, gable roofs, interior center court with three tiers of cells, sides of U-plan. Other rubble two-story buildings for kitchen, workshops in center of U-plan. Prison wall of granite ashlar front and rubble sides and rear; squat battlemented tower at front corners.

Fine example of castellated mode of prison architecture, designed with advanced sanitation and heating system. Built 1832–35; Thomas U. Walter, architect. Ventilation system installed 1849–50; Thomas U. Walter, architect. Workshops built later; rear storage building built 1915; central tower removed later. Vacated 1963; demolished 1968. After 1895 used for detaining prisoners awaiting trial or sentence or serving short sentences. 2 ext. photos (1965),* 7 int. photos (1965),* 1 photocopy of architect's wash drawing (1836);* 2 data pages (1965).*

Philadelphia County Prison, Debtors' Wing
(PA-1097), 1400 S. Tenth St., at S.W. corner Reed St. at Passyunk Ave. Coursed red sandstone ashlar front, sandstone rubble sides and rear, 50'-0½" (three-bay front) × 86'-2", two stories on raised basement with Egyptian distyle entrance porch, gable roof with front cavetto cornice containing carved winged orb, front windows within battered two-story frames with cavetto cornices, central longitudinal corridor.

Outstanding example of Egyptian Revival design and considered the first archaeologically based Egyptian Revival building in America. Built 1836; Thomas U. Walter, architect. Rear extension built 1837–38; vacated 1963; demolished 1968. Portico preserved at Smithsonian Institution, Washington, D.C. Used for confinement of witnesses and prisoners held for proceedings 1841–68, for confinement of women 1868–1963. 7 sheets (1966, including plot plan, plans, elevations, section, details); 4 ext. photos (1965), 2 int. photos (1965), 1 photocopy of architect's drawing (1836);* 6 data pages (1965).*

Philadelphia Fire Department, Engine Company No. 3, and Patrol House (originally known as Weccacoe Engine Company No. 9)

(PA-1610), 117–21 Queen St. (originally 119 Queen St.). Brick, approx. 56' (four-bay front) × 47' with one-story rear extension (originally 19' × 52', later 37' × 67'), two-and-a-half stories (originally three), gable roof with cross-gambrel (originally flat), brick in herringbone pattern between floors, three equipment doors, rectangular plan.

Fine 19th-century fire station whose development reflects changes in architectural design and municipal administration. Built c. 1843; enlarged c. 1858. New front built, patrol house added to western end 1893; possibly by John T. Windrim, architect; Doyle and Doak, contractors. Interior altered 1904; Philip Johnson, architect. Rear altered and building shortened, interior renovated to dwelling and interior-design studio 1969. Volunteer fire hall c. 1843–71; municipal fire station 1871–1957. Certified, PHC 1963. 1 ext. photo (1973),* 2 photocopies of old ext. photos (1896, 1934).*

Philadelphia, Wilmington and Baltimore Railroad Freight Station Train Shed

(PA-1611), S.E. corner Fifteenth and Carpenter sts., at rear of 1000 S. Broad St. Brick with stone trim, approx. 100' (three-bay front) × 230', one story, gable roof with clerestory skylights, overhanging eaves with iron cinquefoil supports, rectangular plan with exposed iron trusses.

Fine example of vernacular railroad architecture and use of trusses to span large space before introduction of three-hinged arch. Built 1876 as train shed with brick two-story head house fronting on Broad St.; head house demolished 1968. Pennsylvania Railroad acquired control of railroad 1881, changed name to Philadelphia, Baltimore and Washington Railroad 1902, sold buildings 1966. Now Semple Co. Warehouse 5 ext. photos (1969),* 3 int. photos (1969),* 2 photocopies of old ext. photos (1914, 1917).*

Powder Magazine

(PA-124), Magazine Lane. Rubble with brick trim, 53'-7" (two-bay front) × 72'-9", one-and-a-half stories, five buttresses on side walls, two barrel vaults run the length of the building. Built by Commonwealth of Pennsylvania 1808; vacated 1874; demolished 1940. 4 ext. photos (1937), 1 ext. photo of two-and-a-half-story, half-gambrel roof, caretaker's house (1937); 2 data pages (1937).

Purves, Hugh, Store
(PA-1612), 626 S. Second St., at N.W. corner Bainbridge St. Brick, approx. 20' (three-bay front) × 40', four stories, flat roof, corner storefront, decorative iron lintels, rectangular plan. Built c. 1851; demolished c. 1968. Hugh Purves, stove manufacturer, had his store on the ground story and leased upper-story dwelling rooms c. 1851–96. 1 ext. photo (1967).*

Queen Street Area Study
(PA-1613), 28–38 Queen St., on S. side Queen St. between Swanson and Front sts. Six contiguous brick houses, each approx. 17' (two-bay front) × 17' with two-story rear ell, two-and-a-half stories on raised basement, gambrel roof (No. 38 gable roof), probably city house plans. A residential community of waterfront workers for nearly two centuries. Built at various times between 1743 and 1793; demolished 1967. Certified, PHC 1957. 2 ext. photos (1966, 1967);* 36 data pages (1963, 1964, including 1763 insurance survey).*

Ralston School
(PA-1614), 625 S. American St., at N.E. corner Bainbridge St. Brick, approx. 60' (six-bay front) × 50' with two-story lateral addition (east end), two stories, hipped roof with cross-gables, name and date stone on south end, ventilator oculus in gable, segmental-arch windows, rectangular plan with four rooms to a floor and front and rear entrances and stairs.

Fine example of post–Civil War public school house continuing the earlier modular plan of Samuel Sloan's "Philadelphia Plan." Built 1869; Lewis H. Eshler, architect; George H. Brinkworth, contractor. Lateral addition built 1928; Francis P. Canavan, architect. Named in honor of Robert Ralston, prominent mid-19th-century merchant; school until 1922. Certified, PHC 1973. 1 ext. photo (1967),* 1 photocopy of architect's plan (c. 1869).*

Ridgway Branch of Library Company of Philadelphia. Illustrated
(PA-1616), 900 S. Broad St., composing block bounded by Broad, Catharine, Thirteenth, Carpenter sts. Brick faced with granite ashlar and with iron columns and beams in book rooms, approx. 220'

(thirteen-bay front) × 105', two stories on raised basement with central Doric octastyle portico and flanking Doric tetrastyle porticoes with pediments, gable roofs with significant skylight system, central-hall plan with stylized Ionic-colonnade gallery.

Often considered the final expression of the Greek Revival in the United States. Built 1873–78; Addison Hutton, architect. Vacated 1966; altered to recreation center 1973. The oldest circulating library in the United States, the Library Company of Philadelphia was founded by Benjamin Franklin 1731 and the Ridgway Branch was built from funds donated by Dr. James Rush in honor of his wife, Phoebe Ann Ridgway Rush. Certified, PHC 1972. 9 ext. photos (1962),* 9 int. photos (1962),* 1 photo of architect's model (1962),* 4 photocopies of architect's plans and elevations (c. 1873).*

Rooming House

(PA-1617), 115 Bainbridge St. Brick with marble trim, approx. 20' (four-bay front) × 53', four stories, flat roof, molded brick trim between sills and lintels at each floor, rectangular plan. Example of late-19th-century rooming house. Built between 1880 and 1888; ground-story front, interior altered to warehouse 1922. 1 ext. photo (1967);* 3 data pages (1973).*

Schuylkill Arsenal. See Arsenal on the Schuylkill

Siddons, William, House

(PA-1618), 851 S. Front St. Brick, approx. 17' (two-bay front) × 25' with two-story rear ell, two-and-a-half stories on raised basement, gable roof. Built after 1785; ground story altered to store late 19th century; new shopfront built 1920; demolished 1967. Certified, PHC 1957. 1 photocopy of ext. photo (1957);* 2 data pages (1961); * HABSI form (1958).*

Singley House. See Bel Air

South Front Street Area Study

(PA-1812), 600–858 S. Front St., W. side Front St. between South and Catharine sts. Sixty-five contiguous brick houses and one church (Church of the Redeemer), two-and-a-half, three, and three-and-a-half stories, gable and flat roofs. Nearly all of the houses built late 18th and early 19th centuries. 4 ext. view photos (1967).*

Spafford, William, House
(PA-1620), 626 S. Front St., at N.W. corner Bainbridge St. Brick, approx. 20' (three-bay front) × 34' with two-story rear wing, three-and-a-half stories, gambrel roof, brick stringcourses, London house plan, notable oval stairwell. Built before 1762; altered c. 1801; ground story altered to tavern 1907. Certified, PHC 1957. 2 ext. photos (1961, 1966),* 2 int. photos (1966);* 13 data pages (1961, including 1762–1873 insurance surveys);* HABSI form (1957).*

Sparks's Shot Tower
(PA-1621), 129–31 Carpenter St. Brick, approx. 30' diameter at base, six stories (originally seven), conical roof. Built 1808; altered after 1913. The first shot tower erected in the United States and a rare extant example. Used as recreation center since 1913. Certified, PHC 1957. 3 ext. photos (1973, 1976);* HABSI form (1971).*

Stephen Girard's Country House. See Gentilhommière

United States Naval Asylum (now United States Naval Home). Illustrated
(PA-1622), S.W. corner Gray's Ferry Ave. and Twenty-fourth St. at Bainbridge St. Complex of four primary buildings on 9 acres that until 1976 served as the only residence facility for retired naval personnel in the United States. Certified, PHC 1956; Pennsylvania Register 1972; designated National Historic Landmark 1975.

Biddle Hall: Pennsylvania marble ashlar with granite ashlar basement, approx. 385' (thirty-three-bay front) × 135' including domed rear chapel, two-and-a-half stories on raised basement with central Ionic octastyle portico, gable and hipped roofs, lateral dormitory wings with balconies on granite piers and iron columns, symmetrical plan with central axial corridor and central hallways through dormitory wings.

A major Greek Revival building designed to be healthy, efficient, and fireproof. Built 1827–33; William Strickland, architect; John Struthers, marble mason; John O'Neill, carpenter. Cellar added c. 1843; attic altered, windows added 1848. Served as Naval Academy 1840–45 and hospital 1833–68. Name changed to U.S. Naval Home 1889. 6 ext. photos (1964, including detail of iron railing),* 7 int. photos (1964),* 14 photocopies of architectural drawings (including 8 by William Strickland 1826, 5 by W. L. Andrews 1843, 1 by G. W. Mackay 1888),* 2 photocopies of plot plans (c. 1824, 1878),* 1 photocopy of oil painting by Thomas Doughty (1828);* 17 data pages (1965).*

Governor's Residence: Approx. 150' N.E. of Biddle Hall. Brick covered with coursed stucco, approx. 47' (three-bay front) × 100' including two-story rear kitchen wing, two stories with two-story front veranda supported by four pairs slender cast-iron columns, hipped roof, central-hall plan. Built 1844; William Strickland, architect. Kitchen remodeled later. 2 ext. photos (1964),* 3 int. photos (1964),* 1 photocopy of architect's drawing (1844);* 7 data pages (1965).*

Surgeon's Residence: Approx. 150' S.W. of Biddle Hall. Brick covered with coursed stucco, approx. 47' (three-bay front) × 100' including two-story rear kitchen wing, two stories with two-story front veranda supported by four pairs slender cast-iron columns, hipped roof, central-hall plan. Built 1844; William Strickland, architect. Interior altered later. 3 ext. photos (1964, including detail of iron railing);* 8 data pages (1965).*

Laning Hall: Approx. 400' N.W. (rear) of Biddle Hall. Brick with brownstone trim, approx. 325' (twenty-five-bay front) × 85', three stories on raised basement, mansard roof, center section with one-story balustraded porch and Flemish gables, lateral wings, brick quoins, central-hall plan. Built 1868; John McArthur, Jr., architect. Served as hospital 1868–1921; rehabilitated 1938. 2 ext. photos (1964),* 1 int. photo (1964);* 2 photocopies of old ext. photos (1908),* 4 photocopies of old int. photos (1938).*

United States Naval Base, Quarters "A" (also known as Commandant's Quarters)

(PA-1623), Davis Ave., approx. 100' W. of Broad St., near entrance to U. S. Naval Base, League Island. Museum. Brick, 34'-9" (five-bay front) × 38'-3" with two-story rear wing and one-story rear addition, two stories with three-story square corner tower, gable roofs, hipped roof on tower, second-story semi-octagonal bay window on east side, round-arch and segmental-arch windows, bracketed cornice, L-plan with attached wing and tower.

Late example of the Italian villa mode. Built 1874–75; porch added to north and east sides 1901; porch enclosed, porte-cochere and rear one-story brick laundry room built later; interior renovated 1960, 1975. Initially housed civil engineer in charge of developing the base, later Inspector of Ordnance; Commandant's Quarters 1900-1902, dwelling of Captain of the Yard 1903–60; Naval Historical

Museum since 1975. Pennsylvania Register 1975; NR. 1 ext. photo (1976).*

Weccacoe Engine Company No. 9. See Philadelphia Fire Department, Engine Company No. 3, and Patrol House

Wharton, John, Houses
(PA-1624), 919–21 S. Front St. Two brick row houses, each approx. 15' (two-bay front) × 33', two-and-a-half stories on raised basement, gable roof, London house plan, notable round-arch entrance with fanlight and pedimented frontispiece on No. 919. Built c. 1795; exterior of No. 921 renovated mid-19th century; demolished 1967. Certified, PHC 1957. 1 ext. photo (1961);* 7 data pages (1961, including 1812, 1848 insurance surveys);* 2 HABSI forms (1958).*

Wharton-Stewart House
(PA-1185), 27 Christian St. Brick, 13'-6" (one-bay front) × 19'-11", two-and-a-half stories, shed roof, hollow diamond of glazed brick on west exterior wall, originally pent eave along west wall, originally one room to a floor.
    Probably a back building built in expectation of a front building. Built between 1745 and 1774; demolished 1967. Certified, PHC 1963. 5 sheets (1966, including plot plan, plans, elevations, section, details); 2 / ext. photos (1966); 2 int. photos (c. 1965); 6 data pages (1960).*

Woolfall-Huddell House
(PA-1625), 9 Queen St. Brick with stone trim, approx. 21' (two-bay front) × 22' with two-story rear ell, two-and-a-half stories on raised basement, gable roof, city house plan. Built between 1763 and 1787; demolished 1967. Certified, PHC 1966. 3 ext. photos (1961, 1966);* 11 data pages (1964, including 1791 insurance survey).*

Workman Place
(PA-133), 742–46 S. Front St. and rear, at S.W. corner Pemberton St. Group of ten houses around a central courtyard, including three dwellings on Front St. built 1812–13 for John Workman, lumber merchant, and seven small tenements to the rear built 1748 for George Mifflin, grandfather of the first Governor of Pennsylvania. Variation of interior court plan by which early Philadelphians broke up large blocks into small living complexes. Owned by Workman

family 1812–1906 and by Octavia Hill Association since 1942. Certified, PHC 1957.

House, 742 S. Front St.: Brick with marble trim, approx. 17' (two-bay front) × 38', three-and-a-half stories, gable roof, side-hall London house plan. Built 1812. 6 data pages (1961, including 1812 insurance survey).*

Houses, 744–46 S. Front St.: Brick with marble trim, approx. 20' (three-bay front) × 38' with rear stair tower, three-and-a-half stories, gable roof, side-hall plan. Built 1812–13; No. 746 altered to store 1875, rehabilitated to dwelling after 1900. 2 ext. photos (1961, 1967);* 7 data pages (1960, including 1813–75 insurance surveys).*

Tenements 1–2 and 3–4, 110–12 Pemberton St., at rear of 742 S. Front St.: Brick, each approx. 17' (two-bay front) × 27', two-and-a-half stores, gable roof, originally one room to a floor, originally two tenements to a building, initials "GM" in black headers on north wall of Tenement 1–2, date "1748" in black headers on north wall of Tenement 3–4. Built 1748; Tenement 1–2 altered to single dwelling 1964. 6 ext. photos (1937, 1961*); 5 data pages (1937, 1961,* including 1850 insurance survey).

Tenement 5–6–7, rear of 744–46 S. Front St.: Brick, each approx. 13' (two-bay front) × 17' with two-story rear wing, two-and-a-half stories, half-gambrel roof, one room to a floor. Built 1748. 1 data page (including 1850 insurance survey).*

Gloria Dei. *Jack E. Boucher photo, 1962.*

Jesse Godley Warehouse. *Thomas M. Osborn, del., 1966.*

Nathaniel Irish House. *Michael Cunningham, del., 1966.*

Nathaniel Irish House, fireplace detail. *James L. Dillon & Co. photo, 1967.*

George Pearson Houses. *Jack E. Boucher photo, 1961.*

Ridgway Branch of Library Company of Philadelphia. *Jack E. Boucher photo, 1962.*

Philadelphia County Prison. *Oil painting by Thomas U. Walter, c. 1835, courtesy Historical Society of Pennsylvania.*

United States Naval Asylum, Surgeon's Residence. *Jack E. Boucher photo, 1964.*

West Philadelphia

Blockley and Kingsessing
Townships

5

Introduction

*K*NOWN AS BLOCKLEY Township and Kingsessing Township in the eighteenth century, West Philadelphia, that part of the city west of the Schuylkill River, was dotted with farms and estates, particularly along the banks of the river. Among the oldest of these buildings is Wynnestay at Fifty-second and Woodbine streets in the city's Wynnefield section.[1] Its two adjoining sections were built in 1689 and 1700 for Dr. Thomas Wynne, an early Quaker convert and missionary, who became William Penn's personal physician and accompanied the Founder to the province in 1682. The first structure was of modest proportions; a pent eave skirted its thick rubble-masonry walls and there was only one room to a floor.[2] With its later additions, however, Wynnestay assumed the appearance of a comfortable early Georgian Pennsylvania country house.[3]

"Of all the Georgian houses in the Philadelphia neighbourhood, none has more striking individuality than Whitby Hall,"[4] which once stood near the present intersection of Fifty-eighth Street and Baltimore Avenue, not far from Cobb's Creek. When Colonel James Coultas, a Philadelphia merchant and man of affairs, acquired his plantation in 1741, a house was apparently already there, but in 1754 he added to it the section commonly known as Whitby Hall.[5] It possessed an unusual combination of architectural elements and building practices. Unlike most country houses, all four of its exterior walls were constructed of coursed ashlar with blank end walls only one room deep.[6] Also, its ridgepole ran the breadth of the house instead of its length so that its gable walls formed the long sides of the building, a practice that was customary for city houses but rarely found in country houses. The stair-and-entry tower was almost cer-

193

tainly an afterthought. It was awkwardly abutted to the north gable end, interrupting the pent eave and cove cornice and overlapping onto a sash window and oculus in the peak. Yet it was a proud addition, pretentiously finished with brick-trimmed tracery windows on the second story, architrave-framed windows on the third floor, a dressed-stone stringcourse in between the floors, and a dentil cornice and three decorative urns at the top.[7] The interior elements were equally rich and more smoothly integrated. "Enrichment tempered with dignified reserve" was the conclusion of the English visitor Nicholas Pickford in 1765.[8] Early in this century the house was dismantled and parts of it were reassembled in nearby Haverford, Pennsylvania, in a manner that belies its former "striking individuality"; most of its interior woodwork was installed at the Detroit Institute of Art.[9]

Not far from the former site of Whitby Hall stands another unique country house that expresses even more directly its owner's personality. The famous naturalist John Bartram built the house in two stages, in 1730–31 and 1770, facing the Schuylkill near the former Darby Road (Woodland Avenue). Constructed of massive blocks of local stone in what a nineteenth-century historian called a "quaint, old-fashioned style of architecture,"[10] Bartram's house reflects the individuality of a Quaker farmer who bravely left both his personal and general callings to become a self-styled deist and botanist.[11] From a distance the house's most striking feature is its elongated Ionic columns, which with their thick irregularly spaced joints rise two stories to form a recessed porch; the second floor was apparently enclosed later with beaded tongue-and-groove siding to give the entrance a pinched quality. An additional touch of rustic grandeur is given by the carved stone crosset-and-volute window surrounds and the stone panels beneath the heavy sills, all of which are adapted from contemporary architectural design books.[12] Juxtaposed with this attempt at worldly sophistication is Bartram's self-conscious proclamation of religious independence; in a second-story stone panel is carved

IT IS GOD ALONE ALMYTY LORD
THE HOLY ONE BY ME ADORD
JOHN BARTRAM 1770.

It was the last word from a man who had lived a running religious debate with his neighbors and had been expelled from the

Darby Friends Meeting for denying the divinity of Jesus Christ.[13] Seven years later he died, leaving behind an impressive contribution to natural history, including the country's first botanical garden, which beginning in the 1920's has been restored by the John Bartram Association.

The grandest eighteenth-century country house of West Philadelphia is Woodlands (illus.). It was the seat of William Hamilton, who inherited the extensive estate along the Schuylkill near Fortieth Street and Woodland Avenue from his grandfather, Andrew Hamilton of Bush Hill, the eminent attorney and designer of Independence Hall. After tactfully sitting out the Revolution and narrowly avoiding the rebels' confiscation of his property, the Anglophile William Hamilton visited Britain and returned to Philadelphia about 1786 to plan an estate befitting the luxurious tastes of a wealthy and hospitable gentleman.[14] His gardens, one of the earliest examples of romantic landscaping in America,[15] have since disappeared, but the house remains as an outstanding American example of the Adamesque-Federal style. In fact, the perambulatory Englishman Nicholas Pickford visited the estate in 1786, and after praising the house's site, design, and appointments, he archly concluded, "I know of no house in England of like Estate where a greater degree of Elegancy and Comfort can be found."[16] In addition to the giant Ionic pilasters that grace the landside terrace and the giant Tuscan portico that faces the river, Hamilton's design incorporated the interplay of surfaces (the Palladian windows recessed within blind arches) and forms (the juxtaposition of the squarish library and study with the oval dining room and parlor, which protrude as exterior bays) that characterized the Adamesque style but was rarely so urbanely executed. After the property became the Woodlands Cemetery in 1843,[17] a caretaker occupied the mansion, and natural growth intruded into the gardens, enhancing the scene in the opinion of contemporaries.[18] Today gravestones and monuments fill the former gardens.

Blockley's rural isolation was broken by the completion of the Lancaster Turnpike in the 1790's and the opening of the Market Street Permanent Bridge on New Year's Day, 1805.[19] The area became increasingly attractive to gentlemen seeking sites for their country estates. They included both newcomers like Italian-born Paul Busti, who moved to his Retreat Farm near Forty-fourth Street and Haverford Avenue about 1799,[20] and established Philadelphians like John Hare Powel, who moved into and renovated Powelton, which had been begun in 1800 near Thirty-second and Race streets.[21] The growth of rural hamlets in the township and small industry along the river, however, began to engulf these estates by mid-century. About 1804 William Hamilton of Woodlands laid out Hamilton Village, which extended north from the Schuylkill to Market Street and west to Forty-first Street.[22] It became an early suburban town and before the Civil War was considered one of the most pleasant villages in the Philadelphia area.[23] About the same time along Haverford Avenue and Spring Garden Street west of the river Judge Richard Peters planned Mantua, whose development was stimulated by the building of the Upper Ferry Bridge in 1812.[24] Thirty-two years later, in 1844, the Philadelphia gentleman George Sidney Fisher visited the neighborhood to view Powelton, which was finally nearing completion. While he praised the house's architecture, he concluded with some regret that "Mr. Powel was foolish to build it. . . . If it were 10 miles from town it would be a delightful residence, but it looks on the coal wharves and mass of brick buildings on the other side of the river & is so near the city that it is constantly liable to trespass & intrusion."[25]

It was during the second quarter of the nineteenth century, while John Hare Powel was overimproving Powelton, that social and charitable institutions began moving into West Philadelphia. The first of these was Blockley Almshouse, designed by William Strickland. Begun in 1830 as a group of four three-story buildings arranged around a large interior courtyard, its grimly gray presence contradicted the optimism and good will that had created it.[26] Beginning in the 1820's the presence of poor people in the midst of a self-consciously democratic and prosperous America posed a challenge, if not an embarrassment, to concerned citizens. Reformers claimed that primary among the roots of poverty were the temptations of a dynamic society in which physical mobility and concomitant urban growth had undermined traditional social sanctions and responsibilities. To remove the indigent from the evils of society and place them in an almshouse where they could be rehabilitated and comforted was thought to be not only humane but also enlightened and practical.[27] Furthermore, if the purpose was to remove the destitute from society, then the farther away they were the better, which accounted for the isolation of Blockley Almshouse on extensive grounds bordering the Schuylkill River south of Thirty-third and Spruce streets.

As the almshouse was being completed, another institution moved to West Philadelphia. Pennsylvania Hospital, which had been caring for the insane since 1794, reflected the enlightened opinion of the times when it was decided in 1831 to build separate quarters for the insane outside the city.[28] The insane asylum of the 1830's and 1840's was not considered a warehouse for lunatics or a last resort for the mentally ill, but a humane institution where psychiatrists were confident mental and nervous disorders could be cured. This confidence was based on the theory that a turbulent and treacherous society caused insanity, and to cure the disease the victim must be removed to a controlled, disciplined environment. The asylum was to be this curative retreat. The problem, however, was to translate psychiatric theory into architectural form. Medical theory dictated the hospital's hundred-acre site on the city's outskirts, since it was argued that if the afflicted must be removed from the anxieties of daily life to the ordered confines of the asylum, then the asylum, in turn, must be removed from the commotion of the community to the tranquility of the countryside.[29] The orthodox plan of the asylum, however, was not fixed until 1836, when the English-trained Isaac Holden won the architectural competition for the Pennsylvania Hospital for Mental and Nervous Diseases (illus.).[30] A pioneer structure of the nineteenth century, it stood near Forty-fourth and Market streets on Paul Busti's former estate. It was the first American hospital built on the echelon, or pavilion-plus-link, plan, a scheme of sprawling attached wings that afforded the best compromise of isolation and communication with a minimal staff.[31] The technical problems of heating and fire prevention led to the installation of twenty-six steam-boiler furnaces and maximum utilization of iron—for columns, stairs, door frames, and window sashes. It is not clear how instrumental Dr. Thomas Story Kirkbride was in deciding the building's plan and appointments, but he certainly became a dedicated booster of the arrangement after he became the asylum's superintendent on its opening in January, 1841. The plan, known as the Pennsylvania School of Hospital Design, was adopted for both insane asylums and general hospitals throughout the United States until after the Civil War.[32]

Other hospitals were erected in the neighborhood during the third quarter of the nineteenth century, but because of their small beginnings, none followed the Pennsylvania School of Hospital Design. The brownstone structure of Christ Church Hospital, which was established in 1772 as a home for the aged, was built from the designs of John M. Gries in 1856–61 on Belmont Plateau near Belmont Avenue and Forty-ninth Street, where its residents could enjoy cool summer

breezes and rural scenery. Presbyterian Hospital began in 1872 at
Thirty-ninth Street and Powelton Avenue, using two houses that had
been renovated for hospital purposes. Its first hospital building, a
modest one-story ward pavilion designed by Joseph M. Wilson, was
ready in 1874, the year that the Hospital of the University of Pennsylvania opened its more extensive facilities at Thirty-fourth and Spruce
streets.[33] In the last quarter of the nineteenth century a number of institutions were established in West Philadelphia, including the Home
for Incurables at Forty-seventh Street and Woodland Avenue, Home
for Indigent Widows and Single Women at Chestnut near Thirty-
sixth Street, Pennsylvania Working Home for the Blind at Thirty-
sixth and Lancaster Avenue, and most notably the Pennsylvania Institution for the Instruction of the Blind (illus.), whose complex was
built from the designs of Cope and Stewardson at the end of the
century.[34]

During the half-century after the opening of the Market Street
Bridge, Blockley's economy shifted from agriculture to manufacturing
and commerce, and its population grew from a meager 882 inhabitants in 1790 to 6,214 by 1840. Consequently, in 1840 the Borough
of West Philadelphia was carved out of Blockley Township by the
Court of Quarter Sessions, but since its legality was questioned, the
process was repeated four years later by the General Assembly. As
the population of the combined borough and township continued to
grow, nearly doubling during the 1840's, the borough's area was approximately tripled in 1852. Kingsessing, on the other hand,
remained rural. In 1840 more than three-fourths of its people were
engaged in farming, and a decade later it possessed fewer than 1,800
inhabitants. Under the Act of Consolidation in 1854, however, the
two townships and borough lost their separate identities, if not their
distinctions, and became the Twenty-fourth Ward of the City of
Philadelphia.[35]

Shortly after the Act of Consolidation, street railways came to
West Philadelphia, and during the next twenty years eleven different
companies established a recticular complex of horse-powered railways over large parts of the area,[36] helping to make it one of the city's
most fashionable suburbs. The model for the antebellum houses that
went up along the horsecar lines was Bartram Hall, Andrew M. East-
wick's nationally known picturesque villa designed by Sloan and
Stewart in 1850–51 on the former site of John Bartram's botanical
gardens.[37] Part of Bartram Hall's visual impact derived from its great
scale and superb site, but part also came from its style, a free adapta-

tion of the Italian villa, whose cubic volumes and projecting towers
best complemented the cultivated rusticity of the area.[38] Its medieval
details, such as a battlemented bay window and free use of corbel ta-
bles, led the architects to call Bartram Hall a "Norman villa." More
common to the area, however, were the flat, bracketed towers and
cornices of the "Tuscan villa," like that of the noted medieval historian Henry Charles Lea (illus.) at 3903 Spruce Street. These towers
were more than picturesque ornaments. The four-story tower of Lea's
house, for example, served as the entrance foyer, walk-in closets on
the upper floors, and a bathroom on the second floor. The well-
furnished bathroom, one of two on the floor, was a mark of the
owner's affluence. In addition to a walnut bathtub lined with
planished copper and fitted with a shower, each bathroom had a cop-
per-lined bidet, a reservoir water closet, and a marble washbasin with
marble skirting.[39] Functional as they may have been, towers were not
mandatory for Italian villas. The proportions, details, and comfortable interior spaces of the style could be attained without towers or
belvederes, as in the case of Samuel Sloan's 1854 design for Joseph
Allison's house at 4207 Walnut Street.[40] Yet towers remained popular
and were retained when the mansard mode came into fashion after
the Civil War.

Block developments also appeared in the wake of the street railways. Again instrumental in setting the pattern was Samuel Sloan,
who in 1854 designed Hamilton Terrace, a group of five villas on
Forty-first Street below Baltimore Avenue.[41] More extensive and better preserved is Woodland Terrace (illus.), which was built between
Baltimore and Woodland avenues on the eve of the Civil War. These
two early terrace developments of large semidetached dwellings
helped to establish the hierarchical pattern of speculative row housing that was followed throughout the century. This was a status-
conscious plan in which the most expensive and picturesque houses
occupied the best sites on corner lots or major thoroughfares, with
lesser edifices filling in the middle of the rows or side streets. This
plan offered monumentality that was not to be had from a continuous
row of identical houses, a more democratic but more monotonous
plan. Similar brownstone dwellings continued to be built in the
neighborhood into the 1860's, but, since most horsecar lines stopped
at Forty-third Street, these developments rarely extended west of
Forty-fifth Street during the nineteenth century.[42] Plenty of open
land, however, remained in West Philadelphia east of Forty-fifth
Street, where as late as the 1890's architects designed many hand-

some houses, such as Wilson Eyre's chaste facade for William Cochran's house at 3511 Baring Street, the Wilson Brothers' Renaissance Revival dwelling for George W. Childs Drexel at Thirty-ninth and Locust, and Will Decker's rusticated Romanesque pile for William J. Swain at 3925 Chestnut Street.[43]

The advent of the automobile after 1900 and the opening of the Market Street Elevated in the spring of 1907 ignited another wave of speculative developments. Instead of the commodious double houses and distinctive mansions of the old streetcar suburb, the West Philadelphia of the auto and Elevated was to be row upon interminable row of two-story dwellings with bay windows set above columned front porches.[44] Apartment buildings, a relatively new housing alternative, were also built near the El, especially in the older parts of West Philadelphia. Hamilton Court, designed by Wilson Brothers and Company in 1901 at Thirty-ninth and Chestnut streets, was one of the area's earliest apartment buildings, but one of the largest was the twelve-story Garden Court Plaza at Forty-sixth and Spruce streets. Built during the late 1920's from the designs of Ralph B. Bencker, it was an up-to-date complex whose parking garage and special radio antenna anticipated future trends. Its name derived from the garden that covered most of the garage's roof.[45] Recent decades have brought updated versions of the row house, either speculative units such as University Mews at Forty-sixth and Spruce streets, or public housing, of which the best example is Louis Kahn's Mill Creek project on Fairmount Avenue between Forty-fourth and Forty-seventh streets.[46]

West Philadelphia's great event after the Civil War was the celebration of the nation's one-hundredth birthday at the International Exhibition of 1876 in nearby Fairmount Park. In an attempt to capitalize on the event, street railways were built in the Park area for the first time, setting off a small real estate boom in the blocks adjacent to the Park. To accommodate the increased traffic, the Pennsylvania Railroad built a new station at Thirty-second and Market streets, and until the Broad Street Station opened in 1881 it remained a major terminal for trains to New York and the West. Most of the physical evidence of the exhibition's direct impact on the area disappeared long ago. The railroad station burned in 1896, and those horsecar lines that did not collapse after the centennial rush were electrified in the 1890's before being integrated into a single urban transit system in 1902.[47] Only Frank Furness's chunky Centennial National Bank at Thirty-second and Market streets remains as a remainder of those fleeting glorious days.

A more lasting impression has been made by the growth of some of the city's great educational institutions. The oldest of these is the University of Pennsylvania, which moved from Ninth and Market streets to Thirty-sixth Street and Woodland Avenue in 1871.[48] Beginning with Thomas W. Richards, who designed College Hall in 1871, the University of Pennsylvania has employed a Who's Who of collegiate architects. The list includes such nineteenth-century greats as Frank Furness, the Victorian Goth who created the massive Library in 1888; Wilson Eyre, Jr., who, in collaboration with Frank Miles Day and Cope and Stewardson during the 1890's, designed the city's finest Creative Eclectic building, the University Museum (illus.); and Cope and Stewardson, who were already famous for their Collegiate Gothic works at Bryn Mawr and Princeton when in 1895 they employed the Jacobethan to produce "a series of architectural adventures" in the Men's Dormitories (illus.) at Pennsylvania.[49] The campus enjoyed another period of expansion after World War II to make its architecture even more diverse. Among the notable names and works of the later era are Eero Saarinen's fortresslike Hill House, with its festive and spacious interior court (1958–60), Mitchell/ Giurgola Associates' monumental poured-concrete parking garage at Thirty-second and Walnut streets (1963), and the great Louis I. Kahn's Alfred Newton Richards Medical Research Building (1957–61), which has been called "one of the greatest buildings of modern times."[50]

Twenty years after the university's arrival in West Philadelphia, Drexel Institute of Art, Science, and Industry became a neighbor. Now called Drexel University, it was founded in 1890 by Anthony J. Drexel, one of the nation's leading bankers, to provide a practical industrial education for young people. It opened its doors at Thirty-second and Chestnut Streets in 1892 after the dedication of its main building, an impressive exercise in terra cotta detailing and interior spatial planning by Wilson Brothers and Company.[51] It remains a *tour de force* of academic architecture that Drexel has not matched in the past eighty-five years. Only two dormitories on Thirty-third Street offer competition: Grant Simon's thirteen-story Sarah Drexel Van Rensselaer Dormitory (1930–31) on Powelton Avenue and Vincent G. Kling's Calhoun Hall (1970–71), with its concave facade on Arch Street.[52]

St. Joseph's College is a relative newcomer to West Philadelphia. It moved to its twenty-three-acre campus west of Fifty-fourth Street and City Line Avenue in suburban Wynnefield during the late 1920's, a time of expansion and migration for a number of the city's colleges.

As a small school with initially only one building (a notable Collegiate Gothic pile begun in 1925 by F. Ferdinand Durang) on a large campus, St. Joe's had minimal impact on its residential neighborhood.[53] The college grew rapidly during the flush years of the 1960's, and most of its open space has since been filled in.

As the city pushed westward along the transit system during the early twentieth century, the neighborhood surrounding Drexel and Pennsylvania lost its suburban charm, and with the concomitant stagnation and blight of the Great Depression evolved into a no-man's-land. West of Forty-fifth Street stretched the rows of houses and east of Thirty-second Street stood the encroachments of the commercial city, most notably the Thirtieth Street Station and the new Bulletin Building.[54] Between the two lay a decaying strip occupied by poor residents, the academic institutions, and roving gangs of hoodlum youths. In an effort to reverse the trend and to enable the area's institutions to execute their planned physical expansion smoothly, the West Philadelphia Corporation was formed in 1959 to work with the Redevelopment Authority and the City Planning Commission.[55] Out of this cooperative effort has evolved a learning and research complex, which includes the two adjacent universities, other nearby institutions, and the new University City Science Center along Market Street. It has substantially restructured the neighborhood, as dwellings have been replaced by institutional high-rises. The area's new name, University City, is visually, socially, and economically appropriate. Nevertheless, nooks and crannies of nineteenth-century West Philadelphia have survived. One of them, north of Lancaster Avenue, is Powelton Village, which is gamely trying to resist Drexel's growth.[56] Another is Spruce Hill, which includes a number of pleasant residential streets like St. Mark's Square. In these remnants of the affluent post–Civil War suburb many mansions, large semidetached houses, and revival style churches[57] still stand on tree-lined streets, handsomely illustrating this stage of Philadelphia's growth.

Catalog

Academic Department of the University of Pennsylvania. See University of Pennsylvania, College Hall

Bartram, John, House

(PA-1132), Bartram Park, S. Fifty-fourth St. between Elmwood and Gibson aves. Historic house museum. Coursed ashlar front and stuccoed rubble sides and rear, approx. 49' (four-bay front) × 27' with one-story lateral wings, two-and-a-half stories, gable roof, full-height Ionic stone columns form recessed porch, carved stone window trim, quoins, center entry room with stairs.

Notable example of Pennsylvania stone house with characteristic exterior door to each room but with unique detailing. Built 1730–31; extended eastward one-room depth c. 1770; wings built later; second story of porch enclosed later; restored 1923–25. House and gardens acquired by Fairmount Park Commission, City of Philadelphia 1891. John Bartram, America's first internationally known botanist, built house and lived here 1731–77. Certified, PHC 1956; designated National Historic Landmark 1960.

8 sheets (1940, including plans, elevation, section) from Survey, Philadelphia Charter, A.I.A. (1932); 4 ext. photos (1938), 7 photocopies of measured drawings (n.d.).*

Bleakley House (also known as Cannon Ball Farm House)

(PA-134), Mud Island, approx. 350' W. of Delaware River, approx. 150' N. of north sallyport of Fort Mifflin (originally on Penrose Ferry Rd., approx. 0.5 mi. S.W. of Schuylkill River, approx. 1.24 mi. N.W. of Delaware River, in Southwest Sewage Treatment Works). Brick,

19'-4" (three-bay front) × 36'-10³/₄", two-and-a-half stories on raised basement, jerkin-head roof with pent eave across gable ends, originally pent eave or porch across rear at second story, unusually large chimney on north end, originally two rooms to a floor with corner fireplaces.

A rare surviving example of Philadelphia's characteristic early architecture. Built between 1714 and 1720; side addition with gable roof built later; interior gutted by fire 1947; house moved to present site, side addition demolished 1975. Site of British batteries during siege of Mud Fort (later Fort Mifflin) 1777, when American cannon ball pierced front and back walls. Acquired by City of Philadelphia 1910, Southwest Sewage Treatment Works built around original site of house 1949–54. Certified, PHC 1956. 10 sheets (1940, including plans, elevations, details); 6 ext. photos (1937, 1940); 1 data page (1937).

Blockley Retreat Farm. See Busti Mansion

Blue Bell Tavern
(PA-131), 7303 Woodland Ave., at N.W. corner Park Rd., approx. 170' E. of Cobbs Creek. Coursed rough-hewn fieldstone front, rubble sides and rear with galleting, approx. 18' (two-bay front) × 26' with one-story rubble rear ell with galleting, two stories, gable roof, date stone with initials "HP" on front, open wooden front and side porch. Built 1766. Three-and-a-half-story, five-bay rubble addition built 1801, demolished 1941. Since tavern served as southern gateway to city, George Washington stopped here often; site of his first welcome to Philadelphia as president-elect and his last farewell to city. Acquired by Fairmount Park Commission, City of Philadelphia 1913. Certified, PHC 1958. 2 ext. photos (1936), 10 photocopies of measured drawings (1916);* 2 data pages (1937).

Burnham, George, House. Illustrated
(PA-1627), 3401 Powelton Ave., at N.W. corner Thirty-fourth St. Random rough-faced granite with carved and dressed sandstone trim, approx. 40' (three-bay front) × 45' with two-story rear wing, two-and-a-half stories on raised basement, hipped and gable roofs with cross-gable, ridge cresting, one rear and three corner porches, balcony above one-story entry porch and vestibule, side vestibule and lateral entry hall to stairhall, notable interior woodwork.

Example of suburban domestic architecture by a popular late-19th-century Philadelphia architect. Built 1886; Theophilus Parsons

Chandler, Jr., architect. Corner porches enclosed 1952. Until 1910 the home of George Burnham, senior partner in the Baldwin Locomotive Works, America's foremost manufacturer of locomotives. Drexel University fraternity house since 1967. Certified, PHC 1959. 2 ext. photos (1973).*

Burnside. See Hamilton-Hoffman House

Busti Mansion (also known as Blockley Retreat Farm, later as Kirkbride Mansion)
(PA-1628), Approx. 300' S. of Haverford Ave. at E. side Forty-Fourth St. on grounds of Institute of the Pennsylvania Hospital. Brick with marble trim, approx. 54' (five-bay front) × 38', two-and-a-half stories, gambrel roof with balustrade, originally open one-story porch on south side and one-bay entrance portico on north side, center-hall plan.

Fine Federal-style country house that survived urban expansion. Built 1794; two-story wing on north side built before 1908, removed 1960; porch on south side removed 1960. Italian-born Paul Busti, General Agent of Holland Land Co. and founder of Buffalo, N.Y., lived here 1799–1826. Property purchased by Pennsylvania Hospital 1836 and served as residence of Dr. Thomas S. Kirkbride, mental hospital superintendent, 1841–83. Acquired by City of Philadelphia 1957 as recreation building and caretaker's residence. Certified, PHC 1956.

3 ext. photos (1958),* 5 int. photos (1958),* 1 photocopy of old watercolor (c. 1820);* 11 data pages (including 1806–1908 insurance surveys).*

Cannon Ball Farm House. See Bleakley House

Centennial National Bank
(PA-1095), 3142 Market St., at S.E. corner Thirty-second St. (and originally Woodland Ave., since closed). Brick with sandstone and black brick trim, approx. 48' (angled three-bay front) × 92', two stories on raised basement (originally one-story interior with two-story facade), hipped and gable roofs, projecting angled entrance bay with squat columnettes and pediment at roof line with crockets and trefoil design enclosing clock, pinched-top windows on ground story, pointed-arch windows on second story.

A landmark work whose three-sided front related to a former three-street intersection and whose design marked a significant development in Frank Furness's style. Built 1876; Frank Furness, architect. Interior altered 1893. Interior remodeled, rear addition built 1899; Frank Miles Day and Bro., architects. Interior altered, exterior simplified 1956; Budd Ross, architect. Branch bank of First Pennsylvania Banking and Trust Co. since 1956. Certified, PHC 1966; Pennsylvania Register 1970; NR. 3 sheets (1965, including plot plan, elevations);* 1 ext. photo (1960).*

College Hall. See University of Pennsylvania, College Hall

Columbia Engine Company
(PA-1629), 3420 Market St. Brick with marble trim, approx. 25' (three-bay front) × 115', three stories, flat roof, round-arch windows at second story, segmental-arch windows at third story, rectangular plan. Built 1867; demolished c. 1969. Built for West Philadelphia Engine Co. but occupied by Columbia Engine Co. 1868–71. 1 photocopy of old ext. photo (c. 1935).*

Cottage
(PA-138), 5901 Woodland Ave. Wood frame with clapboards (gable ends covered with tar paper), 20'-4" (three-bay front) × 14'-2" with one-story rear ell, one-and-a-half stories, gable roof, open front porch, one room with corner winding stairs. Built probably 18th century; rear ell built later; demolished c. 1956. 4 sheets (1940, including plans, elevations, details); 1 ext. photo (1940).

Drexel Institute, Main Building (now Drexel University)
(PA-1630), N.E. corner Thirty-second and Chestnut sts. Museum. Buff brick with rusticated granite basement and terra cotta trim, approx. 200' (eleven-bay front) × 200', three and four stories on raised basement, flat roof, richly decorated giant arched entrance with terra cotta portrait medallions on intrados and statue of Genius of Knowledge on keystone, giant Ionic pilasters, spacious marble entrance hall and large multilevel arcaded central court open to skylight.

Impressive interior space and exterior ornament on a notable late-19th-century academic building. Built 1890–91; Wilson Brothers & Co., architects; Charles McCaul, contractor; terra cotta by New York Architectural Terra Cotta Works. Three-story buff brick and terra cotta Randell Hall built at east end 1901–2; Wilson Brothers & Co., architects; John R. Wiggins, contractor. Drexel Institute was founded 1890 by prominent banker and philanthropist Anthony J.

Drexel to promote technical and vocational education; later known as Drexel Institute of Technology, name changed to Drexel University 1970. Houses Drexel Museum Collection. 3 ext. photos (1973),* 1 photocopy of architectural rendering (1901).*

Fort Mifflin. Illustrated

(PA-1225), Mud Island, W. bank of Delaware River, 0.76 mi. below confluence of Schuylkill and Delaware rivers. Gneiss and brick walls with earth fill, major axis approx. 530', surrounded by moat, flanked by redoubts and demilune, entered from any of three sallyports, wall 11' to 12' high, topped by earthen parapets and bullnose coping, 4' revetments or interior parapet wall, section includes terre plein and ramparts with central parade; star fort plan-type, most gun emplacements along S.W. and S.E. walls, bombproofs beneath east bastion.

Built c. 1772–c. 1798; portion of original stone wall still standing. Certified, PHC 1956; Pennsylvania Register 1970; designated National Historic Landmark 1970. 4 sheets (1970, 1971, including plan, site and location maps, gun emplacement details, bombproof details, wall sections); 18 aerial photos (1970), 6 general view photos (1969, 1970), 4 photos of walls (1970), 11 photos of bombproofs (1969), 5 photos of gun emplacements (1969, 1970), 2 photos of flagpole base (1969), 1 photo of date stone (1969), 1 photo of gun carriage (1969), 27 photos of old maps and views (1777, 1864–66, early 1900's, USGS map 1967, and several n.d.); 3 data pages (1971).

Fort Mifflin, Smith's Shop (PA-1226), Mud Island, W. bank of Delaware river, 0.76 mi. below confluence of Schuylkill and Delaware Rivers. Brick, 22'-8" × 19'-3", one story, gable roof with cornice returns at ends; rectangular one-room plan with herringbone brick flooring, brick and stone forge at S.W. end wall. Built before 1802; restored 1969. 4 sheets (1969, including plan, roof-framing plan, elevations, section, details); 5 ext. photos (1969, 1970, 1971), 5 int. photos (1969, 1970); 2 data pages (1971).

Fort Mifflin, Soldiers' Barracks (also known as Enlisted Men's Barracks) (PA-1227), Mud Island, W. bank of Delaware River, 0.76 mi. below confluence of Schuylkill and Delaware rivers. Brick, 117'-0" (eight-bay front) × 35'-1", two stories, gable roof (superimposed over gambrel roof) with shed roof over one-story colonnade along facade, three gabled dormers on either face of roof; rectangular plan, massive fireplaces of brick and stone. Built before 1800. 5 sheets (1969, including plans, elevations, section, details); 10 ext. photos (1969, 1970), 2 int. photos (1969, 1970); 2 data pages (1971).

Fort Mifflin, Officers' Quarters (PA-1228), Mud Island, W. bank of Delaware River, 0.76 mi. below confluence of Schuylkill and Delaware rivers. Brick, 80'-10" (six-bay front) × 19'-6½", two stories, gable roof with shed roof over two-story porch on facade, colonnaded porch with gallery, iron gallery rail in trellis pattern and iron strap supports for second floor of porch; rectangular plan, row of four rooms on each floor. Built c. 1814; later alterations. 6 sheets (1969, including plans, elevations, sections, details); 12 ext. photos (1969, 1970), 2 int. photos (1970); 2 data pages (1971).

Fort Mifflin, Arsenal (PA-1229), Mud Island, W. bank of Delaware River, 0.76 mi. below confluence of Schuylkill and Delaware rivers. Brick, 4' thick walls, 44'-2" (three-bay side) × 24'-2" (one-bay front), one story, gable roof with east and west walls parapeted, three circular openings on east and west sides with recessed panels above on east side, metal grilles within six circular openings; rectangular two-room plan, openings that are circular on exterior become arched with flat sills to receive rectangular window sashes on interior. Built c. 1816; later alterations. 2 sheets (1970, including plan, elevations, section, isometric detail); 2 ext. photos (1969), 2 int. photos (1969); 2 data pages (1971).

Fort Mifflin, Storehouse (also known as Commissary) (PA-1230), Mud Island, W. bank of Delaware River, 0.76 mi. below confluence of Schuylkill and Delaware rivers. Brick, 55'-8½" (six-bay front) × 20'-4", one story, gable roof, originally one room open to rafters. Built between 1839 and 1851; renovated early 1960's. 2 sheets (1970, including plan, elevations, section); 3 ext. photos (1969, 1970); 2 data pages (1971).

Fort Mifflin, Artillery Shed (PA-1231), Mud Island, W. bank of Delaware River, 0.76 mi. below confluence of Schuylkill and Delaware rivers. Brick on three sides with projecting rubble foundations 1' above grade, original open facade of monolithic gneiss columns, frame addition to facade covered with boards and tar paper, 97'-0" (nine-bay front) × 36'-9", one story with interior deck, hipped roof with shed roof over porch addition, cornice returns on ends of porch; rectangular one-room plan, herringbone brick flooring, wooden deck 7' above floor with hoist. Built c. 1837; later additions and alterations. 5 sheets (1970, including plan, elevations, sections, details); 2 ext. photos (1969, 1970), 5 int. photos (1969); 2 data pages (1971).

Fort Mifflin, Commandant's House (also known as Headquarters) (PA-1232), Mud Island, W. bank of Delaware River, 0.76 mi. below confluence of Schuylkill and Delaware rivers. Stuccoed brick, 70'-2½" (seven-bay front) × 34'-5", one-and-a-half stories, low hipped roof (superimposed over original steep hipped roof), rectangular pavilion on S.E. side of house, octagonal wood cupola with bell-shaped roof, stuccoed pilasters define bays, heavy entablature of cor-beled brick; rectangular plan with two-room pavilion, transverse hall between four-room group with central chimney stack and two-room suite with back-to-back fireplaces. Built c. 1796; later alterations and additions. 8 sheets (1970, including plans, elevations, details); 7 ext. photos (1969), 21 int. photos (1969, 1970); 3 data pages (1971).

Fort Mifflin, Mess House (also known as Hospital) (PA-1233), Mud Island, W. bank of Delaware River, 0.76 mi. below confluence of Schuylkill and Delaware rivers. Brick, 49'-6" (five-bay front) × 27'-4", two stories, gable roof with shed roof over two-story porch on facade, colonnaded porch with gallery, rectangular plan. Built c. 1819; many later alterations. 6 sheets (1970, including plans, elevations, section, details); 3 ext. photos (1969); 2 data pages (1971).

Fort Mifflin, Magazines (PA-1234), Mud Island, W. bank of Dela-ware River, 0.76 mi. below confluence of Schuylkill and Delaware rivers. Includes East and West magazines inside fort, above and below grade magazines in demilune, and below grade and Mortar Magazines in post–Civil War Redoubts; East and West magazines recorded in detail.

Concrete East Magazine with vault 128'-1" × 16'-0¼", brick West Magazine with valut 43'-2" × 15'-1", both magazines: one story, bar-rel-vaulted, beneath earthen mounds 20' high, stepped brick retain-ing walls and heavy semicircular-arched doors at entries, offset passages lead to vaults of rectangular plans. West Magazine built c. 1867; East Magazine built c. 1872–86. 3 sheets for East and West magazines (1970, including plans, elevations, sections); for all magazines, 6 ext. photos (1969, 1970, 1971), 7 int. photos (1969, 1970, 1971); 2 data pages (1971).

Fort Mifflin, Northeast Sallyport (PA-1235), Mud Island, W. bank of Delaware River, 0.76 mi. below confluence of Schuylkill and Delaware rivers. Now principal entrance to fort, passage approx. 10'-9" × 42'-6" including retaining walls, runs through N.E. brick curtain wall beneath parapet, barrel vault 9' high, guard rooms to either side with embrasures to exterior of wall, retaining walls extend beyond face of vault as supports against earth ramparts. Massive iron hardware, 6" thick double doors set in frame within semicircular arch, herringbone brick paving. Built c. 1779–98. 4 sheets (1970, including plan, elevation, section, details); 1 ext. photo (1969), 4 int. photos (1969); 1 data page (1971).

Fort Mifflin, Southeast Sallyport (originally known as Main Gate)

(PA-1236), Mud Island, W. bank of Delaware River, 0.76 mi. below confluence of Schuylkill and Delaware rivers. Stone and brick entrance near east bastion, solid brick wall 9' thick with elliptical arched opening 14'-6" high, splayed on interior side, 18' from parade to top of wall, massive double doors framed into arched opening, exterior faced with chamfered gneiss, walkway over entry raised from level of surrounding wall, retaining wall 7' high and 41'-6" long extending from sallyport toward interior of fort for support of adjacent ramparts. Building begun before 1802, completed 1807. 1 ext. photo (1969), 3 int. photos (1969).

Fort Mifflin, Northwest Sallyport (PA-1237), Mud Island, W. bank of Delaware River, 0.76 mi. below confluence of Schuylkill and Delaware rivers. Brick, T-shaped plan including guard rooms to either side of passage, exterior brick masking, barrel-vaulting, retaining walls extending to interior, passage from exterior of scarp curtain wall to ramparts and beneath parapet, massive double doors set in framing of semicircular arch. Built c. 1779–98. 1 ext. photo (1969), 3 int. photos (1969).

Furness Building. See University of Pennsylvania, Library

George House
(PA-1631), 6099 Drexel Rd., at S.E. corner City Line Ave. Stuccoed rubble, approx. 50' (five-bay front) × 15' with two-and-a-half-story rear ell, two-and-a-half stories, gable roof, open columned front porch. Built in three stages during 18th century; altered later; demolished 1958. HABSI form (1958).*

Hamilton-Hoffman House (also known as Burnside)
(PA-1053), N.E. corner Cobbs Creek Parkway and Sixty-first St. Stuccoed rubble, approx. 40' (five-bay front) × 30' with one- and two-story lateral wings (southwestern and northeastern ends respectively), two-and-a-half stories, gable roof, open front and back porches; center-hall plan, elaborate interior trim, carved Federal-style mantels.

Fine example of early-19th-century country estate. Built between 1791 and 1800; porches built c. 1880; two-story wing added later. Demolished 1960. Living-room mantelpiece given to Philadelphia Museum of Art; other woodwork given to St. Peter's Protestant Episcopal Church, Philadelphia. Gavin Hamilton, Jr., was a prominent snuff merchant; Hamilton family owned house from 1832. 2 ext.

photos (1959), 10 int. photos (1959), 1 photocopy of old ext. photo (c. 1890); 8 data pages (1960).

Institute of the Pennsylvania Hospital. See Pennsylvania Hospital for the Insane, Department for Males

Justi, Henry D., House
(PA-1632), 3401 Baring St., at N.W. corner Thirty-fourth St. Random granite ashlar, approx. 45' (five-bay front) × 35' with three-story stuccoed rear ell and one-story lateral rear wing, two-and-a-half stories on raised basement with square three-story corner tower, gable roof with mansard roof on rear ell, open front porch, and semi-hexagonal front bay window, entry in tower with side stairhall.

Example of suburban villas erected in West Philadelphia after the Civil War. Built c. 1867; rear ell built c. 1875; lateral wing and front porch built c. 1890. Home for displaced children since 1922. Henry D. Justi, a manufacturer of artificial teeth and dental instruments, lived here 1867–1922. 2 ext. photos (1963);* 1 data page (1962).*

Kirkbride Mansion. See Busti Mansion

Kirkbride's. See Pennsylvania Hospital for Mental and Nervous Diseases

Lea, Professor Henry Charles, House. Illustrated
(PA-1633), 3903 Spruce St. Stuccoed brick, approx. 50' (five-bay front) × 55', three stories with square four-story corner tower, flat roof with carved brackets, open balustraded semicircular and rectangular porches, ground-story side bays, quoins; entrance foyer in tower with adjacent stairhall, excellent Italianate interior detailing.

Notable example of Italianate suburban villa. Built c. 1857; demolished 1969. Home of internationally known historian and prominent local publisher, Henry Charles Lea, 1857–69; University of Pennsylvania fraternity house 1924–68. Certified, PHC 1962. 3 ext. photos (1968);* 14 int. photos (1968).*

Mount Moriah Cemetery Gate House. Illustrated
(PA-1634), 6299 Kingsessing Ave., at N.E. corner Cemetery Ln. Connecticut brownstone ashlar, approx. 80' × 30' with one-story stuccoed stone side wings, two buildings connected by triple arcade gateway, each two stories, flat roof (originally hipped) with front

corner turrets on southern building, gable roof with Flemish cross-gables on northern building, battlements and urns.

Early picturesque eclectic design. Built 1855; Stephen D. Button, architect; A. H. Ransom, stone builder. Octagonal battlemented tower on southern building and statuary over gateway removed, side wings built later. 5 ext photos (1975).*

Museum of Science and Art. See University of Pennsylvania, University Museum

Overbrook School for the Blind. See Pennsylvania Institution for the Instruction of the Blind

Pennsylvania Hospital for the Insane, Department for Males (now Institute of the Pennsylvania Hospital)

(PA-1635), 111 N. Forty-ninth St. Stuccoed rubble with granite trim, approx. 470' (thirty-three-bay front) × 225' with two flanking rear one-story E-plan wings, three stories with central dome, gable roofs with cross-gables, Doric tetrastyle portico with flat pediment, two octagonal belvederes each on north and south end buildings, triple E-plan with central hall and intersecting corridors.

Fine example of the "Kirkbride System," a plan to increase individual attention to patients and total operational efficiency; originated by Dr. Thomas S. Kirkbride, hospital superintendent 1841–83, and designed by Samuel Sloan, prominent mid-19th-century architect. Built 1856–59; Samuel Sloan, architect; John Sunderland, superintendent of construction. Enlarged 1929, 1931. Certified, PHC 1957; designated National Historic Landmark 1965. 2 ext. photos (1973),* 12 data pages (including 1861–1908 insurance surveys).*

Pennsylvania Hospital for Mental and Nervous Diseases (also known as Kirkbride's). Illustrated

(PA-1636), N.W. corner Forty-fourth and Market sts. Coursed granite ashlar center building and stuccoed rubble wings and end buildings with stone trim, approx. 443' (forty-one-bay front) × 116', two stories on raised basement, gable roofs with central dome, Doric tetrastyle portico with flat pediment, octagonal belvederes at intersection of wings and end buildings, E-plan with central hall and intersecting corridors.

Pioneer example of mental-hospital architecture using extended wings to permit maximum isolation of wards. Built 1836–40; Isaac

Holden, architect; Samuel Sloan, superintendent of construction. One-story addition to north (men's) lodge 1846–47; addition to south (women's) lodge 1849; north wing (Fisher Ward) enlarged 1872–80, 1906. Demolished 1959; portico and flanking walls preserved on site. Used only for women after 1859. Popularly named for Dr. Thomas S. Kirkbride, hospital superintendent 1841–83 and formulator of advanced methods of treating the mentally ill. Certified, PHC 1957. 4 ext. photos (1958),* 4 int. photos (1958),* 1 photocopy of old ext. engraving (c. 1840);* 14 data pages (including 1840–1908 insurance surveys).*

Pennsylvania Institution for the Instruction of the Blind (now Overbrook School for the Blind). Illustrated

(PA-1637), N.E. corner Sixty-fourth St. and Malvern Ave. Yellow plastered stone with terra cotta trim, approx. 400' (forty-five-bay front) × 200', two and three stories, tiled gable roofs with tiled hipped roofs on corner pavilions and tiled shed roofs on courtyard arcades, square bell towers flank arcaded entry porch to octagonal rotunda with low circular turrets and large circular lantern, round-arch and rectangular windows, rectangular plan with two large inner courtyards.

Rare and exceptional example of the Mission style in eastern United States. Built 1897–1900; Cope and Stewardson, architects; Warner H. Jenkins & Co., contractor. Two-story stone addition to superintendent's house built 1910; Cope and Stewardson, architects. Two-story steel-frame Graduate Cottage with brick curtain walls built 1940–41; Zantzinger and Borie, architects. Auditorium behind rotunda burned 1960, replaced by reinforced-concrete auditorium 1961; Francis, Cauffman, Wilkinson and Pepper, architects. One of the oldest institutions for the blind in the country; founded 1834. Name changed to Overbrook School for the Blind 1948. Certified, PHC 1963. 5 ext. photos (1973).*

Potts, Joseph D., House

(PA-1638), 3905 Spruce St. Brick with tile trim, approx. 46' (five-bay front) × 38'with rectangular rear corner tower and two-story rear ell, three-and-a-half stories, hipped roof, segmental pointed-arch windows, center-hall plan, richly carved interior woodwork and hand-painted interior tile.

Important residential work of Joseph M. Wilson, innovative late-19th-century architect of commercial and railroad structures. Built

1850. Extensively enlarged and remodeled c. 1876; Joseph M. Wilson, architect. Front porch removed 1943. Joseph D. Potts, a wealthy steamship and railroad executive lived here 1876–93. Center for foreign students 1918–59; University of Pennsylvania building since 1960. Certified, PHC 1963. 5 ext. photos (1961, including 1 of stable and carriage house),* 6 int. photos (1961);* HABSI form (1962).*

St. Agatha's Roman Catholic Church

(PA-1639), 3801 Spring Garden St., at N.W. corner Thirty-eighth St. Brownstone ashlar, approx. 70' (three-bay front) × 150', one story on raised basement, gable roof with cross-gables, three-stage center tower with pinnacles and battlements, three-aisle plan, galleries, apsidal chancel.

Fine High Victorian Gothic design by a leading late-19th-century church architect. Built 1874–78; vacated 1976; Edwin F. Durang, architect. Octagonal spire erected 1882–83, dismantled 1909. Chapel built and church interior altered 1901, one-story rear addition built 1912; Edwin F. Durang, architect. Interior extensively remolded 1924–26; Maginnis and Walsh (Boston), architects. Roof and top of tower demolished by fire 1966, replaced 1967. Rectory (3813 Spring Garden St.) built 1892; P. Albert Welsh, architect. 2 ext. photos (1973, including 1 color photo),* 1 photocopy of old ext. lithograph (c. 1880).*

St. Francis De Sales Roman Catholic Church. Illustrated

(PA-1640), 4629–35 Springfield Ave., at N.E. corner Forty-seventh St. Coursed rock-faced limestone ashlar with dressed limestone and marble trim, approx. 90' (three-bay front) × 150', one story with two-story facade, gable roofs, central green, yellow, and white tiled Byzantine dome with arcaded lantern and four small tiled domes at base, arched parapet between corner octagonal minarets with tiled domes, round-arch windows with engaged columns and hoods, large oculus at second story of each facade, sculpture over round-arch entrances, three-aisle plan, rectangular chancel.

One of America's finest examples of Late Victorian Byzantine architecture. Built 1907–8; Henry D. Dagit, architect; Melody and Keating, contractors. Sanctuary elements redesigned to conform with ecumenical reforms 1968; Venturi and Rauch, architects. 4 ext. photos (1973, including 3 color photos),* 1 photocopy of architectural drawing (1907).*

St. James Roman Catholic Church

(PA-1641), 3728 Chestnut St., at S.E. corner Thirty-eighth St. Rough-hewn limestone ashlar with marble trim, approx. 67' (three-bay front) × 157', one story on raised basement, gable roof with cross-gables, twin front four-stage towers with pinnacles, rose window, large superimposed pointed-arch entrance, pointed-arch windows, three-aisle plan, apsidal chancel.

Fine example of High Victorian Gothic church. Built 1881–87; Edwin F. Durang, architect. Spire on northeast corner tower removed after 1900; towers altered 1930. 1 ext. photo (1973),* 1 photocopy of old ext. lithograph (c. 1880, including school),* 1 photocopy of old ext. photo (c. 1900),* 1 photocopy of old int. photo (c. 1900);* 2 data pages (including 1869 insurance survey of school).*

St. Mary's Protestant Episcopal Church, Hamilton Village

(PA-1642), 3916 Locust St. (now closed, known as Locust Walk). Random rough-hewn granite ashlar with limestone trim, approx. 85' × 128' with one-story rough-hewn limestone entrance porch and limestone enclosed cloister leading to rear two-story coursed rough-hewn parish house, one story, polychromatic gable roofs with cross-gables, two-stage square tower with pinnacles and spire at northwest corner, pointed-arch, quatrefoil and trefoil windows, one-story brick addition at southeast corner; three-aisle plan, semihexagonal chancel with notable marble and mosaic high altar, exposed wooden trusses.

Small Gothic Revival suburban church whose architecture and function reflect a century of change in its neighborhood. Built 1872–73; Thomas W. Richards, architect. High altar imported from Rome 1875, exhibited at Centennial Exhibition 1876, installed in chancel 1890. Chancel, western entrance porch built 1890; Charles M. Burns, architect. Parish house built 1897; George Nattress, architect. Tower raised to two stories, spire and terra cotta pinnacles added 1907; Herbert J. Wetherill, architect. Enclosed cloister added, chancel altered c. 1910; parish house renovated after fire damage 1936, renovated 1965; spire removed 1973. Founded 1830 as parent parish of West Philadelphia; Hamilton Village derived its name from Hamilton family of Woodlands and was officially incorporated into borough of West Philadelphia 1844. Certified, PHC 1974. 3 ext. photos (1973).*

Tabernacle Presbyterian Church. Illustrated

(PA-1099), 3700 Chestnut St., at S.W. corner Thirty-seventh St. Granite ashlar with limestone trim, approx. 50' (three-bay front) × 100' with rear two-story chapel and two-and-a-half-story manse on raised basement at southeast corner, gable roofs with cross-gables, four-stage corner entry and bell tower with gargoyles and pinnacles, octagonal stair tower between church and chapel, open Gothic-arch arcade along chapel; four-aisle cruciform plan, galleries, notable exposed roof truss with angels carved on hammerbeams.

Fine examples of late-19th-century Gothic Revival architecture. Built 1884–86; Theophilus Parsons Chandler, Jr., architect; Oliver Bradin, superintendent of construction; Michael Scully, master mason. 11 ext. photos (1963),* 3 int. photos (1963),* 1 photocopy of old ext. photo (c. 1886),* 2 photocopies of old int. photos (c. 1890, c. 1930),* 1 photocopy of architect's drawing (1884);* 7 data pages (1965).*

University of Pennsylvania, College Hall (originally known as The Academic Department of the University of Pennsylvania)

(PA-1643), S. side Woodland Ave. (now vacated) between Thirty-fourth and Thirty-sixth sts. Random green serpentine ashlar with Leiperville stone, brownstone and Ohio stone trim, 254'-0" (twenty-five-bay front) × 102'-4", three and four stories on raised basement, mansard roofs with cross-gables, Gothic tracery windows at second-story center for original chapel, originally two pinnacles on each facade and five-and-a-half-story towers with steep hipped roofs at east and west ends, Gothic entrance porch, E-plan with center entry hall and longitudinal corridors.

Fine example of Collegiate Gothic architecture and one of the country's most advanced academic structures when built. Built 1870–72; Thomas W. Richards, architect; George Watson, builder. Towers and pinnacles removed 1914, 1929. Certified, PHC 1957. 2 ext. photos (1973),* 1 photocopy of architects drawing (c. 1871);* 15 data pages (including 1876 insurance survey and architect's description of plans).*

University of Pennsylvania, Library (now known as Furness Building)

(PA-1644), W. side Thirty-fourth St. S. of Walnut St. (originally at S.W. corner Thirty-fourth St. and Woodland Ave., since closed). Iron and brick with terra cotta and smooth and pecked redstone trim, approx. 140' (eight-bay front) × 80' with three-story lateral book stack and side and rear additions, four stories on raised basement with five-story square battlemented tower, tiled hipped roof with cross-gable on main section with tiled conical roof on apsidal north end and glass gable and shed roofs on book stack, open entrance porch, crockets on dormers and gables, gargoyles on apsidal north end; entry and stairhall with notable iron staircase lead to two original reading rooms and stacks with glass walkways, north room with iron-beam apsidal vaulting, monumental interior detailing.

A major work of Frank Furness, path-making late-19th-century architect, and a masterpiece of library design and function when built; early example of separating reading rooms from book stacks. Built 1888–91; Furness, Evans & Co., architects; terra cotta by New York Architectural Terra Cotta Works. Five-story brick and redstone Duhring Memorial Stack added to book stack 1914–15; Furness, Evans & Co., architects. Two-story reinforced-concrete and brick Henry Charles Lea Library and Reading Room added to rear (along Thirty-fourth St.) 1923–24; Furness, Evans & Co., architects. One-story brick and granite Horace Howard Furness Memorial Library added to front of book stack 1931; Robert McGoodwin, architect. Floor added within main (south) reading room 1922. Duhring Stack (or Wing) altered c. 1947; Harbeson, Hough, Livingston and Larson, architects. Interior renovated 1963. Library and studios of Graduate School of Fine Arts since 1963; name changed to Furness Building in memory of its architect 1963. Certified, PHC 1961. 7 ext. photos (1964),* 3 int. photos (1964);* HABSI form (1962).*

University of Pennsylvania, Men's Dormitories. Illustrated
(PA-1645), S. side Spruce St. at Thirty-seventh St. and Woodland Ave. (since vacated). Brick with sandstone trim, approx. 560' × 42' on Spruce St., approx. 530' × 40' on Woodland Ave., three-and-a-half stories with six-story quadruple entry towers, gable roofs with cross-gables and Flemish cross-gables, balustrades, oriels, arcades, five courts in semitrapezoidal plan.

Integration of architectural detailings, openings, and courts of various sizes and levels into a notable example of Late Victorian Jacobean style. Built 1895–1902; Cope and Stewardson, architects. Enlarged between 1902 and 1910; Cope and Stewardson, architects. Enlarged between 1912 and 1930; Stewardson and Page, architects. Steel-frame additions with brick curtain walls built 1955, 1959; Trautwein and Howard, architects. Certified, PHC 1959. 7 ext. photos (1973, including 1 color photo).*

University of Pennsylvania, University Museum (originally known as Museum of Science and Art). Illustrated

(PA-1646), 3620 South St., at S.E. corner Thirty-third and Spruce sts. Brick with white and colored marble trim, approx. 475' (thirty-eight-bay front) × 190', one, two, and three stories, tiled hipped and gable roofs, round-arch windows, notable sculpture at entrance, U-plan with side and rear extensions.

Notable cooperative work of architecture integrating many historical styles into a building of various levels and units. West court built 1893–99, rotunda behind west court built 1912, middle section and eastward addition to rotunda built 1926–28; Wilson Eyre, Jr., Frank Miles Day and Bro., Cope and Stewardson, collaborating architects; Alexander Calder, sculptor. Planned complex never completed. Five-story reinforced-concrete addition built at southeast end 1969–71; Mitchell/Giurgola Associates, architects. One of the world's leading archaeological museums. Certified, PHC 1959. 4 ext. photos (1973).*

Woodland Terrace Area Study. Illustrated

(PA-1647), 501–19, 500–520 Woodland Terr., E. and W. sides Woodland Terr. between Baltimore and Woodland aves. Eleven brick semidetached houses alternately faced with random brownstone ashlar and stucco, each approx. 32' (four-bay front) × 58' with one-story rear wing, three stories, flat roof, open front and side porches, four-story square side tower on end houses on E. side, transverse entry-hall plan.

Notable example of mid-19th-century speculative terrace housing in the Italianate mode. Built 1861–62; probably by Samuel Sloan, architect. Porches removed from Nos. 500, 520 later; No. 522 demolished before 1963. Paul M. Cret, eminent early-20th-century architect and teacher, lived in No. 516, 1919–45. Certified, PHC 1963; Pennsylvania Register 1971; NR. 8 ext. photos (1973);* 10 data pages (1963, including 1862–63 insurance surveys).*

Woodlands. Illustrated

(PA-1125), S.W. corner Thirty-ninth St. and Woodland Ave., in Woodlands Cemetery. Rubble and stuccoed rubble with brick trim, approx. 86' (five-bay front) × 45', two stories on raised basement, hipped roof, Tuscan tetrastyle portico with pediment on south (river) facade, central stuccoed pavilion with six pilasters and pediment on north facade, circular bays on east and west ends, Ionic frontispiece with fanlight and arched pediment at north entrance, central circular reception hall with stairs to the side. Rubble two-story stable with hipped roof and flanking one-story shed-roof wings approx. 280' north of house.

Notable Adamesque-Federal country house with river and land fronts and the first giant portico on a Philadelphia building. Built c. 1742; extensively enlarged and remodeled for William Hamilton 1787–90. Country seat of eminent Hamilton family until grounds became cemetery 1843; house now superintendent's quarters. Certified, PHC 1956; designated National Historic Landmark 1967. 18 sheets (1940, including plans, elevations, details, plan and elevations of stable) from Survey, Philadelphia Chapter, A.I.A. (1932); 6 ext. photos (1938, including 2 of stable); 1 data page (including 1811 insurance survey).*

Wynnestay
(PA-1648), 5125 Woodbine Ave., at N.E. corner Fifty-second St. Rubble, approx. 55' (five-bay front) × 22' with two-story rear ell (originally approx. 25' × 22'), two-and-a-half stories (originally two), gable roof, pent eave on eastern part, door hood on western end, oculus in west gable end, cornice across gable ends, originally one room to a floor.

Fine example of early Pennsylvania architecture. Built 1689; lateral western extension built 1700; roof of eastern part raised later; rear ell built early 20th century. Built on property of Dr. Thomas Wynne, William Penn's personal physician and Speaker of Provincial Assembly 1683, probably for Wynne's son Jonathan. Certified, PHC 1957. 1 ext. photo (1973).*

George Burnham House. *Jack E. Boucher photo, 1973.*

Church of St. Francis de Sales. *Jack E. Boucher photo, 1973.*

Fort Mifflin, Sally Port. *Cortlandt V. D. Hubbard photo, 1969.*

Professor Henry Charles Lea House. *James L. Dillon & Co. photo, 1968.*

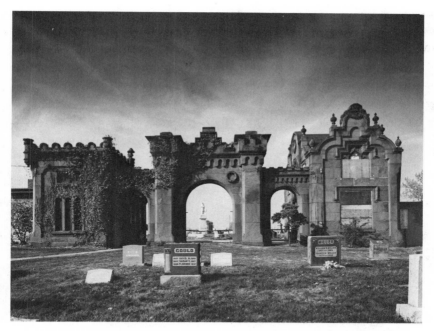

Mount Moriah Cemetery Gate House. *Cortlandt V. D. Hubbard photo, 1975.*

Pennsylvania Hospital for Mental and Nervous Diseases. *Engraving by W. E. Tucker, c. 1840.*

Pennsylvania Institution for Instruction of the Blind. *Jack E. Boucher photo, 1973.*

University of Pennsylvania, Men's Dormitories. *Jack E. Boucher photo, 1973.*

Tabernacle Presbyterian Church. *Jack E. Boucher photo, 1963.*

University of Pennsylvania, University Museum. *Jack E. Boucher photo, 1973.*

Woodland Terrace, *Jack E. Boucher photo, 1973.*

Woodlands. *L. G. Park, del., 1940.*

Fairmount Park

6

Introduction

"**I**S IT POSSIBLE you have never seen Fairmount Park? Believe me, then, that it is the most beautiful place of the whole civilized world . . ." claimed the well-traveled writer Lafcadio Hearn in 1889.[1] Surrounded by a city of nearly two million, Fairmount Park offers more than 4,000 acres of open land dotted with recreational and cultural sites. Its borders extend northward from Fairmount along both banks of the Schuylkill River to the Wissahickon Creek and northward along that stream and its tributary, Cresheim Creek, to the city limits at Northwestern Avenue.[2] Its natural history reaches back to pre-Columbian America to include untouched virgin soil strata, rock outcroppings, and ancient trees. In commemoration of the preservation of this natural environment, the Wissahickon Valley was designated a Registered National Natural Landmark in 1964.

Civilization encroached upon the area during the eighteenth and early nineteenth centuries. The falls and rapids of the Wissahickon made it especially suited for mills, while along the Schuylkill gracious manor houses crowned the heights, and gardens and lawns sloped down to the river's edge. These estates served as nuclei for the park's nineteenth-century development and the houses have been seminal projects in historic preservation. Twenty-six of them still stand, joined by three others moved to the park from various sites in Philadelphia.[3] In recognition of this trailblazing role in America's recreation, preservation, and ecological history, Fairmount Park was put on the National Register of Historic Places in 1972.

The genesis of Fairmount Park in 1812 occurred when the city's waterworks were moved from Center Square to the Schuylkill River at Fairmount, a hill on the western outskirts of the original city. The

Fairmount Waterworks (illus.) initially operated in a large two-and-a-half-story steam-engine house, which still stands on the southern edge of the complex. The steam engines proved troublesome and expensive from the beginning of their operation in 1815, and four years later City Councils decided to switch to water power.[4] The new facility, next to the original steam-powered works, required a great deal of work: purchasing the rights to the water power at the Falls of Schuylkill from the Schuylkill Navigation Company, throwing a dam across the river, blasting from the mount a forebay (from which water would power the wheels), and building the machinery and mill house. It was all accomplished within three years, and the system was operating by the end of 1822.[5] The five acres surrounding the initial Fairmount Waterworks had been landscaped into a public garden, making it probably the earliest planned municipal park in the United States.[6] The garden met with such public favor that the landscaped area grew with the waterworks and by 1828 the small park had nearly quintupled in size and had attained a beauty so striking that even the critical Charles Dickens praised it.[7] The present appearance of the waterworks is largely the results of changes made when the waterwheels were replaced by turbines after the Civil War. The pitch roof of the mill house was covered with a flat terrace, and an ornamental peristyle temple structure and flanking wooden huts were placed between the two original end pavilions.[8]

By the mid-nineteenth century a visit to the park generally included a stroll through Laurel Hill Cemetery, located near the river north of the waterworks. Begun in 1836 on the site of the former country seat of Joseph Sims, Laurel Hill was more than a mere burial ground. It was also a romantically landscaped arboretum and sculpture garden highlighted by a handsome Doric gate house (illus.). The young architect John Notman planned twisting roads through the undulating grounds, and the directors planted a wide variety of valuable trees and shrubs and encouraged the erection of tasteful memorials and monuments to make Laurel Hill one of the finest rural cemeteries in the country.[9] These two dissimilar projects, a classically clothed technological wonder and a naturally landscaped graveyard, served as stimuli for Fairmount Park's rapid growth, which began in 1855. In that year Lemon Hill and its approximately forty-five acres were dedicated to public use. Lemon Hill, the graceful Federal-style country house overlooking the waterworks, had been purchased by the city eleven years earlier in order to preserve the purity of the municipal water supply. Two years later Sedgeley and its thirty-three acres were acquired, and shortly thereafter title was obtained to the land between the waterworks and Lemon Hill. Finally in 1867, just about the time that the city was acquiring the Wissahickon Valley and two large estates on the west bank of the river, the Pennsylvania General Assembly set aside a large area bordering the Schuylkill River "forever as an open public place."[10]

By this time the city was clearly concerned as much for park land as for pure water. The river was already a center for racing sculls, a sport that had been inaugurated on its quiet waters in about 1835. Gunwale barges were initially used, followed by outriggers and eventually by sculls,[11] whose gracefulness inspired many of Thomas Eakins's paintings. By the 1850's the growing barge clubs began replacing their shacks with substantial stone buildings,[12] a process that developed into picturesque Boat House Row, which stands in juxtaposition to the classical waterworks and Museum of Art nearby. Perhaps the most noted boathouse is the Undine Barge Club by Furness and Evans, but the bold peaks of Vesper and Malta also contribute to the irregular composition.[13]

A design competition for the park was held in 1858, although the area officially had not yet been set aside for that purpose. The proposal of Sidney & Adams was adopted but the coming of the Civil War seems to have prevented its completion.[14] Later advice was sought from noted landscape architects Robert Morris Copland of Boston and Olmsted and Vaux of New York, but again no plans were executed, although one of Olmsted's proposals survives.[15] It was not until after the Civil War that the park took on a deliberate design. In 1872 the Fairmount Park Commission adopted modest but romantic plans for East Fairmount Park that had been developed by Senior Assistant Engineer H. J. Schwarzmann. Two years later he became the chief engineer and architect of the International Exhibition of 1876, which was located in West Fairmount Park.[16] The site was but a short distance from the Zoological Gardens, which had opened in 1874 as the first zoo in the United States. Schwarzmann also laid out the zoo's grounds,[17] which were filled with imaginatively picturesque structures, such as the gate houses by Furness and Hewitt and the bear pits (illus.) by Theophilus Parsons Chandler, Jr. Both the zoo and the centennial exhibition were accessible to the city by way of the Girard Avenue Bridge (1874) and the Spring Garden Street Bridge (1875).

As one of the great world fairs, the centennial had a major impact on the development of West Fairmount Park. It created circulation

problems that dictated the design of many of the permanent roadways, and it left behind a number of structures, of which only two
remain, Memorial Hall (illus.) and the Ohio House (illus.) It also encouraged the park's sculpture project, which had begun in 1872 with
the founding of the Fairmount Park Art Association, a private group
dedicated to "promote and foster the beautiful in the City of
Philadelphia."[18] The association has given the city notable works by
such greats as Augustus Saint-Gaudens, Daniel Chester French,
Frederic Remington, and Jacques Lipshitz, and while it was not
directly responsible for the grandiose Civil War monument standing
near Memorial Hall—the gift of Richard Smith, a patriotic and
very successful typefounder—it was charged under the benefactor's
will to select and supervise the sculptors of the project.[19] Considered
"one of the most ambitious public monuments erected in Victorian
America,"[20] Smith Memorial possesses works by some of the leading
American sculptors from the turn of the century, and remains a striking landmark.

The park's charms became accessible to people of modest means
in 1896 when the Fairmount Park Transportation Company inaugurated its six-mile trolley run through the park, crossing the river on
the graceful Strawberry Mansion Bridge (illus.). Operations ceased
fifty years later, another casualty of the automobile.[21] The same automobile, however, brought even more people to the park and
further diversified its recreation role. In the summer of 1930 the Robin
Hood Dell presented its first free concert by the Philadelphia
Orchestra,[22] and in 1952 the Playhouse in the Park began its first
season of summer stock under a tent; a permanent structure now
houses the theater. Meanwhile, more tennis courts, swimming pools,
and picnic grounds were being built and promptly filled, reflecting
the increased leisure of the mid-twentieth century and leading some
to fear that even so large a park as Fairmount may be threatened by
overuse.

Catalog

Art Gallery. See International Exhibition of 1876, Memorial Hall

Belmont Mansion. Illustrated
(PA-1649), Belmont Mansion Dr. Brick and rubble with stone trim, approx. 40′ (three-bay front) × 35′ with attached one- and two-story buildings, three stories (originally two), hipped roof with balustrade, projecting center pavilion with gable, open porch on three sides, center great-hall plan, notable interior details.

Fine example of evolutionary growth of a country house with notable early decorative plaster work. Two-story gambrel-roof rubble cottage west of mansion built before 1742; semioctagonal bay added c. 1744. Two-story gable-roof house at S.W. corner of mansion built 1745. Mansion built c. 1755; rear stair tower, front porticoed porch built c. 1760; ornamental ceiling of great hall installed c. 1762; third story, lattice porch across front built before 1860; porch extended around sides after 1867. Stairway of 1745 house removed 1874; octagonal bay at south end removed 1876. Interiors rehabilitated 1926. One-story brick building at west corner of rubble cottage built after 1931; demolished 1972.

Country house of William Peters, lawyer, jurist, Register of Admiralty 1744–71, and his son Richard Peters, agriculturist, Commissioner of War for Continental Congress 1776–81, member of Pennsylvania Assembly 1788–92, noted federal jurist 1792–1828. Acquired by Fairmount Park Commission, City of Philadelphia 1867. Certified, PHC 1956. 2 photocopies of ext. photos (1931),* 4 photocopies of int. photos (1926);* 4 data pages (1973).*

Boat House Row
(PA-1650), E. River Dr. W. of Main Dr. Ten houses of brick or random rough-hewn stone (one frame with shingles), two, two-and-a-half, and three stories, gable and hipped roofs with cross-gables and turrets. Rare and picturesque assemblage of river-boat clubhouses. Built late 19th and early 20th centuries including: No. 2, Fairmount Rowing Association built early 20th century; No. 3, Quaker City Barge Club built c. 1860 with later alterations; No. 4, Pennsylvania Barge Club built 1892 Louis C. Hickman, architect; No. 5, Crescent Boat Club built c. 1867, alterations and addition 1891, Charles Balderston, architect; No. 6, Bachelors' Barge Club built 1893, Halzehurst and Huckel, architects; No. 7, University Barge Club built 1870, altered and enlarged 1893; No. 8, Philadelphia Barge Club built late 19th century; No. 9, Malta Boat Club built 1870, enlarged 1880, enlarged and remodeled 1901, G. W. and W. D. Hewitt, architects; No. 10, Vesper Boat Club built c. 1865, altered and enlarged 1898, Howard Hagar, architect; No. 11, College Boat Club of University of Pennsylvania built c. 1875; No. 12, Penn Athletic Club Rowing Association (former West Philadelphia Rowing Club) built 1873 with later alterations; No. 13, Undine Barge Club built 1882–83, Furness and Evans, architects; No. 14, Philadelphia Girls Rowing Club (former Skating Club and Humane Society) built 1855; No. 15, Sedgely Club built 1892, Hazlehurst and Huckel, architects; alterations 1902, Arthur H. Brockie, architect. Boat clubs organized during 1850's, led to formation of Schuylkill Navy 1858 to supervise regattas. 1 ext. photo (1973).*

British Building. See International Exhibition of 1876, St. George's House

Callowhill Street Bridge. See Spring Garden Street Bridge

Cedar Grove. Illustrated
(PA-1651), Lansdowne Dr. near Black Dr. (originally at S.W. corner Old Front St. and Harrowgate Ln., Frankford). Historic house museum. Coursed Wissahickon schist ashlar front and rubble sides and rear, approx. 38' (six-bay front) × 50' (originally 19' × 34'), two-and-a-half stories, gambrel roof (orginally gable), open porch on two sides (originally pent eave), notable interior woodwork of three periods of 18th-century architecture.

Fine example of a Philadelphia Quaker farmhouse with furnishings accumulated by five generations of owners. Built c. 1748; rear one-story kitchen wing raised to two-and-a-half stories 1752;

enlarged one-room width c. 1799; porch replaced pent eave c. 1831. Vacated 1888; acquired by Fairmount Park Commission, City of Philadelphia 1926; moved to present site 1926–27; opened to public 1928; maintained by Philadelphia Museum of Art. In possession of Morris family c. 1793–1926. Certified, PHC 1956. 3 ext. photos (1937, 1973*), 1 photocopy of ext. photo (c. 1900),* 1 photocopy of int. photo (1928);* 13 data pages (1962, including 1791–1868 insurance surveys).*

Centennial Exhibition of 1876. See International Exhibition of 1876, Memorial Hall, Ohio State Building, St. George's House

Centennial Guard Box

(PA-1652), Traffic Triangle, at W. end of Benjamin Franklin Parkway and E. side of Thomas Eakins Plaza, in front of Phialdelphia Museum of Art. (Formerly at N.W. corner E. River Dr. and Fairmount Ave.) Wood frame, octagonal plan with 10'-diameter, one story, concave octagonal roof, large pointed-arch window with engaged column on each side. Notable example of a romantic park structure in the Gothic Revival style. Built c. 1873; restored 1973. Moved to present site 1973. Certified, PHC 1976. 1 ext. photo (1973).*

Chamounix Mansion

(PA-1653), Chamounix Dr. Stuccoed rubble, approx. 45' (three-bay front) × 47', two-and-a-half stories, hipped roof (originally with balustrade), semicircular bay on south facade, ironwork porches on east and north sides (originally columned porticoes), wood porch on west side, center-hall plan.

Example of modest Federal-style country house with complementary addition. Built c. 1802; enlarged, interior altered, three ironwork porches added, Gothic Revival carriage house built 1856. West porch replaced by wood porch c. 1875; interior altered 1885, 1887. Carriage house altered for youth hostel 1972. Acquired by Fairmount Park Commission, City of Philadelphia 1868. Youth hostel since 1964. Certified, PHC 1956; Pennsylvania Register 1972; NR. 3 ext. photos (1973, including 1 of carriage house);* 5 data pages (including 1835–87 insurance surveys).*

Civil War Memorial. See Smith Memorial Arch

The Cliffs

(PA-185), Columbia Ave. Dr. Rubble with scored stucco front and rear, 36'-5" (three-bay front) × 22'-3", two-and-a-half stories, hipped

roof with small cross-gables over center bay, pedimented front and
rear frontispieces leading directly into living room.

Fine example of Georgian country house. Built 1753; restored
1929; dormers added later; rehabilitated 1976. Acquired by Fairmount
Park Commission, City of Philadelphia 1868; vacated 1968. Built for
Joshua Fisher, successful merchant, and stayed in possession of this
prominent Quaker family until 1868. Certified, PHC 1956; Pennsylvania Register 1971; NR. 14 sheets (n.d., including plans, elevations,
details); 1 ext. photo (1973),* 1 photocopy of ext. photo (1931),* 2
photocopies of int. photos (1932);* 2 data pages (including 1854 insurance survey).*

Clunie. See Mount Pleasant

Covered Bridge
(PA-19), Thomas Mill Rd. across Wissahickon Creek. Wooden Howe
trough truss with wrought-iron tie rods and cast-iron shoes covered
with board and batten and low-pitch gable roof, rubble abutments,
21'-3" × 96'-0".

Employing the most popular of the 19th-century timber truss
systems, this remains the last extant covered bridge in Philadelphia.
Built c. 1855; reconstructed 1937. Certified, PHC 1976. 1 sheet (1936,
including plans, elevations, sections); 3 ext. photos (1973, including 1
color photo).*

Fairmount Waterworks. Illustrated
(PA-1654), Fairmount, at Schuylkill River near Twenty-fifth St.
Group of six wooden and plastered stone buildings on granite ashlar
bulkheads: wooden Tuscan peristyle temple structure (approx.
40' × 50') flanked by one-story wood frame buildings (approx.
38' × 15') and one-story stone pavilions (approx. 20' × 40') with
Tuscan tetrastyle porticoes on top of former stone mill building (approx. 56' × 238'); at south end three-and-a-half-story, gable-roof
stuccoed stone house (approx. 72' × 48') for steam engines (known as
Greaves Mansion).

Pioneer pumping system of engineering significance when built
that now serves as a foil for the Neoclassical Revival Philadelphia
Museum of Art behind and above it on site of former reservoir.
Steam-engine house built 1812–15; Frederick Graff, engineer and
probable architect; Frederick Erdman, carpenter; John Moore, mason.
Mill house with end pavilions built 1819–22; Frederick Graff, engineer and probable architect. Engine house altered to saloon, gazebo

built at east end of dam 1834. Standpipe with Italianate facade built behind forebay 1852; Frederic Graff (Jr.), architect and engineer. Mill house built on mound at east end of dam 1860–62; H. P. M. Birkinbine, engineer. Level of terrace raised, central peristyle temple structure built, flanking wooden buildings built over mill houses 1867–72; Frederic Graff, architect and engineer. Abandoned as waterworks 1911; standpipe demolished c. 1920. Site of city aquarium 1911–62. Certified, PHC 1956; Pennsylvania Register 1970; designated National Historic Landmark 1976; designated National Engineering Landmark by American Society of Civil Engineers 1975. 4 ext. photos (1973, including 1 color photo);* HABSI form (1970).*

Falls Bridge
(PA-1655), connects E. River Dr. at Calumet St. with W. River Dr. at Neil Dr. across Schuylkill River. Steel with stonemasonry abutments and two stonemasonry piers, approx. 540' × 40', Pratt-type pin-connected trough truss with secondary system of bracing. Built 1894–95; George S. Webster, chief engineer. Designed as double-deck bridge, upper deck never built. 3 photos (1973, including 1 color photo),* 3 photocopies of old photos (1895, 1896),* 1 photocopy of plan (1894).*

Fountain of the Sea Horses (also known as Italian Fountain)
(PA-1656), Aquarium Ln., approx. 310' N.W. of Philadelphia Museum of Art and approx. 200' W. of E. River Dr. Travertine stone with concrete foundation, four sea horses supporting fountain basin with central fountain of circular splayed palmetto forms approx. 10'-8" high, ciruclar pool approx. 155' circumference with inscribed rounded rim.

A modern reproduction that retains a human scale in relation to the nearby Museum of Art. Made c. 1926 as a reproduction of Fontana Dei Cavalli Marini in Borghese Gardens, Rome, by Christoph Untenberger (c. 1770); installed 1928; basin removed later. Gift of Italy to the United States in commemoration of Sesquicentennial of American Independence 1926. 1 photo (1973),* 1 photocopy of old photo (c. 1928).*

Girard Avenue Bridge
(PA-1657), Girard Ave. across Schuylkill River. Wrought-iron quadrilateral Pratt deck truss with four stone piers, approx. 865' × 100', cast-iron railing, lower level for pedestrians, geometric design of structural members.

Considered the widest bridge in the world when it was built,

1872–74; Henry A. Sims and James P. Sims, architects; Clarke, Reeves and Co., engineers; Phoenixville Iron Co., builders. Demolished 1970–71. Parts of iron railing at Smithsonian Institution. 15 photos (1969, 1971),* 1 photocopy of old photo (1906),* 1 photocopy of old stereopair (c. 1880).*

Hatfield House

(PA-1658), N.E. corner Girard Ave. and Thirty-third St. (originally at N.W. corner Hunting Park and Pulaski aves., formerly known as Nicetown Ln. and Clarissa St.). Wood frame with flush board front and random-width beaded-edge clapboard sides and rear, 30'-2" (four-bay front) × 43'-5", two-and-a-half stories with Tuscan five-column portico, hipped roof in front, gable roof in back (original), transverse central-hall plan with entrance on south side, Greek Revival detailing.

Fine example of a small 18th-century house remodeled into a Greek Revival residence. Built c. 1760; enlarged to the front, extensively remodeled c. 1838; open porches built on north and south sides c. 1850. Moved from original site, porches removed 1930. Maintained by Fairmount Park Commission, City of Philadelphia. Certified, PHC 1957; Pennsylvania Register 1970; NR. 6 ext. photos (1938, 1959*), 3 int. photos (1959),* 7 photocopies of old ext. photos (1901, c. 1910, 1929);* 17 data pages (1929, 1958*).

House on Letitia Street. See Letitia Penn House

International Exhibition of 1876, Memorial Hall (also known as Art Gallery). Illustrated

(PA-1659), North Concourse, 0.2 mi. E. of Belmont Ave. Brick with wrought-iron beams and cast-iron columns faced with coursed marble ashlar, approx. 365' (fifteen-bay front) × 210', one story on raised basement with mezzanine at north (rear) end, flat roofs with balustrades and large central square iron and glass dome, on south facade three large round-arch entrances flanked by arcades (originally open), on front corner of main pavilion zinc statues representing Science and Art by A. J. M. Müller (Germany), on top of dome zinc statue of Columbia and at its corners zinc statues of Industry, Commerce, Agriculture, Mining by Müller, originally speed-eagle sculpture on corners of each corner pavilion, handsome Renaissance-style central rotunda with large entry vestibule.

Notable example of Beaux-Arts architecture in United States that influenced many subsequent American and European museum, exposition, and government buildings. Last remaining important Centennial building. Built 1874–76; Hermann J. Schwarzmann, architect; Richard J. Dobbins, contractor. Arcades enclosed, spread-eagle sculpture removed later. Exterior restored, interior rehabilitated 1958–69; Hatfield, Martin, and White, architects. Served as art gallery during Centennial Exhibition 1876; as Pennsylvania Museum of Art (later Philadelphia Museum of Art) 1876–1928; housed some museum collections 1928–1954; used as Fairmount Park Commission offices, park police headquarters, recreational center since 1969. Certified, PHC 1976.

2 ext. photos (1973),* 2 photocopies of old ext. photos (1875, including 1 of dome under construction),* 1 photocopy of old lithograph (1876),* 1 photocopy of plan (1876);* 8 data pages (including 1885 insurance survey).*

International Exhibition of 1876, Ohio State Building (also known as Ohio House). Illustrated

(PA-1660), N.W. corner States Dr. and Belmont Ave. Rusticated sandstone ground story, Dayton stone ashlar second-story pavilion, frame second story with vertical siding and clapboard gables and rear ground story, approx. 40' (five-bay front) × 42', two stories, twin gable roofs with cross-gable, centered gabled pavilion with crockets and one-story entry porch, open side porches, center-hall plan.

Rare example of architectural advertising with names of various Ohio stone dealers, cutters, and quarries carved in stones. Built 1876; Heard and Sons (Cleveland), architects; Aaron Doan and Co. (Philadelphia), builders. Exhibition hall for State of Ohio during Centennial Exhibition 1876; owned by Fairmount Park Commission, City of Philadelphia, and used as dwelling since 1876. Certified, PHC 1963. Rehabilitated 1976. 4 ext. photos (1973, including 2 in color).*

International Exhibition of 1876, St. George's House (also known as British Building)

(PA-1080), W. side States Dr. approx. 0.2 mi. W. of Belmont Ave. Wood frame with applied half-timbering, approx. 90' (eight-bay front) × 65', two stories, gable roofs, picturesque facade, irregular E-plan. Built 1875; Thomas Harris (London, England), architect; J. H. Cundall, superintendent; John Rice, builder. Demolished 1963. 3 ext. photos (1961), 1 int. photo. (1961), 2 photocopies of architectural drawings (1875), 1 photocopy of ext. lithograph (1876); 4 data pages (1964).

Italian Fountain. See Fountain of the Sea Horses

Laurel Hill (also known as Randolph House)
(PA-13), Edgeley Dr. Brick with marble trim, 31'-6" (three-bay front) × 22'-2" with two-story lateral octagonal addition (north end) and one-story lateral wing (south end), two stories on raised basement, hipped roof with gable roof on lateral wing, Doric frontispiece with pediment, pediment over central pavilion, center entrance with stairhall and lateral hall to octagonal end (originally central-hall plan).

Built c. 1748; one-story wing built 18th century; octagonal addition built early 19th century. Acquired by Fairmount Park Commission, City of Philadelphia 1869. Certified, PHC 1956; Pennsylvania Register 1970. Rehabilitated 1976. 10 sheets (1934, including plans, elevations, details); 1 ext. photo (1938); 2 data pages (n.d.).

Laurel Hill Cemetery Gatehouse. Illustrated
(PA-1743), 3820 Ridge Ave. Stuccoed stone, approx. 65' (six-bay front) × 30' with stuccoed brick lateral wings, two stories, flat roof, flat Doric octastyle portico with barrel-vault entrance. One of the earliest and most outstanding rural cemeteries in 19th-century America. Built 1836; John Notman, architect. Second story inserted in gatehouse, one-story kitchens built behind wings 1885; kitchens raised to two stories, balustrade removed later. 2 ext. photos (1973),* 1 photocopy of unexecuted design (elevation) by William Strickland (c. 1836).*

Lemon Hill
(PA-1010), Lemon Hill Dr. Historic house museum. Stuccoed rubble with granite trim, approx. 60' (three-bay front) × 40', two stories on raised granite ashlar basement, hipped roof, round-headed entrance with large fanlight and double in-curving steps, large central oval pavilion at rear, side verandas with walkway extending across rear, central-hall plan, oval parlor and bedroom.

Notable example of Federal-style country house. Built c. 1799; restored under direction of Fiske Kimball, Director of Philadelphia Museum of Art 1925–26. Between c. 1799 and 1838 country seat of Henry Pratt, merchant whose early work with lemons gave estate its name. Acquired by City of Philadelphia 1844, set aside as a common

1855, forming nucleus of Fairmount Park; under jurisdiction of Fairmount Park Commission since 1867. Headquarters of Colonial Dames of America, Chapter II, since 1957. Certified, PHC 1956.

1 sheet (1962, including gutter detail);* 3 ext. photos (1938, n.d.), 1 photocopy of int. photo (1958).*

Letitia Penn House (also known as House on Letitia Street)
(PA-184), Lansdowne Dr. near W. Girard Ave. (originally at 8 S. Letitia St). Brick, 20'-3" (three-bay front) × 30'-0", two-and-a-half stories, gable roof, notable hood with carved corbels over door, cove cornice, two rooms on ground story with corner fireplaces.

Notable example of small early-18th-century Philadelphia dwelling originally built in a court later opened as a street. Built for Thomas Chalkley between 1713 and 1715; probably by John Smart, house carpenter. Acquired by Fairmount Park Commission, City of Philadelphia, and removed to present site 1883. Restored 1931–32. Once believed to have been built for William Penn on lot of his daughter Letitia. Certified, PHC 1956. 4 sheets (1931, including plans, elevations); 2 ext. photos (1938), 1 photocopy of int. photo (1932);* 1 data page (including 1769 insurance survey).*

Memorial Hall. See International Exhibition of 1876, Memorial Hall

Monastery
(PA-183), Kitchen's Ln. on E. side Wissahickon Creek. Coursed Wissahickon schist front and rubble sides and rear, 33'-1" (four-bay front) × 32'-1½" with one-and-a-half-story lateral kitchen wing, three-and-a-half stories, gable roof, originally pent eave at each story, front and rear open porches, two large rooms on ground story without entrance hall.

Notable example of vernacular domestic architecture of 18th-century Germantown. Built c. 1747; interior altered c. 1800, c. 1850; porch added 20th century. Altered to Children's Museum of Philadelphia 1973. Acquired by Fairmount Park Commission, City of Philadelphia 1897. Received name from association with Brotherhood of Seventh-Day Adventists at Ephrata, whose members sometimes stayed here. Certified, PHC 1956; Pennsylvania Register 1970; NR. 23 sheets (n.d., including plans, elevations, section, details); 1 ext. photo (1973).*

Mount Pleasant (originally known as Clunie)

(PA-1130), Mt. Pleasant Dr. Historic house museum. Scored stuccoed rubble with brick trim, 53'-7" (five-bay front) × 30'-5", two-and-a-half stories on raised basement, hipped roof with balustrade, projecting center pavilion with pedimented Doric frontispiece and Palladian window above, flat-arch lintels with keystones, brick quions and stringcourse, blank end walls; central-hall plan, notable interior detailing. Flanked by two stuccoed brick and stone outbuildings, each approx. 22' square, two stories, concave hipped roof.

Notable example of a Georgian country house with finely carved interior woodwork. Built 1761; restored 1926; rehabilitated 1976. Stone stable in forecourt demolished after 1940. Owned for a short time but never occupied by Gen. Benedict Arnold 1779–80. Acquired by Fairmount Park Commission, City of Philadelphia 1868; maintained by Philadelphia Museum of Art since 1926; gardens maintained by Planter Garden Club. Certified, PHC 1956; designated National Historic Landmark 1960.

31 sheets (1940, including plot plan, plans, elevations, details, plan and elevations of outbuildings and stable) from Survey, Philadelphia Chapter, A.I.A. (1932); 18 ext. photos (1938, 1939, 1960,* 1970,* 1971,* including 2 of outbuilding), 6 int. photos (1971),* 6 photocopies of measured drawings (1897);* 2 data pages (including 1835 insurance survey).*

Ohio House. See International Exhibition of 1876, Ohio State Building

Ormiston

(PA-187), Reservoir Dr. Stuccoed brick, 34'-3" (three-bay front) × 40'-11", two-and-a-half stories, hipped roof with balustrade, open front and rear porches, center-hall plan. Built 1798; porches added before 1855. Acquired by Fairmount Park Commission, City of Philadelphia 1869. Certified, PHC 1956; Pennsylvania Register 1970. 9 sheets (n.d., including plans, elevations); 1 ext. photo (1973);* 2 data pages (including 1855 insurance survey).*

Pennsylvania Museum and School of Industrial Art. See Philadelphia Museum of Art

Philadelphia Museum of Art (originally known as Pennsylvania Museum and School of Industrial Art)

(PA-1661), Fairmount. The Plaza, at N.W. terminus of Benjamin

Franklin Parkway and merging of E. and W. River drives. Steel frame with Minnesota Mankato and Kasota ashlar curtain walls and terra cotta trim, approx. 545' × 325', three and four stories on raised rusticated basement, blue tiled gable roofs with crest-tiles, Corinthian octastyle portico on east end and Corinthian hexastyle portico on west end of central pavilion, Ionic hexastyle porticoes on inner courtyard pavilions with notable polychromatic terra cotta sculpture in tympanum of north pavilion, Ionic tetrastyle porticoes in antis on four outer pavilions, acroteria on pediments, polychromatic palmetto cornice; E-plan, large entrance stairhall with polychromatic Ionic colonnade at upper level.

An outstanding example of early-20th-century eclectic Neoclassical design. Located on the site of the former Fairmount reservoir, the Museum serves as a focal point for Jacques Gréber's Benjamin Franklin Parkway, one of the most successful attempts at baroque urban planning in the United States. Built 1919–28; Horace Trumbauer, Charles C. Zantzinger, and Charles L. Borie, Jr., collaborating architects; C. Paul Jennewein, sculptor of north portico sculpture; John Gregory, sculptor of south portico sculpture (never installed); George A. Fuller Co., contractor. One of America's great art museums. Name changed to Philadelphia Museum of Art 1938. Certified, PHC 1971.

1 ext. photo (1973),* 3 photocopies of ext. photos (1924, 1926, n.d.),* 1 photocopy of int. photo (1927, during construction),* 1 photocopy of aerial photo (1966),* 2 photocopies of architectural drawings (1912, 1915).*

Philadelphia Zoological Gardens, Bear Pits (also known as Bear Dens).
Illustrated
(PA-1662), approx. 200' W. of Thirty-fourth St., approx. 925' S. of entrance pavilions at S.W. corner W. Girard Ave. and Thirty-fourth St. Trenton brownstone rubble, three adjoining semicircular enclosures built into knoll with two terraced semicircular protrusions filling areas between curvatures of enclosures, approx. 86' × 30', front at ground level, rear depressed forming pits; front of each pit has stepped gable with pointed-arch doorway, date stone in center gable. Fine example of 19th-century resolution of romanticism and utility in a new building form. Built 1874; Theophilus Parsons Chandler, Jr., architect. 10 photos (1975);* 1 photocopy of old print (c. 1875).*

Philadelphia Zoological Gardens, Entrance Pavilions
(PA-1663), S.W. corner W. Girard Ave. and Thirty-fourth St. Granite
rubble and brick with brick trim, approx. 20' (two-bay front) × 28',
two stories, steep hipped roofs with cross-gables and cross-jerkin-
head roofs, projecting cornices with bold brackets. Notable example
of picturesque design. Built 1875–76; Furness and Hewitt, architects.
The Zoological Society of Philadelphia opened this zoo, the nation's
oldest, in 1874. 1 ext. photo (1973).*

Randolph House. See Laurel Hill

Ridgeland
(PA-1664), Chamounix Dr. Wissahickon schist rubble, approx. 34'
(three-bay front) × 34' with two-story rear frame addition, two-and-
a-half stories, gable roof, Tuscan entrance porch, open rear porch,
center-hall plan. Built c. 1800; rear addition built late 19th century.
Certified, PHC 1956. 3 ext. photos (1959),* 5 int. photos (1959).*

Sedgeley Porter's House (later known as Sedgeley Guard House)
(PA-1665), S.E. corner Sedgeley Dr. and W. Girard Ave. Sandstone
rubble with brick trim and local stone rubble additions, approx. 36'
(three-bay front) × 18' with flanking lateral extensions, one story,
hipped roof, pointed-arch windows and doorway, entrance porch,
originally center-hall plan with cellar kitchen.

Earliest surviving example of the Gothic Revival style in the
United States, exhibiting the classical proportions with the pointed-
arch details that characterize the style's origins. Built c. 1799 as
porter's house in rear of William Cramond's country house Sedgeley;
probably by Benjamin Henry Latrobe, architect of Sedgeley. Sedgeley
demolished 1857. Porch built mid-19th century; lateral wings, cornice
trim added 1897; interior altered later. Acquired by City of
Philadelphia 1857; maintained by Fairmount Park Commission since
1867; guard house 1857–1973, maintenance storage since 1973.
Certified, PHC 1960. 2 ext. photos (1973);* 1 data page (including 1811
insurance survey);* HABSI form (1971).*

Smith Memorial Arch (also known as Civil War Memorial)
(PA-1666), N.W. and S.W. corners North Concourse and Lansdowne
Dr. Two curved forms of smooth rusticated granite with dressed
granite trim and bronze statuary, each form approx. 96' (along seg-
ment) × 16', each with Palladian arch flanked by rusticated pedestals;

each inner pedestal surmounted by giant Doric columns (7'-6" diameter) with colossal standing statues of Maj. Gen. George Meade by Daniel Chester French, sculptor (south side), and of Maj. Gen. John Reynolds by Charles Grafly, sculptor (north side); outer pedestals surmounted by colossal equestrian statues of Maj. Gen. George B. McClellan by Edward C. Potter, sculptor (south side), and of Maj. Gen. Winfield S. Hancock by J. Q. A. Ward, sculptor (north side); standing statue of Richard Smith, type founder and donor of Memorial, at base of northern inner pedestal, niches filled with eight colossal busts including Union generals, admirals, Pennsylvania's Civil War governor, Memorial's architect, and executor of Smith's will; frieze carved with names of 84 prominent Pennsylvania participants in Civil War. Monumental expression of late-19th-century individualism and patriotism. Built 1897–1912; James H. Windrim and John T. Windrim, architects. Sculpture under auspices of Fairmount Park Art Association. 1 ext. photo (1973).*

Solitude
(PA-1127), S.W. corner W. Girard Ave. and Thirty-fourth St., on Philadelphia Zoological Gardens grounds. Coursed stuccoed rubble, approx. 30' (three-bay front) × 32', two-and-a-half stories, hipped roof, open Ionic porch on east side, Ionic frontispiece with pediment on west side, center-hall plan, notable Adamesque interior plasterwork.

Built 1784–85 for John Penn, grandson of William Penn; rehabilitated 1976. Offices for Philadelphia Zoological Gardens since 1874. Certified, PHC 1956. 9 sheets (1940, including plans, elevations, details) from Survey, Philadelphia Chapter, A.I.A. (1932); 8 ext. photos (1939, 1961,* 1962*), 12 int. photos (1939, 1961*), 1 photocopy of old plan print (n.d.),* 3 photocopies of measured drawings (1897).*

Somerton. See Strawberry Mansion

Spring Garden Street Bridge (also known as Callowhill Street Bridge)
(PA-1667), Spring Garden St. and Callowhill St. across Schuylkill River. Iron with stone abutments, approx. 350' × 48', double-decked roadways with cast-iron arches and stone piers on bridge approach, cast-iron arches and cast- and wrought-iron Whipple truss over river. Built 1874–75; Jacob H. Linville, engineer; Keystone Bridge Co., builders. Arches removed c. 1900; balustrades removed between 1904 and 1910; bridge demolished 1964. 1 photo (1963),* 1 photocopy of old

print (1876),* 2 photocopies of old stereopairs (c. 1880),* 6 photocopies of old photos (1874, c. 1890, 1904, 1910).*

Strawberry Mansion (originally known as Summerville, later as Somerton) (PA-1668), near N.W. corner Dauphin St. Dr. and Edgeley Dr. Historic house museum. Stuccoed rubble and brick, approx. 125' (eleven-bay front) × 30', two-and-a-half and three stories, gable roofs, Tuscan entrance porch, center-hall plan.

Fine example of the evolution of a modest country house into a Classical Revival mansion. Stone center section built 1797–98; three-story brick south wing built 1825; three-story north brick wing built c. 1828; open front and rear porches built 1870, removed c. 1926. Restored 1926–31. Acquired by Fairmount Park Commission, City of Philadelphia 1867; used as restaurant until 1926; since then maintained by Committee of 1926 under direction of Philadelphia Museum of Art. Fine collection of Tucker porcelain, America's first commercially successful high-quality porcelain, in Empire Parlor. Between 1819 and 1842 the country home of Judge Joseph Hemphill, politician and businessman who served six terms in Congress between 1801 and 1831 and was an owner of Tucker porcelain firm c. 1829–35. Supposedly the first strawberries in the United States were successfully grown here after 1820, giving mansion its present name.

1 ext. photo (1938), 2 photocopies of ext. photos (1932),* 3 photocopies of int. photos (1962, 1963);* 7 data pages (including 1873, 1880 insurance surveys).*

Strawberry Mansion Bridge. Illustrated

(PA-1669), connects Ford Dr. in W. Fairmount Park with Strawberry Mansion Dr. in E. Fairmount Park across Schuylkill River. Four wrought-iron arches on three stonemasonry piers with three Warren trusses supporting viaducts on east and west approaches, 1240'-6" × 52'. Built 1894–96; Russell Fair, Jr., engineer; Theodore Cooper, consulting engineer; Phoenix Bridge Co., builders. Built as trolley bridge for Fairmount Park Transportation Co. with vehicular lanes and sidewalk; trolleys stopped running, tracks removed 1946. 2 photos (1973, including 1 color photo),* 1 photocopy of old photo (1908).*

Summerville. See Strawberry Mansion

Sweetbrier

(PA-1670), Lansdowne Dr. Historic house museum. Stuccoed rubble, approx. 53' (five-bay front) × 38', two-and-a-half stories on raised basement, hipped roof, round-arch entrance with fanlight and Tuscan frontispiece, quoins, center-hall plan.

Fine example of a country house in the Federal style. Built 1797; restored by Junior League of Philadelphia 1926. Acquired by Fairmount Park Commission, City of Philadelphia 1868; since 1939 headquarters of The Modern Club, which furnished and maintains the house. Samuel Breck, prominent merchant, public servant, politician, member of Congress 1823–25, lived here 1797–1838. Certified, PHC 1956. Renovated 1976. 2 ext. photos (1973),* 3 photocopies of int. photos (1928).*

Woodford

(PA-1307), S.W. corner Ford Rd. and Greenland Dr. Historic house museum. Brick, approx. 45' (three-bay front) × 25' with two-story rear ell and additions, two stories (originally one) on raised basement, hipped roof with balustrade, projecting central pavilion with pediment, center Palladian window, pent eave on four sides, central-hall plan.

Notable example of a Georgian country house. Built c. 1756; second story added c. 1772; restored 1927–30. Acquired by Fairmount Park Commission, City of Philadelphia 1868; served as Park guard house 1887–1927. Has housed Naomi Wood Collection of household articles under direction of Philadelphia Museum of Art since 1930. Certified, PHC 1956; designated National Historic Landmark 1967. 6 ext. photos (1938, 1960*), 4 int. photos (1960),* 20 photocopies of 1897, 1932 measured drawings;* 2 data pages (1954, including 1769, 1772 insurance surveys).*

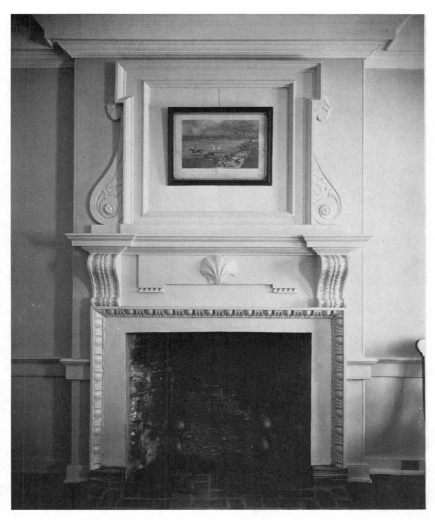

Belmont Mansion. *Photo 1926, courtesy Philadelphia Museum of Art.*

Cedar Grove. *Jack E. Boucher photo, 1973.*

Fairmount Waterworks. *Jack E. Boucher photo, 1973.*

International Exhibition of 1876, Memorial Hall. *Photo 1875, courtesy Philadelphia City Archives.*

International Exhibition of 1876, Ohio State Building. *Jack E. Boucher photo, 1973.*

Philadelphia Zoological Gardens, Bear Pits. *Cortlandt V. D. Hubbard photo, 1975.*

Laurel Hill Cemetery Gatehouse. *Jack E. Boucher photo, 1972.*

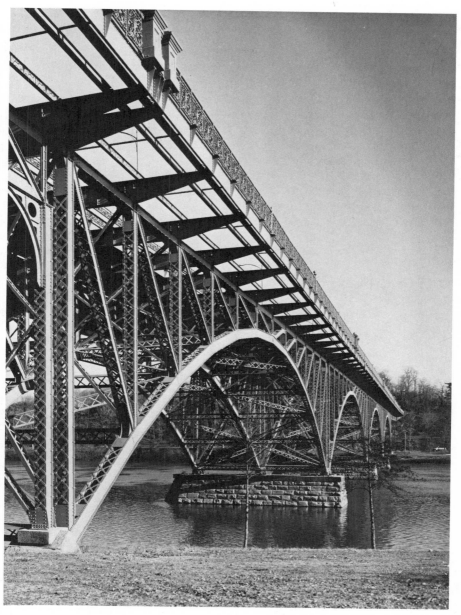

Strawberry Mansion Bridge. *Jack E. Boucher photo, 1973.*

Northwest Philadelphia

Germantown and Roxborough Townships

7

Introduction

*I*N SEPTEMBER, 1748, the Swedish botanist Peter Kalm rode out of
Philadelphia toward the northwest. He passed through a forest,
broken by well-tended fields and orchards, until after about a six-mile
ride he came upon Germantown. "This settlement," he noted, "has
only one street but is nearly two English miles long. It is for the
greatest part inhabited by Germans, who come from their country to
North America and settle here because they enjoy such privileges as
they are not possessed of anywhere else. . . . Most of the houses are
built of stone, which is mixed with glimmer and found everywhere
around Philadelphia. . . ."[1] Kalm's description has stood the test of
time. The oldest, and for many the most fascinating, part of the
ancient town remains the double row of stone houses ranging along
Germantown Avenue, the former Great Road, residual evidence of
Pennsylvania's first linear community.

Germantown has justifiably captured the imaginations of local
historians more than any other section of Philadelphia County. It was
founded in 1683 by German-speaking settlers as an essentially independent province and during the colonial period developed into a
socially separate town, whose material culture has survived to a
degree great enough to justify designating its main thoroughfare,
Germantown Avenue, a National Historic Landmark.

What people have meant by the term "Germantown" has dif-
fered over the years. Initially, it seems to have extended along Germantown Avenue from Roberts Avenue northward to Northwestern
Avenue, and stretched from the present Stenton Avenue westward
to Wissahickon Avenue. After 1707, when the area became German
Township in Philadelphia County, Germantown became known as

the more built-up portion between Wayne Junction and Carpenter Lane, and the present neighborhood designations gradually came into use.[2] Mount Airy apparently got its name from Chief Justice William Allen's country estate, Mount Airy, which was built about 1750 on Germantown Avenue near the present Allen's Lane.[3] References to Chestnut Hill, the area north of Mount Airy, appear as early as 1711. The name was self-explanatory, although there is no evidence that there were any more chestnut trees here than elsewhere in Philadelphia County. It is a hill, however; in fact, it is the highest point between Trenton and Bryn Mawr.[4] The more populous part of the township was organized as Germantown Borough in 1844, and in 1854, when the city and county governments were consolidated, the whole area became the Twenty-second Ward of the City of Philadelphia, and its boundaries became roughly those of the original Germantown.[5] Roxborough Township, presently the Twenty-first Ward, is a natural geographical extension of the former German Township, and in the early years no distinction was made between the two places. The two former townships enjoyed a parallel economic development, and the daily routines of their early inhabitants were often intertwined, particularly in the mills along Wissahickon Creek. Consequently, Northwest Philadelphia includes all of the city north and west of Broad Street and Roosevelt Boulevard, with Broad Street its eastern boundary and the Schuylkill River its southern boundary.

Historians have quibbled about whether the first Germantown settlers were Dutch, German, or Swiss, but the important point is that whatever their ethnic origins (most were apparently Dutch), they were German-speaking and self-consciously called their settlement Germantown. Yet the population was pluralistic in religion almost from the beginning, as newcomers arrived and built primarily along the great road leading to Philadelphia.[6] The earliest settlers were predominantly Quakers, but by 1690 Mennonites were numerous enough to have their own minister. This group, the first Mennonite congregation in America, still worships at 6119 Germantown Avenue in its plain rubble meeting house (illus.) that was built in 1770 on the site of its 1708 log meeting house. Before 1730 congregations of the Church of the Brethren (Dunkers) and of the Lutheran and Reformed churches were established, and some of their early houses of worship still stand, such as the Church of the Brethren at 6613 Germantown Avenue, built about 1770 but enlarged and altered in 1897. As German immigration grew during the eighteenth century, St.

Michael's Lutheran Church became the dominant religious influence in Germantown. Disputes within the congregation led to a host of new churches, such as the more pietistic St. Peter's Lutheran at Barren Hill (1752), the English-speaking Trinity Lutheran (illus.) at Germantown Avenue and Queen Lane (1836), the exclusively German-speaking St. Thomas Lutheran at Herman and Morton streets (1860), and three others in Chestnut Hill and Germantown.[7]

The language disputes at St. Michael's point up a continual tension within the greater Germantown community. Germantown began with a charter assuring political autonomy, but by 1707 an apparently insufficient tax base forced the town into accepting township status and losing political independence.[8] This caused no immediate disruption, since the ethnic distinctiveness of the inhabitants kept the town socially separate from Philadelphia city. By about the middle of the eighteenth century, however, the six-mile trip to Philadelphia no longer assured isolation but only made Germantown far enough removed from the city to be attractive to Philadelphians for summer residences.

Exemplary of these early summer residences is Grumblethorpe (illus.) at 5267 Germantown Avenue, opposite the eastern end of Queen Lane. The German-born Philadelphia merchant John Wister purchased the lot in 1741 and three years later he had his house built,[9] evidently by a local builder, because the structure is a glossary of rural Delaware Valley architectural elements. Like all early Germantown houses, it was built of local Wissahickon schist, a stratified gneiss speckled with mica. The rubble sides and rear and a coursed ashlar front with benches on the stoop were typical of Germantown buildings. Its handling of the pent eave and heavy cornice across the front and one end was repeated in one form or another in a host of Germantown houses, but most explicitly in the Green Tree Tavern, which was built four years later at 6021 Germantown Avenue for Daniel Pastorius, the grandson of the town's founder.[10] Grumblethorpe's balcony, however, has no exact duplicate. The Livesey House (c. 1747) on Wissahickon Creek comes close; it has a balcony but it extends across the entire front, taking the place of a pent eave. Oculi placed in Grumblethorpe's gable near the roof's edge were evidently to provide light and ventilation for the attic. These oculi are probably more evident today in old Pennsylvania barns, but they can be seen in other houses of the period, such as the house at 5434 Germantown Avenue, built c. 1740 and later owned by the noted carriage-maker William Ashmead.[11] The use of two entrances—in the

case of Grumblethorpe one leads to a parlor and the other to a hall—
was apparently a rural German practice and is also found on the
house that was built about 1730 at 6505 Germantown Avenue and
later inhabited by Michael Billmeyer, German printer for the Pennsylvania Assembly.[12] Because of local building traditions, Grumblethorpe stands as an archetype of mid-eighteenth-century Germantown architecture, yet the fact that it was built for a Philadelphian
seeking refuge from the city's summer heat suggests that by the
1740's Germantown was well along the way to becoming an English
town. This point was architecturally reinforced by the town's new
market house, which was erected by 1745 in Market Square and was
nearly identical to its contemporary in Philadelphia, New Market at
Second and Pine streets.[13]

Cultural tensions in Germantown were institutionalized in 1759,
when Germantown Academy was founded. There had been earlier
schools in the township, such as the Beggarstown School at 6669 Germantown Avenue, which provided a rudimentary education for
German-speaking children, but attempts to establish English-speaking public schools were stubbornly resisted by Christopher Sower I,
the renowned German printer and cultural purist. A year after
Sower's death in 1758 a group of men met in Green Tree Tavern to organize what they self-consciously called the Union School of Germantown, and in 1760 ground was purchased on Bensell's Lane,
which has been known as School House Lane ever since the school
building was finished in 1761.[14] It is a large two-story stone building
designed to accommodate both English- and German-speaking
classes, with a small house on each side for the German and English
schoolmasters. It was not long before the school was known as Germantown Academy, a name it retained until 1965. From the beginning, English pupils outnumbered their German counterparts, so it is
not surprising that by 1775 English-speaking residents in the
northern end of Germantown found their numbers increasing fast
enough and the distance to School House Lane great enough to justify building an all-English school on the property of the Upper Burial
Ground at 6309 Germantown Avenue.[15] Concord School (illus.), as it
was euphemistically called, is a rectangular, stuccoed stone structure
with only a central belfry on the roof betraying its original function.
Yet this simple one-room schoolhouse signaled English cultural
dominance in Germantown on the eve of the American Revolution.

About 1750 the newly appointed Chief Justice of the Province of
Pennsylvania, William Allen, built his country house, Mount Airy, on

Germantown Avenue, approximately two miles north of Grumblethorpe. William Allen was not a German; he was an Englishman
and one of the wealthiest and most influential political and business
figures in the colony, in fine, a taste-maker.[16] The fact that such a
prominent man built a summer home in Germantown started a trend.
Spending the summer of 1763 in Allen's Mount Airy, Benjamin
Chew, one of the province's leading attorneys and public servants, so
enjoyed the cool, healthful air that he decided to emulate his friend.
The result was Cliveden (illus.), one of the finest and best documented Georgian country seats in the American colonies.[17] It is a
happy compromise between the English Palladian country house and
the Germantown building tradition. Evidently inspired by country-
house plans to be found in such books as James Gibbs's *A Book of Architecture* (1728), Cliveden consists of a central dwelling flanked to the
rear by two small service dependencies that form a rear court for
formal gardens. The house incorporates some of the finest elements
of Georgian architecture: a dressed sandstone stringcourse, lintels
with keys, a pedimented central pavilion with a Doric frontispiece
and pediment, and dormers with scroll brackets and five ornamental
stone urns distributed across the front of the roof. Yet since Cliveden
was built of local stone by a local master carpenter and mason, it
continues the Germantown tradition of facade architecture (coursed
ashlar front and rubble sides and rear) with gables on the short ends.
Also, since the designer was a provincial gentleman, Benjamin Chew,
the proportions of the central pavilion are rather pinched, and the
handling of the urns and lintels a bit pretentious. The interior is as
grand as the exterior. The entrance hall is the widest room in the
house and nearly half its depth. A screen of four fluted Doric columns
with a finely carved Doric frieze separates the entrance hall from the
rear stairhall, which is flanked by a finely paneled dining room and
parlor. Benjamin Chew succeeded his friend William Allen as the
provincial Chief Justice in 1774, but when the Revolution broke out he
was deported to New Jersey for a year because of his pre-Revolutionary ties to the Tory faction. With his political and economic future
in doubt he sold Cliveden in 1779. Eighteen years later, however, he
regained the estate, and the Chew family resided at Cliveden
continuously until 1972, when it was acquired by the National Trust
for Historic Preservation and opened to the public.[18]

By the time of the Revolution the German era of Germantown
appears to have come to a close. The last significant detached house
to be built in Germantown before the Revolution was the Deshler-

Morris House at 5442 Germantown Avenue, opposite Market Square. It was built in 1772 for David Deshler, a successful Philadelphia importer of English and West Indian goods and the nephew of John Wister, the man who helped to begin the summer trek to Germantown more than a generation earlier. Although Deshler was German-born, his business and charitable activities and architectural taste suggest that he had been anglicized by the time he approached retirement in the early 1770's.[19] His summer dwelling is a fine example of Georgian domestic architecture built on the double-house plan. Although its ample size was more or less standard for its time, the plan, in which the center hall extends through to a back door with stairs off to the side, usually at the rear, was most often reserved for impressive city and country houses, such as the Reynolds-Morris House on South Eighth Street and Mount Pleasant in Fairmount Park. The house is probably best known as Germantown's "White House." In 1793, when Philadelphia was the nation's capital and in the throes of the yellow fever epidemic, President George Washington fled the pestilential city to reside here for about a month. He evidently enjoyed his visit—or perhaps feared a recurrence of the fever—because he returned the next summer for a six-week stay. Washington must have found his days here particularly ironic since the house had served as the headquarters of his victorious opponent, General Sir William Howe, after the Battle of Germantown sixteen years earlier.[20] Samuel Morris acquired the house from his father-in-law, Elliston Perot, in 1836 and for the next 112 years the Morris family owned the property until it was turned over to the National Park Service in December, 1948, and restored as a historic house museum.[21] Today it stands as not only America's earliest "summer White House" and presidential retreat but also as a fine example of a pre-Revolutionary house and garden.

The exodus of government officials and private families from the City of Philadelphia to Germantown during the yellow fever epidemic in 1793 firmly established the town's reputation as a place with healthful air free from the deadly miasmas of the city. Thereafter the number of both town and country houses increased, and since they were executed in the more delicate Federal style, they did much to change the appearance of Germantown. Across Germantown Avenue from Benjamin Chew's six-acre estate, John Johnson in 1798 began building a large two-and-a-half-story house onto a rubble structure that became its rear ell.[22] Later called Upsala (illus.), it is a fine Federal-style country house with a light, porticoed entrance porch and finely modeled dentil-and-modillion cornice, but it still retains a Germantown character in its plan and treatment of materials.

To the south, in Vernon Park at 5860 Germantown Avenue, stands a more formal Federal-style country house known as Vernon. As in the case of Upsala and many other Germantown houses, the main part of Vernon was built onto an earlier rubble farmhouse that then became a rear service wing. The front building was built in 1805 for James Matthews, a cane and whip manufacturer, but the first occupants seem to have been John Wister and his family. This John Wister was the grandson of the John Wister who sixty years earlier had had Grumblethorpe built about half a mile down the road.[23] The contrast between the two houses indicates the degree to which the local builders had acculturated. There are no traces of the vernacular rural house in the new section of Vernon; it is a country house of the eighteenth century. The Germantown builders were now incorporated into the Anglo-American world, yet they remained in the backwash of changing taste. The builder of Vernon exhibited his Adamesque-Federal vocabulary by using the proper details, such as fanlights and dentil cornices, in the proper places, but he did not appreciate the subtleties of the language. The house's form, scale, and proportions are those of the Palladian era. It does not possess the interplay of forms and surfaces that can be seen in such paragons of Adamesque-Federal architecture as Woodlands in West Philadelphia. In fact, conceptually and stylistically, Vernon is a continuation of a house type that was first built in the area about 1728 when Stenton was begun at Eighteenth and Courtland streets for James Logan. Since Logan was the leading political figure in early-eighteenth-century Philadelphia, his fine mansion influenced Germantown's architecture even though it stood on the town's geographical fringe. Of course, Vernon is three-quarters of a century later than Stenton, hence stylistically more sophisticated. Its use of a pedimented central pavilion, continuous stringcourse, and projecting frontispiece give it a classical horizontality and three-dimensionality that is lacking in Stenton. Vernon improves in like manner upon the qualities of Cliveden, the other famous local eighteenth-century country house, yet it retains the latter's basic proportions and many of its details, including the shingling across the top of the pediment's cornice.

Improved transportation facilities in the early nineteenth century tied Germantown even more closely to the City of Philadelphia. Notoriously bad roads had greatly impeded communication between the two places during most of the colonial period, and it was not until 1761 that stage coaches began running between Germantown and Philadelphia and shortly thereafter to Reading and Bethlehem as well.[24] The roads remained wretched, however, and travel was at best uncomfortable until in 1801 the Germantown and Perkiomen Turnpike Company was chartered and given control of Germantown Road from Third and Vine streets on the northern edge of Philadelphia to Perkiomen Bridge in Collegeville, Montgomery County. This step, however, did not always assure a quick, smooth trip between Germantown and Philadelphia, and over the decades conditions failed to improve significantly; in 1874 the town's citizens went to court and forced the City of Philadelphia to acquire and pave the road. Meanwhile, leading citizens of Germantown took action to build a rail connection with both the city and lower Montgomery County. The Philadelphia, Germantown and Norristown Railroad, one of the country's earliest, was incorporated in February, 1831, and construction was begun that summer. By the following fall the road extended to the Germantown Depot, a tavern at Germantown Avenue and Price Street.[25] This tavern was replaced by a two-story station (now the city's oldest railroad station) in 1855, about the same time that the road was extended into Chestnut Hill by leasing the newly completed Chestnut Hill Railroad.[26] These rail lines were supplemented in 1859 by the Germantown Passenger Railway Company, whose horse-drawn streetcars carried an average of 2,500 passengers daily during its first month of operation along Germantown Avenue between Phil-Ellena and Eighth streets.[27]

These developments in transportation heralded another era in Germantown's history, that of garden suburb. The writings of Andrew Jackson Downing helped to popularize the environment and architecture of the kinds of residential neighborhoods that Germantown knew during the last half of the nineteenth century. Ivy Lodge, at 29 East Penn Street, not far from the Penn Street station on the Philadelphia, Germantown and Norristown Railroad, was built about 1850, making it one of the town's first suburban villas. Because of its proximity to Germantown Avenue and the built-up part of the town, its version of the Italianate is more self-contained than many Italian villas with their towers, belvederes, wings, and porches. Yet the static nature of Ivy Lodge's nearly cubic form is relieved by the use of material (rock-faced local stone ashlar), details (octagonal side bay, porches, and elongated cornice brackets), and silhouette (arched dormer set into the cornice). Moving beyond the classical restraint of

Ivy Lodge into the early phases of Picturesque Eclecticism is the Ebenezer Maxwell House (illus.), built in 1859.[28] Its site at Greene and Tulpehocken streets, then a sparsely populated neighborhood with natural plantings, gave the architect the opportunity to develop a design with a rambling plan and irregular silhouette that was more suitable for the setting than a classically balanced dwelling. Its prominently shaped and angulated cross-gables indicate that it was probably meant to be an Elizabethan villa, yet a host of other elements obscure this point. The archivolt treatment of the recessed entrance and the boldly carved porch arcades are reminiscent of the Romanesque; the porch battlements and truncated lancet window of the spindly tower are taken from the Gothic; and the mansard roof suggests French Renaissance. These elements were combined with random local rubble relieved by dressed ashlar quoins and multiple diamond-shaped red sandstone and eight different shapes of windows to create an effect so picturesque that recently neighbors affectionately called the mansion the "Addams House" in reference to Charles Addams, the macabre cartoonist whose witches, ghouls, and monsters often peer from mansarded towers like that of the Maxwell House. This splendid example of High Victorian Eclecticism was nearly lost, however, when in the early 1960's efforts were made to demolish the house to make room first for a service station and then for a rest home. The Philadelphia Historical Commission interceded to prevent this, allowing enough time for a dedicated local group to organize and start the present process of restoring the house into a center for Victorian arts.[29] Next to its preservation, the most pleasant aspect of the Maxwell House is its environment. It is but one star in a galaxy of nineteenth-century suburban villas. Its immediate neighborhood of Tulpehocken Street, Walnut Lane, and Wayne Avenue makes up but one constellation; there are many other picturesque patches to be found bordering such streets as School House Lane and Upsal Street. The houses in a wide range of styles remain remarkably little altered, planted firmly on their large lots along tree-lined byways that are tailor-made for walking tours of Victorian domestic architecture.

Germantown's second railroad, the Chestnut Hill Line of the Pennsylvania Railroad (now Penn Central), began operations west of Germantown Avenue in June, 1884, and almost immediately set off another rash of residential construction along its path, particularly in Mount Airy and Chestnut Hill.[30] A fine example of such an affluent commuter neighborhood is Pelham. Most of its sumptuous Colonial

Revival houses extend along Pelham Street and its tributaries
between Upsal Station, built about 1884 probably by Wilson Brothers
and Company, and the former Pelham Trust Company (now Mount
Airy Branch of the First Pennsylvania Bank), built on Germantown
Avenue in 1907 from the designs of Churchman and Thomas.[31]

Chestnut Hill reflects even more directly the interactions of railroad and suburban development. Henry Howard Houston was the
person most responsible for the orderly development of Chestnut Hill
into what was then called "Philadelphia's prettiest suburb" and is still
acknowledged as "one of the most beautiful and distinctive sections
of the city."[32] Houston was an entrepreneur, one of those
nineteenth-century men who successfully turned their energy and
imagination to business pursuits. His enterprises included wise investments in oil and gold that led to directorships of financial institutions and transportation companies, most notably the Pennsylvania
Railroad, which obligingly built the Chestnut Hill Line through
Houston's extensive land holdings in what was then known as
Wissahickon Heights.[33] In order to give direction to development of
the largest piece of personally owned real estate in the city,[34]
Houston commissioned the noted architects G. W. and W. D. Hewitt
to build two key social centers on Willow Grove Avenue, a short
distance from the former Wissahickon Heights station. One was
Wissahickon Inn, a summer resort hotel that is now Chestnut Hill
Academy, and the other was the Church of St. Martin-in-the-Fields,
for an Episcopal congregation, of course.[35] The neighborhood's environment was at least equally determined by its houses. It was estimated in 1889 that Houston had already erected between eighty and
one hundred dwellings in Wissahickon Heights.[36] All were apparently built for sale, and some, such as the Houston-Sauveur
House (illus.) (1885) at Seminole Avenue and Hartwell Lane, were
initially rented for a few years. The great size and distinctive design of
this robust rendition of the Queen Anne style indicate the extent of
Houston's investment in this real estate venture and help to account
for its stable development. There was no ticky-tacky in Wissahickon
Heights.

Houston's son-in-law, Dr. George Woodward, continued to
contribute to the orderly growth of Chestnut Hill in the early
twentieth century. In addition to freestanding suburban houses,
designed by such practitioners of the Philadelphia suburban style as
Wilson Eyre, Jr., Mantle Fielding, Robert McGoodwin, and Duhring,
Okie and Ziegler, Woodward also built rows, such as the first block of

Benezet Street west of Germantown Avenue, and semidetached
dwellings, of which the best examples were built between 1906 and
1928 around Pastorious Park at the end of Lincoln Drive.[37] French
Village is a fine example of this conscientious development continuing into the automobile age of the 1920's. This picturesque ensemble
of stone dwellings designed by Robert McGoodwin stretches along
two twisting lanes on the edge of the Cresheim Creek extension of
Fairmount Park to make the most of a triangular piece of land on the
corner of McCallum Street and Allen's Lane.[38] Some fine apartment
buildings were also erected in Germantown during the 1920's. Alden
Park Manor on the former Justus C. Strawbridge estate at Wissahickon Avenue and School House Lane is an outstanding complex that is thought to be the country's first high-rise apartment
building planned around open park land in the manner advocated by
LeCorbusier only a few years earlier.[39] Notable dwellings are still being built in the area. Three from the early 1960's are Robert Venturi's
house for his mother and Louis Kahn's design for Margaret Esherick
north of Pastorious Park, and Mrs. Thomas Raeburn White's house
by Romaldo Giurgola on the western fringe of Chestnut Hill at 717
West Glengarry Road.[40]

Since the heights of Chestnut Hill, Germantown, and
Roxborough offered rapidly moving streams and waterfalls as well as
salubrious air, they also possessed attractive sites for mills. Until the
advent of steam power in the last half of the nineteenth century, the
banks of Wissahickon Creek were dotted with all kinds of mills,
including the earliest paper mill in the English colonies. William Rittenhouse, the first minister of Germantown's Mennonites, built his
paper mill about 1690 near the present intersection of Lincoln Drive
and Rittenhouse Street. The mill and its replacement (the original mill
was washed away about a decade after its erection) are now gone, but
the millrace and neighboring buildings remain. Among them is a
two-story rubble dwelling built in 1707 that is probably best known as
the birthplace of William Rittenhouse's great-grandson David Rittenhouse, the noted astronomer, mathematician, and Revolutionary
political figure.[41] Gristmills were even more abundant, but like paper
mills, they could not compete with the larger steam-powered mills
and were abandoned in the mid-nineteenth century, allowed to fall
into ruins, and most have since disappeared. Remnants of one of the
last of these sites, at the mouth of the Wissahickon, was demolished
as recently as 1961. At that time only the house, Shoomac Park, was
left, but a gristmill had been erected on the property as early as 1690

by Andrew Robeson, a former Proprietor of the Province of West
Jersey and a member of the Pennsylvania governor's council. The
mill's site along Ridge Road at the point of a ferry across the
Schuylkill could not have been better. By the 1790's, when Robeson's
great-grandson owned the facilities, the mill was grinding nearly
50,000 bushels of wheat a year.[42] The Livezey farm, dating from the
1740's, near the other end of the Wissahickon, has fared better. The
barn is gone now and little more than the foundations of the gristmills remain, but the house, Glen Fern, still stands as the Valley
Green Canoe Club.

Because of its size and flow, the Schuylkill River could not be
turned to manufacturing purposes until a canal was dug. Such a
project was not launched until 1815 when the Schuylkill Navigation
Company was incorporated to develop a waterway along the river's
108 miles between Philadelphia and the anthracite coal mines around
Pottsville. When the project was completed in 1825, it included 51
miles of canals with 114 locks to overcome a total drop of 610 feet.
Forming part of this system was the Flat Rock Canal, which was
opened in early 1819 along the Schuylkill's east bank in the
northwestern end of Philadelphia County.[43] Finding the area's name,
Flat Rock, too prosaic, residents proposed others, and in the mid-
1820's adopted Manayunk, an apparent derivation from an Indian
word.[44] The canal was to make Manayunk what it has been ever
since—a nineteenth-century mill town with a classic ribbon development.[45] The canal carved out an island that provided two additional
banks for water power. By the end of 1822 nine mills stood along the
canal, and by 1830 the number had nearly tripled.[46] By the mid-
nineteenth century the island and the canal's banks were choked with
mills. Among the most extensive operations were the Economy Mills
of Sevil Schofield, remnants of which still stand on the island and
east bank of the canal above Lock Street.[47] The first street back from
the canal, Main Street, developed into the commercial district and the
primary overland route to the Wissahickon and thence into
Philadelphia. Beyond Main Street stand the houses, which have been
forced by Manayunk's topography to cling to the rocky hillside for
which Manayunk is famous. Nearest to the mills is the modest row
housing for workers, and beyond that the more comfortable single
dwellings of the former managerial class, which are usually far
enough removed from the mills to be in Roxborough. Rising above
the rooftops are the spires and towers of the community's churches.
The most imposing of the lot is the brownstone pile of the Roman

Catholic Church of St. John the Baptist at Cresson and Robinson
streets.[48]

Industry became so firmly planted in this neighborhood that it
easily survived the conversion to steam, which allowed companies to
move their mills away from the crowded riverside and up the hill.
Few went farther up the hill than Shur's Lane Mills of T. Kenworthy
& Bro. at Shur's Lane and Freeland Avenue. Built in two stages, the
Worsted Mill in 1876 and the Shoddy Mill in 1882, the complex has
had small extensions and offices added over the years,[49] but the two
main buildings have barely changed their appearances. The railroad,
which turned neighborhoods such as Germantown into residential
suburbs, served only to expand industrialism in Manayunk. Even the
automobile has not substantially changed the appearance of the
town. While Main Street seems never to have recovered from the
Great Depression and some old mills have fallen into ruins and disappeared, others are still functioning, and two of the city's largest
container manufacturers continue to operate on the canal's island, although the canal itself has not been used since 1916.[50]

Catalog

Armat, Thomas, House
(PA-1671), 5450 Germantown Ave. Coursed Wissahickon schist ashlar front and stuccoed rubble sides and rear, 24'-10" (three-bay front) × 41'-3" with one- and two-story side addition and two-story rear ell (not original), two-and-a-half stories, gable roof, side-hall plan. Built c. 1792; rear brick ell, two-story frame-and-shingle side addition built 19th century; interior altered to shop early 20th century; one-story ashlar addition built in front of side addition 1926; new shopfront, one-story rear concrete-block addition built 1960. Certified, PHC 1957. 2 photocopies of ext. photos (1957, 1960);* HABSI form (1957).*

Ashmead, Albert, House
(PA-1672), 5430 Germantown Ave. Coursed Wissahickon schist ashlar front and rubble sides and rear, 33'-8" (three-bay front) × 32'-1" with two-story rear brick ell and one-story lateral brick addition, two-and-a-half stories, gable roof, side-hall plan. Built before 1796; lateral addition built late 19th century; interior extensively remodeled, frontispiece and triple dormer added 1903. Certified, PHC 1957. 1 photocopy of ext. photo (1957);* HABSI (1957).*

Ashmead, William, House
(PA-1673), 5434 Germantown Ave. Random Wissahickon schist ashlar front and rubble sides and rear, 32'-4" (four-bay front) × 31'-4" with two-story rear ell, two stories, gable roof. Built 1740; rear brick ell built 1906; exterior partially restored, interior altered to bank 1949. Certified, PHC 1957. 1 photocopy of ext. photo (1957);* HABSI form (1957).*

Bank of Germantown. See Clarkson-Watson House

Barron, Commodore James, House
(PA-1674), 5106 Germantown Ave. Stuccoed rubble, 43'-9" (five-bay front) × 22'-5" with two-and-a-half-story rear ell, two-and-a-half stories, gable roof, center-hall plan. Rear ell probably built before 1794; house built between 1794 and 1803; altered to store after 1920. Commodore Barron, commander of the *Chesapeake* when it was attacked by the *Leopard* 1807 and Commandant of Philadelphia Navy Yard 1824–25, 1831–37, owned this house 1839–45. Certified, PHC 1957. 2 photocopies of ext. photos (c. 1900, 1957);* HABSI form (1957).*

Baynton House. See Germantown Historical Society Area Study

Bechtel House. See Germantown Historical Society Area Study

Beggarstown School
(PA-1675), 6669 Germantown Ave., at N.E. corner Springer St. Coursed Wissahickon schist ashlar front and stuccoed rubble sides and rear, 28'-3" (four-bay front) × 18'-3" with one-story rear ell, one story (originally one-and-a-half), gable roof with projecting cornice, one-room plan.
     Rare example of simple colonial schoolhouse. Built c. 1740; interior altered c. 1840; "restored" 1915; rear ell added later. St. Michael's Lutheran Church parish school, which provided basic education. Certified, PHC 1956; Pennsylvania Register 1970; NR. 1 ext. photo (1973).*

Belfield (also known as Charles Willson Peale House). Illustrated
(PA-1676), 5500 N. Twentieth St., at N.E. corner Clarkson Ave. (not cut through). Stuccoed brick, approx. 55' (five-bay front) × 25' with two- and two-and-a-half-story rear ell (not original), two-and-a-half stories in front, three-and-a-half stories in rear, gambrel roof. Built mid-18th century; enlarged, altered later; porch enclosed, three-story rear corner bay built c. 1923. Charles Willson Peale, versatile and prolific early American painter, lived here 1810–25. Certified, PHC 1956; designated National Historic Landmark 1965. 3 ext. photos (1967),* 3 int. photos (1967);* 3 data pages (including 1923 insurance survey).*

Billmeyer, Michael, House

(PA-1677), 6505–7 Germantown Ave., at N.E. corner Upsal St. Coursed Wissahickon schist ashlar front and rubble sides and rear, approx. 40' (four-bay front) × 33' with two-story rear ells, two-and-a-half stories on raised basement, gable roof, front pent eave, two entrances with side-hall plans.

Fine example of Germantown colonial architecture. Built c. 1730. Acquired by Germantown Historical Society 1961. Michael Billmeyer, newspaper and almanac printer and German printer for Pennsylvania Assembly, lived here 1789–1831. Certified, PHC 1957. 1 ext. photo (1973).*

Blair House

(PA-7-5), 6105 Germantown Ave. Stuccoed rubble, 26'-4" (three-bay front) × 36'-2" with two-and-a-half-story diagonal rear wing, two-and-a-half stories, gable roof, round-arch entrance with fanlight and Tuscan frontispiece, side-hall plan. Rear wing probably built before 1806; house built 1806; demolished c. 1950. 7 sheets (1934, including plans, elevations, sections, details); 4 ext. photos (1934); 2 data pages (1936).

Bringhurst House

(PA-1679), 5448 Germantown Ave. Wissahickon schist rubble front and stuccoed rubble sides and rear, 38'-6" (five-bay front) × 28'-0" with two-story rear brick ell, two stories, gambrel roof (originally gable), center-hall plan. Built mid-18th century; rear ell built mid-19th century; gambrel roof added c. 1875; altered to offices later; exterior partially restored 1960. Certified, PHC 1957. 1 photocopy of ext. photo (1957);* HABSI form (1957).*

Chestnut Hill Academy. See Wissahickon Inn

Chew House. See Cliveden

Church of St. Vincent de Paul (Roman Catholic)

(PA-1680), 101–7 E. Price St., at N.E. corner Lena St. Plastered stone with brownstone trim, approx. 46' × 140', one story, gable roofs with central dome, round-arch windows, giant Tuscan pilasters; Greek-cross plan with extended nave, three aisles, semicircular chancel, notable original interior decorations and paintings.

Fine example of reserved Italianate church design. Built 1849–51; Joseph D. Koecker, architect; William A. and Daniel Ruffner, builders. Dome, transept built 1857; interior renovated 1881, 1901; white marble altar restored c. 1945. Exterior replastered to simulate granite 1945; Earley Studio (Rosslyn, Va.), contractors. First Roman Catholic parish in Germantown. Certified, PHC 1972; Pennsylvania Register 1973. 2 ext. photos (1973),* 1 photocopy of old int. lithograph (c. 1880).*

Clarkson-Watson House (also known as Bank of Germantown)

(PA-1681), 5275–77 Germantown Ave. Museum. Stuccoed rubble, 38'-5" (five-bay front) × 32'-3" with two-story rear wings, two-and-a-half stories on raised basement, gable roof, Tuscan frontispiece with pediment, originally front pent eave, center-hall plan. Built c. 1745; pent eave removed, frontispiece added c. 1775; altered to bank and dwelling c. 1825; altered to stores, rear brick ells built c. 1870, c. 1910. Exterior restored to 1793 appearance 1967–70; Henry J. Magaziner, architect.

Country home 1780–95 of Matthew Clarkson, Mayor of Philadelphia 1792–96. Quarters of Secretary of State Thomas Jefferson and Attorney General Edmund Randolph during yellow fever epidemic of 1793. Home of John Fanning Watson, author of *Annals of Philadelphia* (1830) 1825–47. Bank of Germantown 1825–69. Costume Museum of Germantown Historical Society since 1971. Certified, PHC 1957; Pennsylvania Register 1972; NR. 1 ext. photo (1973).*

Cliveden (also known as Chew House). Illustrated

(PA-1184), 6401 Germantown Ave., in middle of block bounded by Germantown Ave., Johnson, Morton, Cliveden sts. Historic house museum. Coursed Wissahickon schist ashlar front, scored stuccoed rubble sides and rubble rear, 53'-10" (five-bay front) × 44'-4" with two-story rubble rear ell, two-and-a-half stories on raised basement, gable roof with front pediment, stone urns on brick pedestals at front corners and pediment and roof ridge, Doric frontispiece with pediment, quoins, central front-hall and rear-hall plan, notable interior woodwork. Flanked at rear by two-story rubble buildings with stuccoed fronts; northern building connected to house by one-story passage (originally arcade open on south side). Two-story rubble barn and stable at rear of property.

Oustanding example of Georgian domestic architecture with notable interiors. Built 1763–67; Jacob Knor, master carpenter; John

Hesser, mason. Arcade enclosed 1856; rear ell built 1867–68. Country house of Benjamin Chew, Chief Justice of Pennsylvania Supreme Court 1774–76 and Judge of High Court of Errors and Appeals 1791–1808; Chew family residence until 1972 when acquired by National Trust for Historic Preservation. Site of the turning point in the Battle of Germantown 1777. Certified, PHC 1956; designated National Historic Landmark 1961.

17 sheets (1972, including plot plan, plans, elevations, sections, details, landscape plan, plan and elevations of barn-stable);* 40 ext. photos (1967, 1972, including battle-scarred door and barn-stable),* 52 int. photos (1967, 1972, including details of lock, servant bells, floor joists),* 5 photocopies of architectural drawings (c. 1763);* 5 data pages (including 1856–68 insurance surveys).*

Compton (also known as John T. Morris Estate)
(PA-1682), Meadowbrook Ave., near S.W. corner Stroud St. Coursed cyclopean-rusticated granite, approx. 75' (six-bay front) × 65' two-and-a-half stories on raised basement with battlemented four-story octagonal tower, hipped, gable, and apsidal roofs with Flemish cross-gables, open porch on two sides, irregular plan with large entrance-stairhall, notable carved interior woodwork. Built 1887–88; Theophilus Parsons Chandler, Jr., architect. Acquired by University of Pennsylvania as part of Morris Arboretum 1932; demolished 1968. 6 ext. photos (1964),* 6 int. photos (1964).*

Concord School. Illustrated
(PA-12), 6309 Germantown Ave. Historic house museum. Stuccoed rubble, approx. 25' (two-bay front) × 37', two stories with open square belfry with spire, gable roof, two side entrances to first-floor schoolroom with enclosed stairs in southeast corner, second-floor library (now caretaker's apartment).

Fine example of an 18th-century schoolhouse. Built 1775; probably by Jacob Knor, master carpenter. Established to provide an English education for children too far distant from Germantown Academy. Maintained by Trustees of the Upper Germantown Burying Ground. Certified, PHC 1956. 6 sheets (1934, including plans, elevations, section, plans and section of bell and belfry, details); 1 ext. photo (1973);* 2 data pages (1934).

Conyngham-Hacker House. See Germantown Historical Society Area Study

Deshler-Morris House

(PA-1683), 5442 Germantown Ave., opposite Market Sq. Independence National Historical Park. Historic house museum. Stuccoed rubble, 36'-2" (five-bay front) × 35'-2" with two-story rear ell (not original), two-and-a-half stories on raised basement, gable roof, Tuscan frontispiece with pediment, central-hall plan, notable interior woodwork, adjoining restored 18th-century garden.

Notable Georgian "double-pile" house, whose central-hall plan is unusual for colonial Germantown houses. Built 1772; rear ell built 1838, enlarged 1856, 1868; interior altered 1868, "restored" 1898; lateral addition built on north end 1909; partially restored by National Park Service 1949–50; restoration by National Park Service completed 1975–76. Gen. William Howe's headquarters after Battle of Germantown 1777. Summer residence of President George Washington 1793, 1794. Built for David Deshler, prosperous merchant; in possession of the prominent Morris family 1836–1948; acquired by National Park Service 1948; opened to public 1950. Certified, PHC 1956; Pennsylvania Register 1971; NR. 2 ext. photos (1973),* 4 int. photos (1950, 1960);* 7 data pages (including 1774–1909 insurance surveys).*

Detweiler House

(PA-1684), 8226 Germantown Ave. Coursed Wissahickson schist ashlar front and stuccoed rubble sides and rear, 26'-7" (three-bay front) × 34'-7" with two-story rear ell, two-and-a-half stories, gable roof, open side porch, side-hall plan. Built c. 1760; new front built c. 1800; rear ell built 1902. Certified, PHC 1957. 1 photocopy of ext. photo (1957);* HABSI form (1957).*

Dorfenille House

(PA-1685), 5139 Germantown Ave., at S.E. corner Collom St. Stuccoed rubble, 25'-6" (three-bay front) × 38'-0" with one- and two-story rear wing, two-and-a-half stories, gable roof. Built c. 1795; rear wing built before 1894; ground story altered to store 1924. Certified, PHC 1957. 1 photocopy of ext. photo (1957);* HABSI form (1957).*

Endt, Theobald, House

(PA-1686), 5222–24 Germantown Ave. Stuccoed rubble, 38'-6" (five-bay front) × 41'-3", two-and-a-half stories on raised basement, gable roof, probably originally center-hall plan. Built c. 1795; rear brick addition built later; altered to store and apartments 20th century. Acquired by Germantown Historical Society 1972. Certified, PHC 1957. HABSI form (1957).*

Fielding, Mantle, House
(PA-1687), 28 W. Walnut Ln. Wissahickon schist rubble, approx. 58' (four-bay front) × 30', two-and-a-half stories, gable roof, Tuscan-column porch and balcony across front, center-hall plan. Early example of adaptive use and taking advantage of a vernacular building's rustic qualities for domestic purposes. Built 1796 as barn on adjoining Wyck property. Remodeled into dwelling c. 1891; Mantle Fielding, architect. Porch enclosed later. Mantle Fielding, noted early-20th-century architect and writer, lived here 1892–1939. Certified, PHC 1972. 1 ext. photo (1973).*

First Baptist Church of Germantown
(PA-1688), 36–42 E. Price St. Stuccoed rubble, approx. 50' × 75', one story on raised basement with Corinthian hexastyle portico, gable roof, three-aisle plan. Fine late example of the Greek Revival. Built 1852–53; Samuel Sloan, architect. Steeple added 1862, removed 1887; lecture room remodeled 1892; interior altered 1897. Polite Temple Baptist Church since 1955. Certified, PHC 1965. 2 ext. photos (1973);* 8 data pages (1965, including 1852–53 news clippings).*

Folwell House
(PA-1689), 5281 Germantown Ave. Stuccoed rubble, 24'-1" (three-bay front) × 33'-3" with two-story rear ell, two-and-a-half stories on raised basement, gable roof, side-hall plan. Built late 18th century; brick rear ell built before 1880. Certified, PHC 1957. 1 photocopy of ext. photo (1957);* 6 data pages (including 1881–1916 insurance surveys);* HABSI form (1957).*

Fromberger, John, Houses (now known as Germantown Insurance Co.)
(PA-1690), 5501 Germantown Ave., at N.E. corner Church Ln., on E. side Market Sq. Brick with marble trim, approx. 70' (nine-bay front) × 75' (originally three row houses, probably each approx. 23' × 34'), two-and-a-half stories, gable roof, round-arch entrance with fanlight and pedimented Ionic frontispiece (not original), originally London house plans.

Built 1795–96; altered many times later; enlarged, altered 1917; renovated after fire 1930. Rehabilitated 1952–54; G. Edwin Brumbaugh, architect. Place of worship for St. Luke's Protestant

Episcopal Church 1813–37; site of (Young) Women's Christian Association of Germantown 1873–1915; Mary Warden Harkness House, boarding home for girls, 1917–41; offices of Germantown Fire Insurance Co. since 1954 whose name changed to Germantown Insurance Co. 1964. Certified, PHC 1956; Pennsylvania Register 1971. 1 ext. photo (1973);* 10 data pages (1965, including 1796 insurance survey);* HABSI form (1957).*

General Wayne Hotel

(PA-1691), 5060 Germantown Ave., at S.W. corner Manheim St. Stuccoed rubble, approx. 32' (three-bay front) × 22' with two-and-a-half story rear wing, two-and-a-half stories, gambrel roof with cross-gambrel (originally gable). Built between 1780–85; enlarged, altered, gambrel roof built 1866; front porch removed, ground story altered later. Certified, PHC 1957. 1 photocopy of ext. photo (1957);* HABSI form (1957).*

Germantown Academy (originally known as Germantown Union School)

(PA-7-4), 110 School House Ln., at S.W. corner Greene St. Main building: coursed Wissahickon schist ashlar front and rubble sides and rear, 67'-2" (five-bay front) × 40'-0" with two-story rear ell and two-and-a-half-story addition, two-and-a-half stories on raised basement with centered square belfry and spire, gable roof, central-hall plan originally with classroom on each side.

Notable mid-18th-century educational complex. Built 1760–61; Jacob Knor, master carpenter. Rear wing built at northeast end 1879–80; James Kinnier and Sons, architects and builders. Sower Hall built onto rear western end of wing 1904; Robeson Lea Perot, architect. Organized by Pennsylvania Germans as private school 1759; chartered as Public School of Germantown 1784, popularly known as Germantown Academy since 1794. Germantown Lutheran Academy 1965–73; Germantown-Stevens Academy since 1973. Hospital during Battle of Germantown 1777. Certified, PHC 1956; Pennsylvania Register 1971; NR. 13 sheets (1934, including plot plan, plans, elevations, section, details, belfry plan, elevation and section); 7 ext. photos (1934, 1960*); 2 data pages (1936).

German Headmaster's House: S.E. of Main Building. Wissahickon schist rubble, 20'-2" (two-bay front) × 28'-0" with rear addition, two stories, gable roof. Built 1760–61; rear addition built later. 3 sheets (1934, including plans, elevations, section, details).

English Headmaster's House: S.W. of Main Building. Wissahickon schist rubble, approx. 20' (two-bay front) × 28', two stories, gable roof. Built 1760–61; altered later. 1 sheet (1934, including details); 1 ext. photo (1934).

Germantown Cricket Club (also known as Manheim Club). Illustrated (PA-1693), 5140 Morris St., at S.W. corner Manheim St. Brick with marble trim, approx. 215' (twenty-bay front) × 60', two-and-a-half stories, gable roofs originally with central balustrade, rear Doric colonnade with Tuscan balcony above, U-plan with large central entry hall.

Important Georgian Revival work by a leading late-19th-century architectural firm. Built 1890–91; Charles F. McKim of McKim, Mead and White, architect; A. S. Tourison, contractor. Wings, addition built 1902, 1907; McKim, Mead and White, architects. Interior altered, three-story brick addition built 1911–12; Mantle Fielding, architect. One-story rear brick addition built 1929; Dreher and Churchman, architects. Roof balustrade removed after 1953. Oldest cricket club in the United States; founded 1854. Certified, PHC 1970. 2 ext. photos (1973).*

Germantown Historical Society Area Study
(PA-1694), 5208, 5214, 5218, 5226 Germantown Ave. Three Wissahickon schist rubble houses and one brick house, approx. 25' and 35' (three- and five-bay fronts) × 20' and 30' with two-story rear ells, two-and-a-half stories on raised basements, gable roofs, side-hall and center-hall plans.

Built between 1742 and c. 1790; altered, rear ells added later. Includes Baynton House, No. 5208; Conyngham-Hacker House, No. 5214; Howell House, No. 5218; Bechtel House, No. 5226, which serve as library, headquarters, costume museum, and textile museum respectively of Germantown Historical Society. Certified, PHC 1957; Conyngham-Hacker and Howell Houses on Pennsylvania Register 1971; NR. 5 ext. photos (1976);* 1 data page (including 1827 insurance survey);* 2 HABSI forms (1957).*

Germantown Insurance Company. See Fromberger, John, Houses

Germantown Union School. See Germantown Academy

Glen Fern (also known as Livezey House)
(PA-14), Livezey Ln. at E. side of Wissahickon Creek. Fairmount Park. Wissahickon schist rubble, 34'-0" (four-bay front) × 37'-2" with

one-and-a-half-story lateral ells (originally approx. 34' × 20'), two-and-a-half stories (originally one-and-a-half), gable roof, balcony across south front, two front rooms and large back room (once center-hall plan).

Fine example of 18th-century Delaware Valley farmhouse. Built between 1733 and 1739; enlarged to rear (north) and raised one story c. 1765; ells built before 1853, altered later. Springhouse remains as only extant outbuilding. Purchased 1747 by Thomas Livezey, farmer, miller, justice of peace and provincial commissioner; owned by Livezey family until acquired by Fairmount Park Commission, City of Philadelphia 1869; Valley Green Canoe Club since 1909. Certified, PHC 1956.

12 sheets (1935, including plot plan, plans, elevations, sections, details, barn and springhouse plans, elevations and details); 1 ext. photo (1973);* 8 data pages (1935, including 1833 insurance survey*).

Green Tree Tavern (also known as Pastorius House)
(PA-1695), 6023 Germantown Ave. Wissahickon schist ashlar front and south end, rubble rear and north end, 42'-4" (five-bay front) × 36'-6", two-and-a-half stories, gable end with cornice returns at ends, pent eave on front and south end, 1748 date stone in south gable, center-hall plan.

Notable example of colonial Germantown architecture. Built 1748 for Daniel Pastorius, grandson of Germantown's founder Francis Daniel Pastorius. Moved northward, entrance exterior altered, interior extensively renovated 1930. Germantown Academy organized at meeting here 1759. Offices and parish house of First United Methodist Church of Germantown since 1907. Certified, PHC 1956. 1 ext. photo (1973);* 4 data pages (including 1797–1932 insurance surveys).*

Grumblethorpe (also known as Wister's Big House). Illustrated
(PA-7-1), 5267 Germantown Ave. Historic house museum. Coursed fieldstone ashlar front and rubble sides and rear, 43'-5" (six-bay front) × 34'-4" with three-story rear ell (originally one-and-a-half stories), two stories, gable roof, pent eave with center balcony, center-hall plan with separate door to front parlor.

Initially a country house, Grumblethorpe is a fine example of Delaware Valley vernacular domestic architecture. Built 1744; rear ell enlarged and extended 1750, 1799, 1806, 1819; house altered 1808, restored 1957–67. Headquarters and site of death of British Brig. Gen. James Agnew during Battle of Germantown 1777. Owned and maintained by Philadelphia Society for Preservation of Landmarks since 1940. Certified, PHC 1956; Pennsylvania Register 1971; NR.

10 sheets (1934, including plot plan, plans, elevations, section, details, plan and sections of springhouse and pump); 6 ext. photos (1934, 1973,* including 1 of pump); 9 data pages (1936, including 1764–1887 insurance surveys*).

Grumblethorpe Tenant House. See Wister's Tenant House

Haines House. See Wyck

Hood Cemetery Entrance (originally known as Lower Burying Ground).
Illustrated
(PA-1697), 4901 Germantown Ave., at N.E. corner Logan St. Marble, approx. 147' front, horseshoe-arch entry between engaged Corinthian columns and beneath bracketed round arch with cartouche, balustraded front wall. Built 1849; William Johnston, architect; William Struthers, marble mason. Part of original Germantown plan; graves date from 1708. Known as Hood Cemetery since William Hood bequeathed money for entrance in 1850. Certified, PHC 1957. 2 ext. photos (1973).*

House

(PA-1698), 6000–6002 Germantown Ave., at N.W. corner Harvey St. Wissahickon schist rubble, 35'-4" (five-bay front) × 30'-8" with two-story rear ell, two-and-a-half stories, gable roof, originally center-hall plan. Built 18th century; altered to store, one-story brick side addition built later. Certified, PHC 1957. 1 photocopy of ext. photo (1957);* HABSI form (1957).*

House

(PA-1699), 6377 Germantown Ave. Stuccoed rubble, approx. 25' (three-bay front) × 40' with one-story rear ell, two-and-a-half stories on raised basement, gable roof, side-hall plan. Built mid-18th century; interior altered c. 1800; altered to store, rear ell added 20th century. Certified, PHC 1961. 2 ext. photos (1961),* 2 int. photos (1961);* 7 data pages (1961).*

Houston-Sauveur House. Illustrated
(PA-1700), 8205 Seminole Ave., at N.W. corner Hartwell Ln. Random Wissahickon schist ashlar with frame-and-shingle third story, approx. 36' (three-bay front) × 42', three stories, gable and hipped roofs

with cross-gables, enclosed semioctagonal sun porch, open front porch with balcony above, center entry-hall plan. Notable example of Queen Anne style. Built 1885; probably by G. W. and W. D. Hewitt, architects. Initially rental property for Henry H. Houston, steam transportation entrepreneur and developer of Chestnut Hill. 2 ext. photos (1973).*

Howell House. See Germantown Historical Society Area Study

Ivy Lodge
(PA-1701), 29 E. Penn St. Coursed rough-hewn Wissahickon schist, approx. 44' (three-bay front) × 38' with two-story rear wing, two-and-half stories, hipped roof, bracketed cornice interrupted by centered round-arch dormer, front rectangular bays and porch, open porch on east side, semioctagonal bay on west side, center-hall plan. Fine example of Italian villa design. Built c. 1850; Thomas U. Walter, architect. Rear wing built later. Certified, PHC 1970; Pennsylvania Register 1970; NR. 1 ext. photo (1973).*

Jacoby, Wigard, House
(PA-1702), 8327 Germantown Ave. Coursed Wissahickon schist ashlar front and rubble sides and rear, approx. 25' (three-bay front) × 36' with rear one-story concrete-block kitchen ell, two-and-a-half stories, gable roof, round-arch entrance with fanlight and pedimented frontispiece, side-hall plan. Built c. 1794; probably by Wigard Jacoby, carpenter. Two dormers added after 1911; ell built 1948. Certified, PHC 1957. 1 photocopy of ext. photo (1957);* HABSI form (1957).*

Johnson House
(PA-7-7), 6306 Germantown Ave., at N.W. corner Washington Ln. Wissahickon schist ashlar front and rubble sides and rear, 41'-6" (five-bay) × 35'-7½" with two-story rear ell, two-and-a-half stories, gable roof, pent eave on front and south side, center-hall plan, notable interior paneling.

Fine example of Germantown vernacular architecture exhibiting German influence in exterior details. Built 1765–68. Owned and maintained by Women's Club of Germantown since 1920. Certified, PHC 1956; Pennsylvania Register 1971; NR. 12 sheets (1934, including plans, elevations, sections, details); 4 ext. photos (1934); 3 data pages (1936).

Keyser Houses

(PA-1704), 5920–26 Germantown Ave., at S.W. corner Haines St. Two contiguous stuccoed rubble houses, each approx. 19' (two-bay front) × 22' with one-story rear wing, two stories, gable and flat roofs. Two stuccoed rubble row houses, each approx. 23' (two- and three-bay front) × 33' with two-story rear wings, three stories, gable roofs. Built mid-18th century; altered to stores later. Certified, PHC 1957. HABSI form (1957).*

Keyser, Jacob, House

(PA-11), 6205 Germantown Ave., at N.E. corner Tulpehocken St. Coursed Wissahickon schist ashlar front and rubble sides and rear, 37'-4" (five-bay front) × 28'-10" with two-story rear ell, two-and-a-half stories on raised basement, gable roof, pent eave, center-hall plan. Built after 1744 (rear ell probably part of an earlier house); demolished 1950. 7 sheets (1934, including plot plan, plans, elevations, cellar sections, details, elevations of barn); 2 data pages (1934).

Livezey House. See Glen Fern

Log House

(PA-143), N.E. corner Courtland and Eighteenth sts. on Stenton grounds (earlier at Friends' Select School, S.W. corner Race and Sixteenth sts.). Squared logs with clapboard gable ends, 31'-9" (four-bay front) × 21'-4" with brick rear ell, two-and-a-half stories, gable roof, two rooms with central chimney.

Probably built as barn c. 1790; converted to house c. 1820. Relocated from Sixteenth St. between Cherry and Race sts. to S.W. corner Race and Sixteenth sts., rear ell built after 1886; clapboards removed c. 1925. Moved to Stenton grounds 1969. Maintained by National Society of the Colonial Dames of America since 1969. Certified, PHC 1957. 4 ext. photos (1940, 1976*).

Loudoun

(PA-1705), 4650 Germantown Ave., at N.W. corner Apsley St. Historic house museum. Stuccoed rubble, 49'-10" (five-bay front) × 46'-3" including two-story stone lateral and brick rear additions (originally approx. 32' × 30'), two-and-a-half stories with Corinthian tetrastyle portico, gambrel and hipped roofs, one-story side (west end) sun porch, center-hall plan.

Germantown's most imposing Federal-style house. Built 1796–

1801; west section and sun porch built 1829; portico added 1850; rear
addition built 1888; rehabilitated 1964. Acquired by Fairmount Park
Commission, City of Philadelphia 1939; opened to public 1966.
Certified, PHC 1956. 2 ext. photo (1973);* 5 data pages (including
1808–88 insurance surveys);* HABSI form (1957).*

Lower Burying Ground. See Hood Cemetery Entrance

Manheim Club. See Germantown Cricket Club

Maxwell, Ebenezer, House. Illustrated
(PA-1098), 200 W. Tulpehocken St., at S.W. corner Greene St.
Museum. Random rough-hewn Wissahickon schist with
maroonstone diamond patterns, 78'-3$^{1}/_{2}$" (seven-bay front) × 45'-
9$^{1}/_{2}$" including lateral kitchen wings, two-and-a-half stories with
square three-story tower, mansard roof with Flemish cross-gables,
two open battlemented porches; center-hall plan with lateral passage
to kitchen wings.
    Fine early example of eclectic suburban villa. Built 1859; probably
by Joseph C. Hoxie, architect. Western kitchen wing raised to two
stories, western porch added later; porch removed 1970. Restored by
Germantown Historical Society as Victorian arts museum 1965– .
Ebenezer Maxwell was a successful Philadelphia dry goods merchant.
Certified, PHC 1964; Pennsylvania Register 1970; NR.
    7 sheets (1966, including plot plan, plans, elevations, details);* 8
ext. photos (1964),* 3 int. photos (1964);* 14 data pages (1964, including 1859 insurance survey).*

Mehl House
(PA-1706), 4821 Germantown Ave. Wissahickon schist rubble, approx. 36' (five-bay front) × 29' with one- and two-story rear ell, two-
and-a-half stories on raised basement, gable roof, center-hall plan.
Built late 18th century; two-story stone rear ell built later; interior renovated 1906; one-story brick ell built 1933. Certified, PHC 1957. 1
photocopy of ext. photo (1957);* HABSI form (1957).*

Mennonite Meeting House. Illustrated
(PA-15), 6119 Germantown Ave., at N.E. corner Herman St.
Wissahickon schist rubble, 30'-1" (three-bay front) × 35'-6" with one-
story rear addition, one story, gable roof, two-room rectangular plan.
Plain style of a German pietist sect. Built 1770; rear addition built

1907. Established in 1688 as the first Mennonite congregation in America. Certified, PHC 1956; Pennsylvania Register 1972; NR. 7 sheets (1934, 1935, including plot plan, plans, elevations, section, details); 1 ext. photo (1973);* 2 data pages (1934).

Morris, John T., Estate. See Compton

Mutual Fire Insurance Company Building
(PA-1014), 5521 Germantown Ave., at N.E. corner School House Ln. Brick with stone and terra cotta trim, approx. 30' (three-bay front) × 74', two-and-a-half stories, tiled gable roof with cross-gables, general office in front with president's room and directors' room in rear.

Fine example of late-19th-century architectural design with rich use of materials, color, and texture. Built 1884; George T. Pearson, architect; James Kinnier's Sons, builder. Demolished 1959. 3 ext. photos (1959), 2 int. photos (1959), 1 photocopy of old ext. photo (c. 1900); 6 data pages (1959).

Pastorius House. See Green Tree Tavern

Peale, Charles Willson, House. See Belfield

Philadelphia and Reading Railroad, Chestnut Hill Line. See Philadelphia, Germantown and Norristown Railroad, Germantown Depot

Philadelphia, Germantown and Norristown Railroad, Germantown Depot (later Philadelphia and Reading Railroad, Chestnut Hill Line)
(PA-1707), 5731–35 Germantown Ave., at S.E. corner Price St. Brick covered with scored stucco, approx. 50' (three-bay front) × 35' with one-story rear additions (originally one-story train shed approx. 38' × 256'), two stories, gable roof, boldly framed round-arch windows, quoins, rectangular plan.

Fine example of early suburban passenger and freight depot, now Philadelphia's oldest surviving railroad station. Built 1855; probably by Joseph C. Hoxie, architect. Altered to store and offices 1902; Armstrong and Printzenhoff, contractors. Rear train shed replaced by present additions 1934–35; Samuel Rothblatt, contractor. This railroad, Philadelphia's first, began operations 1832; acquired by Philadelphia and Reading Railroad 1870. Certified, PHC 1964. 1 ext. photo (1973).*

Rectory of St. Stephen's Methodist Episcopal Church

(PA-1708), 5213 Germantown Ave. Stuccoed rubble, approx. 26'
(three-bay front) × 40' with two-story lateral addition, two-and-a-
half stories, gable roof, round-arch entrance with fanlight, originally
side-hall plan. Built late 18th century; lateral addition, open side and
rear porches built mid-19th century. Rectory since 1856. Certified,
PHC 1957. 1 photocopy of ext. photo (1957);* HABSI form (1957).*

Rittenhouse House

(PA-16) S.W. corner Lincoln Dr. and Rittenhouse St. Fairmount Park.
Whitewashed Wissahickon schist rubble, 44'-0" (five-bay front) ×
18'-4", two stories, gable roof, originally pent eave on north side, two
sections with one room to a floor in each.

Germantown vernacular architecture reflecting strong German
influence. Built 1707. Birthplace of David Rittenhouse, early
American astronomer and instrument-maker and foreign member of
Royal Society. William Rittenhouse, original owner of house, built
nearby first paper mill in British colonies 1690. Acquired by Fairmount Park Commission, City of Philadelphia 1890. Certified, PHC
1956. 7 sheets (1935, including plot plan, plans, elevations, details); 3
ext. photos (1925, 1973*); 1 data page (1935).

Robeson House. See Shoomac Park.

Royal House

(PA-1709), 5011 Germantown Ave., at N.E. corner Garfield St. Stuccoed rubble, 26'-3" (three-bay front) × 36'-0" with two-story rear ell,
two-and-a-half stories, gable roof, side-hall plan. Built probably early
19th century; brick·rear ell added later; altered to store and apartments early 20th century; storefront remodeled 1925. Certified, PHC
1957. 1 photocopy of ext. photo (1957);* HABSI form (1957).*

St. Timothy's (Protestant Epsicopal) Church

(PA-1710), 5720 Ridge Ave. Random rough-hewn Wissahickon schist
with brick trim, approx. 45' × 130' (originally approx. 45' × 38') with
two-story rear parish house, one story with squat battlemented rear
clerestory tower and three-stage square front corner tower, polychromatic gable roof with shed roof over aisles, lancet windows; three-
aisle plan with side entrances, semihexagonal chancel, exposed interior wooden trusses.

Fine synthesis of High Victorian Gothic church design. Built

1862–63; Emlen T. Littell, architect. Corner tower added 1871, nave extended, eastern part of parish house built 1874; probably by Charles M. Burns, architect. Nave extended, clerestory tower built, parish house enlarged and connected to church 1885–86; church and parish house renovated 1931; chancel altered later. Certified, PHC 1974. 5 ext. photos (1973).*

St. Timothy's Working Men's Club and Institute
(PA-1711), 5164 Ridge Ave., at intersection of Terrace and Vassar sts. Random Wissahickon schist ashlar with granite trim, approx. 21' (two-bay front) × 46', two-and-a-half stories with three-story front square entry and stair tower, mansard and jerkin-head roofs, Corinthian cast-iron columns at two corners, semihexagonal second-story frame bay on struts, irregular plan.

Built 1877; probably by Charles M. Burns, architect. Founded 1873 by St. Timothy's Protestant Episcopal Church to provide self-improvement and social facilities for residents of working-class neighborhood. Certified, PHC 1974. 2 ext. photos (1973).*

Schaeffer, Harriet D., House
(PA-1712), 433 W. Stafford St. Wissahickon schist rubble with wood frame second story covered with shingles, approx. 55' (six-bay front) × 35', two-and-a-half stories, hipped and jerkin-head roofs, circular porch with apsidal roof, pointed-arch entrance, vestibule leading to open entry hall. Notable example of Shingle style in cottage mode. Built 1888; Wilson Eyre, Jr., architect. Southern gable end altered c. 1920; Wilson, Harris and Richards, architects. 1 ext. photo (1973).*

Shoomac Park (also known as Robeson House)
(PA-1067), S.E. corner Ridge Ave. and Wissahickon Dr. Stuccoed rubble, 55'-4" (six-bay front) × 38'-3" (originally 55'-4" × 22'-9"), two-and-a-half stories, gambrel roof, originally porch at second story along north and west sides, originally one room deep and three rooms wide with hall between north and middle rooms.

Built c. 1759; enlarged c. 1840; large two-story front and side porch built before 1890; demolished 1961. Woodwork sections, paneled chimney breast, corner cupboard in Architectural Study Collection, Museum Division, Independence National Historical Park. Associated with one of the earliest gristmills in Pennsylvania, Certified, PHC 1956. 5 sheets (1961, including plot plan, plans); 3 ext.

photos (1956, 1961, including 1 of carriage house), 4 int. photos (1961); 9 data pages (1961).

Shur's Lane Mills, T. Kenworthy & Bro.

(PA-1713), 428 Shur's Ln., at N.W. corner Freeland Ave. Two Wissahickon schist rubble factories with brick trim at right angles to each other, three stories, gable roofs; Worsted Mill (facing Pechin St.) approx. 55' (five-bay front) × 150' with lateral elevator shaft, Shoddy Mill (facing Shur's Ln.) approx. 72' (seven-bay front) × 149' with lateral fire tower and one- and two-story rear extensions and one-story rear additions; rectangular plans, interior stone walls with iron doors originally separated more combustible processes from finishing work.

Fine example of steam-powered textile mills built in Manayunk and Roxborough after the Civil War. Worsted Mill built 1876; Shoddy Mill built 1882; later minor alterations and additions, including corrugated iron bridge connecting buildings built c. 1921 and rear cinderblock building built 1954. 1 ext. photo (1973),* 1 printed plan and view (1885).*

Sower, Christopher, Jr., House. See Trinity Lutheran Church House

Stenton

(PA-1714), N.E. corner Courtland and Eighteenth sts. Historic house museum. Brick, approx. 50' (six-bay front) × 38', two-and-a-half stories, hipped roof, plain doorway with side lights, asymmetrical side and rear fenestration, center-hall plan; covered porch connects to detached one-and-a-half-story rear service ell.

Significant Georgian "double-pile" house, prototype of Germantown country houses. Built 1728 for James Logan, William Penn's secretary and agent, Chief Justice of the Supreme Court of Pennsylvania, President of Provincial Council. Occupied by Gen. George Washington before Battle of Brandywine and by Gen. William Howe during Battle of Germantown 1777. Acquired by City of Philadelphia 1908; maintained by National Society of Colonial Dames since 1910. Certified, PHC 1956; designated National Historic Landmark 1965. 4 sheets (1976, including plans);* 7 ext. photos (1960, 1967).*

Stenton Barn. Illustrated

(PA-1715), 4685 N. Eighteenth St., at S.E. corner Wyoming Ave. and intersection of Windrim Ave., on Stenton grounds approx.

200' N. of Stenton. Rubble with used brick incorporated into interior wall fabric, approx. 61' × 36', two stories, gable roof, ventilation slits in walls, oculus in peak, inclined approach to large door at upper level, lower stable level, upper level of threshing floor with flanking mows. Fine example of Pennsylvania bank barn without customary forebay. Built between 1787 and 1798; rehabilitated 1974–76. 1 ext. photo (1976).*

Trinity Lutheran Church. Illustrated

(PA-1716), 19 W. Queen Ln. Stuccoed brick, approx. 55' (three-bay front) × 85', two stories with center octagonal steeple and hexagonal spire on wooden rectangular base, gable roof, pedimented enclosed entry porch, Tuscan pilasters between round-arch windows, three-aisle plan, rectangular chancel.

Fine example of a carpenter-planned Italianate church that dominates neighborhood's skyline. Built 1856–57; Jacob and George A. Binder, designers and builders. Clock, Germantown's first community clock, put in steeple 1858; interior frescoed 1870, remodeled 1886. Incorporated 1837 as English Evangelical Lutheran Church, changed name 1860. Certified, PHC 1957. 3 ext. photos (1973).*

Trinity Lutheran Church House (also known as Christopher Sower, Jr., House)

(PA-1717), 5300 Germantown Ave., at N.W. corner Queen Ln. Stuccoed rubble, approx. 40' (five-bay front) × 25' with two-story rear wing and ell, two-and-a-half stories, gable roof, center-hall plan. Rear ell (southwest corner) built c. 1723; front section built between 1755 and 1760; two sections joined 1795; stuccoed brick rear wing (northwest corner) built 1870; interior altered 1917; house renovated 1950. Jacob Bay and Christopher Sower, Jr., operated first permanent American type foundry here 1772–73. Owned by Trinity Lutheran Church since 1836, its church house since 1950. Certified, PHC 1957. 1 photocopy of ext. photo (1957);* HABSI form (1957)*

Upsala. Illustrated

(PA-1718), 6430 Germantown Ave. Historic house museum. Stuccoed rubble sides and rear; coursed Wissahickon schist ashlar front with marble trim, approx. 49' (five-bay front) × 44' with one- and two-story diagonal rear ell, two-and-a-half stories on raised basement, gable roof, Doric entrance porch with pediment, marble stringcourse and lintels with keystones, central-hall plan, notable interior woodwork.

Fine example of Adamesque-Federal style. Rear ell probably built c. 1755; front section built 1798–1801. Restored 1944– . Headquarters of Upsala Foundation since 1944. Certified, PHC 1956; Pennsylvania Register 1971; NR. 3 ext. photos (1973, including 1 of boot-scraper).*

Valley Green Inn

(PA-1719), W. side Upper Wissahickon Dr. near Valley Green Dr. Fairmount Park. Stuccoed rubble, 60'-9" (seven-bay front) × 17'-0" with one-story rear frame addition, two stories, open front and side porches, pent eave on north end, center-hall plan.

Example of an old roadhouse still operating as a restaurant. Built early 19th century; rear additions built later. In the middle of the Wissahickon Valley, designated a National Natural History Landmark 1964. Certified, PHC 1967. 11 sheets (n.d., including plot plan, plans, elevations, section, details);* 1 ext. photo (1973).*

Vernon

(PA-7-2), 5860 Germantown Ave., Vernon Park. Scored stuccoed rubble, 49'-4¹/₂" (five-bay front) × 23'-2" with two-story rear ell and two-and-a-half story back building, two-and-a-half stories on raised basement, hipped roof, projecting central pavilion with pediment, Tuscan frontispeice with fanlight, originally central-hall plan.

Fine example of expansion of colonial farmhouse into Federal-style country house. Rear ell built before 1741; main house built 1805; back building added to ell later; interior entensively altered 1898, rehabilitated 1962. Acquired by City of Philadelphia 1892. Germantown Branch of Free Library of Philadelphia 1898–1907; quarters of Site and Relic Society (later known as Germantown Historical Society) 1907–27; now a community center. Certified, PHC 1956. 17 sheets (1934, including plot plan, plans, elevations, details); 7 ext. photos (1934, 1975,*); 4 data pages (1936, including 1808 insurance survey*).

Wissahickon Inn (now Chestnut Hill Academy)

(PA-1720), 500 W. Willow Grove Ave., at S.E. corner Huron St. Random rough-hewn Wissahickon schist ashlar with wood frame third story covered with shingles, approx. 235' (twenty-three-bay front) × 225', three stories on raised basement, hipped roofs with cross-gables, square corner turrets originally with steep pyramidal roofs, large entrance porch and circular turret centered on east facade, U-plan with central-hall corridors.

Fine example of late-19th-century suburban summer resort hotel. Built 1883–84; G. W. and W. D. Hewitt, architects; William C. Mackie, builder. Original porte-cochere and open porches removed 1928. Originally owned by Henry H. Houston, steam transportation entrepreneur and developer of Chestnut Hill. Chestnut Hill Academy since 1898. Certified, PHC 1972. 2 ext. photos (1973).*

Wister's Big House. See Grumblethorpe

Wister's Tenant House (also known as Grumblethorpe Tenant House)
(PA-7-6), 5269 Germantown Ave. Wissahickon schist rubble, 31'-2" (five-bay front) × 30'-11" (originally 18'-4 × 28'-3") two stories (originally one), gable roof, center-hall plan (originally side-hall plan), corner fireplaces in original part.

Example of modest mid-18th-century dwelling as later enlarged. Southeastern section built c. 1745; northwestern section built and southeastern section raised one story early 19th century. Owned and maintained by Philadelphia Society for Preservation of Landmarks since 1940. Certified, PHC 1956; Pennsylvania Register 1971; NR. 9 sheets (1934, including plans, elevations, section, details); 4 ext. photos (1934, 1973*); 1 data page (1934).

Wyck (also known as the Haines House)
(PA-7-3), 6026 Germantown Ave. Historic house museum. Stuccoed stone, 79'-7" (eight-bay front) × 29'-0" (originally 36'-5" × 29'-0") with one-story lateral wing, two-and-a-half stories, gable roof, center-hall plan (in eastern section).

Example of early farmhouse enlarged and remodeled into country house. Western section built c. 1690; eastern section built and open passageway between sections enclosed before 1775. Extensively altered 1824; William Strickland, architect. Lateral western wing built before 1845. Oldest extant house in Germantown; served as British field hospital during Battle of Germantown 1777. Haines family residence until presented to Germantown Historical Society 1973. Certified, PHC 1956; Pennsylvania Register 1970; NR.

22 sheets (1934, including plot plan, plans, elevations, sections, details, plan and elevations of granary, springhouse, smokehouse, and pump); 8 ext. photos (1934, 1973*); 5 data pages (1936, including 1845, 1894 insurance surveys*).

Belfield. *Cortlandt V. D. Hubbard photo, 1967.*

Cliveden. *Jack E. Boucher photo, 1972.*

Concord School. *Jack E. Boucher photo, 1972.*

Germantown Cricket Club. *Jack E. Boucher photo, 1972.*

Grumblethorpe. *Jack E. Boucher photo, 1973.*

Grumblethorpe, water pump. *E. F. Hoffman photo, 1934.*

Hood Cemetery Entrance. *Jack E. Boucher photo, 1973.*

Houston-Sauveur House. *Jack E. Boucher photo, 1972.*

Ebenezer Maxwell House. *Jack E. Boucher photo, 1964.*

Stenton Barn. *Jack E. Boucher photo, 1976.*

Mennonite Meeting House. *Jack E. Boucher photo, 1972.*

Trinity Lutheran Church. *Jack E. Boucher photo, 1972.*

Upsala. *Jack E. Boucher photo, 1973.*

North Philadelphia

CHELTENHAM AVENUE

STREET

STREET

N. BROAD

N. 6TH

WINGOHOCKING AVE.

ROOSEVELT BOULEVARD EXTENSION

RIDGE

ALLEGHENY   AVENUE

AVENUE

STREET

STREET

STREET

N. 33RD

COLUMBIA   AVENUE

8

N. BROAD

N. 6TH

VINE   STREET

Introduction

$\mathcal{N}$ORTH PHILADELPHIA is an area without precise historical, political, or social boundaries, partly because its social and economic configuration has been in a more agitated state of flux than has that of almost any other part of the city. Generally, North Philadelphia is considered that part of the city flanking Broad Street between Girard and Lehigh avenues. For the purposes of this catalogue, however, North Philadelphia is considered that area north of the original city, west of Northern Liberties, and east of Fairmount Park and Germantown, and including the former Spring Garden and Penn districts. Its precise boundaries are Vine Street on the south, Sixth Street on the east, and Cheltenham Avenue on the north. Its western boundary is more irregular: Fairmount Park and Laurel Hill Cemetery north to Allegheny Avenue, Hunting Park Avenue between Allegheny Avenue and Broad Street, and thence northward to the city limits at Cheltenham Avenue.

Bush Hill was probably the most prominent of the few widely scattered eighteenth-century country seats in the area. Built in 1740 at what is now Buttonwood Street between Sixteenth and Seventeenth streets, Bush Hill was better known for its celebrated occupants than for its architecture. The first resident was the famous defender of New York printer John Peter Zenger, lawyer Andrew Hamilton, who built the house and was succeeded in it by his son Pennsylvania Governor James Hamilton. The last occupant was Vice-President John Adams, who lived in the house for two or three years in the early 1790's before it became a hospital during the yellow fever epidemic of 1793. Bush Hill as a name and place, however, remained in the neighborhood for another eighty years. After 1808 the fire-gutted relic was converted into an oil-cloth factory, which it remained until 1871.[1]

Another case in which a name survived an estate is Cherry Hill, the country seat of Benjamin Warner. In 1821 the Commonwealth of Pennsylvania purchased the eleven-acre property for the site of the proposed Eastern State Penitentiary (illus.),[2] known locally as Cherry Hill Prison. At that time most of the region north of the city was open farmland. Some small villages had begun to grow along the thoroughfares, as Francisville had on Ridge Road west of Broad Street, but the greater growth was in the District of Spring Garden. By 1809 Spring Garden was sufficiently built up to be afforded the same legal protection from hazardous manufactories as the city enjoyed, and four years later it was organized as a district from Sixth Street west to Broad and north from Vine to Poplar Street. The district was not extended westward to the Schuylkill until 1827, by which time Eastern State Penitentiary was nearing completion at Twenty-first Street and Fairmount Avenue.[3]

Eastern State Penitentiary was established on the Pennsylvania System, a Quaker-inspired theory of penal reform that had good intentions but hellish results. The reformers believed that if a prisoner were removed from the bad influences of compatriots and put by himself to read the Bible, think penitent thoughts, and engage in light handicrafts, he would leave the prison a humanely reformed person.[4] The Commonwealth commissioned the young, English-trained John Haviland to give the controversial philosophy concrete form. Haviland's proposal had two distinctive and widely copied features: the castellated Gothic facade and the radial plan. Both fit well the philosophy of the institution. The lugubrious dark granite walls with the heavy iron portcullis stood as an impregnable fortress of justice whose dungeons held the wrongdoers of society, and the trauma of entering its gates was heightened by a hood being placed over the head of the prisoner until he reached his isolated cell to begin his period of repentance.[5] The seven cell blocks that radiated outward from the central rotunda like spokes from the hub of a wheel afforded maximum isolation and surveillance of the inmates, who lived every hour of their sentences in their eight-by-ten-foot cells and adjoining high-walled private exercise yards. Although the Pennsylvania System was not officially abandoned until 1915, the maddening condition was ameliorated before the Civil War by a more traditional penal condition—overcrowding.[6] By the mid-twentieth century a growing prison population exceeded the limited space and obsolete facilities of the penitentiary, and a neighborhood landmark of 150 years was vacated in 1970 to become an architectural dinosaur—a curious creature of disproven theory, a massive monster from the past in desperate need of imaginative adaptive use.[7]

The same rural remoteness that was suitable for a prison attracted other institutions as well. Two of the more notable ones were Girard College (illus.) at Girard Avenue and Corinthian Street and Preston Retreat (illus.) at Twentieth and Hamilton streets, both bequeathed by private patrons and designed by the same architect, Thomas U. Walter. Girard College was the earlier, larger, and by far the more famous of the two and, as time has shown, the more enduring. Preston Retreat was demolished in 1963, while Girard College still stands and performs the same function it did when it opened on New Year's Day, 1848—the education of fatherless boys.[8]

Girard College was one of the great institutions of its time. It was an unprecedented expression of philanthropy—two million dollars for the education of the underprivileged. Stephen Girard was a French immigrant who lived a legendary rags-to-riches life to become one of the nation's earliest and most eccentric millionaires.[9] He was the school's benefactor, but it was Nicholas Biddle, a controversial financier and tastemaker, who successfully circumvented the founder's intentions and saw the plans of the talented young Walter carried into execution. In spite of Girard's wishes for a plain, utilitarian main building, Biddle, chairman of the college's board of directors, was determined to use Girard's millions to erect the most imposing and archaeologically correct Greek temple in America.[10] The result is Founder's Hall, the peristyle centerpiece of the forty-one-acre campus. Its architectural significance rests not only in its graceful design and overpowering scale, but also on its ingenious construction. Since Girard's restrictions on interior dimensions and construction were not adaptable to the classical style, Walter was forced to design within the temple form a series of pendentive domes, groin vaults, and cantilevered stairs.[11] Walter hurdled all the obstacles and produced one of the great pieces of American architecture, the climax of the Greek Revival style, but his success was qualified. A structure that met the demands of scale, style, and interior arrangement that circumstances made of it could not also provide the acoustics, lighting, and heat efficiency necessary for a good school building, and it has not been used for classroom purposes since 1916.[12] Yet the building's form fit its function, which was primarily not to be utilitarian but to serve as a monument to a magnanimous man, as its name suggests. And like a Greek temple housing the spirit and effigy of its honored god, Founder's Hall encloses both the body and a statue of Stephen Girard.

Preston Retreat, on the other hand, was much more utilitarian and decidedly less symbolic. It was incorporated in 1836 under the will of Dr. Jonas Preston, a Quaker physician who saw the need for a maternity hospital for indigent women.[13] Walter won the architectural competition with a compact design that took advantage of the Retreat's special function. A Doric tetrastyle portico and flanking side wings gave an austere, imposing presence to the marble front, but the building's virtues lay in its plan. Wards and rooms were organized around two intersecting halls with a central nurses' station and opened onto a veranda that extended around the rear half of the building and gave access to water closets at the rear corners.[14] The longevity of the design—it was never essentially altered—bore testimony to its functionalism. The extensive renovations of 1908 introduced elements of twentieth-century technology (electricity, elevators, fire escapes, refrigeration, and larger furnaces), and the building's end was caused less by the obsoleteness of the physical plant than by the inefficiency of a charitable hospital in a welfare state with centralized institutions.[15] In spite of its modest intentions, Preston Retreat did not open its doors as a hospital for thirty years after its founding. Unlike Girard's investments, Preston's had been limited in both scope and extent, and the quarter-million-dollar estate was crippled the year after the benefactor's death by the suspension of specie payment and the failure of a single company. During most of the twenty-six years that the estate's managers were rebuilding the fund the structure was used by the Foster Home Association, giving children rather than mothers and infants the advantages of the fresh country air.[16]

The environmental advantages that these outlying institutions enjoyed were soon reduced when their presence stimulated improved transportation in their direction. A year after Girard College opened, for example, Ridge Road was paved out to its gates, making the area west of Broad Street less inaccessible.[17] Even before this, the region north of the College, near the Falls of the Schuylkill, had emerged as a suburb with sufficient population and wealth to erect one of the most important Gothic Revival churches in America, the Church of St. James the Less (illus.) at Clearfield and Thirty-second streets. In the early 1840's Robert Ralston, a successful merchant and High Church enthusiast with a country home in the area, acquired from the Ecclesiological Society, an English group dedicated to enriching Anglican liturgy and architecture through study of the medieval past, measured drawings of a thirteenth-century Anglican country church. Construction began in the fall of 1846, making St. James the Less the first American church built under the auspices of the ecclesiologists.[18] Most of the development during this decade, however, remained in the Spring Garden District east of Broad, especially along Spring Garden Street itself, which in 1847 was flanked by stores west to Tenth Street.[19] The neighborhood's sophistication was illustrated by the diversity of buildings designed by noted architects. By 1852 the single block of Spring Garden Street west of Thirteenth included the Commissioners' Hall, probably by William L. Johnston, St. Mark's Lutheran Church by John McArthur, Jr., Spring Garden Institute by Hoxie and Button, and the Odd Fellows' Hall by Samuel Sloan.[20]

On the other side of Broad Street Matthias Baldwin's locomotive works had been expanding since 1835, helping to make large parts of western Spring Garden an industrial park.[21] Four noted firms had plants in the early 1850's along the tracks of the Philadelphia and Reading Railroad. The Industrial Works of Bement and Dougherty began in 1851 at Twentieth and Callowhill streets; in 1852 Hoopes and Townsend established their nuts-and-bolts plant on Buttonwood Street east of Broad; the next year Bancroft and Sellers (known as William Sellers and Co. after 1855) built their extensive machine shops on Pennsylvania Avenue between Sixteenth and Seventeenth streets; in 1854 at the western end of Callowhill Street near the Schuylkill, McKeone, Van Haagen and Co. opened the Pennsylvania Soap-Works which by the 1880's had become the largest soap manufactory in the state.[22]

Houses of all types were going up in the area during these two decades. In addition to row houses, whose speculative advantages were well known, there were cottages, such as the Edgar Allan Poe House, along Brandywine Street west of Seventh. Built for families of modest incomes, many of these cottages, including the Poe House, lost their separate identities when larger houses were attached to them along the street fronts, making the former cottages back buildings.[23] Terrace houses, a new development promoted particularly by the noted architect Samuel Sloan, were popular among the middle class. The main feature of these semidetached houses was the small grass plot in front of each dwelling. Woodland Terrace 1861–62) in West Philadelphia possesses the city's best known and best preserved

example of this housing type, but in 1853, Sloan and Stewart had
designed twenty-two terrace houses along Green Street between
Sixteenth and Eighteenth streets.[24]

Many members of the industrial city's managerial and entrepreneurial class wanted something more opulent than row or terrace
houses. It was for them that the North Philadelphia mansions, large
stylish dwellings, were built. They appeared in large numbers in the
1850's, particularly on Broad Street, one of Philadelphia's best addresses for more than fifty years, where the mansions of each decade
were more grandiose than those of the preceding ones. One of the
first of these buildings, Howard Tilden's home at Broad and Brown
streets, set the pattern. The *Public Ledger* considered Tilden's house "a
magnificent residence . . . of the richest style of Corinthian architecture," further "evidence of the taste of the architects [Hoxie and But-
ton], and the growing desire of our wealthy citizens to surpass one
another in the construction of splendid mansions."[25] Neither the architects' taste nor the client's ambition could be called avant-garde,
but both illustrated the resolution of the tensions between tradition
and change to give a new direction to urban domestic architecture.
The house was large—its forty-five-foot front was double that of a colonial town house—but its basic plan of front living quarters and
adjoining back service buildings was traditional. Its style was a successful marriage of old forms and new materials, and might be called
Georgian Brownstone. Its Corinthian frontispiece, Palladian window,
and balustrade were elements long familiar to Philadelphians, but the
brownstone walls, enriched window dressings, and skylighted grand
staircase were sufficiently Italian to be "modern." Tilden also was
operating within a tradition, but one that was increasingly expressed
in material terms, that of individual achievement.[26] His business success brought him money, and he used it to buy one of the costliest
houses in the city.[27]

Tilden's mansion was but one of many houses that went up in
the area during its building boom after 1850. More than 160 houses
were constructed between Poplar and Berks streets during the summer of 1863 alone.[28] Some were finished in granite, like the block of
ten houses that Sloan and Stewart designed in "the New York
style,"[29] but most of the houses were brick, particularly on the lesser
streets. Brownstone dwellings, however, were predominant on
Broad Street and to a smaller degree on Green Street, where many
leading Philadelphians displayed their preference for this somber material for nearly half a century.[30] Brownstone fronts were used on

both the 1854 Italian villa of William Gaul, a wealthy brewer, at Broad
and Master streets,[31] and the 1864 mansarded "Romanesque" mansion of Matthew Baird, a partner in the Baldwin Locomotive Works,
at 814 North Broad Street.[32] The flamboyant French Renaissance
mansion (illus.) of traction magnate Peter A. B. Widener at Broad and
Girard was finished in 1887 in a highly wrought brownstone, and the
stately 1890 mansion (illus.) of financier William H. Kemble at
Twenty-second and Green was built of brownstone, as were many of
its neighbors.[33]

The area's post–Civil War affluence supported better architec-
Banks, stores, market houses, assembly halls, and a rail terminal
went up in Spring Garden during the 1850's and 1860's, until by the
time of the centennial celebration the former district and the old city
were an economic continuum. As a developing fringe of the city,
however, the area initially lacked the capital and predictability
necessary to assure good architectural design for its commercial and
public buildings. Since emphasis was on utility and versatility, most
of the commercial structures were architecturally uninteresting, or at
best undistinguished. Charles Lewars's 1852 building at the southeast
corner of Ninth and Spring Garden streets illustrates this point well.
With stores at the street level and assembly rooms and living quarters
on the upper floors, the property evidently proved to be a lucrative
one for grocer Lewars and his successors, but it was devoid of architectural pretensions; the *Public Ledger* euphemistically spoke of its
"new and chaste pattern."[34]

The area's post–Civil War affluence supported better architecture, such as the Northern Saving Fund, Safe Deposit and Trust
Company (illus.) at the southwest corner of Sixth and Spring Garden
streets. An early and little known work of Furness and Hewitt, it
contains many elements that Frank Furness would later develop more
fully as his distinctive style matured.[35] Because of its early date, the
bank does not assume the massive presence of the architect's later
commissions, and for it, unlike nearly all of Furness's later banks, he
did not exploit the corner site by putting the entrance on a bevel.
Neither did the architects clutter the doorway of the Northern Saving
Fund with the columns, corbels, and overhangs that gave a be-
leaguered appearance to so many of Furness's banks. Instead, the entrance is centered on the building's long Spring Garden Street axis,
and the simple round-arch entrance appears inviting rather than in-
timidating. Other aspects of the design, however, suggest Furness's
future histrionics. The projecting central salient, which is corbeled
outward above the second story and then slides backward into the

crowning tympanum, anticipates the exaggerated examples of Furness's Provident Life and Trust Company (1876–79) and the Kensington National Bank (1877); and the use of contrasting materials,
here dressed and pecked granite, would later be handled more
vividly. Flat triglyph corbels were also used by Furness's contemporaries,[36] but in the customary function of supporting cornices. Furness, on the other hand, used them more daringly to support projecting upper parts of facades, a practice that is suggested here. Other
elements, such as the pinched-top windows and exaggerated keystones and imposts, would appear in very similar forms on Furness's
later buildings. The bank has been a local landmark for more than a
century, and although it has been enlarged on three different occa-
sions, its additions have been stylistically synonymous with the
original structure.[37]

North Broad Street reached its peak in the decade before World
War I. Although the extravagantly rich, like Widener and his close
associate William Elkins, moved out of the city to palatial estates in
suburban counties, splendid mansions were still erected along the
great thoroughfare and its adjacent streets into the twentieth century.
Brownstone finally lost favor and was replaced by marble and
limestone as architects turned to more restrained historical styles: the
Second Renaissance Revival, Beaux-Arts Classicism, and the
Neoclassical Revival. Alfred E. Burk's house at Broad and Jefferson
may be too austere to be the most representative example of the
Second Renaissance Revival, but it is distinguished enough to be included in that long list of buildings wishfully attributed to the great
Stanford White of the New York firm McKim, Mead and White. In
actual fact, however, the house was designed by Simon and Bassett, a
fine Philadelphia firm, a year after White's death.[38]

Burk, a millionaire leather manufacturer, was continuing the
sixty-year-old drift of self-made men toward Broad Street that stimulated a social rivalry between North Philadelphia and Rittenhouse
Square, the more traditionally fashionable neighborhood. Oscar
Hammerstein, probably the foremost impresario of his day, came to
Philadelphia in 1907 and with great bombast exploited the competition by announcing his plans to build an opera house on North Broad
Street to compete with the city's only other center of opera, the
venerable Academy of Music.[39] After commissioning the nation's
leading theater architect, William H. McElfatrick of New York, to
design the massive structure at Broad and Poplar, Hammerstein
made good his promise that the Philadelphia Opera House would be

finished in a year's time, and brazenly planned its grand opening to coincide with the beginning of the Academy's opera season.[40] Opening night was a social and cultural extravaganza, and the newspapers covered the event in the spirit of a political election or an athletic contest. The result was a draw, for both houses were filled. Perhaps Hammerstein won a moral victory, since, contrary to predictions, "social Philadelphia" did go uptown.[41] Pride had its price, however, and five years later the city's largest stage was dark. Faced with a hopeless $400,000 mortgage, Hammerstein sold out to E. T. Stotesbury, who brought New York's Metropolitan Opera Company to the Opera House for three years, and ever since the building has been known as "the Met." Opened for special events for a few years, the Renaissance Revival theater has been a tomb for memories since 1920. Except for a couple of theatrical spectaculars in the mid-1920's and in 1931, the once ornate structure is used primarily for evangelical purposes,[42] its splendor fading as its cornices crumble and its paint peels.

The Opera House's decline anticipated, if it did not parallel, that of its neighborhood. The beginning of the Broad Street Subway in 1924 reinforced the northward trend of the commercial city. Two of the more notable office buildings erected in the southern limits of the area were the Elverson Building for the *Philadelphia Inquirer* and the Terminal Commerce Building for the Reading Company. These two quite different structures face each other across Broad Street above Callowhill. The *Inquirer's* building, a 1924 application of the Italian Renaissance style to a tall commercial structure, is faced with white limestone and terra cotta and ascends in a series of setbacks to a sleek central tower crowned with a lantern and dome.[43] Although it was designed five years later "to harmonize architecturally with the Elverson Building,"[44] the Reading Company's massive edifice appears squat on its site, although its buff brick walls with their colorful terra cotta ornament rise twelve stories above the street.

The subway also brought changes to the educational institutions that lay along its path. Temple University had been growing slowly since its inception in 1884 as a night school, housed in the basement of Russell Conwell's Grace Baptist Church at Broad and Berks streets. Empowered to grant degrees in 1891, Temple immediately began plans for its own building. This was completed in 1894 from the designs of Thomas Lonsdale.[45] More accessible to its commuting student population, Temple enjoyed a growth during the 1920's and early 1930's exceeded only by that of the 1960's, when it burgeoned

into one of the largest and finest universities in the state. [46] Whereas
the presence of the subway encouraged Temple to expand on its old
site, it induced another Broad Street school, LaSalle College, to move
farther north. Limited to an old mansion at Broad and Stiles streets,
LaSalle saw in the cheap rapid-transit system an opportunity to build
a new campus on the undeveloped land surrounding Twentieth
Street and Olney Avenue. The first building was completed in 1929, [47]
and although the campus is outside our arbitrary boundaries for
North Philadelphia, it reflected events within that area and has
played an important role in the cultural life of the Philadelphia neighborhoods of Logan and Fern Rock.

Spurred on by the inexorable urban expansion, by citizens'
hunger for a suburban environment, and by the building of the
subway, housing construction boomed in the northern reaches of the
city. The region north of Columbia Avenue had been developing
progressively during the 1880's, and by 1890 commodious row
houses were being built as far north as Erie Avenue. [48] The area beyond that, near York Road and Rockland Street where J. B. Lippincott, Jr., built his large stone house in 1891, remained a pleasant
suburb, [49] while commuter railroads helped to transform large parts
of Oak Lane into a district suitable for the development of single
homes and twin houses. [50] Yet great open spaces ranged west of
Broad Street at the turn of the century. When Shibe Park (illus.) was
opened at Twenty-first Street and Lehigh Avenue in the spring of
1909 it stood virtually alone, and some critics feared its distant site
might exceed the loyalty of the city's baseball fans. The fears were un-
founded. Rising attendance forced an extension of the stadium within
two years, and before long it was engulfed by open-porched row
houses. [51] By the time the Great Depression put an end to this boom,
North Philadelphia's frontier had been closed. Houses stood in close
order drill, with the domes and steeples of the area's churches punc-
tuating the low skyline. [52] Aglow with gas logs in their fireplaces and
with electric lights to brighten the dark winter nights, with colorful
flowers decorating their grass plots in the bright summer sun, these
modest dwellings were—and remain—material expressions of the
American Dream.

Catalog

Burk, Alfred E., House
(PA-1722), 1500 N. Broad St., at N.W. corner Jefferson St. Brick faced with coursed Green River limestone ashlar, 42'–10" (three-bay front) × 71'–0" with three-story lateral addition, three stories on raised basement, low hipped tile roof with terra cotta cornice, smooth rusticated ground story, large Corinthian frontispiece with balustrade above, two semicircular bays on south facade; central-hall plan with hall open to roof, notable interior details; detached rear limestone conservatory.

Fine example of Late Victorian Italian Renaissance style. Built 1907–9; Simon and Bassett, architects; John N. Gill & Co., contractors. Rear conservatory altered, enlarged for offices 1949–50; Louis A. Manfredi, architect. Three-story steel-frame northern addition with limestone ashlar curtain walls built 1953–54; Louis A. Manfredi, architect. Alfred E. Burk, leather manufacturer, lived here 1909–21; headquarters of Upholsterers' International Union 1945–70; Temple University School of Social Administration since 1971. Certified, PHC 1971. 2 ext. photos (1973);* 2 data pages (including 1908–53 building permits).*

Cast-Iron Sidewalk. Illustrated
(PA-1723), 1907 N. Seventh St. Cast iron, approx. 11' × 53', constructed of hexagonal plates of approx. 1'-diameter. Rare surviving example of mid-19th-century Ferromania. Built c. 1861; Charles Carnell (machinist and iron founder), probable designer and builder. 8 photos (1972);* HABSI form (1970).*

Cherry Hill Penitentiary. See Eastern State Penitentiary

Church of the Gesu (Roman Catholic). Illustrated
(PA-1724), S.E. corner Eighteenth and Thompson sts. (originally at
N.E. corner Eighteenth and Stiles sts., since closed). Brick with
granite trim, approx. 122' (five-bay front) × 252', one and five stories
with two-story facade, gable roof, square towers with low hipped
roofs flank cyma-curved center gable, coupled Doric colonnade at
ground story, coupled Ionic colonnade at second story, curved pedimented doors; three-aisle plan with four chapels along each side,
balconies, apsidal chancel with two side altars, large flattened barrel
vault, notable decorations.

Notable example of a High Victorian Baroque church with
the country's widest unobstructed nave when built. Part of an ecclesiastical complex that included parish school, college (St. Joseph's),
and nearby hospital (St. Joseph's). Masterpiece of an important local
church architect. Built 1879–88; Edwin F. Durang, architect. Towers
finished after 1895. Interior decorated 1918; Br. Francis C. Schroen,
S.J., decorator. Lower half of interior redecorated, renovated 1952–
56; Brs. Frederick E. Barth, S.J., and George M. Bambrick, S.J.,
decorators. Five-story Jesuit Community House built at rear corner
1911; Fr. Charles Lyons, S.J., designer; Thomas Reilly, builder. 3 ext.
photos (1973).*

Church of St. James the Less (Protestant Episcopal). Illustrated
(PA-1725), 3200 W. Clearfield St., at S.W. corner Thirty-second St.
and intersection of Hunting Park Ave. Random granite ashlar, approx. 36' × 62' with one-story rear vestry, one story, gable roof,
pointed-arch windows, open belfry at west end, three-aisle plan, rectangular chancel.

First and influential example of the Ecclesiological Society's (formerly Cambridge Camden Society) providing plans of a Gothic
church to an American congregation, leading to a fine re-creation of a
13th-century English country parish church and churchyard. Built
1846–50; G. G. Place (England), architect; John E. Carver,
superintendent of construction; three windows by Henry Gerente
(Paris). Chancel remodeled 1878; Charles M. Burns, architect. Open
belfry added c. 1885. Rodman Wanamaker Bell Tower built at edge of
churchyard 1908; John T. Windrim, architect. Certified, PHC 1965;
Pennsylvania Register 1974; NR. 3 ext. photos (1973, including 1 of
doorway sculpture).*

Community College of Philadelphia, Campus II. See United States Mint

Connie Mack Stadium. See Shibe Park

Diamond Street Area Study
(PA-1726), 1601–43 W. Diamond St., N. side Diamond St. between Sixteenth and Seventeenth sts. Twenty-two brick row houses with rock-faced brownstone trim, each approx. 18' (two-bay front) × 26' with three-story rear ell (except corner buildings, 26' × 72' without ells), three stories on raised basements, flat roofs, rock-faced brownstone basements and stringcourses, side-hall plans.

Middle-class row house development designed by a leading late-19th-century architectural firm. Built 1887; Furness, Evans and Co., architects; W. D. Huston, builder; Page Brothers, developers. No. 1601 enlarged, raised one story later; Nos. 1629, 1631, 1637 altered in rear later. Certified, PHC 1974. 2 ext. photos (1973).*

Eagle Hotel
(PA-1727), 601–7 W. Girard Ave., at N.W. corner Sixth St. Brick, approx. 84' (twelve-bay front) × 110', four stories, flat roof, interior courtyard for coaches. Built c. 1858; demolished c. 1958. 4 ext. photos (1957).*

Eakins, Thomas, House
(PA-1728), 1729 Mt. Vernon St. Museum. Brick, approx. 20' (three-bay front) × 75', four stories, mansard roof. Built c. 1854; mansard added 1902; restored 1969–70. Thomas Eakins, famous portraitist and predecessor of American modern painting, lived here from the age of thirteen until his death in 1916. Now an Eakins museum and neighborhood art center administered by the Philadelphia Museum of Art. Certified, PHC 1964; Pennsylvania Register 1970; designated National Historic Landmark 1967. 2 ext. photos (1967);* 2 data pages (1964).*

Eastern State Penitentiary (also known as Cherry Hill Penitentiary). Illustrated
(PA-1729), block bounded by Fairmount Ave., Corinthian Ave., Brown, Twenty-second sts. Coursed granite ashlar wall, 35' height, encloses 11.7 acres and eleven granite ashlar cell-block buildings (originally seven), approx. 80' × 250' and approx. 65' × 335', one and two stories, gable roofs, radial plan around central rotunda; short battlemented towers flank pointed-arch entrance topped with hexagonal

battlemented tower, lancet windows in front wall, battlemented hexagonal towers at front corners.

One of the nation's oldest prisons designed by a foremost prison architect. Its plan is a masterful architectural expression of the Pennsylvania System, a penal philosophy emphasizing solitary confinement, and its design was an early expression of the Gothic Revival in the United States. Built 1823–36; John Haviland, architect; Jacob Souder, master mason. Three radial wings added 1877, one wing 1894, one wing 1911. Acquired by City of Philadelphia 1970. Certified, PHC 1958; Pennsylvania Register 1970; designated National Historic Landmark 1965. 6 ext. photos (1967),* 5 int. photos (1967),* 1 photocopy of isometric view (n.d.).*

Gaul-Forrest House

(PA-1730), 1346 N. Broad St., at S.W. corner Master St. Brick with brownstone ashlar front and painted galvanized iron side trim, approx. 53' (five-bay front) × 50'with one-story brownstone lateral addition and three-story brick L-plan rear addition (originally two-story rear ell with veranda), three stories on raised basement, flat roof, projecting lintels on consoles, projecting center second-story window, center-hall plan.

Fine example of Italianate town house and its later remodeling. Built 1853–54; probably by Stephen D. Button, architect. Veranda enclosed, interior rear ell altered 1860; rear ell raised to three stories, bay window added, one-story lateral addition built 1863; ground story altered to restaurant 1876, used for church services 1877–79. Interior extensively altered, one-story addition enlarged, rear ell remodeled, rear addition built 1880; James H. Windrim, architect; B. Ketcham and Son, contractors.

Built for William Gaul, prominent brewer. Edwin Forrest, America's first outstanding actor, noted for his Shakespearean roles, lived here 1855–72. Site of Philadelphia's School of Design for Women (now Moore College of Art), the country's pioneer school of industrial art for women, 1880–1959. Now Heritage House, neighborhood art and music center. Pennsylvania Register 1971; NR. 1 ext. photo (1973);* 15 data pages (1973, including 1854–76 insurance surveys).*

Girard College, Founder's Hall. Illustrated

(PA-1731), Girard Ave. and Corinthian St. Museum. Coursed marble ashlar, approx. 111' × 169', three stories, gable roof, Corinthian peristyle colonnade with octastyle porticoes, four square vaulted rooms to a floor, stairways in corners. Low segmental groined vaults in lower rooms and penditive domes under roof provide structural soundness and maximum space.

Considered one of the most impressive and monumental Greek Revival buildings in the United States, its innovative internal structure makes it a remarkable blend of structural engineering and architectural design. Built 1833–47; Thomas U. Walter, architect; Findley Highlands, marble mason. Central feature of a school for fatherless boys endowed 1831 by Stephen Girard, America's first multimillionaire philanthropist. Houses sarcophagus of Stephen Girard and the Stephen Girard Collection, probably the best-documented group of furnishings owned by an American of the late-18th and early-19th centuries. Certified, PHC 1956; Pennsylvania Register 1970; designated National Historic Landmark 1969. 7 ext. photos (1973, including 1 color photo),* 1 photocopy of architect's perspective drawing (1835),* 1 photocopy of unexecuted design (plan) by Alexander Jackson Davis (n.d.);* HABSI form (1970).*

Green Street Area Study. Illustrated
(PA-1732), 2201–31 Green St., on N. side Green St. between Twenty-second and Twenty-third sts. Ten large brownstone and brick houses, some faced with granite and brownstone fronts, three, four, and five stories, flat and mansard roofs. The dwellings are architecturally unrelated to one another but as a group they serve as an example of a wealthy late-19th-century neighborhood. Built at various times during the last third of the 19th century. Nos. 2219, 2221 demolished 1963. No. 2201–5 (Kemble-Bergdol House) and No. 2213 (Burnham House) certified, PHC 1967. 15 ext. photos (1963, 1973);* 3 data pages (including 1866 insurance survey).*

Met. See Philadelphia Opera House

Northern Saving Fund, Safe Deposit and Trust Company. Illustrated
(PA-1733), 600 Spring Garden St., at S.W. corner Sixth St. Brick with iron joists, faced with coursed Richmond granite ashlar with rusticated and pecked granite trim, approx. 135' (twelve-bay front) × 76' (originally 97' × 22'), one and two stories, flat roofs, central pedimented salient corbeled out over round-headed entrance, ground-story pinched-top windows, second-story round-headed windows, pecked and rusticated quoins and pinnacles, dark rough-hewn water table, banking room in one story on east end.

Early bank design by two leading 19th-century architects who

later developed some of its elements into notable picturesque buildings. Built 1872; Furness and Hewitt, architects. Southern extension
(516 N. Sixth St.) built c. 1888; probably by Furness, Evans & Co., architects. Western addition built 1903; George T. Pearson, architect.
Another southern extension (514 N. Sixth St.) built 1913–14; Stearns
and Castor, architects. Interior altered, entrance lowered to street
level, marquee added 1960. Name changed to Northern Trust Co.
1902; acquired by Provident National Bank 1948. 1 ext. photo (1974).*

Philadelphia Opera House (later known as the Met)

(PA-1734), 1400–1418 Poplar St., at S.W. corner Broad St. Steel frame
with white brick curtain walls and marble and terra cotta trim, approx. 240' (fourteen-bay front) × 160', four and five stories, flat roof,
pedimented central pavilion with open balustraded arcades, simulated smooth rustication on lower stories, originally domes at either
end, originally highly lavish interior.

A formerly elegant opera house by a leading theater architect.
Built 1908; William H. McElfatrick (Brooklyn), architect; John Morrow
and Harry Weichmann, superintendents of construction; Phoenix
Iron Co., steel contractors. Interior destroyed by fire, altered 1948;
frieze, cornice, pediments removed later. Built for Oscar Hammerstein, an internationally famous early-20th-century impresario.
Largest stage in city when built. Opera performances ended 1920;
used for various entertainment purposes until 1955 when it became
Philadelphia Evangelistic Center. Certified, PHC 1970; Pennsylvania
Register 1972. 3 ext. photos (1974),* 1 photocopy of old ext. photo
(1925).*

Poe, Edgar Allan, House

(PA-1735), rear of 530 N. Seventh St., at N.W. corner Brandywine St.
Museum. Brick, approx. 32' (four-bay front) × 15', three stories, shed
roof, center entry with enclosed stairs. Built c. 1841; probably by John
Evans, Jr., house carpenter. Partially restored by Richard Gimbel
Foundation 1964–66. Back building built before front section (1849).
The famous author and editor Edgar Allan Poe lived here 1842–44.
Certified, PHC 1962; Pennsylvania Register 1970; designated National
Historic Landmark 1962. 2 ext. photos (1967),* 4 int. photos (1967);* 4
data pages (1962).*

Preston Retreat. Illustrated

(PA-1736), 500–518 N. Twentieth St., at N.W. corner Hamilton St.
Brick with marble ashlar front and smooth rusticated marble base-

ment, approx. 106' (nine-bay front) × 88', three stories on raised basement (originally two-story facade) with Tuscan tetrastyle portico, hipped roof with large octagonal cupola, T-plan with central hall and transverse corridor.

Important Greek Revival work by Thomas U. Walter, noted architect of classical styles. Built 1837–40; Thomas U. Walter, architect. Used by Foster Home Association 1846–65; operated as maternity hospital for the indigent 1866–1960 as originally intended. Third story raised, pediment added to portico, cupola restored, interior extensively remodeled 1908–9; Edgar V. Seeler, architect. Demolished 1963; portico elements preserved for later construction. Certified, PHC 1956.

3 ext. photos (1963, including 1 of iron gate),* 24 photocopies of architectural competition drawings (1837, including 8 by Thomas U. Walter, 3 by Isaac Holden, 3 by John D. Jones, 5 by William Kelly, 2 by Thomas S. Stewart, 5 by unidentified architect);* 16 data pages (1963, including 1840–1909 insurance surveys).*

Ridge Avenue Farmers' Market Company. Illustrated
(PA-1737), 1810 Ridge Ave., at S.W. corner Ginnodo St. Brick with sandstone trim and cast-iron piers, approx. 93' (five-bay front) × 262', one story, jerkin-head roof with shed roofs along sides, segmental pointed-arch windows. A rare surviving example of a building type that increased in number as open market sheds declined after 1860. Built 1875; Davis E. Supplee, architect. Renovated 1968. Certified, PHC 1968. 4 ext. photos (1973);* HABSI form (1970).*

Shibe Park (later known as Connie Mack Stadium). Illustrated
(PA-1738), 2701 N. Twenty-first St., composing block bounded by Lehigh Ave., Twenty-first, Somerset, Twentieth sts. Reinforced-concrete walls faced with brick and terra cotta trim, wooden roofs on steel trusses, approx. 480' on Lehigh ave. × 525' on Twenty-first St., three stories (originally two-and-a-half) with domed four-story circular corner tower, flat roofs (originally mansard), ground-story terra cotta bands and bas-reliefs and second-story Ionic arcade on grandstand, originally L-plan of corner grandstand and flanking left and right field stands.

First reinforced-concrete baseball park in the country. With a 25,000 seating capacity it was considered a baseball showplace when built and was the oldest park in the major leagues when it was vacated in 1970. Built 1908–9; William Steele and Sons Co., architects and builders. Left and right field stands covered and bleachers built along Somerset St. (north end) 1910, grandstand covered 1912–13; William Steele and Sons Co., architects and builders. Second deck added to left and right field stands 1925; grandstand roof raised, press box and 3500 seats installed 1929. Structure reinforced 1930; Percival M. Sax, contractor. East wall (right field) raised 1935. Lights installed for night baseball 1939; Westinghouse Electric and Manufacturing Co., architects and engineers. Left and right field stands rebuilt 1949; Erny and Nolan, contractor. Electrical scoreboard erected atop right field wall (east end) 1956; infield box seats added 1960. Severely damaged by fire 1971; demolished 1976. Renamed Connie Mack Stadium 1953 in memory of the man who helped to organize Philadelphia Athletics 1901 and managed the team 1901–50, a major league record. Home of American League's Athletics 1909–54, of National League's Phillies 1938–70.

9 ext. photos (1973),* 1 photocopy of old ext. photo (c. 1909),* 1 photocopy of int. photo (1963).* 1 photocopy of aerial photo (1970).*

Spring Garden Institute

(PA-1739), 523–25 N. Broad St., at N.E. corner Spring Garden St. Brick faced with mastic on upper stories (originally rusticated ashlar) and iron sheets simulating rusticated ashlar on ground story, approx. 100' (eleven-bay front) × 57', three stories with domed semicircular bay (not original) above entrance, hipped roof, plain piers rise two stories with arcade at top story, top floor suspended from roof rafters.

Example of institutional application of Italianate mode. Built 1851–52; Hoxie and Button, architects. Northern section, at S.E. corner Broad and Brandywine sts., built as First New Jerusalem Society of Philadelphia 1854. Ground-story stores altered to library 1879; domed bay added 1891; upper stories covered with mastic c. 1891. Four-story steel-skeleton east section with buff brick and terra cotta curtain walls built 1898; Thomas P. Lonsdale, architect. North section occupied by Apprentices' Library, oldest free circulating library in America, 1897–1946; part of Spring Garden Institute 1946–1969. Buildings vacated 1969, demolished 1972. 3 ext. photos (1971);* HABSI form (1970).*

Tanner, Henry Ossawa, House

(PA-1740), 2908 W. Diamond St. Brick with marble trim, approx. 16' (two-bay front) × 28' with two-story rear ell, three stories, flat roof, semi-hexagonal bay at second and third stories covered with aluminum siding. Built c. 1871; Daniel H. Bry, builder. Exterior and interior altered later. Henry Ossawa Tanner, America's leading black painter of the late 19th and early 20th centuries, lived here 1872–88. Property held by Tanner family and descendants until 1950. Pennsylvania Register 1976; designated National Historic Landmark 1976. 1 ext. photo (1976).*

United States Mint (now Community College of Philadelphia, Campus II)
(PA-1741), 1600–1644 Spring Garden St., composing block bounded by Spring Garden, Sixteenth, Buttonwood, Seventeenth sts. Coursed gray granite ashlar with smooth rusticated ground story, approx. 318' (nineteen-bay front) × 200', two and three stories, flat roof with balustrade, central flat Roman Ionic tetrastyle portico in antis, projecting second-story lintels with corbels, gold tile and white marble entrance lobby originally with Tiffany Favrille glass mosaics by William B. Van Ingen, arcaded white marble stairhall leading to central red marble rotunda, originally first floor coining operations with visitors' mezzanine, rectangular plan with ivory-white brick inner courtyards.

Fine example of turn-of-century Beaux-Arts government architecture. Built 1898–1901; James Knox Taylor, architect; Edward A. Crane, superintendent of construction; Allen B. Rorke, foundation contractor; Charles McCaul, terrace-level contractor. Altered 1934, 1941. Interior of front half altered 1972–73; Geddes, Brecher, Qualls, Cunningham, architects. Vacated 1969; acquired by Community College of Philadelphia 1971, opened for classes 1973. Tiffany glass mosaics moved to new U.S. Mint, Independence Mall 1971. The third mint in Philadelphia and finest in the country when built. Certified, PHC 1974. 1 ext. photo (1974),* 1 photocopy of architectural rendering (c. 1900).*

Widener, Peter A. B., House. Illustrated
(PA-1742), 1200 N. Broad St., at N.W. corner Girard Ave. Brownstone ashlar and brick, approx. 53' (six-bay front) × 144', four-and-a-half stories on raised basement, hipped roof with four Flemish cross-gables, ogee conical roofs on corner bays, curvilinear walls, curved double-entry stairway, rusticated basement and first stories, carved stone decoration, central-hall plan, notable interior.

Notable example of picturesque eclectic design. Built 1887; Willis G. Hale, architect; George Herzog, decorator. Two-story brick and iron conservatory built at rear 1892; interior altered 1899 when house became H. Josephine Widener Memorial Library 1900–1946. Widener was a developer of street railway syndicates in Philadelphia and Chicago and later a philanthropist. Since 1970 the quarters of The Council of Black Clergy's Institute for Black Ministries at the Conwell School of Theology. Certified, PHC 1963; Pennsylvania Register 1970. 2 ext. photos (1973);* 4 data pages (1964).*

ast-Iron Sidewalk. *Jack E. Boucher ҇oto, 1972.*

Church of St. James the Less. *Jack E. Boucher photo, 1972.*

Church of the Gesu. *Jack E. Boucher photo, 1973.*

Eastern State Penitentiary. *Cortlandt V. D. Hubbard photo, 1967.*

Girard College, Founder's Hall. *Jack E. Boucher photo, 1973.*

Green Street Area Study (Kemble-Bergdol House). *Jack E. Boucher photo, 1973.*

Northern Saving Fund, Safe Deposit and Trust Company. *Jack E. Boucher photo, 1973.*

FRONT ELEVATION

Preston Retreat. *Drawing by Thomas U. Walter, 1837.*

Ridge Avenue Farmers' Market Company. *Jack E. Boucher photo, 1973.*

Shibe Park. *Jack E. Boucher photo, 1973.*

Peter A. B. Widener House. *Jack E. Boucher photo, 1973.*

Delaware River Corridor

Northern Liberties, Kensington, Richmond,
Frankford, Northeast Philadelphia

Introduction

$\mathcal{S}$IX LARGE TOWNSHIPS existed north of the City of Philadelphia in William Penn's time: Northern Liberties, Oxford, Bristol, Lower Dublin, Moreland, and Byberry. Rural during the colonial period, they were developed during the nineteenth century as activity radiated outward from the city's commercial center.[1] By 1854, when the outlying hegemonies of the county were consolidated with the city, the area north of Vine Street between the two rivers (excluding Germantown and Roxborough) included seventeen separate governmental entities. Nine of them had been carved from the original Northern Liberties Township, which formed the city's northern border, while the two northernmost and hence most remote and most rural of the townships, Byberry and Moreland, had never been subdivided. Although few people today would recognize the names of all the original subdivisions, some of the boroughs and districts retain their old identities and still inspire neighborhood loyalties. Frankford, organized in 1800, is the oldest of these, but Northern Liberties District (1803), Kensington (1820), Richmond (1847), and Bridesburg (1848) are equally well-known and traditional neighborhoods.[2] The Delaware River with its tributaries is the common tie to all of them and significantly influenced the development of the area, hence its designation here as the Delaware River Corridor. Arbitrary boundaries have been assigned to the corridor: the river on the east, Vine Street on the south, Sixth Street on the west, and the city limits on the north.

Open land combined with the Delaware River to make the area attractive for farms and country houses during the colonial period. One could enjoy the virtues of country living without being uncomfortably remote from the center of the colony's political and economic activity, easily accessible by means of waterways, which offered vastly quicker and more comfortable transport than overland routes. William Penn had his country estate Pennsbury, for example, built outside Philadelphia above the town of Bristol. It was a very long horseback ride from the city's commercial center, but Penn traveled in a private river barge and probably made the trip faster and certainly more comfortably than can modern commuters traveling on expressways in high-powered autos.

Two of the finest country houses along the corridor were Chalkley Hall and Port Royal, standing on either side of Frankford Creek. Thomas Chalkley, the sea-going Quaker missionary-merchant, built Chalkley Hall in 1723 on the south side of the creek "in order to be more retired and for health's sake."[3] He appears to have been too restless to enjoy either, however, and died eighteen years later on the island of Tortola during one of his self-appointed business-missionary expeditions. Chalkley Hall assumed the appearance of an eighteenth-century double-pile country seat at the time of the American Revolution, when Chalkley's son-in-law built the main section of cream-colored sandstone, reportedly brought from England as ballast.[4] Port Royal (1761) was named after the Bermuda birthplace of Edward Stiles, its first owner, and was perhaps even more sumptuous than Chalkley Hall.[5] Its classical proportions, rich interiors (some of which are now installed at Winterthur Museum), and the knowledgeable handling of Georgian details made it one of Philadelphia's finest country houses. The advantages of such rural retreats, which Chalkley anticipated in the early eighteenth century, were still evident a century later and poetically proclaimed by Whittier:

> How bland and sweet the greetings of this breeze,
> To him who flees
> From crowded street and red wall's weary gleam;
> Till far behind like a hideous dream
> The close dark city lies![6]

The rural expanse and many streams were attractive to farmers and millers as well as to country gentlemen, of course, and farmhouses once sprinkled the area. Two of the more historic ones, Benjamin Rush's birthplace and Stephen Decatur's farmhouse, disappeared as late as 1969, the former by a perverse combination of overzealous bulldozing and administrative error and the latter for expansion of the North Philadelphia Airport. Similar structures can still be found in some remote parts of the area, particularly along Red Lion Road, but it goes without saying that Philadelphia's farmhouses are becoming increasingly rare and her colonial mills are apparently nonexistent.

Churches to serve the spiritual needs of the inhabitants sprang up almost at once. Quakers began meeting in the Frankford area as early as 1682, but they did not have a meeting house for another two years; and the present Flemish-bond meeting house at Waln and Unity streets was not built until 1775.[7] Baptists organized in 1685 farther to the north at the Pennepack Baptist Church, the oldest Baptist congregation in Pennsylvania and the eighth oldest in the country.[8] The oldest church building in the area, however, is Trinity Church, Oxford (illus.), which was built for Anglicans in 1711.[9] A number of nineteenth-century additions have not disturbed the original part, which is distinguished by its Flemish bonding with vitrified dark headers relieved by bold lozenge-shaped diapering. Architecturally comparable to Gloria Dei, the former Swedish mission church in Southwark, Trinity Church and its peaceful churchyard stand in bold relief to the neighborhood's twentieth-century dwellings.

Rapid changes followed in the wake of the Revolution. The Penn family was replaced by a new, indigenous government, which saw in the removal of Penns' control over the lands north of the city possibilities for both public and private gain. In 1781 the Commonwealth's need for quick revenue led to the sale of 1,400 lots in Northern Liberties.[10] Those with money and able to distinguish between chance and opportunity invested in Northern Liberties real estate. In the next twenty years rows of dwellings went up throughout the area directly north of Vine Street. Built sometimes in pairs and sometimes in rows, they were generally small, squarish houses, often only two-and-a-half stories high with one room to a floor. Understandably called bandboxes, they were usually crowded onto small side streets or kept out of sight in courts and in those small alleys that cut into the large blocks from through streets.[11]

Phillips Row (later New Market Street), six two-and-a-half-story dwellings built between 1808 and 1811 by its merchant-developer William Phillips, is a good example of such a row. All but one of the houses measured 17 feet by 16 feet; the exception had a twenty-foot front. Except for one carpenter, all the original purchasers were

porters.[12] Similar bandboxes appearing on Olive Street were
not only small, 16 feet by 16 feet with a kitchen ell, but also cheaply
constructed, without basements or brick party walls between the
houses at the garret level. They were "finished in the plainest
manner"; simple winding stairs led to the second story, which was
floored with white pine rather than the more durable heart pine.
Olive Street was initially called Equality Court, but a rear alley of
rental dwellings by any other name remains a rear alley. Patriotic
associations notwithstanding, its developer fell victim to a sheriff's
sale, and in 1811 the alley became known as York Court.[13]

These dwellings may appear quaint and cozy to our eyes, but one
former inhabitant of a New Market Street bandbox has confessed that
"it is no use pretending there was any glamour attached to life in the
bandbox. One would not be truthful to assume that he has a nostalgia
for 'those good old days.' . . . The chief trouble with the bandbox
was that you had no privacy. You not only knew what your neighbor
had for dinner, but you heard all his conversation and knew all his
business," and he yours, it might be added.[14] Cramped as these
houses may have been, they were generally soundly constructed, and
laissez-faire attitudes toward housing for the poor allowed them to
survive into the last half of the twentieth century. In the end they fell
neither to decay nor to enlightened housing policies, but to the
automobile, or more precisely to the Delaware Expressway.

Post-Revolutionary real estate development of the Delaware
River Corridor did not reach beyond Cohocksink Creek, leaving rural
the extensive region to the north. Even Frankford Borough, formed in
1800, had large open spaces and was more an agrarian village than a
commercial town for several decades. Residents, for example, did not
begin to pave and curb their sidewalks until 1849.[15] The Religious
Society of Friends considered this natural quietness ideal for their
proposed psychiatric hospital, and in 1813 construction began on the
Asylum for the Relief of Persons Deprived of the Use of Their Reason,
about two miles west of Frankford.[16] The plan of the plastered stone
asylum, opened in 1817, was very similar to that of the Pennsylvania
Hospital, whose elegant center section was finished in 1805
completing a project begun fifty years earlier.[17] Since Friends
Asylum, as it was named in 1888, was the work of a Quaker carpenter
(Israel Maule), it does not possess the architectural finesse of the
Pennsylvania Hospital. It was severely plain and only a small classical
porch marked its entrance. Many later additions, including an 1871
mansard that replaced the original gable roofs, disguise its initial

simplicity.[18] Yet as the country's first private psychiatric hospital, the building's plan and the staff's practices served as precedents for the development of the famous Kirkbride System, and its architectural expression is to be found in the Pennsylvania Hospital for Mental and Nervous Diseases (1836–40) and the Pennsylvania Hospital for the Insane (1856–59). Friends Hospital, as it is known today, still stands at Roosevelt Boulevard and Adams Avenue.[19] Now a complex of buildings, its spacious landscaped grounds serve as a pleasant greensward in the residential neighborhood.

Open land was still abundant on the western fringes of Kensington as late as the 1850's, when the Protestant Episcopal Church of Philadelphia accepted the gift of the Leamy estate at the southeast corner of Front Street and Lehigh Avenue as the site of their proposed hospital.[20] Many argued that this location was too peripheral to be of service to the city, an argument not lightly to be dismissed since Episcopal was only the third general hospital to be built in a city of over 400,000. In the end, however, the force of environmentalism and faith in urban expansion prevailed, and in May, 1860, the cornerstone for the new hospital (illus.) was laid.[21] Its architect, Samuel Sloan, already nationally known for his hospitals for the insane, was to add to his reputation with this work. Although the hospital's construction was interrupted by the Civil War and the final part was not completed until 1875, the nation knew of the hospital before then as a result of a profusely illustrated fund-raising volume published in 1869 and a long article the following spring in Sloan's *Architectural Review.*[22] Because of Sloan's attention to detail and his full execution of the 1778 recommendations of the French Academy, Episcopal Hospital was considered the finest general hospital in the country during the 1860's and 1870's. Its "pavilion" system, which articulated in the building's form any of its interior functions and was borrowed from Sloan's insane asylums, particularly influenced later hospital design. Although its Trenton sandstone walls and irregular silhouette seem lugubrious today in contrast to the sleek walls and clean lines of the complex's more recent buildings, they projected the sweet-melancholy images that Victorians associated with hospitals.[23]

The same waterways and open land that made the Delaware River Corridor so convenient for country gentlemen also offered militarily strategic sites. In 1816 the United States Army purchased more than twenty acres at the mouth of the navigable Frankford Creek as the site for what has since been known as the Frankford

Arsenal. The choice of the site was not sudden and arbitrary. Even
before the four years of internal deliberations leading to the selection
of the site, Army ordnance and muskets had been stored there in a
stone barn, whose walls were incorporated into a building (now
Quarters 2 and 3) erected prior to 1812 when the area served as the
Cantonment on Frankford Creek.[24] In the seven years following the
arsenal's founding, seven major structures were built in an
institutional classical style, and thereafter the arsenal's expansion has
paralleled periods of military activity. Two large tracts of land were
added in 1849 and 1917, the latter giving the arsenal crucial frontage
on the Delaware River when the creek was no longer navigable for
twentieth-century vessels. During the Civil War many large manufacturing buildings with bold Victorian details were added to the
complex, and after 1895, with the beginning of the American empire,
the arsenal gradually expanded, with peaks of activity during the two
world wars. Initially a repair, storage, and distribution depot, the
arsenal shifted to the manufacture of small arms and artillery
ammunition after the Mexican War.[25] Its days are evidently
numbered, unfortunately. The post–World War II symbiotic
relationship between the military and private industry in weaponry
research and development appears to have made the Frankford
Arsenal expendable, and it was scheduled to close in mid-1976.[26]

Almost from the beginning of the European presence in the area,
the many creeks tributary to the Delaware River were seen as sources
of water power, and this eventually became the factor that
determined the configuration of the area between the Old City and
Frankford Creek. Although popular tradition places one Swede's Mill
on Frankford Creek as early as the 1660's, milling was subsidiary to
the area's agriculture during the eighteenth century.[27] With the
beginning of American industrialism about 1800, a host of mills
related to textiles opened along these natural waterways. Globe Mills,
Philadelphia's first extensive cotton mill, began operations in 1804 in
Kensington, then an unincorporated village extending along the
Delaware between Cohocksink Creek and Gunner's Run.[28]
Established by Seth Craige, its first contracts were for girth-web to be
sold in his saddlery and harness shop at 320 Market Street.[29] Another
early mill, the first in Frankford Borough, was begun in 1809 by
English-born Samuel Martin, who manufactured woven woolen
blankets until the mill burned after the War of 1812.[30] The factory
system was firmly ensconced in Kensington and Frankford in the
years after that war, mostly by English immigrants who applied in a

land of opportunity skills learned in the crucible of the Industrial Revolution.[31]

Because these mills were being built in essentially rural settings there was insufficient housing nearby for the workers.[32] Manufacturers like Thomas Holloway met this need by erecting rows of bandboxes (illus.) near his factory. Holloway, Philadelphia's first marine-engine builder, had a row of ten compact dwellings built along Ellen Street on ground that he had acquired in three large purchases between 1829 and 1832.[33] Although the houses were plain, they suggest Holloway's concern for his workers' well-being. Their pleasant classical proportions, paired round-headed doorways, and arched dormers presented a rhythmic streetscape. The interiors were built on the London house plan, a popular one for nineteenth-century speculative builders. This provided two rooms to a floor with the stairs between the rooms and an entrance hall at one side. While this allowed only a ten-by-twelve-foot front room, the houses were still more commodious and more attractive than the tight bandboxes nearby at Hope and Gray streets with but half the depth of Holloway's and without the small backyards.[34] Holloway's own dwelling, a comfortable three-story brick house, was at the end of the row on the northeast corner of New Market Street.[35] Its proximity to his workers' dwellings and his factory is less an indication of paternalism than of the absence of a transit system.

Although Holloway's row has been demolished for the Delaware Expressway, similar dwellings can still be found along Adams Avenue, particularly on the 1500 block where stone and frame dwellings stand on opposite sides of the street. Those across from the Globe Dye and Bleach Works on Worth Street east of Kinsey exhibit the full range of Philadelphia housing types for workers—singles, twins, and short rows.[36] Not all of the mid-nineteenth-century row houses in Kensington and Northern Liberties were built by local industrialists, however. The area's steady growth attracted real estate entrepreneurs such as Joseph Harrison, who was responsible for the construction of two long rows of houses, one with stores below, in the vicinity of Fourth and Jefferson streets.[37]

About the same time that Holloway was building his workers' houses, the Philadelphia and Trenton Railroad was incorporated, and with the almost simultaneous arrival of both factories and railways the destiny of much of the Delaware River Corridor was sealed. By November, 1834, the new railroad was operating between Kensington and Morrisville, spelling the end to the New York-

Philadelphia stages and drastically reducing the influence of the old inns along Frankford Road.[38] No longer merely a passageway between two cities, the area between Northern Liberties and Frankford was to become Philadelphia's industrial heartland as new waves of European immigrants flowed into the city, and the new railroads merged with the old port facilities.

Since the eighteenth century, shipbuilding had been a lucrative trade for independent shipwrights along the Delaware. With the introduction of steam, shipbuilding became more sophisticated, creating opportunities for those with capital and technical specialties, and in 1830 William Cramp started what was destined to become one of the country's foremost private shipyards. Shortly thereafter, one of Holloway's apprentices headed the nation's foremost propeller-engine manufactory, Reany, Neafie & Company at Beach south of Palmer Street. The Kensington waterfront was teeming with activity, but instead of many small shipyards, six major establishments had consolidated the business.[39]

The Philadelphia and Reading Railroad completed its line from the Falls of Schuylkill to Richmond in 1842 in order to carry its prize cargo from the great anthracite coalfields of Pennsylvania to wharves extending 300 feet into the Delaware River.[40] Out of this developed Port Richmond, today the largest privately owned railroad tidewater terminal in the world, with 85 miles of track on its 225 acres.[41]

The variety of factories in the area reflected the city's diversified economy. By the middle of the nineteenth century Northern Liberties could boast of the country's two leading saw manufacturers: Rowland's Saws on Beach Street, the country's oldest, and Henry Disston's Keystone Saw Works (illus.) on Laurel Street, the country's largest.[42] The neighborhood was already an industrial center when Disston began his saw works in 1846. The works grew steadily until it covered eight acres by the time of the centennial. So persistent was its expansion that two fires, in 1849 and 1864, were less business reverses than opportunities to update facilities.[43] The building at the corner of Front and Laurel streets, erected in 1872 after the second fire, illustrated the functional versatility of these industrial structures, although its functions were not readily visible from the street. Its shell was an example of incongruous architectural splendor. Behind arcaded walls with galvanized iron pilasters and window heads and a richly ornamental cornice were coal storage areas, packing and display rooms, and an office. A passage through the middle of the building carried freight cars to the millyard and coal storage facilities on the ground story; the carved oak paneled office was on the second floor.[44]

In addition to these large manufacturing complexes there were a host of smaller factories in the corridor, such as Isaac Pugh's paper-hangings factory at New Market and Pegg streets. Built about 1842 and enlarged after the Civil War, it was a plain brick structure bereft of architectural ornament; standing in stark contrast to the pulchritude of Disston's later building. It appears that Pugh rented the building after 1849, and although he never became the Disston of paper hangings, he did help to establish one of the city's leading firms of the 1850's, Hart, Montgomery & Company.[45]

The water-powered mills and steam-powered railroads quickly transformed the sleepy villages along the Delaware into factory towns that were economic and social extensions of the city. Industrialists' need for wholesale outlets and storage facilities led to the development of a warehouse district between the river and Third Street that physically and commercially linked Northern Liberties to Philadelphia well before their official consolidation in 1854. The warehouses erected during the 1850's set the pattern for the next generation. Generally of four stories, these brick buildings had iron storefronts at the ground floor and often at the second story as well.[46] Later buildings, such as the Massey and Janney Leather Warehouse at Third and Callowhill streets, employed a wider range of architectural ornament and looked less like a warehouse than some of its older neighbors on Leather Row, but it did not differ from them in construction and organization. Designed by Hutton and Ord in 1878, the broad expanse of its side wall was relieved by bands of white and yellow brick, and a second-story arcade graced the front. Slender incised iron piers marked the ground story, and the interior offered the customary warehouse plan of one large room to a floor with a counting room partitioned off on the first floor and a hoist and hatchways at the rear.[47]

As transportation improved and residents of outlying neighborhoods like Kensington and Frankford were drawn toward the vortex of the city, their shopping districts, churches, and cultural and municipal institutions imitated those of Philadelphia. Some institutions, such as the Frankford Lyceum, were more significant for their existence than for their accomplishments. Formed in 1836 and patterned after the Franklin Institute, the Lyceum was intended to provide a technical education for aspiring workingmen, and in 1840 its building was begun. Interest languished rather quickly, however.

The town was apparently too small to support the institution yet too big to be without some expression of cultural pride. In 1866 the Lyceum building was acquired by the Frankford Mutual Insurance Company, an important local firm whose expansion from a small office in the building in 1842 to possession of the whole structure stands as another example of the town's commercial growth.[48]

The Odd Fellows Hall at Third and Brown streets in Northern Liberties, on the other hand, enjoyed a longer life. It was one of many such lodge buildings erected during the mid-nineteenth century, the heyday of private voluntary associations. "Americans form associations for the smallest undertakings," Tocqueville insisted, attributing this phenomenon to the nature of democratic societies in which independent citizens organize in order to overcome their individual sense of incapacity.[49] Modern scholars pinpoint this sense of alienation and see these organizations as attempts to counter the socially disruptive forces of the burgeoning industrial city.[50] When it was completed in 1847, Odd Fellows Hall served as the meeting place for at least eighteen lodges in the northern part of the county. Its Egyptian Revival facade, matched by Egyptian scenery painted on some of the interior walls, was meant to evoke exotic awe from the uninitiated and to hint at those mysteries of the order that were to cement its bonds of brotherhood.[51]

Socially similar to fraternal lodges were the volunteer fire companies. The erection of new fire halls in the 1840's, such as the United States Hose Company No. 14 and the Northern Liberty Hose Company No. 4, further testify to the neighborhood's complexity.[52] As grass-roots institutions that reflected the ethnic, economic, and political composition of their neighborhoods, these voluntary companies "successfully competed with local pubs and workshops for their members' attention and devotion."[53] They also performed a crucial civic service, and in recognition of this they began receiving public appropriations in 1811.[54] As physical expressions of strong neighborhood associations with quasi-municipal functions, their fire halls were often self-consciously finished in a builder-designed high style. Sometimes the company's pride was restrained, as in the case of the large incised name stone and delicately carved door panels of the Northern Liberty Company; sometimes it led to exuberant designs like the awkward and dated Greek Revival of the United States Company. The companies' competitive spirit, however, exceeded socially acceptable limits during the 1840's and 1850's, and after a series of violent confrontations the city established its paid fire department in 1871. Some of the halls served briefly as municipal fire stations before becoming warehouses and community halls.[55]

Tocqueville included religious groups among America's ubiquitous associations, and appropriately so. America's pluralistic, democratic society has historically encouraged the growth of a wide variety of sects, and while their doctrines complemented the secular faith of democracy in the mid-nineteenth century, their congregations generally reflected narrow social, ethnic, and economic biases.[56] If "the creative soil for religion is social anxiety,"[57] then the rapid growth of the southern part of the Corridor provided not only the bodies and souls to make up the congregations but also the uncertain environment that would draw them to the churches. By the 1850's many congregations had grown sufficiently large and wealthy to enable them to commission noted architects to design their new churches. In Northern Liberties, for example, the Fourth Baptist Church had Joseph C. Hoxie design its well-sited Italianate building (1853–55, demolished c. 1970); in Kensington Samuel Sloan supplied the plans for the First Presbyterian Church (1857–59), which initially had a high steeple where the incongruous ogee dome now rests; in Frankford John McArthur, Jr., furnished the awkwardly eclectic design of the First Presbyterian Church (1859–60); in Holmesburg St. Luke's Episcopal Church hired the renowned Richard Upjohn & Son to produce one of their tasteful Gothic Revival works (1860).[58]

In addition to the imposing Protestant churches there appeared a spattering of modest Roman Catholic churches, beginning in 1833–34 with St. Michael's in Kensington. A decade after its completion St. Michael's was attacked by "Native American" rioters who left it in flames and moved southward to deliver the same fate to St. Augustine's in Old City.[59] Undaunted by the hostile atmosphere and strengthened by the growing number of Catholic immigrants who found work in nearby factories, the area's Roman Catholics not only rebuilt St. Michael's in 1846, but a year earlier engaged Napoleon LeBrun to design the German Catholic Church of St. Peter's in Kensington and the year after the riots two additional churches, St. Ann's in Richmond and St. Joachim's in Frankford, were organized.[60] After the Civil War a burgeoning Catholic population demanded more and larger churches, which with their attendant rectories, convents, and schools were built and rebuilt into the twentieth century.[61] Protestant congregations, on the other hand, saw their membership decline. As the Presbyterian Church of Cohocksink and the First Presbyterian Church of Northern Liberties were being dissolved on the eve of World War I, the Second Presbyterian Church altered the old Shunk School on New Market Street into a community center for Russian, Polish, and Ukranian residents. The trend could not be reversed, however, and the number of Protestant churches continued to decline, until by the 1960's Northern Liberties, once the corridor neighborhood with the largest Presbyterian congregations, did not have a single active Presbyterian church. [62]

In 1854 the Delaware River Corridor was united politically with the City of Philadelphia, and the opening of the North Pennsylvania Railroad in 1855 and the Frankford and Southwark Passenger Railway Company in 1858 helped to make the union a physical and economic fact. [63] As mills and factories multiplied so did the banks that catered to their financial needs. Beginning with the sober brownstone Consolidation Bank on North Third Street, chartered in 1855 and built two years later, new financial institutions were formed and old ones moved to new quarters. During the 1860's and 1870's five banks and trust companies were founded in the area, and the two banks antedating the city's consolidation had new buildings erected. [64] The oldest bank in the corridor, the Bank of Northern Liberties, acquired the building of the Manufacturers and Mechanics Bank about 1870 and had it enlarged and extensively rebuilt from the designs of James H. Windrim, then a young architect who had just made his mark as the winner of the Philadelphia Masonic Hall competition. [65] Windrim's concentration of superimposed pilasters, pediments, arched hoods, and carved ornament at the entrance and the window above lent a touch of baroque exuberance to the facade, but the sobriety of the rusticated quoins and granite balustrade prevailed, keeping the building within the Renaissance tradition of bank design. The Kensington National Bank, on the other hand, stood in vivid contrast to this convention, as might be expected of a bank designed by Frank Furness in the 1870's. Since it repeated the form and decoration of some of his earlier banks, its granite walls of contrasting shades and finishes, rugged details, and colorful interior made it one of the area's foremost architectural attractions. [66]

Supporting these banks and in turn supported by them was a burgeoning group of industrial concerns, as old firms expanded and new ones were established in the last half of the nineteenth century. Frankford Dye Works, established in 1820 by Jeremiah Horrocks, was the oldest such establishment in Philadelphia and on the eve of the Civil War the largest dye works outside New England. [67] Although its expansion continued after the Civil War, its primacy was challenged

during the 1870's by new concerns like the Globe Dye Works at
Kinsey and Worth streets.[68] The Globe operation began in 1867 with
five buildings, which unlike many of the Frankford Works structures
were brick rather than frame. In less than seven years seven new
buildings were added, the two original Dye Houses were replaced,
and the Bleaching House was enlarged.[69] By 1876 it had expanded
across Tacony Creek. Further alterations and additions during the
1880's and 1890's made it one of the city's most extensive dye and
bleach concerns; it still flourishes at its original site.[70]

One of the greatest industrial establishments in the corridor was
John Bromley & Sons carpet mill (illus.). Nationally celebrated for
their fine rugs and carpets since before the Civil War, their two large
manufacturing factories in Kensington constituted the largest rug and
carpet complex in the United States by the turn of the century.[71]
Bromley's Lehigh Mills at 201–63 East Lehigh Avenue are especially
noteworthy and stand as one of the handsomest nineteenth-century
industrial buildings to be found anywhere. A massive brick structure
with interior iron columns and beams, it is a U-plan that encompasses
a large city block. The west side was built in 1886, probably from the
designs of Walter H. Geissinger, the city's leading industrial architect
and the architect of the company's other nineteenth-century
elements.[72] Projecting brick piers rise out of a plain ground story to
frame the windows and reduce the heaviness of the walls, while the
dull repetition of this pattern is relieved by corbeled brick parapets
flanked by molded minarets at the middle and corners of each long
side. The focal point, however, is the 1891 office building, which is
firmly planted in the middle of the Lehigh Avenue facade. From the
bold granite arches at the street level through the cylindrical minarets
protruding from the upper stories to the bulbous French roof, it
remains the visual embodiment of vibrant power.

Changing tastes, technologies, and transportation and lower
suburban and southern tax rates have combined to undermine the
corridor's industrial prominence since World War II. Some industrial
giants have closed their doors and quit; others have moved to the
cheaper land and limited-access highways of the suburbs. Their old
factories are either left vacant or let to a variety of tenants who usually
are collectively less productive than the original owners, and because
of age and neglect the buildings are vulnerable to an age-old threat,
fire.[73] Yet these massive, grimy red brick buildings are monuments to
industrial capitalism. Often consuming an entire block and
surrounded by rail spurs and small row houses, they are mute

reminders of an age when work meant insecurity and hard and
dangerous activity relieved by periodic and uncompensated layoffs,
while ownership offered wealth, power, and luxury.

Monumental and lucrative as these factories were, they and the
railroad ravaged the idyllic surroundings along Frankford and Tacony
creeks during the last half of the nineteenth century. The Georgian
mansions were abandoned and fell into ruin, and their stripped and
rotting hulks were finally torn down in the 1940's and 1950's.[74] (One
of Port Royal's dependencies managed to survive because it could be
converted to low-rent housing.) This nineteenth-century industrial
pattern was so well entrenched in the lower part of the corridor that
the twentieth century has brought no significant change. The present
physical culture of the upper region, on the other hand, is more the
product of the automobile than that of any other part of the city, since
large parts of it lay undeveloped until after World War II.

Inland from the waterways a few nineteenth-century suburban
villas remain as testimony to its former status as a haven for the city's
business elite. Burholme (illus.), a picturesque Italianate villa with a
matching carriage house, is one of the finest examples of this building
type, which was first popularized by Andrew Jackson Downing in the
1840's. Its crowning glory is an overwhelming belvedere with
stained-glass windows and attenuated dome that combines with the
arched cross-gable of the hipped roof to give the mansion a bold
silhouette. Built about 1859 for Joseph W. Ryerss, president of the
Tioga Railroad, Burholme stands on high ground, affording a
sweeping view of its forty-eight landscaped acres.[75] The house and
grounds were transferred to the city in 1905 by Ryers's daughter-in-
law, and today they are part of the extensive Fairmount Park system,
which is helping to preserve a splendid survivor of a dying species.[76]

Knowlton falls into the next generation of rural retreats. It was
built in 1879–81 for William H. Rhawn, president of the National
Bank of the Republic, and is even more unusual and even rarer in
some respects than Burholme.[77] While few Italianate villas had the
distinctive qualities of the Ryerss mansion, it was still one of many
such suburban villas of generally similar design built at the time.
Knowlton, on the other hand, is unique. It is the only Philadelphia
survivor of a small number of country houses designed by Frank
Furness, one of the nation's most innovative nineteenth-century
architects. Like Burholme, Knowlton has a matching carriage house
and both project lively picturesque silhouettes, but that is the end of
their similarities. Juxtaposition of living volumes and the bold

massing of richly textured exterior elements set Knowlton apart from the classical balance and order of earlier country houses and qualify it as one of Philadelphia's prized "architectural aberrations."[78]

Improved public transportation after 1890 stimulated real estate development of the middle part of the corridor, especially the Frankford and Wissinoming areas. Trolleys were introduced in Frankford in 1893 and the next year the Reading Railroad completed a commuter line to the former borough. An even more significant event in the corridor's history was the opening of the Frankford Elevated late in 1922.[79] With residents able to travel quickly and cheaply into the city's commercial center, its army of clerks, secretaries, and shopkeepers could now heed Whittier and flee to the northeast "from crowded street and red wall's weary gleam."[80] Open land was subdivided and parceled out in a manner not unlike that practiced in Whittier's "close dark city." Single dwellings with front lawns, pale imitations of an earlier Georgian grandeur, were outnumbered by row houses or semidetached houses built and organized on the row house pattern. Housing construction was stifled by the Depression and World War II, but after 1945 a new generation of consumers hungered for homes. Geared to the automobile, encouraged by cheap fuel, and helped by expressway construction, these urban commuters made possible the explosive development of the great northeast. Weak attempts at architectural individuality were made, the foul and crowded courts of the older areas were not repeated, and streets were laid out in sweeping curves instead of on a rectangular grid, but the nineteenth-century speculative pattern persisted, because it had proved so profitable. Called airlites, these compact, low-maintenance row houses varied little in plan or appearance over two decades.[81]

Among the wave upon wave of mid-brow housing, however, can be found some imaginative attempts at architectural excellence. Named for a young hosiery worker killed during an incident surrounding a 1930 strike,[82] the Carl Mackley Apartments (illus.), on Castor Avenue facing Juniata Park, were in the vanguard on two points when they were built in 1933–34. Their construction was sponsored by the American Federation of Hosiery Workers with the proceeds of a loan of more than a million dollars from the Public Works Administration, making it one of the first low-rent developments built with federal aid.[83] The four buildings in the group are the work of European-trained Oskar Stonorov in association with Alfred Kastner. Although they now look like just another apartment complex (only better), their design was considered "strikingly modern" in the 1930's, and they mark one of the earliest adaptations of the International style to American domestic architecture.[84] Crisp lines, total absence of applied ornament, and conscious arrangement of the buildings in reference to their grounds are clearly European features, but the residents' organization of life within the development—by way of a credit union, cooperative market, and tenants' steering committee—has historical roots in American utopian communities of an earlier, more romantic era.[85]

Catalog

Bank of Northern Liberties. See National Bank of Northern Liberties

Beth Eden House. See Shunk School

Birely House
(PA-1743), 313 Richmond St. Brick with stone trim, approx. 20' (two-bay front) × 28' with three-story rear ell, four stories on raised basement, mansard roof, round-arch entrance with fanlight and carved stone frontispiece, corbel cornice, side-hall plan. Built c. 1859; mansard probably added later; demolished c. 1969. John Birely (occupant) and Theodore Birely (owner) were local shipbuilders. 1 ext. photo (1967); * 6 data pages (1967).*

Blue Dick, The. See United States Hose Company No. 14

Bromley, John, & Sons, Lehigh Mills. Illustrated
(PA-1744), 201–63 E. Lehigh Ave., composing block bounded by Lehigh Ave., A., E. Somerset, E. Gurney, B sts. Brick with granite trim and interior iron beams and columns, front building approx. 500' (fifty-eight-bay front) × 55', western rear wing approx. 66' × 500', eastern rear wing approx. 66' × 300', one, four, five, and six stories, gable roofs with clerestory skylights, bulbous mansard roof on center office building, projecting piers, turrets, and rock-faced round-headed entrance on center building, U-plan with buildings in courtyard.

Notable late-19th century industrial architecture with massive membering. West wing and six buildings in courtyard built 1886–87;

probably by Walter H. Geissinger, architect. East wing and one building in courtyard built 1889–90; Geissinger and Hales, architects.
Center office building and one building in courtyard built 1891; Geissinger and Hales, architects. Northern end of west wing burned and
replaced, front building connecting wings and office building built
1892; Walter H. Geissinger, architect. Boiler house built 1894; Walter
H. Geissinger, architect. Later additions and alterations to buildings
in courtyard.

John Bromley & Sons was one of the country's largest manufacturers of carpets and rugs; now used for various manufacturing and
wholesale purposes. 2 ext. photos (1973),* 4 photocopies of plans and
printed views (1887, 1892),* 1 photocopy of architectural rendering
(1901).*

Brown, Anna S., House and Shop

(PA-1745), 408 Richmond St. Brick with stone trim, approx. 18' (two-
bay front) × 20' with two-story frame ell, two stories, flat roof,
ground-story shopfront with paneled piers and bracketed cornice.
Example of modest nieghborhood shop-dwelling of mid-19th
century. Built c. 1872; frame ell probably built before 1856; demolished c. 1969. Anna S. Brown, widow, confectioner, had her shop
and residence here 1873–78. 1 ext. photo (1967);* 12 data pages
(1967).*

Browne, John C., Houses

(PA-1746), 427–29 Richmond St. Brick with brownstone ashlar front,
each approx. 18' (two-bay front) × 30' with two-story rear ell, three
stories on raised basement, mansard roofs, side-hall plans. Mid-19th-
century brownstone residences built for investment purposes on
inherited land. Built before 1860; cornice, mansard roof added later;
demolished c. 1969. 1 ext. photo (1967);* 7 data pages (1967).*

Burholme (also known as Ryerss Mansion). Illustrated

(PA-186), Burholme Park, at N.W. corner Cottman and Central aves.
Museum. Stuccoed stone, 74'-9" (five-bay front) × 52'-3" with two-
story rear wings, three stories, hipped roof with large arched cross-
gable, central one-story tower with intersecting barrel-vault roof and
tall dome (not original), veranda on three sides, originally center-hall
plan.

A splendid suburban villa whose picturesque Italian style blends
with the rolling landscape of its 48-acre estate. Built c. 1859; two-story

rear brick kitchen built 1888; tower (or belvedere) added after 1888; interior altered c. 1908–10. Acquired by Fairmount Park Commission, City of Philadelphia 1905; opened to public as Robert W. Ryerss Library and Museum 1910. Built for Joseph W. Ryerss, railroad entrepreneur, and willed to city by son of Robert W. Ryerss. Named for ancestral estate in England. Certified, PHC 1957.

10 sheets (n.d., including plans, elevations, section, details, plan and section of tower); 4 ext. photos (1973, including 1 of carriage house, 1 in color);* 8 data pages (including 1872–88 insurance surveys).*

Butler, Anthony, Houses

(PA-1747), 133, 132–34 Olive St. Three brick houses (Nos. 132–34 contiguous), each approx. 16' (two-bay front) × 16' with two-story rear ell, two-and-a-half stories, gable roofs, ground-story alleyways to backyards, city house plans.

Houses were part of a speculative row of eight dwellings built for Anthony Butler, merchant, on each side of a court cut through from Front St. to New Market St. Built c. 1791; demolished c. 1969. Street known as Equality Court before 1810, as York Court 1811–58, as Onas St. 1858–97. 1 sheet (1967, including plot plan, elevation)* courtesy of Pennsylvania Historical Salvage Council; 2 ext. photos (1967);* 16 data pages (1968).*

Carmalt, Thomas, Houses

(PA-1748), 129–31 Brown St. Two contiguous brick houses, each appprox. 16' (two-bay front) × 20', two-and-a-half stories, gable roof, brick stringcourse, probably originally London house plan. Built between 1795 and 1802; altered later; demolished 1970. 1 sheet (1967, including plot plan, elevation);* 1 ext. photo (1967);* 11 data pages (1968).*

Chalkley Hall

(PA-110), 3869 Sepviva St., at S.W. corner Wheatsheaf Ln. Brick faced with coursed sandstone ashlar and granite trim, 57'-8" (five-bay front) × 46'-11" with two-and-a-half-story stuccoed brick and rubble lateral wing with granite trim, two and three stories, hipped and flat roofs, central pavilion with giant Tuscan pilasters and pediment, Tuscan frontispiece, central-hall plan.

Lateral wing built 1723; main section built 1776; two-story rear wing enlarged to width of house later. Vacated before 1907; demolished 1954. Entrance door installed in American Wing, Metropolitan Museum of Art, New York City. Interior elements at William Penn Memorial Museum, Harrisburg, Pa. Earliest part built for Thomas Chalkey, merchant and itinerant Quaker proselytizer; main section built for Abel James, merchant and Chalkley's son-in-law.

24 sheets (1937, including plans, elevations, section, details); 10 ext. photos (1936, 1937), 1 int. photo (1937), 1 photocopy of old ext. photo (n.d.); 11 data pages (1937, including 1833–59 insurance surveys*).

Clarke, Samuel, House

(PA-1749), 536 New Market St., at S.W. corner Nectarine St. Brick, approx. 14' (two-bay front) × 28', two-and-a-half stories, gable roof, round-arch entrance with fanlight, molded brick cornice. One of five row houses built for rental income for Samuel Clarke, retired merchant and naval officer. Built after 1824; demolished 1969. 1 ext. photo (1967);* 5 data pages (1968).*

Commercial Building

(PA-1750), 214–16 Callowhill St., at S.E. corner American St. Brick with stone trim, 39'-7" (five-bay front) × 33'-4", three stories (No. 214 originally two-and-a-half stories), flat roof (No. 214 originally gable roof), window and side-lights set in blind arch in second story of No. 214, rectangular plan. No. 214 built as dwelling between 1814 and 1825; No. 216 built as store-dwelling between 1851 and 1859; two buildings combined into one, ground story altered later; demolished 1969. 1 ext. photo (1967);* 6 data pages (1968).*

Commercial Building

(PA-1751), 305–7 N. Second St. Brick with cast-iron storefront and trim, approx. 35' (six-bay front) × 70', four stories, flat roof, molded cast-iron Corinthian piers on first and second stories, heavy granite lintels on upper stories, rectangular plan. Built before 1859. Two-story brick addition with steel columns and girders at rear of No. 307 built 1927; J. S. Wilds, engineer. Demolished 1973. 1 ext. photo (1967).*

Commercial Buildings

(PA-1752), 405–7 N. Second St. Two adjoining brick buildings with cast-iron storefronts and stone trim, each approx. 22' (three-bay front) × 42' with one-story rear wing, two stories (originally No. 405

three-and-a-half stories, No. 407 four stories), flat roofs (originally No. 405 probably gable roof), rectangular plan. No. 405 built early 19th century; No. 407 built after 1845; ground stories altered to stores before 1859; upper stories altered to commercial use 1909; lowered to two stories 1951–52; demolished c. 1969. 1 ext. photo (1967).*

Commercial Buildings

(PA-1753), 401–3 Richmond St., at N.E. corner E. Columbia Ave. Brick with stone trim, each approx. 18' (two-bay front) × 70' (No. 403 approx. 30' deep), three stories, flat roofs, shopfronts, rectangular plan. Built c. 1850; shopfronts altered later; demolished c. 1969. 1 ext. photo (1967);* 11 data pages (1967).*

Commercial Buildings

(PA-1754), 123–27 Vine St. Three adjoining brick stores with stone trim, each approx. 17' (two-bay front) × 35' with three- and two-story rear ells, four stories, flat roofs, stores on ground story. Built after 1859; No. 123 lowered to two stories 1957. Demolished 1968. 1 ext. photo (1967).*

Consolidation Bank

(PA-1755), 329–33 N. Third St. Brick with brownstone ashlar front, 41'-6" (five-bay front) × 115'-3" with one-story rear addition, three stories, flat roof, round-arch windows, curved pediment over round-arch entrance, projecting piers and recessed spandrels on upper stories, corbel table beneath cornice, rectangular plan.

Fine example of a mid-19th-century bank in Italianate mode. Built 1857; possibly by Stephen D. Button, architect; George Watson, builder. Parapet date stone removed, interior altered c. 1908. Rear brick addition built 1912; Ralph White, architect. Demolished 1972. Became Consolidation National Bank 1865; ceased banking operations 1908. 3 sheets (1968, including plot plan, plans, elevation)* courtesy Pennsylvania Historical Salvage Council; 1 ext. photo (1967);* 5 data pages (1968).*

Day, Michael, House

(PA-1756), 400 Richmond St., at S.E. corner E. Columbia Ave. Brick with stone trim, approx. 18' (two-bay front) × 65', three stories, flat roof, second-story balcony on rear wing. Built before 1866; altered to saloon later; demolished 1968. 1 ext. photo (1967);* 3 data pages (1967).*

Disston, Henry, & Sons, Keystone Saw, Tool and Steel Works. Illustrated
(PA-1757), 1001–5 N. Front St., at N.E. corner Laurel St. Brick with
cast-iron posts and galvanized iron trim, approx. 66' (nine-bay
front) × 166', two stories, flat roof, round-arch windows with bold
lintels, clerestory skylights, rectangular plan with passage through
ground story to millyard.
One building in a complex that composed the largest saw and file
works in 19th-century America. Built 1872; altered c. 1907; demolished 1968. Served as office and packing and show rooms of firm
until 1907 when it became a paper box factory.
7 sheets (1967, including plot plan, plans, elevations, sections,
details)* courtesy of Pennsylvania Historical Salvage Council; 2 ext.
photos (1967),* 4 int. photos (1967),* 1 photocopy of printed view of
Works (1873),* 1 photocopy of Works' plan (1873);* 3 data pages
(1967).*

Episcopal Hospital. See Hospital of the Protestant Episcopal Church of
Philadelphia

Frankford Town Hall
(PA-1758), 4255 Frankford Ave., at S.E. corner Ruan St. Brick, approx. 30' (three-bay front) × 55', two stories, gable roof. Built 1848;
demolished 1960. 1 ext. photo (1959).*

Friendship Engine Company No. 15
(PA-1759), 2200–2204 E. Norris St., at S.E. corner Sepviva St. Brick
with stone trim and cast-iron front at ground story, 37'-10" (four-bay
front) × 84'-0", four stories (originally three), flat roof, quoins, rectangular plan. Built c. 1860; fourth story installed later by dividing tall
second story. Served as Hook and Ladder Company C 1871–78. 1
photocopy of old ext. photo (c. 1935);* 1 data page (1963).*

Goodwin Building
(PA-1760), 317–19 N. Second St. Brick with cast-iron storefront and
iron and granite trim, approx. 34' (four-bay front) × 58' with one-
story rear wing, four stories, flat roof, molded cast-iron piers on
ground story, engaged clustered cast-iron piers and low-pitch segmental pointed arches on second story, originally skylights in rear
wing, rectangular plan. Example of mid-19th-century wholesale
store. Built between 1854 and 1859. Demolished c. 1973. 1 ext. photo
(1967).*

Griffith-Peale House

(PA-1761), 8100 Frankford Ave., at N.W. corner Welsh Rd. (originally known as Bristol Turnpike and Mill St.). Stuccoed rubble, approx. 24' (three-bay front) × 36' with two-story rear ell, two-and-a-half stories, gable roof, round-arch entrance with Tuscan frontispiece, transverse center-hall plan.

Modest Federal-style town house. Built between 1807 and 1810; interior altered, ell built later. Built for Thomas Hockley Griffith, gentleman, who sold the house in 1811. Home of Joseph Temple, merchant and patron of arts 1845–57, Col. John Clark, railroad contractor and politician 1857–72, Dr. James Burd Peale, physician and grandson of painter Charles Willson Peale 1877–80. Owned by Peale's descendants until 1944. Certified, PHC 1960. 3 ext. photos (1959);* 6 data pages (1960, 1962, including 1813 insurance survey).*

Harrison House

(PA-1458), Point No Point, or Port Richmond (street address unknown). Brick, approx. 40' (five-bay front) × 25' with one-story rear wing and frame side addition, two-and-a-half stories, gambrel roof, open porch across the front (probably replacing earlier pent eave), one interior end chimney, probably center-hall plan. Built late 18th century; rear and side additions, front porch built later; demolished after 1936. 2 ext. photos (1936).

Helffenstein, Dr. Abraham, House

(PA-1762), 1008 Shackamaxon St. Brick with brownstone and marble trim, approx. 20' (two-bay front) × 27' with two-story rear ell, four stories, flat roof, smooth rusticated brownstone ground story, wrought-iron balcony on carved stone consoles at second story, alleyway through ground story to backyard, side-hall plan. Example of mid-19th-century town house. Built c. 1849; demolished 1968. 1 ext. photo (1967);* 9 data pages (1967).*

Holloway, Thomas, Houses. Illustrated

(PA-1763), 125–31 Ellen St. Four brick row houses, each approx. 16' (two-bay front) × 28', two-and-a-half stories, gable roof, ground-story alleyway between alternate houses, side-hall London house plan. Part of a row of ten small tenement houses built for a steam-engine and machine manufacturer whose home and factory were nearby. Built c. 1832; demolished 1968. 2 sheets (1967, including elevation, plans)* courtesy of Pennsylvania Historical Salvage Council; 1 ext. photo (1967);* 6 data pages (1967).*

Hospital of the Protestant Episcopal Church in Philadelphia (now Episcopal Hospital). Illustrated

(PA-1764), S.E. corner Front St. and Lehigh Ave. Random Trenton sandstone ashlar, approx. 258' (thirty-one-bay front) × 256' (center building and chapel) and 200' (wings), two-and-a-half and three-and-a-half stories on raised basements (chapel one story), gable roofs (later altered to gambrel roofs on south end of wings), two four-story towers with concave roofs on wings, minarets, chapel on south end of center building, originally E-plan with central longitudinal halls and transverse corridor.

Considered the best general hospital design in the United States when built and had a great effect on subsequent American hospital architecture. Center building, chapel, west wing built 1860–62; Samuel Sloan, architect; James H. Windrim, superintendent of construction. East wing built 1873–75; Samuel Sloan, architect; William A. Armstrong, builder. Iron fire escapes added to south end of wings 1885; wings vacated 1967.

Three-story sandstone Harrison Memorial House of Incurable Patients built at east end 1889–91; G. W. and W. D. Hewitt, architects; George F. Payne & Co., contractors. Two-and-a-half-story sandstone Ingersoll Receiving Ward built at west end 1892–94; G. W. and W. D. Hewitt, architects; Thomas Little & Son, contractors. North end of center building demolished 1933, replaced by ten-story steel-frame Tower Building with brick curtain walls 1933–35; Day and Zimmerman, architects. Harrison Memorial House demolished 1965, replaced by six-story brick and reinforced-concrete Potter-Morris Building 1964–66; Vincent G. Kling and Associates, architects. Name changed to Episcopal Hospital 1964. Certified, PHC 1957.

4 ext. photos (1973),* 3 photocopies of old ext. photos (1869),* 2 photocopies of old int. photos (1869),* 2 photocopies of old prints (1859),* 2 photocopies of plan (1859, 1869),* 1 photocopy of architectural rendering of Receiving Ward (1893).*

House

(PA-1765), 705 New Market St. Wood frame with clapboards, approx. 18' (two-bay front) × 25' with one-story rear ell, two-and-a-half stories, gable roof, two rooms to a floor. Built after 1858; demolished 1969. 1 sheet (1967, including plot plan, plans, elevation)* courtesy of Pennsylvania Historical Salvage Council; 1 ext. photo (1967).*

House

(PA-1766), 720 New Market St., at S.W. corner Olive St. Brick, approx. 17' (three-bay front) × 35' with two-story rear ell, two stories (originally three-and-a-half stories), flat roof (originally probably gable). Built late 18th century. Lowered to three stories and converted to garage 1919; Isadore W. Levin, architect. Lowered to two stories 1942; demolished 1969. 1 ext. photo (1967).*

House

(PA-1767), 106 Produce St. Brick, approx. 20' (three-bay front) × 18' with three-story rear ell (originally two-story rear ell), three-and-a-half stories, gable roof, brick stringcourse at second and third stories, originally ground-story arched alleyway to backyard, probably originally city house plan. Built mid-18th century; rear ell raised one story late 19th century; altered to garage-workshop 20th century; demolished 1969. 1 ext. photo (1967).*

House on Old Turnpike

(PA-1429), Frankford Ave. (street number unknown) Scored stuccoed rubble with brick trim, approx. 22' (three-bay front) × 20' with two-story scored stucco side wing, two-and-a-half stories, gable roof, recessed and paneled entrance with simplified Adamesque frontispiece, brick quoins, brick string-course on wing, probably side-hall plan. Built early 19th century; demolished after 1936. 2 ext. photos (1936).

Houses

(PA-1768), 1035–37 Frankford Ave. Two frame houses with wood sheathing and asbestos shingles, each approx. 14' (two-bay front) × 30' with rear ell, two-and-a-half stories, gable roof. Built after 1828; demolished 1969. 1 ext. photo (1967).*

Houses

(PA-1769), 142–50 Nectarine St. Five adjoining brick houses, each approx. 16' (two-bay front) × 16' with two-story rear ell (three westernmost houses with more attenuated proportions), three stories, gable roofs, alleyways through ground story of alternate houses.

Example of sidestreet dwellings of 19th-century artisans. Nos. 142–44 built between 1823 and 1830; Nos. 146–50 built between 1792 and 1803. Demolished 1969. Street known as Artillery Lane until c. 1785, as Duke St. c. 1785–1858, as Dana St. 1858–97. 1 ext. photo (1967);* 26 data pages (1968).*

Houses and Livery Stable

(PA-1770), 149–55 Noble St. Adjoining brick houses (Nos. 149–51) approx. 16' and 20' (two- and three-bay fronts) × 18' with two-story rear ells, three-and-a-half stories, gable roofs, ground-story alleys to backyards, side-hall plans; brick livery stable (Nos. 153–55) approx. 30' (three-bay front) × 65', two stories, flat roof, rectangular plan. Houses built after 1807; No. 149 by Moses Lancaster, house carpenter. Livery stable built after 1837. Demolished 1969. 1 ext. photo (1967);* 14 data pages (1968).*

Independent Order of Odd Fellows Hall

(PA-1771), 800 N. Third St., at N.W. corner Brown St. Brick covered with plaster, approx. 90' (seven-bay front) × 50', four-and-a-half stories, flat roof, windows with battered surrounds continue over three stories surmounted by corbel-arch windows, polychromatic cavetto cornice, discontinuous floor plans and stairways, third-story truss studding carries second-story auditorium ceiling.

Fine surviving example of Egyptian Revival architecture. Built 1846; possibly by John Haviland, architect. Interior altered 1891; Mettler Brothers, contractors. Destroyed by fire 1976 Lodge hall until 1932; later used for light manufacturing. Certified PHC 1966; Pennsylvania Register 1970; NR. 3 ext. photos (1961),* 1 int. photo (1961);* 8 data pages (1963, including 1849 news article).*

Keen, James, House

(PA-1772), 1015 Shackamaxon St., at N.E. corner Emery St. Brick with stone trim, approx. 20' (two-bay front) × 30' with two-story rear ell, two-and-a-half stories, gable roof, fanlight in gable curtain wall between twin chimneys, richly carved pent eave (not original). Built after 1815; ground story, cornice altered c. 1900; demolished 1968. James Keen, a Kensington ship-joiner and later steamboat inspector, lived here until 1860. 1 ext. photo (1967);* 7 data pages (1967).*

Kensington National Bank

(PA-1773), 2–8 W. Girard Ave., at S.W. corner Frankford Ave. Rock-faced granite with dressed granite trim, approx. 85' (eight-bay front) × 43' with one-story lateral wing, two stories on raised basement, flat roof (originally with crenelation), entrance on bevel with second-story balcony and pinched-top window, boldly carved stone details, decorative wrought-iron window grilles.

Early bank design by an innovative late-19th-century architect. Built 1877; Frank Furness, architect. Western addition built 1920;

Frank R. Watson, architect. One-story southern addition built 1941–42; Charles H. Ingle, engineer. Interior extensively altered 1954; Howell Lewis Shay, architect. Kensington Office, First Pennsylvania Banking and Trust Co. since 1947. 1 ext. photo (1974);* HABSI form (1962).*

Keyser-Wainwright Building
(PA-1774), 336 Richmond St., at S.W. corner E. Columbia Ave. Brick with stone trim, approx. 40' (six-bay front) × 20', two stories, flat roof, bracketed cornice over corner shopfront, rounded corner, rectangular plan. Example of mid-19th-century neighborhood retail store. Built between 1861 and 1867; ground-story shopfront altered later; demolished c. 1969. 1 ext. photo (1967);* 7 data pages (1968).*

Knight Building
(PA-1775), 301–3 N. Second St., at N.E. corner Vine St. Brick with cast-iron storefront and trim, approx. 30' (four-bay front) × 92', four stories, flat roof, cast-iron balcony at second-story front, ornamented cast-iron lintels, rectangular plan. Built between 1851 and 1859; demolished 1973. 1 ext. photo (1967).*

Kramer-Rommel Houses
(PA-1776), 915–17 N. Hope St., at N.E. corner Gray St. Two contiguous brick houses, each approx. 15' (two-bay front) × 13', three stories, flat roof, one room to a floor. Early-19th-century expression of an earlier tenement-building type. Built between 1828 and 1832; demolished 1968. 1 sheet (1967, including plot plan, plans, elevation)* courtesy of Pennsylvania Historical Salvage Council; 2 ext. photos (1967);* 5 data pages (1968).*

Lawrence, Charles, House
(PA-1777), 400 N. Front St., at N.W. corner Callowhill St. Stuccoed brick, approx. 20' (three-bay front) × 27' with three-story rear wing, four stories (probably originally three-and-a-half), mansard roof (originally probably gable), bold bracketed cornice. Built between 1773 and 1781; altered to tavern before 1867; rear wing, cornice, mansard added later. 1 ext. photo (1967);* 6 data pages (1968).*

Lynfield
(PA-132), 4601 Rhawn St., at S.E. corner Ditman St. Coursed fieldstone ashlar and rubble, approx. 38' (five-bay front) × 38' (originally 38' × 23') with two-story side wing, two-and-a-half stories, gable and

hipped roofs, projecting pavilion with pediment and Adamesque frontispiece, open wooden rear porch, center-hall plan.

Fine example of rural house enlarged into a country house. South ashlar section built c. 1760; enlarged c. 1800 with new north rubble section becoming the front; side wing added mid-19th century; demolished 1942. Entrance in storage, parlor installed as Chippendale Room, William Penn Memorial Museum, Harrisburg, Pa. 3 ext. photos (1937); 1 data page (1937).

McGee, Ann, Houses

(PA-1778), 128–30 Brown St. Two contiguous brick houses, each approx. 11' (two-bay front) × 29', three stories, flat roof, round-arch entrances with fanlights, ground-story alleyway between houses, London house plan without entrance hall. Built between 1830 and 1837; demolished 1969. 1 sheet (1967, including plot plan, plans, elevation);* 1 ext. photo (1967);* 10 data pages (1968).*

Mackley, Carl, Apartments. Illustrated

(PA-1779), block bounded by Castor Ave., Bristol, M, Cayuga sts., on S. side Juniata Park. Four parallel concrete-block units faced with tan tile, each approx. 480' (thirty-four-bay front) × 33', three stories, flat roofs with pavilions, recessed central pavilions, recessed balconies on upper stories; contain 272 apartments.

Notable early example of International style employed on American domestic architecture. Built 1933–34; Oskar Stonorov and Alfred Kastner, architects; W. Pope Barney, superintendent of construction. Named in honor of Philadelphia hosiery worker killed during 1930 strike. 2 ext. photos (1976).*

Maguire-Howell House

(PA-1780), 976 N. Front St. Brick, approx. 18' (two-bay front) × 28' with three- and two-story rear ell, flat roof, round-arch entrance, alleyway through ground story to backyard, side-hall plan with rear stair tower. Built between 1831 and 1844; demolished 1968. 1 sheet (1967, including plot plan, elevation)* courtesy of Pennsylvania Historical Salvage Council; 6 data pages (1968).*

Manderson, Andrew, Houses

(PA-1781), 117–19 Fairmount Ave. Brick with stone trim, each 17'-6" (three-bay front) × 18'-6" with one- and two-story rear ell, three-

and-a-half stories, gable roof, brick stringcourse above first and second stories, dentil cornice, round-arch doorway with fanlight, round-arch alleyway between houses to rear yard, city house plan.

Built between 1801 and 1828; rear ells extended 1833. Certified, PHC 1971. 2 sheets (1967, including elevation, plans)* courtesy of Pennsylvania Historical Salvage Council; 1 ext. photo (1967);* 7 data pages (1967, including 1828–33 insurance surveys).*

Massey & Janney Warehouse

(PA-1782), 355 N. Third St., at S.E. corner Callowhill St. Brick with bands of white and black brick, approx. 20' (three-bay front) × 115', five stories, flat roof, rectangular plan with rear office. Notable example of late-19th-century warehouse. Built 1878; Hutton and Ord, architects. Demolished 1973. Massey & Janney, prominent leather merchants, were here until 1896. 3 ext. photos (1971);* 15 data pages (including architects' specifications and 1878 insurance survey).*

Mount Sinai Cemetery Chapel

(PA-1783), N.E. corner Bridge and Cottage sts. Rock-faced granite and brick with pecked and carved red terra cotta trim, approx. 42' (three-bay front) × 60', one story, intersecting hipped and gable red tile roofs with hipped cross-gables and copper cornice, horseshoe-arch windows, semihexagonal side bay; three-aisle plan, exposed wooden trusses, rear vault.

Richardsonian window and roof motifs mark this as one of the first and best designs by Frank Furness during his declining years. Built 1892; Furness, Evans & Co., architects. Certified, PHC 1974. 5 ext. photos (1973).*

National Bank of Northern Liberties

(PA-1784), 300–302 N. Third St., at N.W. corner Vine St. Brick faced with coursed granite ashlar, approx. 35' (three-bay front) × 94' with two-story lateral addition, two stories, flat roof, pedimented entrance, round-arch windows, quoins, balustrade. Built c. 1835. Enlarged, extensively rebuilt c. 1870; James H. Windrim, architect; George Watson, builder. Addition built c. 1887; probably by James H. Windrim, architect; Allen B. Rorke, contractor. Chartered as Bank of Northern Liberties 1814, it became a national bank 1864. 3 ext. photos (1963),* 1 photocopy of old ext. photo (n.d.);* 2 data pages (1970).*

Northern Liberty Hose Company No. 4 (also known as The Snappers)

(PA-1785), 714 New Market St. Brick with granite trim, approx. 20'
(two-bay front) × 55', three stories, flat roof, carved and paneled apparatus doors, date and name stone in middle of facade, rectangular
plan. Fine example of mid-19th-century volunteer fire hall. Built 1846;
demolished 1969. Name stone at Philadelphia Fire Museum. Served
as Philadelphia Fire Department, Engine Company No. 21 1871–75.
Certified, PHC 1964. 2 ext. photos (1963, 1967);* 8 data pages (1964,
1967).*

Pennypack Creek Bridge

(PA-1786), 8300 block Frankford Ave. across Pennypack Creek.
Random local stone ashlar, approx. 38' (originally 18') × 110', three
round-arches with buttresses. Built 1697–98; eastern (upstream) addition built 1893. Oldest bridge in continuous use in United States.
Certified, PHC 1970; designated National Historic Civil Engineering
Landmark by American Society of Civil Engineers 1970. 3 photos
(1973);* HABSI form (1971).*

Philadelphia Fire Department, Engine Company No. 21

(PA-1787), 826–28 New Market St. Brick with sandstone trim, approx. 27' (four-bay front) × 85', two stories, flat roof, originally elliptical-arch engine doors capped by straight and segmental-arch dentil
cornice, tall round-arch windows, heavy straight and segmental-arch
iron cornice, parallelogram plan.

   Fine example of late-19th-century municipal fire station. Built
1875; ground-story front replaced mid-20th century. 2 sheets (1967,
including plot plan, plans, elevation)* courtesy of Pennsylvania Historical Salvage Council; 1 ext. photo (1967),* 1 photocopy of old ext.
photo (1896);* 1 data page (1967).*

Phillips Row

(PA-1788), 903–13 New Market St. Six contiguous brick houses, each
approx. 17' (three-bay front) × 16' with two-story rear ell, two-and-a-
half stories, gable roofs, ground-story alleyway through alternate
houses, city house plan. Row of artisans' homes built on a plan by
William Phillips, merchant. Built c. 1810; altered later; demolished
1968. 1 sheet (1967, including plot plan, plans, elevation, section)*
courtesy of Pennsylvania Historical Salvage Council; 1 ext. photo
(1967);* 24 data pages (1967).*

Port Royal

(PA-111), S. side Tacony St. between Church and Duncan sts. Brick with stone trim, approx. 54' (five-bay front) × 31' with two-story rear ell, two-and-a-half stories on raised basement, hipped roof, central pavilion with pediment, round-arch entrance with fanlight and Doric frontispiece, stone quoins and stringcourse, open rear porches, central-hall plan.

Notable Georgian country house. Built 1761–62; demolished c. 1962. Main entrance, doorway, windows, exterior details, plaster ceiling, and entrance hall, parlor, dining-room woodwork installed in H. F. duPont Winterthur Museum, Delaware. 7 sheets (1937, including plans, elevations, details); 5 ext. photos (c. 1900, 1937, including 1 of barn); 5 data pages (1937, including 1770 insurance survey*).

Potts, Horace T., & Co. Warehouse

(PA-1789), 316–20 N. Third St., at N.W. corner Wood St. Steel frame, brick curtain walls with terra cotta trim, approx. 64' (three-bay front) × 176', four stories, flat roof with projecting cornice, pointed-arch windows, glazed brick diaperwork at top story, rectangular plan. Notable example of Venetian Gothic design for a utilitarian building. Built 1896–97; Frank Miles Day & Bro., architects; George Watson & Son, contractors. Interior altered 1917–19; Addison H. Savery, architect. Destroyed by fire 1976. 3 ext. photos (1963, 1974).*

Pratt, Henry Houses

(PA-1790), 229–33 Wood St. Three contiguous brick houses with stuccoed fronts, each approx. 15' (two-bay front) × 17' with two-story rear wing, three-and-a-half stories, gable roofs, probably originally London house plans. Built c. 1800; demolished c. 1970. Investment properties of merchant Henry Pratt, whose country seat was Lemon Hill. 1 ext. photo (1967);* 8 data pages (1968).*

Preisendanz, Christian A., Wagon Works

(PA-1791), 520–26 New Market St. Brick with stone trim, 51'-10$\frac{1}{2}$" (six-bay front) × 110'-6", three stories, flat roof, segmental-arch windows, projecting brick piers with corbel-table frame end bays, canted brick string-course on third-story end bays, U-plan with alley through ground story. Built c. 1888; demolished 1969. 1 ext. photo (1967);* 2 data pages (1968).*

Pugh, Isaac, Paper Hangings Factory

(PA-1792), 440 New Market St., at N.W. corner Pegg St. Brick, approx. 42' (four-bay front) × 95' with wing on north side (originally approx. 42' × 73' with one- and two-story front additions), three stories, flat roof, segmental-arch windows, trapezoidal plan.

Example of mid-19th-century factory. Built c. 1842; extended 22' to front between 1880 and 1886; south side (Pegg St.) ground-story windows altered, iron lintels inserted later; demolished 1970. 1 ext. photo (1967);* 5 data pages (1968).

Reybold-Paul House

(PA-1793), 617 New Market St. Brick with marble trim, approx. 20' (three-bay front) × 20' with two-story rear ell, three-and-a-half stories, gable roof, round-arch entrance with fanlight and Adamesque frontispiece, brick stringcourse at second and third stories, sidehall plan. Built between 1803 and 1810; demolished 1969. 1 ext. photo (1967),* 1 photocopy of old ext. photo (1931); * 6 data pages (1968).*

Rich, Comly, House

(PA-1794), 4276 Orchard St. Wood frame with tongue-and-groove siding, approx. 12' (three-bay front) × 15' with one-story rear addition, two stories, gable roof, one room to a floor. Example of a Frankford artisan's dwelling on a deep lot. Built c. 1826; rear wing built later. First house in the United States financed through a savings and loan association 1831. Certified, PHC 1960. 3 photocopies of measured drawings (1974),* 1 photocopy of ext. photo (1960).*

Rotan, William, Houses

(PA-1795), 325–27 Richmond St. Brick with stone trim, each approx. 19' (two-bay front) × 32' with two-story rear ell, two-and-a-half stories, gable roofs, alleyway through ground story to backyard. Example of dwellings for families whose livelihoods were associated with river commerce. Built between 1833 and 1836; demolished c. 1969. William Rotan, Kensington shipwright, rented one house and lived in the other (No. 325) until his death 1875. 1 ext. photo (1967);* 8 data pages (1967).*

Rush, Benjamin, House (also known as Benjamin Rush Homestead)

(PA-1796), N. side Red Lion Rd. between Academy and Knight rds. (later at S.E. corner Keswick and Rayland sts. when streets cut through). Coursed fieldstone ashlar, approx. 30' (two-bay front) × 22' with two-and-a-half-story ashlar and three-story clap-boarded frame lateral additions, two-and-a-half stories, gable roof, originally pent eaves on front and back, open front porch (not original), center-hall plan (originally probably one room to a floor).

South end (left) built c. 1690; center part built probably before 1765; roofs rebuilt, porch added early 19th century; north frame addition built mid-19th century. Demolished 1969. To be rebuilt as museum and community center on Philadelphia State Hospital grounds, Byberry. Birthplace of Benjamin Rush, "father of American psychiatry," signer of Declaration of Independence, Physician General of Continental Army, first professor of chemistry in America's first medical school (University of Pennsylvania), cofounder of America's first abolitionist society, founder of Dickinson College and Franklin and Marshall College. Certified, PHC 1958. 2 ext. photos (1959, including 1 of springhouse),* 1 int. photo (1959, including 1 of mortise-and-tenon joint);* 1 data page (1959).*

Ryerss Mansion. See Burholme

Schaible, Charles, Store and House
(PA-1798), 144 Fairmount Ave. Brick with marble trim, approx. 16' (two-bay front) × 25' with three- and two-story rear ell, three stories, flat roof, wooden storefront with sash doors and bulk window on ground story, arched alley to rear. Example of mid-19th-century store-dwelling. Built c. 1865; two-story addition built early 20th century. Demolished 1969. 1 sheet (1967, including plot plan, elevation)* courtesy of Pennsylvania Historical Salvage Council; 1 ext. photo (1967);* 4 data pages (1968).*

Searle-Bond Houses
(PA-1799), 123 Laurel St. and 1002–4 N. Hope St., at N.W. corner Hope and Laurel sts. Three contiguous brick row houses, each approx. 13' (two-bay front) × 20', two-and-a-half stories, hipped and gambrel roofs, one room to a floor, cellar of corner houses extends under Hope St. sidewalk. Built between 1815 and 1819; demolished c. 1974. Representative of early-19th-century dwellings rented to artisans. 2 sheets (1967, including plot plan, plans, elevations)* courtesy of Pennsylvania Historical Salvage Council; 1 ext. photo (1967)* 6 data pages (1967).*

Shunk School (later known as Beth Eden House)

(PA-1800), 807 New Market St. Brick with marble trim, approx. 40' (three-bay front) × 64', two stories, gable roof, projecting lintel on plain corbels over entrance (originally window) and center second-story window, name and date stone in center of gable, rectangular plan with four rooms to a floor.

Fine example of a mid-19th-century public school. Built 1852; Samuel Sloan, architect; Jacob Jones, contractor. Interior altered, reinforced 1916; Louis H. Rush, architect. Front window converted to door, interior altered 1923; Louis H. Rush, architect. Demolished 1969. Named in honor of Francis R. Shunk, educator and public official, who served as Governor of Pennsylvania 1845–48. Beth Eden House, settlement house of Second Presbyterian Church in Philadelphia, 1916–68. Certified, PHC 1967.

3 sheets (1967, including plot plan, plans, elevations)* courtesy of Pennsylvania Historical Salvage Council; 2 ext. photos (1967);* 9 data pages (1967).*

Singerly, Joseph, Houses

(PA-1801), 120–22 Fairmount Ave. Brick with marble trim, each approx. 13' (two-bay front) × 33' with one-, two-, and three-story rear ells, three-and-a-half stories, gable roof, round-headed doorway, side-hall plan with rear stair tower. Example of perseverance of 18th-century town house plan. Built between 1831 and 1836; Joseph Singerly, house carpenter. Demolished 1969. 2 sheets (1967, including plot plan, plans, elevation, basement fireplace elevation and details)* courtesy of Pennsylvania Historical Salvage Council; 1 ext. photo (1967);* 6 data pages (1968).*

Smith, John B., House

(PA-1802), 1026 Shackamaxon St. Brick with brownstone trim, approx. 19' (two-bay front) × 25' with two-story rear ell, two stories on raised basement, flat roof, rusticated brownstone watercourse, molded galvanized metal cornice with small end minarets, ground-story alleyway, side-hall plan. Built c. 1898; demolished 1968. 1 ext. photo (1967);* 5 data pages (1967).*

Snappers, The. See Northern Liberty Hose Company No. 4

Swope-Weissman Houses

(PA-1803), 527–29 N. Second St. Two contiguous brick houses with stone trim, each approx. 20' (three-bay front) × 30' with two-story rear ell, three-and-a-half stories, gable roofs, probably originally side-hall plan. Built c. 1819; ground stories altered to stores before 1859; ground story of No. 529 bricked up 20th century; demolished c. 1969. Rear ell of No. 529 originally three tenements. 2 ext. photos (1967);* 7 data pages (1968).*

Trinity Church, Oxford (Protestant Episcopal). Illustrated

(PA-17), 6900–02 Oxford Ave., at S.W. corner Disston St. (formerly Church Ln.) and Oxford Ave. Brick, 34'-11" × 75'-0¹/₄" (originally 25'-2¹/₂" × 36'-4³/₄"), one story, gable roof, three-stage corner entry and bell tower with octagonal roof, round-arch windows, diamond patterns of glazed headers on original walls, one-aisle cruciform plan with rectangular chancel, originally probably one-aisle rectangular plan.

Example of an early Anglican church incorporating Delaware Valley vernacular building techniques. Built 1711; pews installed 1759; flooring completed, door moved from north side to west end 1807; transepts added 1833; tower (now chancel) built 1839; tower lowered to one story, present corner tower built 1875. Second oldest congregation in Philadelphia and oldest known Episcopal church in Pennsylvania in which continuous services have been held. Certified, PHC 1956.

6 sheets (1934, 1935, 1936, including plot plan, plan, elevations, elevation rendering from old drawing, details, 1709 gravestone rubbing); 3 ext. photos (1973, including 1 color photo),* 2 photocopies of ext. sketch and watercolor (n.d.); 4 data pages (1936).

United States Hose Company No. 14 (also known as the Blue Dick)

(PA-1804), 423 Buttonwood St. Brick covered with coursed stucco with marble trim, approx. 20' (three-bay front) × 50', three stories (originally with square frame observation tower), flat roof, recessed second-story balcony with marble Ionic colonnade in antis and ornamental iron fence containing name "United States," marble-pier ground story, originally sculpture of water pump in third-story center niche.

Example of Greek Revival volunteer firehouse. Built 1845; William L. Grubb, carpenter; Charles Twaddell, bricklayer. Parapet, sculpture removed after 1870; demolished 1953. 1 photocopy of old ext. photo (c. 1935).*

Weaver, John, House

(PA-1805), 134 Fairmount Ave., at S.W. corner New Market St. Brick, approx. 20' (two-bay front) × 43', two-and-a-half stories, gable roof, brick stringcourse above first and second stories. Built after 1802; altered to store before 1859; altered to tavern before 1867; altered to store again late 19th century. Demolished 1969. 1 ext. photo (1967);* 6 data pages (1968).*

Whitton, Abednego J., Houses

(PA-1806), 1018–20 Crease St., at S.W. corner Salmon St. Two contiguous frame houses with asbestos siding, each approx. 16' (two-bay front) × 16' with two-story rear ell, two-and-a-half stories, mansard roof, ground-story alleyway between houses, side-hall plan. Built between 1825 and 1830; mansard roof added later; demolished c. 1969. 1 ext. photo (1967);* 7 data pages (1967).*

Wiedersum, George, House

(PA-1807), 405 Richmond St. Brick with marble trim, approx. 18' (two-bay front) × 30', three stories, flat roof, probably originally side-hall plan. Built c. 1848; ground story altered to store later; demolished c. 1969. Southernmost house in a row of eight contiguous houses. 1 ext. photo (1967);* 8 data pages (1967).*

Wildes-Sonder Houses

(PA-1808), 455–57 N. Second St. Two contiguous brick houses with stone trim, each approx. 20' (three-bay front) × 34' with one- and two-story rear wings, three-and-a-half stories, gable roofs, stone stringcourse at third story.

Buildings' history reflects neighborhood's change over two centuries. Built between 1797 and 1799; No. 455 probably by Joseph Wildes, bricklayer; No. 457 probably by Jacob Sonder, bricklayer. Altered to stores before 1859; storefront of No. 455 remodeled 1923; interior of No. 457 altered 1926. Rear wings added before 1886, enlarged between 1922 and 1931. Demolished c. 1969. 1 ext. photo (1967);* 12 data pages (1968).*

John Bromley & Sons, Lehigh Mills. *Jack E. Boucher photo, 1973.*

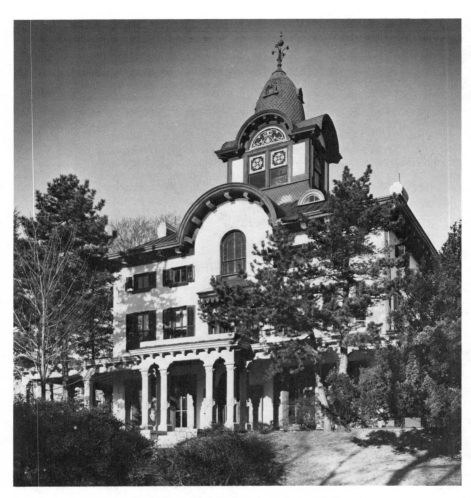

Burholme. *Jack E. Boucher photo, 1973.*

Henry Disston & Sons Keystone Saw, Tool, and Steel Works. *Lithograph 1873, Hexamer General Surveys, courtesy Free Library of Philadelphia.*

Thomas Holloway Houses. *E. McFarlin, del., 1967, courtesy Pennsylvania Historical Salvage Council.*

Hospital of the Protestant Episcopal Church in Philadelphia. *Jack E. Boucher photo, 1973.*

Carl Mackley Apartments. *Jack E. Boucher photo, 1976.*

Trinity Church, Oxford. *Jack E. Boucher photo, 1972.*

Addendum

Penn's City: Society Hill

Apartment Building
(PA-1316) 113–17½ South St.

Nos. 115–17½ interiors altered, molded metal bays replaced by lath-and-stucco bays 1976–c. 77.

Eastburn Mariners' Bethel (Presbyterian) Church (also known as Mariners' Bethel)
(PA-1327), 328–30 S. Front St., at S.W. corner Delancey St.

Demolished 1977 after roof, parts of walls collapsed.

Holy Trinity (German) Roman Catholic Church
(PA-1336), 601–9 Spruce St., at N.W. corner Sixth St.

Certified, PHC 1956.

Palmer, John, House
(PA-1353), 117 Lombard St.

Exterior rehabilitated, interior altered 1978–.

Pennsylvania Hospital
(PA-1123), N.W. corner Eighth and Pine sts.

Center section surgical amphitheater and center hall restored, second-floor offices altered 1976–77; Bartley, Long, Mirenda and Reynolds, architects.

Reed Houses
(PA-1615), 518–20 S. Front St.

Fronts restored with identical pedimented Doric frontispieces and fanlights on both houses, interiors rehabilitated as offices and garret apartments 1977–79; Zimmers Associates, architect. Certified, PHC 1958.

Richardson, Nathaniel, House
(PA-1360), 524 S. Front St.

Rehabilitated 1969. Certified, PHC 1958.

Spruce Street Area Study
(PA-253), 700–714 Spruce St., S. side Spruce St. W. of Seventh St.
Seven contiguous brick houses with Schuylkill marble trim, each ap-

prox. 24'-6" (two- and three-bay fronts) × 52' (195'-8" total length), four stories, flat gable roofs; majority have double-door entrances with marble frontispieces, side-hall plans, notable interior wood and plaster work, marble mantelpieces.

Row of Greek Revival houses. Nos. 700–702 built 1835–36 as Roman Catholic Society for Educating and Maintaining Poor Orphan Children; Thomas U. Walter, architect. Nos. 704–12 built between 1835 and 1839. Nos. 700–702 connected to No. 704 c. 1881, fourth story added 1888, interior altered 1914, one-story rear addition built 1915. Nos. 708, 710 connected 1907; No. 710 interior altered c. 1900 as dormitory for Church Training and Deaconess House of the Diocese of Philadelphia; No. 714 interior altered 1891. Demolished 1978 with facades retained as front of five-story steel-frame ambulatory health care building for Pennsylvania Hospital. Certified, PHC 1957. 4 sheets (1978, including site plan, plan, elevations, cross section); 12 ext. photos (1977), 15 int. photos (1977), 1 photocopy of 1970's photo; 30 data pages (1977, 1979).

Spruce Street Baptist Church (now Society Hill Synagogue)
(PA-1370), 426 Spruce St., at S.W. corner Lawrence St.

Main sanctuary altered 1971. Exterior restored 1978–; Herbert W. Levy, architect.

Stocker, John Clement, House
(PA-1068), 402 S. Front St. (Street number changed to 404 in 1978).

Exterior restored, interior rehabilitated as two-family dwelling 1978–; Roland C. Davies and Associates, architects. Certified, PHC 1960.

Water Trough and Fountain
(PA-1379), E. side Ninth St. between Spruce and Pine sts., opposite Clinton St.

Certified, PHC 1971.

Williams-de La Forest House
(PA-1383), 427 Spruce St.

Interior rehabilitated, partially restored 1977–. Antoine René Charles Mathurin de La Forest, French Consul General, lived here 1791–93. Don Jose de Jaudenes, Spanish Commissioner to the United States, lived here 1795–c. 1805.

Penn's City: Old City

Athenaeum of Philadelphia
(PA-1389), 219 S. Sixth St., at S.E. corner St. James St., on E. side Washington Sq.

Designated National Historic Landmark 1976.

Ayer, N. W., & Son, Inc., Building (later N. W. Ayer & Company)
(PA-1390), 204–12 S. Seventh St., at S.W. corner St. James St., on W. side Washington Sq.

Certified, PHC 1974; NR.

Brock, John, Sons & Co. Warehouse
(PA-1395), 242–44 N. Delaware Ave. and 243–45 N. Water St.

Severely damaged by fire 1977; exterior iron elements dismantled and stored by Fairmount Park Commission.

Chestnut Street Area Study
(PA-1402), 213–43 Chestnut St., on N. side Chestnut St. between Strawberry and Third sts.

Interior of Nos. 223–27 altered as Museum for United American Indians of Delaware Valley 1979. All buildings certified, PHC 1976.

Commercial Exchange (also known as Chamber of Commerce)
(PA-1406), 135 S. Second St., at S.E. corner Sansom St.

Scheduled demolition halted by court order 1976. North wall collapsed 1977, building demolished 1977–78.

Cooper, Jacob, House
(PA-1407), 118 Cuthbert St.

Rear two-story addition built 1974.

Drexel and Co. Building
(PA-1411), 34 S. Third St.

Demolished 1976.

First German Reformed Church Area Study
(PA-1418), 129–51 N. Fourth St., between Cherry and Race sts., and 322–30 Race St.

Church built 1836–37; Andrew D. Caldwell, architect. Dwellings (Nos. 129–43) rehabilitated 1969–78; dwelling (No. 151) rehabilitated as parish house 1969–72. Nos. 129–33, 151 certified, PHC 1965; Nos. 141–43, church certified, PHC 1966.

First National Bank
(PA-1011), 315 Chestnut St.
   Certified, PHC 1970; NR.

Franklin Institute (now Atwater Kent Museum)
(PA-121), 15 S. Seventh St.
   Air conditioning installed 1972, interior stairway altered 1976.

Janney Building
(PA-1228), 121–23 Market St. Brick with marble trim, cast-iron ground story with depressed-arch windows, approx. 40' (six-bay front) × 102', six stories, flat roof, segmental-arch windows on second through fifth stories, round-arch windows on sixth story, terra-cotta bosses on piers, rectangular plan.
   Built c. 1885 for Benjamin S. Janney, Jr.; elevator installed 1945; demolished c. 1977. 1 sheet (1976, including elevation, details).*

Leland Building
(PA-1086), 37–39 S. Third St.
   Original ground-story exterior destructively altered 1973; ground story of No. 37 partially restored 1980.

Lit Brothers
(PA-1438), 701–39 Market St., composing block bounded by Seventh, Market, Eighth, Filbert sts.
   Lit Brothers dissolved, vacated buildings 1977; all tenants vacated buildings 1980. Certified, PHC 1970; Pennsylvania Register 1977; NR.

McClare-Hutchinson Building
(PA-1439), 20 S. Third St.
   Interior rehabilitated 1975. Certified, PHC 1977.

North Front Street Area Study
(PA-1448), 2–66 N. Front St., on W. side Front St. between Market and Arch sts.
   Nos. 2–8 demolished c. 1977. Upper floors of Nos. 62–66 rehabilitated 1980. Nos. 14–44, 56–66 certified, PHC 1977, 1979. 1 sheet (1976, including elevation, details of No. 8).*

North Third Street Area Study
(PA-1450), 17–63 N. Third St., E. side Third St. between Church and Arch sts.

Upper floors of Nos. 23–25 rehabilitated as apartments 1979. Nos. 27–29, 33, 42–47, 51–57, 61–63 certified, PHC 1980.

Philadelphia Bourse
(PA-1456), 11–21 S. Fifth St., composing block bounded by Fifth, Ludlow, Fourth, Ranstead sts.

Interior extensively renovated 1978–.

Philadelphia Fire Department, Engine Company No. 8 (now known as Fireman's Hall)
(PA-1459), 149 N. Second St., at N.E. corner Quarry St.

Front restored, two-story rear addition built 1976. Certified, PHC 1980.

St. Charles Hotel
(PA-1472), 60–66 N. Third St.

Exterior restored, interior upper floors rehabilitated as apartments, interior ground floor rehabilitated as stores 1979–81. Certified, PHC 1980.

Singer, John, Warehouse
(PA-1478), 319½ Market St., at rear of 319 Market St.

Destroyed by fire 1975.

Stone-Penrose House (also known as Meredith House)
(PA-1483), 700 Locust St., at S.W. corner Seventh St., on S. side of Washington Sq.

Exterior facade, interior stairs restored, basement renovated 1977–78. British Consul General vacated premises 1980. Certified, PHC 1957; NR.

Tutleman Brothers & Faggen Building
(PA-1485), 56–60 N. Second St., at N.W. corner Cuthbert St.

Interior upper floors rehabilitated as apartments, interior ground floor rehabilitated as stores 1978–79. Certified, PHC 1977.

Penn's City: Center Square

Arch Street Methodist Episcopal Church
(PA-1494), S.E. corner Broad and Arch sts.
    Certified, PHC 1964.

Arch Street Opera-House (also known as The Troc)
(PA-1495), 1003–5 Arch St.
    The Troc closed 1978. Exterior restored 1978–79; H. Reed Longnecker, architect. Interior rehabilitated, partially restored as Chinese movie theater 1978–79. Certified, PHC 1973; NR.

Bellevue-Stratford Hotel
(PA-1226), 200–216 S. Broad St., at S.W. corner Walnut St. Steel frame, brick curtain walls faced with smooth-rusticated limestone on ground and second stories, coursed dressed terra cotta on third story, coursed smooth-rusticated terra cotta on fourth through tenth stories, dressed terra cotta on eleventh through nineteenth stories; approx. 185' (fifteen-bay front) × 180' (originally approx. 185' × 130'), nineteen stories, highly enriched straight-sided and bulbous mansard roofs, eastern entrance with two engaged enriched Roman Doric columns and balustrade (originally stylized Composite tetrastyle flat portico with balustrade), semi-hexagonal oriels on east and west sides between third and tenth and between twelfth and thirteenth stories, iron balconies, giant enriched Ionic twelfth- and thirteenth-story pilasters, large enriched corbels and swags at fourteenth story; squarish ground-floor plan (originally rectangular) with two parallel rows of four light wells above second and third stories to form E-plan for upper floors; large and lavish lobby, ball rooms, restaurants.
    One of America's most elegant hotels and an outstanding example of the late Victorian French Renaissance style. A famous local landmark and site of exclusive social events and important political events, it has hosted all U.S. presidents from Theodore Roosevelt to Gerald Ford. Built 1902–4; G. W. and W. D. Hewitt, architects. Enlarged at west end (rear) 1910–11; Hewitt and Paist, architects. Basement, ground floor altered 1943–44; new tile bathrooms installed 1944; original entrances replaced by cantilevered marquees 1955; interior altered, decorations simplified 1954–59; vacated 1976. Rehabilitated, partially restored 1978–79; Day and Zimmermann Associates, architects. Reopened as Fairmont Hotel 1979, changed name

back to Bellevue-Stratford Hotel 1980. Certified, PHC 1973; Pennsylvania Register 1977; NR. 10 ext. photos (1976),* 27 int. photos (1976).*

Cope, Edward Drinker, Houses
(PA-1500), 2100–2102 Pine St., at S.W. corner Twenty-first St.
Both houses certified, PHC 1973.

Delancey Street Area Study
(PA-1501), 1800–1836 Delancey St., on S. side Delancey St. between Eighteenth and Nineteenth sts.
Interior No. 1828 altered 1977; interior No. 1812 altered 1980. Certified, PHC 1972.

Drexel & Company
(PA-1503), 135–43 S. Fifteenth St., at N.E. corner Walnut St.
Exterior refurbished, door cut into east end of south wall, interior rehabilitated to commercial use 1980–. Certified, PHC 1971; NR.

Federal Reserve Bank of Philadelphia
(PA-1506), 921–39 Chestnut St., at N.E. corner Tenth St.
Interior altered 1979–. Certified, PHC 1961; NR.

Girard Trust Corn Exchange Bank
(PA-1510), 34–46 S. Broad St., at N.W. corner Chestnut St.
Interior clear plastic entrance vestibule installed 1975; interior partitions erected 1978. Certified, PHC 1976.

Harrison Building II
(PA-550), 1001–5 Market St., at N.W. corner Tenth St. Probably steel frame, brick curtain walls with terra-cotta trim and marble first and second stories (not original), approx. 66' (seven-bay front) × 200', seven stories, flat terne plate roof, three giant arches with terra-cotta bands and terra-cotta medallions in spandrels on north end (also originally on south end), recessed rectangular triple windows with terra-cotta frames on front third through fifth stories, sixth-story arcade with terra-cotta voussiors and engaged columns, squarish seventh-story windows with terra-cotta frames, terra-cotta dentil and egg-and-dart frieze with modillion cornice capped by lion's heads and antefixae, rectangular plan.
Fine example of late-19th-century use of terra-cotta ornament. Built 1893–94; Cope and Stewardson, architects; Louis D. Havens,

contractor. New ventilating system installed 1898; basement, stairways altered 1905; minor interior alterations 1915, 1916, 1919; interior ground and second floors altered, fenestration altered and dressed marble facing applied to ground and second stories on south (front) and east sides 1941; demolished 1979. 5 ext. photos (1979),* 1 int. photo (1979);* 8 data pages (1980).*

Land Title Building
(PA-1514), 100–118 S. Broad St., between S.W. corner Chestnut St. and N.W. corner Sansom St.

Southern twenty-two-story building built 1902; D. H. Burnham & Co., architects; Horace Trumbauer, associated architect. Interior alterations to first, third through sixth, twelfth floors, one door on south exterior wall closed on southern building 1978. Certified, PHC 1973; NR.

Leidy, Dr. Joseph, Jr., House
(PA-1515), 1319 Locust St.

Poor Richard Club vacated premises 1979; headquarters of District 1199C, National Union of Hospital and Health Care Employees, since 1979.

Moore, Clarence B., House
(PA-1521), 1321 Locust St., at N.E. corner Juniper St.

Exterior restored, interior rehabilitated as headquarters of District 1199C, National Union of Hospital and Health Care Employees, 1979–.

Pennsylvania Institution for the Deaf and Dumb (now Philadelphia College of Art)
(PA-1526), 320 S. Broad St., composing block bounded by Broad, Pine, Fifteenth, Delancey sts.

Exterior restored, interior rehabilitated 1980–.

Philadelphia and Reading Railroad, Terminal Station (also known as Reading Terminal)
(PA-1528), 1115–41 Market St., at N.E. corner Twelfth St.

Certified, PHC 1980; designated National Historic Landmark 1976.

Philadelphia City Hall

(PA-1520), Penn Square, intersection of Broad and Market sts.

Certified, PHC 1957, Pennsylvania Register 1976; NR; designated National Historic Landmark 1976.

Philadelphia Saving Fund Society Building (also known as PSFS Building)

(PA-1533), 12 S. Twelfth St., at S.W. corner Market St.

Designated National Historic Landmark 1976.

Portico Square (later known as Portico Row)

(PA-1534), 900–930 Spruce St., composing block bounded by Ninth, Spruce, Tenth, Cypress sts.

No. 900 exterior restored, interior rehabilitated as three apartments 1977–; No. 902 restored to 1867 appearance, interior rehabilitated as three apartments 1979–; No. 906 severely damaged by fire 1976, exterior partially restored, interior rehabilitated as nine apartments 1977–80; Nos. 908–10 exterior restored, interior rehabilitated as six apartments in each 1979–; Nos. 912–14 rehabilitated as eight apartments in each 1980; No. 924 exterior restored, interior rehabilitated as eight apartments 1978–80; No. 926 restored as Wurts House, 19th- and early-20th-century historic house museum, 1978–; No. 930 damaged by fire 1978, exterior restored, interior rehabilitated as twelve apartments 1978–. Pennsylvania Register 1977; NR.

Restaurant and Apartment Building

(PA-1536), 110 N. Ninth St.

Ashlar facade removed 1976, replaced with stucco 1977. Certified, PHC 1974; decertified 1977.

St. Stephen's Protestant Episcopal Church

(PA-1576), 19 S. Tenth St., at N.E. corner Ludlow St.

Pennsylvania Register 1978; NR.

Schuylkill Hose, Hook & Ladder Company No. 24

(PA-1577), 1227 Locust St.

Scott-Wanamaker House

(PA-1578), 2032 Walnut St.

Rehabilitation not executed; severely damaged by fire 1978.

Sims-Bilsland House (originally known as 2 Franklin Row)

(PA-1186), originally 228 S. Ninth St., now 236 S. Eighth St.

Restoration not executed; house moved to 236 S. Eighth St. 1978, rehabilitated 1980–.

Spruce Street Area Study
(PA-1579), 2009–47 Spruce St., on N. side Spruce St. between Twentieth and Twenty-first sts.

Twelfth Street (Friends) Meeting House (also known as Meeting House of Central Philadelphia Meeting of Friends)
(PA-1622), 20 S. Twelfth St., at N.W. corner Clover St.

Union League of Philadelphia
(PA-1626), 140 S. Broad St., at S.W. corner Sansom St.

Wanamaker, John, Store
(PA-1692), 1300–1324 Market St., composing block bounded by Market, Thirteenth, Chestnut, Juniper sts.
Grand Court renovated 1976; Crystal Tea Room renovated 1980. Grand Court, Crystal Tea Room certified, PHC 1974; designated National Historic Landmark 1978.

West Arch Street Presbyterian Church (now Arch Street Presbyterian Church)
(PA-1696), 1726–32 Arch St., at S.E. corner Eighteenth St.

Western Saving Fund Society
(PA-1703), 1000–1008 Walnut St., at S.W. corner Tenth St.

White Tower
(PA-1721), 159 N. Broad St., at S.E. corner Race St.

South Philadelphia

Bel Air (also known as Belleaire, Singley House, Lasse Cock's Manor House)
(PA-1124), S.W. corner Twentieth St. and Pattison Ave.
Rehabilitated 1975–76.

Bird, Joseph, Houses
(PA-1543), 813–15 S. Hancock St.
Rehabilitated 1977.

Ely-Osbourn Houses and Stores
(PA-1557, 136–38 South St., at S.W. corner Hancock St.
   Rehabilitated c. 1979–81.

Flickwer-Williamson Houses
(PA-1561), 809–11 S. Hancock St.
   Rehabilitated 1978.

Fullerton, John, Houses
(PA-1563), 606–8 S. Front St.
   Rehabilitated 1977–78.

Harper, William, Jr., Houses
(PA-1567), 621–23 S. American St., at N.E. corner Harper's Pl.
   Rehabilitated, front facade stuccoed 1976.

Houses
(PA-1583), 123–25 League St.
   Exterior No. 123 restored 1977.

Hutton, Nathaniel, House
(PA-1586), 814 S. Front St.
   Destroyed by fire 1975.

Little, John, House
(PA-1591), 618 S. Front St.
   Exterior restored 1973; interior altered 1973, 1977.

McDowell-Fritz House
(PA-1594), 808 S. Front St.
   Rehabilitated, two-story rear addition built 1976–78.

Marshall-Morris House
(PA-1599), 774 S. Front St.
   Upper stories demolished 1976, ground story demolished 1978.

Moore, John, House
(PA-1605), 734 S. Front St.
   Exterior partially restored, kitchen and bathroom altered 1976.

Pearson, Anthony, House
(PA-1608), 806 S. Front St.
Interior extensively altered 1976–77.

Powder Magazine
(PA-124), Magazine Lane.
2 sheets (1936, including plan, elevations).

Ridgway Branch of Library Company of Philadelphia
(PA-1616), 901 S. Broad St., composing block bounded by Broad, Catharine, Thirteenth, Carpenter sts.

United States Naval Asylum (later United States Naval Home)
(PA-1094), S.W. corner Gray's Ferry Ave. and Twenty-fourth St. at Bainbridge St.
Vacated 1976.

Woolfall-Huddell House
(PA-1625), 9 Queen St.
Exterior restored, interior rehabilitated 1971–72.

West Philadelphia

Bartram, John, House
(PA-1132), Bartram Park, S. Fifty-fourth St. between Elmwood and Gibson aves.
Exterior restored, interior mechanical systems improved 1980–.

Drexel Institute, Main Building (now Drexel University)
(PA-1630), 3101–99 Chestnut St., at S.E. corner Thirty-second St.
Interior of third, fourth floors altered 1978–79. Certified, PHC 1972.

Fort Mifflin
(PA-1225), Mud Island, W. bank of Delaware River, 0.76 mi. below confluence of Schuylkill and Delaware rivers, Marine and Penrose Ferry roads.
Built c. 1779–98; portion of c. 1772 stone wall from earlier fort still standing. 9 sheets (1970, 1971, including plan, site and location maps,

gun emplacement details, casemate details, northeast sallyport details, wall sections); 10 aerial phots (1971), 8 general view photos (1937, 1969), 4 photos of walls (1969), 6 photos of northeast sallyport (1969), 3 photos of northwest sallyport (1969), 5 photos of southeast sallyport (1937, 1969), 6 photos of gun emplacements (1969), 1 photo of guard room (1969), 1 photo of chimney, east bastion (1969), 10 photos of casemates (1969), 2 photocopies of c. 1922 photos of general views, 1 photocopy of 1915 photos of southeast sallyport, 13 photocopies of historic maps from 1777, c. 1778, 1807, 1815, 1839, 1868, 1901; 124 data pages (1971, 1974, 1979); field records.

Fort Mifflin, Guard House (also known as Arsenal) (PA-1225 A). Built 1815–16. 2 sheets (1970, including plan, elevations, section, isometric detail); 3 ext. photos (1937, 1969), 2 int. photos (1969), 1 photocopy of 1915 ext. photo; 5 data pages (1974, 1979); field records.

Fort Mifflin, Artillery Shed (PA-1225 B). Built 1837. 5 sheets (1970, including plan, elevations, sections, details); 1 ext. photo (1969), 5 int. photos (1969), 1 photocopy of undated ext. photo; 5 data pages (1974, 1979); field records.

Fort Mifflin, Commandant's House (also known as Headquarters) (PA-1225 C). Severely damaged by fire 1980. 8 sheets (1970, including plans, elevations, details); 8 ext. photos (1937, 1969, 1970), 21 int. photos (1969), 4 photocopies of undated and c. 1922 ext. photos; 11 data pages (1974, 1979); field records.

Fort Mifflin, Storehouse (also known as Commissary) (PA-1225 D). Built 1842; renovated 1960. 2 sheets (1970, including plan, elevations, section); 4 ext. photos (1937, 1969), 1 photocopy of undated ext. photo; 4 data pages (1974, 1979); field records.

Fort Mifflin, Soldiers' Barracks (also known as Enlisted Men's Barracks) (PA-1225 E). Built before 1802. 5 sheets (1969, including plans, elevations, section, details); 11 ext. photos (1937, 1969, 1970), 2 int. photos (1969), 3 photocopies of undated and 1915 ext. photos; 7 data pages (1974, 1979); field records.

Fort Mifflin, Officers' Quarters (PA-1225 F). 6 sheets (1969, including plans, elevations, sections, details); 12 ext. photos (1937, 1969, 1970), 2 int. photos (1969), 3 photocopies of undated and 1915 photos; 7 data pages (1974, 1979); field records.

Fort Mifflin, Powder Magazines (also Torpedo Casemate) (PA-1225 G). Includes West Magazine and Torpedo Casemate (East Magazine) inside fort. Torpedo Casemate (East Magazine) with concrete vault 12' × 16'. West Magazine built c. 1866; Torpedo Casemate built c. 1875. 8 data pages (1974, 1979); field records.

Fort Mifflin, Smith's Shop (PA-1225 H). 4 sheets (1969, including plan, roof-framing plan, elevations, section, details); 6 ext. photos (1937, 1969), 5 int. photos (1969), 1 photocopy of c. 1922 ext. photo; 5 data pages (1974, 1979); field records.

Fort Mifflin, Hospital (also known as Mess House) (PA-1225 I). Brick, 50'-6" (five-bay front) × 26'-5", two stories. 6 sheets (1970, including plans, elevations, section, details); 4 ext. photos (1937, 1969); 6 data pages (1974, 1979); field records.

Fort Mifflin, Frame Guard House (PA-1225 J). Frame with clapboarding, 30' (three-bay front) × 16' with 7'-wide porch across front, one story, gable roof, one off-center chimney; two rooms. Probably built c. 1798; demolished between 1922 and 1935. 1 photocopy of c. 1922 ext. photo.

Potts, Joseph D., House
(PA-1638), 3905 Spruce St.

Interior third floor altered to University of Pennsylvania radio station 1970–71; ground floor damaged by fire 1976; interior altered to offices, new stairs built, windows on north wall bricked in 1977.

Fairmount Park

Boat House Row
(PA-1650), E. River Dr. W. of Main Dr.

No. 10, Vesper Boat Club one-story brick women's locker room addition at northwest corner planned 1981. No. 11, College Boat Club of University of Pennsylvania interior renovated, two-story stucco-finish steel-and-concrete women's addition built on upriver side 1981–. No. 12, Penn Athletic Club Rowing Association second-floor stuccoed concrete-block locker-room addition built at northwest corner 1979–80.

Hatfield House
(PA-1658), N.E. corner Girard Ave. and Thirty-third St.

Kitchen altered 1975.

International Exhibition of 1876, Memorial Hall (also known as Art Gallery)
(PA-1659), North Concourse, 0.2 mi. E. of Belmont Ave.

Pennsylvania Register 1976; designated National Historic Landmark 1976.

Laurel Hill (also known as Randolph House)
(PA-13), Edgeley Dr.
    Partially restored 1975.

Laurel Hill Cemetery Gatehouse
(PA-1811), 3820 Ridge Ave.
    Certified, PHC 1980; NR.

Lemon Hill
(PA-1010), Lemon Hill Dr.
    Restored 1975–76; mechanical systems improved 1981.

Letitia Penn House (also known as House on Letitia Street)
(PA-184), Lansdowne Dr., near W. Girard Ave.
    Partially restored 1975.

Monastery
(PA-183), Kitchen's Ln., on E. side Wissahickon Creek.
    Alteration to Children's Museum not executed, house remains
vacant.

Ormiston
(PA-187), Reservoir Dr.
    Rehabilitated 1975–76.

Philadelphia Zoological Gardens, Bear Pits
(PA-1662), approx. 200' W. of Thirty-fourth St., approx. 925' S. of
entrance pavilions at S.W. corner W. Giard Ave. and Thirty-fourth
St.
    Dismantled, stone stored by Fairmount Park Commission 1977.

Philadelphia Zoological Gardens, Entrance Pavilions
(PA-1663), S.W. corner W. Girard Ave. and Thirty-fourth St.
    Certified, PHC 1980.

Solitude
(PA-1127), S.W. corner W. Girard Ave. and Thirty-fourth St., on
Philadelphia Zoological Gardens grounds.
    Interior plasterwork restored 1975–76.

Strawberry Mansion (originally known as Summerville, later as Somerton)
(PA-1668), near N.W. corner Dauphin St. Dr. and Edgeley Dr.
>   Rehabilitated 1975–76.

Strawberry Mansion Bridge
(PA-1669), connects Ford Dr. in W. Fairmount Park with Strawberry
Mansion Dr. in E. Fairmount Park across Schuylkill River.
>   Certified, PHC 1978.

Sweetbrier
(PA-1670), Lansdowne Dr.
>   Restored 1975–76.

Woodford
(PA-1307), S.W. corner Ford Rd. and Greenland Dr.
>   Restored by Naomi Wood Estate 1927–30; air conditioning
equipment installed in attic 1978. Open under auspices of Trustees of
Naomi Wood Estate, housing Naomi Wood Collection of household
articles since 1930.

Northwest Philadelphia

Church of St. Vincent de Paul (Roman Catholic)
(PA-1680), 101–7 E. Price St., at N.E. corner Lena St.
>   Interior altered to conform with ecumenical reforms 1978–79.

Folwell House
(PA-1689), 5281 Germantown Ave.
>   Second (northern) dormer added after 1924; rehabilitated to four
apartments and store 1980.

Schaeffer, Harriet D., House
(PA-1712), 433 W. Stafford St.
>   Certified, PHC 1972.

Valley Green Inn
(PA-1719), W. side Upper Wissahickon Dr. near Valley Green Dr.
Fairmount Park.
>   Front porch restored, minor interior improvements 1976.

Wissahickon Inn (now Chestnut Hill Academy)
(PA-1720), 500 W. Willow Grove Ave., at S.E. corner Huron St.
   Pennsylvania Register 1979; NR.

North Philadelphia

Burk, Alfred E., House
(PA-1722), 1500 N. Broad St., at N.W. corner Jefferson St.
   Interior altered 1975.

Cast-Iron Sidewalk
(PA-1723), 1907 N. Seventh St.
   Elements stolen 1978; sidewalk removed 1979, part of it installed
in floor of enclosed rear porch of Ebenezer Maxwell House, 200 W.
Tulpehocken St., Philadelphia (PA-1098) 1978–80. Certified, PHC
1966.

Diamond Street Area Study
(PA-1726), 1601–43 W. Diamond St., N. side Diamond St. between
Sixteenth and Seventeenth sts.
   No. 1601 demolished c. 1978.

Green Street Area Study
(PA-1732), 2201–31 Green St., on N. side Green St. between
Twenty-second and Twenty-third sts.
   No. 2223 certified, PHC 1974; Nos. 2225, 2229–31 certified, PHC
1979.

Northern Saving Fund, Safe Deposit and Trust Company
(PA-1733), 600 Spring Garden St., at S.W. corner Sixth St.
   Southern extension (516 N. Sixth St.) built 1888; Frank R. Watson, architect. All additions demolished 1978. Original surviving 1872
building vacant since 1978. Certified, PHC 1978; Pennsylvania Register 1977; NR. 5 sheets (1978, including plans, elevation, section); 8
ext. photos (1974, 1979), 5 int. photos (1979); 1 data page (1980).

Poe, Edgar Allan, House
(PA-1735), rear of 530 N. Seventh St., at N.W. corner Brandywine St.
   Rehabilitated 1977–80. Acquired by Independence National His-
torical Park 1980.

Tanner, Henry Ossawa, House
(PA-1740), 2908 W. Diamond St.
  Certified, PHC 1970.

Widener, Peter A. B., House
(PA-1742), 1200 N. Broad St., at N.W. corner Girard Ave.
  Destroyed by fire 1980.

Delaware River Corridor

Bromley, John, & Sons, Lehigh Mills
(PA-1744), 201–63 E. Lehigh Ave., composing block bounded by Lehigh Ave., A, E. Somerset, E. Gurney, B sts.
  Destroyed by fire 1979.

Brown, Sarah, Houses (formerly listed as Houses)
(PA-1768), 1035–37 Frankford Ave.
  Two frame houses with wood sheathing and asphalt shingles.

Burholme (also known as Ryerss Mansion)
(PA-186), Burholme Park, at N.W. corner Cottman and Central aves.
  Rear kitchen wing demolished, rear museum extension built, interior renovated c. 1920. Exterior restored, interior rehabilitated 1977–80; Day and Zimmermann Associates, architects. Certified, PHC 1972; Pennsylvania Register 1976; NR.

Harrison House
(PA-1458), Point No Point, or Port Richmond (street address unknown).
  2 data pages (1936).

Kensington National Bank
(PA-1773), 2–8 W. Girard Ave., at S.W. corner Frankford Ave.
  Certified, PHC 1980.

Meyer-Kessler House (formerly listed as House)
(PA-1765), 705 New Market St.
  Built between 1793 and 1806.

Potts, Horace T., & Co. Warehouse
(PA-1789), 316–20 N. Third St., at N.W. corner Wood St.
  7 sheets (1976, including plans, elevations, details);* 19 ext. photos (1963, 1974, 1976).*

Rich, Comly, House

(PA-1794), 4276 Orchard St.

4 sheets (1977, including plot plan, plans, elevations, sections).*

Searle-Bond Houses

(PA-1799), 123 Laurel St. and 1002–4 N. Hope St., at N.W. corner Hope and Laurel sts.

Not demolished, vacant since c. 1974.

Stetson, John B., Company Hat Manufactory

(PA-1227), 1716–60 N. Fourth St., at N.W. corner Cadwallader St. (closed off as private street); 1745 N. Fourth St., at S.E. corner Montgomery Ave.; 1801 N. Fourth St., at N.E. corner Montgomery Ave.; 1801 Germantown Ave., at N.E. corner Montgomery Ave. (originally 1748–54 N. Fourth St.)

Nine brick and steel-frame industrial buildings that were part of a twenty-building industrial complex built between 1874 and 1930. For nearly a century John B. Stetson Company was America's most noted hat manufacturer, famous in particular for its "Western" (cowboy) hats. Stetson was also known for his paternalistic concern for employees, establishing for them a building and loan association, hospital, non-denominational Sunday school, auditorium, library, and citizenship classes (for immigrants). Factory closed, buildings vacated 1971; acquired by City of Philadelphia 1977; some buildings demolished c. 1979, others (Nos. 10–13) destroyed by fire 1980.

Building No. 10 (1740–44 N. Fourth St.): brick with interior iron columns, 52' (seven-bay side) × 84' (S. side) and 110' (N. side) (originally approx. 18' on W. side × 45'), five stories (originally four), gable roof, rectangular windows on original section, segmental-arch windows on later section, irregular octagonal plan. North end built between 1874 and 1877; raised one story 1878; east section, south end built with interior iron columns c. 1882; destroyed by fire 1980.

Building No. 11 (1736–38 N. Fourth St.): brick with stone trim, approx. 36' (four-bay side) × 68' (S. side) and 84' (N. side), five stories (originally four), gable roof, segmental-arch windows with stone imposts and polychromatic brick voussoirs, irregular hexagonal plan. Built 1881; raised one story 1884; destroyed by fire 1980.

Building No. 12 (1726–34 N. Fourth St.): brick with stone trim, approx. 82' (ten-bay side) × 40' (S. side) and 68' (N. side), five stories (originally three), gable roof, third-story segmental-arch windows with stone imposts and polychromatic brick voussoirs, rectangular ground-story windows with corbeled stone hood-moulds, iron-frame fourth and fifth stories with giant pilasters and wreathes on recessed spandrels, irregular pentagonal plan. Built 1885 with first-floor east reading room and west carriagehouse; raised two stories after 1892; destroyed by fire 1980.

Building No. 13 (1716–24 N. Fourth St.): brick with stone trim, approx. 18' (S. end) × 55' (seven-bay E. side) and approx. 40' (N. side) × 50' (W. side), six stories with eight-story elongated semi-octagonal clock tower at S. end, hipped roof, clock tower with enriched copper square Gothic-revival-style clock spire and concave pyramidal roof, stone stringcourses and narrow quarreled windows on tower, two-story molded copper-faced iron passageway (to Building No. 12) with quarreled windows at E. side second and third stories, round-arch fifth-story windows connected by stone stringcourse at imposts, paired sixth-story round-arch windows, brick corbel cornice, truncated triangular plan. Built 1892 as library, reading room, dispensary, auditorium, Sunday school room, armory, gymnasium. Destroyed by fire 1980, bell salvaged.

Building No. 19 (1745 N. Fourth St., at S.E. corner Montgomery Ave.): steel frame with brick curtain walls, approx. 127' (six-bay W. front) × 103' (originally approx. 62' × 103'), five and six stories, flat roof, rectangular plan, enclosed fourth- and fifth-story bridge over Montgomery Ave. to Building No. 27, enclosed third-, fourth-, fifth-story bridge over Fourth St. to Building No. 21. Five-story south section built before 1906; six-story north section built 1906. Demolished 1979.

Building No. 21 (1746–60 N. Fourth St., at S.W. corner Montgomery Ave.): steel frame with brick curtain walls, approx. 140' (seven-bay side) × 100' (S. side) and 167' (N. side), eight stories with two-story penthouse on west side, flat roof, rectangular steel-sash triple windows, irregular pentagonal plan with large central light well, enclosed third-story bridge over Montgomery Ave. to Building No. 23, enclosed third-, fourth-, fifth-story bridge over Fourth St. to Building No. 19. Built c. 1905; probably by J. Oliver Potts, architect. Demolished 1979.

Building No. 23 (1804–32 Cadwallader St.): steel frame with brick curtain walls, approx. 165' (twenty-seven bays) × 100', five stories (originally two), flat roof with seven sawtooth skylights, rectangular steel-sash triple windows on top three stories, rectangular plan, enclosed third-story bridge over Montgomery Ave. to Building No. 21.

Built 1906 as Stetson Auditorium; possibly by George T. Pearson, architect. Raised three stories c. 1915; demolished 1979.

Building No. 24 (1801 Germantown Ave., at N.E. corner Montgomery Ave.): steel frame, brick curtain walls with marble trim, splayed U-plan, S. wing approx. 211' (twenty-two-bay side) × 50', W. side approx. 138' (fourteen-bay front) × 75', N. wing approx. 190' × 50', eight stories, flat roof, marble Ionic flat portico in antis on S. side, quoins on lower two stories, marble flat-arch windows with prominent keystones. Built 1909–10; possibly by George T. Pearson, architect. Demolished 1979.

Building No. 27 (1801–23 N. Fourth St., at N.E. corner Montgomery Ave.): steel frame with brick curtain walls, approx. 54' (six-bay front) × 198', eight stories, flat roof, rectangular steel-sash triple windows, rectangular plan, enclosed fourth- and fifth-story bridge over Montgomery Ave. to Building No. 19. Built 1912; J. Oliver Potts, architect. Driveway through first floor removed, interior first floor altered 1928; J. Oliver Potts, architect. Demolished 1979.

16 ext. photos (1980),* 6 int. photos (1980).*

Notes

Abbreviations used in notes:

AABN   *American Architect and Building News*

Building Permit   City of Philadelphia, Department of Licenses and Inspection, Construction Unit

Deed Book   City of Philadelphia, Department of Records

FFI   Franklin Fire Insurance Company

FLP   Free Library of Philadelphia

HABS   Historic American Buildings Survey

Historic Philadelphia   *Historic Philadelphia from the Founding until the Early Nineteenth Century,* Transactions of the American Philosophical Society 43, Part 1 (1953)

HSP   Historical Society of Pennsylvania

INA   Insurance Company of North America

JSAH   *Journal of the Society of Architectural Historians*

LCP   Library Company of Philadelphia

MA   .Mutual Assurance Company

PC   Philadelphia Contributionship

PHC   Philadelphia Historical Commission

PL   *Public Ledger*

PMHB   *Pennsylvania Magazine of History and Biography*

PRERBG   *Philadelphia Real Estate Record and Builders' Guide*

Registry Unit   City of Philadelphia, Department of Records

Penn's City: Society Hill

1. Frances Wright d'Arusmont, *Views of Society and Manners in America* (London: Longman, Hurst, Rees, Orme, and Brown, 1821), pp. 83–84.

2. John F. Watson, *Annals of Philadelphia* (enlarged, rev. ed.; Philadelphia: Leary, Stuart Co., 1927), 1:12; J. Thomas Scharf and Thompson Westcott, *History of Philadelphia, 1609–1884* (Philadelphia: L. H. Everts & Co., 1884), 1: 87, 89, 202.

3. Edwin Iwanicki, Brief of Title, 117 Lombard Street, Philadelphia (1961), PHC; PC 918 (March 24, 1764), photocopies at HABS, PHC. For a fuller presentation of the houses and institutions of Society Hill, see Elizabeth B. McCall, *Old Philadelphia Houses on Society Hill, 1750–1840* (New York: The Architectural Book Publishing Co., 1966).

4. Richard S. Fuller, Brief of Title, 220 Spruce Street, Philadelphia (1960), PHC; Iwanicki, Brief of Title for 117 Lombard Street, PHC; rehabilitation plans for 220–22 Spruce Street in PHC files.

5. Brief of Title, 217 Delancey Street, Philadelphia (c. 1957), PHC; Gregory B. Keen, "The Descendants of Jöran Kyn, the Founder of Upland," *PMHB* 5 (1881): 96–97; Henry D. Biddle, "Colonial Mayors of Philadelphia: Samuel Rhoads, 1774," *PMHB* 19 (1895): 64–71.

6. The story of this detailed map, the Clarkson-Biddle Map of Philadelphia, is related by Martin P. Snyder in *City of Independence: Views of Philadelphia Before 1800* (New York: Praeger Publishers, 1975), pp. 62–64, 73–74.

7. Harold Donaldson Eberlein, ed., "Further Passages from the Diary of Nicholas Pickford Esquire, Relating to His Travels in Pennsylvania in 1786," *The Architectural Review* 48 (July 1920): 28.

8. Carl and Jessica Bridenbaugh, *Rebels and Gentlemen: Philadelphia in the Age of Franklin* (New York: Oxford University Press, 1962), p. 109. The Powel House was built in 1765 for Charles Stedman, a merchant who suffered business reverses and sold the property to Powel in 1769. Professor George B. Tatum has written the definitive study of this house and some of its contemporaries: *Philadelphia Georgian: The City House of Samuel Powel and Some of Its Eighteenth-Century Neighbors* (Middletown, Conn.: Wesleyan University Press, 1976). For information of its early ownership, see pp. 4–16, 25–30.

9. Fiske Kimball, "Interior from the Powel House," *Pennsylvania Museum Bulletin* 21 (January 1926): 68; Kimball, "Drawing Room From the Powel House, Philadelphia, 1768," *Pennsylvania Museum Bulletin* 23 (March 1928): 29.

10. This housing form is discussed in William John Murtagh, "The Philadelphia Row House," *JSAH* 16 (December 1957): 9.

11. Brief of Title, 236 Delancey Street, Philadelphia (c. 1957), PHC; MA 2234–35 (June 1806); PC 4745 (March 12, 1830), photocopies at HABS, PHC.

12. Physical evidence shows that an earlier house, built in 1769, was incorporated into the house. PC 1328 (August 24, 1769), photocopy at PHC; Brief of Title, 321 South Fourth Street, Philadelphia (c. 1958), PHC. Hill's biographical sketch appears in William H. Egle, "The Constitutional Convention of 1776: Biographical Sketches of Its Members," *PMHB* 3 (1879): 441–42.

13. Robert E. Cooper, "John Clement Stocker House," HABS Report, PA-1068.

14. Margaret B. Tinkcom, "The New Market in Second Street," *PMHB* 82 (October 1958): 379–96.

15. Edward B. Krumbharr, "The Pennsylvania Hospital," *Historic Philadelphia*, pp. 237–43; George B. Tatum, *Penn's Great Town* (Philadelphia: University of Pennsylvania Press, 1961), pp. 51, 77, 165–66; pl. 35. The most thorough work on the institution's

early years is William Henry Williams, *America's First Hospital: The Pennsylvania Hospital, 1751–1841* (Newark, Del.: University of Delaware Press, 1976).

16. For a brief discussion of the importance of the church to nineteenth- and twentieth-century blacks, see Theodore Hershberg, "Free Blacks in Antebellum Philadelphia," in *The Peoples of Philadelphia,* ed. Allen F. Davis and Mark F. Haller (Philadelphia: Temple University Press, 1973), pp. 120–21.

17. "Richard Allen and Mother Bethel African Methodist Episcopal Church" (Philadelphia: Bethel African Methodist Episcopal Church, 1972), n.p. Allen's auto-biography accompanies his biography in R. R. Wright, Jr., *The Bishops of the African Methodist Episcopal Church* (Nashville, Tenn.: The A.M.E. Sunday School Union, 1963), pp. 46–76.

18. *PL,* October 27, 1890.

19. Richard S. Fuller, Brief of Title, 240 South Fourth Street, Philadelphia (1959), PHC; MA 4871 (June 1830), photocopies at PHC; Harold Donaldson Eberlein and Cort-landt Van Dyke Hubbard, *Portrait of a Colonial City* (Philadelphia: J. B. Lippincott Co., 1939), p. 301.

20. Wright d'Arusmont, *Views of Society and Manners in America,* p. 83.

21. *PRERBG* 15 (October 24, 1900): 681; Registry Unit 3S7–23, 2S11–70.

22. A favorable discussion of this process is in Hugh Scott, "Society Hill: Renewal's Mudder Hits the Home Stretch," *Today: The Inquirer Magazine,* March 30, 1969, pp. 6–10, 12, 14–18. A more scholarly examination of the plan and its execution is in Valerie Halverson Pace, "Society Hill, Philadelphia: Historic Preservation and Urban Renewal in Washington Square East" (Ph.D. dissertation, University of Minnesota, 1976).

23. Edmund N. Bacon, the man responsible for the "design structure" of Society Hill, discusses its development in *Design of Cities* (New York: Viking Press, 1967), pp. 243–49.

Penn's City: Old City

1. *The National Register of Historic Places, 1974 Supplement* (Washington, D.C.: U.S. Government Printing Office, 1974), pp. 452–57. The historic districts are Old City His-toric District and Elfreth's Alley Historic District. The other National Historic Landmarks are Carpenters' Hall, Christ Church, Elfreth's Alley, Musical Fund Society Hall, Philosophical Hall, Reynolds-Morris House, and Walnut Street Theatre. The major buildings in Independence National Historical Park were designated National Historic Sites in 1948 and earlier. *U.S.S. Olympia* was moved downstream to Penn's Landing Project in June 1976.

2. The Old Court House is similar to that of Amersham, Buckinghamshire, Eng-land, 1682. See Horace Field and Michael Bunney, *English Domestic Architecture of the XVII and XVIII Centuries* (London: G. Bell and Sons, 1905), pl. 48. The early political his-tory of the city and county is in J. Thomas Scharf and Thompson Westcott, *History of Philadelphia, 1609–1884* (Philadelphia: L. H. Everts & Co., 1884), 1:157–90. The effort to remove the market houses is related in *Journal of the Common Council of the Consolidated City of Philadelphia* (Philadelphia: W. H. Sickels, 1859), pp. 372–74, 392.

3. Evidence of the building's honored place in America's iconography is the great number of copies or near-copies that have been built. See John Maass, "Architecture and Americanism, or Pastiches of Independence Hall," *Charette* 49 (September 1969): 4–7. The most thorough historical and architectural studies of Independence Hall were

done by the National Park Service during the 1960's; they are called Historic Structures Reports: Independence Hall; and may be obtained from Independence National Historical Park headquarters, 313 Walnut Street, Philadelphia. Its architecture is also evaluated by Hugh Morrison, *Early American Architecture* (New York: Oxford University Press, 1952), pp. 532–37; and George B. Tatum, *Penn's Great Town* (Philadelphia: University of Pennsylvania Press, 1961), pp. 32–33.

4. John Maass, "Philadelphia City Hall: Monster or Masterpiece?" *Journal of American Institute of Architects* 43 (February 1965): 24.

5. For twentieth-century commentary on the violation of Penn's original plan, see John W. Reps, *The Making of Urban America* (Princeton: Princeton University Press, 1965), pp. 167–69; Joseph Jackson, *America's Most Historic Highway: Market Street, Philadelphia* (Philadelphia: John Wanamaker, 1926), pp. 4–5. Nineteenth-century observers were aware of this change in Penn's plan, as noted in John F. Watson, *Annals of Philadelphia* (Philadelphia: Edwin S. Stuart, 1884), 1:225; "Journal of John Mair," *American Historical Review* 12 (October 1906): 80; Charles William Jansom, *The Stranger in America, 1793–1806* (New York: The Press of the Pioneers, 1935), p. 183; Frances Wright d'Arusmont, *Views of Society and Manners in America* (London: Longman, Hurst, Rees, Orme, and Brown, 1821), p. 84. Although eighteenth-century descriptions are rare, late-eighteenth-century and early-nineteenth-century descriptions with references to the waterfront's earlier condition can be found in the following books: J. P. Brissot de Warville, *New Travels in the United States of America, 1788*, trans. Mara Soceanu Vamos and Durand Echeverria (Cambridge, Mass.: Belknap Press of Harvard University Press, 1964), pp. 254–55; John M. Duncan, *Travels through Parts of the United States and Canada in 1818 and 1819* (New York: W. B. Gilley, 1823), 1:188; Wright d'Arusmont, *Views of Society and Manners in America*, p. 84; Jansom, *The Stranger in America, 1793–1806*, p. 183. Reps also discusses the development of the city's plan into the nineteenth century; see *The Making of Urban America*, pp. 160–74. For a thorough, cross-cultural analysis of the evolution of the plan of Philadelphia during the colonial period and the democratic era following the American Revolution, see Anthony N. B. Garvan, "Proprietary Philadelphia as Artifact, " *The Historian and the City*, ed. Oscar Handlin and John Burchard (Cambridge, Mass.: MIT Press, 1963), pp. 177–201. A brief discussion of the extended control of First Purchasers and a reproduction of Surveyor General William Parsons's "Plan of Philadelphia" (c. 1748) showing early ownership of city lots can be found in Nicholas Wainwright, "Plan of Philadelphia," *PMHB* 80 (April 1956): 164–226.

6. Mrs. Charles J. Maurer, Executive Assistant to the Chairman of the Philadelphia Historical Commission, to Stanhope S. Browne, Esq., Chairman of the Committee to Preserve Philadelphia's Historic Gateway, February 9, 1966; Stanhope S. Browne, Esq., to Mrs. Charles J. Maurer, March 24, 1966, copies at PHC.

7. MA 2105 (December 1805), photocopies at PHC and HABS.

8. MA 5889 (December 3, 1870), photocopy at PHC; Morrison, *Early American Architecture*, p. 37.

9. PC 2803–2804 (February 10, 1797), photocopy at PHC; HABS drawings of Warehouse, 329 S. Water Street (July 1966), sheet 2, Frank Sanchis, del.; PC 5228 (April 18, 1837); HABS drawings of Jesse Godley Warehouse, 19–27 Queen Street (July 1966), sheet 2, Thomas M. Osborn, del., copies at HABS, PHC. These buildings are also cited by Margaret B. Tinkcom, "Southwark, A River Community: Its Shape and Substance," *Proceedings of the American Philosophical Society* 114 (August 1970): 339. Brick partition walls also were not uncommon in early-nineteenth-century factories, such as Bazel Graves's soap and candle manufactory on Spruce Street between Front and Second, MA unnumbered (no policy issued) (February 1823), photocopy at PHC.

10. MA 2105 (December 1805).

11. Girard's house is described in John Bach McMaster, *The Life and Times of Stephen Girard* (Philadelphia: J. B. Lippincott Co., 1918), 1: 278–79. The Dowers-Okill House is described in PC 1229 (March 3, 1767). These two dwellings were not exceptions. Of the nine buildings on the east side of Water Street between Arch and Race streets that were surveyed by the Philadelphia Contributionship between 1757 and 1783, four were dwellings, one a dwelling with an adjoining store, and two with stores below, one a tavern with rented rooms above, and one a granary and bake house. PC 377 (June 7, 1757); PC 541 (October 7, 1760); PC 626 (February 16, 1761); PC 1229 (March 3, 1767); PC 2063, 2064, 2065 (September 2, 1783); PC 624 (February 16, 1761); PC 2066, 2067 (September 2, 1783); PC 625 (February 16, 1761), photocopies at PHC.

12. One lintel was displayed at "See What They Sawed, An Exhibition on the Occasion of the 200th Anniversary of Building Carpenters' Hall," Visitors' Center (then First Bank of the United States), Independence National Historical Park, 1970–73.

13. Thompson Westcott, *The Historic Mansions and Buildings of Philadelphia* (rev. ed.; Philadelphia: Walter H. Barr, 1895), pp. 68–78; PC 179 (1763); PC 1767–69 (November 2, 1773), photocopies at PHC.

14. Printer and bookseller Eleazer Oswald kept his shop here until July, 1789, when James Stokes began renting it for his fancy hardware store. Francis White, *The Philadelphia Directory* (Philadelphia: Young, Stewart and McCullogh, 1785), p. 54; James Stokes' Ledger, 1783–1801, pp. 25, 79, Paumgarten Collection, MSS, HSP. Joseph Jackson, *Encyclopedia of Philadelphia* (Harrisburg, Pa.: National Historical Association, 1933), 4: 955–57. By 1854 there were two shops on the ground story, a cooper's ware room in the cellar, and storage on the upper floors of the former coffee house. An old photo (c. 1855) in City Archives shows it to have fallen from its former high fashion as described in Watson's *Annals*, 1:222; PC 179 (Re-Surveys 1842, 1845), photocopy at PHC.

15. Sam Bass Warner, Jr., *The Private City* (Philadelphia: University of Pennsylvania Press, 1968), pp. 49–58.

16. The most thorough discussion of the building's architecture and use is by Agnes Addison Gilchrist, "The Philadelphia Exchange: William Strickland, Architect," *Historic Philadelphia*, pp. 86–95. Updating her research are insurance surveys: PC 11807 (March 1873, August 1903), and FFI 22234 (March 1855), photocopies at HABS, PHC; PRERBG 6 (October 7, 1891): 639; 16 (November 20, 1901): 764.

17. Demolished in the 1850's, the City Tavern has been reconstructed by the National Park Service. PC 1767–69 (November 2, 1773) (Re-Survey November 20, 1834); Mark Forest, "City Tavern to Be Rebuilt," *Today: The Inquirer Magazine*, March 1, 1959, pp. 7–8; *Philadelphia Inquirer*, February 23, 1976.

18. Gilchrist, "Philadelphia Exchange," pp. 86–95; *PRERBG* 16 (November 20, 1901): 764; PC 11807 (August 1903).

19. Scharf and Westcott, *History of Philadelphia*, 3:2344–45; *PRERBG* 7 (April 20, 1892): 1099; *PL*, March 25, 1896, March 8, 1901, April 29, 1901, May 2, 1901; *Philadelphia Record*, April 27, 1901.

20. The building of the Bourse was one of the feature architectural and business events of the day. It was begun in 1893 and finished two years later; G. W. and W. D. Hewitt were the architects. A thorough discussion and architectural rendering of the proposed structure appears in *PL*, May 10, 1893. See also PC 10851 (October 1933), photocopy at PHC.

21. In 1849 John Riddell, architect, designed a store for Faust, Winebrenner and Co. on North Third Street and a five-story store at the southwest corner of Third and

Spring streets in this manner. *PL,* April 17, 1849; *McElroy's Philadelphia City Directory for 1858* (Philadelphia: Edward C. and John Biddle, 1858), p. 238.

22. PC 4669 (April 1829); PC 4752 (June 1830); PC 4956 (August 1833); FFI 1654 (September 1836); PC 6060 (November 1844), photocopies at HABS, PHC.

23. PC 4956 (August 1833).

24. The four-story warehouses were at 110–12 Church Alley. PC 4865 (January 1832), PC 4872 (January 1832), photocopies at PHC. Construction of the Naval Asylum began in 1827, was suspended between 1829 and 1832, and completed in 1833. Agnes Addison Gilchrist, *William Strickland: Architect and Engineer, 1788–1854* (Philadelphia: University of Pennsylvania Press, 1950), pp. 7–8; William B. Bassett, "United States Naval Asylum, Biddle Hall," HABS Report, PA–1094, p.l.

25. Richard G. Carrott, "The Architect of the Pennsylvania Fire Insurance Building," *JSAH* 20 (October 1961): 138–39; Harold N. Cooledge, Jr., "A Sloan Checklist, 1849–1884," *JSAH* 19 (March 1960): 36; Samuel Sloan, *City and Suburban Architecture* (Philadelphia: J. B. Lippincott Co., 1859), pl. 56; *PL,* August 28, 1854.

26. Henry-Russell Hitchcock, *Early Victorian Architecture* (New Haven: Yale University Press, 1954), 1:347.

27. Winston Weisman, "Philadelphia Functionalism and Sullivan," *JSAH* 20 (March 1961): 3–19.

28. Agnes Addison Gilchrist, "Jayne Building, Philadelphia, Pa.," HABS Report (PA–188), p. 2. Another source may have been New England, specifically Boston and Providence. Weisman ("Philadelphia Functionalism," p. 6) points out that "structural design involving skeleton stone construction originated in the New England area in the early 1820's" as seen in Alexander Parris's Quincy Market Stores, Boston, and William Holden Greene's Granite Block, Providence, both built in 1824. Since Joseph C. Hoxie and Stephen D. Button, two architects who figure prominently in the use of the utilitarian Italianate, were born and raised in Rhode Island and Connecticut respectively, and Button was married to a Massachusetts woman, it is possible that they brought the new mode to Philadelphia independently. Sixth Census, 1840, Hudson County, New Jersey, MSS, New Jersey State Library; "Biographical Sketch of Mr. S. D. Button, Architect, Philadelphia," *AABN* 37 (July 16, 1892): 37–38.

29. *PL,* July 10, 1852, February 9, 1854, January 22, 1856; Casper Souder, "A History of Chestnut Street" (n.d.), pp. 40–41, MSS, HSP; Registry Unit 1S2–213.

30. M. Field, *City Architecture* (New York: G. P. Putnam & Co., 1853), p. 34.

31. *Ibid.,* p. 17.

32. *PL,* February 9, 1854; January 22, 1856.

33. PC 9439 (c. 1854); PC 4956 (August 1833). Skylights were used on one-story rear buildings without exposed walls during the 1830's, but skylight systems such as that of the Leland Building were not employed until about 1850, when some became quite special, such as the one designed by G. Runge for Morris L. Hallowell & Co., which admitted only "pure northern light" (*PL,* December 20, 1853). An early one-story skylight was at 52 South Second Street (MA 5340, February 1834, photocopy at PHC). Also, iron sliders were used as early as 1833 on the Trotter warehouse, but iron shutters were much more common before the 1850's. Among two contemporary stores on Chestnut Street, numbers 217 and 223, and six on North Third Street between Market and Arch, another wholesale dry goods district, the average dimensions of fireproofs were 7 feet by 6 ½ feet, and five of them were one story and three were two stories. MA 6350 (May 11, 1853); PC 9956 (December 4, 1857); PC 8688 (September 20, 1851); PC 8683 (November 3, 1851); PC 5570 (February 21, 1854); PC 9336 (February 28,

1854); PC 8146 (August 17, 1850); PC 10505 (January 2, 1861), photocopies at PHC.

34. *McElroy's Philadelphia Directory for 1855* (Philadelphia: Edward C. & John Biddle, 1855), pp. 774–75.

35. PC 2381 (December 1, 1789), photocopy of PHC; Deed Books AWM 48–106, AWM 59–453; *McElroy's Directory 1855*, p. 264.

36. Deed Book TH 61–470; *PL*, January 16, 1854. For a history of this famous firm, see Scharf and Westcott, *History of Philadelphia*, 3:2101–2, and Burton Alva Konkle, "Francis Martin Drexel and Philadelphia Leadership in International Finance," *The Girard Letter* 14 (December 1933): 1–2.

37. *PL*, January 12, 1855; July 31, 1855; *McElroy's Directory 1858*, pp. 774–75.

38. MA 6415 (June 6, 1854), photocopy at HABS, PHC.

39. MA 6499 (July 15, 1855); PC 9571 (August 9, 1854), photocopies at PHC.

40. MA 6499 (July 15, 1855); PC 9571 (August 9, 1854); MA 6415 (June 6, 1854), photocopies at PHC.

41. The early history of the Bank of North America is reviewed by Scharf and Westcott, *History of Philadelphia*, 3:2089–93. The most thorough history of the First Bank of the United States is James O. Wettereau, "The Oldest Bank Building in the United States," *Historic Philadelphia*, pp. 70–79.

42. The Second Bank's history is given by Bray Hammond, "The Second Bank of the United States," *Historic Philadelphia*, pp. 80–85. Its architecture is evaluated by Talbot Hamlin, *Greek Revival Architecture in America* (New York: Oxford University Press, 1944), pp. 75–77, and Tatum, *Penn's Great Town*, pp. 65–66.

43. Gilchrist, *William Strickland*, p. 4.

44. *PL*, April 12, 1849.

45. Tatum, *Penn's Great Town*, pp. 194–95, pl. 119, illustrates and gives the basic historical data for Bank Row.

46. Quoted from FFI 22148 (February 17, 1855), photocopy at HABS, PHC. Construction began in 1854. Insurance Policy 252 (February 11, 1854), MSS, Archives Department, INA.

47. FFI 22148 (February 17, 1855).

48. Ibid; Poulson's Scrap-books 7:159, MSS, LCP. For later alterations see *PRERBG* 18 (January 7, 1903): 1; Building Permits 4910 (1917), 5679 (1919).

49. For the history of this banking house, see Nicholas Wainwright, *The Philadelphia National Bank* (Philadelphia: Philadelphia National Bank, 1953).

50. Harold B. Dickson, *A Hundred Pennsylvania Buildings* (State College, Pa.: Bald Eagle Press, 1954), pl. 67.

51. Poulson's Scrap-books 9:34–35, MSS, LCP. For later alterations see *PRERBG* 7 (June 8, 1892): 1212; 7 (November 9, 1892): 1587; 18 (May 6, 1903): 278.

52. George E. Thomas and James F. O'Gorman, "Catalogue of Selected Buildings," in James F. O'Gorman, *The Architecture of Frank Furness* (Philadelphia: Philadelphia Museum of Art, 1973), pp. 110–15.

53. Tatum, *Penn's Great Town*, pp. 194–95.

54. *PL*, July 22, 1872; William A. Armstrong, Account Book, 1867–75, MSS, HSP; Elizabeth Biddle Yarnall, *Addison Hutton: Quaker Architect, 1834–1916* (Philadelphia: Art Alliance Press, 1974), p. 70; *AABN* 8 (September 18, 1880): 144. For the bank's nineteenth-century history, see Harrison S. Morris, *A Sketch of the Pennsylvania Company for Insurances on Lives and Granting Annuities* (Philadelphia: J. B. Lippincott Co., 1896).

55. Included with the Provident Trust and Guarantee Trust would be the National

Bank of the Republic, 313 Chestnut Street, by Furness and Evans in 1884. Thomas and O'Gorman, "Catalogue," *Architecture of Frank Furness,* pp. 150–51.

56. *PL,* August 10, 1893; *PRERBG* 8 (August 16, 1893): 521; PC 14103 (June 1894), photocopy at HABS, PHC.

57. Personnel Office, Minute Book of the Building Committee, MSS, First Pennsylvania Banking and Trust Company.

58. See Nicholas Wainwright, *A Philadelphia Story* (Philadelphia: Philadelphia Contributionship, 1952), for the company's history; pp. 96–128 deal with the erection of the present building.

59. Thomas U. Walter to Directors of Philadelphia Contributionship, July 4, 1835, MSS, PC, photocopies at HABS, PHC.

60. Minutes of the Board of Directors of Philadelphia Contributionship, From 1859, May 18th to 1866, December 16th, pp. 125, 128, MSS, PC, photocopies at HABS, PHC; MA 8908 (December 1898), photocopies at HABS, PHC.

61. MA 8908 (December 1898); *PL,* June 22, 1898.

62. James C. Massey, "Frank Furness in the 1880's," *Charette* 43 (October 1963): 25; Spring Garden Insurance Company, see *AABN* 8 (September 18, 1880): 144.

63. Building Permit 4731 (1911).

64. Building Permit 6442 (1928).

65. Building Specifications, July 24, 1835, MSS, PC, photocopies at HABS, PHC.

66. Bill of Thomas U. Walter, January 3, 1837, MSS, PC; Building Permit 4731 (1911).

67. For praise of this imaginative piece of architecture, see Thomas Hine in *Philadelphia Inquirer,* February 28, 1975; Nessa Forman in *Sunday Bulletin,* August 18, 1974; see also "Penn Mutual Building, Philadelphia," *The Architectural Record* 149 (April 1971): 42.

68. DeWitt C. Baxter, *The Baxter Panoramic Business Directory* (Philadelphia: DeWitt C. Baxter, 1879), n.p.; Francis James Dallett, *An Architectural View of Washington Square* (Philadelphia: By the author, 1968), pp. 28–31.

69. *PL,* April 14, 1852; January 24, 1853; "Horstmann Factory," *Gleason's Pictorial Drawing-Room Companion* 6 (January 21, 1854): 48; Building Permits 1506, 2908 (1934).

70. *Illustrated Philadelphia* (New York: American Publishing Co., 1889), p. 152; *Gopsill's Philadelphia City Directory for 1872* (Philadelphia: James Gopsill, 1872), p. 1164.

71. *PL,* March 26, 1857; August 31, 1857; *Philadelphia Shopping Guide and Housekeeper's Companion for 1859* (Philadelphia: S. E. Cohen, 1859), p. 51; Poulson's Scrapbooks 10:9, MSS, LCP; Nicholas Wainwright, *Philadelphia in the Romantic Age of Lithography* (Philadelphia: Historical Society of Pennsylvania, 1958), p. 153.

72. Jackson, *Market Street,* pp. 220–21; Campbell Scrapbook, vol. 54, MSS. HSP; *PL,* July 27, 1872.

73. *PL,* January 9, 1899, relates the store's early development.

74. *PL,* January 11, 1895, January 6, 1907, March 22, 1907; *PRERBG* 8 (February 8, 1893): 79; 9 (December 26, 1894): 643; 11 (August 12, 1896): 657; 12 (July 7, 1897): 423; Building Permit 1279 (1907); PC 13860 (October 17, 1907) MSS, HSP. The North Seventh Street extension was built in 1917–18, Simon and Bassett, architects; Building Permit 3720 (1917).

The older stores, 709–27 Market, that stand between the end pavilions by Collins and Autenreith were incorporated into the department store during this time with Collins and Autenreith doing the design work. *PL,* September 30, 1898; *PRERBG* 13 (November 16, 1898): 745; 13 (November 23, 1898): 763; 15 (January 3, 1900): 1; 15 (January 17, 1900): 37.

The report that has led to the unquestioned acceptance of Lit Brothers as a cast-iron building appears to have originated in Theo B. White et al., *Philadelphia Architecture in the Nineteenth Century* (Philadelphia: University of Pennsylvania Press, 1953), pl. 72.

75. Hannah Benner Roach, "Elfreth's Alley" (Philadelphia, Elfreth's Alley Association pamphlet, 1972); PC 578 (February 1761); PC 611, (May 1761); PC 1107 (September 3, 1766); PC 2147 (September 1784); PC 2148 (September 1784); PC 2765 (June 30, 1796); PC 2783 (December 2, 1796); MA 1660 (September 1803); PC 6118 (March 7, 1845); PC 6192 (June 4, 1845); PC 6450 (January 8, 1846); PC 7048 (August 30, 1847); PC 475 (Re-Survey April 1811); Fire Association Insurance policy 8862 (April 4, 1844), photocopies at HABS, PHC. Briefs of title of each property by Hannah Benner Roach at PHC.

76. Roach, "Elfreth's Alley."

77. Nos. 113–15 and 121 were new in 1811. MA 3197, 3198 (December 1811); PC 3427 (October 1811).

78. MA 175 (February 1788). The school was built in 1761. Drawing of Old German School-House by D. J. Kennedy (1860), Society Collection, MSS, HSP.

79. PC 1269 (February 1769); PC 1459 (December 1770); Deed Books I1–421 (1763), I10–158 (1771), G8–426 (1747), D12–137 (1762), AWM 73–100 (1848).

Although pent eaves were common during the colonial period, they were built later, as in the case of 131 North Fourth Street, whose pent eave between the second and third floors must have been put up c. 1800 when the third story was added. See PC unnumbered (no policy issued, May 1819), photocopy at PHC. It describes the house with a third story and a pent (neither of which was mentioned in the 1770 survey) and a roof two-thirds worn. Since cedar shingles lasted about thirty years, the pent and third floor were added c. 1800.

80. Census of Philadelphia, 1790, MSS, National Archives, microfilm copy at FLP; County Tax Assessment Ledger, Lower Delaware Ward, 1795, MSS, Philadelphia City Archives.

81. Tatum, *Penn's Great Town*, p. 164, pl. 33; Talbot Hamlin, *Benjamin Henry Latrobe* (New York: Oxford University Press, 1955), p. 152; William John Murtagh, "The Philadelphia Row House," *JSAH* 16 (December 1957): 8.

82. H. M. Pierce Gallagher, *Robert Mills, Architect of the Washington Monument, 1781–1855* (New York: Columbia University Press, 1935), p. 3.

83. Kenneth Ames, "Robert Mills and the Philadelphia Row House," *JSAH* 27 (May 1968): 140–42.

84. MA 191 (November 20, 1795), photocopies at HABS, PHC; Arnold Nicholson, "The Church's White House," *The Episcopalian* 132 (December 1967): 17–19.

85. Murtagh, "Philadelphia Row House," p. 12.

86. PC 4744 (March 9, 1830), photocopies at HABS, PHC.

87. PC 8474 (November 1879; Re-Survey January 1901).

88. It is interesting to note that these patriots evidently dated the nation's birth from the first session of the Continental Congress and the outbreak of hostilities in 1775, not from the signing of the Declaration of Independence. For a discussion of early Quaker meeting houses, see Edwin B. Bronner, "Quaker Landmarks in Early Philadelphia," *Historic Philadelphia*, pp. 210–16. The history of the Free Quakers is presented by Charles Wetherill, *History of the Religious Society of Friends Called by Some the Free Quakers* (Philadelphia: By the author, 1894). Excellent architectural histories of the two buildings under discussion are Lee H. Nelson and Penelope Hartshorne Batcheler, "An Architectural Study of Arch Street Meeting House," (report for

Philadelphia Yearly Meeting of the Religious Society of Friends, 1968), and Charles E. Peterson, F.A.I.A., "Notes on the Free Quaker Meeting House," (report for Harbeson, Hough, Livingston and Larson, AIA, 1966).

89. Donald Richard Friary, "The Architecture of the Anglican Church in the Northern American Colonies: A Study of Religious, Social, and Cultural Expression" (Ph.D. dissertation, University of Pennsylvania, 1971), 1:339, 368; Morrison, *Early American Architecture*, pp. 537–38; Tatum, *Penn's Great Town*, pp. 28–30; Robert W. Shoemaker, "Christ Church, St. Peter's, and St. Paul's," *Historic Philadelphia*, 187–90.

90. Alexander Mackie, "The Presbyterian Churches of Old Philadelphia," *Historic Philadelphia*, pp. 217–22; Tatum, *Penn's Great Town*, pp. 27, 39–40, 69, 160–61, 174 and pls. 23, 61; Theodore Sizer, "Philadelphia's First Presbyterian Church by 'Mr. Trumbul,' " *JSAH* 9 (October 1950): 20–22. For descriptions of the interior appointments of the first two Second Presbyterian churches, see PC 901–3 (June 7, 1763), MA 5516 (September 2, 1837), photocopies at PHC.

91. Tatum, *Penn's Great Town*, pp. 30–32, pl. 13; Scharf and Westcott, *History of Philadelphia*, 2: 1418–21.

92. David Van Horne, *A History of the Reformed Church in Philadelphia* (Philadelphia, 1876); Daniel Miller, *Early History of the Reformed Church in Pennsylvania* (Reading, Pa.: By the author, 1906), pp. 29–31; John T. Faris, *Old Churches and Meeting Houses in and around Philadelphia* (Philadelphia: J. B. Lippincott Co., 1926), pp. 67–75.

93. Fred Pierce Corson, "St. George's Church: The Cradle of American Methodism," *Historic Philadelphia*, pp. 230–36.

94. The erection of Mikveh Israel synagogue and the discriminations the group quietly endured are described by Edwin Wolf 2nd and Maxwell Whiteman, *The History of the Jews of Philadelphia from Colonial Times to the Age of Jackson* (Philadelphia: The Jewish Publication Society of America, 1956), pp. 117–21. For St. Joseph's and St. Augustine's, see Arthur J. Ennis, *Old St. Augustine's Catholic Church in Philadelphia* (Philadelphia: St. Augustine's Catholic Church, 1965), pp. 9–15; Dennis C. Kurjack, "St. Joseph's and St. Mary's Churches," *Historic Philadelphia*, pp. 199–203. The most thorough analysis of the destructive "Native American" riots is Michael Feldberg, *The Philadelphia Riots of 1844: A Study of Ethnic Conflict* (Westport, Conn.: Greenwood Press, 1975). Scharf and Westcott, *History of Philadelphia*, 1: 664–74 describe the riots; and Sam Bass Warner, Jr., *The Private City: Philadelphia in Three Periods of Its Growth* (Philadelphia: University of Pennsylvania Press, 1968), pp. 125–27 discusses the causes of a series of riots between 1834 and 1849.

95. Probably the best account of the early years of the American Philosophical Society is Brooke Hindle, *The Pursuit of Science in Revolutionary America* (Chapel Hill: University of North Carolina Press, 1956), pp. 127–45. For a history of the hall, see William E. Lingelbach, "Philosophical Hall: The Home of the American Philosophical Society," *Historic Philadelphia*, pp. 43–69. PRERBG 5 (June 11, 1890): 337; PL, August 16, 1890.

96. Charles E. Peterson, "Library Hall: Home of the Library Company of Philadelphia, 1790–1880," *Historic Philadelphia*, pp. 96–128; PC 2414, 2415 (November 1790), photocopy at PHC.

97. The most recent and thorough history of the institute is Bruce Sinclair, *Philadelphia's Philosopher Mechanics* (Baltimore: Johns Hopkins Press, 1975). Its architecture is discussed by Tatum, *Penn's Great Town*, p. 70, and Matthew Baigell, "John Haviland in Philadelphia, 1818–1826," *JSAH* 25 (October 1966): 206.

98. The early history of the institution is given by Arthur M. Kennedy, "The Athe-

naeum: Some Account of Its History from 1814 to 1850," *Historic Philadelphia*, pp. 260–65. For its architecture, see Robert C. Smith, *John Notman and the Athenaeum Building* (Philadelphia: Athenaeum of Philadelphia, 1951); Tatum, *Penn's Great Town*, pp. 92, 98, 184; Dallett, *Architectural View of Washington Square*, p. 20; a copy of Notman's printed specifications (1845) are at HABS; MA 7394 (1868), photocopies at HABS, PHC.

99. Arthur Hobson Quinn, "The Theatre and the Drama in Old Philadelphia," *Historic Philadelphia*, pp. 313–17; Harold Kirker, "The New Theatre, Philadelphia, 1791–92," *JSAH* 22 (March 1963): 36–37; George B. Tatum, "The Early Theatres of Philadelphia," *Bulletin of the Philadelphia Old Town Historical Society* 1 (October 1971): 11–12.

100. Tatum, "Early Theatres," pp. 11–16; Derek Naabe, "Philadelphia's Theatre Heritage: The Arch Street Theatre," *Germantowne Crier* 18 (December 1966): 107–10; Derek Naabe, "Philadelphia's Theatre Heritage: The Walnut Street Theatre," *Germantowne Crier* 22 (Winter 1970): 14–18; Stuart B. Smith, "The Walnut Street Theater, 1809–1834" (M.A. thesis, University of Delaware, 1960), pp. v-vi, 1, 5–7, 16–18; Gilchrist, *William Strickland*, p. 65; Tatum, *Penn's Great Town*, p. 187; Miscellaneous Early Papers, Musical Fund Society Collection, MSS, HSP; *PRERBG* 6 (May 13, 1891): 289; *Philadelphia Record*, August 4, 1893; Building Permit 342 (1946); F. J. Burghart, "Formal Concert Hall," *Today: The Inquirer Magazine*, June 7, 1970, 11.

101. MA 2307 (September 1806, May 1848, June 1881, December 1937); *Biographies of Successful Philadelphia Merchants* (Philadelphia: James K. Simon, 1864), pp. 40–41; *PL*, August 28, 1850, January 21, 1851; PC 2299, 2300 (December 1781), photocopies at HABS, PHC. Briefs of Title for 112–16 Cuthbert Street at PHC. For a study of the area's cast-iron architecture, see Antoinette J. Lee, "The Rise of the Cast Iron District in Philadelphia" (Ph.D. dissertation, George Washington University, 1975).

102. The mall project has been controversial. For a generally favorable evaluation, see Roul Tunley, "Comeback of a Shabby City," *Saturday Evening Post*, December 5, 1959, pp. 32–35, 75–78. Lewis Mumford has praised the decision of Charles E. Peterson, the federal government's chief architect on the project during the 1950's, to preserve more than colonial buildings in Independence National Historical Park, but he has been critical of the mall for imposing on Independence Hall "an aesthetic burden that only a vast palace . . . could hope to carry off." See Mumford's "The Skyline: Historic Philadelphia," *The New Yorker*, November 17, 1956, pp. 138–40, 143–48, February 9, 1957, pp. 100–106, April 6, 1957, pp. 132–41, April 13, 1957, pp. 155–62. The first of the large office structures has proven the best: the Rohm and Haas Building, designed by Pietro Belluschi in collaboration with George M. Ewing Company. "Independence Mall Development," *The Architectural Record* 134 (July 1963): 12; James Van Trump, "Elegance on the Mall: The Rohm and Haas Building in Philadelphia," *Charette* 46 (April 1966): 6–7.

103. The Penn's Landing Project is described in *Third Annual Report to the Board of Directors* (Philadelphia: OPDC Penn's Landing Corporation, 1974).

Penn's City: Center Square

1. John Ord succeeded McArthur, but he apparently had a dispute with some members of the Commission and was replaced in 1894 by W. Bleddyn Powell, who, early in his career, had been associated with Thomas U. Walter. Minutes of the Commissioners for the Erection of the Public Buildings, 1887–1897, MSS, Philadelphia City

Archives; Letter Book of the City Architect, 1901–1906, pp. 14, 54, 65 in ibid. John Maass has written the building's architectural history: "Philadelphia City Hall," *Charette* 44 (January 1964): 23–26; "Philadelphia City Hall: Monster or Masterpiece?" *Journal of the American Institute of Architects* 43 (February 1965): 23–30. For an investigation of the Byzantine politics surrounding the building's erection, see Howard Gillette, Jr., "Philadelphia's City Hall: Monument to a New Political Machine," *PMHB* 97 (April 1973): 233–49. The building's statistics are in Frederick Faust, *The City Hall, Philadelphia* (Philadelphia: F. Faust, 1897), pp. 1–2, 5.

2. City Hall's sculpture is discussed by George Gurney in *Sculpture of a City*, ed. Nicholas B. Wainwright (New York: Walker Publishing Co., 1974), pp. 94–109. Each statue, bas-relief, ornament, and railing is illustrated in *Sculptures and Ornamental Details in Bronze and Iron of the New City Hall*, 5 vols. (Philadelphia, 1883).

3. A Friends meeting house stood on the southwest corner of the square as early as 1687, when it was assumed that the city's plan would be developed more or less uniformly. When this expectation failed to materialize the building was dismantled c. 1700. George B. Tatum, *Penn's Great Town* (Philadelphia: University of Pennsylvania Press, 1961), p. 25.

4. Ibid., pp. 57–58; Talbot Hamlin, *Benjamin Henry Latrobe* (New York: Oxford University Press, 1955), pp. 157–67.

5. Kenneth Ames, "Robert Mills and the Philadelphia Row House," *JSAH* 27 (May 1968): 140–42.

6. Robert Ennis, "Thomas Ustick Walter," Lecture to Philadelphia Chapter, Society of Architectural Historians, December 13, 1973; Letter Book of the City Architect, 1901–1906, p. 54, MSS, Philadelphia City Archives.

7. Tatum, *Penn's Great Town*, p. 71, pl. 64; William John Murtagh, "The Philadelphia Row House," *JSAH* 16 (December 1957): 13.

8. Tatum, *Penn's Great Town*, p. 94.

9. See briefs of title in files of PHC. FFI 24376–79 (July 7, 1856), photocopies at HABS, PHC.

10. See briefs of title in files of PHC.

11. Elisabeth B. Walton, "The Building Art of Wilson Eyre: A Study of 'Queen Anne' Motifs in American Architecture" (M.A. thesis, Pennsylvania State University, 1962), p. 71; Building Permit 8964 (1923).

12. Registry Unit 4S1–162–68, 4S1–173.

13. Tatum, *Penn's Great Town*, pp. 93–94, 185, pl. 94; Harold N. Cooledge, Jr., "A Sloan Check List, 1849–1884," *JSAH* 19 (March 1960): 36.

14. Edward Teitelman and Richard W. Longstreth, *Architecture in Philadelphia: A Guide* (Cambridge, Mass.: MIT Press, 1974), p. 92; Julian Millard, "The Work of Wilson Eyre," *The Architectural Record* 14 (October 1903): 285, 311–12.

15. James C. Massey, "Frank Furness in the 1870's," *Charette* 43 (January 1963): 16; George E. Thomas and James F. O'Gorman, "Catalogue of Selected Buildings," in James F. O'Gorman, *The Architecture of Frank Furness* (Philadelphia: Philadelphia Museum of Art, 1973), p. 99.

16. *Philadelphia and Its Environs* (Philadelphia, 1875), p. 70; Registry Unit 2S23–8, 2S23–233; MA 8545, (September 22, 1883), PC 14047 (March 29, 1894), photocopies at HABS, PHC.

17. *PRERBG* 11 (June 10, 1896): 463; 11 (July 29, 1896): 619; Moses King, *Philadelphia and Notable Philadelphians* (New York: Moses King, 1902), p. 62.

18. Will Book 182 (1895), p. 358, City of Philadelphia, Department of Records; In-

ventory Book 23 (1895), p. 295 in ibid; Orphans' Court, Marriage License No. 99814 (1898); *Gopsill's Philadelphia City Directory for 1894* (Philadelphia: James Gopsill's Sons, 1894), p. 216.

19. *Sunday Bulletin,* April 28, 1974, August 18, 1974; *Philadelphia Inquirer,* October 5, 1974.

20. Norman J. Johnston, "The Caste and Class of the Urban Form of Historic Philadelphia," *Journal of the American Institute of Planners* 32 (November 1966): 334–38.

21. Agnes Addison Gilchrist, *William Strickland: Architect and Engineer, 1788–1854* (Philadelphia: University of Pennsylvania Press, 1950), pp. 34, 62.

22. Phoebe B. Stanton, *The Gothic Revival and American Church Architecture* (Baltimore: Johns Hopkins Press, 1968), pp. 115–25; Jonathan Fairbanks, "John Notman, Church Architect" (M.A. thesis, University of Delaware, 1960), pp. 74–79, 111–33.

23. Alfred Mortimer, *S. Mark's Church, Philadelphia, and Its Lady Chapel* (Philadelphia: By the author, 1909), pp. 22–33.

24. Both churches are documented and discussed by Fairbanks, "John Notman," pp. 88–89, 171–204.

25. May Lilly, *The Story of St. Clement's Church, Philadelphia* (Philadelphia: St. Clement's Church, 1964), p. 5.

26. *Evening Bulletin,* September 10, 1968, September 11, 1968, September 17, 1968, October 10, 1968; *Philadelphia Inquirer,* September 8, 1968, September 15, 1968, September 19, 1968; *Preservation News* 8 (October 1968): 1.

27. *PL,* August 4, 1853, October 7, 1853, November 18, 1870. The First Baptist Church is given as an illustration of the early Romanesque Revival by Carroll L. V. Meeks, "Romanesque before Richardson in the United States," *The Art Bulletin* 35 (March 1953): 17–33. The Arch Street Methodist Church measures up well in comparison with other noted Gothic Revival churches in Philadelphia. See James D. Van Trump, "The Gothic Fane," *Charette* 43 (September 1963): 61. The Arch Street Church is shown in Elizabeth Biddle Yarnall, *Addison Hutton: Quaker Architect, 1834–1916* (Philadelphia: The Art Alliance Press, 1974), pls. 9–10.

28. *PL,* March 9, 1898, April 20, 1898, May 16, 1898, June 23, 1898, December 3, 1898.

29. *PL,* March 10, 1853; *The Presbyterian,* May 28, 1853; Teitelman and Longstreth, *Architecture in Philadelphia,* pp. 94, 102.

30. George Frisbie Whicher, *This Was a Poet: A Critical Biography of Emily Dickinson* (New York: Charles Scribner's Sons, 1936), pp. 99–112. This theory is severely questioned by David Higgins, in *Portrait of Emily Dickinson* (New Brunswick, N.J.: Rutgers University Press, 1967), pp. 79–84.

31. "The Cash Book of the Treasurer of the Building Committee" (1852–1856), MSS, Arch Street Presbyterian Church.

32. *PL,* October 12, 1855.

33. Theo B. White et al., *Philadelphia Architecture in the Nineteenth Century* (Philadelphia: University of Pennsylvania Press, 1953), pp. 27–28, pls. 38, 39; Tatum, *Penn's Great Town,* pp. 94, 186.

34. Haviland's biographer sees the old Pump House, which still stood on Center Square during the 1820's, as the probable source for the institution's elements and composition, which Haviland integrated into a flat planar facade. Matthew Baigell, "John Haviland in Philadelphia," *JSAH* 25 (October 1966): 205–6.

35. The motivations for founding the Academy of Music and the details of the competition are explained by James V. Kavanaugh, "Three American Opera Houses:

The Boston Theatre, The New York Academy of Music, The Philadelphia American Academy of Music" (M.A. thesis, University of Delaware, 1967), pp. 52–60, and Tatum, *Penn's Great Town*, pp. 186–87. The hall's acoustics are still praised; the acoustician Leo L. Beranek considers the Academy "unquestionably the finest opera house in the United States" (*Music, Acoustics and Architecture* [New York: John Wiley & Sons, 1962], p. 165).

36. Tatum, *Penn's Great Town*, p. 95.

37. O'Gorman, *Architecture of Frank Furness*, pp. 32, 38.

38. Thompson Westcott, *The Official Guide Book to Philadelphia* (Philadelphia: Porter and Coates, 1875), p. 260; *PRERBG* 11 (July 1, 1896): 523.

39. The Philadelphia Club is the oldest city club not only in Philadelphia but also in the United States; started in 1834, it is two years older than New York's Union Club. See *The Philadelphia Club, 1834–1934* (Philadelphia, 1934). An engaging discussion of Philadelphia clubs is found in Nathaniel Burt, *The Perennial Philadelphians* (Boston: Little, Brown and Co., 1963), pp. 256–70.

40. Because of its size and function, the building has had only minimal changes during the club's tenure. MA 5520 (October 12, 1837; November 24, 1850; November 15, 1858; March 13, 1889), photocopies at PHC; brief of title in PHC files.

41. That distinction is now history; in late 1975 the club agreed to admit Democrats to membership. *Philadelphia Inquirer*, December 12, 1975; Westcott, *Official Guide*, pp. 247–49; *Sunday Bulletin*, February 11, 1962. For the club's history see Maxwell Whiteman, *Gentlemen in Crisis: The First Century of the Union League of Philadelphia, 1862–1962* (Phildelphia: Union League of Philadelphia, 1975).

42. Tatum, *Penn's Great Town*, p. 107.

43. Alfred Bendiner, *Bendiner's Philadelphia* (New York: A. S. Barnes and Co., 1964), p. 16.

44. *PRERBG* 23 (September 16, 1908): 597; 24 (February 10, 1909): 84; 25 (April 27, 1910): 256; 25 (November 9, 1910): 755; Building Permit 60 (1911).

45. A thorough study of the Masonic Temple's architectural competition is John C. Poppeliers, "The 1867 Philadelphia Masonic Temple Competition," *JSAH* 26 (December 1967): 279–84. For a layman's tour, see Jeannie Autret, "The Sumptuous Clubhouse," *Today: The Inquirer Magazine*, April 28, 1974, pp. 32–33, 35. A contemporary description is "The New Masonic Temple, Philadelphia," *The Architectural Review and American Builders' Journal* 1 (July 1868): 71–73.

46. Tatum, *Penn's Great Town*, p. 117; PC Surveyors' Reports Book 3 (February 25, 1888), p. 57.

47. *Evening Public Ledger*, October 24, 1940; *Philadelphia Record*, March 24, 1946; *Keystone Motorist* 38 (March 1946): 1.

48. *Philadelphia Inquirer*, December 17, 1975; *The New Paper*, January 3, 1976.

49. Richard J. Webster, "Stephen D. Button: Italianate Stylist" (M.A. thesis, University of Delaware, 1963), p. 87.

50. Thomas Hine paid tribute to these stores in *Philadelphia Inquirer*, August 18, 1974.

51. Westcott, *Official Guide*, p. 164; *PL*, August 24, 1875.

52. *PRERBG* 6 (August 6, 1890): 466; *PL*, August 9, 1890; DeWitt C. Baxter, *Baxter's Panoramic Business Directory of Philadelphia* (1880); King, *Philadelphia and Notable Philadelphians*, p. 23.

53. Joseph W. Appel, *The Business Biography of John Wanamaker* (New York: The Macmillan Co., 1930), pp. 74–91. Herbert Adams Gibbons, *John Wanamaker* (New York: Harper and Brothers, 1926), 1:212–39.

54. These two stations are discussed by Carroll L. V. Meeks in *The Railroad Station: An Architectural History* (New Haven: Yale University Press, 1956), pp. 103–4.

55. Tatum, *Penn's Great Town,* pp. 112, 196, pl. 121.

56. *PRERBG* 9 (April 4, 1894): 157; 9 (June 13, 1894): 277; 9 (August 1, 1894): 373; 9 (August 15, 1894): 399; *PL,* January 5, 1895, April 2, 1902.

57. *PRERBG* 8 (July 5, 1893): 413; 8 (August 2, 1893): 489; 8 (October 25, 1893): 653; *Philadelphia Record,* October 7, 1893.

58. Exhaustive descriptions of the Reading Terminal can be found in *PL,* October 14, 1893; *PRERBG* 7 (March 16, 1892): 1020; Walter G. Borg, *Buildings and Structures of American Railroads* (New York: John Wiley & Sons, 1893); and Joseph M. Wilson's eloquent and thorough description in *Transactions of the American Society of Civil Engineers,* 34 (August 1895): 115–84. The balloon shed's technology is explained by Carl W. Condit in *American Building Art: The Nineteenth Century* (New York: Oxford University Press, 1960), pp. 215–18, 329.

59. *PL,* June 9, 1897, May 3, 1898.

60. Carl W. Condit, *The Chicago School of Architecture* (Chicago: University of Chicago Press, 1964), p. 113, pl. 68; Thomas S. Hines, *Burnham of Chicago* (New York: Oxford University Press, 1974), pp. 288, 291.

61. King, *Philadelphia and Notable Philadelphians,* p. 14.

62. Tatum, *Penn's Great Town,* pp. 123, 200, pl. 131. *Golden Book of The Wanamaker Stores* (Philadelphia: John Wanamaker, 1911) contains many illustrations of the new store. A discussion of how its design and technology overcame engineering problems is in "A Modern Department Store: The Construction and Equipment of the Philadelphia Wanamaker Building," *The Architectural Record* 29 (March 1911): 277–88.

63. Tatum, *Penn's Great Town,* p. 200; *Philadelphia Inquirer,* January 21, 1972.

64. George E. Thomas claims that Frank Furness was responsible for the design and that McKim, Mead and White did only the details: "An Essay in Commercial Taste," Lecture at Philadelphia Art Alliance, February 12, 1976. The building is favorably evaluated in relation to its time and place by Tatum, *Penn's Great Town,* pp. 124, 200–201. Excellent photos and drawings of the bank are in *A Monograph of the Work of McKim, Mead & White, 1879–1915* (New York: The Architectural Book Publishing Co., [1915]), 4: pls. 329–31. It is praised in relation to contemporary banks in "Recent Bank Buildings of the United States," *The Architectural Record* 25 (January 1909): 8, 20–21.

65. This unintentional architectural irony does not alter the fact that the Crash and the subsequent Great Depression were disastrous for all associated with the construction industry. The number of issued building permits, which were required for additions, alterations, and demolitions as well as for new construction, plummeted from a high of 11,006 in 1927 to a low of 4,672 in 1933. After that the number climbed to 9,023 in 1937, but fell during the next year's economic downturn and continued to decline during World War II to only 2,945 building permits issued in 1944. It was not until the mid-1950's that the number of permits again reached that of 1927.

66. Tatum, *Penn's Great Town,* pp. 201–2; Agnes Addison Gilchrist, "The Classic Essence of Paul Cret," *Charette* 44 (January 1964): 40–43.

67. Theo B. White, *Paul Philippe Cret* (Philadelphia: The Art Alliance Press, 1973), pp. 21–31.

68. Paul Cret, "The New Building for the Federal Reserve Bank of Philadelphia," *The 3-C Book* 14 (September 1932): 35–36; Cret, "The New Federal Reserve Bank Building," *The 3-C Book* 15 (February 1934): 168–69; Cret, "Sculptural Decoration on Our New Building," *The 3-C Book* 16 (March 1935): 209–10.

69. For two of the most complete discussions of the building, see Robert A. M.

Stern, *George Howe: Toward a Modern American Architecture* (New Haven: Yale University Press, 1975), pp. 108–30; and William H. Jordy, *American Buildings and Their Architects: The Impact of European Modernism in the Mid-Twentieth Century* (New York: Doubleday & Co., 1972), pp. 87–164.

70. Building Permit 1084 (1932).

71. Tatum, *Penn's Great Town*, pp. 125–27, 201, pl. 133. The stages of the Parkway's development are illustrated in *The Fairmount Parkway* (Philadelphia: Fairmount Park Art Association, 1919).

72. A critique of the parkway by Michelle Osborne appeared in the *Evening Bulletin*, October 29, 1965; November 5, 1965; November 12, 1965. Lewis Mumford's acerbic commentary is in "The Sky Line: Philadelphia-I," *The New Yorker*, April 28, 1956; pp. 122–23.

73. James Reichley, "Philadelphia Does It: The Battle for Penn Center," *Harper's Magazine*, February 1957, pp. 49–56. "Philadelphia's Hour of Decision," *Architectural Forum* 96 (June 1952): 118–25.

74. *Penn Center: Redevelopment Area Plan* (rev. ed.; Philadelphia; Philadelphia City Planning Commission, 1952), p. 5.

75. *Progressive Architecture's* First Design Award of 1962 was presented "to the architect Vincent G. Kling *and* his client," the City of Philadelphia, for the MSB, as the Municipal Services Building is known: "Ninth Annual Design Awards," *Progressive Architecture* 43 (January 1962): 114–20. For an illustrated presentation of the building's plan and function, particularly the serviceable space of its lobby and concourse, see "M.S.B.: A Diamond in Philadelphia's Center City?" *Progressive Architecture* 46 (December 1965): 109–16.

76. Mayor's Committee on the Efficient and Appropriate Housing of City Functions, Survey of Municipal Facilities in Center City Area (October 1957).

South Philadelphia

1. For an excellent discussion of the relationship between the material culture of London and Philadelphia, see Margaret B. Tinkcom, "Urban Reflections in a Trans-Atlantic Mirror," *PMHB* 100 (July 1976): 287–313. For the early history of Southwark see J. Thomas Scharf and Thompson Westcott, *History of Philadelphia, 1609–1884* (Philadelphia: L. H. Everts & Co., 1884), 1:256; 3:1175.

2. Henry D. Paxson, *Where Pennsylvania History Began* (Philadelphia: By the author, 1926), p. 30.

3. Scharf and Westcott, *History of Philadelphia*, 1:7.

4. Amandus Johnson, *The Swedish Settlements on the Delaware* (Philadelphia: University of Pennsylvania Press, 1911), 1:117, 182–86; 2:581–616.

5. Hugh Morrison, *Early American Architecture* (New York: Oxford University Press, 1952), pp. 506, 509–10.

6. Paxson, *Where Pennsylvania History Began*, p. 55.

7. Joseph Jackson, *Encyclopedia of Philadelphia* (Harrisburg, Pa.: The National Historical Association, 1932), 3:911, 4:967.

8. Scharf and Westcott, *History of Philadelphia*, 1:684.

9. Before the oldest part of Southwark was demolished in the late 1960's for Interstate–95, an excellent study of the area was made through the cooperation of the American Philosophical Society, Historic American Buildings Survey, and the Philadelphia Historical Commission. See Margaret B. Tinkcom, "Southwark, A River

Community: Its Shape and Substance," in *Proceedings of the American Philosophical Society* 114 (August 1970): 327–42. Hereafter cited as Tinkcom, "Southwark."

10. Edwin Iwanicki, Brief of Title, 770 South Front Street, Philadelphia (1961), PHC; PC 4030 (July 28, 1818), photocopies at HABS, PHC.

11. William John Murtagh, "The Philadelphia Row House," *JSAH* 16 (December 1957): 9.

12. *Philadelphia Inquirer*, June 10, 1969.

13. Will No. 70 (May 16, 1758), Inventory of Estate of George Mifflin, (1759), MSS, City of Philadelphia, Register of Wills.

14. MA 6183 (June 26, 1850), photocopies at HABS, PHC.

15. MA 6184 (June 26, 1850), photocopies at HABS, PHC.

16. MA 3272 (June 1812); MA 3425 (April 1813); MA 3426 (April 1813), photocopies at HABS, PHC; Richard S. Fuller, Brief of Title, Workman Place (1961), PHC.

17. Octavia Hill Association, Inc. leaflet (1961), copy at PHC.

18. Beatrice H. Kirkbride, "Nathaniel Irish House," HABS Report (PA–1013), p. 1.

19. Peter Kalm, *The America of 1750: Peter Kalm's Travels in North America. The English Version of 1770 revised from the Original Swedish with a Translation of New Material from Kalm's Diary Notes*, ed. Adolph B. Benson (New York: Dover Publications, 1966), 1: 99–100.

20. James Mease, *The Picture of Philadelphia* (Philadelphia: B. & T. Kite, 1811), p. 33. He lists 1,466 frame dwellings as compared to 834 brick houses.

21. Survey 2729 (February 13, 1803), MSS, Archives of INA.

22. The LaTour Warehouse was a block north of Southwark in Society Hill, but it was representative of early-nineteenth-century storehouses in the maritime neighborhood. James C. Massey, James Glen Carr and Osmund R. Overby, "John LaTour Warehouse," HABS Report (PA–1056), p. 1.

23. Scharf and Westcott, *History of Philadelphia*, 1:490, 3:2339–40.

24. *Aurora*, October 20, 1808; Stephen N. Winslow, *Biographies of Successful Philadelphia Merchants* (Philadelphia: James K. Simon, 1864), p. 142; M. Antonia Lynch, "Southwark," *Philadelphia History* 1 (1917): 104; Registry Unit 6S12–45. Description, plan, and view of the Shot Tower are in *Hexamer General Surveys* 16 (1880): pl. 1491.

25. Registry Unit 4S22–81, 315, 350; Building Permit 707 (1922).

26. The need for a professional municipal fire department by 1871 is illustrated by the turbulent history of the fierce competition among the volunteer companies. See Andrew J. Neilly, "The Violent Volunteers: A History of the Volunteer Fire Department of Philadelphia, 1736–1871" (Ph.D. dissertation, University of Pennsylvania, 1959), pp. 70–84, 179–82. For a discussion of the social and political roles of Southwark's fire companies, see Bruce Laurie, "Fire Companies and Gangs in Southwark: The 1840's," in *The Peoples of Philadelphia*, ed. Allen F. Davis and Mark H. Haller (Philadelphia: Temple University Press, 1973), pp. 71–88.

27. Hope Engine Company Minutes, 1847–1857, Fire Company Records, MSS, HSP. A brief discussion of the Hoxie and Button partnership and a list of their works are in Richard J. Webster, "Stephen D. Button: Italianate Stylist" (M.A. thesis, University of Delaware, 1963), pp. 54–61, 84–86, 95–97.

28. Registry Unit 5S15–249; *First Annual Message of William S. Stokley, Mayor of the City of Philadelphia, with the Accompanying Documents, June 26, 1873*, pp. 554–56, 663–707. Hereafter mayors' annual messages cited by name and year.

29. *PL*, May 15, 1893; *PRERBG* 8 (September 6, 1893): 569. Two early views of the fire house are cited in Nicholas B. Wainwright, *Philadelphia in the Romantic Age of Li-*

thography (Philadelphia: Historical Society of Pennsylvania, 1958), pp. 108, 220. A lithograph showing both the 1840's fire house and the enlarged building of the late 1850's is at the Insurance Company of North America Museum. Unfortunately, the 1890's sashes were replaced by simplified single-pane or one-over-one sashes during the building's rehabilitation in 1969.

30. Franklin Davenport Edmunds, *The Public School Buildings of the City of Philadelphia from 1868 to 1874* (Philadelphia: By the author, 1925), pp. 21–24; Building Permit 1502 (1928); Harold N. Cooledge, "Samuel Sloan and the "Philadelphia Plan,' " *JSAH* 23 (October 1964): 151–54.

31. *Historical Sketches of the Catholic Churches and Institutions of Philadelphia* (Philadelphia: Daniel H. Mahoney, 1895), p. 67; Scharf and Westcott, *History of Philadelphia*, 1: 669–71; 2: 1392; *PRERBG* 12 (October 20, 1897): 671; 12; (December 8, 1897): 795; *PL*, October 28, 1897.

32. *Philadelphia Inquirer*, October 1, 1974.

33. James C. Massey, "Frank Furness in the 1870's," *Charette* 43 (January 1963): 16.

34. *Evening Bulletin*, January 10, 1964.

35. These conclusions are based on a study of the house made by Professor Herbert A. Richardson, Glassboro State College, Glassboro, N.J.

36. William B. Bassett, "Stephen Girard's Country House," HABS Report (PA–140), pp. 1–2.

37. Scharf and Westcoff, *History of Philadelphia*, 2:1014–15, 3:2339.

38. Ibid., 1:361–64.

39. It should be noted that the motivation for building the magazine in South Philadelphia was not solely, or even primarily, war fears but that people living near the old magazine at Twenty-third and Walnut streets were apprehensive about its safety. Paxson, *Where Pennsylvania History Began*, p. 62.

40. Agnes Addison Gilchrist, *William Strickland: Architect and Engineer, 1788–1854* (Philadelphia: University of Pennsylvania Press, 1950), p. 73; Edward Shippen, "Some Account of the Origin of the Naval Asylum at Philadelphia," *PMHB* 7 (1883): 129.

41. William B. Bassett, "United States Naval Asylum," HABS Report (PA–1094), p. 3.

42. George B. Tatum, *Penn's Great Town* (Philadelphia: University of Pennsylvania Press, 1961), p. 80.

43. Alan Gowans, *Images of American Living: Four Centuries of Architecture and Furniture as Cultural Express* (Philadelphia: J. B. Lippincott Co., 1964), pp. 291–301.

44. For discussions of the source and symbolism of the Egyptian Revival, see Frank J. Roos, Jr., "The Egyptian Style: Notes on Early American Taste," *Magazine of Art* 33 (April 1940): 218–33, 255; Richard G. Carrott, "The Neo-Egyptian Style in American Architecture," *Antiques* 90 (October 1966): 482–88.

45. John Daly and Allen Weinberg, *Genealogy of Philadelphia County Subdivisions* (2d ed.; Philadelphia: Department of Records, 1966), pp. 64, 84.

46. George Morgan, *City of Firsts* (Philadelphia: Historical Publication Society in Philadelphia, 1926), p. 308.

47. *Philadelphia: A Guide to the Nation's Birthplace* (Philadelphia: William Penn Association of Philadelphia, 1937), pp. 98–106.

48. Thomas Nolan, "Some Recent Philadelphia Architecture," *The Architectural Record* 29 (March 1911): 235.

49. *PL*, May 8, 1876; September 6, 1901; March 10, 1902; April 5, 1902; April 26, 1902; *PRERBG* 17 (April 16, 1902): 241; 27 (May 8, 1912): 303; James D. Van Trump,

"The Column and the Cross in Philadelphia: Three Victorian Classical Churches by Edwin F. Durang," *Charette* 48 (January 1967): 9–12.

50. The city acquired the properties between 1898 and 1900, but a plan was not chosen until 1911. Work was interrupted in 1912, however, when the courts declared unconstitutional the issuance of the supplemental contracts. That matter was resolved by 1917, and the project was begun again only to be delayed by World War I. The public bathing beaches were opened in the summer of 1922 and the final plantings were made and pathways were paved the next year; land for the golf course was purchased between 1927 and 1930. Deeds to City Property, Box No. 93–M, MSS, Philadelphia City Archives; *First Annual Message of Rudolph Blankenburg, 1911,* p. 286; *Second Annual Message of Rudolph Blankenburg, 1912,* p. 14; *Second Annual Message of Thomas B. Smith, 1917,* 2:132–34; *Third Annual Message of J. Hampton Moore, 1922,* p. 119; *Fourth Annual Message of J. Hampton Moore, 1923,* p. 227; [Second] *Annual Message of W. Freeland Kendrick, 1925,* pp. 13–19.

51. *Philadelphia: A Guide to the Nation's Birthplace,* p. 449.

52. Ibid., p. 447.

53. Ellis Paxson Oberholtzer, *Philadelphia: A History of the City and Its People* (Philadelphia: S. J. Clarke Publishing Co., 1911), 2:407–9; Theo B. White, *Philadelphia Architecture in the Nineteenth Century* (Philadelphia: University of Pennsylvania Press, 1953), pp. 31–32.

54. The erection of the railroad's passenger station at Broad Street and Washington Avenue in 1857 seemed to promise economic vitality for the neighborhood, but in time the tracks running east to the Delaware River proved to be more of a barrier than a gateway. *Nineteenth Annual Report of the President and Directors to the Stockholders of the Philadelphia, Wilmington and Baltimore Railroad Company* (Philadelphia, 1857), p. 28.

55. A brief history of the Library Company's stay in its Broad Street quarters and the arguments for its removal are presented in *Why the Library Company Should Move* (Philadelphia: Library Company of Philadelphia, 1960).

56. For a readable account of the social changes being wrought by the renaissance of Southwark, see Carol Byrne, "Queen Village Comes Out of the Closet," *Philadelphia Magazine,* July 1974, pp. 86–91, 158–59, 163–69.

57. Some observers fear, however, that success has spoiled South Street, that during the mid-1970's rising rents east of Sixth Street forced out of the neighborhood many colorful and unconventional shopkeepers that gave the street a bohemian atmosphere. See Kit Konolige, "The Saviors of South Street," *Today: The Inquirer Magazine,* January 27, 1974, pp. 8–14; *Philadelphia Inquirer,* March 7, 1976.

West Philadelphia

1. The first house reputed to have been built in West Philadelphia was John Warner's mansion on or near the present site of Sweetbrier in Fairmount Park. It was dismantled in the 1790's and its timbers were used in building Colonel Edward Heston's house near Fifty-second Street and Lancaster Avenue; the latter dwelling was demolished in 1901 during expansion of the Pennsylvania Railroad. M. Laffitte Viera, *West Philadelphia Illustrated* (Philadelphia: Avil Printing Co., 1903), p. 103.

2. Harold Donaldson Eberlein and Cortlandt Van Dyke Hubbard, *Portrait of a Colonial City: Philadelphia, 1670–1838* (Philadelphia: J. B. Lippincott Co., 1939), pp. 81–84.

3. Hugh Morrison, *Early American Architecture* (New York: Oxford University

Press, 1952), p. 519. A photograph of the house before restoration appears in Viera, *West Philadelphia Illustrated*, p. 92.

4. Eberlein and Hubbard, *Portrait of a Colonial City*, p. 245.

5. Robert Patterson Robins, "Colonel James Coultas, High Sheriff of Philadelphia, 1755–1758," *PMHB* 11 (1887): 50–57.

6. Blank end walls are rare but not unique in Philadelphia country houses. Mount Pleasant (1761) in Fairmount Park has blank end walls two rooms deep, and Bel Air (c. 1714–29) in South Philadelphia has blank end walls one room deep.

7. The only other Philadelphia dwelling known to have urns on it is Cliveden in Germantown. See Margaret B. Tinkcom, "Cliveden: The Building of a Country Seat, 1763–1767," *PMHB* 88 (January 1964): 10. Both the exterior and interior of Whitby Hall are illustrated in Harold Donaldson Eberlein, "Three Types of Georgian Architecture: The Evolution of the Style in Philadelphia," *The Architectural Record* 34 (July 1913): 73–77.

8. Harold Donaldson Eberlein, ed., "Passages from the Diary of Nicholas Pickford Esquire, Relating to His Travels in Pennsylvania in 1765," *The Architectural Review* 47 (June 1920): 145–46.

9. Eberlein and Hubbard, *Portrait of a Colonial City*, pp. 246, 249. Charles E. Peterson, F.A.I.A., tracked down the location of Whitby Hall's woodwork in the fall of 1975.

10. Thompson Westcott, *The Historic Mansions and Buildings of Philadelphia* (rev. ed.; Philadelphia: Walter H. Barr, 1895), p. 182.

11. Ernest Earnest, *John and William Bartram: Botanists and Explorers* (Philadelphia: University of Pennsylvania Press, 1940), pp. 28–33, 60–67; Brooke Hindle, *The Pursuit of Science in Revolutionary America* (Chapel Hill: University of North Carolina Press, 1956), pp. 20–27.

12. For example, see James Gibbs, *A Book of Architecture* (London, 1728), pl. 91; Batty Langley, *The City and Country Builder's and Workman's Treasury of Designs* (London, 1750), pls. 50, 80, 82, 85, 89; Abraham Swan, *The British Architect* (London, 1758), pls. 51, 53, and perhaps the most logical source, *The Rules of Work of the Carpenters' Company of the City and County of Philadelphia, 1786*, annotated by Charles E. Peterson (Princeton: Pyne Press, 1971), pl. 27.

13. Earnest, *John and William Bartram*, pp. 66–67.

14. Eberlein and Hubbard, *Portrait of a Colonial City*, pp. 448–50; Westcott, *Historic Mansions*, pp. 416–22.

15. Sarah P. Stetson, "William Hamilton and His 'Woodlands,' " *PMHB* 73 (January 1949): 26–27.

16. Harold Donaldson Eberlein, ed., "Further Passages from the Diary of Nicholas Pickford Esquire, Relating to His Travels in Pennsylvania in 1786," *The Architectural Review* 48 (July 1920): 30–31.

17. Deed Book RLL 37–139. The cemetery company acquired additional Hamilton property in 1853 and 1867. Deed Books TH 173–546, JTO 32–446.

18. "Hamilton Mansion," *Gleason's Pictorial Drawing-Room Companion*, April 15, 1854, p. 232.

19. The bridge was called permanent because it replaced a form of pontoon bridge, not because of its expected longevity. In fact, the builder, Timothy Palmer, estimated its life expectancy as only thirty or forty years, yet it survived until 1875, when a fire ended its service. David B. Steinman and Sara Ruth Watson, *Bridges and Their Builders* (New York: Dover Publications, 1941), p. 118; Carl W. Condit, *American Build-*

ing Art: The Nineteenth Century (New York: Oxford University Press, 1960), pp. 80–82; Joseph Jackson, *Market Street, Philadelphia: America's Most Historic Highway* (new ed.; Philadelphia: John Wanamaker, 1926), p. 33.

20. Busti was general agent for the Holland Land Company, which received about five million acres of land in western Pennsylvania and New York from the federal government in lieu of a money payment for a loan to the Continental Congress during the Revolutionary War. "Notes and Queries," *PMHB* 7 (1883): 107–8. Although Busti called his estate a farm, the interior elements as well as the columned southern veranda (or piazza) and northern porch were those of a late-eighteenth-century country house rather than a farmhouse. MA 2149 (March 15, 1806), photocopies at HABS, PHC.

21. John Hare Powel, born John Powel Hare, was the nephew and heir of the eminent merchant Samuel Powel, who served as the city's mayor under both the Crown and the new republic. For the nephew's biography, see Henry Simpson, *The Lives of Eminent Philadelphians* (Philadelphia: William Brotherhead, 1859), pp. 808–19. An evaluation of him as a proper Philadelphian who "did nothing, and did it well" is in Nathaniel Burt, *The Perennial Philadelphians* (Boston: Little, Brown and Co., 1963), pp. 156–57. The main section of Powelton was built for Samuel Powel's widow in 1800–1802; John Hare Powel was responsible for the notable Doric pediment, designed by William Strickland in 1825, and the wings, which were finished in the mid-1840's. Charles B. Wood III, "Powelton: An Unrecorded Building by William Strickland," *PMHB* 91 (April 1967): 147–48, 151–55.

22. Townsend Ward, "A Walk to Darby," *PMHB* 3 (1879): 165–66.

23. Jackson, *Market Street*, p. 332.

24. Joseph Jackson, *Encyclopedia of Philadelphia* (Harrisburg, Pa.: The National Historical Association, 1932), 3:868. J. C. Sidney, *Map of the City of Philadelphia* (Philadelphia: Smith and Wistar, 1849).

25. Nicholas B. Wainwright, ed., *A Philadelphia Perspective: The Diary of Sidney George Fisher Covering the Years 1834–1871* (Philadelphia: Historical Society of Pennsylvania, 1967), p. 169.

26. The hospital of the almshouse received patients during the cholera epidemic of 1832, but the complex was not finished until 1835. There were a number of later additions, beginning with a workshop in 1860. Agnes Addison Gilchrist, "Additions to William Strickland: Architect and Engineer, 1788–1854," *JSAH* 13 (October 1954): Supplement, 4; Charles Lawrence, comp., *History of the Philadelphia Almshouses and Hospitals from the Beginning of the Eighteenth to the Ending of the Nineteenth Centuries* (Philadelphia: By the author, 1905), pp. 110–12, 116–18, 134–36, 256; *Philadelphia Hospital Reports* (Philadelphia, 1890), 1:91–106. For a glimpse of life in the institution, see Alexander Ames Bliss, *Blockley Days: Memories and Impressions of a Resident Physician, 1883–1884* (Philadelphia: By the author, 1916).

27. David J. Rothman, *The Discovery of the Asylum: Social Order and Disorder in the New Republic* (Boston: Little, Brown and Co., 1971), pp. 155–89.

28. J. Thomas Scharf and Thompson Westcott, *History of Philadelphia, 1609–1884* (Philadelphia: L. H. Everts & Co., 1884), 2:1671.

29. Rothman, *Discovery of the Asylum*, pp. 130–38, 141.

30. Harold N. Cooledge, Jr., has made a case for Samuel Sloan as the architect responsible for the plan and form of the nineteenth-century insane asylum, but Sloan was evidently emulating Holden, since Sloan's 1856 Pennsylvania Hospital for the Insane at Forty-ninth and Market streets was nearly identical in plan, design, and appointments to Holden's hospital at Forty-fourth and Market streets, where the young

Sloan superintended the construction. Furthermore, Holden's building possessed in the 1840's those features that the Association of Medical Superintendents considered fundamental in 1851, two years before Sloan's first independent commission for an insane asylum. Sloan was certainly the propagator of the style, as the thirty-two insane asylums from his designs and a number of articles from his pen testify, but Holden appears to have been the author. Holden lost his opportunity to become America's hospital architect when he returned to England in 1838. Harold N. Cooledge, Jr., "Samuel Sloan and the Philadelphia School of Hospital Design," *Charette* 44 (June 1964): 6–7, 18; Thomas G. Morton, *The History of the Pennsylvania Hospital, 1751–1895* (Philadelphia: Times Printing House, 1895), pp. 165, 174–76; PC 5602 (October 16, 1840), PC 10331–33 (March 6, 1861), photocopies at HABS, PHC; Rothman, *Discovery of the Asylum,* p. 135; Wainwright, ed., *Philadelphia Perspective,* pp. 440–41.

31. Robert C. Smith, "Two Centuries of Philadelphia Architecture, 1700–1900," *Historic Philadelphia,* 301.

32. PC 5602 (October 16, 1840), photocopies at HABS, PHC; Cooledge, "Samuel Sloan and the Pennsylvania School," pp. 6–7. Rothman, *Discovery of the Asylum,* p. 134.

33. James C. Massey, ed., *Two Centuries of Philadelphia Architectural Drawings* (Philadelphia: Philadelphia Museum of Art, 1964), pp. 64–65; Thompson Westcott, *The Official Guide Book of Philadelphia* (Philadelphia: Porter and Coates, 1875), pp. 217–18, 224–25; Scharf and Westcott, *History of Philadelphia,* 2:1676, 1682; *First Annual Report of the Presbyterian Hospital in Philadelphia* (Philadelphia, 1872), pp. 5–9; *Third Annual Report of the Presbyterian Hospital* (Philadelphia, 1874), pp. 52–56.

34. Scharf and Westcott, *History of Philadelphia,* 2:1684; *PL,* April 21, 1886; April 28, 1886; August 16, 1890; April 2, 1897; July 3, 1897; *Philadelphia Record,* August 2, 1893.

35. The contrasting nature of the two townships is illustrated by the fact that in 1840, when 61.1 per cent of the people of Blockley were engaged in manufacturing and commerce, 77.3 per cent of the people of Kingsessing were farming. Scharf and Westcott, *History of Philadelphia,* 1:676, 697, 713; *Heads of Families at the First Census of the United States Taken in the Year 1790: Pennsylvania* (Washington, D.C.: Government Printing Office, 1908), p. 10; *Sixth Census or Enumeration of the Inhabitants of the United States, as Corrected at the Department of State, in 1840* (Washington, D.C.: Blair and Rives, 1841), p. 151; *The Seventh Census of the United States: 1850* (Washington, D.C.: Robert Armstrong, Public Printer, 1853), pp. 178–79; John Daly and Allen Weinberg, *Genealogy of Philadelphia County Subdivisions* (2d ed.; Philadelphia: City of Philadelphia, 1966), p. 64.

36. Harold E. Cox, "Horse Passenger Railways of Philadelphia," *Pennsylvania Traction,* May, 1963, pp. 1–18.

37. Harold Norman Cooledge, Jr., "Samuel Sloan, Architect" (Ph.D. dissertation, University of Pennsylvania, 1963), pp. 50–55.

38. For a discussion of the innovative and picturesque qualities of the Italian villa, see Alan Gowans, *Images of American Living: Four Centuries of Architecture and Furniture as Cultural Expression* (Philadelphia: J. B. Lippincott Co., 1964), pp. 316–27; and George B. Tatum, *Penn's Great Town* (Philadelphia: University of Pennsylvania Press, 1961), pp. 92–94.

39. PC 12021 (July 20, 1874), photocopies at HABS, PHC; Registry Unit 20S9–4; Edward Scully Bradley, *Henry Charles Lea: A Biography* (Philadelphia: University of Pennsylvania Press, 1931), pp. 79–80.

40. *PL,* January 2, 1854; Robert A. Corrigan, Brief of Title, 4207 Walnut Street, Philadelphia (1959), MSS, PHC.

41. Cooledge, "Samuel Sloan, Architect," p. 65.

42. *PL*, March 14, 1863; Cox, "Horse Passenger Railways," pp. 9–11.

43. *PRERBG*, 6 (June 3, 1891): 338; 6 (August 5, 1891): 495; *PL*, May 30, 1893; Moses King, *Philadelphia and Notable Philadelphians* (New York: Moses King, 1902), pp. 68–69; Julian Millard, "The Work of Wilson Eyre," *The Architectural Record* 14 (October 1904): 307–8.

44. Housing construction began west of Forty-fifth Street shortly after the twentieth century began. For example, in the spring of 1901, 222 houses, both twins and singles, were begun on the block bounded by Fifty-first, Fifty-second, Brown, and Parrish streets, and in the same year Wilson Brothers and Company designed twenty-eight row houses for the neighborhood of Fifty-eighth and Arch streets. *PL*, March 19, 1901; May 21, 1901.

Building activity in the area significantly increased after work on the El began in 1903 (see *PL*, April 7, 1903). A month after the El's inauguration, developers were running half-page illustrated ads announcing that their row houses were within two-and-a-half blocks from the Elevated and only ten minutes away from City Hall (see *PL*, April 6, 1907). The Market Street Elevated opened, March 4, 1907, running between Sixty-ninth and Fifteenth streets. A year and a half later it was extended to Second Street (*PL*, March 4, 1907; March 5, 1907; August 3, 1908).

45. *PL*, August 24, 1901; *Building* 9 (July 1929): 7–8. Philadelphia's first apartment hotel, the Gladstone, was erected at Eleventh and Pine streets, 1889–90. George Morgan, *The City of Firsts* (Philadelphia: The Historical Publication Society in Philadelphia, 1926), p. 309; *PRERBG* 4 (November 20, 1889): 549; 5 (January 29, 1890): 37.

46. Vincent Scully, Jr., *Louis I. Kahn* (New York: George Braziller, 1962), pp. 22, 31–32.

47. Cox, "Horse Passenger Railways," pp. 7–8; *PL*, April 19, 1896.

48. Edward Potts Cheyney, *History of the University of Pennsylvania, 1740–1940* (Philadelphia: University of Pennsylvania Press, 1940), pp. 261–63.

49. Annie Gardiner Richards, "Thomas W. Richards and College Hall," *The General Magazine and Historical Chronicle* 53 (Summer 1951): 193–98; Tatum, *Penn's Great Town*, pp. 118–22; George E. Thomas and James F. O'Gorman, "Catalogue of Selected Buildings," in James F. O'Gorman, *The Architecture of Frank Furness* (Philadelphia: Philadelphia Museum of Art, 1973), pp. 165–71; *PL*, May 11, 1897; July 3, 1897. For a generally favorable evaluation of the university's architecture by America's foremost architectural critic of the early twentieth century, see Montgomery Schuyler, "Architecture of American Colleges, V: University of Pennsylvania, Girard, Haverford, Lehigh and Bryn Mawr," *The Architectural Record* 28 (September 1910): 183–200.

50. Quote from Scully, *Louis I. Kahn*, p. 26. Except for Horace Trumbauer's Irvine Auditorium (c. 1926) at Thirty-fourth and Spruce streets, the important architectural works on the Pennsylvania campus are identified in Edward Teitelman and Richard W. Longstreth, *Architecture in Philadelphia: A Guide* (Cambridge, Mass.: MIT Press, 1974), pp. 188–93. Hill House, the women's dormitory at Thirty-fourth and Walnut streets, is not one of Saarinen's greatest works, but it does rate brief commentary: "Court for Coeds at the University of Pennsylvania," *Architectural Forum* 114 (February 1961): 120–21; Allan Temko, *Eero Saarinen* (New York: George Braziller, 1962), p. 117; Rupert Spade, *Eero Saarinen* (London: Thames and Hudson, 1971), p. 123.

Mitchell/Giurgola Associates completed a second poured-concrete parking garage for the university at South Street and Civic Center Boulevard in 1969. The interior organization and treatment of the two structures are similar, and they almost make driving into a parking garage pleasurable, but because of their sites their exterior appearances differ. The isolation of the earlier garage allows an independent boldness, but the proximity of Franklin Field to the latter apparently pressured the architects to employ a symmetry and monumentality of scale that leaves its design less imposing than its predecessor. "University Parking Garage for University of Pennsylvania," *Progressive Architecture* 45 (December 1964): 146–51; "Parking Garage de l'Université de Pennsylvanie, Philadelphie," *Architecture d'Aujourd'hui* 35 (March 1965): 46–47; *Evening Bulletin,* November 26, 1965; May 23, 1969.

The Richards Building is acclaimed for its functional expression and economical use of prestressed reinforced concrete. The blank brick service towers, which project above the flat roofline and contrast with the slender concrete columns and cantilevered spandrels, give the building its dynamic quality, actually a nineteenth-century picturesqueness. For a discussion of the evolution of the building's design and a bibliography of the building, see Scully, *Louis I. Kahn,* pp. 27–31, 124–25.

51. After the death of his father Francis W. Drexel in 1863, Anthony J. Drexel (1826–1893), who had been a partner in Drexel and Company since 1847, continued the family's esteemed name in investment banking in Philadelphia, while his brother Joseph W. formed Drexel, Harjes and Company in Paris, and Francis A. moved to New York where he made J. P. Morgan a junior partner in Drexel, Morgan and Company. Scharf and Westcott, *History of Philadelphia,* 3:2101–2; Burton Alva Konkle, "Francis Martin Drexel and Philadelphia Leadership in International Finance," *The Girard Letter* 14 (December 1933): 1–2. For the construction of the school's main building, see Edward D. McDonald and Edward M. Hinton, *Drexel Institute of Technology, 1891–1941* (Philadelphia: Drexel Institute of Technology, 1942), pp. 18–26, 43–45; *PL,* April 19, 1890; April 23, 1890; January 13, 1892.

52. Building Permit 5079 (1930).

53. St. Joseph's College began in 1851 on Willing's Alley in an addition to the parish house of St. Joseph's Roman Catholic Church. After a brief tenure on Center Square, at the northeast corner of Filbert and Juniper streets, the college in 1868 became part of the notable Jesuit complex around Eighteenth and Stiles streets in North Philadelphia, and it was from that site that it moved to Wynnefield. Francis X. Talbot, *Jesuit Education in Philadelphia: St. Joseph's College, 1851–1926* (Philadelphia: St. Joseph's College, 1927), pp. 36–38, 51–52, 73–77, 128–41.

54. Grandiose, if not grand, the Thirtieth Street Station was built in 1927–34 from the designs of Graham, Anderson, Probst, and White, but its washed-out classicism, as Carroll L. V. Meeks noted, "was old-fashioned before it left the drafting board." *The Railroad Station: An Architectural History* (New Haven: Yale University Press, 1956), p.103. The Bulletin Building was designed in 1953 by George Howe in collaboration with Robert Montgomery Brown. Although its appearance—a gray brick block, with strips of windows, that rests on a glass and stainless-steel loggia—is indebted to Mies van der Rohe, its critical reception has been mixed. Some Philadelphians simply don't like it (Burt, *Perennial Philadelphians,* p. 364), but Lewis Mumford, who found a lot of little things wrong with it, concluded that "it vies with William Strickland's old Custom House as one of the best examples of the classic tradition in Philadelphia" ("The Skyline: Philadelphia—II," *The New Yorker,* May 26, 1956, p. 127).

55. Leon S. Rosenthal, *A History of Philadelphia's University City* (Philadelphia: West Philadelphia Corporation, 1963), pp. 73–80.

56. See Thomas Hine's "Surroundings" column in *Philadelphia Inquirer*, February 8, 1976, for a statement of the problem; for its resolution, see Jan Schaffer's article in *Philadelphia Inquirer*, May 29, 1976.

57. Churches were as much a part of Victorian residential neighborhoods as front porches and grassy plots, and occasionally were part of the development plan. When William Hamilton, for example, laid out Hamilton Village he reserved a lot on Locust Street west of Thirty-ninth Street for what was to become St. Mary's Episcopal Church, which has been in a state of almost continuous evolution since its second structure was begun in 1872. The erosion of residential West Philadelphia and the growth of University City threaten the survival of such architectural gems as Edwin F. Durang's St. Agatha's Roman Catholic Church (1874–78) at Thirty-eighth and Spring Garden Theophilus Parsons Chandler's Tabernacle Presbyterian Church (illus.) (1884–86) at Thirty-seventh and Chestnut streets, Charles M. Burns's Church of the Saviour (1889, rebuilt after 1902 fire) at Thirty-eighth and Ludlow streets, Frank R. Watson's Tabernacle Baptist Church (1896–97) near Fortieth and Chestnut streets, and Carrère's and Hastings's (with T. E. Blake) First Church of Christ Scientist (1909–10) at Fortieth and Walnut streets. The Mary Elizabeth Patterson Memorial Church at Sixty-third and Vine Streets, an imaginative interplay of screened spaces and robust forms by Chandler (1885, 1895–97), got a new lease on life in 1975 when the Church of Christ congregation took over the structure. Still abandoned and facing an uncertain future in 1976 is the Philadelphia Divinity School chapel, a chaste twentieth-century Gothic design by Zantzinger, Borie and Medary (1925–26) that takes advantage of its elevated site on Spruce Street west of Forty-second.

Fairmount Park

1. Quoted in John Maass, *The Glorious Enterpise* (Watkins Glen, N.Y.: American Life Foundation, 1973), p. 24.

2. The most comprehensive work on the park is Esther M. Klein, *Fairmount Park: A History and a Guidebook* (Bryn Mawr, Pa.: Harcum Junior College Press, 1974). Also useful is Theo B. White, *Fairmount Park* (Philadelphia: Philadelphia Art Alliance, 1975).

3. *Antiques* magazine devoted its November 1962 issue to the Fairmount Park houses. There are fully illustrated, well-researched articles on the history and architecture of six of the more notable houses: Cedar Grove, Lemon Hill, Mount Pleasant, Strawberry Mansion, Sweetbrier, and Woodford. There are vignettes about the other houses, as well as articles on some owners of park houses and their portraits and the origins of the park. A scholarly investigation of the interior woodwork of some of these houses is Martin E. Weil, "Interior Architectural Details in Eighteenth-Century Architectural Books and Philadelphia County Houses" (M.A. thesis, University of Delaware, 1967).

4. Nelson Manfred Blake, *Water for the Cities* (Syracuse: Syracuse University Press, 1956), pp. 36–39, 78–79; George B. Tatum, "The Origins of Fairmount Park," *Antiques* 82 (November 1962): 502–3.

5. *Report of the Watering Committee, Read January 9, 1823* (Philadelphia, 1823), p.7; *Annual Report of the Watering Committee, for the Year 1852* (Philadelphia, 1852), pp. 28–29; Thomas Wilson, *Picture of Philadelphia, in 1824* (Philadelphia: T. Town, 1823), pp. 26–34; Harold Donaldson Eberlein, "The Fairmount Waterworks, Philadelphia," *The Architectural Record* 62 (July 1927):65.

6. J. Thomas Scharf and Thompson Westcott, *History of Philadelphia, 1609–1884* (Philadelphia: L. H. Everts & Co., 1884), 3:1853; George B. Tatum, *Penn's Great Town* (Philadelphia: University of Pennsylvania Press, 1961), pp. 63–64.

7. Scharf and Westcott, *History of Philadelphia,* 3:1854; Tatum, "The Origins of Fairmount Park," pp. 503–4; Tatum, *Penn's Great Town,* p. 64, pl. 52; Charles Dickens, *American Notes* (London: Oxford University Press, 1957), p. 98.

8. Eberlein, "The Fairmount Waterworks, Philadelphia," pp. 65–66; *Annual Report of the Chief Engineer of the Water Department of the City of Philadelphia, 1868* (Philadelphia, 1868), p. 8. These reports hereafter cited as *Annual Report. Annual Report,* 1869, pp. 5–7; *Annual Report, 1873,* p. 6; *PL,* July 25, 1872.

9. Laurel Hill ranked with Cambridge's Mount Auburn Cemetery and Brooklyn's Greenwood Cemetery, and was particularly praised for its plantings and river view. The concept of rural cemeteries originated abroad with the Père-Lachaise near Paris and the General Cemetery Company at Kensal Green near London; Notman's plan was based on the latter. For a discussion of the cemetery's sculpture, see George Thomas, "The Statue in the Garden," in *Sculpture of a City,* ed. Nicholas B. Wainwright (New York: Walker Publishing Co., 1973), pp. 36–44; Tatum, *Penn's Great Town,* p. 87, pl. 88; *Guide to Laurel Hill Cemetery near Philadelphia* (Philadelphia: Laurel Hill Cemetery Co., 1844), p. 53; R. A. Smith, *Smith's Illustrated Guide to and through Laurel Hill Cemetery* (Philadelphia: W. P. Hazard, 1852); *Rules and Regulations of Laurel Hill Cemetery of Philadelphia* (Philadelphia: Laurel Hill Cemetery Co. 1892), pp. 8–10; Theo B. White, *Philadelphia Architecture of the Nineteenth Century* (Philadelphia: University of Pennsylvania Press, 1953), pls. 31, 32.

10. Tatum, *Penn's Great Town,* p. 88; Scharf and Westcott, *History of Philadelphia,* 3:1855–58.

11. Klein, *Fairmount Park,* p. 56.

12. Scharf and Westcott, *History of Philadelphia,* 3:1871.

13. George E. Thomas and James F. O'Gorman, "Catalogue of Selected Buildings," in James F. O'Gorman, *The Architecture of Frank Furness* (Philadelphia: Philadelphia Museum of Art, 1973), pp. 143–45. G. W. and W. D. Hewitt were responsible for the present appearance of the Vesper and Malta boathouse. *PL,* March 2, 1901; April 1, 1901.

14. Tatum, "The Origins of Fairmount Park," p. 507. One plan from the competition, that of civil engineer Andrew Palles, has survived (Tatum, *Penn's Great Town,* pl. 88). It included both sides of the river between the waterworks and the Philadelphia and Columbia Railroad Bridge. Visual evidence—comparison with a more extensive 1871 plan by Frederick Law Olmsted—suggests that the east part might have been executed (George F. Chadwick, *The Park and the Town* [New York: Frederick A. Praeger, 1966], p. 203). Olmsted's plan is unlike Palles's except for the lower east park, at which point the two plans are almost identical, suggesting that Olmsted was restricted in this older section of the park to what was already there.

15. Maass, *The Glorious Enterprise,* pp. 18, 21; Chadwick, *The Park and the Town,* p, 203; Frederick Law Olmsted, Jr., and Theodore Kimball, *Frederick Law Olmsted: Landscape Architect, 1822–1903* (New York: Benjamin Blom, 1970), p. 15.

16. Maass, *The Glorious Enterprise,* pp. 22–23.

17. Tatum, "The Origins of Fairmount Park," p. 507; Thompson Westcott, *The Official Guide to Philadelphia* (Philadelphia: Porter and Coates, 1875), pp. 185–90; Maass, *The Glorious Enterprise,* p. 22.

18. Wainwright, *Sculpture of a City,* p. 1.

19. Lewis Sharp, "The Smith Memorial," in *Sculpture of a City*, ed. Wainwright, pp. 168–79; George Morgan, *City of Firsts* (Philadelphia: Historical Publication Society, 1926), p. 200; *AABN* 89 (March 31, 1906): 115.

20. Sharp, "The Smith Memorial," p. 179.

21. *Sunday Bulletin*, September 1, 1968.

22. A new indoor-outdoor concert facility, Robin Hood Dell West, opened in June 1976 on George's Hill near Fifty-second Street and Parkside Avenue. Free concerts are still offered, but the best fidelity is enjoyed by the paying customers under the copper-alloy canopy. The older concert shell, Robin Hood Dell East, is still used, but not by the Philadelphia Orchestra. *Philadelphia Inquirer*, June 13, 1976; June 15, 1976; June 16, 1976.

Northwest Philadelphia

1. Peter Kalm, *The America of 1750: Peter Kalm's Travels in North America. The English Version of 1770 Revised from the Original Swedish with a Translation of New Material From Kalm's Diary Notes*, ed. Adolph B. Benson (New York: Dover Publications, 1966), 1:48–49.

2. Edward W. Hocker, *Germantown, 1683–1933* (Philadelphia: By the author, 1933), pp. 21, 29, 51.

3. S. F. Hotchkin, *Ancient and Modern Germantown, Mount Airy, and Chestnut Hill* (Philadelphia: P. W. Ziegler & Co., 1889), p. 349.

4. John J. MacFarlane, *History of Early Chestnut Hill* (Philadelphia: City History Society of Philadelphia, 1914), p. 21.

5. John Daly and Allen Weinberg, *Genealogy of Philadelphia County Subdivisions* (2d ed.; Philadelphia: City of Philadelphia, 1966), pp. 26, 64.

6. Harry M. Tinkcom, Margaret B. Tinkcom, and Grant Miles Simon, *Historic Germantown* (Philadelphia: American Philosophical Society, 1955), pp. 5–6.

7. Ibid., pp. 91, 112; Hocker, *Germantown*, pp. 26–28, 61–67.

8. Hocker, *Germantown*, pp. 51–53.

9. E. Perot Bissell, "Wister's Big House," HABS Report (PA–7–1), p. 2.

10. Tinkcom, Tinkcom, and Simon, *Historic Germantown*, p. 84.

11. Naamen H. Keyser, C. Henry Kain, John Palmer Garber, and Horace F. McCann, *History of Old Germantown* (Philadelphia: Horace F. McCann, 1907), p. 302; John F. Watson, *Annals of Philadelphia* (rev., enlarged ed.; Philadelphia: Leary, Stuart Co., 1927), 2:65–66.

12. Tinkcom, Tinkcom, and Simon, *Historic Germantown*, p. 110; Hocker, *Germantown*, p. 124.

13. For a thorough discussion of Germantown's Market Square and its market house, see Margaret B. Tinkcom, "Market Square," *Germantowne Crier* 19 (September 1967): 69–75.

14. Joseph Jackson, *A History of the Germantown Academy* (Philadelphia: Germantown Academy, 1910), pp. 1–2, 35–40, 43–47;

15. Keyser et al., *History of Old Germantown*, pp. 82–84.

16. An engaging account of William Allen, "the great giant," is given by Carl and Jessica Bridenbaugh, *Rebels and Gentlemen: Philadelphia in the Age of Franklin* (New York: Oxford University Press, 1962), pp. 184–91.

17. Margaret B. Tinkcom, "Cliveden: The Building of a Philadelphia Countryseat, 1763–1767," *PMHB* 88 (January 1964): 3–4. Based on Benjamin Chew's papers at Cliveden, this article is an exceptional discussion of the construction of an eighteenth-

century country house, tracing the evolution of the owner's ideas to the finished structure. For discussions of the house's furnishings, see Alice Winchester, "Living with
Antiques: Cliveden, the Germantown home of Mr. and Mrs. Samuel Chew," *Antiques*
76 (December 1959): 532–36; Nicholas B. Wainwright, "Cliveden and Its Furniture,"
The University Hospital Antiques Show Catalogue, 1970 (Philadelphia, 1970), pp. 66–69;
Raymond V. Shepherd, Jr., "Cliveden," *Historic Preservation* 24 (July–September 1972):
4–11.

18. Burton Alva Konkle, *Benjamin Chew, 1722–1810* (Philadelphia: University of
Pennsylvania Press, 1932), pp. 133, 145–51, 189–91, 264; "National Trust Acquires
Cliveden in Germantown," *Preservation News* 12 (March 1972): 1, 6.

19. Townsend Ward, "Germantown Road and Its Associations: Part Sixth,"
PMHB 6 (1882): 141–42; Karl Theis Weger, "The Deshler Story," *Germantowne Crier* 7
(September 1955): 7–9, 27.

20. Charles F. Jenkins, *Washington Visits Germantown* (Philadelphia: Germantown
Historical Society, 1932), pp. 53–59, 66–68.

21. Brief of Title, 5442 Germantown Avenue, Philadelphia (n.d.), PHC; "Morris
House Presentation: May 16, 1950," *Germantowne Crier* 2 (June 1950): 12.

22. Tinkcom, Tinkcom, and Simon, *Historic Germantown*, pp. 104–5.

23. E. Perot Bissell, "Vernon," HABS Report (PA–7–2), p. 1; MA 2742 (October
1808), photocopies at HABS, PHC; Harold Donaldson Eberlein and Cortlandt Van
Dyke Hubbard, *Portrait of a Colonial City: Philadelphia, 1670–1838* (Philadelphia: J. B.
Lippincott Co. 1939), pp. 520–21.

24. Watson, *Annals of Philadelphia,* 2:28. J. Thomas Scharf and Thompson Westcott, *History of Philadelphia, 1609–1884* (Philadelphia: L. H. Everts & Co., 1884), 1:496.

25. Hocker, *Germantown,* pp. 137–39, 163–73, 253.

26. *Report of the President and Managers of the Philadelphia, Germantown, and Norristown Rail Road Company, to the Stock & Loan Holders for the Year Ending 31st Oct., 1854*
(Philadelphia: John Duross, 1854), p. 5. Hereafter cited as *Report of the Philadelphia, Germantown, and Norristown Rail Road. Report of the Philadelphia, Germantown, and Norristown
Rail Road, 1855,* p. 7.

27. Hocker, *Germantown,* pp. 223–25.

28. Richard S. Fuller, "200 West Tulpehocken Street," *Germantowne Crier* 16
(December 1964): 111–12.

29. *Philadelphia Inquirer,* November 12, 1964; *Evening Bulletin,* November 19, 1964;
January 28, 1965; *New York Times,* January 31, 1965.

30. *Chestnut Hill: An Architectural History* (Philadelphia: Willard S. Detweiler, Jr.,
1973), p. 23.

31. Campbell Scrapbooks, vol. 38, MSS, HSP; *PL,* January 19, 1907; February 28,
1907.

32. *PL,* August 30, 1887; *Chestnut Hill: An Architectural History,* p. 22; John Francis
Marion, *Bicentennial City: Walking Tours of Historic Philadelphia* (Princeton: Pyne Press,
1974), p. xii.

33. E. Digby Baltzell, *An American Business Aristocracy* (New York: Collier Books,
1962), pp. 141, 234.

34. Frank C. Roberts, Jr., *The Houstons of Philadelphia* (New York: The Newcomen
Society in North America, 1954), pp. 11–13.

35. Hotchkin, *Ancient and Modern Germantown,* pp. 403, 425.

36. Ibid., p. 471.

37. Herman L. Duhring, Jr., R. Brognard Okie, and Charles A. Ziegler, "A
Practical Housing Development: The Evolution of the 'Quadruple House' Idea," *The*

Architectural Record 34 (July 1913): 47–50; C. Matlack Price, "Architecture and the Housing Problem," *The Architectural Record* 34 (September 1913): 241–47; George Woodward, "Another Aspect of the Quadruple House," *The Architectural Record* 34 (September 1913): 51–55; Harold Donaldson Eberlein, "Pastorius Park, Philadelphia, and Its Residential Development," *The Architectural Record* 39 (January 1916): 24–39.

38. Edward Teitelman and Richard W. Longstreth, *Architecture in Philadelphia: A Guide* (Cambridge, Mass.: MIT Press, 1974), p. 240; Marshall B. Davidson, *The American Heritage History of Notable American Houses* (New York: American Heritage Publishing Co., 1971), pp. 344–45.

39. Edwyn Rorke was the architect and K. M. deVos & Co. the contractor of these twelve-story buildings whose reinforced-concrete construction is sheathed in red brick and terra cotta. The Strawbridge mansion, built in 1885 from the designs of Addison Hutton, serves as a restaurant in the midst of the group. Building Permit 8242 (1926); Lewis Mumford, "The Skyline: Philadelphia-I," *The New Yorker*, April 28, 1956, pp. 121–22; Elizabeth Biddle Yarnall, *Addison Hutton: Quaker Architect, 1834–1916* (Philadelphia: The Art Alliance Press, 1974), p. 56.

40. *Chestnut Hill: An Architectural History*, p. 94.

41. For Rittenhouse's paper mill, see Horatio Gates Jones, "Historical Sketch of the Rittenhouse Paper Mill: The First Erected in America, A.D. 1690." *PMHB* 20 (1896): 315–33. Brooke Hindle has written the latest and probably the best biography of the famous astronomer, *David Rittenhouse* (Princeton: Princeton University Press, 1964). In addition to the colonies' earliest paper mill, Germantown could also boast of Pennsylvania's first gristmill; Scharf and Westcott, *History of Philadelphia*, 3:2295–96. For Mention of late-eighteenth-and early nineteenth-century Germantown mills, see Townsend Ward, "Germantown Road and Its Associations: Part Eighth," *PMHB* 5 (1881): 365–67; "Notes and Queries," *PMHB* 6 (1882): 128; Harrold E. Gillingham, "Calico and Linen Printing in Philadelphia," *PMHB* 52 (1928): 109–10.

42. Susan Stroud Robeson and Kate Hamilton Osbourne, eds., *Historical and Genealogical Account of Andrew Robeson of Scotland, New Jersey and Pennsylvania and of His Descendants from 1653 to 1916* (Philadelphia: J. B. Lippincott Co., 1916), pp. 6–10; Duc de LaRochefoucauld-Liancourt, *Travels Through the United States of North America, the Country of the Iroquois, and Upper Canada, in the Years 1795, 1796, and 1797* (London: R. Phillips, 1799), 1:7; John Frederick Lewis, *The History of an Old Philadelphia Land Title: 208 South Fourth Street* (Philadelphia: By the author, 1934), pp. 86–87.

43. Joseph Starne Miles and William H. Cooper, *A Historical Sketch of Roxborough, Manayunk, Wissahickon* (Philadelphia: George Fein & Co., 1940), pp. 105, 107.

44. Charles V. Hagner, *Early History of the Falls of Schuylkill, Manayunk, Schuylkill and Lehigh Navigation Companies, Fairmount Waterworks, etc.* (Philadelphia: Claxton, Remsen, and Haffelfinger, 1869), p. 81.

45. John Coolidge, *Mill and Mansion: A Study of Architecture and Society in Lowell, Massachusetts, 1820–1865* (New York: Columbia University Press, 1942), p. 23.

46. Hagner, *Early History of the Falls of Schuylkill*, pp. 75–79.

47. Plans, views, and construction and operations data of many of these mills were recorded by E. Hexamer and Son in the *Hexamer General Surveys*. For Schofield's Economy Mills see 8 (1873): pls. 711–12; 12 (1877): pls. 1131–32; 19 (1883): pls. 1809–10.

48. P. C. Keely of Brooklyn designed the church in 1886; it was dedicated in 1894. Eugene Murphy, *The Parish of St. John The Baptist: The First One Hundred Years* (Philadelphia, 1931), pp. 224, 235–36; Miles and Cooper, *Historical Sketch of Roxborough, Manayunk*, p. 177.

49. *Hexamer General Survey*, 20 (1885): pl. 1948.

50. During the mid-1970's what might be called a comeback has been mustered along Manayunk's Main Street, and the neighborhood's convenient location and low-cost housing have attracted young newcomers. Old-time residents, however, are reluctant to see this activity bloom into a renaissance that could drastically change the area's character. See Mary Walton, "Manayunk: New Settlers, Old Ethnics," *Today: The Inquirer Magazine*, March 7, 1976, pp. 10–12, 16, 18. The closing of the canal is cited in Miles and Cooper, *Historical Sketch of Roxborough, Manayunk, p. 112.*

North Philadelphia

1. Thompson Westcott, *The Historic Mansions and Buildings of Philadelphia* (rev. ed.; Philadelphia: Walter H. Barr, 1895), pp. 415–23.

2. Deed Book IH2–279; Thomas B. McElwee, *A Concise History of the Eastern Penitentiary of Pennsylvania* (Philadelphia: Neall & Massey, 1835), pp. 5–6.

3. Other villages would include Rising Sun, Jacksonville, and Nicetown along Germantown Road east of Broad Street. Townsend Ward, "The Germantown Road and Its Associations," PMHB 5 (1881): 18; J. C. Sidney, *Map of the City of Philadelphia* (Philadelphia: Smith and Wistar, 1849); J. Thomas Scharf and Thompson Westcott, *History of Philadelphia, 1609–1884* (Philadelphia: L. H. Everts & Co., 1884), 1:872–73.

4. McElwee, *A Concise History of the Eastern Penitentiary,* pp. 5–15, 41, 51–56.

5. Norman B. Johnston, "John Haviland, Jailor to the World," *JSAH* 23 (May 1964): 101–5; Negley K. Teeters and John D. Shearer, *The Prison at Philadelphia: Cherry Hill* (New York: Columbia University Press, 1957), pp. 56–59; Matthew Eli Baigell, "John Haviland" (Ph.D. dissertation, University of Pennsylvania, 1965), pp. 92–100.

6. Thompson Westcott, *The Official Guide Book of Philadelphia* (Philadelphia: Porter and Coates, 1875), p. 110; Robert W. Kotzbauer, "Echo from the Cells," *Discover: The Sunday Bulletin Magazine,* October 20, 1974, p. 16.

7. *Sunday Bulletin,* January 25, 1970.

8. The best history of Girard College is Cheesman A. Herrick, *History of Girard College* (Philadelphia: Girard College, 1927). Founder's Hall is thoroughly and statistically described in Henry W. Arey, *The Girard College and Its Founder* (Philadelphia: C. Sherman, 1872), pp. 44–56. Preston Retreat was demolished in the spring of 1963 after a long struggle to save it. *Philadelphia Inquirer,* April 28, 1963; May 10, 1963.

9. The most complete history of the man is John Bach McMaster, *The Life and Times of Stephen Girard* (2 vols.; Philadelphia: J. B. Lippincott Co., 1918).

10. Biddle's influence on the design of Founder's Hall is presented by Agnes Addison Gilchrist, "Girard College: An Example of the Layman's Influence on Architecture," *JSAH* 16 (May 1957): 22–25.

11. For an explanation of this great work of masonry that "goes far beyond anything the Greeks attempted," see Carl W. Condit, *American Building: Materials and Techniques from the Beginning of the Colonial Settlements to the Present* (Chicago: University of Chicago Press, 1968), p. 68.

12. Herrick, *History of Girard College,* p. 113.

13. Westcott, *Official Guide,* p. 211; Scharf and Westcott, *History of Philadelphia,* 1:647–48.

14. See HABS photocopies of Walter's drawings and Fire Association 6361 (July 1840), INA 669 (July 1840), PC 5423 (July 16, 1840), copies at HABS, PHC.

15. *PL,* February 10, 1908; *PRERBG,* 23 (July 15, 1908): 455; MA 7150 (June 14, 1909); *Sunday Bulletin,* May 29, 1960.

16. Westcott, *Official Guide*, p. 211; Scharf and Westcott, *History of Philadelphia*, 2:1617, 1680; *Philadelphia Inquirer*, June 11, 1957.

17. *PL*, March 14, 1849.

18. Phoebe B. Stanton, *The Gothic Revival and American Church Architecture* (Baltimore: Johns Hopkins Press, 1968), pp. 3–29.

19. *PL*, March 3, 1847.

20. Samuel Laird, "St. Mark's Evangelical Church: Historical Sketch" (pamphlet, n.d.), MSS, Lutheran Theological Seminary; *PL*, June 12, 1851; July 8, 1851; November 15, 1852; *First Annual Report of the Board of Managers of the Spring Garden Institute* (Philadelphia, 1852), p. 4. This block is illustrated in Nicholas B. Wainwright, *Philadelphia in the Romantic Age of Lithography* (Philadelphia: Historical Society of Pennsylvania, 1958), p. 175.

21. In less than fifty years the Baldwin Locomotive Works extended along Broad Street between Spring Garden and Hamilton streets and westward to Eighteenth Street. The company moved to Eddystone in 1925 but it was another twelve years before the buildings were demolished. Scharf and Westcott, *History of Philadelphia*, 3:2255–57; *Philadelphia: A Guide to the Nation's Birthplace* (Philadelphia: William Penn Association of Philadelphia, Inc., 1937), p. 460.

22. Scharf and Westcott, *History of Philadelphia*, 3:2263–67; *PL*, May 3, 1853; August 31, 1854; Edwin T. Freedley, *Leading Pursuits and Leading Men: A Treatise of the Principal Trades and Manufactures of the United States* (Philadelphia: E. Young, 1856), p. 11; *Royal Road to Wealth* (Philadelphia: Samuel Loag, 1869), pp. 5–20.

23. Transfers of property indicate that the Poe cottage was built between September 1840 and August 1842, and biographers have established that Poe lived there in 1842. Deed Books GS20–415, GS44–194; Hervey Allen, *Israfel: The Life and Times of Edgar Allan Poe* (New York: Farrar & Rinehart, 1934), pp. 428–31. The first mention of the front building was in a title transfer, May 1849. It evidently was not built before then, which explains why this property was assessed in 1847 for $2,000 less than the adjoining lot with its three-story house (532 North Seventh Street). Deed Book GWC53–231; Guardians of the Poor, Poor Tax Register, 1847, p. 30, MSS, Philadelphia City Archives.

24. Poulson's Scrap-books, 7:137, MSS, LCP.

25. *PL*, June 7, 1850.

26. Robin Williams, *American Society* (2d ed., rev.; New York: Alfred A. Knopf, 1960), pp. 417–21.

27. *PL*, June 2, 1853.

28. Ibid., June 12, 1863; July 29, 1863; October 19, 1863.

29. Raised basements and bay windows with balconies above seem to have made these houses on Broad Street near Columbia Avenue in "the New York style." *PL*, July 4, 1853.

30. *PL*, March 11, 1852; July 4, 1853; May 1, 1863; June 13, 1863; September 26, 1863.

31. Gaul's house is better known for its second owner, Edwin Forrest, the great tragedian, who acquired the partially completed house in 1855. James Rees, *The Life of Edwin Forrest* (Philadelphia: T. B. Peterson & Brothers, 1874), pp. 379–81; Richard Moody, *Edwin Forrest* (New York: Alfred A. Knopf, 1960), p. 331. The house is described in FFI 20072 (January 31, 1854); PC 9546 (September 18, 1854), photocopies at HABS, PHC.

32. FFI 31634 (October 5, 1864), MSS, HSP; *PL*, June 2, 1863; October 3, 1864.

33. For a description of the eclectic Widener House, see *Philadelphia Record,* November 28, 1899; August 22, 1943; and *Philadelphia Telegraph,* November 30, 1899. Since the Bergdols, a family of prominent brewers, moved into the Kemble house in 1907, it is generally known as the Kemble-Bergdol House; James H. Windrim was the architect. *PRERBG* 4 (July 3, 1889): 306; 5 (April 19, 1890): 193; 5 (August 13, 1890): 481; *Gopsill's Philadelphia City Directory, 1907* (Philadelphia: James Gopsill's Sons, 1907), p. 204.

34. *PL,* August 13, 1852. Lewars had his grocery in the corner store, evidently rented meeting rooms above it, and lived over the adjacent shop. *McElroy's Philadelphia Directory for 1853* (Philadelphia: Edward C. & John Biddle, 1853), p. 236; *Cohen's Philadelphia City Directory for 1860* (Philadelphia: Hamelin & Co., 1860), p. 546; *McElroy's Philadelphia City Directory for 1865* (Philadelphia: A. McElroy, 1865), p. 401; *Gopsill's Philadelphia City and Business Directory for 1868–69* (Philadelphia: James Gopsill, 1868), p. 962.

35. For a discussion of the development of Furness's mature style, especially in relation to banks, see James F. O'Gorman, *The Architecture of Frank Furness* (Philadelphia: Philadelphia Museum of Art, 1973), pp. 35–45. The building was erected in 1872, but since the bank did not acquire the property until December 11, 1871, it is unlikely that the architects started the design before early 1872. *PL,* July 18, 1872; Registry Unit 4N8–52.

36. See Addison Hutton's Provident Life and Trust Company Building on Fourth Street below Market (1872) and James H. Windrim's Philadelphia Trust, Safe Deposit and Insurance Company Building at 415 Chestnut Street (1873–74). Both are illustrated in O'Gorman, *The Architecture of Frank Furness,* p. 44.

37. Registry Unit 4N8–55; *PRERBG* 6 (November 4, 1891): 704; 18 (July 1, 1903): 407; 18 (July 29, 1903): 483; 28 (August 20, 1913): 544; 28 (December 17, 1913): 816; Castner's Scrapbooks, 8:10, MSS, FLP.

38. The misattribution of buildings to socialite-architect Stanford White is a popular sport, as Brendan Gill illustrates in "True White from False," *The New York Times Magazine,* October 19, 1975, pp. 14–16, 66. Documentation and contemporary description of the Burk House are found in the sources that follow: *PL,* May 3, 1907; *Philadelphia Record,* September 19, 1909; Building Permit 4548 (1908); Thomas Nolan, "Some Recent Philadelphia Architecture," *The Architectural Record* 29 (1911): 227–29.

39. *PL,* March 5, 1907; March 10, 1907; September 8, 1907; March 28, 1908; March 29, 1908.

40. Building Permit 3806 (1908); *PL,* September 1907; *PRERBG* 23 (April 1, 1908): 209.

41. *PL,* November 18, 1908.

42. *Philadelphia: A Guide to the Nation's Birthplace,* p. 463.

43. Rankin, Kellogg, and Crane were the architects. Ibid., p. 458; Building Permit 12502 (1923).

44. The Reading Company's building is interesting in many respects. With a million square feet of floor space, it was the largest commercial structure in the country at the time. It was uniquely sensitive to both the automobile and railroad. Erected on stilts over the Reading's tracks, it became the second "air right" property in Philadelphia and the only one in the world with a public freight station beneath it. At the same time a vehicle concourse extending the width of the building gave access to the city's first underground parking garage. William Steele and Sons were the architects and builders. *Building* 9 (January 9, 1929): 9–10; Building Permits 4246 (1929), 868 (1930).

45. Temple became a university in 1907. Castner's Scrapbooks, 27A:94, MSS, FLP; *PRERBG* 6 (October 21, 1891): 672; 6 (December 30, 1891): 843; 8 (April 26, 1893): 253; *PL*, August 20, 1893; May 4, 1894.

46. *Philadelphia: A Guide to the Nation's Birthplace*, pp. 466–67.

47. *Building* 9 (February 1929): 22, 36.

48. J. W. Anshutz, for example, designed forty-seven two- and three-story brick houses with brownstone trim and turrets at Broad Street and Erie Avenue in 1890. *PL*, April 28, 1890.

49. *Philadelphia Inquirer*, May 9, 1891.

50. T. Henry Ashbury, president of the Enterprise Manufacturing Company, was Oak Lane's primary developer; Amos J. Boyden was his architect. S. F. Hotchkin, *The York Road, Old and New* (Philadelphia: Binder & Kelly, 1892), pp. 71–73.

51. *PRERBG* 23 (February 23, 1908): 131; *PL*, February 26, 1908; April 2, 1908; April 4, 1908; Letter from James Smart, *Evening and Sunday Bulletin*, to Richard J. Webster, July 25, 1972. Some of the houses were begun on the eve of the stadium's construction. For example, 202 two-story row houses were built on the square west of Shibe Park in 1907. *PL*, March 28, 1907.

52. There are many architecturally significant houses of worship in North Philadelphia. A list of the more important ones would include North Broad Street Presbyterian Church, Broad and Green streets, probably by Samuel Sloan (1862–64); (Roman Catholic) Church of the Gesu, Eighteenth and Stiles streets, by Edwin F. Durang (1879–88); (Episcopal) Church of the Advocate, Eighteenth and Diamond streets, by Charles M. Burns (1890–92); St. Francis Xavier Roman Catholic Church, Twenty-fourth and Green streets, by Edwin F. Durang (1893–95, rebuilt after fire 1906–8); (Roman Catholic) Church of St. Edward the Confessor, Eighth and York streets, by Henry D. Dagit (1908); Rodeph Shalom Synagogue, Broad and Mt. Vernon streets, by Simon and Simon (1928); (Roman Catholic) Church of the Holy Child, Broad and Duncannon streets, by George I. Lovatt (1929); Ukranian Catholic Cathedral of the Immaculate Conception, Franklin and Parrish streets, by Julian J. Jastremsky (1964–66); Zion Baptist Church, Broad and Venango streets, by Walter R. Livingston, Jr. (1973).

Delaware River Corridor

1. Stuart M. Blumin, "Residential Mobility within the Nineteenth-Century City," *The Peoples of Philadelphia*, ed. Allen F. Davis and Mark H. Haller (Philadelphia: Temple University Press, 1973), p. 43; Anthony N. B. Garvan, "Proprietary Philadelphia as Artifact," *The Historian and the City*, ed. Oscar Handlin and John Burchard (Cambridge, Mass.: MIT Press, 1963), pp. 197–98.

2. John Daly and Allen Weinberg, *Genealogy of Philadelphia County Subdivisions* (2d ed.; Philadelphia: City of Philadelphia, 1966), pp. 6–10, 51; Ellis Paxson Oberholtzer, *Philadelphia: A History of the City and Its People* (Philadelphia: J. S. Clark, 1911), 2:308–9.

3. Harold Donaldson Eberlein and Cortlandt Van Dyke Hubbard, *Portrait of a Colonial City* (Philadelphia: J. B. Lippincott Co., 1939), p. 152.

4. Ibid.

5. Guernsey A. Hallowell, "Edward Stiles," in *Papers Read before the Historical Society of Frankford* (1909), 2:12.

6. In the summer of 1838, during a temporary stay in Philadelphia, Whittier made many visits to the Frankford area and the former home of Thomas Chalkley. It moved him to write "Chalkley Hall," whose first verse is quoted from *The Complete Poetical Works of John Greenleaf Whittier* (Boston: Houghton Mifflin, 1894), pp. 220, 636.

7. John F. Watson, *Annals of Philadelphia* (rev., enlarged ed.; Philadelphia: Leary, Stuart Co., 1909), 1:140–41; Thomas Creighton, *Frankford: A Good Place to Live in* (Philadelphia, 1909), p. 3; Caroline W. Smedley, "Historical Sketch of Frankford Meeting," in *Papers Read before the Historical Society of Frankford* 2 (1916): 221.

8. The church building at Meeting House and Krewstown roads was rebuilt in 1805. Robert T. Tumbleston, *Old Pennepack Baptist Church* (Philadelphia, 1938), p. 15.

9. E. Perot Bissell, "Trinity Church, Oxford," HABS Report (PA-17), p. 1; Edward Y. Buchanan, *Two Discourses Relating to the Early History of Trinity Church, Oxford, Philadelphia* (Philadelphia: Porter and Coates, 1885), pp. 16, 57.

10. Garvan, "Proprietary Philadelphia," pp. 197–98.

11. William John Murtagh, "The Philadelphia Row House," *JSAH* 16 (December 1957): 9.

12. Wendy H. Robbins, Briefs of Title for 903–13 New Market Street (1967), PHC.

13. Fire Association 1857 (October 3, 1827), photocopy at PHC. Wendy H. Robbins, Briefs of Title for 132–34, 133 Olive Street (1968), PHC; *Philadelphia Directory for 1811* (Philadelphia: James Robinson, 1811), pp. xxxvii, xlvii.

14. Albert Mordell, "Men and Things: Life in a Band Box a Generation Ago," *Evening Bulletin*, July 21, 1937.

15. Josephine Hedges Ewalt, *As It Was in the Beginning* (Chicago: United States Savings and Loan League, 1956), p. 40; *PL*, March 12, 1849.

16. PC 3748–49 (March 1, 1817), photocopy at PHC; *153rd Annual Report, Friends Hospital* (Philadelphia, 1970), p. 11. The building's architectural history can be traced in resurveys of PC 3748 (June 3, 1829; March 30, 1835) and PC 8905 (March 17, 1852; June 2, 1873; February 3, 1880), photocopies at PHC. A brief description of additions to the main building and the erection of additional structures on the grounds is chronologically presented in *Friends Asylum for the Insane, 1813–1913* (Philadelphia, 1913). The lodestone of information on the institution's architecture is the "Minute Book of the Contributors of the Asylum for Persons Deprived of the Use of Their Reason," Friends Collection, Haverford College, Haverford, Pa. This invaluable volume was uncovered at Friends Hospital by Edward Teitelman, M.D., who has done a great deal of research on the institution's architecture.

17. *Friends Asylum for the Insane, 1813–1913*, pp. 65, 95; George B. Tatum, *Penn's Great Town* (Philadelphia: University of Pennsylvania Press, 1961), p. 165, pl. 35; Theo B. White et al, *Philadelphia Architecture in the Nineteenth Century* (Philadelphia: University of Pennsylvania Press, 1953), p. 22, pl. 1. See HABS Drawings of Pennsylvania Hospital, PA–1123, Library of Congress.

18. *153rd Annual Report, Friends Hospital*, p. 11; *Friends Asylum for the Insane, 1813–1913*, pp. 17–18; PC 8905 (June 2, 1873), photocopy at PHC.

19. *153rd Annual Report, Friends Hospital*, p. 1; Harold N. Cooledge, Jr., "Samuel Sloan and the Philadelphia School of Hospital Design, 1850–1880," *Charette* 44 (June 1964):6–7, 18; Edward Teitelman and Richard W. Longstreth, *Architecture in Philadelphia: A Guide* (Cambridge, Mass.: MIT Press, 1974), p. 165.

20. The Hospital of the Protestant Episcopal Church in Philadelphia was chartered on July 18, 1851; it accepted the generous gift of Miss Ann Leamy and her sister Mrs. Elizabeth H. L. Stout in December 1852. Edward F. Leiper, "The Episcopal Hospital," *Medical and Surgical Reports of the Episcopal Hospital* (Philadelphia: William J. Dornan, 1913), 1:19–20.

The legally defined western border of Kensington District in 1820 was Sixth Street; enlarged in 1848, the district spilled above Lehigh Avenue and westward to Germantown Avenue, which ran diagonally into Sixth Street. Although the area has been officially in Philadelphia since 1854, residents still consider it Kensington. Nowadays, however, Kensington's borders are socially rather than legally determined, leading many to consider Front Street the present western boundary. Laws of Pennsylvania, Chapter 52, March 6, 1820; J. Thomas Scharf and Thompson Westcott, *History of Philadelphia, 1609–1884* (Philadelphia: L. H. Everts & Co., 1884), 1:689; Rod Townley, "Pride and Prejudice in Kensington," *Today: The Inquirer Magazine*, June 16, 1974, pp. 27, 31; Peter Binzen, *Whitetown, U.S.A.* (New York: Random House, 1970), p. 86.

21. Beginning in 1853 patients were treated in the Leamy House, the country seat that had been altered to hospital purposes. By 1860 there was a daily average of twenty-eight patients in the house. Besides Episcopal Hospital there were in the early 1850's only the venerable Pennsylvania Hospital and Philadelphia Hospital, and the latter was essentially a public almshouse. There were also four dispensaries and the Wills Hospital for the blind and lame, but they were small and specialized. Leiper, "The Episcopal Hospital," pp. 19–21.

22. Cooledge, "Philadelphia School of Hospital Design," pp. 6, 18; *The Hospital of the Protestant Episcopal Church in Philadelphia: Its Origins, Progress, Work and Want* (Philadelphia: J. B. Lippincott Co., 1869); *The Architectural Review and American Builders Journal* 2 (March 1870): 514–23; *Report of the Board of Managers of the Hospital of the Protestant Episcopal Church in Philadelphia* 24 (January 1876): 10–11.

23. Cooledge, "Philadelphia School of Hospital Design," p. 18.

24. *Frankford Arsenal: Historical Highlights* (Philadelphia, [c. 1971]), p. 1; Gwen D. Hollahan, *Frankford Arsenal's 150 Year Heritage* (Philadelphia, 1966), pp. 3, 6; Odus C. Horney, *Frankford Arsenal, 1816–1926* (Philadelphia, 1926), p. 1.

25. Hollahan, pp. 8–9, 11–12; Horney, pp. 2–3; Joseph M. Colby, *Frankford Arsenal, 1916–1956* (Philadelphia, 1956), p. 3; *Frankford Arsenal: Historical Highlights* (Philadelphia, [c. 1971]), p. 4; Scharf and Westcott, *History of Philadelphia,* 2:1015.

26. *Philadelphia Inquirer,* June 18, 1969; April 11, 1975.

27. Creighton, *Frankford,* p. 3. There were some industries unrelated to agriculture, such as a glass works that was established in 1771 at the mouth of Gunner's Run. It apparently was not a very large or profitable enterprise, however, until it was taken over by Dr. Thomas W. Dyott in 1833. Charles H. Cramp, "Old Richmond District and Its Memories," *PL,* January 10, 1909.

28. Kensington was laid out and named in 1730 by Anthony Palmer, president of Council in the 1740's. Initially it extended southward along the river from Hanover street to Gunner's Run and westward to near Frankford Road. Formed as a district in 1820, it was extended northward in 1848 to Lehigh and Germantown avenues. Laws of Pennsylvania, Chapter 52; Scharf and Westcott, *History of Philadelphia,* 1:689.

29. Scharf and Westcott, *History of Philadelphia,* 1:522; Joseph Jackson, *Market Street, Philadelphia* (Philadelphia, 1918), p. 207; *The Philadelphia Directory for 1810* (Philadelphia: James Robinson, 1810), p. 83; *The Philadelphia Directory for 1817* (Philadelphia: Edward Dawes, 1817), p. 127.

30. George Castor Martin, "Samuel Martin, Proprietor of the First Textile Mill in Frankford," in *Papers Read before the Historical Society of Frankford* 2 (1916):243–44.

31. Of the first six mills begun in Frankford between 1816 and 1820, five were established by English-born entrepreneurs. The activities included cotton mills, a block

printing plant, dyeing and bleaching works, and a pottery. William B. Dixon, "Frankford's Early Industrial Development," *The Pamphlet of the Historical Society of Frankford for 1911* (1912), pp. 50–59.

32. As late as the 1860's mills along Frankford Creek were surrounded by farmland and meadows. See, for example, the Frogmore Mills at Frankford Creek and Powder Mill Road, Frankford, in *Hexamer General Survey*, 3, (1867–71): pl. 242.

33. Wendy H. Robbins, Brief of Title for 125–31 Ellen Street (1967), PHC; Edwin T. Freedley, *Philadelphia and Its Manufactures* (Philadelphia: Edward Young, 1859), pp. 317–18.

34. E. McFarlin, Pennsylvania Historical Salvage Council Drawings (B–613), 125–31 Ellen Street (September 1967); (B–514), 915–17 Hope Street (November 1967), copies at HABS, PHC.

35. *McElroy's Philadelphia Directory for 1846* (Philadelphia: John & Edward C. Biddle, 1846), p. 164. Will Book 30, Will No. 92, March 31, 1853, MSS, City of Philadelphia, Register of Wills. Ernest Hexamer and William Locher, *Maps of the City of Philadelphia* (Philadelphia: Hexamer and Locher, 1859), 4:pl. 52. Holloway's house measured 27 feet 6 inches on New Market by 52 feet on Ellen Street.

36. Some of these houses date before 1867, and all were completed by 1874. *Hexamer General Survey*, 4 (1867–71):pl. 334; 6 (1874): pl. 504; 12 (1876): pls. 1065–66; 17 (1881): pls. 1598–99.

37. The houses included eleven dwellings with stores below on Fourth Street north of Jefferson in 1849 and ten dwellings on Lawrence south of George, and twelve on Poplar Street east of Lawrence in 1848. J. and G. A. Binder, popular local builders, built the structures. *PL*, March 30, 1849.

38. The Philadelphia and Trenton Railroad was incorporated in February 1832. The Philadelphia-New York stages stopped running in 1836. Scharf and Westcott, *History of Philadelphia*, 3:2183; Guernsey A. Hallowell, "Transportation," *Frankford: Direction of a Greater Philadelphia* (Philadelphia, 1922), pp. 54, 64.

39. David Budlong Tyler, *The Bay and River Delaware: A Pictorial History* (Cambridge, Md.: Cornell Maritime Press, 1955), p. 132; Freedley, *Philadelphia and Its Manufactures*, pp. 317–18; *PL*, May 7, 1849, April 25, 1851.

40. Scharf and Westcott, *History of Philadelphia*, 3:2185. The rail and wharves complex between Huntington and William streets east of Richmond Street (then Point Road) was already well developed by 1849. See J. C. Sidney, *Maps of the City of Philadelphia* (Philadelphia: Smith & Wistar, 1849).

41. *Port Richmond, Philadelphia* (Philadelphia: Reading Company, 1956), p. 1.

42. Freedley, *Philadelphia and Its Manufactures*, pp. 329–30; *McElroy's Philadelphia Directory for 1856* (Philadelphia: John & Edward C. Biddle, 1856), p. 694; Scharf and Westcott, *History of Philadelphia*, 3:2267.

43. *Philadelphia and Popular Philadelphians* (Philadelphia, 1891), p. 133. Disston began his business earlier on a very small scale near Second and Arch streets. Scharf and Westcott, *History of Philadelphia*, 3:2267.

44. *PL*, July 30, 1872; *Hexamer General Survey*, 8 (June 18, 1873): pls. 693–94; Gray Kirk and E. McFarlin, Pennsylvania Historical Salvage Council Drawings (B–611), 1001 North Front Street (1967). This passage was partly filled in after the building became a paper box factory in 1907. *Boyd's City Directory, 1907* (Philadelphia: C. E. Howe Company, 1907), p. 204; George W. and Walter S. Bromley, *Atlas of the City of Philadelphia* (Philadelphia: G. W. Bromley & Co., 1910), pl. 13.

45. Wendy H. Robbins, Brief of Title for 440 New Market Street (1968), PHC;

McElroy's Philadelphia Directory for 1849 (Philadelphia: John & Edward C. Biddle, 1849), p. 158; *McElroy's Philadelphia Directory for 1859* (Philadelphia: John & Edward C. Biddle, 1859), p. 298; Freedley, *Philadelphia and Its Manufactures,* p. 372; *PL,* February 27, 1851; Nicholas B. Wainwright, *Philadelphia in the Romantic Age of Lithography* (Philadelphia: The Historical Society of Pennsylvania, 1958), p. 146.

46. Three well-preserved examples from the 1850's recorded by the Pennsylvania Historical Salvage Council were the Knight Building at the northeast corner of Second and Vine streets, its neighbor at 305–7 North Second, and the Goodwin Building, 317–19 North Second Street. Registry Unit, 2N18–63, 64; 2N18–71, 149; 2N18–111, 112.

47. FFI 56618 (June 24, 1878). The drawings are at the Historical Society of Pennsylvania, copies at PHC.

48. Robert T. Corson, "The Frankford Lyceum," in *Papers Read before the Historical Society of Frankford* 2 (1910): 90–94.

49. Alexis de Tocqueville, *Democracy in America,* trans. Henry Reeve (New York: Schocken Books, 1961), 2:129–30.

50. The "combined effects of Philadelphia's rapid growth—the endless grid streets, the scattering of churches, stations, and factories, and flood of immigrants, the novelty, the sheer size, and pace of the big city—" are cited by Sam Bass Warner, Jr., *The Private City: Philadelphia in Three Periods of Its Growth* (Philadelphia: University of Pennsylvania Press, 1968), p. 61. An added factor, high residential mobility, has been noted by Stuart M. Blumin, "Residential Mobility within the Nineteenth-Century City," pp. 37–52.

51. The erratic organization of the interior—irregularly shaped rooms, discontinuous floor levels and stairs, gigantic false doors, and one room without windows—leaves no doubt about its ceremonial function, and the presence of seven meeting halls suggests that more than one lodge used the building at the same time. The Odd Fellows vacated the hall in November 1932. *Public Ledger and Daily Transcript,* November 5, 1847; Denis B. Myers, "Independent Order of Odd Fellows Hall," HABS Architectural Report (1963), pp. 1–6; Fred R. Korman, Grand Secretary of Grand Lodge of Pennsylvania, Independent Order of Odd Fellows, to Richard J. Webster, June 18, 1974.

52. Deed Book GS 17–369 (August 22, 1840). A limestone plaque in the middle of the facade of the Northern Liberty Hose Company contained the date of 1846. United States Hose Company, Minutes, 1837–1845, 1845–1848, MSS, HSP; Wainwright, *Philadelphia Lithography,* pp. 88, 234.

53. Bruce Laurie describes changes in the social composition and roles of Southwark fire companies, and although he deals with a section south of the city, his conclusions can be related to Northern Liberties, a section just north of the city and with a similar population: "Fire Companies and Gangs in Southwark: The 1840's," in *The Peoples of Philadelphia,* p. 77.

54. Scharf and Westcott, *History of Philadelphia,* 1:551.

55. Northern Liberty Hose Company served as Philadelphia Fire Department, Engine Company No. 21 until 1875 when a new fire station was built at 826–28 New Market Street. Friendship Fire Company No. 15 at Norris and Sepviva streets was rented by the city for Hook and Ladder Company C until 1878. For a time after that it was known as Friendship Hall. Scharf and Westcott, *History of Philadelphia,* 3:710, 836; *Mayor's Annual Report. Annual Report of Board of Fire Commission* (1875), (1878); George W. and Walter S. Bromley, *Atlas of the City of Philadelphia* (Philadelphia: G. W. Bromley & Co., 1887), 4: pl. K.

56. Kurt B. Mayer, *Class and Society* (New York: Random House, 1955), p. 44; Liston Pope, "Religion and the Class Structure," *Annals of the American Academy of Political and Social Science* 256 (March 1948): 84–91; Tocqueville, *Democracy in America*, 2: 128–29; Max Lerner, *America as a Civilization* (New York: Simon and Schuster, 1957), pp. 711–12; Ralph Henry Gabriel, *The Course of American Democratic Thought* (2d ed.; New York: The Ronald Press, 1956), pp. 26–39; Norman J. Johnston, "The Caste and Class of the Urban Form of Historic Philadelphia," *Journal of the American Institute of Planners*, November 1966, pp. 334–38.

57. Lerner, *America as a Civilization*, p. 710.

58. *PL*, April 20, 1853; Poulson's Scrap-books, 4:16, MSS, LCP; Ernest N. Feind, *A History of the First Presbyterian Church of Kensington, 1814–1939* (Philadelphia, 1939), p. 10; Kathryn I. Welliver, *A History of the First Presbyterian Church of Kensington in Philadelphia* (Philadelphia, 1964), p. 5; Trustees' Records, 1853–1873, pp. 60–62, MSS, Frankford Presbyterian Church. A drawing of the First Presbyterian Church of Frankford, signed by McArthur, is in the possession of the church. For an interior description see Fire Association 43232 (December 17, 1866), photocopy at PHC; Teitelman and Longstreth, *Architecture in Philadelphia*, p. 169.

59. *Historical Sketches of the Catholic Churches and Institutions of Philadelphia* (Philadelphia: Daniel H. Mahoney, 1895), pp. 56–59; Scharf and Westcott, *History of Philadelphia*, 1:666.

60. Joseph Jackson, *Early Philadelphia Architects and Engineers* (Philadelphia, 1923), pp. 236–37; *Historical Sketches of Catholic Churches*, p. 81; *St. Joachim's Church: A History* (Philadelphia, [c. 1974]), n.p.

61. St. Peter's, for example, was rebuilt as a large stone church in 1895–97; St. Michael's was enlarged with a new facade and towers at the turn of the century and a new rectory and a school were finished in 1892; a new St. Ann's was built in 1866–69 and its interior was renovated in 1909, and a new St. Joachim's was built in 1874–80, with its convent and school built in 1866 and 1885 respectively. (The present convent dates from 1921.) *Historical Sketches of Catholic Churches*, pp. 56–59, 81; *History of St. Ann's Church* (Philadelphia, 1920), n.p.; *St. Joachim's Church*, n.p.

62. Robert F. Scott, "Historic Presbyterian Churches of Kensington and the Northern Liberties," Address at 14th Annual Meeting of Friends of Old Pine Street Church, April 28, 1964; Franklin Davenport Edmunds, *The Public School Buildings of the City of Philadelphia from 1845 to 1852* (Philadelphia: By the author, 1915), p. 169; Building Permits 6112 (1916), 7224 (1923).

63. *PL*, February 2, 1854; *Evening Bulletin*, June 21, 1921; Scharf and Westcott, *History of Philadelphia*, 3:2187, 2202.

64. The new institutions were Second National Bank, Frankford (1863), Eighth National Bank (1863) and Shackamaxon Bank (1873) in Kensington, and Security National Bank (1870) and Northern Saving Fund, Safe Deposit and Trust Company (1871) on the boundary of the former Spring Garden District. Thompson Westcott, *The Official Guide Book to Philadelphia* (Philadelphia: Porter and Coates, 1875), pp. 155–61.

65. The Bank of Northern Liberties became a national bank in 1864. Westcott, *Official Guide Book*, p. 155; *Philadelphia and Popular Philadelphians*, pp. 9, 226; Scharf and Westcott, *History of Philadelphia*, 3:2111.

66. George E. Thomas and James F. O'Gorman, "Catalogue of Selected Buildings," in James F. O'Gorman, *The Architecture of Frank Furness* (Philadelphia: Philadelphia Museum of Art, 1973), pp. 95, 117.

67. William B. Dixon, "Frankford's Early Industrial Development," *The Pamphlet of*

the *Historical Society of Frankford for 1911* (1912), p. 53; Freedley, *Philadelphia and Its Manufactures*, p. 250; *Hexamer General Survey*, 4 (1867–71): pl. 311; 18 (December 23, 1882): pls. 1729–30.

68. Between 1871 and 1882 the following changes were made: an oil house was added to the Drug Room, the office was enlarged, an extension was built onto the Blue Dyehouse, the Main Building and adjoining buildings were altered on the interior, a boiler house was added to the Engine Room, and the Cylinder Drying Room was altered. *Hexamer General Survey*, 4 (1867–71): pl. 311; 18 (December 23, 1882): pls. 1729–30.

69. Only one building was left unchanged from 1867, and that may have been altered on the inside since an office appears to have been added after 1867. *Hexamer General Survey*, 4 (1867–71): pl. 334; 6 (February 8, 1874): pl. 504.

70. *Hexamer General Survey*, 12 (November 1876): pls. 1065–66; 17 (October 10, 1881): pls. 1598–99; 29 (February 4, 1895): pls. 2843–44.

71. Freedley, *Philadelphia and Its Manufactures*, p. 239; Moses King, *Philadelphia and Notable Philadelphians* (New York: Moses King, 1902), p. 44. The mills' operation is described in *Philadelphia: A Guide to the Nation's Birthplace* (Philadelphia: William Penn Association of Philadelphia, 1937), pp. 518–20.

72. *PL,* April 7, 1886; April 17, 1886; September 12, 1894; *PRERBG* 1 (April 19, 1886):174; 1 (May 31, 1886):244; 4 (August 7, 1889):367; 6 (March 11, 1891):145; 6 (April 15, 1891):226; 7 (April 6, 1892):1067; 7 (April 20, 1892):1099; *Philadelphia Record*, September 12, 1894. For twentieth-century additions and alterations, see Building Permits 970 (1907), 8983 (1909), 582 (1910), 6722 (1912), 9965 (1923), 494 (1924), 921 (1939), 2019 (1941), 2221 (1941).

73. When one of these buildings ignites, it often sets off a multiple alarm fire. In 1975 the former North American Lace Company (1903) at Glenwood and Allegheny avenues fell victim to a nine-alarm fire, and the former Philadelphia Tapestry Mills (c. 1900 and later) at Allegheny Avenue and Mascher Street was consumed in a seven-alarm fire. *Philadelphia Inquirer*, March 1, 1975; August 15, 1975.

74. Carl W. Gatter, a local resident who has done a great deal in researching and documenting Frankford area's historic structures, took photos of Lynfield (c. 1760, c. 1800) during its demolition in 1942, and of Chalkley Hall (1723, 1776) during its demolition in 1954. Port Royal (1761) was demolished c. 1962.

75. Joseph W. Ryerss acquired the property in January 1859 with a messuage on it, but it was evidently a farm building and not the mansion, which nineteenth-century writers say he built. It was Ryerss's country home, probably used only in the summer; his year-round residence was at 922 Walnut Street. Deed Book ADB 48–82 (January 1, 1859); S. F. Hotchkin, *The York Road, Old and New* (Philadelphia: Binder & Kelly, 1892), p. 424; S. F. Hotchkin, *The Bristol Pike* (Philadelphia: George W. Jacobs & Co., 1893), p. 11; *McElroy's Philadelphia City Directory, 1867*, p. 788;

76. *PL,* October 17, 1907.

77. Rhawn did not become president of the bank until 1884, after the house was completed. Hotchkin, *York Road*, p. 416; O'Gorman, *Architecture of Frank Furness*, pp. 50–51, 125.

78. O'Gorman, *Architecture of Frank Furness*, p. 50, quotes this label, which was evidently first used in the *Architectural Record* at the turn of the century.

79. The Frankford Elevated was begun in 1915 with a scheduled completion date of 1918. It opened in November 1922, its construction costs more than twice the original estimate; both the delay of construction and rise in cost were attributable to World War

I. The El proved popular, and it drew enough business from the railroad to force the closing of the Frankford Station of the Reading Railroad, June 30, 1928. Hallowell, *Frankford*, pp. 3, 68; Walter M. Benner, *Frankford Goes to Town* (Philadelphia: Third Federal Savings and Loan Association, [c. 1960]), pp. 10–11.

80. Whittier's poem was quoted in part earlier. Promotions for new houses in Frankford can be found in Hallowell, *Frankford*.

81. Measuring approximately 16 by 36 feet on lots about three times as deep, these two-story brick houses were modern fusions of the eighteenth-century city house plan and mid-nineteenth-century terrace houses. Henry Berg is said to have designed many of them but so did J. W. Lewin and G. Harold Murphy. Yet it mattered little who the architects were; the result was always similar, uninteresting facades, as seen on the 3100 block (by Murphy in 1946) and the 2200 block (by Lewin in 1950) of Friendship Street. *Philadelphia Inquirer*, September 28, 1975; Murtagh, "The Philadelphia Row House," pp. 11–12; Building Permits 4364–67 (1946), 1961–65, 1970–73 (1950).

82. Mackley, 22, was shot in the head by workers of the H. C. Aberle Company while he was waiting for a green light at the intersection of Rising Sun Avenue and Roosevelt Boulevard. The fatal gun shot climaxed an argument between fellow strikers in Mackley's car and nonstriking workers in an adjacent car. *Philadelphia Inquirer*, March 7, 1930, p. 8. Plaques in memory of five other men and women who died in hosiery strikes during the 1930's are placed on the exterior walls of the buildings.

83. The complex fills a city block, bounded by Castor Avenue, Cayuga, M, and Bristol streets, affording ample interior space for lawns, gardens, and even a swimming pool. Construction began in January 1934 and tenants started moving in a year later. It is appropriate that the houses were built for textile workers, because at the time approximately one-fourth of the city's industrial workers were employed in textile factories that were concentrated in this area. *Philadelphia: A Guide to the Nation's Birthplace*, pp. 515, 525–26.

84. William Pope Barney directed the erection of the buildings. Tatum, *Penn's Great Town*, p. 203; Teitelman and Longstreth, *Architecture in Philadelphia*, p. 164; *Philadelphia: A Guide to the Nation's Birthplace*, p. 526.

85. The community's organization in the 1930's is briefly described in *Philadelphia: A Guide to the Nation's Birthplace*, pp. 526–27.

Index

General Index

Street Index

Numbered streets are listed separately at the end of this index.